THE HUNDRED YEARS WAR
VOLUME I
Trial by Battle

THE MIDDLE AGES SERIES

Ruth Mazo Karras, General Editor
Edward Peters, Founding Editor

A complete list of books in the series is
available from the publisher

THE
HUNDRED YEARS
WAR

JONATHAN SUMPTION

VOLUME I
Trial by Battle

PENN

University of Pennsylvania Press
Philadelphia

First published 1990 by Faber and Faber Limited
First published in the United States 1991
by University of Pennsylvania Press
First paperback edition 1999
Copyright © 1990 Jonathan Sumption
All rights reserved

10 9 8 7 6 5 4 3 2 1

Published by
University of Pennsylvania Press
Philadelphia, Pennsylvania 19104-4011

Library of Congress Cataloging-in-Publication Data

Sumption, Jonathan.
The Hundred Years War: trial by battle / Jonathan Sumption.
p.   cm. — (Middle Ages series)
originally published; London: Faber and Faber, 1990.
includes bibliographical references and index.
ISBN 0-8122-1655-5 (pbk.: alk. paper)
1. Hundred Year's War, 1339-1453.   2. France—History—House of
Valois, 1328-1589.   3. Great Britain—History—Medieval period,
1066-1485.   4. France—History, Military—1328-1589.
5. Great Britain—History, Military—Medieval period, 1066-1485.
I. Title.   II Series.
DC96.S86   1991   91-25816
944 025—dc20   CIP

A CIP record for this book is available from the British Library

Maps drawn by John Flower

Contents

Maps and Plans

Preface

This book is intended to be the first volume of a history of the Hundred Years War, from its outbreak in the 1330s until the final expulsion of the English from France in the middle of the fifteenth century. This succession of destructive wars, separated by tense intervals of truce and by dishonest and impermanent treaties of peace, is one of the central events in the history of England and France, as well as in that of their neighbours who were successively drawn into it: Scotland, Germany, Italy and Spain. It laid the foundations of France's national consciousness, even while destroying the prosperity and political pre-eminence which France had once enjoyed. It formed her institutions, creating, in the effort to control anarchy and defeat invasion, the germ of the absolute state of the seventeenth and eighteenth centuries. In England, it brought intense effort and suffering, a powerful tide of patriotism, great fortune succeeded by bankruptcy, disintegration and utter defeat.

I have written about England and France together, almost as if they were a single community engaged in a civil war as, in some respects, they were. I have tried to describe not only what happened, but why it happened and how it affected those who experienced it, whether they were close at hand, like the soldiers in the field and the inhabitants of countless burned-out villages and towns, or saw it at a distance, like the bankers, war contractors, bureaucrats and tax-payers, and the readers of newsletters and proclamations. But this book is a narrative. The sweep of events provides its framework. I make no apology for that. Although narrative history has not always been fashionable, the facts sometimes explain themselves better than any analysis of them could possibly do. Moreover, while there have been many valuable monographs on this or that aspect of the Hundred Years War, some fine histories of isolated incidents and campaigns, and one magnificent account of a single ruler (Charles V of France), no general history of the war has been written on the scale which it deserves. The best account remains that of the great French historian and anglophile, Edouard Perroy, written without access to books while the author was working with the French resistance in the later years of the Second World War. But in a single volume covering 120 years not even Perroy, with his profound knowledge of both English and French sources, could convey more than the outline of events, or penetrate behind the screen to observe the lives of men who never pretended to call the order of events but were only spectators and victims.

My approach has been to work primarily from the record sources of England and France, printed and unprinted. Later volumes will draw on the archives of Italy and Spain also. The chroniclers have an important but subordinate place. They have much to say about the character of the war and their anecdotes are often very revealing. They provide insights into the aristocratic mentality which the records can rarely offer. Depending upon the quality of their sources, they can be reliable guides to the course of events. But most of them are episodic, prejudiced, inaccurate and late. Froissart is particularly unreliable. Moreover, being essentially journalists, the chroniclers were also snobs. They rarely showed much interest in events in which no duke, earl or count participated. So, except for the tremendous battle at Sluys in 1340, they said almost nothing about the war at sea, which was waged by lowly men. Gascony was virtually ignored until 1345, when the first earl fought there. But the records throw a flood of light on these events, unselfconscious evidence, written by clerks who had no idea of recording history. I have identified in the notes the authorities for what I say in the text. But with rare exceptions I have not discussed conflicts of evidence or debated the divergent opinions of scholars. I have simply resolved the differences to my own satisfaction, and I hope to yours.

J.P.C.S.
Greenwich
May 1989

l.t. and *l.p.* stand respectively for *livres tournois* or pounds of Tours, and *livres parisis* or pounds of Paris. The pound sterling was generally worth five *l.t.* and four *l.p.* Unless otherwise stated *livres* are *livres tournois*.

CHAPTER I

France in 1328

Charles IV, the last Capetian King of France, died on 1 February 1328 at the royal manor of Vincennes, east of Paris. The burial of a king in the early fourteenth century was already an elaborate ceremony, marking off with a studied symbolism the end of a reign and the beginning of another. The body of the dead King, imperfectly preserved with vinegar and salt and aromatic spices, lay in state in Notre-Dame Cathedral, clothed in heavy robes of gold cloth and ermine, the crown at its head, the face exposed and the hands holding the regalia of office, the sceptre, ring and staff of justice as if in a macabre reversal of the coronation ceremony. On the following Friday, 5 February, the body was carried on an open bier to the mausoleum of the French monarchy at Saint-Denis, accompanied by a procession in which precedence assigned his exact place to every man. The Bishop of Paris, his fellow bishops, the chapter of Notre-Dame and the clergy of the city preceded it; the royal family and the principal noblemen followed behind; at the rear came the leaders of the rich citizenry of Paris dressed in black with large hoods covering their faces; and close around the bier the poor of the city for whom the funeral of a king was an occasion for the distribution of largesse, a formality which no royal will omitted.

The route from Notre-Dame to Saint-Denis passed through the streets of Paris for scarcely 2 miles before emerging into open country to the north. Yet the Paris of 1328, although it covered but a fraction of the area of the modern city, was the largest, most densely populated city of northern Europe and the richest. Within its walls and in the new suburbs to the north, more than 100,000 people lived, at a time when London probably had less than 40,000 inhabitants. Its citizens were packed into a dense mass of tall, narrow wood-frame houses, separated by a warren of irregular alleyways which Jean de Jandun from the calm of the university quarter on the south bank likened to the 'hairs of a multitude of heads, ears of corn piled up after a plentiful harvest, or leaves in a dense forest'.[1] They lived every day with the indescribable din of raucous cries, rumbling carts, driven cattle, clanging bells and shouts of 'gare à l'eau' as slops fell into the street from upper windows. Only the proximity of the open country outside can have saved from perpetual epidemic a city which had no sewer until 1374 and only three public fountains, all of them north of the Seine, a place where the more fastidious emptied the contents of their latrines weekly into carts to be dumped outside the walls, where pigs, dogs and rats rooted among the piles of garbage, butchers slaughtered their animals in the streets and lepers wandered at large.

No city renewed itself naturally in the unhealthy conditions of the middle ages, and Paris had long drawn its expanding population from immigrants attracted by the wealth, fame and freedom of the capital. An increasingly bureaucratic monarchy had established its courts and record offices there. The great noblemen of the realm, the counts of Burgundy, Brittany, Flanders and Champagne, the princes of the royal family and the more important bishops and abbots visited the city on official business accompanied by crowds of servants and hangers-on, accommodating them in substantial mansions within the walls. Rapid fortunes were made by commodity speculators, bankers and food wholesalers, giving rise to stark contrasts of wealth and poverty, and supplying a market for the luxury trades for which Paris was famous throughout Europe: painters, jewellers, goldsmiths, furriers. A large community of Florentine and Sienese bankers had grown up in the mercantile quarter on the right bank of the Seine. On the left bank, the University attracted an unruly clerical underworld, several thousand strong. And beneath all these came the tide of salaried journeymen, domestic servants and mendicant poor, the ballast of every medieval city. Survival was not easy, and comfort rare.

Notre-Dame in 1328 looked very much as it does today. But it would have been seen not squarely at the end of a wilderness of concrete but in glimpses through the streets around it. Emerging from the darkness of the cathedral, the funeral procession would have come out into a narrow porticoed square populated by beggars, hawkers and ecclesiastical book-sellers. A few feet away from the sculpted portals of the cathedral the funeral procession would already have buried itself in the streets and lanes of the Ile de la Cité, passing into the rue Neuve Notre-Dame, a broad straight street which the chapter of the cathedral had opened up in 1163 to accommodate the heavy wagons of materials for its buildings. But this was as far as town planning went in medieval Paris. The rue Neuve Notre-Dame came to an abrupt end at the Marché Palu, one of the main thoroughfares of the Ile de la Cité leading south towards the Petit Pont and the south bank. To the left, towards the bridge, lay the squalid quarter to which the beggars, wastrels and prostitutes had been banished by royal order ever since they had become a menace to respectable Parisians in the 1250s. On the right lay the southern entrance to the Juiverie, the short street where those other outcasts the Jews had had their stalls and their synagogues until their expulsion from France only two decades earlier. Passing along the rue de la Calandre (now obliterated by the police barracks and Préfecture) the funeral procession reached the east wall of the royal palace. Occupying the whole of the western end of the island on the present site of the Palais de Justice and the Conciergerie, the huge, rambling, ill-planned palace to which each monarch had made his own additions had come to resemble a small city of itself, gathered beneath the spire of its own cathedral, the Sainte-Chapelle. Marking off the palace from the city lay the wing which the dead King had himself added to house the officials of the royal treasury. Charles IV's modest building enterprise was at least uncontroversial. As his bier approached the Seine by the Barillerie (now the Boulevard du Palais) it was carried past the King's Great Hall, that 'marvellous and costly work', now misnamed the Conciergerie and known principally for having housed the victims of the Revolution. Enguerran de Marigny, the unscrupulous Finance Minister of Philip the Fair, had put it up some twenty years before, a fact which was still remembered with bitterness by citizens whose houses and water mills along the river's edge had been expropriated.

The procession crossed the Grand Pont, a broad wooden bridge lined on either side with shuttered booths, the premises of the silversmiths and money-changers who traded there until the eighteenth century and gave the bridge its modern name, the Pont-au-Change. On other days the bridge was the hub of the city's life, perpetually blocked, because it carried the main road through the capital, by crowds of shoppers and loiterers, carriages and herds of cattle. At the northern end of the bridge the procession crossed over the strand. The Seine was not embanked in 1328. Instead, the ground gradually rose out of the river and merged with the city streets forming a mire of intermingled land and water, in summer the site of a long ribbon of shopkeepers' stalls, in winter an invitation to floods. Looking back from the right bank of the river one could see the stumps of the old Grand Pont, the fine stone structure carried away by the floods of 1296. The Parisians had constructed water-mills on the piers, connected by ramshackle wooden gangways. By the central pier a mass of barges waited in the queue to pay the toll exacted by the municipality or to discharge goods on the strand, the proprietors offering samples to onlookers standing above them.

3

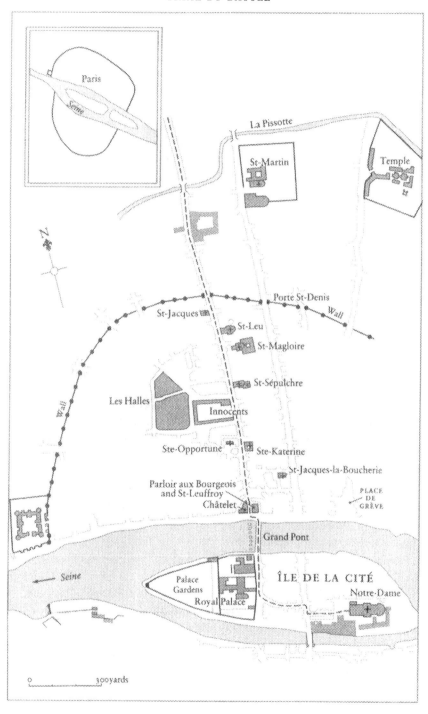

1 Paris in 1328

Once it was clear of the bridge, the funeral procession filed past a curious communal warehouse built out on piles over the river, and then squeezed into a narrow street under the wall of the Châtelet. The Châtelet was a venerable building, a small fortress dating back to the early twelfth century (and not demolished until 1810) which had once guarded the entrance to Paris. Now, deprived of its function by the outward spread of the city, it had become a state prison and a block of offices, the seat of the provost (or governor) of the capital. Hemmed in against it on the eastern side, the procession passed on the right the Parloir aux Bourgeois, a cramped and irregular group of buildings which accommodated the municipality of Paris until it moved to its present site in the Place de Grève in 1357. Adjoining it on the north side, the church of St Leufroy, once the first suburban church of Paris, was now embedded in the busiest part of the city and had been turned over, like its neighbours, to official use. It housed the block of stone which served as the standard measure of the mercantile community, the rough precursor of the universal kilogram of platinum. Leaving the Châtelet behind them, the mourners passed on their right the obscure entrances to the foul-smelling quarter where the butchers of Paris had their premises around the parish church of St Jacques-la-Boucherie. Here were the heavy, violent men, organized into the oldest and most privileged of the city's guilds, who were to supply the mob leaders in a century of Paris revolutions to come.

The procession entered the Grand' Rue (known from the end of the fourteenth century as the rue Saint-Denis) at a point marked today by the north-west corner of the Place du Châtelet, where many of the armourers of Paris carried on their trade. Overshadowed since 1858 by the roaring Boulevard de Sebastopol, this famous street was once the main thoroughfare of the capital, crowded with hawkers and gapers, with carts bringing goods to Les Halles on Fridays, and occasionally with the tumbrils passing in the opposite direction and the great mobs which escorted criminals to the gallows in the plain north of Paris. This was the royal road from the palace of the Ile de la Cité to the abbey of Saint-Denis, scene of the triumphal entries and funeral processions of generations of French kings, the street by which the army of Philip VI was to march to its destruction at the battle of Crécy. The Grand' Rue revealed much of the character of Paris. The city's wealth was flaunted in its paving, a rare luxury in medieval cities. Its solid bourgeois mansions housed some of its richest citizens. A parade of churches and religious foundations created an ecclesiastical atmosphere which today is entirely lost: 'wonderfully provided with monasteries and churches, handsomely constructed and crowned with tall steeples', as an Irish traveller had described it five years earlier.[2] The Grand' Rue was the axis along which Paris had moved northward in the twelfth and thirteenth centuries, spreading out in new and smart suburbs on the great monastic estates situated on either side of the road. The character of the city had changed in the process. Medieval cities never entirely lost their rural atmosphere. The principal charity hospital, the Hôtel-Dieu, had once kept pigs next to the refectory within ten yards of Notre-Dame. There had been famous vineyards on the left bank, opposite the Cité. Townsmen had sown their grain in the suburbs and raised fruit trees under the city walls. However, the distinction between town and country hardened as the spreading wash of buildings put all this further out of reach, except for those religious houses whose jealously enclosed orchards, walled vineyards and vegetable gardens were by now the only reminders of a rural past.

Passing through the salt merchants' district at the south end of the modern rue Saint-Denis the mourners reached the cloistered foundation of St Catherine at the point where the road is now crossed by the rue des Lombards. Its monks and nuns were charged with the burial of travellers found dead on the roads. Directly opposite stood the apse of the church of St Opportune, a house of secular canons which maintained an important hospice for pilgrims. Between the doorway of St Catherine's and the cemetery of the Innocents a little further on, the mourners filed through streets on normal days impassable for the hawkers and itinerant merchants of bric-à-brac who had made this quarter their pitch.

The Innocents, a great walled enclosure halfway between the Grand Pont and the northern gate, was for centuries the principal cemetery of Paris, its largest open space and on weekdays its busiest food market, a place famous for its crowds and noise on occasions less solemn than this one. Beside the small chapel which served it, the Fontaine des Innocents provided the public water supply for much of northern Paris, the ancestor of what is now the grandest fountain of the city. West of this quarter, glimpsed by the mourners as they walked along the Grand' Rue, a warren of narrow streets led back to Les Halles, where Philip Augustus 150 years before had established the main market of Paris for eight centuries. Just north of the cemetery along the processional route the church of the Holy Sepulchre, still incomplete, stood shrouded in builders' scaffolding. Edward II of England had contributed to its funds, and his estranged wife and son, the future conqueror of much of France, had attended the laying of the foundation stone only two years earlier. The tide of church-building was not yet over. But the end of two centuries of expansion was not far away, and the pilgrims' hospice which it was destined to serve was never built.

Behind the houses which extended northward along the street from St Sepulchre, there stood the undistinguished but magnificently endowed abbey church of St Magloire, surrounded by a spacious enclosure, the landlord to most of the district. Only recently the church-going population of the surrounding streets had been able to make do with a side altar in the abbey dedicated to St Gilles and St Leu. Now their pressing numbers required a parish church, and the church of St Gilles and St Leu, forty yards north of the old abbey, had been put up within the last ten years. St Leu has been much altered since its apse was found, in the 1850s, to be out of alignment with the Boulevard de Sebastopol, but it remains the only building in the rue Saint-Denis which the mourners of Charles IV would recognize today.

The last hundred yards of the processional route towards the gate of Paris brought the King's body into a district only recently built over, which had become the artists' quarter of the city, a district not of bohemian scroungers but of small workshop proprietors more notable for output than originality. The house of the fraternity of St James, another pilgrims' foundation, stood on the left as the cortège approached the formal limits of the city. It had been completed only the year before, dedicated to the service of God by Jean de Marigny, Bishop of Beauvais, a man who was to spend the declining years of his life fighting against the English in south-western France. Behind the buildings of the hospice could be seen the roofs of the Hôtel d'Artois (soon to become the Hôtel de Bourgogne), a cluster of buildings all dating from the past half-century which was the home of the formidable old Countess of Artois. It was one of the grandest aristocratic mansions in Paris, its rooms lit by great glass windows and supplied with piped water laid on from the Fountain of the Innocents a few hundred yards away, two of the greatest luxuries available to rich men of the fourteenth century.

The procession reached the formal limits of the city at the ramparts of Philip Augustus. When Philip built them at the end of the twelfth century only two groups of buildings of any importance lay outside. The fortified suburb of the Knights Templar lay in the middle of an insalubrious marsh about half a mile north-east of the new walls, just south of the modern Place de la République. Almost directly north of the city, at about the same distance, lay the less formidably defended enclosure of the wealthy Cluniac priory of St Martin-des-Champs. Neither place retained its dignified isolation now. Although the monks still looked out to the north of their buildings on fields and vineyards, to the south a continuous line of houses stretched out along the rue Saint-Denis and the rue Saint-Martin, and other buildings were moving into the side roads to fill the tract of land between their own walls and those of the capital. When the mourners emerged from the Porte Saint-Denis, at the point where the rue Saint-Denis now crosses the rue de Turbigo, they would have found little to distinguish the crowded suburbs from the city which they had just left. The ramparts had long ago lost their military significance and in a century of peace Parisians had grown accustomed to the fact. Philip Augustus had let out towers and gates to private tenants from the moment it was built. The outer wall of the Porte Saint-Denis, an austere fortified gateway flanked by two fortified towers, was now incongruously decorated with an elegant pointed window at its first-floor level, and a statue of the Virgin Mary. The true boundary of Paris lay well north of it, marked by a stagnant stream known as La Pissotte de St Martin, where the city's sewage was dumped.

At about the point where the rue Saint-Denis now crosses the rue Réaumur near the Réaumur-Sebastopol Métro station, the procession came into open country, crossing a broad belt of land around the north of the city whose marshy ground and fetid streams were a sufficient deterrent to potential settlers. But it was fit enough for the undesirables who lived there. Half a mile away to the east stood the monumental tricornered gibbet of Montfaucon. Closer at hand, a little way past the Pissotte on the left, the Filles-Dieu housed 200 redeemed prostitutes, the quality of whose lives was a familiar Parisian joke. A few hundred yards further north around the chapel of St Lazare lay the huts and refectory of the principal Parisian leper colony side by side with the lodge in which the kings of France customarily spent the night before making their triumphal entries into Paris. The juxtaposition of squalor and splendour was typical of the age and place. Both of these foundations had been the work of rich citizens of Paris applying their wealth in a fashion set by the older nobility. It was an assertion of status as conspicuous as those other pretensions of the patrician families of Paris, the country estate, the patent of nobility and, two years after Charles's death, the tournament held in the plain over to the right beyond the abbey of St Martin-des-Champs, where the gorgeously dressed sons of Paris merchants re-enacted in mock battle the wars of Troy and the deeds of the knights of the Round Table.[3]

The marsh gave way to firmer ground, and for more than 4 miles the procession trailed across the rich, empty plain of Saint-Denis. On the left a low line of hills followed the Seine as it wound round to the north of Paris, prominent among them the hill of Montmartre, then crowned by a tiny country village and a nunnery of which the name of the Place des Abbesses is now the only relic. Extending down to the edges of the low-lying villages, rows of vines marked out a district which was famous for its wine until Paris engulfed it in the nineteenth century. The royal household drew its supplies not from Bordeaux but from Clignancourt, St Ouen and Argenteuil:

> le plus digne
> Par sa bonté, par sa puissance
> D'abrever bien le roi de France

as a thirteenth-century poet sang.[4]

By the end of the morning, the funeral procession would have reached La Chapelle, a small wine-growing village whose identity is still preserved by the survival of its parish church (in the rue de la Chapelle) where a hundred years later Joan of Arc would pray before unsuccessfully attempting the capture of Paris from the English. At its northern edge lay the boundary of the domain of the abbey of Saint-Denis, a point marked on the road by a leaning cross. Here the procession was met by the abbot and monks, a moment which emphasized the dignity which their abbey derived from its long connection with the French monarchy. The Bishop of Paris had no jurisdiction beyond this point, and was required to admit as much in a sealed document before removing his robes of office. He and all his clergy and fellow bishops with him entered the land of Saint-Denis in plain religious garb. The pall-bearers were replaced and the procession formed up behind the community of Saint-Denis for the last 3 miles of the journey through the mild countryside today desolate with industrial ugliness. As the line of mourners passed into the town of Saint-Denis and approached the abbey enclosure, most of the laymen and lesser clergy fell away, leaving the monks, a few ecclesiastical grandees and more important royal princes and household officers to their privilege of burying the royal dead.

France in 1328 occupied a position of apparent strength but real weakness. Charles IV had ruled a territory somewhat smaller than that of modern France. To the north it included the whole of the county of Flanders and the western part of what is now Belgium. But in the east the kingdom extended no further than the Meuse, the Saône and the Rhône. Hainault, Lorraine, part of Burgundy, the Dauphiné, Savoy and the whole of Provence lay outside it, although much of this territory was French-speaking and their rulers moved in the political orbit of France. Lyon had been French for barely twenty years when Charles IV died, and east of

9

Lyon lay territory which was still ostensibly part of the German Empire. A lawyer–Pope writing to the King of France in 1265 might well wonder whether Viviers, a cathedral city on the west bank of the Rhône, was in France or the German Empire. 'We find the boundaries between your kingdom and the Empire nowhere recorded in writing, and we have no idea where they run.'[5] France was not Gaul.

Nevertheless she was beyond question the richest and most populous European country. In 1328 a census of taxable households compiled by officials of the royal treasury enumerated 2,469,987 households divided between nearly 24,000 parishes. The great fiefs and princely appanages (which the King did not tax) were excluded, and techniques of enumeration were no doubt less refined than those misleadingly precise figures would suggest. Even so, France in 1328 can scarcely have had less than 16 million inhabitants, which was about three times the population of contemporary England.

This population, impressively dense for the period, was supported by agricultural resources which had unceasingly expanded for 300 years. In the second half of the thirteenth century the countryside had been at the height of its prosperity. The cultivated area had reached its greatest extent, the result of a prolonged assault on the heathland, forest and marsh which had once covered much of the kingdom. In Froissart's evocative words: 'At that time, France was gorged, contented and strong, its people rich and prospering, and not one of them knew the word war.'[6]

In retrospect, it is possible to see that this society had already passed its apogee. The pattern differed from province to province. The peak of the boom may have been reached as early as the 1260s, although it was not for many years after that that the symptoms of economic change became apparent to contemporaries. In much of France the countryside had become not only populous but crowded. The assault on the forest could go no further without encroaching on woodlands needed for grazing animals, hunting and growing timber. Towards the end of the thirteenth century the expansion of the cultivated area came to a halt. But the population continued to grow. Real wages faltered and then declined. The rise of prices accelerated. Average expectation of life, never very high in the poorly nourished rural communities of the middle ages, fell back to about twenty years. To begin with these strains affected chiefly the towns and the poor. Proprietors and tenant farmers prospered mightily. Food prices reached a peak during the famines of 1315–17 never attained before. Or afterwards. It was the turning point of their fortunes. Agricultural prices began to fall sharply in the 1320s and did not recover even when the hunger returned. Rents fell with them. Thus began the long agricultural depression of the fourteenth century. Aristocratic incomes fell, and in some provinces fell catastrophically. Beyond the crosses which marked the boundaries of each community, in untidy shanty villages of hastily erected cabins, there grew up the communities of rootless poor who took a subsistence by begging and hiring themselves out to work the fields at harvest time. In 1320 and 1321 the discontent of these outcasts, and others thrown among them by circumstance, had erupted in a rash of localized rebellions accompanied in some places by virulent attacks on the Church and massacres of Jews. Between 1323 and 1328 a civil war of unparalleled savagery was fought between the landowners and peasants of western Flanders. These events were harbingers of graver problems to come.

Some men simply fled from their problems. Smallholdings shrank or vanished, their former owners drifting to the towns. However, the capacity of the towns to take them depended on a delicate economic balance which had already shown signs of failing. The population of the towns had grown in the course of the twelfth and thirteenth centuries even faster than the population of the rest of France. The greater towns had thrown their limits outwards in successive campaigns of wall-building. Others, which marked their limits less grandly with ditches and joined-up façades at the edges, added new streets like concentric rings around the hearts of ancient trees, or spread themselves in rambling suburbs which merged gradually with the fields around. In the south the greater princes and ecclesiastical corporations laid out several hundred new towns (*bastides*) where settlements had never been. In the old towns men crammed themselves into the squalid quarters where immigrants were traditionally found, making them more insanitary than they had ever been and aggravating still further the difficulties of supplying them. It is easy to under-estimate how great these difficulties were in an age in which carrying bulky supplies overland called for supreme effort if it were possible at all. A typical provincial town of some 3,000 inhabitants consumed more than 1,000 tons of grain a year, requiring a cultivated district of about 8,000 acres in which to grow it. Larger towns could not hope to feed themselves from their own districts, and depended upon provisions brought from a considerable distance. Flanders, the most heavily urbanized region of France, was dependent for its food supply on road and river lines extending far beyond the boundaries of the province into northern France, Hainault, Brabant and the Rhineland. Paris was provisioned by a corporation of privileged wholesalers, the Hanse des Marchands de l'Eau, who enjoyed powers by royal grant to control the commercial traffic of the whole valley of the Seine from Nogent to the sea, together with much of the valley of the Oise.[7] It was a miracle of commercial organization, but it was not enough. The first warning came with the famine of 1305 when the bakers of Paris had to board up their shops against mobs. Then came the famines of 1315–17 and the epidemics of the 1320s and 1330s. Some northern cities lost a tenth of their population to the plague. In Flanders, the death rate was higher. The denser the population, the greater the distress. Périgueux, which was among the most densely populated cities of southern France, lost a third of its inhabitants during the famines of the 1330s. War was another scourge to complete the misery of such places. They were much more vulnerable to it than they would have been a century before. Their swollen suburbs were liable to be demolished by friends or burned by enemies. A road or river cut might mean hunger for weeks; a harvest burned, starvation for the best part of a year.[8]

The industrial wealth of France was heavily concentrated in one industry, textiles, and in one region, the north-west: Flanders, Artois and Picardy and a small number of towns in the neighbouring provinces of Normandy and Champagne. In Flanders the textile industry had caused great towns to grow up from little more than villages in an explosion of commercial activity which had few parallels in European history before the nineteenth century. Ghent, with about 60,000 inhabitants, was the largest city of northern Europe after Paris. Arras, Douai, Bruges, Ypres and Lille, although smaller, were very substantial by the standards of any other region. In this confined corner of the kingdom was packed the teeming proletariat which manufactured broadcloth, the staple of international trade, and throughout the middle ages the only industrial product made in quantity for export. Production on this scale required regimentation and considerable capital. Both were provided by a small class of merchants, who also constituted in almost every case the governing oligarchy of the city. They brought the raw wool in England, and sold it to self-employed artisans to be woven, cleaned and dyed in many small workshops. Quite frequently the merchant also supplied the equipment and rented out the premises. At the end of the process, he bought back the finished product and sold it on to middlemen, principally Italians, for distribution as far afield as Spain, Russia and the Near East. Great fortunes were made.

Contrasts of wealth and poverty were not easily concealed in the close environment of medieval towns. In crowded houses within the walls and in sprawling shanty towns of thatched huts outside, the artisans lived in conditions no more squalid perhaps than those of the average northern peasant but bitterly resented for being experienced side by side with the close-fistedness and ostentatious wealth of the financiers on whom they depended. In 1280 there were risings in Ypres, Bruges and Douai. In 1301 a far graver rebellion broke out in Bruges and Ghent under the leadership of a 'genial and smooth-talking' weaver, Peter Koninck, and succeeded for a time in supplanting the government of the commercial oligarchy. These events proved to be the first of a series of urban revolutions in Flanders which gravely damaged France's only important industry. Some of the trade which Flanders lost moved south to older, more peaceful cities such as Amiens and Rouen. But much of it moved beyond the frontiers of the kingdom to the imperial territories of Hainault and Brabant.

These events had greater consequences for France than the ruin of some Flemish capitalists and the displacement of the oligarchies of the northern cities. The looms of Flanders had drawn across eastern France one of the major trade routes of Europe. Thirty years before Charles IV died, the international fairs of Champagne held successively at Lagny, Bar-sur-Aube, Provins and Troyes had been the hub of European banking where the cloth merchants met the Italian dealers who financed the trade. But by 1328 the fairs had lost their banking business, and their importance as an exchange of goods was waning rapidly. It was in part the natural consequence of geographical changes which could not have been avoided: new patterns of trade over the Alpine passes drew the main routes further east, and the opening up by the Italians of the sea route to northern Europe by the straits of Gibraltar by-passed France altogether. But the process was accelerated by the troubles of Flanders and the policies of the French Crown. The kings repeatedly prosecuted their disputes with the counts of Flanders by impounding the goods of their subjects. The Flemings had lost their goods throughout France in 1297. They had been banned from the fairs by Philip the Fair between 1302 and 1305 and again by his son in 1315. They stayed away. The Italian traders, whose own nascent cloth industries in Florence and Milan were beginning to compete with those of Flanders, increasingly found their opportunities elsewhere. Philip the Fair hastened their departure by subjecting them to persecution, forced loans and discriminatory taxation.[9]

Toll-gates are eloquent witnesses of economic decline. South of Arras, at the cross-roads of Bapaume which long ago had marked the frontier of Flanders, a great toll-gate stood across the main roads from Paris to the industrial cities of Flanders and east from the cities of Champagne to the Atlantic ports. The tolls fell by two-thirds in the immediate aftermath of the troubles of Flanders in 1302 and again, although by less, in the crisis of

1313–15. The toll collectors at the approaches to the Alpine passes told the same story of erratic but persistent descent from the golden years of the late thirteenth century.[10]

In spite of the visible strain which the troubles of the early fourteenth century inflicted on French society, few contemporaries could have foreseen the political catastrophes of the next two reigns. They stood as much in awe of France in 1328 as they had ever done. They still saw the rich glow of the golden thirteenth century, the century of St Louis, of the *Roman de la Rose* and of the great Gothic cathedrals and abbeys, founded in a mood of earnest opulence which the chronicler Joinville had likened to the illumination of a manuscript in azure and gold. The University of Paris was truly, as an Irish visitor described it in 1323, 'the home and nurse of theological and philosophical science, the mother of the liberal arts, the mistress of justice and the standard of morals, the mirror and lamp of all theological virtues'. The architecture of the Ile de France had conquered the native traditions of every western European country and for a while had taken complete possession. Italian noblemen studied French sartorial fashions and learned to speak French, which they described as the most beautiful language in existence. Dante's commentator, Benvenuto of Imola, who tells us this, was one of the many contemporaries who resented the intrusion of French manners, just as the poet himself had resented the money and brute force by which France had established herself in Italy during the thirteenth century.[11]

The German prince who railed against 'prating Frenchmen always sneering at other nations than their own'[12] had been worsted in diplomacy, but in using the occasion for an outburst against Gallic swaggering he was voicing the feelings of many of his contemporaries as well as paying an implied tribute to the power which had made the swaggering possible. In the course of the thirteenth century French armies had fought in England and the Low Countries, in Spain, in Italy and in the Middle East. French dynasties ruled in Provence, Naples, Navarre, Cyprus and Greece, and within recent memory they had ruled in Sicily and Constantinople. The papacy was installed in Avignon at the outer gate of France, governed by a succession of French popes and a college of cardinals in which Frenchmen held an overwhelming majority. 'The government of the earth', Jean de Jandun announced in his eulogy of Paris, 'belongs rightfully to the august and sovereign House of France.'[13]

By the standards of fourteenth-century European states, France's military strength was prodigious. The army available to its rulers for field service was conventionally estimated at between 20,000 and 25,000 men, one-quarter of them cavalry. The armies planned for the invasion of Flanders in 1304, the proposed crusade of 1323 and mooted campaigns in Gascony in 1326, 1329 and 1330 were all of this size. But from time to time much larger forces could be raised. An army of 50,000 was planned for 1339 (the third year of the war with Edward III) and about that number, divided between two fronts, actually served in the following year in addition to 20,000 men mobilized for the fleet. By comparison the English, although they were able on one occasion in the fourteenth century to collect together 32,000 men, only rarely succeeded in fielding as many as 10,000. The sheer numerical strength of French armies was particularly marked in cavalry, the prestige arm of every medieval army. At the peak of their military achievement (in September 1340) the French deployed more than 27,000 cavalrymen. Again a comparison with England is revealing. The largest number of cavalrymen that England deployed at any one time was about 5,000. Numbers of course, are not everything, and by the beginning of the fourteenth century the great age of medieval cavalry was past. What the numbers do, however, reveal is the extent of France's resources, the strength of her military tradition and the quality of her institutions. The assembling and direction of an army was the greatest collective enterprise which a medieval society ever undertook.[14]

The French state as it existed in 1328 was the creation of the fourteen Capetian kings who had successively ruled France since 987. Alone among the great dynasties of medieval Europe they had been able to survive for three centuries, each monarch leaving a male heir to carry on his work. Fortune had favoured them. Most of these rulers had been men of conspicuous ability. None had been manifestly incompetent. Anointed with holy oil at their coronations, gifted by the propagandists of the monarchy with powers of miraculous healing, proclaimed in official documents as the superior of every other mortal, the kings of France had already adopted the trappings of absolutism. 'Being placed by the grace of God above all other men, we are bound to the will of Him who has made us thus pre-eminent'.[15] Yet the reality of power was more elusive than the formulae. At the beginning of the eleventh century Robert II, in whose name these words were uttered, exercised direct power in less than a tenth of his kingdom, a compact lozenge of land stretching from Paris in the north to Orléans in the south. Here he was the immediate feudal lord. Elsewhere he was merely king, compelled to rule through vassals who exercised the royal power for him but did so in their own names and with an independence which reduced the monarchy to a portentous honorary dignity. The princes could and quite frequently did make war upon him and upon each other, as well as maintaining direct relations with the papacy and foreign powers.

Three centuries passed between the death of Robert II in 1031 and that of Charles IV in 1328, during which the monarchy had ceaselessly increased both the territorial extent of the royal domain and the power which they could bring to bear within it. Piecemeal acquisitions continued throughout the period, but by far the most significant were the three huge accessions of territory which in the course of the thirteenth century extended the domain of the Capetian kings for the first time to the Atlantic and the Mediterranean. The first was the work of Philip Augustus and his son Louis VIII, who between 1202 and 1224 destroyed the continental empire of the Angevin kings of England, annexing Normandy, the Loire provinces, Poitou and Saintonge. South of the Dordogne, the Albigensian crusades had ruined the princes of the house of Toulouse, once 'the peers of kings' as the Englishman Gervase of Tilbury had called them at the beginning of the thirteenth century. In 1271 a combination of juridical technicality, good fortune and armed force finally brought this great inheritance into the hands of the Crown. Three years later the male line of the counts of Champagne and Brie became extinct and their territories, embracing some of the richest agricultural land in France as well as the towns which accommodated the fairs of Champagne, passed to the Crown by a series of dexterous marriages. To these spectacular gains were added many lesser territories, filling the interstices of the existing domain or planting the seeds of future expansion. Philip the Fair alone, who reigned between 1285 and 1314, acquired Chartres, Beaugency and Montpellier by purchase, Mortagne and Tournai by confiscation, the counties of La Marche and Angoulême by foreclosing on a mortgage. Along the eastern march of his kingdom, he acquired Lyon and the imperial free county of Burgundy, and gradually insinuated his officials into the Barrois.

Although these acquisitions, and others which followed them, proved in retrospect to be the foundation of the nation state, it is unlikely that the Capetian kings saw them in that light. They were advancing the interests of their family which they only indistinctly identified with the nation. And they gave out with one hand even as they drew in with the other. The doctrine that the royal domain was inalienable did not become an overt principle of royal policy until the Edict of Moulins in 1566. Louis IX restored to the English dukes of Aquitaine a large part of what his father had taken from them not, as he told the councillors who had opposed it, because he was bound to do so 'but so that there may be love between my children and his, who are cousins'. It was a private act as much as a public one. Not only Louis but most rulers of his dynasty treated the royal domain as a source of patronage, granting away rights and immunities in a manner which horrified some of the civil service. The kings were not hoarders of land as the Church was. They gave away whole regions of France to their brothers and sons to be ruled by them and their heirs forever as appanages, principalities for many purposes independent of the Crown. Louis VIII, who died in 1226, had added more to the royal domain than any Capetian king, but in his will he left Artois to his second son, Poitou and Auvergne to his third and Anjou and Maine to his fourth. The heir to the throne inherited little more than the old domain of the Ile de France plus Normandy. Philip the Fair was almost as prodigal with his sons at the beginning of the fourteenth century, and they in turn alienated great tracts of their inheritance. The Crown was saved from the natural consequences of its largesse only by the extraordinary good fortune that the younger branches of the Capetian dynasty were as short-lived and infertile as the older branches were prolific and healthy.

In 1328 the area directly governed by the Crown had reached the full tide from which it was to ebb back in a century and a half of political disintegration, civil war and foreign occupation. It covered about two-thirds of the French kingdom: Paris and the Ile de France; Picardy; Normandy and Maine; Anjou, Touraine and the Orléanais in the Loire valley; the central provinces of Poitou, Limousin and most of Berry; and Languedoc in the south. The French kings governed the rest of France in some cases indirectly, in others not at all. There were, first of all, the three 'great fiefs' of Flanders, Brittany and Aquitaine, virtually autonomous principalities governed by independent dynasties whose princes only inter-mittently formed part of the French political community. Then there were the appanages created by past kings for their younger sons: in 1328 the dukes of Burgundy and Bourbon and the counts of Artois, Alençon and Evreux. They were run on similar lines, with many of the same freedoms, but by men whose links with the Crown, links of blood, sentiment and political interest were so close as to make them at most times part of the government of the realm. This was true even of the oldest of them, Burgundy, which had been severed from the royal domain for 300 years but whose dukes remained among the closest associates of the kings of France until the extinction of their line in the middle of the fourteenth century. A few much smaller territories, although they were not appan-ages, enjoyed very similar privileges of self-government: the territories of the counts of Blois, the lords of Montmorency, Joinville and Coucy; the rather special case of the county of Ponthieu, around Abbeville, which the kings of England had acquired by marriage at the end of the thirteenth century; and the Pyrenean territory of Foix-Béarn, which was too distant for effective royal interference and perhaps too valuable as an ally against the English dynasty in Aquitaine.

In principle the difference between these august princes and the lesser nobility of the royal domain was that the King's judges had no jurisdiction and his officials no power over the inhabitants of their territories. The holders of the great appanages and self-governing fiefs recognized their feudal obligations to the Crown, obligations defined and limited by custom and by the terms of their grants and their acts of homage. But they kept their own courts and maintained their own civil services, which were generally exact miniatures of the contemporary organization of the royal government. They passed their own legislation. Some of them coined their own money. If they were liable to do military service (which was sometimes a vexed question), they received the King's summons and recruited their own armies at their own pay, levying their own taxes to pay for it. They were in effect an intermediate level of government whose obligations were prescribed by law rather than administrative practice. However their status, although high, was less peculiar than it seemed. Even within the royal domain lords who held directly of the Crown had many of the same rights on a smaller scale as the greatest of the land. They too held their own courts. They signalled their authority by erecting gallows at the edges of their territory. They taxed their vassals and answered the King's summonses to military service not only in their own persons but with their vassals and retainers. 'Every lord is sovereign in his own lordship,' as Beaumanoir wrote.[16] It is true that their judges and officials had to work side by side with those of the King and were liable to be called before the royal courts to answer for their neglects and misdeeds, an uneasy coexistence which steadily undermined their authority. But this, increasingly, was the lot of the officers of the great fiefs and appanages also.

The administration of the French kings on the eve of the Hundred Years War was the creation of many hands. But one reign had fixed on it an imprint which it did not lose until the end of the middle ages, that of Philip the Fair, who died in 1314 after a reign of nearly thirty years. In spite of the length and importance of his reign, almost nothing is known of the character of this remarkable man save that he was cold, taciturn and spare with confidences. 'He is not man or beast,' one of his enemies asserted, 'he is a graven image.'[17] Philip surrounded himself with a small circle of professional advisers, senior civil servants of whom many were low-born, ambitious, able and therefore unpopular. Whether the King was the author of the policy or the tool of his advisers is a question on which even his contemporaries were unable to make an informed judgement and historians have no more than their guesses to go by. What is clear is that Philip (or perhaps it was his advisers) had a fervent, almost religious belief in the significance of his royal office. 'The King stands above the law, above all customary right and private privilege,' an official pamphleteer wrote in reply to Pope Boniface VIII, who had ventured to challenge his right to tax the clergy; 'it is his prerogative to make law or to amend or abrogate it as he may deem fit after taking counsel of his subjects.'[18]

Philip the Fair had the advantage of well-prepared foundations, the work for the most part of his ancestors Philip Augustus and St Louis, who had begun the creation of the most impressive civil service in medieval Europe. The old royal court had formed itself gradually into five principal departments whose functions were only vaguely defined and whose staff overlapped. These were the royal household and Chancery, which still travelled around the country with the King, and the treasury, Chambre des Comptes and Parlement, which were directed by professional administrators working from Paris. During the reign of Philip's sons and the first Valois king, Philip VI, the Chancery, which served as a general secretariat for the whole operation of government, gradually became a sedentary department based in Paris like the judicial and financial organs of the state. The royal palace of the Cité was bursting with clerks, lawyers and officials. Philip the Fair and his sons enlarged the palace threefold to contain them, and expenditure on administrative salaries increased by leaps and bounds. Some statistics presented to Philip VI in the early years of the war with England present a striking picture of the inexorable expansion of the functions of government and the size of the central bureaucracy. Between 1314 and 1343 the number of principal judicial officers of the various royal courts in Paris increased fourfold; the number of notaries by about the same; the 'sergeants' who enforced compliance with the orders of the King's ministers and judges increased sevenfold. In 1326 the royal Chancery used no less than a ton and a quarter of wax for sealing documents.[19]

The broad lines of royal policy were determined in the Great Council, so called not for its size but because it dealt with the great affairs of the kingdom. It was in fact quite small, consisting of a clique of influential administrators and friends of the King and a fluctuating body of grandees, the princes of the royal family and the great noblemen and ecclesiastical lords whose presence close to the King was sanctified by tradition and expected by popular prejudice. In the course of Philip's reign the professional element largely displaced these grandees, a policy which caused unfavourable comment not only among the grandees themselves, and was reversed in the time of his successors. Most of the professionals came from the lowest level of lay society in which literacy could be expected, from the ranks of the gentry of the provinces, men whose families had often been left behind in the prosperity of the thirteenth century and who owed everything to the King. Philip's two great chancellors, Pierre Flote and Guillaume de Nogaret, both began their careers obscurely as civil lawyers in the south. Flote was a younger son of a minor knightly family from the Velay. Nogaret was a provincial judge who came from a bourgeois family of Toulouse. Enguerran de Marigny, Philip's chamberlain and in his last years virtually chief minister, was the son of an undistinguished Norman seigneur. For him, royal service meant power and fame, a portrait painting and a statue in the royal palace, a fortune accumulated by more or less questionable means, laid out on large estates and on the fine collegiate church and curious collection of religious statuary, both of which can still be seen at his home town of Ecouis in Normandy. Marigny and his kind earned their high rewards. They brought to the royal service intense loyalty, professional skills and, in some cases, acute political judgement. Without them a government growing in size and importance would have passed out of the King's control, as indeed under his successors it showed signs of doing.

The provincial bureaucracy of the Crown was in some ways more remarkable because local administration tended to be the weak point of even the best-organized medieval governments. The regions directly governed by the Crown were divided into thirty-six administrative districts known as *baillages* (in the old royal domain) or *sénéchaussés* (in the newly acquired provinces of the centre and south). The King's interests in these districts were entrusted to *baillis* and seneschals. Alongside them other officials performed subordinate or specialized functions: judges, lieutenant-bailiffs, provosts of towns, viscounts and receivers, and those ubiquitous minor functionaries of the royal administration, the 'sergeants' (*servientes*), who executed the orders of the others with such force as was required. *Baillis* and seneschals were men of consequence, and they were well paid. Many of them, like their superiors in the central administration about the King, were making a career which would not have been open to them in any other walk of life. Barthélemy de Montbrison, who became the lieutenant-*bailli* of Lyon in 1336, was for ten years the most powerful man in the city, dealing on equal terms with the Archbishop and the commune; yet if he had not left his native city in his youth to study law he would in all probability have become a skinner like his father.[20] In a few districts, those close to the frontier or newly acquired by the Crown, they exercised political functions of great importance. The *bailli* of Vermandois represented the King in the political turmoil of Flanders. The seneschals of Périgord and (later) Agen did the same in Aquitaine. But their regular functions were more humdrum. They enforced public order. They collected the revenues of the domain. And they exercised that peculiar mixture of public and private rights which was the substance of sovereignty in the middle ages: the mass of miscellaneous jurisdictions and privileges which the Crown had inherited or acquired from former feudal lords and which had to be exercised in competition with others still in private hands, accretions built up in layers over the centuries and discovered like the revelation of some complicated archaeological site. Assertiveness was a substitute for clarity. Provincial officials commonly became more royalist than the King, trespassing beyond their jurisdiction in the effort to make good their claims and ignoring royal grants of privilege and immunity. By intervening in other men's quarrels, by offering the loser a right of appeal from some lesser jurisdiction, by extending the royal protection to those who had rightly or wrongly fallen foul of the great of the province, by grinding diligence such men could gnaw away at seigneurial rights until they fell into desuetude or were conquered by those of the Crown.

The great achievement of the lawyers of the last five Capetian kings, who reigned between 1270 and 1328, was to build from the Crown's disparate medley of rights a coherent notion of public law and of the state's authority. Still no more than an ambition, it was not to be justified by political facts before the seventeenth century. But there was one area where these ideas had practical consequences of enormous importance even in 1328. Since the middle of the thirteenth century the jurists of the Crown had developed the novel doctrine that the King could hear appeals even from those parts of the kingdom to which his power did not yet extend whenever it was alleged that the local judges had 'denied justice' by misconducting their proceedings or committed an error of law. The manner in which this doctrine was applied was deeply offensive to the holders of the surviving seigneurial jurisdictions. For a litigant who appealed to the King's court was entitled to the protection (*sauvegarde*) of his officers. For the purposes of his suit the litigant had removed himself from the authority of his immediate lord and placed himself immediately under that of the King. His land became an island of extra-territorial jurisdiction flying the King's banner and marked out with the symbolic gallows emblazoned with the fleur-de-lys. So, with the right to hear appeals, there penetrated into the remaining private lordships and busy royal officials, clerks, notaries and sergeants who protected appellants, made the necessary inquiries, settled documents and invited others who had failed in the accustomed forum to shop for a better one.

The ultimate beneficiary of this constant jockeying for jurisdiction was the Parlement of Paris, not a parliament in the English sense but a supreme court hearing appeals in the growing number of cases which the King's servants claimed as his own. Ostensibly the King's Council sitting in a judicial capacity, the Parlement was in the process of being taken over by full-time professional jurists. By the death of Charles IV the Parlement sat in several divisions, accumulating measureless archives and served by an army of functionaries. In the Salle des Pas Perdus of the royal palace in Paris, surrounded by the statues of the kings of France, gathered the crowds of litigants and petitioners whose concern to put their cases before the King's own court had in parts of the kingdom reduced the proceedings of the seigneurial courts to the status of mere formal preliminaries to a battle carried on elsewhere. The appellants had become so numerous that periodic attempts were made to refer the less important causes of dispute back to the bailiffs and seneschals. But the solution ultimately adopted was a further increase in the size of an already ungainly tribunal. The *rapporteurs* of the Chambre des Enquêtes, who were responsible for assessing the evidence before the trial, were four in number during the reign of Philip the Fair; there were thirty-three of them under his son Philip V. The principal division of the court, which heard appeals involving 'grave cause ... grande personne, grands hommes' had no less than twenty-three judges in 1319.[21]

The middle ages were litigious. Their institutions were rent by competition for jurisdiction pursued with a passion which is apt to seem pointless and absurd. But contemporaries did not see it like that. The administration of justice was not only an important source of revenue; it was the highest attribute of sovereignty. Those servants of the Crown who purposefully set about making the enforcement of law a royal monopoly have a better claim to be regarded as the founders of the French state than the soldiers and politicians whose contribution, because it was more heroic, is better known.

Because the servants of the state were articulate propagandists for their cause, it is easy to gain the impression that they completely succeeded. In fact their success was only partial. It is true that the bureaucracy which they created enabled a Parisian monarchy to retain control in normal conditions of one of the largest and most diverse countries of Europe. It is true that in spasms of exertion it was capable of spectacular displays of executive power. The simultaneous arrest of almost all the Templars in France on 13 October 1307, which had been planned in secrecy in Paris for some weeks, would have been beyond every other European state of the fourteenth century. But although the agents of the state held the advanced positions, the ground behind them had not yet been occupied. There had not been the same thoroughgoing change in the attitude of the governed as there had in that of their masters.

Attitudes to public order were revealing. 'The King's peace is the peace of the whole kingdom; and the peace of the kingdom is the peace of the Church, the defence of all knowledge, virtue and justice,' a propagandist declared from his pulpit; '. . . therefore, whoever acts against the King acts against the whole Church, the Catholic faith, and all that is holy and just.'[22] Perhaps under the strain of the Flemish war (the occasion for this sermon) the audience was receptive. The notion of public authority which made civil violence an offence against the state had been well developed in England since the twelfth century but it was only intermittently recognized in France before the fifteenth. Rebellion was simply politics by other means. The thought that it might be treason took a long time to penetrate even official circles. The stages of its penetration can be traced in the manner in which unsuccessful rebels were treated. In the twelfth and thirteenth centuries it was extremely rare for them to be executed as traitors. Guy of Dampierre, Count of Flanders, for example, went almost unpunished although he waged public war on Philip the Fair and fell into the power of his enemy. The first nobleman to be drawn and hanged for treason was Jourdain de l'Isle-Jourdain, a robber baron from the south-west 'noble in lineage but ignoble in deed' who was executed in Paris in 1323. Some of the leaders of the rebellions of Flanders were tortured to death in 1328. During the first decade of the Hundred Years War, when Philip VI had to deal with a serious crisis of public order and the dissolution of natural loyalties in the face of political and military defeat, he resorted to such public executions with gruesome regularity. These spectacular assertions of sovereignty reflected the government's fear and insecurity. They were a substitute for real authority. There were many who could not share Philip's abhorrence of treachery even under the strain of war. The executions were regarded as strange and shocking. The chroniclers reported them in tones of horrified fascination. They added substantially to the unpopularity of the government.[23]

*

The uncertain limit of the state's natural authority was a problem of which the chief symptom was the growing financial embarrassment of the Crown. Like most medieval kings the King of France was expected by orthodox theorists to pay for his government from the income of his private estates and from the profits of justice and feudal incidents which he enjoyed as lord of his own domain. At the end of the 1320s these sources produced between 400,000 and 600,000 l.t. per year, which was three or four times the ordinary income of the King of England.[24] Nevertheless, it was barely equal to the burden of supporting an expanding bureaucracy and wholly inadequate to meet the cost of fighting wars. This was not a difficulty peculiar to France. It was the experience of almost every western European state, as bureaucracies staffed by clever and ambitious men began to experiment with more pervasive, more intense styles of government. Structural deficit became a regular feature of their accounts, and was endemic in France from the last two decades of the thirteenth century. Philip III's unsuccessful attempt to conquer Aragon in 1285 cost him three times his annual income and brought him close to bankruptcy. His son Philip the Fair was brought under unbearable financial pressure between 1293 and 1303, when he was attempting to fight wars simultaneously in Flanders, in Gascony and at sea. His troops on the northern front mutinied in 1303 for want of pay.

There were several reasons for the growing difficulty which French governments experienced in paying for their wars. They fought them more often and on a larger scale than St Louis had done. Philip the Fair supplied armour and weapons to many of his troops. Even his successors (who abandoned this practice) were obliged to replace horses and equipment lost in their service. There was, moreover, the heavy burden of the royal arsenals at Narbonne and Rouen, which were founded in the last two decades of the thirteenth century to make France for the first time into a significant seapower. But much the most significant reason for the rise of the war expenditure of the Crown was the final abandonment during the last thirty years of the thirteenth century of the ancient system of military recruitment, which had depended on the free service of the holders of military fiefs and the inhabitants of certain towns. It had always been a very unsatisfactory system. It had been difficult to enforce; it had produced troops of variable quality and enthusiasm; and it was hedged about by qualifications and exceptions based on local custom or contract. In the fourteenth century service remained obligatory (unless it was commuted for money); but whereas previously wages were generally due only to those who were serving far from their homes or beyond their customary time, they were now due to all troops throughout the campaign. The result was to create armies which were larger, better disciplined and more enthusiastic, but also a great deal more expensive.

What was wanting was an ordered system of national taxation. The nearest that the French government approached to such a thing in the early fourteenth century was the system for taxing the Church, admittedly by far the largest and richest landowner of the realm. The French Church was regularly taxed with the consent of ecclesiastical councils or (more commonly) of the Pope. Whichever method was chosen the great advantage of ecclesiastical taxation was that there was no need for any further consent. Usually the tax was conscientiously paid, and it made a variable but regular contribution to the royal budget, amounting during the 1320s to about a fifth of receipts.[25] Most of the royal revenues, however, necessarily came from laymen and there was no system at all for taxing them, but only a succession of haphazard expedients.

There were halting attempts at improvement before the storm broke. Civil lawyers had for many years been advancing the theory that because the King had a public duty to safeguard the interests of the realm he might levy taxes by public right from all his subjects. The great moral philosopher Thomas Aquinas had reached the same conclusion by a different route. In his opinion taxes levied at moderate rates were always permissible when 'an unforeseen situation arises and it is necessary to increase expenditure in the common interest, or to preserve the dignity of the court if the ordinary revenues and taxes are not enough.'[26] Not many Frenchmen, however, would have agreed, and the practice was certainly very different. The orthodox view was that the King could demand 'aid' on his own knighthood or that of his son and on the marriage of his daughter, but that was all. Even these could only be levied of the King's own direct vassals. When Philip the Fair attempted, on his own knighthood in 1285, to collect from his subjects generally there were vigorous and on the whole successful protests. Money collected from rear-vassals was returned.[27]

A more promising line was taken during the Flemish wars. After the rebellion of Bruges in 1302 Philip revived the ancient military summons known as the *arrière-ban*. Drawing on an ill-defined but incontestable right of earlier kings, he summoned to the army at Arras 'all manner of men noble or not noble whether holding of ourselves or of other lords.'[28] Philip had no desire to see the whole nation in arms assembled at Arras. The nobility was expected to furnish cavalry. Selected contingents of non-nobles, drawn mainly from the towns, were required to fight as archers or infantrymen. The rest were expected to buy exemption at a price of 2 per cent of their property or more if the collectors could exact it. The yield was gratifyingly large. The experiment was therefore repeated in the following year and again in 1314. The proclamation of the *arrière-ban* began to assume a powerful psychological significance as marking the moment when war began in earnest. But resistance to it, or at least to its financial implications, grew. Noblemen could not be made to pay. They were entitled to fight in person with their retinues in order to keep status and earn wages of war. Moreover, they looked to their subjects to contribute to their considerable expenses and objected to their impoverishment by the King's collectors. Many of the towns felt that they had discharged their duty to the defence of the realm by repairing and defending their own ramparts. Others were unwilling to recognize a summons to defend some far-off region of France from perils which were no concern of theirs. Moreover, it proved difficult to revive the *arrière-ban* without reviving the nice legal distinctions which went with it. One of these was that the device could be used only when war had already begun. Preparation for war, however imminent, required other sources of revenue. The King could never plan far ahead.

In the face of these difficulties Philip responded on several occasions by simply demanding his subjects' property on the ground that he needed it. Those who asked for better reasons were told, like the clergy of Tours in 1305, that they were part of the body politic of the realm, that they owed it to their fellows to contribute to the common interest, and that they might pay their money or have it taken from them by force.[29] In general, however, the King did not levy taxation without at least the semblance of consent from his subjects. This was not a constitutional scruple. He had no choice. Without it no tax could in practice have been collected. The state did not have enough information to assess each subject, nor the officials and soldiers who would have been required to levy a compulsory tax against the vigorous opposition of tax-payers. Noblemen assessed themselves when they paid tax at all. Taxes on towns were collected by the townsmen. Duties on the transactions of Lombard merchants were enforced by the Lombards. Since the King could not do without the co-operation of the tax-payers, there was plenty of room for negotiation about the terms and amount of every assessment. In this haggle for countless individual consents, the King's hand was not a strong one. Consent could be delayed even if it was forthcoming in the end. But the King had probably raised his army already. He needed the money immediately and could not afford to delay its collection by appearing unreasonable or tyrannical. This was why Philip's officials were instructed to approach tax-payers with 'douces paroles et suasions', to point out to them how great was the King's need, how modest were the demands made of the poor and how just the impositions on the rich.[30] Yet if these blandishments failed to win consent, there was very little that could be done about it. The name of the recalcitrant baron or city would be recorded and the opportunity of visiting the King's disfavour upon them might soon afterwards arise. But on the other hand it might not.

It was necessary to soften such obduracy by propaganda. Pamphlets and proclamations explained the justice of the King's cause in his disputes with the Flemings or the Pope. Assemblies drawn from the towns and provinces of the realm were summoned to be harangued by ministers about the government's policies and needs. There is a detailed account of one of these assemblies, which met in 1314 in the royal palace in Paris on the occasion of a renewed crisis in Flanders. Enguerran de Marigny reviewed the whole history of the King's dealings with the Flemings and explained the need for the new tax. When he had finished, the King rose from his seat to see which of those present would decline to help him. One of the richest citizens of Paris promised, in a carefully managed intervention, that those present would each help according to their means.[31] Yet like its predecessors, this assembly had come only to listen. They had no power to bind their constituents. Their approval was simply another argument available to the collectors on their travels. There was still the interminable round of negotiations with every baron and city of the kingdom. After the crisis had passed in September 1314 it proved increasingly difficult to collect the tax. The consuls of Nîmes would not pay anything, even after being imprisoned for their obstinacy. In October the tax was being remitted in much of southern France. In November it was cancelled altogether. Yet the King had already committed himself to the expenditure.

In the Iberian kingdoms, in Sicily, in parts of Germany and above all in England Parliamentary assemblies with power to bind the nation had made possible the slow development of a system of national taxation, thereby improving immeasurably the financial situation of their governments. But what was possible in small, relatively homogeneous and centralized societies was less easy in a large and diverse country like France. It was the country in which representative assemblies appeared latest and developed least. The ultimate outcome was that the kings dispensed with representative institutions, levying taxes by prerogative alone. The absolutism of the seventeenth century was born in the fourteenth. But these were distant consequences. The immediate result was to paralyse the French government at every moment of crisis. The King's capacity to tax his subjects always depended on his personal prestige and on the strength of his political position at the time. Philip the Fair could get away with much in the 1290s which proved impossible in his later years. When the news of his disastrous defeat at Courtrai in 1302 spread through the French provinces it became necessary to increase sharply the exemption limits of the property tax in order for it to be collected at all.[32] In this way, defeat fed on defeat and minor reverses provoked catastrophe.

To stave off bankruptcy, the government was driven to a variety of short-term expedients: cynically contrived confiscations of rich private fortunes; more looting of unpopular minorities; the succession of confiscations from the Jews before they were finally expelled in 1306, the arrests of Lombard and Cahorsin usurers, the dissolution of the Templars and the sequestration of their assets; almost every year huge and more or less forced loans; and the ruthless use of royal justice for financial ends by sending commissioners round the provinces of the royal domain researching into the myriad minor infractions of the law which might justify the imposition of a fine or the sale of a pardon.

Even graver in its consequences for the internal well-being of France was the King's manipulation of the coinage, which was becoming one of the principal sources of war finance. The technique was to reissue the coinage from time to time at a new value (generally lower) fixed by decree, thereby making work for the King's mints. At the same time the *monnayage* (the difference between the face value of the coins and their intrinsic silver value) was increased so as to generate large coinage profits. Repeated devaluations between 1295 and 1306 reduced the silver value of the coinage by about two-thirds. The yield was enormous. At one point in the 1290s the profits of the royal mints supplied two-thirds of the treasury's receipts and filled most of the deficit caused by the war with England. In strict legal theory Philip was probably right in believing that the coinage was the personal property of the King, with which he could do as he pleased. His dealings with the coinage were, however, for all practical purposes a tax but without the need for consent and without the same difficulties of collection. They also caused great distress to those who lived on fixed incomes measured in money of account, including much of the nobility. They added to the existing strains on the French economy. And they provoked intense hatred of the government. Philip temporarily abandoned the device in 1306 under pressure from the Church. But it was too valuable a source of emergency finance to be forgotten. There was another devaluation in 1311. In 1313, with the onset of a fresh crisis in Flanders, the *monnayage* rose to more than 30 per cent, its highest rate ever.[33]

Philip the Fair died in November 1314. His reign had brought the French state to the zenith of its power but also to the limits of its capacities. Already in the weeks before his death aristocratic leagues had formed throughout northern and central France to resist the loss of their exemptions and privileges to an expansive government. In Burgundy, the leaders of the local nobility joined with the higher clergy and the representatives of the towns to press their grievances. They formed a permanent organization with regular meetings, officers and a standing committee. They concluded alliances as between sovereign states with similar associations in other provinces stretching across France north of the capital: Champagne, the Beauvaisis, Artois and some regions of Picardy. The men of Normandy organized themselves independently. In the Midi, leagues were formed in Languedoc and the Rouergue. The encroachments of the royal courts, the exactions of royal tax collectors and the proclamation of the *arrière-ban* to their vassals were prominent among the lists of grievances which these bodies presented to Philip's successor, Louis X. His short reign (1314–16) was almost wholly devoted to submitting to their demands in a succession of placatory charters of privilege. He promised to return to the stable currency of St Louis after the unscrupulous manipulations of the past two decades; the number of royal officers in provinces would be reduced; the encroachments of the King's judges on the surviving seigneurial jurisdictions would cease; taxes would be levied only in cases of urgent need; in Burgundy the King's servants were even to swear to observe the charter and his subjects dispensed from the duty to obey them if they did not. The dead King's principal advisers were thrown into prison and their wealth distributed among the princes of the royal court. Enguerran de Marigny was hanged from the common gibbet at Montfaucon. Assertive governments are rarely popular, but there was more to the protests of the nobility than surly resentment of the constraints of law. The rebellions of 1314 and 1315 opened an age of tension between the Crown and the most significant of its subjects, intensified by the prolonged wars and internal crises of the fourteenth century.

The nobility was a large, amorphous section of the population comprising probably between 1 and 2 per cent of French households. In principle it was clear who was noble and who was not. The nobility consisted of the whole chivalrous class: men defined by their military purpose, the elite of heavy cavalrymen who fought as knights and the much larger number who were qualified to become knights by their fortune, by their way of life, and above all by their birth. Beaumanoir, writing in the 1280s, already regarded nobility as the privilege of those who inherited it 'like kings, dukes, counts and knights', an almost closed caste. The financial officials of the monarchy took the same view, for narrow fiscal reasons. But lawyers habitually deal in absolutes. At the margins distinctions were blurred. Noblemen fell on hard times and could no longer afford the visible marks of their status. 'There are plenty of men, noble by descent', as the Chambre des Comptes informed collectors in 1318, 'who have been living for many years as merchants dealing in cloth, grain, wine, and other goods, or have taken up trade and become skinners, ropemakers, tailors or the like.' Other noble families became extinct, victims of high mortality and low fertility or casualties of war. The best available statistical evidence suggests that more than half of all noble families died out in the male line every century. They were replaced by parvenus: men ennobled for services or money by the king or one of the great princes; or who simply acquired fiefs and began in the fullness of time to call themselves nobles and to be recognized as such. The myths of nobility survived: the new men naturally conformed to them.[34]

There was not much in common between the Count of Champagne, whose income in the late thirteenth century was more than 40,000 *l.t.* per year, and the man with the 200 *l.t.* per year regarded as the bare minimum to support the estate of knighthood.[35] One of the things, however, which almost all of the nobility had in common was that they were encountering mounting financial difficulties from the second half of the thirteenth century onward, difficulties which were mainly attributable to the problems of the French agricultural economy but which the government exacerbated. The pressure on them came from several sources. In almost every case they suffered from a severe and continuous rise in their cost of living. A man-at-arms had to equip himself. He needed up to six warhorses depending on his rank. Apart from his lance, he needed a sword, a helmet and body armour, the latter increasingly expensive as plate armour replaced leather and mail. He needed a crew of attendants to ride with him into battle or to tournaments in peacetime. He needed the leisure to practise his skills, which meant employing expensive servants and administrative staff. Moreover, his way of life, particularly in the upper reaches of the aristocracy, had become progressively more expensive even in peacetime. The great noblemen maintained town houses, employed enormous retinues, travelled incessantly, adorned themselves and their ladies with beautiful jewellery, entertained splendidly. When they died they left directions for tremendous funerals, and wills which beggared their heirs by extravagant bequests to the Church. On the whole the resources of these men were efficiently administered by professionals and they were more successful than any other class of French society (except the Church) in raising their incomes to meet their growing expenditure. But, even so, the dukes of Burgundy were obliged to pledge part of their revenues to moneylenders from Italy or Cahors. Robert II of Burgundy (d.1306) haggled with his Jewish creditors in person. Philip the Fair's brother Charles of Valois (d.1325), who regularly overspent his large income by a substantial margin, borrowed from several hundred sources including the King, the Lombards, the Templars, the Jews and numerous French usurers. The Count of Flanders, Louis of Nevers, was reported in 1332 to be spending money at the rate of 80,000 *l.t.* a year and to have accumulated debts of 342,000 *l.t.*[36]

The lot of lesser men was worse. Their style of life was no doubt more modest, but they too wished to stand out in their smaller communities. They did not have the ear of the great when they needed protection from their creditors and they were not in a position, as Charles of Valois and the dukes of Burgundy were, to obtain lucrative gifts and favours from the Crown in their moments of embarrassment. Moreover their standards of estate management were lower and their capital minimal. No class of rural society had benefited less from the agricultural boom of the thirteenth century than these minor noblemen who had once been its leaders. Their main problem had been the smallness of their holdings, the result of generations of pious bequests and family partitions. Primogeniture was never rigidly applied even in the west and north of France, where it was theoretically the rule of law. Elsewhere, it was not even accepted in principle. As a result, by the beginning of the fourteenth century the holdings of much of the lesser nobility had been reduced to barely workable parcels. Inflation and the devaluation of the coinage completed the disaster. Some of these men mortgaged their land for ready money, availing themselves of a privilege which the law was just beginning to devise for men in their plight. Others sold out to rich peasants or the proprietors of the neighbouring great estates. In the Ile de France the number of seigneurial families had been dwindling for more than a century, their lines extinguished or their sons merged with the peasantry about them, as the pressures of falling income and rising expenditure intensified. Of the noble vassals of the Parisian abbeys and the Crown (the only ones of which much is known) at least a quarter had an annual income of less than ten *livres*, which was approximately the price of a barrel of wine.[37] The jurist

Beaumanoir survived by taking service in a great household. He might, like many of his age and class, have entered the service of the King or the Church, or embarked on the degrading search for minor heiresses among the bourgeoisie of the towns. In the century to come the survivors of this pauperized gentry would turn to war for their living and finally to brigandage.

On the face of it the nobility achieved nothing by the rebellions of 1314 and 1315. Within three years their impetus had failed and Louis X's concessions stood as mere statements of good intention which were only occasionally observed. Although Louis was constrained to remove many of the professional civil servants who had been prominent in the government of his predecessor, his two brothers who reigned between 1316 and 1328 were advised by men of very much the same kind except that experience taught them caution.

Nevertheless the anger and frustration of a whole class made its mark on the government, which lost some of its former self-confidence. One consequence was that the creation of a proper system of taxation was postponed for more than three decades until it was forced on government and people alike by the prospect of military catastrophe. The King's need for new sources of regular income was as great as ever, but for the moment the means of satisfying it were beyond reach. Although Louis X's campaign against the Flemings in 1315 enjoyed widespread support, the tax which was expected to pay for it was a failure. Four years later Philip V had the same experience when he tried to make war in Flanders. In 1321 he asked for a subsidy to enable him to strengthen the administration of his domain and carry out a number of eminently sensible internal reforms. In spite of the careful preparation of public opinion it was almost everywhere refused. When the great war with England began in 1337 there had been no general taxation in France for eight years. Since the government had to be carried on, there was an even heavier reliance on windfall sources of revenue than hitherto. In particular the kings were obliged to return to the coinage policy of Philip the Fair when they came under the same financial pressures as he had. Charles IV financed his wars with England much as his father had done thirty years earlier. Philip VI, during the first decade of the Hundred Years War, was to preside over an abuse of the coinage worse than any for which his predecessors had been responsible.

The leagues of 1314 revealed another abiding weakness of France when they formed themselves by provinces. Provinces long engulfed by the expansion of the royal domain remained nations in themselves, sustained by traditions rooted in recent history and geographical fact. Paris was infinitely remote from most of France at a time when a mounted messenger could cover only 30 miles a day in the best conditions. Convention and conservatism isolated these communities even when geography did not. Strangers were to be ejected from parish churches, as the statutes of provincial synods never ceased to declare. Villagers marked out their territory with rows of stakes and crosses. Beyond these frontiers, there lay the cathedral city, the market town, the shrine of a local saint, little else. In the larger towns the government's views on matters of state could sometimes be discovered from the loyal sermons which the clergy were required to deliver at moments of political crisis. News of national events filtered through slowly, often in garbled form. It was not enough to create a sense of national community in a territory divided by the varied custom of a dozen regions and the charters of privilege of several hundred towns, a territory without a common coinage, a common law or a common language. These divisions were less formidable in 1328 than they had been. But a bishop of Viviers could still threaten to disinherit his nephews if they spoke French instead of the 'language to which I was born and my father before me'. Pope John XXII was born in Cahors, was educated at Orléans and reigned in Avignon, but he was nevertheless unable to understand a letter which the King had addressed to him in French.[38]

A nation, according to the eighteenth-century authors of the dictionary of the Académie Française, meant 'all the inhabitants of a single state living in the same territory, under the same laws and speaking the same language.' By that test France was not a nation in 1328. A loyal servant like Guillaume de Nogaret, steeped in the statist traditions of Roman law, might declare his willingness to die 'for king and fatherland',[39] but in the Midi where he was born the idea would have struck most people as over-zealous. In this and other regions of France, effective government by the King was too fresh an experience. When political crisis weakened the government's hand, there was little that sentiment could achieve. Why should the inhabitants of Poitou or the Rouergue pay for the quarrels of a Parisian king with the Count of Flanders? Why should they concern themselves about his wars with the King of England until they were themselves engulfed by them?

There remained, moreover, three provinces of France where differences of culture and tradition corresponded to marked political divisions. Flanders, Brittany and Aquitaine were the last survivors of the large feudal principalities which had once covered most of France. They were no longer organized on feudal lines. Resourceful local dynasties had created in them miniature states modelled on the government of the Capetians themselves, weakened certainly by their status as vassals of the French crown but for many purposes independent of it. The men of these three provinces were the principal actors and victims of the Hundred Years War. Their existence posed in its most acute form the problem of the French Crown and explains much that seems extraordinary in the unconcern with which many Frenchmen viewed the occupation of parts of their country by English armies.

'There is no doubt', a lawyer wrote in 1341 about Brittany, 'that the duchy was once a kingdom and still enjoys the status of a kingdom in its subjects' eyes.'[40] Assembled from the ruins of the Angevin empire after the defeat of King John, Brittany owed its strength and independence to the four counts who had ruled it between 1213 and 1305. Between them these men had dispossessed the independent lords of the north and west of Brittany, whose lands they had annexed to their own domains. By purchase and by conquest they had made themselves the direct lords of most of their territory. They had established a centralized administration based on local officials supervised by a tight-knit body of lawyers and bureaucrats. The comital council held formal judicial sessions which were soon to be dignified by the portentous title of 'Parlements'. This elaborate and expensive government was financed partly by the efficient exploitation of the Count's personal domain and partly by selling certificates in the Atlantic ports of France which exempted the holders from the Count's right to claim their cargoes if they should be wrecked on the rocky Breton foreshore. By the beginning of the fourteenth century the system had become in effect a toll levied on the seaborne trade of the Atlantic coast, a regular source of wealth which had made the counts of Brittany far more important than their small, relatively poor territory might have warranted. Philip the Fair recognized their achievement in 1297 when he endeavoured to draw them more deeply into the business of his court by elevating them to the status of dukes and peers of France.

During the thirteenth century the French government made occasional attempts to encroach on the autonomy of the Breton state. Philip himself attempted to levy taxes within the duchy. He purported to nominate bishops to Breton sees. Moreover there was a tendency for the royal *baillis* of Tours and Coutances to hear Breton disputes and for the Parlement of Paris to hear Breton appeals. These attempts were resented by the dukes, who treated appeals by their subjects to the King's courts as acts of rebellion. But because Philip the Fair was unwilling to take on Brittany as well as Flanders and Aquitaine, the dukes were able to arm themselves with charters excluding the jurisdiction of the Parlement. By comparison with other French princes, their efforts to preserve the autonomy of their courts were remarkably successful. By 1328, the French Crown exercised practically no direct jurisdiction in Brittany.

Between Brittany and England there were ancient connections which made the dukes uncertain friends of France for all their exalted status in the French peerage. It could scarcely have been otherwise, their geographical situation being what it was. It was not only that England was an important market for Breton exports, principally salt, canvas and cloth, nor even that the duchy lay across the communications between England and Aquitaine. As earls of Richmond in Yorkshire the princes of the ducal house were entitled to a place in the scheme of English politics. They had held estates scattered across England from Durham to East Anglia ever since William the Conqueror had granted them to Alan of Brittany for his services in the invasion of 1066. These estates yielded an income which cannot be quantified but probably exceeded the revenues of their Breton domains.[41] Members of the ducal family were frequent and welcome visitors at the English court. John of Brittany, the uncle of the Duke, who held the honour of Richmond from 1305 until his death in 1334, had passed most of his life in the service of the kings of England. He sat in the House of Lords; he took a prominent part in the civil wars of the reign of Edward II; he fought with English armies in Scotland and led them in Aquitaine against the generals of Philip the Fair; he stood godfather to the future Edward III. Few of his family identified themselves so completely with the political causes of England, but they maintained an ambivalent position which was almost as helpful to successive English governments.

In Flanders, conditions were quite different from those which prevailed in Brittany. An advanced industrial economy made the northern county a more tempting prize, and the social conflict which went with it made it an easier one. But it had in common with Brittany a close dependence upon England which gave it an interest of its own in the Anglo-French war. The counts of Flanders had been allies of the kings of England as often as they had quarrelled with those of France; Guy of Dampierre, who became count in 1280, was a pensioner of Edward I. Yet the bonds between the two countries were stronger than these friendships of momentary convenience. Ever since the industrialization of Flanders in the twelfth century, England had supplied almost all the raw wool used in the looms of Flanders, and had bought back some of the finished product. The political leverage which this circumstance conferred upon the English kings was well understood by them. Since the beginning of the thirteenth century economic sanctions had been England's principal means of bringing pressure to bear on the population of France's richest province. The threat of confiscating the large stocks of Flemish merchants in England had been enough, in 1208, to wrest the alliance of Saint-Omer, Ghent, Bruges, Lille, Douai and Ypres from the King of France. In 1270 there was a veritable trade war between England and Flanders. The English government was well enough pleased with the results to renew them in the 1290s and later during the reign of Edward II, when Flanders next wavered between England and France in a quarrel with which it had no direct concern.[42] It was above all the individual artisans, laid off at each shortage or forced to pay high prices for scarce wool, who felt the effects. After the urban revolutions of the early fourteenth century these men could not be taken for granted, and their influence was increasingly thrown into the scales on the English side.

Sustained by the industrial wealth of the great cloth towns, the counts of Flanders had long conducted their own foreign policy, married into the royal families of Europe, led crusading expeditions to the Middle East and maintained themselves in royal state. Like the dukes of Brittany, they had aped the administrative practices of the Capetians, ruling through local *baillis* and a council of professional accountants, lawyers and administrators which also acted as the highest court of appeal. Their resources ought to have guaranteed them success. But their efforts, unlike those of the dukes of Brittany, were defeated by rival ambitions within their own family and by social conflict outside it. The kings of France watched their opportunities well. The royal *bailli* of Vermandois, based at Laon, and his colleague at Amiens made it their business to supervise almost every apsect of the Count's government. They intervened incessantly in the working of the Count's courts, issuing peremptory instructions through officials as lowly as the Provost of Saint-Quentin and even, on occasion, through ordinary sergeants. In 1289 Philip the Fair went so far as to command that litigation in the Count's courts be conducted in French instead of Flemish when his officials were present 'so that they may be able to send us accurate reports of the proceedings.'[43]

More dangerous than mere inquisitiveness was the King's alliance with the patrician oligarchies of the towns whose pretensions the counts had sought to restrain by championing the cause of the common citizens. In 1289 the town council of Ghent carried its opposition to the Count to the point of lodging an appeal with the Parlement of Paris, an act which in one of the great self-governing fiefs still amounted to rebellion in the eyes of its ruler. The lodging of the appeal immediately placed the town under

Philip's protection. He appointed a guardian. The fleur-de-lys was raised above the highest belfry of the town. Royal troops were sent to protect the appellant burgesses. The Count's jurisdiction was temporarily suspended. Other towns and even discontented individuals followed suit. Guy of Dampierre found himself summoned to the Parlement to account for himself before a self-important gathering of low-born lawyers.

In Flanders the conflict between burgeoning royal absolutism and the independence of the surviving princely fiefs was to be resolved by battle. In Brittany and Aquitaine there was a continued attempt to resolve it by diplomacy and by the incessant argument of moot points in the Parlement of Paris. The rival rhetoric of feudal rights and public law obscured the fact that the three territorial princes of western France were seeking to achieve exactly the same object locally as the King nationally, and by very similar methods. They wanted to replace the masaic patterns of overlapping rights and duties within their principalities by a single public authority vested in themselves. The King wished to apply the same principles to them. These dissonant ambitions could not exist together. In regions endowed with geographical unity, local languages and law and the tradition of political independence, the ultimate consequence of what the territorial princes were doing was the secession of their territories from the kingdom of France. This indeed is what happened in Flanders in the early part of the Hundred Years War and again in the fifteenth century.

The Hundred Years War was more than a war of nations. Its roots lay in the internal policy of France. The three principalities of the Atlantic coast, one of which was ruled by the King of England and other two bound to England by political convenience and economic interest, were not only the bridgeheads by which the English entered France. They were the parties to a French civil war in which ancient territories sought to challenge the imposing constitutional edifice which the French kings had begun to erect in the twelfth and thirteenth centuries. They were aided in their adventure by shifting coalitions of lesser noblemen and a few greater ones in the French interior who seized the occasion to escape from the constrictions of poverty and bureaucratic centralization. It is only in retrospect that the attempt seems foredoomed to failure. AT the time it very nearly succeeded. As it was, the creation of a unitary French state was postponed for a hundred years and was even then achieved only at the expense of appalling destruction and suffering.

CHAPTER II

The England of Edward III

In 1327, when Edward III came to the throne, England and France were nations growing apart. The Norman conquest and the century of aristocratic immigration which followed it had impressed England with the stamp of French manners and French institutions and had given it a governing class which was as much at home in France as in England. The barons who told King John in 1204 that their hearts were with him even if their bodies were beyond the Channel with his enemies had put their finger on an important truth: most Anglo-French wars before the middle of the thirteenth century had something of the character of civil wars.[1] A hundred years later, this was no longer true. The last important wave of French immigrants had been the contemporaries of Simon de Montfort, a minor nobleman from the forest of Rambouillet who died in 1265 fighting in an English civil war. Some Englishmen still had important interests in France in the following century. Aymer de Valence, Earl of Pembroke, took his name from the city on the Rhône, held extensive lands in central France and twice married into the families of important French noblemen. In the last decade of his life he visited France at least ten times. A few French laymen and a larger number of French monasteries still owned significant estates in England. It was the pattern of the past age.

A strong sense of national identity already existed when Edward began to rule. The sons of great noble families received English Christian names like Edward, Humphrey and Thomas, and protested when Edward II proposed to call his heir Louis after his French uncle. The English did not like foreigners, and a crude insularity united most classes of men. There was periodic agitation against alien advisers of the King, alien merchants trading in English towns, alien clergymen provided by the Pope to English benefices, and alien priories whose members were thought to be preparing themselves to assist an invasion. Edward I adopted English national myths as official history, opening up the tomb of King Arthur and Queen Guinevere at Glastonbury in 1278 and reinterring their bones before the high altar. To the Pope, who had ventured to suggest that he had no claim to Scotland, Edward addressed a short history of Britain beginning with its occupation by refugees of Troy in the time of the prophets Eli and Samuel. Much of this was wartime propaganda, but myths are propagated because the audience is believed to be receptive. Edward must have thought that he was striking a responsive note when in 1295 he accused the French King of planning to eradicate the English language. He was almost certainly right.[2]

Language was an important symbol. According to Froissart it was a well-known trick of English diplomats to evade embarrassing questions by pretending not to understand them.[3] But how far was this pretence, and how far was it the undiplomatic reality? Earlier generations of the nobility and higher clergy would have spoken French as a matter of course. However, surviving handbooks of French grammar suggest that, even among the well-born, French was an acquired language in England by the end of the thirteenth century. Although it remained the language of public affairs for another half-century it was already, long before Chaucer, spoken after the school of Stratford-at-Bow. English had become the language of prayer, of business, of light reading and polite conversation.

It was not a uniform English, any more than the French of France was a uniform French. That firm patriot Ranulph Higden held it 'a marvel that the proper language of Englishmen should be made so diverse in one little isle in pronunciation'. The accent of Yorkshire and Northumberland was 'so sharp, slitting and frotting and unshaped that we southern men may that language [hardly] understand.'[4] Nevertheless, England was a small country and by continental standards a remarkably homogeneous one. Provincial differences and regional loyalties, although they undoubtedly existed, did so at a relatively superficial level: accent, dress, tenure. England's political institutions operated uniformly over almost all the country, and her politicians and administrators thought of themselves as belonging to one community. Their sense of identity was intensified by the consciousness of enemies without. The sea defined the frontiers of the kingdom on the south and east and separated it from its most powerful rivals. On the west and north it was bounded by alien societies still largely pastoral and tribal, only intermittently at peace and the object of crude contempt and venomous detestation.

It was an overwhelmingly rural society, even by comparison with France. A population of perhaps five or six million people was concentrated in the east and south Midlands, East Anglia, and in the south-east from Hampshire to Kent, regions of fertile lowland, intensively farmed. Towns were numerous but small. Even London, which was by far the largest of them and the only English town to stand comparison with the cities of continental Europe, probably had less than 50,000 inhabitants. Extensive disafforestation, a favourable climate and expert land management had brought high yields and enabled a population denser than that of France and less evenly distributed to be fed throughout the thirteenth century.

To foreigners, England sometimes seemed a land of wealth and plenty. The chronicler Jean le Bel, camping with the English army near York in 1327, 'never ceased to wonder at such abundance', a continual flow of cheap victuals from the villages around, washed down with wine brought in by sea from Gascony and the Rhine.[5] But he was fortunate and his curiosity superficial. There were great and visible fortunes. But they reflected not so much the wealth of the kingdom as its uneven distribution, which was even more marked in England than it was in France. The proprietors of the major agricultural estates had prospered mightily in the boom of the thirteenth century. They had the acreage and the capital as well as the foresight to take advantage of a revolution of land management. Their manors were surveyed and valued, increased and rounded out by judicious purchases, their rights recorded and systematically enforced, their production targets assessed and their accounts prepared and audited with minute exactness by the corps of professionals which sprang up to meet the demand from these great agricultural businesses. But the general level of prosperity was probably rather lower than it was in most parts of France. Overpopulation and intense demand for fertile land had progressively reduced the size of the smallholdings by which most Englishmen lived. In central and southern England, where the mass of the population consisted of unfree peasants, more than half of them had only the minimum acreage necessary for subsistence, or less. They survived on the uncertain chances of earning wages or by selling off small parcels of their land. The free landowners and minor gentry had fewer burdens and more land, but even they were excessively vulnerable to harvest failure, natural disaster and economic depression. Their fortunes were always delicately balanced between profit and loss.

During the first three decades of the fourteenth century the balance often failed. In 1315 and 1316 the first of a series of rural catastrophes brought famine, unemployment and epidemic disease among men and animals. A run of terrible harvests continued well into the 1320s. Stocks of sheep, cattle and plough-beasts did not recover in some areas until twenty years later. Agricultural yields began to fall. Prices and rents declined. Marginal land went out of cultivation. There were unmistakable signs of soil exhaustion. In these respects, the economic history of England mirrored that of France. Both countries entered the war with fragile economies which the opening blows shattered.

There were no great industries in England to absorb the impoverished population of the countryside as those of Flanders and northern France to some extent did. There were important deposits of coal and of metal (iron, lead and tin), but production methods were inefficient and technically backward, and the scale of operations was small. Salt-making generated a modest export trade and sea fishing supported a large number of harbours along the east and south coasts. Cloth-making, the major industrial activity carried on in England, had a bright past and future but was probably at its nadir in this period: under-capitalized, dispersed and inefficient, and driven from much of its home market by the competition of the great industrial cities of Flanders.

England's principal economic asset was wool. The country was Europe's main producer of high-grade wool. A large part of the Italian cloth industry and substantially the whole of the industries of the French and German Low Countries depended on it. The barons who told Edward I in 1297 that wool accounted for half the nation's wealth were making a political point and they were exaggerating. But it undoubtedly had a special place in English life. Sheep-farming suffered its share of misfortunes, but it sustained a large number of people, from Henry de Lacy, Earl of Lincoln, who owned 13,400 sheep in 1303, to Chaucer's 'powre widowe somdel stope in age' with just one, as well as the army of middlemen, merchants and shipowners who organized the trade. Its political importance was even greater than its economic value. Of all the diverse components of the English national income, the profits of the wool trade were the most easily diverted in the government's interest. Wool was a bulky commodity which was collected for export in a small number of ports. Its immediate destination could be controlled so as to cut out the King's enemies. Licences to export it could be sold for cash grants or loans on favourable terms. Without an excessively large bureaucracy it could be exorbitantly taxed, or compulsorily purchased and exported for the King's account. For a short period in the 1290s and again after 1337, English foreign policy was to be substantially financed by one and sometimes all of these devices.

In the thirteenth century England's foreign trade had been almost entirely controlled by foreigners. The wool trade had been dominated by the great Flemish merchants and the bankers of Lucca and Florence, who alone had the capital to finance the export of large cargoes and their distribution on the continent. But by the end of the century, Edward I's numerous trade wars in Flanders had more or less squeezed out the Flemings. The Italians survived but in conditions which were increasingly unfavourable to them. At the time of Edward III's accession, the business was gradually being gathered into the hands of privileged companies of English merchant capitalists who flourished as never before in an age when the King's licence was the basic instrument of commerce. Their rise to fortune is chronicled in the customs records. The accounts of the customs of Hull for 1275–6, an isolated survival, showed that less than 4 per cent of what left England from this important wool port had been exported by Englishmen; but between 1304 and 1311 the average proportion was more than 14 per cent, and between 1329 and 1336 it was nearly 90 per cent. It was at this place and in these years that William Pole, 'second to no merchant in England and first citizen of Hull' accumulated the fortune that made him one of Edward III's foremost bankers and war contractors and his descendants earls of Suffolk until 1504, the oldest English noble house to have been built on mercantile wealth.[6]

The takeover of English commercial life by native businessmen was a general phenomenon of the early fourteenth century marked out in the case of wool only by the speed and completeness with which it happened. It was part of the process by which against a dismal economic background industrial and commercial wealth was progressively concentrated in fewer hands, just as for quite different reasons the profits of agriculture had been for more than a century. John Pulteney, draper, wool trader, urban land-lord, four times Mayor of London, and sometime war financier, had begun life as the son of an obscure Sussex squire, but when he died in 1349 he owned twenty-three manors in five counties. He built Penshurst Place in Kent and owned two palaces in London, one of which was subsequently the city residence of the Prince of Wales. Pulteney's loans to Edward III more than justified the knighthood and royal pension conferred on him in 1337. Men like him had an important place in the financial manipulation which was becoming a normal part of the financing of war.

The English constitution already revealed its characteristic division between form and substance. 'The best-governed land in the world' was what Froissart said about England.[7] The institutions of the English state were outwardly impressive. The country had been governed as one territo-rial unit since the eleventh century. There was a highly developed notion of public authority, the right of the state as such being acknowledged in theory long before it received any measure of recognition by public opinion in France. In dealing with rebels, spies and traitors the English kings resorted to the state trial and the horrible penalties of treason long before these became regular spectacles in France. Their authority was not limited to the King's domain or to his own immediate tenants, but in principle extended to all places and men. The common law was common to all England. The King's courts at Westminster and those of his itinerant justices in the counties were open to all free men, and some matters were reserved to them exclusively. These included civil litigation about the possession of freehold land, by far the commonest source of civil dispute and disorder, and most prosecutions for crimes of violence.

The principal organs of the state were the Chancery and the Exchequer. They had existed in a recognizable form for two centuries when Edward III came to the throne and had reached a high degree of bureaucratic perfection. The Chancery, in England as in France, acted as the secretariat for most operations of government. Its executive staff consisted of a body of long-serving clergymen with a strong professional *esprit de corps*, many of whom were protégés of a particular chancellor, living in his house and receiving robes, board and lodging from him. Individual Chancery clerks developed specialized functions and expertise, for example in the field of diplomacy. A few achieved positions of much inconspicuous influence. The Exchequer was the audit department of the state to which all spending and collecting officials were eventually called to account. Neither of these great offices was concerned with what might be called politics. They never achieved the pervasive, autonomous influence or the remarkable sense of direction of the French bureaucracy. Their strength was that they were meticulous and accurate and no more cumbersome than they had to be in an age of slow communications.

Like the principal departments of the French government they had become larger and more immobile. When the Exchequer was moved to York during the Scotch wars of the 1330s, fifty carts were needed to bring it back again. The exercise was not repeated. A mile from London across open country, suburban gardens and a few grand mansions, a capital was forming within the walled enclosures of the abbey and palace of Westminster. In William Rufus's Great Hall clerks transacted the administrative business of the Chancery around a long marble table, the noise competing with that of the King's Bench and the court of Common Pleas a few yards away. In two small buildings off, the Exchequer made up its accounts on the great checkered tablecloth that gave the department its name. Outside, a spreading suburb housed the ephemeral population of lawyers, suitors, litigants and officials.

The political functions of the government were concentrated in the royal household, a mobile city of constantly changing population which lodged wherever the King was. In the Council the King had a small body of personal advisers: the Chancellor, the principal household officers, the more influential of the King's retained knights and confidential clerks, all of them men who owed their position to his friendship. Their numbers were swollen as the occasion required by experts from lower down the bureaucratic hierarchy and by bishops and nobleman from outside it whose opinion was valued or feared. These last became distinctly more numerous and influential during the reign of Edward III, who attached more importance than his father and grandfather had done to involving the great of the land in his affairs. Even in his reign, however, government was conducted on an intimate scale, dependent on the King's personality and on his energy. The King's private office, the Wardrobe, was the pivot of the administration. It saw to the issue of warrants under the privy seal which set in motion the distant and formal procedures of the Chancery and the Exchequer, enabling the King to govern from his tent. In periods of crisis and war, the Wardrobe became the main spending department, collecting money directly from customs posts, royal manors, collectors of the Parliamentary subsidies, or wherever else it could be found, and dispensing it under the immediate control of the King.

The main strength and weakness of the English state lay in the provinces, where most of its measures had perforce to be applied, where taxes were raised and soldiers recruited. England had an ancient system of local government, more elaborate than that of France and penetrating further into the recesses of provincial life; but it was not wholly under the King's control. In the twelfth century the kings of England had enjoyed through the sheriffs a degree of control over the affairs of each county which although imperfect was far in advance of anything to be found on the continent. Upon the sheriffs and their staff of deputies, bailiffs, jailers and clerks huddled in a wing of the royal castle by the county town, fell all the humdrum concerns of the central government in the shires: the collection of royal revenues, the execution of numberless writs, the custody of castles, the recruitment of troops, the maintenance of public order. An ordinance of 1326, inaugurating the latest unsuccessful measure of reform, recited without exaggeration that the orderly conduct of the King's government depended on the proper performance of these unglamorous functions.[8] But by now this was wishful thinking. The sheriff's grip had loosened during the thirteenth century. Many large landowners had acquired by obscure means the right to perform the sheriff's functions through their own officials within defined enclaves ('liberties'). Many towns including almost all large ones had acquired by royal grant rights of self-government which effectively removed them from the jurisdiction of the county officials. Power was fragmented. Even in the territory which was left to him, the sheriff was no longer the formidable representative of the central government which he had once been. Concessions had been made under the pressure of local opinion and recurrent political crisis. The typical sheriff of the early fourteenth century was not an experienced administrator in the confidence of the King's ministers but a local landowner with interests of his own in the county which would outlive his term of office and did not necessarily coincide with those of the government. He received no salary from the Crown but drew his remuneration from traditional fees and exactions, and he often held office reluctantly. In deference to his reluctance, and to the unpopularity of any sheriff who was hardened by too much experience of office, he was soon relieved and replaced by another. Similar developments affected other local officials. They were all local men serving for short periods. Behind them stood the landowning community of the county, men linked by elaborate ties of residence, kinship and interest and by bonds of patronage. They gathered at periodic meetings of the county court to transact the judicial business of the county, and see to the election of coroners and Parliamentary knights, the swearing in of local officials, the reading out of statutes and royal proclamations, the assessment of contributions to the county's expenses and increasingly the airing of collective opinions and grievances. They were a political community.

None of this meant that local government was free of central control, but it did mean that that control was spasmodic. All local officials with financial responsibilities had to account regularly at the Exchequer and were relentlessly pursued for their deficiencies. Their more serious misdeeds and omissions could be investigated and punished by a variety of judicial commissions. At best these procedures discouraged abuses. They did not promote enthusiasm. English local officials could hardly have been less like the overburdened but zealously loyal provincial officers of the French monarchy. The difference, however, was not necessarily a disadvantage. The English King's government was heavily dependent on the support of the local communities, it is true. Their power of obstruction was enormous. But so was the support which they could bring to a government of whose enterprises they approved. At the height of their powers, Edward I and Edward III were able to draw more from their subjects than any French government of the fourteenth century. On the other hand Edward II at the nadir of his prestige could do almost nothing.

The limits of the state's power, in England as in France, depended ultimately on money. The ordinary revenues of the kings of England consisted only of those which, like any nobleman, the King received as a landowner and feudal lord, and those which he derived from the operations of government such as fines and fees and the uncertain profits of the royal mints. In the 1330s these were producing between £15,000 and £20,000 a year, which was rather less than a sixth of the revenues which the kings of France drew from the same sources. They had remained more or less stable at this level since the 1280s. To some small extent the King's ordinary revenues could be increased by legal but irregular devices. The English kings did not, as the French kings did, manipulate the coinage. But they taxed the manors and towns of their demesne; they compulsorily purchased goods for their households at a low price, paid late ('purveyance'); they took money for not insisting on the more irksome obligations of their subjects. The revenues which such measures produced were uncertain and the political cost was high. As Sir John Fortescue observed in the following century, 'the greatest harm that cometh of a King's poverty is that he shall by necessity be [forced] to find exquisite means of getting goods.'[9] None of these means, however exquisite, was equal to the burden of financing an ambitious foreign policy.

What differentiated the English public finances from the French was the existence of a reasonably effective system of national taxation. The most important element of the English government's tax revenues was the customs, which were the only permanent tax levied in either realm. The so-called 'Great and Ancient Custom' was an export duty on wool, skins and hides, the major part of England's exports, which had been devised by Edward I's officials in 1275 and approved by an assembly of the merchants in the same year. A supplementary duty was levied on foreign merchants after 1303. This extended to goods of every description and to imports as well as exports. The yield of the customs varied with the state of the wool crop and the prosperity of the trade. But it was substantial and regular. In the early years of Edward III's reign the customs brought in an average of about £13,000 a year. This could be increased by supplementary grants to high levels. The normal rate was 6s. 8d. per sack, but rates exceeding £3 had been levied in the crisis of the 1290s and well over £2 was to be charged in the early part of the Hundred Years War.

In the result there was just enough to cover the ordinary peacetime operations of government. A particularly parsimonious king like Edward II in his last years could even accumulate a surplus. But there was not enough to pay for largesse on any scale nor for significant capital expenditure (for example on fortresses or ships). Faced with onerous and occasionally urgent commitments abroad and only a modest income arriving at measured intervals at home, the English kings from Edward I onwards resorted to heavy borrowing not only from their own subjects but from the nascent banking systems of Flanders, the Rhineland and above all Italy. The scale of Edward I's financial operations and the systematic way in which they were administered and secured was something new among European governments of the middle ages, foreshadowing the juggling with public credit of Renaissance and post-Renaissance states. Edward I's conquest of Wales was paid for in the first instance almost entirely by his bankers. Between 1272 and 1294 the chief of them, the Riccardi partnership of Lucca, lent him £392,000, part of which came from their own deposits and part from syndicates of lenders great and small which they organized. Of this sum nearly £19,000 was still outstanding in 1294 when the King quarrelled with them.[10] The Riccardi were the first of a succession of Italian bankers to be ruined by tying their fortunes too closely to a north European government. There were plenty of others to take their place. The Frescobaldi of Florence lent some £150,000 to Edward I and Edward II before they too were ruined in the baronial revolution of 1311.[11] They were succeeded by a Genoese, Antonio Pessagno, whose loans pound for year exceeded those of any previous creditor of the Crown. Pessagno financed the Bannockburn campaign of 1314, whose ignominious failure was certainly not due to lack of money. The Bardi of Florence, who gradually took over in the 1320s, where so closely associated with Edward II that their London headquarters was sacked by the mob in the revolution of 1326. But they were also significant creditors of his enemies, and were eventually to break themselves by their loans to his successor.

Credit operations, however sophisticated, were not a substitute for tax revenues. They were no more than a means of anticipating them. They enabled the English government to raise money faster than the French could, and they spared it the debilitating problem which successive French kings found in paying for war expenditure at a time when war taxes had still to come in. The bankers usually had to be secured by an assignment of specific revenues. The revenues of the customs were regularly assigned to the King's major creditors and their actual management and collection was on several occasions handed over to them. In the last resort, however, extraordinary expenditure could only be paid from general taxation levied on the population of England.

The machinery of assessing and collecting general taxes was orderly by the imperfect standards of the middle ages, and certainly compared well with the unpredictable and heterogeneous methods of taxation used in France. Taxes were levied as a proportion of value of each taxpayer's movable property, usually a tenth in the towns and a fifteenth in the counties. It was an arbitrary measure, but made for ease of assessment. During the early part of the Hundred Years War collection was based on a particularly careful assessment which had been carried out in 1334 by high-ranking clergymen and permanent officials, in place of the corruptible local men who had traditionally acted as assessors. The principle was to fix a sum as the King's due from each community, leaving local men to apportion the burden among themselves, a method which for all its vices in other directions had the advantage of producing a reasonably predictable yield. There were few exemptions: the Cinque Ports, which did naval service in lieu; the palatine counties of Chester and Durham, which were taxed by their proprietors; the spiritual endowments of the clergy, which were separately taxed by the authority of the Pope or the Convocations of the two ecclesiastical provinces.

General taxation could not be levied at will in England any more than it could in France. It was an emergency measure for which it was necessary to obtain the consent of the community of the realm. The twelfth article of Magna Carta provided: 'No tax is to be levied in our realm except by the common counsel of our realm.' It is true that it was the duty of subjects to assist the King once he had demonstrated (in the time-honoured phrase) the 'evident and urgent necessity' of their doing so. However, what was necessary was a matter on which opinions could and did differ. Taxation was refused for more than twenty years in the reign of Henry III until the King's government was bankrupt. In 1297 the attempt of Edward I to collect a tax with nothing more than the support of his Council provoked one of the seminal constitutional crises of the late middle ages. 'Some people of our kingdom', Edward declared when he capitulated to the opposition in October 1297, 'are fearful that the aid and taxes which they had paid to us out of liberality and goodwill, and because of our wars and other needs, may in future become a servile obligation for them and their heirs.'[12] That was indeed the fear, and it was what was ultimately to happen in France, but the events of 1297 showed that it was unlikely to happen in England.

The difference was that the precocious development of Parliament enabled the English kings to obtain the consent of their subjects to taxation in a form which was recognized as universally binding, and dispensed them from the need to haggle for help with one community after another as the crisis unfolded behind them. The reign of Edward I was the decisive stage in this development as it was in so much else that decided the fortunes of fourteenth-century England. At the time of his accession in 1272 Parliament had been a predominantly official body, a solemn meeting of the King's Council augmented by judges and senior civil servants and by the principal lay and ecclesiastical magnates. Its composition and most of its functions were in many respects similar to those of the Parlement of Paris. It was the pressure of Edward I's wars, the great volume of legislation and controversial public business which his abrasive government generated, and the King's insatiable need for taxes, which made it a more overtly political assembly. The dominant role was played by the Lords: some sixty earls and Parliamentary barons, twenty-one diocesan bishops and about thirty abbots (all of whom received personal summonses to attend), together with a fluctuating body of permanent councillors, generally about a dozen strong. They were the only members of Parliament whose advice was sought on matters of state. The Commons comprised the knights, usually two for each of the thirty-seven shires, and the representatives of more than seventy Parliamentary boroughs. They were a great deal less influential. They were summoned to the earliest Parliaments as mere silent witnesses of what the Lords decided on behalf of the realm and their role remained a subordinate one throughout the fourteenth century. But there was one area in which the Commons had a central role. That was the granting of taxes. By the beginning of the fourteenth century it had become recognized constitutional principle that no general subsidy could be imposed without their consent, which might be dependent on the King's willingness to grant their petitions. Their petitions, which occupied a large part of the proceedings, included not only local gripes and pleas for special interests, but complaints about royal officials, about the general condition of the realm and occasionally about the King's misgovernment of it.

In spite of the vigour of some of these complaints Edward III and his contemporaries did not look upon Parliament as a natural source of opposition. They regarded it as a source of strength, with good reason. At the end of the thirteenth century the disgruntled author of a radical tract, the *Mirror of Justices*, declared that the powers of Parliament in matters of taxation had made it a tool of oppression 'called by the King's order to enable him to exact taxes and hoard money'.[13] What this man had perceived was that Parliament was primarily an instrument of the King's will, a means of extending the power of the government from the centre to the periphery at the cost of some limitations on its freedom of action. How severe these limitations were depended on the personality of the King and on his skills as a propagandist and political manager. Edward I inaugurated a tradition of high taxation which persisted in England throughout the middle ages. He raised more than half a million pounds from Parliamentary subsidies for his wars in Wales, Scotland and Gascony. A third of this sum was voted during the crisis years between 1294 and 1297, a burden of taxation which was quite unprecedented and could not have been achieved without Parliamentary authority. By comparison Philip the Fair was having to finance the war from his side largely from the uncertain profits of coinage devaluations.

The bonds that joined Englishmen together in one community were, by contemporary European standards, very strong. Yet, in spite of these advantages, what struck foreigners most forcibly was the country's chronic political instability. The English deposed four of their kings in the fourteenth and fifteenth centuries, one of them twice. By comparison, in France the deposition of a king seems never to have been seriously contemplated, even in the case of the captive John II and the cretinous Charles VI. England was famous for the brutality and turbulence of its political life. There was no place, Froissart wrote, where the mass of men were so 'fickle, dangerous, arrogant and rebellious'. There were plenty of Englishmen who recognized this portrait as just, and some who took a perverse pride in it. 'It is not poverty that keepeth Frenchmen from rising,' thought the fifteenth-century Chief Justice Sir John Fortescue, 'but it is cowardice and lack of heart and courage, which no Frenchman hath like unto an Englishman.'[14]

Froissart, like others of his contemporaries writing at the end of the fourteenth century under the shadow of the Peasants' Revolt of 1381, attributed this to the mutual antagonisms and class hatreds of Englishmen, the first of countless foreigners over the centuries to diagnose class divisions as the source of English debility. The real problem, however, was the wide distribution of power and the divisions within the political community which exercised it. Power in England was uneasily shared between the Crown and the higher nobility of the realm, two forces which did not always work in harmony. It was the higher nobility, whose influence in Parliament was paramount, on whom the Crown depended for its ability to raise armies and levy taxation. It was on them and on their clients and allies in the shires that the Crown depended for the enforcement of its orders on the mass of the population.

The English nobility was still, in the early fourteenth century, a fluid group whose boundaries were marked by few formal distinctions. Earldoms, of which there were nine in 1331, were the only hereditary dignities until 1337, when Edward III created the first English duke. The Parliamentary peerage comprised another forty or fifty laymen who received personal writs of summons. But these summonses reflected the personal qualities of the individuals who received them and, although the list of those called became increasingly standard in the course of the century, a man called to one Parliament could not yet count on being called to the next and his heir might not be called at all. Beyond the Parliamentary baronage the nobility shaded imperceptibly into the lesser baronage and the gentry of the shires. Among this large and differentiated class of men, perhaps 150 or 200 families were identifiable, for all the difficulties of formal definition, as 'magnates' entitled to a place in the political affairs of the nation. Men used the term according to their subjective impressions, based on the three cardinal virtues of medieval nobility: ancestry, royal favour and money.

The greatest of these was money. The great lay magnates of England stood at the zenith of their economic power in the opening decades of the fourteenth century. They had been the main beneficiaries (after the Church) of the agricultural boom of the past century, and of the concentration of wealth that had gone with it. Primogeniture, still generally applied in England, had conserved their gains to a degree unthinkable in most parts of France. The minimum income necessary to support a knight was conventionally reckoned at £40 per year. By comparison the pensions which Edward III conferred on the new earls whom he created in 1337 suggested that £1,000 per annum was thought to be the least that was necessary to maintain their dignity. Most earls and a substantial number of magnates who were not earls were much richer. Thomas, Earl of Lancaster, who was certainly the richest subject of Edward II, enjoyed an annual income from land of about £11,000. 'By the size of his patrimony you may gauge his influence' was what a contemporary said about him.[15]

The household of a great nobleman was a miniature of the King's: an administrative organization directed at the centre by a tight council consisting not only of bureaucrats and professional advisers but also of those men of substance whose advice and influence were thought to be valuable. In place of the strictly feudal relationship between a great lord and his tenants (a system never perfectly in force and long since obsolete) there had grown up a network of more personal bonds based on contract and mutual self-interest, pervading the fabric of provincial life. A nobleman's contract retinue was not only, or even mainly, a private army corps, the means by which he satisfied his military obligations to the King. It was first and foremost an instrument of local government and, occasionally, of the pervasion of local government for powerful private interests. Justices of the Peace, bailiffs of liberties, members of Parliament for the shires, freeholders of the county court, commissioners for the countless occasional concerns of the Crown were all likely to be associated with an aristocratic household greater than their own. They saw to their lord's interest in their localities, and he for his part offered them the support of his other retainers in the same district as well as his own influence at court, benefits worth far more than the liveries and modest fees mentioned in the formal agreements. After the fall of Mortimer in 1330 the Gloucestershire magnate Sir Thomas Berkeley was accused by a distant cousin of stealing his cattle. There was no justice to be had in Gloucestershire, this man said, because Sir Thomas had too many friends in the county and the ear of the great minister at court. He 'would not allow the sheriff or his bailiff or other ministers to do justice, they being his retainers holding his fees and livery and being of his household'. In this sentence is summed up what mattered to contemporaries about retinues. Sir Thomas retained twelve local knights for terms of years, each of whom contracted to serve with his squires and a page, not to speak of the host of cooks, clerks, grooms, messengers and heavies. 'I am confident', declared the seventeenth-century steward who wrote the family's history from its documents, 'that the mouths of his standing house each day fed were three hundred at least.'[16]

One peculiarity of the English nobility, at least by comparison with the French, was noted by Froissart with surprise after his travels in England in the 1360s. 'The lands and revenues of the barons [he said] are scattered about from place to place.'[17] There were few exceptions. The most significant of them were the earls of Lancaster, who were the descendants of Edmund Crouchback, the youngest son of Henry III. During the half-century after Edmund's original endowment in the 1260s he and his descendants built up by purchase, exchange, inheritance and marriage a formidable block of territory in the Midlands and north-west of England and in north Wales. On account of their birth and wealth they occupied a unique place in English political life, the natural leaders of the higher nobility, and the patrons of a remarkable number of clients and protégés not only among the baronage and gentry of the provinces but in the central administration of the Crown. The earls of Lancaster, however, were in a class of their own. The only other consolidated territorial lordships of any importance were the lordships of the March of Wales whose possessors had held the border since the end of the eleventh century and who continued to enjoy a degree of political autonomy even after the conquest of Wales by Edward I had removed their original *raison d'être*. Edward II's favourite Hugh Despenser the Younger, Roger Mortimer of Wigmore, who governed England during the minority of Edward III, and Edward III's friend and contemporary Richard Fitzalan, Earl of Arundel, all passed their careers in building up powerful territorial interests in eastern and southern Wales to serve as a power-base for political activity in England. But this kind of regional empire-building was exceptional and its results usually short-lived. England had few territorial magnates after the French model. The ordinary pattern was represented by Aymer de Valence, Earl of Pembroke, who died in 1324 owning land in nineteen English counties from Northumberland to Kent, as well as in Ireland and five regions of Wales. Pembrokeshire accounted for less than a tenth of the value of his land.[18] The assets and influence of a great nobleman were likely to be distributed over a large area and in every region where he had friends so, in all probability, did his enemies.

The ablest and richest of these men were more significant forces in national politics than their counterparts would have been in France. It was not an accidental difference. The organic development of the French nation by the gradual coalescence of ancient provinces with disparate traditions had no parallel in England, where the Norman conquest had created a more or less unitary state with an alien aristocracy. The higher nobility of England could hardly ever identify their interests with those of any one region, but were bound to defend them by their influence at the centre of affairs. They readily thought in terms of national politics. So did the lesser men who, although their assets were more concentrated and their horizons closer, were bound to the political fortunes of the great. In Wales and much later on the march of Scotland distinctly regional interests did emerge and occasionally generated unrest and rebellion. But in general the political vision of the nobility, although often partial and self-serving, was not limited by provincial particularism of the kind which had destroyed the aristocratic rebellions of 1314 in France and was later to divide the French in the face of foreign invasion.

However, the interest of the English in national politics brought them into frequent conflict with the King. The baronial rebellions of the thirteenth and fourteenth centuries were much more than the coalitions of private interests which had been characteristic of the twelfth. Although greed and rancour never lost their power to provoke rebellion, during the later years of the reign of Henry III (1215–72) the leaders of the baronial opposition developed a coherent constitutional doctrine to justify their acts. 'Lex stat; rex cadit.' 'The law holds; the King falls,' as the author of a famous radical pamphlet pungently put his precocious notion of fundamental law, a body of principle binding as much on the King as on his subjects.[19] Moreover, the nobility were able to draw on a wide body of support outside their own ranks. Simon de Montfort's propagandists included some influential and articulate churchmen whose opposite numbers in France would not have dreamed of supporting a baronial putsch. The Londoners expelled the King's forces from their city, and their lead was followed in many other towns and even in quite small villages. After Prince Edward's victory over Simon de Montfort on the battlefield, the great rebel continued to enjoy a popular following. His grave became the object of a pilgrimage where 'vain and fatuous' stories of his miracles were related.[20]

This tradition of baronial populism repeatedly returned to plague Henry III's successors during the following two centuries. Edward I's skilful combination of ruthlessness and charm enabled him for twenty years to multiply his revenues by a factor of three, and to maintain huge costly and conscripted armies which he kept in the field for long periods far from home. These efforts were accompanied by an onslaught on private liberties and a great expansion of the machinery of government. Yet when it came to the point Edward's government failed as his father's had done. There was no revolution. But the war with France which began in 1294 and coincided with crises in Wales and Scotland forced him to make large concessions to a well-organized baronial opposition. Only Edward's dignity and his political talents saved him from abject humiliation. Even so, the remaining decade of his reign was soured by the resentment and suspicion of much of the nobility as well as by military stalemate in Scotland and mounting public disorder in England. The brunt of the barons' resentments were left to be borne by his son.

Edward II, who had none of his father's virtues and lacked his powerful presence, had hardly been crowned before the baronage formally asserted that rebellion was a constitutional right, not a symptom of anarchy. Their reasoning was very similar to that of their forbears in the time of Henry III. The act of allegiance, they said, bound them to the Crown and not to the person of any particular king. 'So that if, in his conduct of the Crown's business, the King is not guided by reason, his subjects are bound to guide him back to reason.' Since the King could not be challenged in his own courts it was proper to challenge him by force. In 1311, three years after this pronouncement, the greater part of the baronage imposed on Edward II by force forty-one ordinances as to the manner in which he should govern his kingdom, including one which required baronial consent for the appointment of all the principal officers of state. There were undoubtedly some who would have liked to see these measures permanently embedded in the constitution. But the unity of purpose which produced them was short-lived. The ultimate outcome in Edward II's reign was the same as it had been in Henry III's, a civil war and a royal victory in battle. The Earl of Lancaster, Edward II's principal antagonist, became a popular miracle-worker after his violent death, as Simon de Montfort had done before him, and guards had to be placed on his tomb to turn away pilgrims.[21] London did not rise in 1322 as it had done for Simon, but in the closing weeks of 1326 it exploded in a violent revolution which destroyed Edward's government. Echoes of the ideas which had justified Lancaster's rebellion and the deposition of Edward II were to be heard in 1341 and again, with refreshed violence and bitterness, during the dotage of Edward III and in the reign of his ill-starred grandson Richard II.

Edward II's victory over his enemies at the battle of Boroughbridge in 1322 gave him and his friends control over the government, but did nothing to make his power effective at a distance. A government weakened by the confrontations of thirty years could not enforce its will in the counties. An aristocracy divided by politics and the effort of self-preservation could do little to impose order upon anarchy. At the centre the formalities of justice were duly observed and the splendid system of civil and criminal courts still functioned. But mounting disorder made a mockery of them. The embers of civil war still glowed in the counties several years after the armies had dispersed. The Despensers and other favourites of the king protected bands of brigands who hunted down the remnants of the Earl of Lancaster's party. And these responded by resorting to banditry, attacking the estates of the Despensers and their friends and murdering royal servants such as Sir Roger Belers, the chief baron of the Exchequer, who was cut down by a gang of fifty men near Leicester in January 1326. In the Midlands and the West Country large, well-organized criminal bands led for the most part by dispossessed or impoverished minor gentry, engaged in highway robbery, kidnapping, extortion and murder for political ends or for the interest of anyone who cared to hire them to prosecute their private quarrels. It is some sign of the degree to which violence had tainted a generation of English gentry that of those who represented Bedfordshire in Parliament in the first decade of

Edward III's reign at least a third had previously been convicted of violent crimes ranging from housebreaking to murder. Bedfordshire was certainly not exceptional. This was the condition of England only ten years before she embarked on a major war with the principal European power.[22]

Foreign observers like Jean le Bel and Froissart, both of whom had visited England, found it hard to make sense of these events and even harder to explain how the anarchic England of Edward II became the conqueror of France under Edward III. Their explanation, that it was the chivalrous qualities and high renown of Edward III, sounds superficial. But it is substantially right. Edward III was the first English king for a century and a half to forge a close and durable bond between the Crown and the nobility. The King's personal qualities had a great deal to do with this.

For far from being a united body of natural rebels, the baronage had divergent interests and jealousies, as any group of intelligent and powerful men is bound to do. Few of them were hungry for political power or wanted to participate in the daily business of the central government. Their main interest in it was as a source of patronage. All of them depended to a greater or lesser degree on the Crown's rich store of favours: not only for gifts of money, land and revenues, but for privileges and exemptions, wardships, rich marriages, loans on favourable terms and many other valuable benefits. They needed these things not only for themselves but for their retainers, dependants and clients. It made them natural allies of the Crown. They took power out of the King's hands only when the government had manifestly broken down, as it did in the later years of Henry III; or when they conceived that power had already been taken out of his hands by others who were monopolizing his favours in their own interest, which was the substance of Gaveston's offence in the reign of Edward II. Edward II was deposed not because he was a tyrant but because, in the words of the articles of accusation against him, he was 'incompetent to govern in person'. He had been 'controlled and governed by others'. The higher nobility were remarkably consistent about this. The main source of England's political instability was not the baronage but the monarchy, which in England more often than in France fell into the hands of men incapable of controlling the elaborate and pervasive machinery of government in a manner which inspired confidence among those who depended on it and, to a substantial extent, operated it in the provinces. Edward III and that other great paradigm of medieval kingship, Henry V, were men with limited power to command who succeeded because they were their own men, and because they learned the limits of their power and knew that beyond those limits government was a matter of friendships and patronage, dependent on the reputation of the King and his skills in persuasion and bluff.

The problem for a ruler who knew the business of government was not so much the danger of rebellion as the formidable power of the nobility to resist by sheer inertia any great enterprise of the Crown. 'The baronage is the chief limb of the monarchy', an unfriendly contemporary biographer of Edward II wrote; 'without it the King can do nothing of any importance.'[23] For more than a century the principal weakness of England as a European power had been the nobility's limited interest in warfare or indeed in any aggressive foreign venture. Almost all of them had lost their own possessions in Normandy and western France in the disasters of King John's reign and none had significant interests in Gascony. They did not share the attitude of Henry III and Edward I, who had retained the outlook of great continental princes, drawing to their court friends, advisers and protégés from many countries and maintaining as best they could their claim to play a leading role in the political life of France and her neighbours. In 1242 the baronage had refused to contribute to Henry III's plans for reconquering his lost dominions in France, the last occasion before the mid-fourteenth century when this was seriously contemplated. In the 1250s, when Henry III conceived an absurd scheme for making his son king of Sicily with the assistance of the Pope, the baronage refused to have anything to do with it and twice declined to contribute to its cost.

The constitutional crisis which paralysed Edward I's efforts to defend his continental dominions in the 1290s was due mainly to the opposition of influential noblemen who declined either to serve in his armies or to support taxation to pay for them. In 1295 several noblemen had to be forced by threat of confiscation to go to Gascony, even though they were being offered wages. Two years later, the Constable and the Marshal, Edward's most senior military officers, refused to go to either Gascony or Flanders. 'By God, Earl, you shall go or hang,' Edward is supposed to have said to the Marshal: 'By the same oath, King, I shall neither go nor hang,' he replied.[24] The story is ancient but probably apocryphal. Rather later, when the King attempted to collect a tax to finance the expeditions, the two earls appeared armed in the Exchequer Chamber to protest. The reason for this attitude was not simply that the nobility disliked paying taxes or serving in the army, although this certainly weighed with some of them. It was that they were profoundly insular and did not regard an ambitious foreign policy as being of any interest to the English community. Their view was exactly expressed in the ordinances which they forced on Edward's successor in 1311.

Because the King ought not to make war against anyone or leave his kingdom without the general assent of his baronage, on account of the many perils that could happen to him and his kingdom, we ordain that henceforth the King shall not leave his kingdom or make war without the general assent of his baronage given in Parliament, and if he does otherwise and has his feudal host summoned for the purpose, then the summons shall be void.[25]

It is not particularly surprising that, except for a handful of adventurers who made their names elsewhere the English had a low reputation as warriors, which persisted until they began to win striking victories over the French during the 1340s. By comparison successive French kings were able to promote the adventures of the house of Anjou in Italy, and Philip III of France could lead an enormous French army at ruinous expense into Catalonia in 1284 in the hope of making his son king of Aragon, a venture which had much in common with the Sicilian scheme of Henry III. It was enterprises like these, quixotic and unsuccessful as they were, which had earned the French their reputation as the pre-eminent martial race of thirteenth-century Europe.

The transformation of the baronial attitude to warfare and the changes which made the English the most feared soldiers of late-medieval Europe took contemporary observers by surprise because they occurred out of sight as the gradual result of half a century of persistent warfare within the British Isles, against the Welsh and the Scots and against the rival factions of Edward II's civil wars. There was some truth in the observation of the fifteenth-century Berry Herald that the English had become so good at fighting because they practised so often on each other.[26]

When, in July 1277, Edward I invaded north Wales to force his will on the most powerful of the Welsh princes, it was the first stage in a process which, rather later, Edward conceived as the unification of Britain under his own rule. Five years later, in March 1282, a second war broke out which lasted for more than a year and resulted in the conquest of the whole of Wales and its permanent occupation by English garrisons, officials and colonists. Wales was a relatively easy prize, weak, economically impoverished and politically fragmented. Nevertheless, these enterprises had called for very large armies. Between 18,000 and 20,000 men served in the Welsh war of 1277. Twenty-four thousand men crushed the short-lived rebellion of south Wales in 1287, and three armies comprising between 35,000 and 40,000 men altogether were sent to deal with the rising of 1294, the last and greatest Welsh rebellion for more than a century. By the standard of the past century these were very large armies, and some of them were raised at remarkably short notice. As feats of military organization the subsequent occupation of Wales and the construction of the great Edwardian castles there were scarcely less impressive. Even so, the effort and expenditure involved was dwarfed by the scale of Edward's wars in Scotland, which were longer and more expensive and, principally because they failed, had a seminal effect on the course of England's history in the next two centuries.

Scotland, a land settled, as its leaders proclaimed in the Declaration of Arbroath (1320), 'at the uttermost ends of the earth', was a community divided by history and geography. In the lowlands south of the Forth and along the east coast from the Forth to the Moray Firth were concentrated all of Scotland's significant towns, almost all her cultivable land and the greater part of her population. These regions had been persistently infiltrated since the eleventh century by immigrants from England and north-western Europe who had brought with them their languages, their law, their ecclesiastical and political institutions, and many economic links with the world from whence they had come. The west and north, and the inhospitable highlands and islands, on the other hand, were inhabited by shifting tribal communities living by sheep farming, largely Gaelic-speaking, one of the most inaccessible regions of Europe. Englishmen, and some Scots, already spoke of the 'wild' Scots and the 'tame' ones, of 'governed' and 'ungoverned' Scotland.

The institutions of the Scotch government were modelled on those of England but they operated on a more intimate scale. They depended even more heavily on the personality of the monarch, on a few officers of the royal household and on a very small itinerant civil service. The authority of the Scotch kings within their realm as well as their strength outside it was severely limited: by the small scale of its institutions, by the power of the great territorial lords, and above all by the poverty of a country always sparsely populated, whose soil was either barren highland or heavy undrained valley bottoms. Scotland could never produce the high tax revenues required for sustained and organized warfare or for major campaigns of fortress construction, and although its nobility included some of the great paladins of the age, their country could not afford to mount and arm impressive armies of knights.

Nevertheless the Scots were among the most persistent and effective antagonists of the English throughout the fourteenth and fifteenth centuries. This venomous hostility was a problem which the English had brought upon themselves. In 1290, when the direct line of the kings of Scotland became extinct, Edward I seized the opportunity to revive an ancient but ill-defined claim of past English kings to the superior lordship of Scotland. There is no reason to doubt Edward's own explanation of his acts, given to the magnates who accompanied his army into Scotland in the following year: that he intended to absorb Scotland into his realm as he had already absorbed Wales.[27] It is consistent with all that subsequently happened. During 1291 Edward occupied the country, took oaths of loyalty from its leading men and from all the claimants to the throne, and set up a tribunal to decide the difficult legal and constitutional question which of them was entitled to be king. In November 1292 the 'auditors' of Edward's tribunal pronounced in favour of John Balliol.

But having once set Balliol up Edward pulled him down. He diminished his stature in Scotland and provoked him into rebellion by openly treating him as a subordinate princeling, hearing appeals from his courts and summoning him to perform military service in English armies. It is hard not to see in these proceedings a cruel parody of the treatment which Edward himself, as Duke of Acquitaine, had received at the hands of Philip the Fair and the Parlement of Paris. In October 1295, after Balliol had defaulted in his defence to one of these appeals, Edward I required him to forfeit three castles, and in the spring of the following year he crossed the Tweed with an army to take them. Balliol tried to resist, but his ill-organized supporters were defeated. He himself surrendered and was ceremonially deposed and sent off into captivity in England. Robert Bruce, lord of Annandale and head of one of the great Anglo-Norman noble houses of Scotland, had been John Balliol's principal competitor before the tribunal of 1292, and when Balliol quarrelled with the English King the Bruces had declared for Edward. They expected to gain the throne in Balliol's place. But Edward had other plans. He rudely dismissed them when they came for their reward. The regalia of the kings of Scotland were confiscated. The famous stone of Scone on which they were traditionally enthroned was removed to Westminster.

The expulsion of the English from Scotland occupied more than thirty years. Successive Scotch rebellions, bravely and skilfully led but poorly supported, were brutally put down by the English King between 1297 and 1305. However, in the following year, 1306, Robert Bruce (the grandson of the claimant of 1292) seized the Abbey of Scone with a handful of kinsmen and friends and had himself enthroned on a substitute stone by Isabella, Countess of Buchan. Bruce's coup must have seemed doomed in its opening weeks. Most of the Scotch nobility were either indifferent or hostile. His men were ill equipped to face the heavily armed horsemen of the English army, and he lacked the great siege engines which were essential for the capture of the stone fortresses of the English. During the summer of 1306 his hastily assembled army was overwhelmed by the English and their Scotch auxiliaries. He himself was driven into hiding while his family fell victims to a venomous reign of terror. Bruce's cause was saved from extinction by events elsewhere. In July 1307 Edward I died at Burgh-on-Sands on the Solway Firth, leading a fresh army into Scotland. The first and characteristic act of his successor was to march south again after a brief and empty demonstration. As the English turned their energies to constitutional conflict and civil war, Bruce gradually extended his authority over most of Scotland. Between 1307 and 1313 he recovered all the major English fortresses except Berwick, Bothwell and Stirling.

In the autumn of 1313 Bruce besieged Stirling. Its English governor, Sir Philip Mowbray, agreed to surrender it unless he was relieved by mid-summer 1314. Edward II rose to the challenge. He raised a new army and entered Scotland in June a few days before the deadline expired. On the last day allowed for the relief of the castle his troops were attacked at Bannockburn while they were still caught in the loops and marshes of the Firth and before they could be drawn up in proper battle array. The English were defeated with terrible slaughter. The battle consolidated Bruce's hold on his kingdom and brought over to his side most of the prominent Scots who had remained on the sidelines while the issue was uncertain or had even actively assisted the English. What was left of the English position in Scotland quickly collapsed. Stirling surrendered at once and Bothwell soon afterwards. Berwick survived but was betrayed (by an Englishman) in March 1318. The English government could not bring themselves to recognize Bruce's tenure as permanent, but they recognized their own defeat. In 1323 a truce was made for a period of thirteen years, until June 1336.

In the three centuries which followed Edward I's deposition of John Balliol there was no period when Scotland was not a potential enemy at England's rear, the source of continual friction and violence interrupted by periodic truces and major campaigns, of which the last did not occur until the Flodden campaign of 1513. The change profoundly affected both countries. By the 1320s Scotland had already acquired a degree of cohesion and a strength of national feeling unthinkable thirty years before. 'For so long as there shall be but a hundred of us left alive,' the representatives of the Scotch nobility declared at Arbroath in 1320, 'we shall never consent to be ruled by the English.' After many years in which Scotland had developed along largely English lines, the two nations grew apart. Cross-holdings of land in England and Scotland virtually disappeared. Scotch clerics graduated abroad at Paris or Orléans instead of Oxford. The law and institutions of Scotland developed in their own way.

In England, a larger country with wider concerns, the impact of the Scotch wars was less resonant, but there were two respects in which the hostility of the Scots was to shackle the conduct of English foreign policy during the fourteenth and fifteenth centuries. The first was the continual drain of wealth and manpower occasioned by the border wars even in times of formal truce. From 1296 onwards the Scots regularly mounted small-scale raids on the northern counties in addition to the occasional major invasion, crossing the Tweed without warning on their light horses, burning villages, rounding up cattle, plundering the land and buildings of the rich northern churches and towns such as Carlisle, Hexham and Durham. The raiders reached a new peak of effectiveness after the battle of Bannockburn. A highly organized system was instituted for extracting protection money from the towns and churches of the north and despoiling those who would not pay. It generated considerable revenues for the Scots and set in train the secular decline of the economy of the north of England. This was the country which Jean le Bel, travelling with the English army in 1327, had called a 'savage land full of desolate wastes and great hills, and barren of everything except wild beasts'.[28] The north of England contributed little or nothing to the long wars of Edward III against France except to hold the border. The border counties, Cumberland, Westmorland and Northumberland, had regularly to be excused the payment of taxes on account of their poverty. The progressive depopulation of the north made it increasingly difficult to recruit soldiers there and virtually impossible to recruit them for service in the south or on the continent. The normal practice in the early years of the Hundred Years War was to recruit no troops for foreign armies north of the River Trent. This meant that in prosecuting its wars against France the English government was deprived of the services of something like a fifth of its population.

The second abiding consequence of the wars of England and Scotland was the 'auld alliance' between Scotland and France, which remained the cardinal element of Scotch foreign policy until the end of the sixteenth century and in one sense can be said to have lasted until 1745. The first formal treaty, which was made under the threat of imminent invasion in October 1295, contained all the classic elements. Philip the Fair promised that if Scotland were invaded by the King of England he would 'give them help by distracting the said King in other places'; while the Scots for their part would invade England 'as widely and deeply as they can, waging war, besieging towns and wasting the country' as soon as the King of England embarked for the continent with an army. If Philip the Fair himself was sometimes cavalier in his observance of his obligations to the Scots, his successors took them very seriously. Charles IV formally renewed the alliance by the treaty of Corbeil in April 1326. Philip VI's refusal to abandon the Scots in the 1330s, even when they appeared to be on the brink of destruction, was one of the principal causes of the great Anglo-French war which began in 1337, a war in which the Scots were to have a prominent part. It is often forgotten that in 1346 the English had to fight a Scotch army in the north as well as a French one at Crécy, and that the Scots fought as private adventurers with the French army at Poitiers (1356) and in organized contingents in French armies of the fifteenth century.

The wars of the English in Scotland and the north had another, equally important result. They created, during the fifty years before the beginning of the Hundred Years War, a military society of a kind which had not existed in England since the twelfth century.

The main difficulty of the English in fielding armies equal to their enemies was a shortage of heavy cavalrymen. There were fewer of them in England than there were in France even in proportion to the country's population. It was the result of a perceptible shrinking of the number of men who possessed the landed wealth to sustain the status of a knight and the horses, equipment and leisure which cavalry service demanded. The class of men capable of fighting as knights in the early fourteenth century was probably no more than 3,000 strong. This included not only dubbed or 'belted' knights but squires, who were usually men of equivalent social status but either unable or unwilling to take on the full burdens of knighthood. It was about half the number which had been available to Henry II in the second half of the twelfth century. Not all of them were able to fight: age, illness and hard times were common excuses. The numbers were made up to some extent by recruiting men of lower condition, sergeants-at-arms and other men-at-arms. Even so, Edward III, who raised larger numbers of heavy cavalry than either his father or grandfather, never succeeded in collecting more than 5,000 in one place and that in an exceptional year. This was about one-sixth of what in optimum conditions the French government could find. Of belted knights there were rarely more than 500 together in one army at any time in the reign of Edward I. Under Edward III, whose reputation and patronage greatly

increased enthusiasm for knighthood, there may have been about twice
that number. This was in spite of vigorous and frequent measures known
as 'distraint of knighthood' designed to force men with sufficient wealth
and status to become knights on pain of confiscation of their goods.

One consequence of the shortage of knights and other cavalrymen in
England was that it was necessary to make particularly heavy use of those
that there were, giving them an intensity and continuity of experience
which was rare. The other, and in the long run more significant, consequence was that the English government came to rely more heavily on
infantry than any other western European monarchy.

To recruit infantry on any scale it was necessary to devise a system of
general military conscription more efficient than anything that had existed
hitherto. In principle every Englishman aged between sixteen and sixty
was liable to do military service for the defence of the realm and for the
occasional large-scale police operation. It was his duty to have the
weapons appropriate for his wealth and status according to an ancient and
elaborate code re-enacted in the reign of Edward I in the statute of
Winchester. But this ancient *levée en masse* was not a practical tool of
warfare. From the 1280s onwards the practice was to require a selection of
the 'best and strongest' for the King's armies in Wales and Scotland. Later
it became usual to specify how many men were required in each category,
how many archers, how many pikemen and so forth. The work was
carried out by officers known as commissioners of array, local knights
appointed in each county as they were required. The men whom they
recruited were inspected and listed, then arranged in twenties under the
command of a 'vintenar' and hundreds under the command of a 'centenar'
(usually a cavalryman), and marched at the appointed time by their leaders
to the assembly point of the army. The system was in practice rather less
impressive than the succession of administrative commands which brought
it into operation. Arrayers were often corrupt. Villagers conspired to
present feeble fellows and armed them poorly or not at all. Experience
suggested that only half to two-thirds of the numbers called for could be
expected to appear, a factor which was no doubt taken into account in
preparing the arrayers' instructions. Desertion was a serious and perennial
problem, both before and after the muster. Nevertheless, the results were
impressive by the low standards of medieval governments.

Conscription was taxation in kind. The circumstances in which it should
be permitted gave rise to some dispute during the reign of Edward I and to
intense controversy under Edward II, who experimented with a variety of
unconventional schemes for requiring infantry service without pay. The

whole question of compulsory infantry service was considered in detail in the first Parliament of Edward III, in 1327. From the petitions of this assembly and the King's generally accommodating answers to them, and from trial and error in the following years, a consensus emerged. Conscripted men could not be required to serve without pay except for the defence of the realm against foreign invasion or with the consent of Parliament; but if pay were offered they could be required to serve wherever they were sent. The towns and county communities generally provided them with food, clothing, weapons and horses, and paid them wages until they passed the county boundary (or, in the north, until they reached Newcastle or Carlisle). Thereafter, their pay and expenses were the responsibility of the King. Obviously this informal compromise was subject to the overriding rule of sound government in any medieval community, that the King should not push even his lawful demands too far. No administrative mechanism could prevail over any widespread and deep-seated sense of grievance, and none could raise large armies for an unpopular war. Moreover, popular indifference, even if it could not prevent the recruitment of an army, could significantly delay it. Propaganda was an essential tool of war. Edward I learned this lesson very well, and his grandson better still.

Edward I had recruited huge infantry armies, but had shown no particular skill in using them and on some notable occasions had failed to use them at all. There was a considerable improvement in the time of his son and grandson. By the 1330s the English system of military conscription was producing smaller numbers of troops of much higher quality than the rather haphazard methods used at this stage in France. Moreover, English commanders devised highly effective methods of deploying them, a particular weakness of French military practice for much of the fourteenth century. The great teachers of the English were the Scots. They had wisdom forced on them. Unable to field large cavalry armies of their own, they fought off the massed cavalry of their enemies by drawing up infantry in squares ('schiltrons'), their pikes embedded in the ground in front of them, pointed outwards towards the approaching horsemen. The suicidal charge of the English cavalry against the Scotch infantry formations at Bannockburn had been an awesome lesson and it provoked much reflection among the English. It was 'unheard of in our time', one of them wrote, 'for such an army to be scattered by infantry, until we remember that the flower of France fell before the Flemings at Courtrai'.[29] The English learned from the Scots what the French had failed to learn from the Flemings. Disciplined infantry in well-prepared positions were more than a match for heavy cavalry.

At the battle of Boroughbridge (1322), the principal engagement of the civil wars of Edward II's reign, the King's army was commanded by Sir Andrew Harclay, a Cumberland knight who had passed much of his life fighting against the Scots on the western march of Scotland. He 'sent all the horses to the rear, drew up his knights and some pikemen on foot ... and formed up other pikemen in squares after the fashion of the Scots ... in order to resist the cavalry in which the enemy was placing all their trust.' The Earl of Lancaster's cavalry were massacred. The Earl of Hereford, 'the flower of solace and comfort and of courtesy', was hacked to death on the ground by a footsoldier.[30] The use of infantry formations stiffened with dismounted cavalry became the hallmark of English battle tactics. Five years later, in 1327, the English government announced at the outset of its campaign against the Scots that even the greatest noblemen of the land would have to be ready to fight on foot.[31]

There was another lesson that the English learned from the Scots. Faced with the problem that infantry armies moved slowly and could rarely seize the initiative, the Scots had adopted the practice of mounting part of their infantry on low-grade horses, the 'little nags' observed by Jean le Bel on the border in 1327. Their raiding forces, although they were commonly followed by great hordes of unmounted men, were led by a handful of men-at-arms and a much larger number of fast-moving mounted infantry, covering long distances within a day, dismounting to fight, and swiftly escaping any encounter on unequal terms. The English had already begun to experiment with similar mounted infantrymen (known as 'hobelars') in the last years of the thirteenth century. But it was once again Andrew Harclay who was responsible for their regular use. The border army which he commanded on the march of Scotland in the years after Bannockburn was composed of a small troop of knights and a much larger number of lightly armed horsemen. Hobelars were employed in growing numbers in the 1320s not only in the borderlands.[32]

At about the same time the English armed their infantry with the six-foot longbow, a weapon peculiar to the British Isles which was to give them the decisive advantage on European battlefields until the middle of the fifteenth century. Archery was an old skill, but for some reason the longbow had not traditionally been used as an infantry weapon on any scale. Like his predecessors, Edward I had begun by using crossbowmen, in spite of their high wages and expensive equipment and although he had had to find most of them abroad. But in the course of his wars in Scotland the longbow gradually displaced the crossbow and during the 1320s and 1330s longbowmen began to displace other infantry troops. In the latter part of this period they tended increasingly to be mounted men, like the hobelars. It is not at all clear why the English woke up so suddenly and so late to the military potential of the longbow, but there is no doubt of the importance of the change once it had occurred. Longbowmen needed great strength and training, and an aptitude which could not be acquired overnight. But they were extremely effective en masse. Volleys loosed in rapid succession into the sky came down over the heads of the opposing army, and on their lightly protected limbs and shoulders, breaking up infantry and cavalry formations, causing carnage in their tightly packed ranks and terror among the horses. The great English victories of the 1330s and 1340s, Dupplin Moor, Halidon Hill, Sluys, Crécy and Neville's Cross, were all won by archers.

A hobelar was a good deal more than the proletarian thug who was traditionally regarded as the raw material of infantry armies. He needed a horse, a jacket of hardened leather, a steel helmet and throat-piece, and a pair of metal gauntlets as well as his sword, knife and lance. In the 1330s the government reckoned that the typical hobelar would need land worth at least fifteen pounds a year to support him, which was the income of a substantial farmer. A mounted archer, with similar armour, was thought to need the same. Even the humble foot-archer with his sword and knife, his bow and his quiver of two dozen arrows, was reckoned to be a two-pound man, which placed him among the more substantial peasants.[33] Only the Welsh, most of whom fought as unmounted pikemen, were still recruited in the indiscriminate fashion of an earlier age. What had happened was not so much the conscription of the masses as the creation of a larger military class composed of men who, without having the social standing of the knights and squires, acquired something of their discipline and aptitude for war.

Much had changed since Simon de Montfort claimed to have taught the English elementary battle-drill. The changes were part of a revolution of English attitudes to war which extended a long way beyond the recruitment and deployment of armies. The major campaigns of Edward I and Edward II had required a prodigious bureaucratic organization charged with all the mundane tasks needed to maintain men in the field: the requisitioning of transport, the purveyance, storage and distribution of victuals and fodder, the maintenance of field pay and account offices, the carriage of equipment and supplies on carts overland and by ship around the coast, the mass production of arrows and bow-staves, the construction of prefabricated bridges and siege artillery.

'In my youth', the poet Petrarch wrote (he was born in 1304), 'the

English were regarded as the most timid of all the uncouth races; but today they are the supreme warriors; they have destroyed the reputation of the French in a succession of startling victories, and men who were once lower even than the wretched Scots have crushed the realm of France with fire and steel.' The chronicler Jean le Bel, although he was a great deal better informed than this expatriate Italian, and had marched with an English army against the Scots in 1327, was equally astonished. The English 'did not count' in the 1320s but had become the most celebrated soldiers in Europe by 1350s. Perception lagged behind reality. Even before the great victories of the 1340s and 1350s Richard of Bury, Bishop of Durham, a loyal Englishman but no flag-waver, had concluded that the days of France's martial fame were passing.[34]

CHAPTER III

Gascony

A ribbon of coastal territory never more than 50 miles wide, stretching from the mouth of the River Charente in the north to the Pyrenees in the south, was all that remained in 1328 of the great continental empire of the Angevins. Gascony had never been the most highly regarded part of the splendid dowry which Eleanor of Aquitaine had brought to Henry of Anjou on their marriage in 1152. Poitou had been the heart of Eleanor's duchy, Poitiers its capital and La Rochelle its major port. The natural resources of Gascony seemed poor by comparison. Between the two major maritime cities of Bordeaux and Bayonne there stretched the bleak marshes of the Landes, occasionally relieved by patches of windswept grassland on which a sparse population eked out a living by growing millet and raising pigs. Between this sombre wasteland and the hills further east lay a flat, thickly wooded territory cultivated in irregular swatches marked out of the forest, by the broad river valleys, by a few roads of execrable quality and by the clearances of the *bastides* and greater monasteries.

The main source of its prosperity and the link which joined it to England for 350 years was wine. Until the thirteenth century Bordeaux had been only another local wine. The favourite wine of the English kings in the twelfth century was that of Poitou, which was shipped from La Rochelle. In this they shared the tastes of their subjects, for when King John attempted in 1199 to enforce maximum prices for all French wines sold in England, Poitou had pride of place and Bordeaux was not mentioned. The capture of Poitou and the fall of La Rochelle to the French in 1224 was therefore an event of central importance in the life of the region. It deprived Europe's principal wine-importing nation of its main source of supply, and made the fortune of Bordelais. By the beginning of the fourteenth century more than 80,000 tons of wine were being exported every year from the ports of the Gironde. At least a quarter of this was landed in England, giving rise to complaints in Parliament that the country was being drained of gold to pay for it and invaded by Gascon merchants and usurers. The vineyards of Gascony ceaselessly expanded to meet the demand, filling the Graves south of the city of Bordeaux, spreading over the river into Entre-Deux-Mers and extending through the river valleys into the hinterland. [1]

Aquitaine was a formless duchy whose inhabitants were conscious of the differences which separated them from other Frenchmen. But they were not unduly attached to old loyalties. They were fickle men, Froissart thought; 'a very captious and unreliable people' Edward I called them, whose promises should always be recorded in writing.[2] The unifying agents and the sources of English strength in the duchy through three centuries were the cities of Bordeaux and Bayonne, which stood at the estuaries of the two great river systems of south-western France and, although turbulent and independent-minded, remained fundamentally loyal to the English Crown until the end of the middle ages. This was particularly true of Bordeaux, which was the seat of the administration. The city inherited the mantle of Poitiers, decorating itself (as Poitiers had done two centuries earlier) with the grand architecture of a true capital. The nobility of the province established residences there, as other notables were doing in London and Paris. Fortified by a succession of charters of privilege, Bordeaux raised taxes, concluded treaties and issued bombastic statements sealed with its own seal. Its wealth had drawn a ceaseless flow of immigrants for most of the latter part of the thirteenth century, pushing out the crowded population into more than a dozen suburban parishes. A new line of ramparts, built at the beginning of the fourteenth century, enclosed three times the area of the old ones, themselves barely a century old.[3]

Bordeaux owed its political and economic importance chiefly to its incomparable position at the head of five river valleys. The inland towns depended for their trade on the passage of the rivers which joined up in the estuary of the Gironde. Bordeaux held them in a tight and much resented tutelage. No grower might sell his wine until the citizens of Bordeaux had first sold theirs. Growers and merchants bringing in wine from upriver towns found it difficult to sell except through Bordeaux merchants. The government of the duchy had their own reasons for conniving in this system. The duties which they levied on the traffic of the Gironde were a potent political weapon as well as a profitable source of revenue. Discounts were offered to loyal inland towns and to favoured communities in the neighbouring parts of the French King's dominions, privileges far less extensive, it is true, than those of Bordeaux itself, but enough to give them the edge over their own neighbours. Saint-Macaire, La Réole and Agen on the Garonne, Moissac on the Tarn, and Cahors on the Lot were all the

market towns of fertile wine-growing regions which had to send their
goods past the walls of Bordeaux on the best terms which they could
obtain. The wines of the Dordogne, which by-passed Bordeaux itself,
were stopped and assessed to duty near the sea at the outpost of
Castillon. Even the tiny village of Castelsagrat, situated on a barely
navigable tributary of the Garonne more than a hundred miles from
Bordeaux, did not dare to plant vines on the empty lots within its walls
without petitioning Edward I for a discount on the customs of
Bordeaux.[4]

Since the loss of Normandy at the beginning of the thirteenth century
the English kings had rarely visited their continental dominions. Edward I
visited Aquitaine twice. He spent two years there at the very beginning of
his reign, and three years between 1286 and 1289, highly productive
times during which he impressed his seal on the province in the
businesslike manner which had become familiar to his English subjects.
But although he lived until 1307 and his successors governed their duchy
until the middle of the fifteenth century, no reigning King of England ever
visited south-western France again. In spite of the distance from England
(the journey was usually made overland to avoid the dangers of the Bay
of Biscay) the government of Aquitaine was kept on a tight reign by its
English master. Royal lieutenants with viceregal powers visited the
province at fairly frequent intervals to make investigations or perform
specific duties. At Westminster there grew up a group of record clerks
and diplomatic officials, specialists in the affairs of south-western France,
who were expert even when they were not wise. In Bordeaux, the
government was carried on by a close group of officials in the Château de
l'Ombrière. The Seneschal, usually an Englishman, was the chief military
and administrative representative of the King–Duke. The Constable,
notwithstanding his martial title, was usually a clergyman seconded from
the English civil service to superintend the finances of the duchy. He was
answerable directly to the Exchequer at Westminster. These two august
personages controlled a surprisingly small bureaucracy, far smaller in
relation to its burdens than the imposing bureaucratic machine which
was growing up in England and in the provinces directly governed by the
kings of France. In the outlying regions there was a small body of district
officials, sub-seneschals, provosts and bailiffs, a few castellans and
resident tax collectors. There were very few Englishmen. Almost all the
subordinate officials of the duchy, and the great majority of the higher
ones as well, were native Gascons. Except for the personal retainers of
the Seneschal there were usually no English troops in Gascony, and even

in moments of crisis military expeditions from England were small and infrequent. It was certainly not a colony.

There were good political reasons for the retentive interest which the English kings took in their continental dominions. Except in wartime, when it had to be expensively defended, Aquitaine had usually been an asset. Gascons were born fighters and skilled crossbowmen who commanded high wages as mercenaries. Large contingents of them had fought in the Welsh and Scottish wars of Edward I, swaggering intolerably as an English chronicler complained. The commissioners sent by Edward II in 1315 to assess the contribution which the duchy could make to his Scottish wars found that there were about 100,000 households (say half a million inhabitants) from which to draw recruits. There was no system of regular taxation in Gascony and very little in the way of ducal domain land, features of the duchy's government which were to become a major source of weakness in wartime. But other revenues, the proceeds of the sale of offices, tolls and dues, and above all duties on river traffic, had traditionally made a large contribution to the budget of the English dynasty. In January 1324 a report presented to Edward II estimated his net receipts from the duchy at £13,000, which was roughly equal to the entire revenues of the English customs.[5]

Yet the retention of Aquitaine was more than a political calculation. The kings of England were French noblemen, sharing the tastes and conventions of the French aristocracy from which they had sprung. Aquitaine was part of their inheritance, the preservation of which was a duty owed to their family, part of the *pietas* of every medieval aristocrat. In the twelfth century, Henry II of England had ruled more of France than did the King of France. He had asked to be buried in an abbey in the Loire valley. His English subjects had been quite unable to converse with him without the assistance of an interpreter. Most of Henry's empire had vanished, but French remained the first language of his descendants until the middle of the fourteenth century. Henry III and Edward I took most seriously their status as peers of France. It is true that their sense of being part of a common political community was badly dented in the Anglo-French wars of the 1290s, but it was many years after that before English kings stopped regarding themselves as princes of France, and a frustrated desire to be recognized as such was certainly one element of the bitterness which affected King Edward III's relations with his second cousin Philip VI.

The peculiar status of the English kings in the French political order dated back to the treaty of Paris of 1259. Before that treaty the dukes of Aquitaine had acknowledged no superior on earth. They had performed no homage to the kings of France since the confiscation of their continental dominions had been proclaimed by Philip Augustus at the beginning of the thirteenth century, an act which they regarded as unlawful and which they refused to recognize. It was an unsatisfactory stalemate which the parties proceeded to replace in 1259 with an even more unsatisfactory compromise. The treaty doubled the size of the duchy, suddenly extending its boundaries from the coastal plain to the steep valleys of the interior and into regions which had not known English rule for half a century. But the surrender of these great territories was hedged about by qualifications and exceptions. The English dynasty recovered certain ill-defined rights in the 'three bishoprics' of Limoges, Périgueux and Cahors. Subject to equally ill-defined conditions, they were also promised the return of the diocese of Agen and parts of Saintonge and Quercy. There was no comprehensive territorial settlement of south-western France. All that was finally settled in Paris in 1259 was that the Duke held his lands there as the vassal of the King of France and owed him liege homage, the feudal bond to which all other loyalties yielded. On 4 December 1259 Henry III performed the act of homage in a fine ceremony in the garden of the royal palace in Paris, but what were the territories for which he was doing homage and what were his rights within them were questions which were left for his successors to argue out with increasing vehemence in the courts of successive French kings and finally on the battlefield. It was 'a defiance of good sense' as an Archbishop of Canterbury acidly observed twenty years later, and more than any other act it earned Henry his place in that region of Dante's Purgatory reserved for children and negligent kings, 'il re de la semplice vita'. Posterity has generally endorsed these verdicts, but neither of them is entirely fair to the ageing King who had greater problems both at home and abroad than the precise definition of indefinable rights. His intentions were defeated not only by casual draftsmanship but by two changes which occurred after the treaty was sealed and which he could scarcely have foreseen.[6]

The first was a sudden transformation in the political geography of France which resulted from the death in August 1271 of Alphonse of Poitiers followed within a few days by that of his wife. Alphonse, a younger brother of Louis IX, had ruled the whole of Saintonge, Poitou and the Rouergue as his appanage. His wife was the last representative of the house of Toulouse, whose territories included substantially the whole of Languedoc and the Agenais together with much of Quercy. Their marriage had been childless. The whole vast inheritance therefore fell to Philip III of France. Part of that inheritance, the Agenais, Quercy and the southern part of Saintonge, consisted of territories which had been somewhat indistinctly promised to Henry III in 1259. The Agenais in particular was much coveted by the English because it was essential to the successful defence of Gascony from the east. Probably for that reason Edward I, who succeeded his father in 1272, had the greatest difficulty in enforcing the promises of 1259 and recovered these territories only by several years of diplomacy, litigation and menaces of war. By the Treaty of Amiens in May 1279, Philip III surrendered the Agenais. After seven years of further disputation, Edward obtained southern Saintonge in a supplementary agreement signed in Paris in August 1286. Quercy was never recovered.[7]

These were substantial gains, but Edward's secure possession of them was undermined by the far greater gains which the French Crown made by Alphonse's death. By occupying Languedoc, the kings of France had turned the flank of the dukes of Aquitaine, completing a march on the Mediterranean and the Pyrenees which had begun with the Albigensian wars sixty years earlier. When Henry III of England had signed the treaty of Paris in 1259, his neighbour to the north and east had been an avaricious but unaggressive younger son of the French royal house, who could be expected to beget heirs and found an independent local dynasty. Whatever ambition the French monarchy might have to recover by stealth what it had yielded by treaty was restrained by distance and geography. Henry's heirs were less comfortably placed. They had to assert their rights against a government whose officials were solidly installed in the neighbouring cities of Périgueux and Toulouse.

The ambitions which these officials nursed for the aggrandizement of their master's domains was the second factor which Henry III could be forgiven for not foreseeing. Both the kings who signed the Treaty of Paris had been brought up in a world which had profoundly respected the feudal bond, more profoundly perhaps than its waning economic and military significance warranted in the thirteenth century. They felt no need or desire to see its legal effect defined with pedantic precision. 'He was not my man before; now he has entered into my homage', Louis IX told his confidant Joinville, who had ventured to criticize the treaty.[8] While the personal relations of the English and French kings remained close, this was a good enough answer. But it was not good enough for the lawyers and civil servants of what, in the course of the late thirteenth and early fourteenth centuries, was becoming an increasingly impersonal monarchy. Their notion of royal sovereignty had little place for rights and obligations founded on the sentiment and tradition of an older governing class. In their hands the bond of personal homage lost much of its meaning as soon as the King of France and the Duke of Aquitaine made it the cornerstone of their relations.

The extent of the English dynasty's problems became apparent within a decade of Louis IX's death, when it lost control of Limousin without a blow being struck for its retention. In Limoges, the capital of a region ceded to the English dynasty in 1259, the Bishop, the Viscount, the Abbot of St Martial and the citizenry were all local powers with independent minds and incompatible ambitions. The Bishop was the King's man, in keeping with the royalist traditions of the French episcopacy. The Abbot had done homage to the Duke of Aquitaine in 1261, but his successor changed sides in the following year. The citizens were at war with the Viscount, the former looking to the King–Duke and the latter clinging to his allegiance to the Crown. Neither the King of France nor the Bordeaux government were manipulating their protégés. Indeed the King of France thought that Limoges ought to do homage to the King–Duke. But here, as elsewhere, they found themselves drawn into the quarrels of others, the rivalry of their officials lightly superimposed upon ancient grudges and jealousies in small self-sufficient communities. Treaties had little substance. Possession was not the gift of rulers but the prize of local politicians. In 1274 Edward abandoned the contest and Limoges became the fief of the French King's nephew. It was a characteristic failure.[9]

The loss of Limoges was a severe blow to the Duke's efforts to hold his own in the northernmost of the 'three bishoprics' which had been ceded in 1259. Less dramatic events were equally surely depriving him of what he had in the other two. Many of the French King's vassals in the 'three dioceses' had privileges requiring their assent before their homage could be transferred to another, privileges of long standing in some cases but in others acquired in great haste on the very eve of the signature of the treaty. Their allegiance was not therefore in the gift of the French kings. They included some important territorial magnates: all three bishops, some of the largest lay and ecclesiastical lords and frontier towns such as Figeac, Brive, Périgueux and Sarlat. Few of them consented to the transfer of their homage. Their reasons were understandable. They wanted to be left alone, and preferred the more distant power. Those who did agree to the transfer of their homage often had to be bought by offers of privileges and immunities which made the Duke's lordship in places little more than a nominal dignity. The Viscount of Turenne, one of the principal lords of Périgord, was brought into the Duke's allegiance only by a handsome pension and a promise that the Duke would exercise only very limited jurisdiction in his lands. Another privileged vassal, the Count of Périgord, accepted the Duke's lordship on restrictive terms in the 1260s and renounced it in the 1270s with the connivance of the Parlement of Paris.[10]

In southern Périgord, along the valley of the Dordogne and south of it, the English dynasty remained a powerful force until the 1320s, chiefly on account of the construction of the *bastides*. The more important of them were all foundations of the King–Duke and his officers: Puyguilhem, Fonroque, Beaulieu, Lalinde, Molières, Beaumont, Monpazier. The inhabitants of these places were men with no political past, colonists carving new land out of forest. They depended directly on the ducal government from whom their freedom and their privileges were derived. For much the same reasons, the English dynasty was able to hold its own in the Agenais, another territory heavily colonized by *bastides*. But elsewhere, in northern Périgord, in Limousin and in much of Saintonge, all of them regions controlled by ancient and powerful families and ecclesiastical corporations with penetrating networks of clients and dependants, the situation was very different. The ducal government faded away.

There was very little that could be done about the persistent erosion of the Duke's jurisdiction even in the core territories of the duchy. A permanent and ubiquitous military occupation was out of the question. A limited military presence was possible, confined to the major strategic points, fords and bridges and the confluences of rivers. But even this was achieved with difficulty in a territory which until 1259 had extended no further than the coastal plain. The King–Duke had garrisoned citadels at Bordeaux, Bourg, Fronsac, Cubzac, Saint-Émilion, Pujols and La Réole, all in the old heartland of the duchy. There were also garrisons at Bayonne and Dax on the southern march. In the interior, military strongholds had to be acquired gradually and expensively over many years. Edward I devoted much thought and considerable resources to this task. He bought, built or restored a number of fortresses and acquired a share in others by private treaty. Some *bastides* were founded for specifically military purposes and were built with powerful walls. These acquisitions provided some sinew with which to control the more distant limbs of Edward I's continental dominions. But even he never succeeded in controlling more than about one in six of the strongholds of his duchy.[11]

There were regions where the Duke's power was more noticeable than it was elsewhere. But nowhere was it possible to draw a line marking off the duchy from the outside world. Instead the changing fortunes of France and Aquitaine had in the course of two centuries left numberless scattered rights of the one to be surrounded by the territory of the other, like rock-pools after an ebb-tide. As one moved eastward from the Bordelais along the river valleys into the interior, the territory of the Duke merged imperceptibly with that of the King. There were islands of strength, the occasional privileged town or garrisoned fortress. There were periodical assizes, interruptions in the life of the small market towns at which itinerant officials did justice in the Duke's name. There were obscure rights, often dormant, often contested, often ignored. Sovereignty was not power but a multitude of personal loyalties based on private bargains and the evanescent necessities of local politics.

It was probably true, as that shrewd old francophobe Boniface VIII told a French ambassador in 1298, that the Gascons would prefer to be ruled by the English dynasty than by the kings of France. But what they really wanted, he went on to say, was to have 'a multitude of lords so that they may never be touched by any of them'.[12] The right of appeal from the King–Duke's courts to the Parlement, which was firmly established by the 1270s, was the perfect instrument for their purpose and the source of most of the ducal government's political difficulties. Appeals from the duchy to Paris were very numerous. They were also extremely slow. They were heard only on certain days of the year. Quite frequently the plaintiff was not ready on the appointed day or failed to appear, in which case, there was almost invariably an adjournment. During this time the appellant might continue to enjoy the protection of royal sergeants sent from Toulouse and Périgueux. The courts of the principality were paralysed and, in some cases, the government as well.

In these conditions malcontents appealed for great and small causes alike. A vigorous seneschal like Luke of Thanet, otherwise an able and energetic servant of the Duke, could provoke some thirty appeals in the course of a few years until the government at Westminster was obliged to recall him in 1278. The malcontents could not lose, even if they did not win. But very often they did win. The profound suspicion which the councillors of the Parlement felt for the authority of any prince but their own had more important consequences than the abrupt summonses served on local notaries whose deeds were dated after the regnal years of the King of England, or the petty complaints about the circulation of coins bearing Edward's image. There was a time (it lasted barely three decades) when such difficulties could be resolved by tact on one side and restraint on the other. Edward I got on well with his cousin Philip III and at first with Philip the Fair, who succeeded him in 1285. While the Parlement was still feeling its way in matters of substance as well as procedure, important cases could be decided informally in the still open atmosphere of the

French royal court. When the notaries of the Agenais were summoned to answer for the dating of their deeds, the Seneschal of Gascony could help them out by appearing before the court to claim responsibility, and then settling the matter behind the scenes with the more influential royal councillors. The most celebrated and dangerous appeal of Edward's reign, which concerned his great Pyrenean vassal Gaston of Béarn, was never resolved judicially. Edward prevailed upon Philip III to bring pressure on Gaston. The appeal was ultimately withdrawn. The appellant was forced to surrender himself to his lord and passed some time in prison at Winchester.[13]

The development of French jurisprudence and the hardening policy of Philip the Fair made future disputes less easily resolved by those diplomatic pressures which Edward I's government was so skilled in applying. In the mid-1270s Edward's officers in the duchy endeavoured to discourage appeals by applying a variety of sanctions to appellants, and particularly to unsuccessful ones. In 1285, according to a decree of the Parlement denouncing the practice, the King–Duke's officers were in the habit of seizing the property of litigants shortly before judgement was given in his courts, a measure designed to prevent a potential appellant from placing his domains under the protection of the King of France. The Duke did not need to go so far in order to make his displeasure felt. The many charters in which unsuccessful appellants were readmitted to the Duke's favour on terms testify to the years of bureaucratic cold-shouldering which a litigant could expect if he appealed and failed. These sanctions became progressively more severe. In 1289 some citizens of Bordeaux appealed in the name of the city against the contempt of their privileges shown by Edward's officers. Edward's response on this occasion was to seize all cargoes of wine arriving in England which were not accompanied by a certificate attesting the loyalty of their owners. The appellants (who were probably in a minority in the city) resisted for eighteen months under the leadership of one Vidal Pansa, assisted by a commissioner appointed by the French King for their protection. But when resistance failed in 1291 the appeal was withdrawn, the commissioner was deported and Vidal Pansa drawn through the streets on a hurdle and hanged.[14]

Such quarrels were very damaging to the fabric of English government in Aquitaine and Edward attempted to avoid them by a careful observance of legal niceties which must itself have made the work of his officers more difficult. Increasingly, those officers tended to be lawyers. In Paris too Edward retained a permanent corps of lawyers and kept an office to deal with the steady flow of litigation involving the government of his southern dominions. In the spring of 1289, a few weeks before Edward's return to England after a prolonged sojourn in Gascony, he issued a remarkable series of ordinances from the small town of Condom. In addition to formulating methodical regulations for the conduct of the government by his representatives, Edward required the appointment of regional officials whose business it was to attend the ducal courts and keep an eye out for the government's interest in cases which might culminate in an appeal to the Parlement. In the same document, Edward took a number of measures designed to protect himself against the accusation of denying justice to his subjects and at the same time to make appeals to himself or his officers more congenial to local litigants. The greater part of the litigation of the duchy was assigned to professional judges (itself an innovation) sitting in various local centres, whose judgements might be challenged by appeal to a newly created Court of Appeals in Bordeaux.[15]

Whether this interesting experiment could have succeeded is a question which cannot now be answered. Probably no juridical reorganization could have stemmed the flow of appeals whose origins had always been more political than juridical. In the event it was not given time to succeed, for within five years the duchy was in the hands of the King of France. The sudden collapse of English government in Aquitaine in the 1290s bore out the worst of the gloomy prognostications which Edward had for some years been receiving from his most experienced Gascon counsellors.

The origin of this disaster lay in a ferocious private war between the seamen of Bayonne and those of the ports of Normandy which, although it was begun without reference to either ruler gradually embroiled most of the maritime communities of England and France and eventually their governments also. In a manifesto directed at Edward I's Gascon subjects, the French King accused them of insensate hatred of the French language and every man who spoke it. There is no doubt that at some times and places during 1292 and 1293 this extravagant accusation was justified. In Bordeaux and Bayonne lynch mobs had attacked every man of Norman origin whom they could find. At Fronsac on the Dordogne, four French customs officials had been lured on to a merchantman and murdered.

Philip the Fair had been looking for a quarrel with the King of England for at least a year. There was a powerful war party at his court, gathered round his brother Charles of Valois, an ambitious soldier who looked forward to a more decisive resolution of the tortuous disputes of twenty years of diplomacy and legal argument. On 4 May 1293, Philip sent his officers to proclaim the peace in the streets of Bordeaux and Bayonne. When this was followed, not long afterwards, by some particularly serious attacks on Philip's subjects, the French King ordered the Seneschal of Gascony to deliver up the malefactors to his officers, including all the principal dignitaries of the city of Bayonne. The Seneschal refused. The case was brought before the Parlement of Paris, which pronounced the sequestration of the greater part of the duchy and sent a number of unarmed sergeants to take possession. They were curtly dismissed. Accordingly, on 27 October 1293, Edward I was summoned to appear before the Parlement to answer for the contumacy of his officials. A date was fixed in January 1294. 'And we shall proceed against you as justice requires, whether you appear or not.'[16]

Edward I had not sought this crisis. His resources were heavily committed in his own kingdom and in Scotland. He was also genuinely willing to compromise. So he commanded his subjects to keep the peace with the Normans and declared himself ready to bring all the malefactors within his own dominions to justice if Philip would do likewise in his. Alternatively, Edward proposed arbitration. These offers Philip professed to find 'dishonourable to himself and to his realm'. They would have required him to deal with Edward on terms of equality as between one monarch and another, whereas this was a matter which concerned the juridical rights of his Crown against a subject. He therefore proposed to decide it in his own courts. In the autumn of 1293 Edward sent his brother Edmund of Lancaster to negotiate with Philip in Paris. Edmund had many friends at Philip's court. His wife (whom he brought with him) was the mother of the French Queen. But he was too trustful, and there is no doubt that he was elaborately duped. Philip told him that Edward was technically in contempt of the Parlement. He could not withdraw the citation without losing face before his more aggressive councillors. Therefore it would be necessary for Edward to suffer a short, nominal occupation of his French territories. A secret agreement was made. 'One or two men' of the King of France would be admitted to the principal strongholds of Aquitaine, but real control would remain with the existing garrisons. After a decent interval (forty days was suggested) there would be a formal treaty. Philip would withdraw the citation and graciously restore the duchy. Edmund agreed to this plan. In February 1294 a draft treaty was drawn up, and instructions were sent to the Seneschal of Gascony to admit the French officers. Over the weeks which followed 'one or two men' were joined by many more. In Paris, the English negotiators became anxious. In April they reminded Philip of his promises and received a soothing answer. There was some opposition among his councillors, Philip told them. If he seemed harsh in his public pronouncements it was only for their ears. Reassured by this, the English ambassadors listened with equanimity as the King told his council that the citation would not be withdrawn without their consent. But on 5 May 1294 Philip unexpectedly entered the chamber of the Parlement and had Edward's name called. Edward's retained lawyers scrambled to the front to discover what was happening and to seek an adjournment. It was refused and Edward was declared a defaulter. On 19 May the duchy was forfeited. In the south Philip's officers closed their grip on the principal towns and castles.[17]

The French remained in Aquitaine for nine years. From the distance of his English capital Edward I discovered the strategic difficulties of fighting a war in the duchy against a power which was perpetually at its borders. A French army could be gathered in Périgord and Languedoc within a few weeks. The English response took much longer. Edward's vassals were not obliged to serve him beyond the seas, and if they consented to do so at all they had to be well paid. Transports had to be requisitioned in the ports of southern England. Victuals had to found. The winds were not always favourable. It was a very slow and expensive process. The war in Gascony, although it was desultorily fought and lasted but four years, cost Edward I about £400,000, more than he had spent on the larger armies which he had raised to fight in Wales and Scotland, and much more than the same war cost Philip the Fair.[18]

In spite of his difficulties, Edward succeeded in dispatching a small army to Aquitaine in October 1294. It sailed up the Garonne under the command of John of Brittany and recaptured some important strongholds including Bourg, Blaye and Rions. Bayonne was recovered in January 1295 with the help of its citizens. By the spring, much of the southern part of the duchy was once again in English hands. But reinforcements were slow in coming. Pay fell into arrears. And supply presented formidable problems for an army which was fighting on the territory of friends and could not live off the land. John of Brittany was repulsed at Bordeaux, where there was a strong French garrison. In March 1295 Charles of Valois arrived in the duchy with a fresh French army. The English troops at Rions mutinied and Charles retook the town on Palm Sunday, 'not processionally with palms but violently with lances', says the chronicler. The French quickly re-established their position in the Garonne valley. Another English army, smaller than the first, arrived in 1296 under the command of Edmund of Lancaster, but he was no more able than his predecessor to capture Bordeaux. Within very few weeks of the army's arrival, its funds were exhausted and its commander was dying. Edward had preserved a foothold in Aquitaine but little else had been achieved.[19]

From these humiliating events some interesting conclusions were drawn, the source of one of the great strategic orthodoxies of successive English governments during the fourteenth century. The fate of Aquitaine, according to this view, could be decided only in the north, the political heart of France where the French King was most vulnerable to pressure and where the English were best placed to apply it. Edward I's first essay in this direction was an expensive failure but it became, nevertheless, the inspiration of his grandson's strategy at the beginning of the Hundred Years War. During 1294 English agents had created a great alliance among the territorial princes of the German Empire whose lands bordered on France to the north and north-west. These men had grievances of their own against the acquisitive French monarchy and were readily persuaded to mount a co-ordinated invasion of northern France in return for the generous subsidies which Edward was offering. However, when the moment came none of them did anything except for Edward's son-in-law the Count of Bar. He invaded Champagne in 1297 and suffered a convincing defeat. The German King, Adolf of Nassau, accepted the bribes of both sides.

Edward I found a somewhat better instrument for his purpose in the Count of Flanders, Guy of Dampierre, an impressionable vacillating man now in his seventies, not an ideal ally but a prince with a stronger vested interest than the Germans had in fighting Philip the Fair. In June 1296, the long litigation in the Parlement of Paris between Guy and the oligarchy of Ghent, which Philip had allowed to sleep for some years, had suddenly been revived. Philip had summoned his vassal before the tribunal and at the same time announced that he was taking the Flemish cities of Ghent, Bruges, Ypres and Lille under his protection. The sequence of events was uncannily similar to the one which had led to the forfeiture of the duchy of Aquitaine two years earlier. Unlike Edward I, however, the Count of Flanders appeared. The occasion was deeply humiliating for him. In front of the representatives of his subjects, he was made to submit to a fine and to surrender his territories into the King's hands to receive them back out of grace. When he returned to Flanders in the autumn of 1296 he at once entered into negotiations with the King of England. A military alliance was concluded on 7 January 1297. Edward paid him £6,000 on account. Guy formally renounced his homage to the French King two days later.

The enterprise ended in disaster. Edward could not live up to his promises. At home his demands for money and men provoked open resistance and eventually a grave constitutional crisis. The French army invaded Flanders in June 1297, before the English forces could arrive, and when eventually they landed on 23 August the campaign had already been lost. The only fighting in which the English engaged was some rioting against their Flemish allies in Ghent. Edward hastily abandoned Flanders and when, in 1300, the French invaded what was left of Guy's territory he left the Count to his fate. Philip's armies occupied Flanders without difficulty. Guy was arrested and locked up in the castle of Compiègne.

The English King made a serious attempt to resolve the dispute by arbitration before the Pope. But these proceedings, like most litigation, served only to reveal the irreconcilable differences of the two protagonists. Edward's plenipotentiaries boldly challenged the entire juridical basis on which Aquitaine had been held by the English dynasty since 1259. They argued that Gascony had always been held free of any feudal obligations; alternatively, if the Treaty of Paris was an answer to that, the French Crown had repudiated it and lost whatever rights it had once conferred on them.[20] The arguments deployed by the French have not survived, but they can readily be imagined. Boniface VIII, who scarcely troubled to conceal his dislike of the French, once asked the French Chancellor, Pierre Flote, whether it was not Philip's real intention to drive the English dynasty out of Aquitaine as his ancestors had driven them out of Normandy. The Chancellor smiled: 'Of course,' he replied.[21] Whether this really was Philip's intention has sometimes been doubted, but there is scarcely room for doubt. The great noblemen of Philip's court probably had some sympathy for Edward I. His problems were theirs writ large. But it was to Flote that the French King listened. The Pope was realistic enough to perceive this, and his award when it appeared was unexpectedly anodyne. He declared that Edward should do homage for such lands as Philip might be persuaded to restore to him. But Philip was not persuaded to restore any lands to Edward until 1302, and what persuaded him then was not the abstract reasoning which two very law-minded kings submitted to a lawyer–Pope. In May 1302 there was a popular revolution in Bruges. The French garrison there was massacred and with them many of Philip's allies among the governing oligarchy of the city. On 11 June 1302 a hastily recruited army of fullers, weavers and peasants, poorly armed and without cavalry but ably led by a grandson of Guy of Dampierre, destroyed the French army beneath the walls of Courtrai. Some 20,000 Frenchmen were left dead on the field. Pierre Flote was one of them.

The battle of Courtrai created a considerable sensation in Europe. Boniface VIII's attendants did well to wake him in the middle of the night to tell him the glad news. The French King's authority never entirely recovered. The defeat also did great harm to Philip's credit in an age when solvency was largely a matter of bluff. The second part of Philip's reign was a story of successive financial crises. And not only financial crises. After the news had reached Bordeaux the citizens rose and expelled the French garrison. Without Bordeaux Philip could not hold Gascony. With his resources fully committed in the north he could not afford to allow Edward I to remain an enemy. So he made peace with him on 20 May 1303. Edward I got most of what he had fought for in vain in Flanders and in Aquitaine. He agreed to do homage for the duchy, and Philip restored it to him. Edward's son, Edward of Caernarvon, was betrothed to Philip's daughter Isabella, the origin of the disputed succession which justified a greater war a generation later.[22]

A few days after the treaty had been sealed in Paris the representatives of Philip the Fair formally transferred possession of Aquitaine to the English commissioners before a crowd of lawyers, witnesses and onlookers assembled at Saint-Émilion. But Edward never fully recovered what he had lost in 1294. Some French officials in the remoter parts of the duchy were particularly tardy in leaving, and disputes on this score were to continue for many years. In the western foothills of the Pyrenees French troops hung on to the castle of Mauléon until 1307. The incoming officials of the King–Duke found their master's affairs in a state of disarray which was still evident ten years later. Many of his rights had been sold off. Others were appropriated by powerful local interests who had taken advantage of the confusion to assert forgotten claims or invent new ones. Others were encumbered with debt and with the consequences of a decade of misman-agement. A number of Gascon noblemen had been bribed or coerced into declaring for Philip the Fair, including most of the dominant families in the south-east of the duchy bordering on Languedoc. The counts of Foix and Armagnac were among them. Freed of the heavy hand of Edward I and his officials, they had made the southern part of the duchy the theatre of a destructive private war. Elsewhere, in the valleys of the Dordogne and the Garonne whole districts were given over to anarchy and brigandage. In the Landes, the lord of Albret had usurped a variety of ducal prerogatives and had made his family almost immune from the government's control. 'There is no king in Gascony but he,' one of Edward's correspondents reported in 1305.[23]

The most significant consequence of the war was the change wrought in the attitudes of those who made English policy. Before the war Edward I had taken issue with some of the more irritating manifestations of French royal policy, but he had never challenged his cousin's sovereignty. He had sought to define the powers of the Parlement and if possible to limit them. But he had not denied that those powers existed. On 5 June 1286, when Edward I had performed his homage to Philip the Fair, his Chancellor Robert Burnell had delivered a speech in the great hall of the royal palace in Paris in which he had darkly referred to more abrasive possibilities. Edward, said Burnell, might well have chosen to contest the French King's rights if he had not had confidence in his justice. There were 'plusieurs de son conseil' who would have supported such a move. The manner in which the French King and his Parlement had treated him in 1294 was a shock. Probably the 'plusieurs' became the majority. The ingenious arguments addressed to the Pope in 1298 may have been advanced as bargaining counters, but they were in the process of becoming principles of English policy. Towards the end of Edward's reign his clerk, Philip Martel, an experienced diplomat who had borne the brunt of the negotiation of the treaty of 1303, recorded his thoughts in a confidential memorandum. In the immediate future the King–Duke should endeavour to recover what he had lost in three decades of French encroachment and one of open war. Islands of French jurisdiction within the duchy should be suppressed and the constant intervention of French courts brought to an end. Until these conditions were satisfied, Martel thought that Edward should refuse to do homage to the King of France. But he had met Philip the Fair. He could see that these were terms which would not be countenanced by any French king cast in Philip's mould. They were but temporary expedients, the preliminaries of larger ambitions. The great object, Martel thought, was to enable the English King at a convenient moment to repudiate the Treaty of Paris 'without untoward consequences and without dishonour in the eyes of God or man'. It was a reservation characteristic of this ageing ecclesiastical lawyer trained in the patient way of the English civil service who would not live to see his views applied by force of battle.[24]

How far Edward I was privy to these thoughts is impossible to say, but it is hardly conceivable that Martel had not discussed them with him. By the terms of the treaty Edward was bound to do homage in person, and a date had been appointed for the purpose in September 1303. But the homage was never performed. A variety of excuses was offered. There is little doubt that the real reason was the Edward was not willing to do homage for Aquitaine until his rights within the duchy had been defined by treaty and those of the King of France reduced to nominal obeisances. Still less was Edward inclined to swear the traditional oath of fealty. Philip Martel said as much to the French King's ministers in the course of a stormy interview at Vernon in February 1306.[25]

*

Certainly there were signs that Edward II, who succeeded his father in 1307, was impatient of the constraints which his feudal obligations to the French King placed upon him. On 31 December 1308 he did his homage in person at Boulogne. For a man who was king in his own land the ceremony was an uncomfortable humiliation and Edward II was unfortunate in the number of occasions on which he was called upon to repeat it. Philip the Fair died in 1314 and was succeeded by his three short-lived sons. Each of them required an act of homage, and one of them, Louis X, rubbed in the point by summoning Edward to sit as a judge in the court of peers and to perform military service in Flanders. Edward was able to resist all of Louis X's demands until the latter died prematurely in 1316. Under Philip V the evil moment was put off for four years. Homage was eventually performed in Amiens cathedral in July 1320, but it was done with ill grace and without the oath of fealty. The ceremony was accompanied by a gratuitous lecture on French breaches of the treaty and was followed by a number of disputatious meetings in which the participants dispelled whatever goodwill the act of homage had created. When Edward II was next called upon to do homage by Charles IV in August 1323, he rudely dismissed the French ambassadors and informed his 'dear and beloved brother' by letter that he was too busy.[26]

Edward II's relations with the French court would have been better if he had been a more courteous diplomat and a more capable politician, but in the nature of things they would not have been close. Behind the posturing at Amiens there lay real grievances. In returning to his old dominions in 1303 Edward I had returned to his old problems, and these problems Edward II had now inherited. The mosaic pattern of competing jurisdictions was still there. The boundaries were not fixed. Ancient disputes were not resolved. In 1311 the English government made a determined attempt to define once for all the respective rights of the two kings in southern France. The device chosen was a standing commission to which each side would refer all outstanding grievances. It was a failure. Four English commissioners and three French ones met in January in the convent of the Franciscan friars in Périgueux. For five months they exchanged elaborate documents drafted by lawyers in which each side accused the other of misconstruing and disregarding the four treaties which their governments had made since 1259. There were articles of complaint tendered by the English, followed by the Responses of the French, the Replications of the English and the succession of statements and counter-statements borrowed from the elaborate procedure of the civil courts in which most of the participants had been trained. On 2 June 1311 the English walked out.

'These proceedings', they told the French commissioners, 'clearly show that you have no intention of respecting the treaties and it is therefore quite useless for us to stay here.' With goodwill and another procedure something might have been achieved. But the jurisdiction which French courts claimed in Aquitaine was a problem which could never have been resolved at the conference in Périgueux, for Philip the Fair had insisted on excluding it from the commissioners' terms of reference. They were not proper matters for diplomacy, he said, for they concerned the relations between king and subject. In such matters Edward II was a subject.[27]

French officials had already resumed the inexorable encroachment upon Edward II's southern duchy after the ten-year interruption brought about by the war. There were renewed attempts to make notaries date their documents by the regnal years of the French kings. From time to time the French government attempted to legislate for Aquitaine, issuing commands to the government in Bordeaux now to expel Jews from the duchy, now to banish English coins from circulation, now to refrain from taxing the traffic of the Garonne. French sergeants were reported at one point to be touring Saintonge and the Agenais demanding to know of the inhabitants whether their allegiance was to the English or to the French King and uttering menaces if they received the wrong answer.[28]

The weakness and incompetence of Edward II's government, punctuated by its occasional outbursts of aggressive energy, offered an irresistible temptation to appeal to the Parlement in Paris. English officials complained that these appeals gravely aggravated their difficulties in imposing order on the duchy. Appellants committed every kind of crime while their appeals were proceeding, knowing that they were for all practical purposes immune from the jurisdiction of the Duke. Pope John XXII said much the same thing in the course of several thoughtful letters about the condition of the English duchy. It was true. In one notorious case the Parlement itself was constrained to agree that the lord of Navailles had prosecuted his appeal in the most dilatory fashion for eleven years while engaging in violence against his enemies 'daily'. This was in June 1319. After passing judgement upon him the Parlement expressed its hope that the French Seneschals in Toulouse and Périgueux would suppress acts of theft, rape and murder among eleven other prominent Gascon noblemen who were 'temporarily exempt from the Duke's jurisdiction as appellants from the judgements of his officers'.[29]

It is unlikely that this warning was heeded. When the French King's relations with England were good he might listen with sympathy to his complaints. The practice of appealing directly to Paris without the

preliminary formality of seeking redress in the ducal courts was unorthodox, Philip the Fair had agreed in 1310, and would have to stop. Further
concessions had been made in 1313 when the two kings met at Boulogne.
French officials in the south-west were ordered to restrain their enthusiasm, and a serious attempt was made to prevent abuses of the protection
afforded to appellants. It was to be conferred only in urgent cases with
Philip's personal permission and then only on the appellants themselves
and their immediate families, not on a host of followers and dependants.[30]
Nevertheless, these concessions were generally disregarded by the royal
officers on the spot and they were forgotten by the kings themselves when
their relations became less cordial. In 1324 there were some forty appeals
pending in the Parlement involving several hundred separate disputes.
Many of these appellants had been enjoying royal protection for years. On
one occasion a liveried sergeant of the French King was arrested in Bordeaux, where he had apparently been distributing letters of protection
freely to potential appellants. 'The Court of France is encroaching on your
jurisdiction day by day,' the city Council observed when reporting this
affair to the government at Westminster.[31]

For their part Edward II and his officials in the duchy resorted to
increasingly high-handed measures against appellants. The King wrote to
the Abbot of Cluny threatening to confiscate the possessions of the order
in England if the Cluniac priory of St Eutrope in Saintes did not abandon a
particularly embarrassing appeal. His officers in Saintes beat up members
of the community. It was by no means the worst case. It was also entirely
ineffective. The policy of bullying appellants provoked much more litigation in the Parlement than it prevented.[32]

The *causes célèbres* of these years were the successive appeals of the lord
of Albret between 1310 and 1324. His prolific family, the most powerful
in Gascony, dominated the Landes south of Bordeaux and enjoyed
influence and alliances penetrating throughout south-western France.
There is little doubt about Albret's motives. He wanted to pursue his
ferocious vendettas against rival Gascon clans free of the inhibiting hand
of the King–Duke's judges and officials. Some of his quarrels with the
English seneschals were provoked on trivial grounds for the deliberate
purpose of exempting himself from their jurisdiction. Others arose directly
from the attempts of the Bordeaux government to bring him to order.
Albret's appeals against the Seneschal in 1312 involved the protection of
his dominions in the Landes by a small French army: in 1312 there were
50 cavalry and 200 infantry. Edward II was obliged to buy off the appeal
in the following year for a large sum. But in spite of the settlement, and in

spite of their situation in the heart of the duchy the Albrets continued to move away from the orbit of the kings of England and into that of the French.[33]

Almost as serious as the defection of the lord of Albret was the secession of one of the other great noble families of the south-west, the house of Béarn. Béarn was a small territory on the north slopes of the Pyrenees around Oloron and Pau whose ambitious rulers were extending their influence and power down the river valleys into the lowlands of southern Gascony. It was one of those mountain regions at the periphery of the wars of the fourteenth century which were destined to play a central role in them: Béarn, Navarre, Savoy, Wales. They were all territories densely populated for their sparse resources by clans of farmers and mountain-dwellers who took naturally to war and to the wages and occasional fortunes as well as the violence which war offered. The viscounts of Béarn had for many years been vassals of the dukes of Aquitaine and their subjects were spread across the territories of the king–dukes, pasturing their sheep, serving as administrators, soldiers and captains, trading as moneylenders and merchants. But as the result of a marriage alliance and the extinction of the old line of viscounts, Béarn had been merged since 1290 with the county of Foix, which was a fief of the Crown of France. Thereafter its rulers had veered uneasily between England and France according to the fortunes of politics and war. It was in Edward II's reign that Béarn was lost to the English dynasty and, apart from a short period in the middle of the century, finally lost. The circumstances are obscure, but the Parlement of Paris certainly played a crucial role. It began to assume jurisdiction in disputes between the viscounts and their vassals of Béarn, displacing the court of the dukes of Aquitaine at Saint-Séver. In the course of one such dispute, in 1318, the Parisian tribunal ordered the temporary confiscation of Béarn. Four years later, in 1322, the regent of Béarn herself invoked the jurisdiction of the Parlement against Edward II's officers and brought in French troops to defend her territory while the litigation continued. When the young Count of Foix, Gaston II, came of age in 1323 there was no doubt about his allegiance. He never did homage to a king of England. Throughout his life, until perhaps the very end of it, he remained a firm supporter of the French dynasty, and a sharp thorn in the southern flank of the duchy.[34]

Edward II was more vulnerable to this kind of problem than his father, and much less skilful in dealing with it. Preoccupied by constitutional crisis and civil war in England and constantly threatened by the renascent power of Robert Bruce's Scotland, Edward's government was of little account in his continental dominions. The revenues of the duchy were mortgaged first to an Italian banking house and then to the Pope. In the outlying districts seigneurial castles sprang up like mushrooms after rain, while the strongholds which Edward I had patiently and expensively acquired were allowed to fall into the hands of the local nobility or abandoned for want of money to garrison and repair them. It was a characteristic caution which moved the government, in 1320, to order that the garrison of Saint-Puy should be paid 'as little as we can get away with', although Saint-Puy was the only castle which Edward held in the territory of the powerful counts of Armagnac. Four years later its walls were reported to have collapsed in several places. At Blaye, the major fortress on the north shore of the Gironde, the roof work of the citadel had fallen in and squatters had built themselves houses in the main court. 'And this', said the official who reported it in 1324, 'has happened for want of money.'[35]

A bankrupt administration in Bordeaux watched impotently as Philip the Fair appointed commissioners to investigate 'violence, looting, rapine and anarchy' in Aquitaine. This was in 1313. Although Philip was certainly not averse to stirring that troubled pot no one doubted that the symptoms listed were real and not imagined. Pope John XXII, himself a native of Quercy, expressed himself in stronger terms. The ambush of a papal legate near Valence d'Agenais in 1318 provoked from him a jeremiad in which Edward's Gascon subjects were berated for permitting every kind of atrocity. There was, he said, 'no king, no law' there. Private war between rival coalitions of noblemen, which had always been endemic in Gascony, now reached its most ferocious pitch. That nicely judged combination of bribery, bullying and tact by which Edward I had governed was beyond the resources of his son's officials and beyond the ability of some of them. In the course of Edward's reign there were no less than nineteen seneschals of Gascony in as many years, some scandalously insufficient or cynically self-interested. None had time to accumulate experience of an office which more than any other in Edward's gift required experience. There was nothing surprising in the English government's appointment of a commission in 1320 to investigate the corruption of Edward's servants in the duchy; nor in the fact that another commission was charged with exactly the same duty only four years later.[36]

The failure of diplomacy left Edward's officials in Aquitaine with no defence against the constant gnawing of their territory from outside, except a policy of reprisal. The danger of such a policy was not that it would lead to war: Edward's advisers were resigned to that. It was that the war would come at a moment of the French King's choosing. When it came, with the war of Saint-Sardos in 1324, the English were unprepared. Characteristically, Edward II was drawn into it by a local dispute which he had not desired and could not control.

Until 1322 Edward II had probably never heard of Saint-Sardos. It was a small village in the Agenais, situated in the wedge of territory in the angle of the Lot and the Garonne which was at once the most lawless part of the duchy and the key to its eastern defences. By the village there was a Benedictine priory. The priory was within the jurisdiction of the dukes of Aquitaine, but it was a daughter-house of the abbey of Sarlat, which was not. It was a lawyer's delight. The Abbot of Sarlat had on several occasions petitioned the Parlement of Paris to declare that Saint-Sardos was exempt from the King–Duke's jurisdiction. These proceedings had not been taken very seriously and they had always been inconclusive. The matter was mentioned and then forgotten at the conferences at Périgueux in 1311. In 1318 the Abbot renewed his attempt and endeavoured to interest Philip V in it by suggesting that if Saint-Sardos were exempt a royal *bastide* might be built there in partnership with the monks. Philip invited the Parlement to pronounce on the question, but did very little to push the proceedings on. Then, in December 1322, the Parlement pronounced in the Abbot's favour. On 15 October 1323 a sergeant dispatched by the French Seneschal at Périgueux, arrived at Saint-Sardos and drove into the ground a stake bearing the arms of the King of France.[37]

Edward was preoccupied by the problems of England in 1323, and he was in no position to do anything about it. But the Abbot's plans had enemies closer at hand. The citizens of Agen believed that the privileges which were habitually granted to *bastides* would injure their trade. Local landowners feared that settlers would be drawn from their estates. One of them was Raymond-Bernard, lord of the castle of Montpezat, 3 miles away. Raymond-Bernard had himself, in his time, been a thorn in the flesh of the ducal government. He had had an appeal pending in the Parlement for the past five years. But necessity called for new alliances. On the night of 15 October 1323 he raided Saint-Sardos, burned the village, and hanged the French sergeant at the royal stake which he had just erected. The Seneschal of Gascony at this time was Ralph Basset, a Staffordshire knight hardened in the treacherous politics of England but without experience of Aquitaine. He had been in office for only four months. Unfortunately, he was staying in the vicinity when the incident occurred, and had conferred with Raymond-Bernard only two days earlier. The French believed that he was privy to the crime, and they were probably right. Suddenly Saint-Sardos was the centre of European affairs.[38]

The news of the incident took more than five weeks to reach Edward II and it arrived at an unfortunate moment. Edward had just sent an embassy to France to make further excuses for his failure to do homage. He appreciated the significance of the incident even if his Seneschal in Gascony did not. A letter of abject apology was prepared, in which Edward assured the French King that he had had nothing to do with the incident and promised that if the rumours were true ('which God forbid') the malefactors would be found and punished. This letter was sent post haste after the ambassadors and reached them in Paris in only five days. The ambassadors had found the capital in a mood of great excitement. A commission had been appointed to investigate the facts and Ralph Basset had been summoned to appear before it at Bergerac. He had declined to attend, sending in his place some unconvincing excuses which, as English spies reported, were 'ungraciously received'. Charles IV himself was not in the capital but at Tours, where he had held a meeting of the Great Council. Provisional arrangements had been made to assemble an army at Toulouse after Christmas. Anti-English feeling ran high. On 21 December 1323 Edward II's chief advocate in the Parlement was abruptly seized in the precincts of the court and imprisoned in the Châtelet.[39]

The English ambassadors caught up with the French King at Limoges, where he had spent Christmas. Charles was disposed to accept Edward's personal excuses, but not those of Ralph Basset and Raymond-Bernard de Montpezat. Both of them were ordered to appear before the King at Toulouse on 23 January 1324 together with several other Gascon officials. Basset sent a message stating that the summons had been improperly made out, adding that in any event he was the representative of Edward II, who was a peer of France and could be tried only in Paris before the Great Chamber of the Parlement. The other officials claimed benefit of clergy. Raymond-Bernard said nothing. None of them appeared. In February they were outlawed and their property declared forfeited to the Crown. The French seneschals of Toulouse and Périgueux were ordered to enter the duchy and take possession of the castle of Montpezat by force. It was an order of doubtful legality and it proved to be impossible to carry out. Edward II ordered Raymond-Bernard to hold the castle in his name. Trenches were dug round the outer walls. Every Gascon of military age was summoned to arms. The officers sent to execute the judgement of the French court were turned away at the beginning of March by a garrison of

600 men. When the commander of the royal corps of archers attempted to read out the court's judgement he was seized and held for ransom.[40]

In England the conduct of affairs was in the hands of the Chamberlain, Hugh Despenser the Younger, Edward II's ruthless and greedy favourite. Despenser was an able and clever man, and hard working, in these respects quite unlike Edward's other favourites. But he lacked judgement. After the first robust response, English policy was lost in the confusion of conflicting decisions and uncertain intentions. In March 1324, Ralph Basset was recalled. On 7 March it was announced that the Archbishop of Dublin and the King's brother Edmund of Woodstock, Earl of Kent, would lead a new embassy to the French court. Their instructions, however, were rambling and unclear. There was a number of appeals pending in the Parlement which they were to mention to the French King. As to the matter of Saint-Sardos, Edward II was willing in principle to make amends. They were to suggest that the incident called for a lengthy investigation and could perhaps more profitably be discussed when the two kings met on the occasion of Edward's homage. However, the principal object which the ambassadors were to achieve was the postponement of that meeting at least until July, and if possible until the following year, to which end they were to employ 'such subtle and clever devices as they could think of'. This was a serious misjudgement. The homage had already been repeatedly put off with excuses which Charles IV had declared to be inadequate, as indeed they were. Coming at such a time this request was bound to sow suspicion even in the mind of so correct and uncynical a ruler as Charles IV.[41]

Edward's ambassadors performed their difficult duty with the greatest possible ineptitude. They sailed from Dover on 8 April 1324 and arrived in Paris a fortnight later. They were met there by Elias Joneston, an experienced professional diplomat who had been in the capital since December. It was already clear to him that the French government was about to confiscate the duchy. Charles, it appeared, had summoned his army to muster at Moissac on the confines of Aquitaine on 10 June 1324. Joneston was dispatched to carry this portentous news back to England. The Earl and the Archbishop went on to the royal manor of Vincennes, where the King was staying. They were received frostily in the presence of the whole royal Council. After they had spoken their piece they were banished to a waiting room while the matter was discussed, and when they were recalled it was to hear an angry harangue from the French Chancellor. Charles, he said, was astonished by their impertinence in proposing a compromise in the matter of Saint-Sardos as if a king could compromise with a subject about the performance of his public duties. The conduct of Edward's Gascon officials and the incident at Montpezat were acts of treason and insulting to the Crown. They could not be overlooked without dishonour. So the Chancellor continued until the ambassadors at length endeavoured to adjourn the proceedings to the following day when tempers might perhaps have cooled. But the proceedings were not adjourned. Instead the ambassadors were required to promise at once that the contumacious officials of the duchy would be delivered up to the French government and the castle of Montpezat forthwith surrendered. The ambassadors asked for twenty days to take instructions from Edward II and beseeched the French King to postpone the muster due on 10 June. Both requests were refused. The muster would be brought forward unless an answer was forthcoming within four days. The ambassadors dispatched a messenger to England but before the answer could return they would have to choose between a declaration of war and a complete surrender. Edmund of Woodstock was not the man to wrestle with difficulties such as these. He was weak and malleable and awed by the French King. The news from the south-west was not encouraging. Letters received from the government in Bordeaux indicated that prominent vassals of the King–Duke could not be relied upon. None was in the mood for war. The ambassadors therefore gave Charles what he wanted. They promised that the guilty officials would be given up; Montpezat would be surrendered; and Edward would come to Amiens on 1 July to do homage. Then they hurriedly left for Bordeaux to see to the fulfilment of their agreement.[42]

When they reached the duchy they found that support for Edward II was rather stronger than they had been led to believe. Charles IV's conduct at Vincennes seemed to have aroused real indignation. The Earl recovered his courage among friends and when the French officials arrived to take possession of Montpezat they were told that this would be contrary to the customs of the duchy and the privileges of its inhabitants. They went away empty-handed.[43]

In England Edward II's advisers agonized. The King's immediate reaction, when the news of the Vincennes agreement reached him in mid-May, was to disown his ambassadors. What they had done had been beyond their powers and extorted from them by duress. Then, at the beginning of June, Edward changed his mind. Yet more ambassadors were appointed, this time led by the Earl of Pembroke, a venerable elder statesman with good connections and many friends in France. His instructions were to persuade Charles IV to put off the homage and to this end he was to promise to surrender Montpezat until homage had been duly performed.

This new proposal came at a very late hour. The homage had been fixed for 1 July and the French court was already making its way to Amiens for the ceremony. Speed was of the essence, but the ambassadors did not leave before 20 June. Then, on the 23rd, while they were lodging near Saint-Riquier, the Earl of Pembroke had a sudden heart attack and died. The rest of the embassy, consisting of royal clerks, did not reach Amiens until 1 July. The King was not there. He had already declared the duchy forfeit a week earlier when it became clear that Edward II would not appear. After fours days the two royal clerks found him at Anet-sur-Marne. They arrived on his wedding day. Three days passed before they could obtain an audience and then it was a short one. The King told them that Edward had failed to punish the authors of the crime of Saint-Sardos and therefore he could not take seriously Edward's protestations that he had had nothing to do with the incident. He then dismissed them. Edward did not give up. He appointed yet another embassy and wrote to Charles IV asking for the necessary letters of safe conduct. The ambassadors waited in vain at Dover for the safe conduct to arrive. No reply came from France.[44]

In August 1324 the French King's uncle, Charles of Valois, invaded Aquitaine for the second time in his long career.[1] In spite of the slow development of the crisis the ducal government was quite unprepared. Montpezat was fully garrisoned and victualled. So was Penne, the principal royal castle of the Agenais. There were also 200 men at Agen. But elsewhere the castles were well below their full strength and some important places were not garrisoned at all. No troops had arrived from England, although attempts were being made to assemble an expeditionary force at Portsmouth. In Bordeaux Edward's administration had no resources and few friends. Some of the most prominent noblemen of the duchy had joined Charles of Valois. They included the Count of Foix, who had hurried to Paris at the outset of the dispute to promise his support, and the lord of Albret, who finally deserted the cause of the English dynasty. Those who remained loyal had good reason to feel betrayed by their leaders. The new Seneschal had fallen ill immediately after his arrival and his servants reported that he could not be moved. Edward's senior representative in the duchy was his indecisive brother, the Earl of Kent, and the Earl's fellow Ambassador Alexander Bicknor, Archbishop of Dublin. They shut themselves up with an armed force in the fortress of La Réole at the eastern edge of the Bordelais and remained there until the campaign was over.

It was over in less than six weeks. The French army numbered about 7,000 men. It had no difficulty in overrunning the undefended valley of the Dordogne in Périgord. In the Agenais Penne held out, but Montpezat was captured in the first few days and razed to the ground. Agen surrendered without a blow, having first expelled its garrison. The citizens of numberless small walled towns took their cue from Agen. They wanted a quiet life, and the anarchy of the past twenty years had left them little reason to feel grateful to Edward II's government. Charles of Valois was at La Réole by 25 August, the twelfth day of the campaign. In this great fortress on the Garonne, only 30 miles from Bordeaux, the Earl of Kent hoped to resist until help could arrive from England.

At first it seemed that he might succeed. Attempts to take the place by storm failed ingloriously and cost Charles of Valois the lives of several of his best commanders. But within the castle all was not well. It was not victualled for a long siege. Morale was low. The loyalty of the townsmen could not be counted on. The gates were in disrepair and in years of impecunious neglect the moats had been allowed to fill with debris. In England the promised reinforcements had assembled but they were bottled up in their ports by southerly winds. The garrison of La Réole felt that the government of the Despensers, Hugh the Younger and his father, had forgotten them. There were others who had more radical objections to this able but unscrupulous pair who monopolized power and favour under the benevolent eye of an incapable King. The Archbishop of Dublin was one of these. When recriminations were exchanged after the war, he was said to have preached against the wickedness of the royal favourites and to have declared himself ready to fight a duel with the younger Hugh had he not been restrained by the dignity of the cloth. Thus were the political squabbles of fifteen years of English civil wars revived within the close confines of a besieged castle in France. The Earl of Kent was still loyal to his brother, but he was a weak man, heavily reliant on the Archbishop's advice. The Archbishop advised him that La Réole should be surrendered. On 22 September 1324, after only five weeks of the siege, the Earl surrendered and made a truce with the conquerors. Each party was to hold its present positions in the duchy for six months. For the English there were few positions to hold. They had lost everything except the districts of Bordeaux and Bayonne and the coastal strip in between, the city of Saintes and a few castles on the eastern marches of the duchy where garrisons isolated by the speed of the campaign looked out on hostile territory as far as the eye could see. In the occupied towns those who had demonstrated their loyalty to the English King were elbowed out of power and privilege by the many more who had been treacherous, cowardly or indifferent. 'Nous sumes trays, nous sumes venduz,' they complained to powerless officials in Bordeaux.

As the winter truce continued, the French made preparations for its expiry. In December the French army was ordered to assemble at Bergerac on 1 May 1325. A two-pronged attack was planned, one force invading Saintonge and capturing Saintes, while the other invested Bordeaux and the Gironde ports. A formidable siege-train was prepared at Toulouse and Moissac, and a fleet of barges was assembled to carry it downriver. All this activity suggested, at any rate to the beleaguered English representatives in the duchy, that a decision had been made to finish with the English presence in France.[46] There were plenty of Frenchmen who would have supported such a decision. There would be no hope of peace in France while the kings of England had a foothold there, one of them told Charles's successor four years later. Let the sea mark the frontier:

> Soit la mer borne et dessevrance
> De l'Angleterre et de la France.[47]

Yet the ambitions of Charles IV himself were not as straightforward as this. He was the son of Philip the Fair, but he did not have Philip's ruthlessness or cynicism. His closest advisers were not lawyers and officials with their ambitious notions of French territorial sovereignty, but the princes of his family and in particular that conservative old war-horse Charles of Valois. They were men who shared with Edward II himself the outlook of great territorial magnates. Charles was no doubt glad to annex some of the frontier provinces of Aquitaine. But although he was attached to forms and stiff-necked in the defence of his prerogatives, he had no particular wish to exploit them for larger political ends.

Towards the end of the year, Charles IV let it be known to the Pope that if Edward would cede the Agenais to him and do homage for the rest of the duchy he would not insist upon enforcing the total forfeiture which had been pronounced in June. These hints were duly passed on to the English government. The Pope also passed on another hint which the French King had let drop. Charles, so it seemed, would be more easily persuaded if Edward appointed his Queen Isabella as his ambassador. It was a strange suggestion. This formidable and evil lady was twenty-nine years old in 1325. Since she was Charles IV's sister she could claim some influence at the French court if any English ambassador could. But it was notorious that she hated and despised her husband and his homosexual friends. She had loathed Gaveston, and her loathing of the younger Hugh Despenser was scarcely less intense. Isabella had in the past engaged in some desultory intrigue of her own with Despenser's many enemies. One of them was Roger Mortimer, lord of Wigmore, a political rival of long standing who, after a short spell of imprisonment in the Tower of London, had escaped in August 1323 and fled to France. He was now living at the French court and was rumoured to have offered his services to Charles IV for the invasion of Gascony. As a result, when the war broke out, Isabella was treated in England as an enemy alien. In September 1324 all her lands and castles were confiscated and her private household (most of which was French) was disbanded on Despenser's instructions. Isabella's final indignity was to be placed in the custody of Despenser's wife, who confiscated her seal and censored her correspondence. This then was the suggested agent of reconciliation. The French King's proposal was put to an assembly of magnates at Winchester at the beginning of March 1325. They had misgivings about it. But in the interests of peace they suggested that the Queen should be allowed to go on condition that Roger Mortimer was first extradited from France. In the event the condition was never satisfied, but the Queen went nonetheless. She departed on 9 March 1325.[48]

For the first few weeks of her sojourn in France. Isabella worked under the careful eye of her husband's ministers and officials, a substantial number of whom were now in almost permanent residence at the French court. In Aquitaine, the promised reinforcements from England had still not arrived and when they did so in the course of the negotiations they immediately mutinied for want of victuals and set fire to parts of Bordeaux.[49] In Paris the English made what they could of their declining bargaining power. But it was not much. A fresh truce was agreed on 31 March 1325 and a provisional agreement followed in May. According to this document, Charles IV was to be allowed to go into nominal occupation of what was left of the duchy of Aquitaine. French officials would be installed in the seaboard towns and by this means the French King's honour would be saved. Real control would remain with Edward II's garrisons. When Edward had done homage for the duchy those parts of it which he still held would be formally restored to him. But the parts which the French had conquered by force of arms in the previous year would not be restored until some outstanding disputes had been dealt with; and then only on payment of reparations for a war which the French government had found more costly than it had expected. These were severe terms. They involved the tacit recognition of the loss of most of the duchy, including substantially everything that the English had held in Périgord and the Agenais. Indeed, so severe were they that Edward attempted once again to disown his ambassadors. But the prelates and lay barons who were consulted on the point advised him in the clearest terms that the treaty was within the wide words of the ambassadors' authority and was binding.

Accordingly, Edward II was bound to ratify it and he reluctantly did so. Charles IV remained in possession of his conquests.[50] Whether he would ever voluntarily have surrendered them cannot now be known, for it shortly became unnecessary for him to do so. The humiliating conclusion of the war and the unexpected sequel of Isabella's embassy destroyed Edward II's government in England.

CHAPTER IV

Crises of Succession

Edward II had agreed to do homage at Beauvais on 15 August 1325. In early August he travelled to the coast. Shipping was ordered for his passage of the Channel. But as the day approached the Despensers became nervous of allowing the King to leave the country when so many enemies were waiting to prize the government from their grip. At the last moment the plans were changed. A few miles from Dover in the Premonstratensian abbey of Langdon the royal Council met and resolved to tell the French King that Edward had fallen ill. Regrettably, it would be necessary for Edward's twelve-year-old son, the future Edward III, to be invested with the duchy in his father's place.[1]

For the English King and his friends this decision proved to be a serious mistake. The young Prince was placed in the charge of the Bishop of Exeter, Walter Stapledon, an experienced civil servant whose loyalty was beyond question. They left for France on 10 September 1325. A fortnight later Prince Edward did homage to his uncle at Vincennes in the presence of his mother and an assembly of officials and noblemen from both countries. The sequel was less satisfactory. Walter Stapledon's visit to the French court opened his eyes to some alarming truths. It became clear to him that Isabella had no intention of returning to an England dominated by the Despensers. Nor did she propose to let Stapledon bring the heir to the throne back to his father. Worse than this, it appeared that Edward II could no longer rely on those whom he had sent on diplomatic business to Paris. Many of them nursed private grievances of their own which the freer atmosphere of a foreign capital encouraged them to declare openly. The bishops of Winchester and Norwich and the Earl of Richmond had all decided not to return at the conclusion of their mission, but to remain with the Queen. The Earl of Kent, Edward's brother, who had been in France throughout the crisis, was about to throw in his lot with them. Roger Mortimer himself, 'our mortal enemy' as Edward had it, was openly to be seen among the Queen's household. He had become Isabella's principal adviser and was shortly to become her lover. In this ugly atmosphere

Stapledon found himself denied access to the Queen and the Prince and threatened with violence by her entourage. In mid-November he fled from Paris in secret and took ship for England disguised as a common traveller.[2]

A more calculating schemer than Charles IV might have welcomed this turn of events. Charles certainly refused to comply with the importunate and increasingly hysterical requests which Edward II addressed to him demanding the extradition of his wife and son to England. But he was a strait-laced man. He was genuinely shocked when Isabella's liaison with Mortimer became public knowledge and embarrassed when in the first six months of 1326 she began to recruit mercenaries among the French nobility. What she envisaged was nothing less than an armed invasion of England for the purpose of replacing Edward II on his throne by his son. In May 1326, Isabella showed off her strength at the coronation of the new French Queen. She appeared with a large and showy retinue in which Mortimer held the foremost place, a fact which scandalized onlookers and was duly reported to Edward II by his spies. Shortly after this incident Isabella was banished from the French court and her military preparations in France brought to an end.[3]

In August, she took up residence outside French territory at Valenciennes in the Imperial county of Hainault. Edward was not reassured. He ordered the removal of French monks from English monastic houses and imposed restrictions on the movements of Frenchmen travelling in and out of England. The French government retaliated by ordering the arrest of all English men and women in France and the confiscation of half their property. On 16 August 1326 the officers of the *baillages* came for them without warning, knocking up some in their beds in the early hours. They were 'Christians, labourers, craftsmen of many trades, merchants and good men like the rest of us', a Parisian lawyer grumbled. Many had taken French spouses. Edward II replied in kind as soon as he heard the news.[4]

At Valenciennes Isabella and Mortimer began to remake their plans. They proposed to the Count of Hainault, William I, that Prince Edward should be betrothed to his daughter Philippa in return for military assistance. William accepted this offer with alacrity. He had no ties to Edward II and had no objection to making his daughter a queen. He was willing to provide a port of embarkation and a force of some 700 men.[5] The men were volunteers, raised by the Count's brother John. They sailed from Dortrecht on 23 September 1326 and arrived the following day in the Suffolk port of Orwell.

It was a tiny force which should have been defeated without difficulty. But no one was willing to fight for Edward II. The seamen of the southern ports had refused to guard the coasts for hatred of the Despensers. Others joined forces with Isabella and Mortimer and their foreign army. London proclaimed its support for the Queen and erupted into mob violence. Bishop Stapledon was lynched in Cheapside by her partisans. As for Edward II and the Despensers, they were obliged to flee westwards pursued by Isabella and a growing pack. For Mortimer, it was an occasion to avenge five years of defeat, imprisonment and exile. The elder Despenser was caught at Bristol. He was drawn, hanged and quartered. The younger Despenser, having failed to escape to Lundy Island, was tracked down in Glamorganshire. He was perfunctorily tried and executed in the same barbarous fashion as his father. Edward was captured with him. He was kept under guard at Kenilworth while Parliament was summoned to decide what should be done with him. On 13 January 1327 it was resolved that he should be deposed. A few days later he was brought into the hall of Kenilworth Castle to meet his enemies. There, half fainting, his voice stifled by his own groans and tears, he abdicated in favour of his fourteen-year-old son. Real power fell to Mortimer and his mistress.

Among the faults of which Edward II had been accused by the Parliament which deposed him was the neglect of Aquitaine. They said that it was 'as good as lost by negligence and bad counsel.' This was hypocrisy. In the last months of Edward's reign English policy in Gascony had shown fresh vigour. There had been a serious attempt to bully Charles IV into making the final territorial settlement which had been promised in 1325. A new seneschal, Oliver Ingham, had even succeeded in raising an army of Gascons and Spanish mercenaries to invade Saintonge and the Agenais. He had taken a number of strongholds in the name of Prince Edward as Duke of Aquitaine, who was even then residing at the court of France. The abandonment of Aquitaine was in reality the work of Isabella and Mortimer, whose government had greater preoccupations than the prosecution of a distracting, expensive and distant war. They hastened to make peace with France on whatever terms were available. When the final treaty was made on 31 March 1327, it appeared that the English government had bound itself not only to restore Ingham's conquests but also to pay reparations of 50,000 marks to Charles IV. Of the greater part of the duchy which the French had occupied since 1324 nothing was said. The loss of all but the coastal strip was accepted in silence. To most contemporaries the loss of even that shrunken remnant seemed to be no more than a matter of time.[6]

Thus inauspiciously began the reign of Edward III. The life of Edward II still had a few more months to run. In April 1327 he was removed to

Berkeley Castle and held there until, at the end of September, it was unexpectedly announced that he had died. There is little doubt that he had been smothered on the instructions of Mortimer and with the approval of Queen Isabella. So, when France's own age of political crisis began in February 1328 with the death of Charles IV the French government had the good fortune to see its principal rival paralysed by the bitter memory of recent disputes and the weakness of illegitimate rulers.

Philip the Fair had left three healthy adult sons when he died in 1314, but a combination of circumstances and misfortune wiped out the whole of his line within fourteen years. Louis X died of pneumonia only eighteen months after his father, leaving an infant daughter behind him. His brother, Philip V, was struck down in 1322 by dysentery, the endemic disease of insanitary medieval palaces. He too left only daughters. The third brother, Charles IV, had reigned for only six years when he died from some unknown affliction in February 1328. As the only son of Philip the Fair to survive into his thirties Charles had had a better chance to beget a large family, but he had not done so. His first wife had been put away for adultery after a famous scandal and, although his second wife gave birth to a son in 1324, both mother and child died within a few days. His third wife, Joan of Evreux, was seven months pregnant when Charles died. For the first time in more than three centuries there was no obvious male heir to succeed a king of France.

The splendid obsequies of Charles IV ended on 5 February 1328. A few days afterwards there occurred a fateful meeting in Paris of the great men of the kingdom. The surviving family of the late King was represented by his first cousins the counts of Valois and Evreux, and by the agents of the King of England, who was the son of the dead man's sister as well as Duke of Aquitaine. There were five other peers of France present, three of whom, the dukes of Brittany, Burgundy and Bourbon, had married into the royal family. Others were bound to it by more distant connections of blood and clientage, the cement of every medieval community. The occasion must have lacked intimacy, but it was as much a family gathering as a council of state. Ostensibly their purpose was limited to the choice of a regent to govern France for the last two months of the Queen's pregnancy. Yet, although the succession to the throne was not on the agenda it can hardly have been excluded from the discussion, for it was by now clear that if the Queen gave birth to a daughter the child would not inherit the crown.

Although subsequent tradition invested this rule with the force of

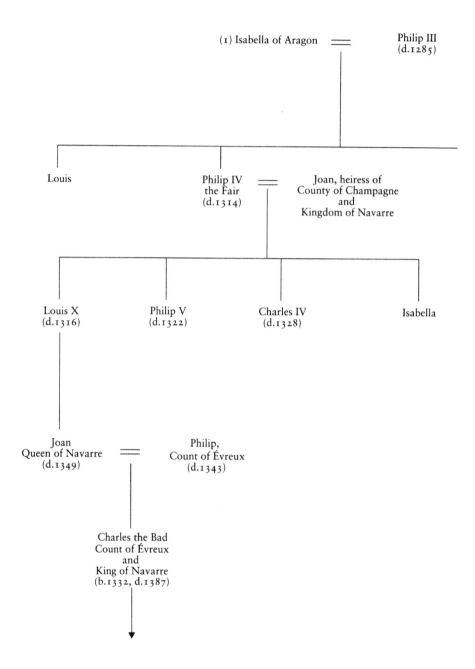

2   The French royal succession

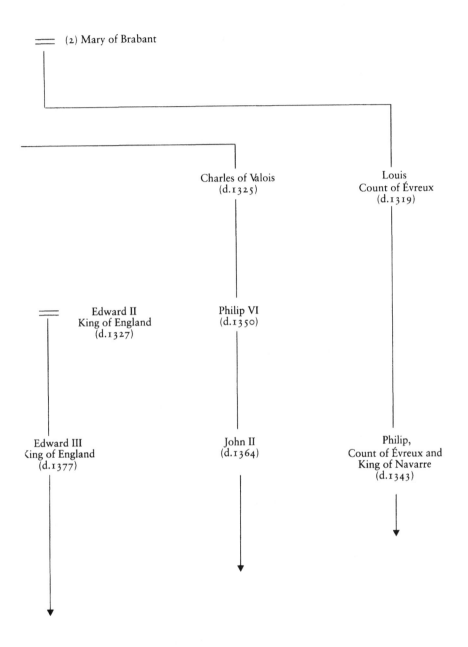

immemorial antiquity it was a rule of force rather than principle, and one of recent origin. For many years, Frenchwomen had held noble fiefs in their own right without objection, and outside France they had succeeded to kingdoms, including Hungary, Naples and Navarre, which were ruled by cadet branches of the Capetian dynasty. It was therefore far from obvious to contemporaries that Philip V should have become King of France in 1316 instead of the infant daughter of his predecessor. The fact that he did so was due more than anything else to a forceful personality and a large armed following. Even so, Philip had had to buy off his niece's claims and the protests of some important noblemen with the promise of an expensive endowment. By contrast, in 1322, when Philip himself died his daughters were pushed aside without question. Practice had hardened into law. The question at issue in 1328 was more elusive: if a woman could not inherit the crown, could she nevertheless transmit the right of inheritance to her descendants? The closest male relative of Charles IV was the King of England, who was the only surviving male descendant of Philip the Fair but was descended through his mother, Isabella. The closest male relative after Edward was Philip, Count of Valois, who was Philip the Fair's nephew and descended from Philip III in unbroken male line. If the rule excluding women from the French throne was justified by their incompetence to govern the state, then there was no reason why that objection should extend to their sons. But perhaps it was justified by some more spiritual attachment to the notion of succession in the uninterrupted male line. Philip of Valois and his supporters asserted that it was. They also demanded that the Count, as the senior male in the line of succession to the throne, should become regent.

Although the question of principle did not have to be decided in February of 1328, those who remembered the events of 1316 knew quite well that if the Count of Valois became regent it would be difficult to prevent him from making himself king should Joan of Evreux give birth to a girl. The English knew this too. Their representatives (probably Edward III's permanent attorneys at the Parlement of Paris) vigorously pressed their master's claims to the regency as well as to the succession. There were many 'learned in civil and canon law' who agreed with them. But they were silenced. Edward III seems to have had no supporters among those who mattered. None of the princes of the blood espoused his cause. Even his father-in-law, William of Hainault, supported his rival. Philip therefore became regent and when, on 1 April 1328, Joan gave birth to a daughter, he at once assumed the title of king. The only overt opposition to Philip VI's assumption of the crown came from the turbulent Flemings, now in the last stages of a bloody rebellion. They in their desperation sent the Burgomaster of Bruges to England to offer Edward III their support. The proposal came to nothing, and for his indiscretion the Burgomaster was mutilated, drawn and hanged by order of the French government.

'The mother had no claim, so neither did the son,' the chronicler of Saint-Denis judiciously observed. Yet the magnates of 1328, although no doubt glad of a legal basis for their decision, scarcely needed one. There was rather more truth in the chronicler's other explanation that the French were uneasy about the prospect of a foreign ruler. Edward, although a Frenchman in his own eyes, was certainly foreign to the French. Moreover, he had other things against him. His appointment as regent would have been perverse while he himself was a minor. His accession as king would have brought real power in France to his mother, whose misconduct there was a recent memory. By comparison, Philip of Valois was a man of thirty-five whose father, Charles of Valois, had been a great hero among the higher nobility of France, a pillar of the state and the head of a considerable political connection. By birth, Philip of Valois was entitled to a place at the centre of French political life, while his rival was by birth no more than Philip the Fair's grandson, an outsider to all but genealogists.[7]

Whether Philip VI had any other advantages than birth and age was a question often debated in his own day. His early manhood had been passed beneath the shadow of an overpowering father. Charles of Valois had been a man of great energy and unlimited but frustrated ambitions, a life-long soldier commanding French armies in the Low Countries and Gascony and an adventurer for his own account in many other places. An invasion of Italy in 1302 had won him nothing more than an obscure corner in Dante's *Inferno*. Designs upon the Holy Roman Empire and ambitions to revive and rule the Latin Empire of the east had been only the most spectacular of his many failures, symptoms of a romantic, impulsive temperament and an utter want of political judgement. At home, he was recklessly generous, maintaining an impressive retinue and dying heavily in debt. Some of these qualities were inherited by Philip VI. Although moody, irresolute and unpredictable, in these respects quite unlike Charles, Philip shared his father's reckless impulsiveness and romantic ambitions. He was also prone to long bouts of nervous uncertainty, insecurity and depression, moods in which his decisions were unusually erratic, even incomprehensible. These depressions seem to have been provoked more often than not by the difficulties of his family life: a strident wife and sickly children of whom he was extravagantly fond. Unfortunately his advisers did not make up for his failings. Philip did not have the Capetians' talent for choosing subordinates and friends. 'He was always ready to accept advice from fools,' said Froissart.[8]

Contemporaries exaggerated the King's sensuality and self-indulgence and were certainly wrong to accuse him of lacking interest in affairs of state. Philip was an intensely serious man. What he lacked was judgement and experience. He had not been brought up to be king. His background and interests were those of a great territorial nobleman. His attendances at court and in council had been few, and separated by long periods in his lands in western France. Moreover the new King, although he was a competent knight and had some experience of field service, was not made to be a commander of armies. He was capable of great personal courage, as those who saw him at Crécy could testify. But he was increasingly obese and unfit, and temperamentally averse to the discomforts of campaigning and the uncertainties of the battlefield. His father had bequeathed his most famous sword not to Philip but to the younger brother.[9] It was a significant choice. Philip was a thoroughly bad soldier, more so than any other medieval King of France except, perhaps, for the mentally defective Charles VI.

What became plain at a very early stage was that Philip VI was not entirely the master of his own government and needed to tread delicately in a way which had not been required of his predecessors. He owed too much to others for his accession. He owed it to the Count of Flanders to restore him by force to the control of his county. He owed it to the rest of the higher nobility to consult them at length before doing any such thing. He owed it to his friends to order the judicial murder of Pierre Remi, his predecessor's efficient but low-born, greedy and unpopular finance minister. He owed it to them too to distribute grants of land and cash which even the enormous forfeited estates of the disgraced minister were inadequate to supply. He owed it to countless allies great and small to find jobs for themselves and their protégés in the public service, which consequently underwent an enormous and costly expansion not all of which was warranted by the burden of its work. An English diplomat perceived an important truth when he told his government in 1329 that there would be no change in French policy towards Gascony without the approval of the peerage, the King's power was 'so far hedged about'.[10]

The new King reacted to these pressures in a way which was perhaps predictable, but left him vulnerable when things went wrong. He visibly distrusted his gossiping and often disloyal court and his huge, unwieldy bureaucracy with its constricting procedures. He governed secretively, delegating little, confiding only in his immediate family and a handful of trusted ministers and officials, avoiding public discussion, by-passing the great departments of state as far as he could by the informal cabal, the personal warrant, the private interview. The image of him left by an Aragonese ambassador who was at court in the winter of 1330–1 is telling, and wholly characteristic: the withdrawal into a small room by the great hall, the King's cousin slipping in behind, the Constable of France locking the door, Philip himself seated with his back to the fire talking freely as the embers glowed in the ambassador's face, the insistence on absolute secrecy when the decision was made. The contrast with Edward III was striking.[11]

Subsequent events made the rejection of Edward III's claim to the French throne seem more significant than it really was. At the time, it aroused neither surprise nor indignation in England, where the French interests of the royal house had traditionally been viewed with indifference or suspicion. Only the Queen Mother, Isabella, felt strongly about the issue and her indignation drew its intensity from her own special position as the sister of Charles IV of France. The discarding of her son was a slight all the more galling for having come from her closest blood relations. It was certainly at her instance that in the middle of May 1328 the bishops of Coventry and Worcester were dispatched upon a futile expedition to the French court to claim the Crown in the name of their fifteen-year-old master. They never performed their mission. Upon their arrival in France, they were subjected (so they said) to ugly threats by supporters of Philip VI and left hastily after swearing a notarial protest which recorded what had happened. Later in the year, Philip sent an embassy to England led by the Abbot of Fécamp, a polished rhetorician who later became Pope Clement VI. The Abbot, whose instructions were to summon Edward III to do homage for Aquitaine to the new French King, received a surly response from the Queen Mother, 'typical of a woman' says the chronicler. According to one report Isabella said that Edward 'was the son of a king and would not do homage to the son of a count'. The Abbot remained in England for some time in the hope of a more measured response, then returned home.[12]

If Philip VI had had his way the duchy would have been confiscated at once. But he was dissuaded from this extreme course by his Council, who no doubt had in mind the threat of their own security implicit in a frontal attack on a peer of France. Instead, a more circumspect course was proposed. Two commissioners, including the Abbot of Fécamp, were sent to the south-west to sequester the Duke's revenues until such time as Edward III should agree to do homage. At the same time a further embassy was sent to England to threaten Edward with more extreme measures.

This put the English in a more realistic frame of mind. Gascony was manifestly indefensible. The enormous treasure which Edward II had hoarded up in his last years had been dissipated. And in the aftermath of two civil wars, public opinion was in no mood to pay for an ambitious foreign policy. When Philip's second embassy arrived in England in January 1329 Parliament was about to meet at Westminster, an occasion for reviewing past policies and raising taxes to pay for future ones. The advice of the lords of Parliament was unequivocal. Edward's claim to the French Crown was unsustainable and it was his duty to do homage for his French territory. Edward therefore told the French ambassadors that he would do as Philip asked. He wrote to the French King himself regretting that the pressure of business had prevented him from doing so earlier.[13]

The English government did not surrender gracefully. They assembled from every department of state an enormous collection of 'bulls, charters, instruments, rolls and memoranda' relevant to the act of homage and past dealings with France. The fruits of this research were sent off in advance of the royal party together with a force of lawyers and diplomats to haggle with the French on the exact ramifications of the ceremony. So when Edward III performed his homage to Philip VI in the great Gothic choir of Amiens cathedral on 6 June 1329, he did it in a manner which raised as many new disputes as it resolved old ones. At the high point there was a wrangle reminiscent of the homage of Edward II to Philip V in 1320. Edward III's ministers wanted him to do homage not only for the lands which he held in southern France but also for those which he ought to hold, by which was meant the ones which had been occupied by French troops since the war of Saint-Sardos. For their part, Philip's spokesmen declared that homage would not be accepted on these terms. The occupied provinces had been 'justly acquired by right of war'. The conflict was resolved by an untidy compromise, tolerated only because there was no time to devise anything better. Edward did homage according to the French formula making no reference to the lost provinces. But his spokesman, the Bishop of Lincoln, was allowed to make a short speech of protest, reserving all his master's rights and handing over a document setting out the homage which the English government thought ought to have been done. Moreover, Edward's homage was not unqualified. He refused to join his hands between Philip's, the ceremonial distinction which marked out 'liege' homage from simple homage: Edward was recognizing Philip as king of France, but he was recognizing the King of France as his landlord and not as his sovereign. Meanwhile, away from the light of publicity, the English were given private assurances by Philip that all would, in due course, be resolved to their mutual satisfaction. The studied vagueness of the arrangement had the sole advantage of allowing the ceremony to take place and the kings to part on something resembling friendly terms. In the tournament outside Amiens which celebrated their reconciliation the English King, now sixteen years old, carried off all the honours. It was only mock-war.[14]

The recovery of the conquered territories remained the first priority of English diplomacy throughout the 1330s. These territories included the whole of the Agenais, all the English possessions in southern Périgord and most of Saintonge. Their loss had been a catastrophe for the duchy, as both sides knew. It had severed the main fortresses which were necessary for its defence on the east. It had deprived it of much of its best agricultural land, on which the population depended for their supplies of grain and other foodstuffs. It had removed a large part of the patronage and revenues at the disposal of the Seneschal, severely weakening the government in the face of an unscrupulous and land-hungry nobility. From being a net contributor to the royal revenues, the duchy became a dependency. In the most recent treaty between the two crowns, that of 1326, the French King's predecessor had promised that he would do what was just with regard to these lands. That, in the opinion of the English, meant nothing less than their restoration without condition.

Perhaps this was asking for too much of one whose filial piety was as strong as Philip's. He had no intention of disgorging the lost provinces and no intention of allowing matters to rest with the partial homage of June 1329. Within weeks of Edward's return, Philip gave him a fixed date by which he was to recognize that he owed liege homage for his duchy or submit to the loss of the rest of it. For their part the English government, still controlled by Mortimer and Isabella, sent a number of embassies to France with instructions to put off the evil moment for as long as they could. They also endeavoured to strengthen the defences of Gascony. There was an air of mounting desperation about these attempts. Just after Christmas 1329, the government held a Great Council of magnates at the King's manor of Eltham where some support was obtained. In the following March, Parliament met at Winchester and deliberated upon the defence of the duchy with results that are difficult to discover from the surviving sources but cannot have been very encouraging. Certainly, no tax was voted, but the peers were buttonholed individually and some of them promised to make personal contributions. Further support was obtained from the towns after a certain amount of bullying. By this means it was possible in April 1330 to send Edward's thirteen-year-old brother to

Gascony as royal lieutenant, together with a decent escort and forty ships.[15]

At the end of August 1330 negotiations broke down. Edward III had technically been in breach of his feudal obligations since 28 July, when the latest deadline for doing homage had expired. An important embassy, led by the devious Bishop of Norwich, William Ayrmin, had been at the French court for a month and had wholly failed to extract any further postponements from the French King. Edward was declared to be in default. The measured procedure of the Parlement of Paris entitled him to two more summonses before he could be judged in his absence. Philip gave him until 15 December 1330.[16]

William Ayrmin returned to England to find the court at Nottingham. He reported on the dismal results of his embassy on 6 September 1330. The decision seems to have been taken at once not to yield. On the same day a Great Council of the English peerage was summoned for mid-October to consider further measures for the reinforcement of Gascony. Edward's Seneschal there was warned to expect from the north either a group of officials come to sequester the duchy or an armed invasion. In the former case, the officials were to be humoured 'debonerement par bel parler' until more vigorous steps were possible; in the latter, the government in Bordeaux was to resist with all its strength.[17]

It was upon the latter course that Philip VI resolved. At the end of the year 1330, his brother Charles, Count of Alençon, marched south with an army. There was some doubt, even at the time, about the Count's precise instructions but none about his actions. At some time in the new year, probably in February, he attacked Saintes, the northernmost of the major strongholds defending the approach to Bordeaux. Saintes was defended by a large and well-supplied garrison, but it was taken, apparently without much difficulty, and sacked.[18] Rather later it suited Philip VI to say that he had not authorized this attack and had ordered his brother to desist as soon as he had heard about it. But Philip cannot really have expected his brother to hold his army in a state of suspended animation while political developments unfolded in the north, a task quite beyond the organizational resources of a medieval military staff. The real reason for the change of orders was a change of policy in England, the result of another *coup d'état* which brought Edward III to power in place of his mother and Mortimer.

Edward II had been overthrown by a coalition of interests which had nothing else in common than contempt of him and hatred of the

Despensers. Once they were in power, this proved to be a fragile foundation for government. The body nominally in control was the Council of Regency, which had been invested by the baronage with power to govern in the King's name. Its president was the Earl of Lancaster, the brother of the great rebel of Edward II's reign and the natural leader of a powerful baronial caucus, but ageing and gradually going blind. Partly because of his ineffective stewardship, the Council of Regency had been edged aside by Mortimer and Isabella. They had possession of the young King and were able to install their own protégés in important parts of the administration. The two of them proved to be even more rapacious in their own interests than the Despensers had been. Isabella received an enormous increase in her dower allowance. Mortimer made himself Earl of March in 1328 and built on his own ancestral lands and those forfeited by the Despensers to form what amounted to a private principality in Wales and the western marches. The wealth which came with this sudden access of power was spent on lavish display and on building a party of clients and dependants, the essential foundation of political power. At his 'Round Table' tournaments, Mortimer entertained the entire nobility and disported himself like a king. The comparison occurred to more than one contemporary.

But Mortimer's power was insecure and he knew it. In the winter of 1328–9 he had to suppress an incipient rebellion. The Earl of Lancaster gathered round himself at Bedford an army comprising the King's uncles, the earls of Kent and Norfolk, and much of the baronage. The two earls, however, were lured away by Isabella and the rebellion collapsed. Many of its supporters fled to France. The motives of the royal uncles in rejoining Mortimer and Isabella can only be guessed: loyalty to the young King, misgivings about another baronial coup. But they were not friends to be relied upon. The following year, the Earl of Kent, a dignified but stupid man, was persuaded by *agents provocateurs* that his brother Edward II was still alive, and gave his support to a plot to release him. Since the Earl had been one of the army which deposed Edward, his opinion at least had turned full circle. Kent was arrested at the Winchester Parliament of March 1330 and hurriedly condemned to death. Although the Earl was not particularly popular, it was necessary to find a condemned criminal to carry out the sentence; no one else would kill so august a nobleman.

However, the greatest threat to Mortimer's survival was untouchable: Edward III, who, although a minor, was ceasing to be a cypher. It would be interesting to know what kind of man this remarkable ruler was. But although much was written about Edward III in his lifetime, it was written according to glossy conventions drawn from the received stereotypes of knightly virtue. These conventions completely obscure Edward's personality just as they do those of his rivals Philip VI and John II of France. For Froissart, Edward was the 'mighty and valiant King Edward who lived and reigned so nobly and courageously'.[19] But a man with such a genius for friendship, who could inspire such extravagant personal loyalty must have been more than the cardboard figure described by Froissart's phrase. He was a literate, although not a bookish man. He was already a famous horseman, and an enthusiastic participant in tournaments. His triumphs there were recognized even by French chroniclers, sufficient evidence that they were not only due to the deference of his competitors. Much care had evidently been lavished on Edward's education, but experience must have counted for more than education in Edward's personality. Five years of being carried about in his mother's baggage train, first to France, then to the Low Countries and finally in the relentless pursuit of his father across England had given Edward an intensity of experience unusual even by the standards of an age which did not shelter children from violence and cruelty. Edward's royal dignity had been his mother's principal asset in bargaining with foreign princes during her exile, and in ruling England after her return. He had become profoundly conscious of it himself, both from training and by reaction against the grubby humiliations of these early years.

Edward married Philippa of Hainault in January 1328, an event which made it necessary to provide him with a household more than nominally his own. Its officers were appointed by the government, but ambition as well as personal sympathy identified some of them with the King himself. His virtual exclusion from official business and the strict tutelage of his mother and Mortimer became increasingly irksome both to him and to them. In September 1329 William Montagu, an ungrateful protégé of Mortimer, was dispatched by the government on a diplomatic mission to the papal court at Avignon. While he was there he took the opportunity to warn the Pope in the course of a secret audience that Edward was not his own master. As a result of this interview Edward's tutor and amanuensis, Richard Bury, supplied the Pope with a specimen of Edward's handwriting and a code word ('Pater Sancte') by which the Pope could distinguish letters which embodied the King's own desires from those which were dictated by Mortimer and Isabella.

The summer of 1330, a time of mounting tension in foreign affairs, was also one of intensifying suspicion and unease in England. Mortimer tightened his grip upon the King. Access to him was restricted. Attendants of

Mortimer's choice were appointed to wait upon him, and spies planted among them to report upon his doings. At the beginning of September 1330 Mortimer and Isabella moved to Nottingham, the principal royal fortress of the Midlands, where they installed themselves and a large bodyguard in the keep. Edward was with them and remained under constant observation. In mid-October there was a humiliating public scene. Mortimer had the principal members of Edward's household interrogated before the Council. He told them that Edward (who was present) was untrustworthy, and accused them of abetting him in a plot against the government. All of them denied it except Montagu, who replied with an evasion. He said that he would do nothing inconsistent with his duty.[20]

On the night of 19 October 1330 Montagu, leading an armed band of some two dozen companions, penetrated the inner bailey of the castle through an underground culvert with the connivance of the garrison commander. Together with the King, they invaded the Queen Mother's apartment where they found her preparing for bed. Mortimer was in a nearby room with a handful of adherents. There was a fight. Two of Mortimer's men were killed and a number of others were wounded. 'Fair son, have pity on gentle Mortimer,' the Queen Mother is supposed to have cried. Mortimer was taken unharmed, but he was kept under guard and sent to London while a decision was made about what to do with him. On the following morning his supporters were rounded up in their lodgings about the town, the final stage of an enterprise as effortlessly successful as the one which had placed Mortimer himself in power in 1327. Edward issued a proclamation repudiating the acts which Mortimer and Isabella had done in his name and announcing his intention of governing in his person according to 'justice and reason'.[21] It is worth noticing the ages of those who helped Edward III to seize power in 1330, many of whom were to become his closest friends and collaborators in three decades of war. The oldest members of the band who can be identified were Robert Ufford (later Earl of Suffolk), who was thirty-two; and John de Nevill, a former retainer of the Earl of Lancaster, who was thirty. Most were much younger. Montagu, the leader, was twenty-eight. John Moleyns must have been in his mid-twenties. Humphrey Bohun, who later became Earl of Hereford and Constable of England, was twenty-one and his two brothers Edward and William were still in their teens. Edward himself was not yet eighteen.

Parliament met in London at the end of November and condemned Mortimer unheard. On 29 November 1330 he became the first person ever to be executed at Tyburn. His adultery with the Queen Mother was an embarrassment best forgotten. Isabella was compelled to surrender the riches which she had accumulated in four years of power and retire to a life of comfortable obscurity at her manors of Hertford and Castle Rising. There, she kept a large establishment and occupied herself in entertaining, hawking and pious works. Decent fictions were scrupulously observed. When she died in 1358, at the age of sixty-six, she was buried in the mantle of red samite lined with yellow silk which she had worn at her wedding.[22]

These events jolted the course of relations between England and France. The Great Council which Mortimer and Isabella had summoned to consider the defence of Gascony had duly assembled in the great hall of Nottingham Castle on 15 October 1330. But it had disbanded inconclusively on the 19th, only a few hours before the coup. The sequel was a period of paralysis, followed by a change of policy. Intransigence in the face of French threats had been a policy particularly associated with the Queen Mother, and its execution with diplomats such as the bishops of Worcester and Norwich, who were her protégés. At the beginning of November 1330, Edward ordered John Shoreditch, a Chancery clerk who was one of the government's principal experts on Aquitaine, to prepare a dossier on the current state of negotiations with France to be presented to Parliament at the end of the month. Presumably it was duly presented, but the result is not recorded. It would be surprising if Parliament were enthusiastic about the prospect of further quarrels with France. What is clear is that by the beginning of 1331, probably as a result of the dispatch of Charles of Alençon to the south-west, Edward decided to give Philip VI what he wanted. There is no reason to suppose that his heart was not in it. Edward did not yet have his mother's grudge against the French King, and the immediate problem was to avoid the complete loss of what was left of the duchy for a principle which did not seem to matter. A particularly grand embassy left England in February 1331. It was led by the bishops of Worcester and Norwich and three household knights in Edward's confidence, including William Montagu. Evidently the surrender was to be a dignified affair. Negotiations took place in Paris under severe pressure. The Count of Alençon was already in the south-west and was thought to be besieging Saintes (the news that he had captured it had not yet arrived). The next line of defence was the Gironde itself, and the fortress towns of Bourg and Blaye on its north shore. Terms were quickly agreed. On 30 March 1331 Edward issued letters explaining that he had not done liege homage in 1329 because he had been advised that there was some doubt about whether he was obliged to do so. But now, having been appraised of the true position, he desired that the homage at Amiens should be treated as liege homage and promised that he and his successors would do homage in due form in future.

The surrender of the English was almost as complete when it came to the territorial dispute. Philip VI promised that he would pardon Edward for his dilatoriness in the matter of liege homage and would revoke the decree of confiscation made in the Parlement. He also promised to lift the sentence of banishment which had been imposed on the individuals concerned in the outrage at the *bastide* of Saint-Sardos. What Philip did not do was pardon Edward's father for his conduct in that obscure affair. There was to be another joint judicial commission after the model of the process of Périgueux, which had so acrimoniously failed. The commissioners were to be ordered to effect a mutual restoration of territories seized by force of arms in Aquitaine since the war of Saint-Sardos. But that was as far as Philip would allow the clock to be turned back. The conquests made by the French in the war itself were studiously ignored. All that was said about them was that Edward III might apply to Philip for their restoration at some future time, in which case the French King would do what his predecessor had promised to do in May 1325, namely whatever seemed to him to be proper. Philip had already made it clear what he considered proper. In his view, Edward's father had been condemned by the due process of law and the lost provinces were held by right of conquest.[23]

The ambassadors had evidently agreed in Paris that the two kings would meet. But for some reason Edward did not wish this to be generally known. He embarked with the Bishop of Winchester at Dover on 4 April 1331 in conditions of the greatest secrecy, dressed as a merchant and accompanied by only fifteen knights. He left behind him letters patent announcing that he had gone to fulfil a vow of pilgrimage and to do 'certain other things touching the well-being of ourselves and our kingdom'. Philip VI met Edward at Pont-Sainte-Maxence, a short distance north of Paris, and they rode together to the French King's hunting lodge at Saint-Christophe in the forest of Halate. The French King was surprisingly accommodating. Edward was spared a fresh act of homage, Philip declaring himself satisfied with an exchange of letters defining the effect of the earlier ceremony. Philip had already recalled his army in the south and promised to indemnify Edward for the sack of Saintes by the Count of Alençon. Alençon had exceeded his authority, it was explained; letters ordering him to desist had unfortunately arrived too late. Some minor bones of contention were removed. Edward expressed his interest in joining with Philip in a crusade against the Spanish Moslems. Philip was duly gratified. The two kings parted friends, or at least 'not enemies' as the French official annalist put it.[24]

The annalist's doubts were well founded. Only the quarrels of the immediate past had been patched up. The more intractable problems which dated back to 1259 were left untouched. Both sides were well aware of this. When Parliament met at Westminster in September 1331 the Chancellor, John Stratford, delivered in his opening address a magisterial summary of the alternatives available. There were three ways, he said, of settling matters with the King of France: first by submitting all the outstanding disputes to the arbitration of the peers of France and abiding by their decision, as Philip had apparently offered to do; secondly by negotiations leading to a marriage alliance and a permanent treaty; thirdly by war. The lords advised that arbitration and war were both too risky. They suggested that negotiations should resume, and then turned to other business.[25]

No imaginative compromise was likely to emerge from the cumbrous diplomatic procedures of the early fourteenth century. In this dawn of international relations governments were only beginning to place their relations on a regular footing, to apply themselves continually to the business of keeping their friendships in repair instead of doing so spasmodically and late when the occasion arose. There were no permanent embassies to study from close at hand the hopes and fears and changing moods of their adversaries, to report to their governments where there was room for manoeuvre and where there was not. The English kings usually maintained a small corps of lawyers in Paris to transact their extensive business in the Parlement, and latterly some of them had been Englishmen. But while these men could be relied on to report the more public occurrences affecting their master, they were far removed from the political mood of the French royal court. The French kings themselves did not even have this measure of contact with their principal north European rivals.

Instead, negotiations of any importance were conducted by the irregular dispatch of 'solemn' ambassadors. This meant stately dignitaries, generally bishops or great noblemen, accompanied by great retinues of servants and hangers-on, and by a small number of permanent officials, sharp and disputatious clerics with satchels of documents. These magnificent affairs were required by the conventions of the time and by the self-esteem of the rulers concerned. But they were usually an unproductive hindrance to good diplomatic relations. Their arrival was attended by great publicity, and although they often had secret as well as public messages to deliver, these rarely remained secret for long. An embassy which failed, failed publicly. The rebuff was the more humiliating for being inflicted before the world, and to such exalted men. If communications had been better, such failures might more often have been avoided. But news travelled slowly, and the reactions of governments were slower still. Solemn embassies moved at a dignified pace while events happened fast. Instructions, which had to be prepared well in advance, were usually fairly narrowly limited. If they were found to be inappropriate, further instructions had to be obtained from home. For these reasons, it was occasionally suggested that important business should be transacted by confidential clerks who could ride post haste without losing face and without exhausting the store rooms of hospitable monasteries on the route. But these occasions were rare, and called for embarrassed apologies. The consequences for Anglo-French relations were serious. The muddle and inconsistency, the unintended tactlessness and ill-timed intransigence, which had propelled the affair of Saint-Sardos to its crisis, had been very largely due to Edward II's complete ignorance of the way in which his beloved cousin in France was thinking. Both governments were to make similar mistakes in the 1330s, for similar reasons.

The disappearance of most of the archives of the medieval French government makes it difficult to say whether there was anyone charged with the permanent function of watching the progress of the King's relations with foreign powers. Individual royal councillors were employed on diplomatic missions on an *ad hoc* basis. None of them was continuously concerned with England, or even with foreign affairs. In the first few years of Philip VI's reign his main advisers on relations with England were two high-ranking ecclesiastics, Andrea Ghini, successively Bishop of Arras and of Tournai, and Pierre Roger, Abbot of Fécamp, then Archbishop of Rouen. Ghini was a Florentine, a civil lawyer who had worked his way up through the financial service of the French government. At the time of the war of Saint-Sardos he had been Charles IV's private secretary. He had been to England once, in the autumn of 1323, to threaten Edward II with the forteiture of Aquitaine, and had received the rough end of Edward's tongue. Thereafter, he was concerned in every significant diplomatic exchange between the two countries until 1334.[26] Pierre Roger, who received a very similar rebuff from Queen Isabella in 1328, was a more considerable figure, and his was probably the face which was most familiar to successive English ambassadors. He was a theologian and in his day a famous orator who was often employed as a public spokesman for the

French government's views. It fell to him, on a memorable occasion in the audience hall of the papal palace at Avignon, to make the protest of France at the outset of the Hundred Years War, which he did in cogent and colourful language.[27] This was advocacy, and advocacy in time of war by a loyal servant of the French state. At a time when war might still have been avoided, Pierre Roger had been in favour of compromise, but he had been overruled by others whose judgement had been more strongly influenced by law and pride. Moreover, he was a practising bishop, not a permanent royal official, and he had other concerns even when he was at court. He attended to diplomatic occasions as they arose and then passed on to other things.

The English kings were slightly better served. Although there was no department of the government with special responsibility for foreign affairs, a number of individual Chancery clerks were almost continuously employed in seeing to the King's concerns abroad. Between about 1304 and the outbreak of the Hundred Years War an official known as the Keeper of Processes and Memoranda was responsible for accumulating, preserving and cataloguing a great collection of documents dealing with the problems of Aquitaine and of England's relations with France. In spite of his nondescript title, this personage was much more than an archivist. Elias Joneston, who held the office in 1331, had been Keeper for twenty-five years and before that had been the clerk of his predecessor. This immensely patient, profoundly pessimistic, rather blinkered man had advised the royal Council at every crisis of Anglo-French relations. He had written numerous and sometimes penetrating summaries of diplomatic problems, had drafted the instructions of most of the important embassies and had accompanied not a few of them in person.[28] At a lower level of bureaucratic existence, the same long-serving confidential clerks constantly reappear as the authors of reports prepared for the Council or Parliament, as members of the staff of English embassies to France and occasionally as diplomatic agents in their own right. Here were true experts who had done much for the continuity of English foreign policy in three decades of domestic disturbance.

However, for all their expertise these men had a serious shortcoming which was common to both English and French diplomacy. They were lawyers and antiquarians, students of precedent and form. They possessed an encyclopaedic knowledge of the ancient and complex territorial disputes of England and France. They saw to it that ambassadors were briefed on the precise juridical status of particular castles in the Agenais, on the correct method of setting up joint commissions of enquiry, on the peremptory exceptions that could be taken to proceedings in the Parlement of Paris, on the diplomatic history of every clause in the treaties of Paris and Amiens and the *ipsissima verba* of every homage which an English king had ever done to a French one. In some of their memoranda one can detect a real relish for the arcane complexities of Gascon affairs. They rarely rose above the technicalities. Except in moments of great stress, when legal forms were obviously beside the point, they looked upon the differences of the two nations not as a political problem calling for a political answer, but as a quest for justice calling for sustained forensic skill. From their superiors, the bishops and noblemen who led the principal embassies, rather more might have been expected. But they were part-time diplomats who depended for their understanding on their clerks, and on their instructions, which were often drafted by their clerks. In 1315 a Chancery clerk prepared a memorandum for Edward II which dealt with the qualities to be looked for in an ambassador to the French court. This man expressed the outlook of this kind when he remarked that, apart from tact and high rank, the main requisite of an ambassador was that he should know his country's rights.[29]

Philip VI's response to the offer of negotiations which Edward III made at the end of 1331 on Parliament's advice was very casual. The English messengers learned that Philip would consider making concessions of his grace, but not yet and probably not at the request of mere diplomats. Edward would have to come and seek his favour in person. Edward toyed with the idea of making another visit to France, his third since his accession, but then thought better of it and stayed at home. There was very little to be done. Edward had nothing to offer to the French King which was worth the concessions he was demanding. A marriage alliance was offered, but proved to be of little interest. An attempt was made to invite the Pope to determine the dispute as supreme judge, which the Pope declined to do without Philip's consent. Edward was still not taken entirely seriously in France, and his kingdom must have been viewed by Philip's councillors as unstable, anarchic and ineffective. Edward had to tread delicately. He was well aware of the constitutional difficulties which earlier Anglo-French wars had provoked, and many of the diplomatic memoranda prepared for him in this period reminded him in case he had forgotten. When Parliament next met, in March 1332, the lords spiritual and temporal were told about Philip's suggestion of a meeting but expressed no great interest. Edward, they advised, might go to France if that was thought useful, and when his affairs allowed.[30]

Edward's ministers were not minded to press the point. The most influential of them by far was the cautious John Stratford, Bishop of Winchester, whom Edward had appointed chancellor almost immediately after the fall of Mortimer. Stratford was a career civil servant, a clever and ambitious ecclesiastical lawyer, not over-scrupulous, who must have been in his early forties when he took office. To the eighteen-year-old King he became a father figure, the phrase which Edward himself used when years later the two men fell out. Stratford was a restraining influence on English policy. He had lived through the disasters of the war of Saint-Sardos as one of the inner circle of Edward II's advisers. He had been present when Edward III had done homage to the French King at Amiens in 1329 and again at the surreptitious negotiations between the two kings in the forest of Halate. And although the years of diplomatic frustration and immobility were eventually to nurture in his breast a deep distrust and hatred of France, there is little doubt that the evasions and hesitations of these years represented Stratford's own preference and little doubt that he was right to prefer them. A war in the early 1330s could have ended only in disaster. The prospect was inaction in France and frustrated resignation in England.

The event which disturbed the ordained course of Anglo-French relations was an unexpected but fierce war in Scotland. The war progressively choked off any serious negotiations about Aquitaine. It generated an exaggerated but very real fear that the French would invade southern England. It gave the English aristocracy a taste for fighting and some experience of it. And it produced a weather change in English public opinion, a venomous resentment of France and, for a time, a willingness to indulge it by force of arms and at great expense.

CHAPTER V

War in Scotland
1331–1335

The treaty of Northampton, which was ratified by the English government in May 1328, brought an end to thirty-six years of war between England and Scotland. It was laid before Parliament and presumably approved by them. But it was not popular. The chroniclers who denounced it as the 'turpis pax', 'the cowardice peace' of a tyrannical government, were expressing the view widely held even among those in the north who had suffered most from the border war. It was also the view of Edward himself. The peace was associated with one of the most humiliating episodes of his youth. The Scots had deliberately repudiated the truces shortly after the deposition of his father and set about forcing a permanent settlement on the new rulers of England while they were still finding their feet and weakened by well-publicized dissensions. In this they were entirely successful. The short war which preceded the peace had been a fiasco. Mortimer and Isabella recruited a large army in England and a troop of cavalry several hundred strong in the Hainault. But the foreign horsemen and the English infantry fought each other in the streets of York with heavy casualties on both sides. The combined army cut off the Scots on the Wear but failed to bring them to battle or to stop them from escaping unscathed to Scotland. The young King, who had been taken up north in the baggage of his guardians, was seen weeping tears of anger and frustration. His discomfiture was completed by the events which followed: raids launched with persistence and impunity into the northern counties of England, then prolonged and tortuous negotiations from which he was excluded. The treaty renounced all of Edward's claims to overlordship in Scotland, and finally recognized Robert Bruce as king. In July 1328 Bruce's heir, the future David II, married Edward's sister. The Scots paid £20,000 by way of reparations for the harrying of the north, most of which was quickly slipped into the money-chests of Mortimer and Isabella. During the 1330s royal propagandists put it about that the peace had been imposed on an unwilling King in his minority, and was not binding on him in his maturity. This was bad law, but it was probably good history.[1]

The peace had serious defects of a less personal kind. The first of them was that it left in being the formidable threat of a concerted attack on England by France and Scotland. The treaty which the Scots had made with France at Corbeil in 1326 had provided that, in the event of a war between England and France, the Scotch King should invade England and make war there 'to the utmost of his power'. In their treaty with England, the Scots expressly reserved their right to comply with this obligation. After four decades of fear, suspicion and war, it was perhaps unreasonable to expect them to lay down their guard entirely by abandoning their only ally. But the reservation had dismal consequences for them. It meant that any English king who envisaged a violent quarrel with France would wish to deal firmly with Scotland first in order to protect his rear. The English civil service had a long memory and an obsessive interest in the lessons of the past. There were still officials who remembered the terrible year 1295 when the Scots had made common cause with the French for the 'disherison and destruction' of the English people.

The second grave defect of the 'shameful peace' proved to be the immediate cause of its undoing. It failed to deal with the claims of very many English and Scotch noblemen who had been expropriated from their Scotch lands after the battle of Bannockburn. The English had been long enough in Scotland before their expulsion for families like Percy, Wake and Beaumont to set down roots and long enough for many Scots to conclude that the future lay with the invaders. When the English were expelled, these men lost everything they had in Scotland. Some of them could fall back on extensive lands and interests in England. Others had nothing left except their claims against Robert Bruce and his heirs. The peace of 1328 appeared to mark the end of these claims. A few cases were taken up by the English government in desultory and fruitless diplomatic exchanges; some favoured individuals were rewarded by modest pensions from the Exchequer; most were ignored, a betrayal which was profoundly shocking to English aristocratic sentiment and had added to the already swollen ranks of Mortimer's enemies.

One of the 'disinherited' was Henry Beaumont, an able soldier and adventurer of French origin who had once been among the greatest lords of the English-occupied lowlands, holding the earldom of Buchan in right of his wife and the office of Constable of Scotland. At some time in 1331 Beaumont conceived a bold plan to recover his losses. This involved nothing less than an invasion of Scotland by a private army to be raised by Beaumont himself with the assistance of other prominent 'disinherited'. The greatest of these, who had lost more by the English defeats in Scotland than anyone, was Edward Balliol. Balliol was the eldest son of the hapless King John. He was a forgotten figure who had for some years been living a penurious existence on his heavily mortgaged estates in France. But he was a good soldier and the owner of a valuable name, and he had nothing to lose. So, in the winter of 1331–2 he came to England and settled in Yorkshire. There, preparations were set in train for a seaborne expedition to Scotland. Beaumont and Balliol and their friends set sail from three Yorkshire ports on 31 July 1332, a mixed band of aggrieved Scotch exiles, out-of-pocket Englishmen and mercenaries a few hundred strong.

They were fortunate, or perhaps shrewd, in the moment that they chose. Robert Bruce had died in June 1329, leaving as his heir a five-year-old child, David II. For the first three years of the new reign the government was in the hands of the Guardian, Thomas Randolph, Earl of Moray, a capable and vigorous old soldier who had commanded the Scotch centre at Bannockburn. Moray was well aware of Beaumont's preparations and had made his own plans for countering them. But he was a sick man and on 20 July 1332 he died in the castle of Musselburgh on the south shore of the Firth of Forth, where he had chosen to await Balliol's descent. On 2 August, while the small armada of the disinherited was making its way up the coast, the Scotch leaders gathered at Perth and chose Donald, Earl of Mar, to succeed him. The choice of the Earl of Mar was inevitable, for he was the King's closest kinsman of full age. But it was unfortunate in every other respect, for he had few political skills and little military experience. He was, moreover, a man of ambiguous background and uncertain loyalty who had lived most of his life in England as friend and courtier of Edward II. That there were misgivings at Perth upon his election, 'dissensions and disputes' according to the Scotch chronicler, was not surprising.[2]

Mar was not destined to govern Scotland for long. On 6 August 1332, Beaumont's band landed in Fife. Five days later, on the 11th, they destroyed a Scotch army many times larger than their own at Dupplin Moor. The battle was even more significant than its political consequences. The Scots had attacked the invaders in gallant disorder, led by Lord Robert Bruce, bastard son of the great Bruce. The 'disinherited' had disposed their small forces according to the formula which a succession of English victories in the Hundred Year War was to make classic. The men-at-arms stood dismounted along a narrow front with fixed pikes in front of their line, while their horses were held at the rear for pursuit or flight. The archers were disposed in looser formation at the flanks, slightly forward of the centre, from where they poured a rain of arrows into the advancing Scotch host. There was a terrible massacre. Some thousands of

Scots died of arrow wounds or were suffocated under the piles of corpses. Most of them never reached the lines of the enemy. Mar, Bruce and many of the leading noblemen of Scotland were among the dead.[3]

Edward III's role in these events was obscure, as without doubt he intended it to be. His situation was not an easy one. He was formally at peace with the King of Scotland who, indeed, was married to his sister. On the other hand he had scores to settle with the Scots, and many friends among the 'disinherited' who had helped him to seize power from Mortimer. Beaumont and Balliol certainly consulted Edward III and asked his permission to attempt the reconquest of Scotland. There are varying reports of Edward's answer. According to the most reliable evidence Edward refused to countenance an invasion across the Tweed, which would be too easy to associate with him; but he was willing to turn a blind eye to the plans of the 'disinherited' on the understanding that they entered Scotland from the sea, and that if the enterprise ended in disaster he would publicly disavow them and confiscate their English lands. After his victory, Balliol issued a number of proclamations suggesting that before his departure he had secretly done homage to the English King for the realm of Scotland. He even quoted the exact words used. It is probably what happened. At the end of March 1332 Edward informed the sheriffs of the northern counties that he had received several reports that armed men were gathering to invade Scotland in breach of the peace of 1328, which conduct was to be stopped at once and the perpetrators arrested. Since it could quite easily have been stopped and was not, it may be assumed that these writs had been prepared for consumption in Scotland and were accompanied by oral instructions to do no such thing.[4]

Balliol's extraordinary success came as a surprise. Parliament had been summoned to Westminster for 9 September 1332 to consider the affairs of Ireland, but Ireland's troubles were relegated to the background by the snippets of news which arrived daily from Scotland. On the second day of the session, the lords and the knights of the shires emerged from their deliberations to volunteer the advice that Edward should proceed at once to the north of England without even waiting for the conclusion of Parliamentary business at Westminster. For the safety of the realm against incursions from Scotland, they voted him a tenth and fifteenth. It seems that the prevailing wisdom at Westminster was that, in spite of his remarkable victory, Balliol's enterprise was still likely to fail and that the main danger was of retaliatory raids by a revived and strengthened government of Scotland. But after the dispersal of Parliament good news continued to arrive from the north. A second Scotch army, which had been making its way from the south while the battle of Dupplin Moor was being fought, had made a half-hearted attempt to besiege Balliol in Perth and had then melted away. Galloway, where Balliol's family had once possessed important interests, had rallied to his cause. It seemed that he would soon extend his rule over most of central and southern Scotland if only by default of organized opposition. Edward III left London in the third week of September 1332 and reached York in mid-October. There he was greeted by the news that Balliol had been crowned at Scone as king of Scotland in the presence of a mixed assembly of armed Englishmen and Scotch malcontents and trimmers. This had happened on 24 September. Since then, Balliol had moved south with his supporters into the Scotch lowlands and installed himself in the huge, partly ruined border fortress of Roxburgh. There he received a steady trickle of submissions and waited upon events.[5]

Edward Balliol desperately needed English assistance in holding his insecurely won kingdom. At the end of November 1332 he made it clear how much he was prepared to concede in order to get it. He issued two open letters acknowledging in glowing terms his debt to England. These began by announcing that, with the help of the King of England and some good Englishmen, Balliol had reconquered his own. He acknowledged that Scotland was and always had been a fief of England. Then came promises for the future. Edward was to have 2,000 librates of land next to the border, to include Berwick-on-Tweed, the gateway for any English army entering the lowlands of Scotland. Moreover, for the rest of his life, Balliol would faithfully serve Edward III with 200 men-at-arms for at least six months in the year wherever Edward had need of them, including Gascony 'and elsewhere where the King may hold lands or claim rights and where others may seek to prevent him by force from enjoying them'.[6] These remarkable letters were brought to York by Balliol's emissaries, and provided the main talking point at the meeting of Parliament which opened there on 4 December 1332.

It was a disorganized and inconclusive affair. York was far away and most of the lords failed to attend. After two adjournments for stragglers to come in, the main proceedings opened on 8 December with a speech from Geoffrey Scrope, Chief Justice of the King's Bench. Scrope was a rich Yorkshire parvenu, a lawyer of strong martial tastes who was becoming one of Edward's principal advisers on foreign affairs. He explained to the half-empty benches that the peace of 1328 could be ignored. It had been made by others who had taken advantage of the King's youth. That being so, he continued, there appeared to be two ways in which the present situation could be exploited. Edward might claim the kingdom for himself; or he might support one of the rival parties within Scotland in exchange for homage and feudal services. Scrope made it quite clear that the government was not wedded to the cause of Edward Balliol. He reminded his audience that Balliol's father had forfeited his kingdom to Edward I. As for David II, his representatives, who were present, were briskly told that Edward was not bound to restrain his subjects who had been disinherited in Scotland in the cause of himself and his predecessors and had now begun to reconquer what was theirs. The Lords were asked to deliberate about Scrope's 'two ways' and to give the King their advice, but it was evident that Edward had already decided what advice he wished to hear. He wished to be told to annex Scotland to his crown. In this he was disappointed. After deliberating for an unusually long time by the standards of medieval parliaments, the Lords told Edward that it was too weighty and difficult a matter for so small a gathering, that only five ecclesiastics (all northerners) were present, and that the best thing was to do nothing until an adjourned session could be held in January.[7]

By the time the adjourned session took place the King's problem had been simplified by a collapse of Balliol's fortunes as swift and violent as his triumph of August. At some time towards the end of October 1332, the new Guardian of Scotland, Archibald Douglas, had made a truce with Balliol, ostensibly to enable the Scotch Parliament to assemble and decide who was their rightful king. The truce caused Balliol to relax his guard. He dismissed most of his English soldiers and left the relative security of Roxburgh for Annan on the north shore of the Solway Firth. Douglas attacked him there in the early hours of 17 December. Most of his companions were killed in their beds. He himself escaped through a hole in the wall and fled half-naked on an unbridled horse until he reached Carlisle.[8]

In the evolution of Edward III's policy, Balliol's sudden expulsion was decisive. The adjourned meeting of Parliament on 20 January was as sterile as the previous one in December and dispersed at the end of the month without proffering any advice to the monarch. Clearly there were misgivings about the King's new ambitions even in an assembly which had traditionally favoured firm measures against the Scots. But these misgivings, whatever they were, did not trouble Edward's Council. They had decided to fight in Scotland whatever was said in Parliament. The last public business before Parliament dispersed was the announcement by Chancellor Stratford that Edward had appointed a special committee of six councillors to assist him in the matter of Scotland. They, according to the author of the *Scalacronica*, were 'enterprising and warlike men, keen to repair their dented prestige'. They knew that the King had already gone too far for there to be any prospect of patching up relations with the Scots loyal to David II. They also had an eye on France as English policy-makers always did when dealing with Scotland. Edward's hands were tied in France for as long as the Scots remained independent and hostile. There was unlikely to be a better moment for taming them than the present. It was therefore resolved to invade Scotland in force.[9]

The affair showed Edward III at his worst, devious, impulsive and incapable of looking beyond the events of the moment. Even the events of the moment he saw in purely military terms. It is surprising that a ruler whose subordinates plied him so assiduously with historical lessons should have supposed that the battle of Dupplin Moor would be as decisive on the political plane as it had been on the military one, or that the Scots would accept the loss of most of the lowlands and the introduction of a new class of anglophile landowners descended from the expelled interlopers of an earlier generation. These misjudgements were not made for want of advice. But Edward chose his advisers and although they were neither cyphers nor mediocrities they were generally of the same mind as he was.

Whatever illusions Edward III may once have had about the size of the task before him were dissipated now. For the next four years the administrative capital of the kingdom was transferred to York. The Chancery was already installed with its bulky archives in the Chapter House of the cathedral. The normally sedentary offices of the Exchequer and the Court of Common Bench arrived at about the same time and were settled in York Castle. North of the castle the large Franciscan convent became the headquarters of the royal household. A host of clerks, household troops, dignitaries, suppliers and hangers-on as well as suitors in the royal courts crammed themselves into such private accommodation as could be found in the confined triangle between the Ouse and the Foss. York became, briefly, a boom town suffering all the hustle, congestion and disturbance that belonged with prosperity. In the cathedral close, work on the half-completed nave was suspended as zealous royal officers requisitioned horses, carts and materials. Westminster was abandoned to monastic regularity and tawdry indigence.[10]

The English invasion of Scotland achieved nothing, but militarily it was a complete success.[11] Edward divided his forces into two armies, the first of which, commanded by Edward Balliol, entered the western lowlands from Carlisle in March 1333. The second, under Edward himself, marched north from Newcastle at the end of April. The objective of both forces was Berwick, the powerful fortress-town which guarded the north shore of the estuary of the Tweed. Edward reached the south bank of the Tweed opposite the walls in the second week of May and found Balliol's force already in place on the north bank. By the end of June, much of the town had been destroyed by catapults and fires, and the garrison weakened by repeated assaults. On 28 June the Warden of the town agreed to surrender in two weeks unless by then he had been relieved.

At first the Scotch Guardian tried to relieve Berwick by mounting diversions south of the border in the destructive tradition of the Scots. Tweedmouth, opposite Berwick on the south shore, was burned. Queen Philippa was besieged in Bamburgh Castle, 15 miles away. In the face of these threats to his subjects and his wife, Edward displayed the ruthlessness and constancy of purpose which became characteristic of him. The Scots were left to do their worst in Northumberland. When Berwick failed to surrender on the appointed day, Edward began to hang hostages, beginning with the son of the garrison commander and continuing at a rate of two a day, 'and so he wolde teche them to breke their convenauntz.' In the third week of July, Douglas was forced to take the step which every Scotch commander since the early days of Edward I's wars had learned to avoid at all costs. He recrossed the Tweed and offered battle to the English army. It was the only hope of relieving the town, but it meant a battle on ground of Edward's choosing and at a time which suited him.

The ground was at Halidon, a hill 2 miles north-west of Berwick about 500 feet high. It lay across the only route by which the Scotch army could reach the beleaguered town. On 19 July 1333, Douglas attacked the English army there. Edward III's tactics were the same as those which had won Dupplin Moor for Balliol. He arranged his army with dismounted cavalry at the centre and archers placed slightly forward of them at the flanks. The horses were held at the rear. The object was to remain on the defensive for as long as possible while the enemy pressed through a rain of arrows to break themselves on the English lines. This was exactly what the Scots did. After the battle, the carnage wreaked by the English archers was completed by a relentless pursuit of the fleeing Scots. Seeing the outcome of the battle, their camp followers had fled with the horses. Some of the troops ran for five miles before they were killed. Others threw themselves into the sea. The number of dead is impossible to disentangle from the exaggerations of the chroniclers, but there must have been several thousand. They included the Guardian and five Scotch earls. The few prisoners who had been taken were put to death on Edward III's order, a final act of savagery for which there is no rational explanation. English casualties were light.

'And so', said one Englishman, 'men freely declared that the Scotch wars had been brought to their close, that nothing remained of the Scotch nation which was willing or able to defend or govern itself. Yet they were wrong, as the sequel showed.'[12] These words were written about five years after the battle. The immediate sequel did not show that they were wrong. Berwick opened its gates to the besiegers on the following day, and was at once annexed to the English Crown together with the county of which it was the head. Balliol set up his capital at Perth, where he ruled in theory all of Scotland and in fact the greater part of it, including Fife and most of the English-speaking lowlands. The young David II and his Queen fled to Dumbarton Castle on the Clyde and clung on there while the tidal wave passed over them. Elsewhere, less than half-a-dozen castles held out for David's cause.[13]

It now fell to Balliol to perform his magnificent promises of the previous year. There was some delay and indications of backsliding. Balliol knew how much those concessions would cost his reputation among the Scots. His situation was a difficult one as Edward III, intoxicated by the verdict of the battlefield, failed to recognize. In February 1334, however, Balliol summoned the Scotch Parliament to Holyrood Abbey outside Edinburgh to ratify the arrangement which he had made with the English King. It was an ill-attended assembly, there being present a respectable number of bishops but scarcely any lay magnates apart from Balliol's long-standing friends among the 'disinherited' and Englishmen holding land in Scotland. Edward III compromised on some points to make the pill sweeter for the Scots. He agreed not to hear appeals from Scotland and not to require Balliol's attendance at English parliaments. But on the main point there was no compromise. Balliol met Edward III in Newcastle in June 1334 and ceded to him most of the English-speaking lowlands of Scotland, eight counties lying south and east of a line from Linlithgow on the Firth of Forth to Wigtown on the Solway Firth. On 19 June, in the Dominican convent of Newcastle, he did homage to Edward III, this time in public, for what was left of his kingdom.[14]

The battle of Halidon Hill marked an important point in Edward III's development as a soldier and as a ruler. It was his first taste of victory, a source of measured confidence, perhaps over-confidence, in dealing with more formidable enemies. Edward had taken advice from his friends before the campaign and he was characteristically generous to them afterwards. William Montagu, who had been one of the closest of them, received the grant of the Isle of Man and a royal manor in the Tweed valley. At a humbler level, soldiers who had distinguished themselves in the fighting and merchants and civil servants who had kept the army supplied and paid saw their services recognized by grants of money, land or privileges.[15] He was doing what was expected of a king in a world which valued largesse more than good housekeeping. Edward's capacity to behave as he was expected to may have come easily to a man of conventional temperament, without cynicism or humour. It was the key to his successful management of public opinion. The Parliament of January 1333, in failing to support an ambitious military adventure by an untried king, had almost certainly reflected widespread unease even among those who hated the Scots:

> Of Ingland had my hert grete care
> When Edward founded first to wer

sang the patriotic poetaster Lawrence Minot in his jubilant celebration of the slaughter of Halidon Hill. Royal propaganda saw to it that the jubilation was spread well beyond the northern counties. In London the citizens and clergy processed with their relics from St Paul's to Trinity Church by Aldgate and back. There was no doubt of the spontaneity of such demonstrations, harbingers of a more militant England.[16]

In France the troubles of Scotland had been followed with growing concern but imperfect understanding. This was, perhaps, inevitable given the speed of events and the paucity of the French government's sources of information. Philip VI had interests at once more distant and more compelling than Scotland. Ever since 1329, perhaps even earlier, Philip had been anxious to lead a great crusade against the infidel. Initially, his interest was focussed on Spain, where the Islamic kingdoms were being driven further into their southern heartlands. But in 1331, Philip resolved to mount an expedition to the Middle East for the liberation of the Holy Land, the first such expedition since the ill-fated crusade of Louis IX, which had ended with his death in 1270. On 2 October 1332, the French King had announced his intentions to an assembly of notables gathered at the Sainte-Chapelle, and exactly a year later he formally took the cross in a great ceremony in the Pré-aux-Clercs outside the Parisian abbey of St Germain. Given the uncertainties of the King's political position within France, it was a courageous, perhaps foolhardy decision. Yet there seems to have been no significant opposition. No one said to Philip that his enthusiasm would be better applied to the needs of his kingdom, as Suger had said to Louis VII in the twelfth century and Joinville to Louis IX in the thirteenth. The crusade was still a predominantly French affair: *Gesta Dei per Francos*, 'the deeds of God, performed by the French' as a twelfth-century chronicler had it. Acre, the last outpost of Christianity on the east Mediterranean mainland, had fallen in 1291, and the only surviving remnants of the crusading states were now Rhodes, which belonged to the predominantly French Hospitallers, and Cyprus, which was ruled by the French Lusignan family. The French nobility had always looked beyond their own frontiers for adventure, riches and atonement. For them the crusading ideal had a reality which it lacked in other classes and other countries. Certainly it was real enough for Philip VI, who bent most of his energies to its preparation for five years from 1331 to 1336. Spies were sent to examine the walls and gates of Levantine cities. The Queen's physician wrote a treatise on siege engines and the other armaments which would be required. The alternative routes were debated in the royal Council. Arrangements were made with the Venetian Republic for the transport of a great army and its supplies by sea. In the Mediterranean ports of France, preparations were put in hand for the accumulation of a large fleet of war galleys. Commanders were appointed and a date was eventually fixed: August 1336.[17]

Scotland was an unwelcome distraction. The news of Balliol's victory at Dupplin Moor must have reached Paris in about October 1332, at about the same time as the French King was describing his plans to the assembled soldiers and bishops in the Sainte-Chapelle. None of Philip's advisers seems to have appreciated the significance of the battle. It is quite probable that they did not know how much had been contributed to it by Englishmen, including some close associates of Edward III. If so, their eyes were shortly to be opened. By January 1333 there had been two meetings of the English Parliament at York, at which Edward had made no secret of his ambitions or of the means by which he proposed to achieve them.

The news presented Philip VI's government with a dilemma. The Treaty of Corbeil imposed obligations on France in such circumstances which were loosely defined but not so loosely that they could be ignored. On the other hand it was dangerous to antagonize Edward III, and unthinkable for a French king to sail for the eastern Mediterranean with the flower of his army leaving a hostile England behind him. Philip even hoped that Edward III would join his expedition. Accordingly, he responded as mildly and unprovocatively as his Chancery knew how. A letter was sent to Edward III the text of which has not survived but which appears from subsequent correspondence to have consisted of gentle complaints coupled with requests for information about what was happening. Another letter, in stronger terms, was sent in March 1333 at about the time that Balliol's army was leaving Carlisle.[18]

Edward took the implied threat of French intervention in Scotland seriously, and humoured Philip VI with some skill. A number of routine embassies visited France at this time, but none was empowered to discuss Scotland. The English Chancery maintained a vigorous correspondence with the French court, dealing at length with every other subject. The omission was quite deliberate. 'We have received the letters of the King of France,' Edward wrote to Stratford during the siege of Berwick, 'but it seems to us and to those of our Council who are about us that it would not be desirable to give any clear answer about the matter of Scotland.' Instead the French King's letter was answered with a long complaint about the seizure of some cargoes of wheat and the problems of Aquitaine. French diplomatic agents in England were kept away from the war area for some time by the simple device of delaying the provision of escorts, and when at length they did reach Edward's camp at Berwick they were kept there until all was over. The only information about Scotland which Philip received officially from Edward was that the Scots had broken the peace of 1328, launching raids on northern England for the destruction of Edward's subjects and their property, a repetition of Edward's war propaganda in England which he addressed to the French court on 7 May 1333. Apart from a dark reference to certain 'remedies' which were proposed, this letter contained no information about Edward's plans.[19]

By the time it reached Paris, Philip's Council had become aware that he was besieging Berwick and had already proceeded to robuster measures. A fleet of ten ships was fitted out and sent to Berwick with arms and food for the defenders. The fleet left Dieppe, but encountered fierce northern gales and was compelled to take refuge in the Flemish port of Sluys. There, the cargoes were sold off or pilfered. The English probably never heard about it.[20]

The closing stages of the siege of Berwick were witnessed by a small group of Frenchmen from the English camp. They were members of an embassy which had come to discuss the English King's participation in the crusade. They had left France before the English campaign had got under way and by the time of their arrival their instructions were grievously out of date. Their leader, Raoul de Brienne, Count of Eu and Constable of France, was known to be *persona grata* at the English court, the owner of large estates in England and Ireland, and one of the few Frenchmen about Philip VI who had more than a passing acquaintance with English affairs.

But in spite of an intelligent choice of principal, this mission achieved nothing except to discover that victory had made Edward III stickier in his dealings with France. Edward reminded the ambassadors that on the occasion of his homage at Amiens in 1329 Philip had promised that he should enjoy all his rights in France. In Edward's opinion, those rights were much more extensive than any which Philip had yet conceded. Nothing less would do than a complete reappraisal of the treaties and conventions which related to Aquitaine. 'You shall tell your master', Edward is reported to have said, 'that when he has kept his promises I shall be even more ready than he is to go on the crusade.' This response was brought back to the French King together with the news of the destruction of his Scotch allies.[21]

The policy behind it, trading Edward's participation in the crusade for real concessions in Aquitaine, remained the keystone of English policy for three years from 1333 to 1336. If it had been vigorously pursued in the immediate aftermath of Halidon Hill it might well have succeeded, for Philip VI was undoubtedly attracted by the idea. As it was, English diplomacy unaccountably marked time for several months after the battle, during which Edward's enemies were actively sowing doubts about the finality of the victory and the durability of Edward Balliol's government. A trickle of distinguished Scotch refugees found their way to the French court, including the teenage John Randolph, Earl of Moray, who had commanded a division of the Scotch army in the battle, as well as some of the less pliable Scotch bishops. They tried to persuade Philip that it was his duty to intervene in Scotland. Philip hesitated and initially did nothing. But he did agree, it may be unaware of the significance of his act, to offer asylum to the ten-year-old King of Scotland in France. David II's position on the isolated coast of Dumbarton was becoming untenable. His capture by Edward Balliol would have been a serious blow to any prospects of Scotch recovery. And so, early in 1334, Philip VI paid 1,000 marks to the Earl of Moray to fit out and arm a ship to carry the diminutive Scotch court to safety in France. In May 1334, they landed in Normandy.[22]

This event forced on the French King a decision which he had been avoiding for almost a year. It came at a particularly delicate moment. There had recently arrived in France an English embassy of which Edward III had high hopes. It was the most exalted that Edward had yet sent to Philip's court. It consisted of John Stratford, now Archbishop of Canterbury, William Montagu, William Clinton and Chief Justice Scrope, all men who were very much in the King's personal confidence (two of them had taken part in Edward's *coup d'état* of 1330). Their instructions were to negotiate a final resolution of the dispute about Aquitaine on the basis of the restitution to Edward III of the territories which his father had held before the war of Saint-Sardos. To this end, Edward had empowered them to commit him to join the crusade. The ambassadors were met by Philip VI and his court at Senlis, a small walled city of the Ile de France just north of Paris, whose castle was used as a base for royal hunting parties. French sources are more or less agreed about what happened next. According to their account, which is probably accurate, the Englishmen arrived to be frigidly received by Philip's courtiers. Philip himself, however, was anxious (or persuaded by some of his advisers) that the negotiations should succeed. A committee of three councillors was deputed to talk to them: the Count of Eu, Pierre Roger, Archbishop of Rouen, and the Marshal Matthieu de Trie. All of these men had experience of the English position and probably some sympathy for it. They rapidly came to an agreement. A treaty was agreed in principle on terms which have not survived but which must have embodied significant concessions to Edward III. The English formally took their leave of all the French councillors and returned to their lodgings in the town.

This was probably the point at which Philip learned of the arrival of the Scotch court in Normandy; if not, it is certainly the moment at which it dawned on him that a peace with England which left the Scots to their fate would now be impolitic and embarrassing. As the criers were proclaiming the treaty from street corners, the English were recalled from their lodgings. When they arrived in the King's presence, they were told that it was of course to be understood that the Scots and their exiled King would be included in the treaty. They were aghast. Nothing had previously been said about Scotland. They had no instructions on the question. As far as their master was concerned the only King of Scotland was Edward Balliol. Indeed, although they probably did not know it, Balliol was at about that very time in the Dominican Convent at Newcastle making the final arrangements to subordinate his kingdom to England and to cede a large part of it in perpetuity. The ambassadors at Senlis did their best, but seeing that their protests cut no ice they left empty-handed for England. Philip's last words to them were that it seemed that there 'would never be friendship between England and France until the same man is king of both', a *bon mot* whose finality made a firmer impression on the English than perhaps was intended.[23] Philip meanwhile welcomed David II and his Queen and installed them in Château-Gaillard, the great fortress of the lower Seine which an English king had built a century and a half before to defend another French duchy from the encroachments of the Capetians.

Here they were to live for seven years sustained by irregular remittances from their supporters in Scotland and by subsidies from Philip VI, drawing dignity from their surroundings and from a small court of Scotch ecclesiastics and officials.[24]

The affair exemplified all the classic vices of the 'solemn embassy': ambassadors ill informed, instructions overtaken by events, failure humiliating and public. The history of Stratford's embassy and the maladroit manner of its ending became fertile sources of national misunderstanding and resentment. On his return, the Archbishop gave a graphic account of it to a gathering of dignitaries in London, and the parting words of Philip VI passed onto the mythology of French intransigence. English popular opinion believed that Philip had said: 'There will be no perfect Christian peace until the King of France sits in the midst of England in judgement over the three kingdoms of England, France and Scotland.' The French for their part believed that Edward had responded that he would 'never rest until he had Scotland under his heel'. The consequences were serious enough even without patriotic exaggerations. Up to this point, Philip VI had never refused point-blank to consider restoring Edward to his lost dominions in Aquitaine. He had now in effect refused because he had imposed a condition which Edward could not meet without undoing Balliol and surrendering his gains in the Scotch lowlands. What Philip was demanding would not have been tolerated by the English baronage even if Edward himself had been inclined to concede it. Months afterwards, a French ambassador at the papal court tried to explain to the Pope that Philip could not without dishonour escape the obligations which his predecessor had assumed by the Treaty of Corbeil. The Pope replied to this with words of chilling percipience. France was rich, he said, and her riches were coveted. Was there not some risk that Edward III would take a leaf out of Philip's book, finding allies among the many malcontents within her border and outside?[25]

In southern France the atmosphere was abruptly altered by the failure of Stratford's embassy and the quarrel over Scotland. The Anglo-French commission appointed under the terms of the treaty of 1331 had been progressing slowly with its enormous task in the spacious surroundings of the Dominican convent of Agen. The proceedings had been surprisingly friendly. Indeed, the commissioners had jointly proposed to their governments that their terms of reference should be altered to allow them to do justice to those inhabitants of Aquitaine, who had been displaced during the war of Saint-Sardos, and not only those displaced afterwards. This proposal was very beneficial to Edward III, as the English commissioners were quick to point out to him. Although it would not put him in possession of the lost provinces, it would put his subjects back in possession of their estates there, giving him friends and allies in a region which he was hoping sooner or later to prize from Philip's grip. Before the unfortunate Stratford embassy, Philip had agreed to appoint new commissioners with the necessary powers, and with evident reluctance he actually did so at the beginning of July 1334, about a fortnight after Stratford had left. No doubt he had been told that there were other ways of obstructing the commission's work.[26]

The new commissioners met on 29 September 1334 in the Carmelite house of Langon and at once fell to bickering on matters procedural and substantive. Were the commissioners' letters of appointment drawn up in due form? Did their powers extend to all of Aquitaine or only to the Agenais? What should be the order of their proceedings? Some of these matters were trivial but by no means all of them were. At the outset, the French commissioners interested themselves in the case of the castles of Blanquefort and Veyrines, which belonged by inheritance to the Count of Armagnac. The Count had been prevented from taking possession of them in 1325 ostensibly because Edward II had wished to consider the validity of the last owner's will, in fact because Armagnac, whose principal lands lay outside the duchy, was thought to be a troublemaker and a friend and ally of the French Crown. The French commissioners demanded the surrender of both places. It was a small dispute presenting in its classic form the dilemma of the English government of Gascony. Edward III was plainly in the wrong and his own Seneschal advised him to give way. But Blanquefort was an important fortress, recently strengthened, on the northern outskirts of Bordeaux. There could be no question of allowing the chances of inheritance to put such a place into the hands of a potential enemy. The affair brought chaos to the commission's proceedings. In October 1334, one of the French members was said to be on his way to Paris to arrange for the confiscation of Edward III's county of Ponthieu until the two places were given up. His colleagues were later reported to be extorting oaths of allegiance to the King of France by threats of expropriation, banishment and death. Evidently, as Edward III wrote to the English commissioners, their French colleagues were guided 'more by their own caprices than by judicial reasoning'.[27]

On 15 November 1334 Edward addressed a gentler protest to the King of France. He was, he said, as anxious for a lasting peace as any man but it was unrealistic to hope for peace unless Philip was prepared to consider his complaints and those of his subjects. What was required was a complete reappraisal of the existing treaties and conventions between the two kings as well as a resumption of the more detailed work of the joint commission in Aquitaine. The letter reveals a growing perception on Edward's part and that of his advisers of what had gone wrong with previous diplomatic efforts.[28] Philip's reply has not survived, but it was probably of a piece with his actions. He did not see any need to concede what his law did not require. The work of the commission limped on into the following year and then ended. A large number of reports had been compiled and provisional arrangements made for some disputed properties, but no actual restitution had been ordered. It was a complete failure. The consequences of the impasse were potentially very serious. For by one of the more improvident clauses of the treaty of 1331 any deadlock in the joint commission was to be resolved by referring disputed cases to the Parlement of Paris. Hitherto Philip had made a real effort to restrain the Parlement's enthusiasm for hearing Gascon appeals. But from 1335 onwards Gascon disputes were to find their way there in growing numbers.[29]

Edward's hands were now tied by an unwelcome revival of the Bruce cause in Scotland, encouraged and, it was believed, financed by France. There is no way of testing the belief, but it is plausible. In July 1334 there was an insurrection in the south-west between the Clyde and Solway Firth. The Bruces had always been powerful in this region, where the English-speaking lowlands merged with the Gaelic communities of the coasts and islands. The leaders of the new rebellion, both men with powerful interests there, were Robert Stewart, the head of his family, and John Randolph, Earl of Moray. The first warning of it was a sudden seaborne attack by Stewart on Dunoon Castle, which fell almost immediately. Rothesay fell soon afterwards to a spontaneous uprising of the Stewart tenants on Bute. In July, the Earl of Moray, who had recently returned from France to Dumbarton, crossed the Clyde and raised most of the rest of the south-west. At the time of these events, Stewart was only eighteen years old. Moray was even younger, 'a youth not yet full grown'. Together, these two set themselves up as joint regents of Scotland and began to construct the semblance of a government.[30]

Edward III was now to learn, as he would learn again in France, how much easier it was to win territory than to hold it. Medieval armies usually kept the field for short campaigns, determined by the seasons and the weather. Governments lacked the money and the administrative resources to keep them in the field for longer. Balliol's friend David of Strathbogie might disport himself as Steward of Scotland, feasting Robert Stewart's tenants at Renfrew and receiving in state the keys of his castles, but among the dispersed, pastoral population of Scotland whose loyalties were still largely tribal the governing class could not be changed overnight. Had not Galloway risen for a Balliol in 1332 after an absence of nearly forty years? Where towns were few and small and generally unwalled, possession depended on the garrisons of isolated fortresses. Between them, Balliol and Edward III now controlled rather more than a dozen of these, concentrated in the southern lowlands close to the border, in Fife and in the east-coast plain beyond the Tay. But their garrisons were kept at very low strength and controlled no more land than they could see. Even within the walls, loyalties were uncertain.

Balliol was at Stirling when the news of the rebellion arrived, and at once sent to England for help. But events moved faster than the English could do. By the middle of August, the revolt had spread to most parts of Scotland. In the next few days Balliol's kingdom disintegrated before his eyes. His Council was rent by bitter disputes about the distribution of land, some of which was no longer his to distribute. On 24 August 1334 his closest associates refused to make common cause against the rebels and dispersed to their castles to resist individually. Some were captured before they got there; some were besieged in their strongholds. Those who could hope for any favour from Bruce's friends joined them. Balliol himself fled to English territory at Berwick, narrowly escaping a raiding party which had been sent to intercept him.[31]

Edward III was in serious financial difficulty in the summer of 1334. The Halidon Hill campaign of the previous year had been expensive and Parliamentary subsidies had not closed the gap. The Westminster Parliament of September 1332 had voted Edward one tenth and fifteenth to finance a campaign which was expected to be much more limited and more defensive than the one which occurred. Moreover, its yield had been disappointing: depressed by corrupt under-assessment, late to come in, and partly eaten up by the peculation of local officials. The next Parliament, which had met in York in December 1332 and January 1333, had done nothing to improve Edward's financial position except to give their grudging consent to a supplementary duty on wool exports. As a result, Edward had become heavily dependent on his bankers. For some months in 1332 there was a complete stop on payments to any other creditors.[32] Parliament's obvious lack of enthusiasm seems to have deterred Edward from seeking further assistance in that quarter. But by good fortune

Parliament was actually in session at Westminster in September 1334 when the news arrived of Balliol's second expulsion from Scotland and the maltreatment of his English followers. A new subsidy, the first for two years, was voted forthwith. Its yield was about 10 per cent up on its predecessor in spite of the ravages of the weather and a deepening agricultural recession. These measures went some way towards relieving the government's financial embarrassment. The two provinces of the Church, which had resisted demands for taxation for at least a year, were subjected to intense pressure by the King's ministers. They were induced to make their own grant shortly after the Parliament had done so. At the same time Edward began to increase the scale of his borrowing. He made a long-term arrangement with the Bardi by which the firm advanced him a monthly sum, initially 1,000 marks, against an assignment of future customs revenues, a scheme which lasted in some shape or form for two years, when it was superseded by a more ambitious one. The Italians had already set out on the road which was to lead them to the most spectacular of all medieval commercial bankruptcies, and Edward had partly refilled his war-chests for what proved to be a debilitating succession of campaigns.[33]

The King invaded Scotland for the second time in November 1334. On this occasion the Scots avoided giving battle, the old policy of Robert Bruce which would be completely vindicated in the succeeding years. Edward's first objective was Roxburgh, the great border fortress on the Tweed which had lain in ruins since Bruce had demolished it in 1314 'lest the English should ever again rule the land by holding castles'. A large corps of builders whom Edward had brought with him set about rebuilding it while the King waited for reinforcements from the south. Edward had only about 4,000 men with him, consisting mainly of his own household and the retainers of the nobility. His larger plans were dependent on the arrival of the shire levies. What these plans were was not, however, revealed for they were never put into effect. Shortly after the English reached Roxburgh, the snow began to fall and freezing winds howled across the moorland, blowing it in the soldiers' faces. It was the worst winter for many years. In England, floods and gales added to the misery, destroying buildings, uprooting trees and killing animals. Indifference, bureaucratic inertia and winter combined to prevent more than a trickle of reinforcements from reaching the army.

The Scots stayed well away. After Christmas, Edward conducted a military promenade through the forest of Ettrick in the hope of finding the enemy. Balliol, who had led a separate and smaller force up from Carlisle, conducted an equally fruitless hunt in Peebles. Between them, they laid waste to large tracts of the western lowlands, destroying houses, animals and grain stores, killing those whom they found in their way. Balliol's ancestral lands in Galloway were spared, but no other attempt was made to distinguish between friend and foe. At the beginning of February 1335 they returned to England. Edward had almost certainly run out of money.[34]

Philip VI learned of Balliol's expulsion from Scotland almost as soon as the King of England did, for one of the first acts of the newly constituted Guardians of Scotland was to send him an urgent appeal for help. In late November 1334 Philip notified Edward III of his intention to send ambassadors to him to discuss the matter of Scotland. His original intention had been to send Andrea Ghini, whose past experience of the English question eminently qualified him for the job. But when the embassy arrived in England in January 1335 its leader was found to be the Bishop of Avranches, a worthy but inexperienced Norman whose main claim to fame was the authorship of an index to a well-known encyclopaedia. He was waiting with his colleagues at Newcastle on 18 February 1335 when Edward III returned in an ugly mood from his unsuccessful campaign. The Bishop's message was straightforward and unwelcome. According to a summary made by an English clerk he wished to know 'why the English King's advisers had prevailed upon him to help Edward Balliol, a man who had no right in Scotland, against David and indeed against his own sister David's wife, who held the kingdom by possession, by the conquest of Robert Bruce and by the treaty with Edward III himself'. Edward did not answer this question, as his father would have done, with oaths. He said that he would consider his reply and deliver it through ambassadors whom he would be sending at some later date to the court of France. The Chancery clerks who were with him did indeed draft a rather disingenuous reply, but it appears not to have been used. Edward had no desire to bring his dispute with Philip VI to a head.[35]

The French ambassadors asked to be allowed to act as intermediaries to negotiate a truce between the English and the Scots. Edward was more than willing to let them try. Seeing that there were now virtually no English troops in the northern counties and no money in the treasury with which to raise another army, Edward wanted time to prepare and finance his next assault on Scotland more thoroughly than the last. Three lesser members of the French embassy were therefore permitted to proceed into Scotland to negotiate with the Scotch leaders at Perth, while their principals retired to the less warlike atmosphere of Gedling in Nottinghamshire to await events. The outcome of these exchanges was a truce which carried

Edward's hard-pressed government through from Easter to midsummer 1335. The ostensible object was to enable the French ambassadors to negotiate a final peace between Edward and David II's supporters in Scotland. The French were almost certainly serious about this.[36]

They knew even less about the condition of Scotland than they did about the personality and ambitions of Edward III. The two young Guardians had by now fallen out and gathered round themselves competing parties of jealous and resentful Scotch noblemen. There were old personal rancours and disagreements about the form of a renascent Scotch government, while such government as there was fell apart around them. Each Guardian seized whatever royal revenues he could lay hands on.[37] No serious negotiation would have been possible in these conditions even if there had been a will in England. But there was not. Edward had no intention of making a permanent peace with his enemies. Arrangements for a major summer campaign in Scotland had been put in hand almost as soon as Edward had returned from Roxburgh. On 6 March 1335, the recruiting officers of thirty-seven counties were warned to be ready to meet the King's need for troops as soon as the order should be given them. The final decision to reinvade Scotland appears to have been taken by a council of noblemen and ecclesiastical magnates at Nottingham on 26 March 1335. On the following day writs were issued calling for all contingents to be in arms at Newcastle on 11 June 1335. Throughout the life of the truce, these preparations continued without abatement, except that the date of the muster was postponed so as to coincide with its expiry.[38] The Scots themselves had no illusions. They were making their own plans for the threatened invasion. Religious communities obtained from Edward III certificates of immunity from the coming destruction. For others there were harder decisions. In April, the Scotch leaders met at Dairsie in Fife and although they were divided by bitter personal antagonisms they appear to have agreed to abide by the traditional Bruce policy of avoiding battle. It was decided to evacuate the inhabitants of the lowland villages with as many as possible of their goods and animals to the safety of the hills.[39] When the English Parliament met at York on 27 May 1335 Edward III announced his aggressive plans for the summer, and the Lords and Commons endorsed them. As the assembly dispersed, two members of the French Ambassador's staff left York for France to report to their government. It must have been an unhappy report. The truce still had a month to run, but it was now apparent that they had been duped.[40]

The return of fair weather and the minatory tone of Edward's letters to his recruiting officers did their work. By the second week of July 1335, three weeks late, he had more than 13,000 men under arms, three times as many as he had been able to muster for the Roxburgh campaign. It was the largest army with which Edward ever entered Scotland. The plan was for a threefold attack on the heartlands of the Scotch national cause in the south-west of the country. Part of the army, under the King's command, was to march north from Carlisle while the rest, commanded by Balliol, made its way west from Berwick. The two groups were to meet on the Clyde. Meanwhile a third, seaborne force was to be collected in Ireland and to land men in the Clyde estuary. The latter part of the plan was a suggestion of Edward Balliol's, an intelligent strategic idea but dependent on an exactness of timing difficult to achieve given poor communications and slow recruitment and supply. In the second half of July 1335 Edward's force marched almost unopposed through south-western Scotland, destroying everything in their path and propelling refugees in their thousands to the hills and borderlands. Balliol's force, advancing from the east, met virtually no opposition. Edward and Balliol joined forces at Glasgow towards the end of July and, seeing that they were beating the air in the south-west, they turned north in search of an enemy. Edward installed himself at Perth while his army looted and destroyed the country around.[41]

At the court of Philip VI they were waiting with mounting irritation for the answer which had been promised to the Bishop of Avranches back in February. In the interval French foreign policy had acquired a coherence and sense of direction which had been noticeably lacking before. It also acquired a new hardness of mood. Both tendencies were associated with one man, Mile de Noyers, a nobleman from northern Burgundy who had acquired a dominant place in the French royal Council at the beginning of 1335. Mile de Noyers was a determined and overbearing man with a strong interest in foreign policy and a clear, uncompromising view of where French interests lay. His value to Philip VI in this as in other fields arose from the confident certainty of his advice as well as from his great experience of the machinery of government. In the course of a long career (he was sixty-five in 1335) he had held important positions in the royal service almost without interruption. 'No one doubts that the Crown may take whatever territory it requires to preserve the public interest and the security of the realm.' The sentiment itself, and its public announcement must have reminded many contemporaries of Guillaume de Nogaret, the great minister of Philip the Fair. Mile de Noyers had some, although not very much, experience of the diplomatic details of the English problem. He had taken part in some negotiations in 1330 and 1331 and had been addressed by Edward III on one occasion as his 'dear friend'. But a man of his instincts could not feel much sympathy for Edward's position as Duke of Aquitaine, nor was he likely to compromise his master's rights for larger political ends.[42]

To this change of mood in France, other more personal factors contributed. The French King was experiencing one of his periodic moods of destructive self-doubt, a sense that God was punishing him for the false policies of the past. The occasion, as so often in Philip's life, was the health of his family. Since his accession Philip had lost six sons either still-born or dead within a few days of birth. The survival of his line depended upon the only surviving son, John, Duke of Normandy, a sickly boy now sixteen years old, whose progress was watched with obsessive concern by his father. In the middle of June 1335 John fell suddenly and seriously ill. In all parts of France processions and public prayers were organized for the boy's recovery. From Paris the clergy walked barefoot with their relics 20 miles to the village of Taverny, where he was lying. It was not until the following month that John began to recover, and for a long time after that Philip's conduct of his government was coloured by his gratitude for divine mercy and his abiding fear of a relapse. It was in this tense and lugubrious atmosphere that a decision had to be made about Scotland. It was not a time for cynical political calculation of costs and benefits, nor for casuistic interpretations of France's treaty obligations to the Scots.[43]

At the beginning of July 1335, as the English armies were gathering at Newcastle and Carlisle, the French royal Council decided to send a seaborne force of 6,000 French soldiers including 1,000 men-at-arms to Scotland. Philip made no secret of his plans. The Pope was told about them. The Parlement of Paris was informed on 22 July. On the 31st, Pierre Roger, Archbishop of Rouen, announced the decision in an official sermon preached before a crowd of functionaries in the courtyard of the royal palace in Paris. The Archbishop reminded his audience of the treaties which French kings had made with the Scots in 1295 and 1326, and of the shameful conduct of Edward III in disinheriting his own brother-in-law. In these circumstances Philip, although he had nothing to gain personally, intended to restore David to his throne. The enemy was also informed. The Scots, Philip wrote to Edward III, had been asking for his help 'frequently, continually, insistently'. Placed thus upon his honour, Philip had been obliged to promise that they should have it. An open breach between England and France would certainly involve the cancellation of the crusade, and in the hope of avoiding this misfortune the English government was invited to submit its quarrel with David of Scotland to the impartial arbitration of the Pope and Philip himself. This letter was written on 7 July 1335, the day on which John of Normandy was pronounced to be out of danger. It was brought to Edward III on 20 August 1335 when he was at Perth. The French messengers must have travelled for 150 miles through country which Edward's army had devastated. The letter was answered at once. The problems of Scotland would not imperil the crusade, Edward said, because he would soon have pacified that country effectively and permanently. Moreover, since Edward was Philip's cousin and his vassal it was perhaps surprising that Philip should appear to be on the side of the Scots rather than the English. The suggestion of arbitration was obnoxious because Edward was dealing in Scotland with his own subjects and vassals. It was as complete a rebuff as could have been drafted.[44]

Philip had already started supplying arms and victuals to the Scots. This had been known to the English since at least the beginning of February when a large foreign ship was seen discharging a cargo of wine and armour at Dumbarton Castle. The traffic cannot have been easy to sustain. With English garrisons holding important coastal towns in eastern Scotland and the strength of the Scotch Guardians concentrated in the west, French supplies had to travel for 800 miles from the ports of Flanders to the Clyde, navigating for much of the journey from headland to headland and running the gauntlet of the southern and western ports of England. In February 1335, ships were being requisitioned in Bristol, Falmouth, Plymouth and Southampton to search for them. But the supplies got through, and must have contributed greatly to the morale of the Scots.[45]

Help of a more effective kind could be given by creating diversions further south, additional demands on Edward's stretched resources which might force him to unhand the Scots. In the spring of 1335 French and Scotch privateers were permitted to use the Channel ports of France, a grave threat to the small, unwalled and barely defended towns of the south coast of England as well as to their shipping. On 20 April 1335 an English ship, the *Little Lechevard* of Southampton, was attacked in the estuary of the Seine by a Scotch privateer, called John of St Agatha, with a mixed crew of Scots and Frenchmen. They killed the ship's master and some of the crew, took the cargo off at Honfleur and then scuttled her. It was not unknown for the seamen of the Norman ports to pursue their private vendettas by attacking English and Gascon shipping. But the sequel of this incident suggested official tolerance if not support. The *baillis* of Rouen and the Pays de Caux seized the plundered cargo at the request of its English owners, but John of St Agatha defended his conduct as a legitimate act of war. The *baillis* accepted this defence and returned the goods to him. Their actions were endorsed by Philip VI. John was thus enabled to pursue his career of plunder until later in the year when he was killed in a brawl with some Newcastle men in the Flemish port of Sluys. There was no shortage of others to take his place.[46]

In the middle of July 1335, as Edward was about to enter Scotland, he received a report that raiding parties of Scotch and other foreign troops were gathering in the ports of Normandy and Flanders. Warships and transports were being requisitioned by royal officers in the French Channel ports from Sluys to Mont-Saint-Michel. This intelligence was almost certainly provided by spies who had been sent to Calais at the beginning of June 1335. Even allowing for the fact that spies must earn their pay, there had plainly been naval preparations in France too extensive to have been financed and organized by the unaided efforts of the Scots. The prevailing view, which had geography and common sense in its favour, was that there would be an attempt to land in southern England, closer at hand and far away from Edward's army. Castles were ordered to be surveyed and repaired throughout southern England and Wales, and especially in the Isle of Wight and the Channel Islands, vulnerable targets for smash-and-grab raids launched from the French coast. Beacons were prepared on hill tops to warn the towns and villages of the coast. Although there had already been heavy recruiting for Scotland, the barrel was scraped for fresh recruits for the defence of the realm against the new threat. During August 1335 a scheme of national defence was proposed. The country was divided into three sections: north of the Trent (including Lincolnshire); south of the Trent; and Wales and the Marches. Assemblies of local notables gathered in each sector to plan their response to a French invasion. Special captains were appointed in each to see to the requisitioning of shipping, and keepers of the coasts organized for sea watches.[47]

In spite of these measures about eight ships penetrated the Solent during August. Three of them succeeded in landing soldiers ashore who burned some coastal villages. At least two of the ships were taken by men of Southampton and their stranded landing parties killed or captured.[48] It was not a great campaign, but it brought the communities of southern England closer to the rancours of war than the periodic visits of tax assessors and recruiting officers could do. Edward made the most of his opportunity for propaganda. 'Because it is easier to win hearts by flattery than by threats,' Edward wrote to the Welsh bishops, 'we desire that our subjects should have evidence of our favour and affection for them, that their hearts should be fired with loyalty to ourselves and enthusiasm for the defence of our realm.' In breathless and repeated instructions from the north his subjects were told about the foreign allies who stood behind the Scots. In some quarters it was believed that Philip VI had more than 700 ships ready to fall on England.[49]

Edward himself was still marking time in Perth awaiting events which never happened. The Scots remained quiescent, a mixture of disorganization and policy. The government which had formed itself in the aftermath of the rising of 1334 finally ceased to exist. In early August 1335 the Earl of Moray, who despite his youth was the most level-headed of the Scotch leaders, was captured near the border in a skirmish with a party of English garrison troops.[50] This left as the effective leader of the Scotch cause David of Strathbogie, Earl of Atholl, an ambitious and unscrupulous trimmer who had fought with Balliol at Dupplin Moor and Halidon Hill and then deserted him when his star waned; and the courageous but immature Robert Stewart. Strathbogie, true to his equivocal past, submitted to Edward III at Perth, bringing after him some two dozen Scotch noblemen. Robert Stewart submitted rather later at Edinburgh. On the face of it these were notable political successes, but it was the dissensions of the Scots and not Edward's armies which had produced them.[51]

Edward's long-awaited Irish contingent left Dublin at least a month late in the last week of August 1335. The object was almost certainly to capture Dumbarton Castle. But the Irishmen never reached it. Instead they landed on the Isle of Bute and lost much time attempting to take Rothesay. In the middle of September, threatened with the onset of the northern winter, they returned home. In eastern Scotland, the main army was already on its way south to be paid off and disbanded. Public opinion was not impressed. It was certainly a poor return for the 'immense labours and hardships' which Edward had told the King of France that he was expending in the cause of peace.[52]

At the end of September 1335 the surviving leaders of the Scotch resistance gathered at Dumbarton, still the most secure Bruce stronghold, and chose Sir Andrew Murray as Guardian of Scotland. This formidable warrior, a brother-in-law of Robert Bruce, was one of the very few Scotch magnates who had never even briefly submitted to Edward Balliol. He proved to be the first Scotch leader with ruthlessness and force of personality to match Edward's own. Closely associated with Murray was a guerrilla leader of genius, Sir William Douglas, the future 'Knight of Liddesdale' a man of strong, undying antagonisms who had never found it easy to get on with those such as David of Strathbogie whose support for the Scotch cause was intermittent and self-serving. The two men had one interesting point in common. They had both been captured in the opening months of the war and had passed some time in English prisons. Douglas had been held in irons in Carlisle Castle for a year. Edward had allowed them to ransom themselves in 1334. Later he learned to be more cautious in the matter of prisoners, irrespective of the conventions of the knightly class.[53]

The new Scotch leadership inherited a disastrous legacy, a country without a king, partly occupied and laid waste in its richest regions. Nevertheless, they almost immediately re-established the Scotch cause and won for it the first significant victories since the start of the war.

Murray began by dividing his enemies. In mid-October he made contact with Edward III and suggested a truce so that negotiations could be begun. A truce was duly granted until 12 November and extended from time to time until Christmas. In the first week in November 1335 there were talks between the two sides at Bathgate, not far from Edinburgh.[54]

Edward Balliol did not participate in the talks, and his supporters were not protected by the truce. Shortly after they had begun, David of Strathbogie, one of Balliol's few allies in Scotland, embarked upon a ruthless campaign of murder, destruction and eviction in the coastal lowlands between Perth and Aberdeen designed, he said, to reduce the Scots to obedience. The news was brought to Murray at Bathgate that Strathbogie had laid siege to his castle at Kildrummy in the Don valley. His wife, Lady Christian Bruce, was making 'stowt and manly resistance' there. Murray withdrew from the conference at Bathgate and marched north. His forces were absurdly small, his own retainers and those of his friends including Douglas, about 800 men at the most. Strathbogie was warned, presumably by the English. He raised the siege of Kildrummy, marching south to meet the approaching troops with his own men. On St Andrew's Day 1335, Murray and Douglas fell upon them by the River Dee in the forest of Culblean and routed them. Strathbogie's troops fled into the forests. He himself took his stand by an oak tree and fought until he was killed, the end of an eventful and self-serving existence. He was twenty-six years old.[55]

It was a major reverse for the English cause. In addition to intangible losses, the boost which it gave to Scotch morale at an important moment, Murray's victory left Balliol with virtually nothing north of the Tay. Moreover, it was followed up by attacks on other enclaves of Balliol's power. David of Stratbogie's widow had fled after the battle to the island fortress of Lochindorb, leaving her money and most of her wardrobe behind her. There she and 'other ladyis that were luvely' were besieged by the Scots. Murray himself crossed the Tay and laid siege to Cupar, the strongest castle in Fife.[56]

By grinding persistence Edward III could have reduced Scotland to obedience as completely as his grandfather had reduced Wales. But his main concern now was to hold the eight counties which Balliol had ceded to England. These were being transformed into huge military regions governed by English barons from strong reconstructed fortresses: Percy at Jedburgh, Montagu in Peebles and in the forests of Ettrick and Selkirk, Bohun at Lochmaben at the head of the Solway Firth. A strong garrison and an army of masons and carpenters were in the process of rebuilding Edinburgh Castle from the stumps which Robert Bruce had left of it.[57] Any ambitious enterprises beyond the eight counties would serve only to set Edward Balliol a little less precariously on his throne. This seemed an increasingly pointless objective. Balliol had no significant support in Scotland except in eastern Galloway and among the survivors of the 'disinherited' who had brought him there. He had no resources with which to build a following or sustain himself by force, because he had had to cede the richest part of his kingdom to Edward III. Not only were the ceded counties relatively rich, but they contained most of the anglophone population of Scotland, among whom Balliol's quest for friends would ordinarily have begun. In northern and western Scotland, even after the government of the Guardians had collapsed, the government of Edward Balliol remained part of the baggage train of successive English armies. When the English returned to Berwick in the autumn of 1335, Balliol returned with them and passed the winter with his companions in the security of Holy Island off the Northumberland coast, running up large bills which he was unable to pay. In the chronicler's phrase, he 'did not possess a place in Scotland where he could live in safety'.[58] This must have been as clear to Edward III and his advisers as it was to Balliol himself. In future, English policy north of the Forth was to consist in defending the pools of ground controlled by English garrisons, and in launching punitive raids against Balliol's enemies with small forces and for short periods at unpredictable moments. In strictly military terms there was no other way of dealing with an enemy who never showed himself at an appointed time.

Edward's exchange with the French King in August marked a change of priorities. He was becoming concerned about the intensifying hostility of France and about Gascony, concerns which are reflected in a growing volume of memoranda from his experts warning him of the circumstances in which the French King might feel able to seize the duchy without too gross a violation of his own law. Edward cared more about Gascony than he did about Scotland, and if this seems a perverse defiance of historical logic it would have seemed obvious to him: the natural preference of any medieval nobleman for the lands which belonged to his family by inheritance over those which he held by the operations of force or fortune.

CHAPTER VI

The Failure of Diplomacy:
The Threat at Sea
1335–1337

History has dealt harshly with the Avignon popes, and few things have aroused more controversy than their relations with France. It is true that the French kings, including Philip VI, frequently behaved as if the Pope were a spiritual arm of French foreign policy. It is also true that most of the fourteenth-century popes before the Great Schism of 1378 enjoyed closer relations with France than with any other country. This was not surprising. The popes were Frenchmen. Most of them, even if they were born in territory ruled by the dukes of Aquitaine, had been formed in the royalist tradition of the French Church. They lived at Avignon, in Imperial territory but under the shadow of the great tower of Philip the Fair at Villeneuve on the French side of the Rhône. Moreover, they had political concerns of their own which made them natural allies of France, the most powerful European country, whose protection and support were a factor in almost every political calculation which they were called upon to make. But these matters, important as they were, did not make the papacy a possession of France, and in dealing with the delicate subject of Anglo-French relations most of the Avignon popes were careful to preserve their neutrality. Indeed there were times when Philip VI, admittedly a neurotic and insecure ruler, believed that the papacy was in league with the English. Edward III was an important prince, as John XXII felt obliged to point out in response to one such accusation; his wishes could not be disregarded simply at the behest of the French government.[1]

In 1335 the Pope was Benedict XII. Of all the Avignon popes he was the least sympathetic to French interests. He was a Cistercian, a theologian and a former Inquisitor, a man of austere life and rigorous intellect whose characteristic monument is the gaunt mass of the north court of the papal palace at Avignon. His words, a cardinal wrote, 'carried no hint of human weakness.' Such a man was not likely to feel the pull of French patriotic sentiment. Benedict ascended the papal throne in December 1334 and his relations with the French King were frigid from the start. He resented the high-handed manner of the French government and despised Philip VI for his naivety and want of judgement. He particularly disliked Mile de Noyers, who had once abused him to his face.[2]

When Benedict was informed, by a more ingratiating ambassador, of Philip's intention to invade Scotland, he was not encouraging. He readily admitted that he had not studied the Scotch problem in any detail, but he had formed certain provisional views which were not welcome to the French government. In the first place, the Pope said, he did not agree that Philip VI was bound by treaty to go to the rescue of the Scots, and thought that he had not given enough thought to the consequences of his decision. Not only was it plain that the crusade would have to be cancelled if Philip invaded Scotland, but the mere attempt was bound to weaken the French King in his own realm and cost him more money than he had. Moreover, as Benedict delicately hinted, Edward III was likely to win in Scotland whatever Philip did. As to the proposal (which had already been made to the English) that Benedict and Philip should act as joint arbitrators, the Pope tartly told Philip that he was disqualified by his overt support for one of the protagonists. He proposed to undertake the work of mediation himself.[3] These icy sentiments appear to have had some effect on Philip for he took no further steps to invade Scotland until April 1336. The intervening period was occupied by Benedict's valiant but unavailing attempt to bring Edward III and David Bruce to terms.

The Pope appointed two mediators, 'discreet and judicious men with great experience of difficult negotiations'. The description was just. Hugh d'Aimery, the senior of the two, was a Provençal bishop who had been employed for many years on delicate missions of conciliation. Indeed, between 1324 and 1326 he had spent frustrating months in England trying to reconcile Edward II and Charles IV in the aftermath of the incident at Saint-Sardos. On that occasion Hugh had demonstrated his instinct for the face-saving device and the large compromise which the parties and their legal advisers had been unable to suggest for themselves. But he had also demonstrated how short-lived such arrangements must be in the face of real grievances.[4] Ten years older, he was now condemned to watch history repeating itself. He and his fellow mediator (a papal official) travelled to Paris where they collected the views of the French King, and then moved on to Amiens where they waited to be collected by an escort sent from England. They did not reach Newcastle until 1 November 1335. At the same time there arrived a French embassy, of no particular eminence, whose principal function seems to have been to watch for the interests of their own government and to act as a channel of communication with the Scots.

The negotiations which followed lasted for more than four months, in the course of which the Pope's mediators earned their reputation for discretion. Only the distant outline of events is known. The mediators held a succession of interminable meetings at Newcastle and Berwick with the representatives of all three parties in an atmosphere of tension heightened by the pressure which Edward III applied to bring them to a quick decision. He conceded extensions of the truce with difficulty and for short periods. In the background was the bustle of preparations for fresh raids into Scotland which were being planned for the contingency of failure.[5] On 26 January 1336, five days before the expiry of the current truce, a measure of agreement was finally reached. The threat of a new attack on Scotland was lifted. The truces were prolonged to the middle of April and in effect extended to the whole of Scotland. The Scots agreed to lift the sieges of Lochindorb and Cupar, the only significant military operations in progress in Balliol's part of the country. For the longer term, a controversial draft treaty was drawn up. The central point of this document was that Edward Balliol, who was unmarried and entering middle age, was to be recognized as king of Scotland and David II would be recognized as his heir. It was also agreed that while David waited for his turn he would withdraw from the malign influence of France and would live in England. This ingenious solution seems to have been approved by the leaders of the Scots in Scotland including, presumably, Andrew Murray himself. But it required the consent of David II, who was still in Normandy, as well that of the English Parliament. A party of Scots crossed the Channel to put the proposal to David at Château-Gaillard. They were expected to return with his answer before Parliament met in March.[6]

The proposal was a failure. Parliament had been summoned to Westminster for 11 March 1336, but when it met the Scotch ambassadors failed to appear. They sent messengers of low status to announce that David II had rejected the draft agreement and was not interested in further truces. English public opinion, only indistinctly informed about the affair, turned quickly from optimism to indignation. A fresh subsidy was voted for the continuation of the war, and on 7 April 1336 Edward announced that as soon as the truces expired his troops would invade Scotland 'in great numbers'. Most people blamed Philip of France for inducing David to reject the draft agreement. This was probably right. Philip had no more reason than did David himself to accept an arrangement so obviously in the interests of the King of England. The same messengers who brought Edward the news of the failure of his negotiations with the Scots also carried messages from Philip proposing a meeting of the two kings. But a meeting at such a level was bound to lead to loss of face if it failed to produce an agreement, and the prospect of agreement did not look good. Edward rejected it. The two papal emissaries told Benedict XII that there was nothing more to be done, and he recalled them.[7]

While the English Parliament was learning of the failure of the only serious attempt to date to compromise with Scotland, the French King was at Avignon experiencing disappointment of his own. Philip had a long secret audience with Benedict XII at the beginning of March 1336, from which all witnesses were excluded, a very unusual circumstance, frustrating for Edward III's agents in the city. Benedict had now learned of the failure of Hugh d'Aimery's mission, and in the course of the interview and the conferences which followed it he told the French King that he proposed to cancel the crusade. There were several reasons for the decision, some more candidly declared than others. The preparation of the venture was not going well. There had been disagreements about Philip's powers as secular leader of the expedition. Recruitment had been poor. There were now, moreover, insuperable political difficulties which Benedict outlined in a *tour d'horizon* of European affairs. Germany and northern Italy, he said, were in turmoil. The Angevin kingdom of Naples was on the verge of war with the Aragonese in Sicily. Above all, Philip himself was embroiled in a war between England and Scotland. Within France the Pope knew that Philip had enemies who were waiting for their opportunity. The Pope's reasoning was faultless, but the decision was a grave blow to Philip's pride as well as to his very real hopes of liberating the Holy Land. For some months he clung to the hope that Benedict would relent, and that the cancellation might prove to be no more than a postponement. In mid-March 1336 he left Avignon to visit Marseille, where his personal galley was being prepared for the expedition. Here he was entertained by a mock battle in the roads in which ships bombarded each other with oranges. The Pope was more realistic. The decision, as he reminded Philip later in the year, had been taken after very careful thought and the King should reflect upon the reasons for it. Benedict had formed a firm view of Philip VI. He thought that the French King was a child.[8]

The cancellation of the crusade had much more serious consequences for Edward III than any injury to his pride or dreams of immortality. At one stroke, the Pope had deprived Edward of his most valuable diplomatic bargaining counter, namely the indistinct and probably dishonest promise that he would participate in it. At the same time French resources were liberated for aggressive ventures elsewhere. On his way north, Philip celebrated Easter at Lyon, where he was met by representatives of the Scots. They told him that the truces in Scotland had only five weeks to run, until 5 May 1336, and reminded him of his earlier promises of help. Philip repeated them.

In the previous winter the French royal Council had made contingency plans for a seaborne expedition to Scotland in the summer of 1336. A commander, the Count of Eu, had been appointed, and some supplies had been laid in. These plans were now dusted off and arrangements made to put them into effect. They were conceived on an ambitious scale. It was proposed to embark an army of 1,200 men-at-arms, 5,000 crossbowmen and 20,000 infantry on 200 transports. This great fleet, together with sixty fishing boats carrying victuals and an escort of thirty war galleys, was to proceed from the ports of Normandy and Flanders to the east coast of Scotland, there to restore David Bruce to his throne. The authors of the plan were well aware of the difficulties. It would have been the largest amphibious operation since the assault on the Nile Delta by the fifth crusade in 1218. Ships would be hard to find in sufficient quantities and would have to make several round trips in order to carry the whole of the army to its destination. The cost would be enormous. But they were not deterred.[9]

The naval tradition in France was short. Until the end of the thirteenth century the only significant naval forces deployed by France had been those required for occasional crusading expeditions in the Mediterranean. They had generally been acquired by hiring ships together with their crews in Italy, mainly from the republic of Genoa, which was then one of the principal maritime powers of the western Mediterranean. The first attempt to build a powerful French war fleet was not made until 1284, when Philip III decided to invade Aragon and Catalonia. To do this, he needed to supply his army, south of the Pyrenees, by sea in the face of the very strong navy of Aragon and its Sicilian allies. He embarked at breakneck speed on construction and purchase of a fleet of up to 100 galleys and some 200 large transports. Many of these ships were built at a royal arsenal which was specially created at Narbonne. The venture was a disaster. In two battles off the Mediterranean coast of Spain the new French fleet was almost entirely destroyed by the Aragonese. The arsenal of Narbonne was subsequently abandoned. But the idea of a permanent royal fleet survived. In 1293, Philip the Fair conceived the plan of building an Atlantic fleet to contest with England control of the Channel and the Bay of Biscay routes to Gascony. Philip's most significant decision was the construction of a great naval arsenal, the Clos des Galées, in the Richebourg quarter of

Rouen by the south end of the city bridge, the only establishment of its kind in northern Europe. The main purpose of the arsenal was the construction, storage and repair of war-galleys, vessels whose essential features barely changed from classical times to the eighteenth century: long, narrow, oared hulls with low freeboards, powered by a single tier of thirty oars on each side and carrying a crew of 180 rowers, three at each oar. The Genoese design, which the French adopted, also included a single mast with a lateen sail which provided the motive power when the vessel was cruising. The arsenal was not abandoned when Philip the Fair's war with England came to an end in 1303. Instead it was retained on a care-and-maintenance basis throughout the reigns of his sons, and in times of tension would spring to life, as it did during the crises in Gascony and Flanders in the mid-1320s. Acres of timber would once more be requisitioned by royal officers in the Cotentin and bands of southerners speaking their own arcane dialect would pour into Rouen. The crews, like the builders, were generally Provençals or Narbonnais with Genoese officers, acknowledged experts in handling fighting galleys.

To these traditional warships others of a different kind, specially designed for Atlantic conditions, were added during the 1330s. They were clinker-built Norman barges with a rather higher freeboard, up to 90 feet long and powered by oars and a single square sail not unlike the old Viking barges of the ninth and tenth centuries. They carried timber castles fore and aft and a complement of between 100 and 200 men.[10]

Most of the thirty warships required for Philip VI's Scotch expedition were already available, although they were in the wrong places. There were eight large newly constructed galleys at Rouen and La Rochelle, and five smaller ones. There were twelve large galleys in the Mediterranean, either at Marseille or in the last stages of construction at Beaucaire on the Rhône. All these ships, which had been intended for the crusading fleet, were now available for the Atlantic, and orders were given to bring them round to the Channel ports.[11]

Transports, a more intractable problem, could be obtained only by requisitioning merchantmen. The French merchant marine had a number of advantages for this purpose. It was large. A high proportion of its ships were of the biggest kind with high freeboards for fighting at sea and ample deck space for carrying men and horses. A comparison with the English merchant marine is difficult to make, but a plausible guess based on the requisitioned fleets of the early part of the Hundred Years War suggests that, although the number of merchant ships available to each side was about the same, the average tonnage of French requisitioned merchantmen was greater. Moreover, the French merchant marine, unlike the English, was geographically concentrated. It was drawn almost entirely from the ports of Normandy, Picardy and the Boulonnais (Flanders and Brittany, being autonomous principalities, contributed nothing). Several of these ports, and in particular Calais, Boulogne and Dieppe, had long piratical traditions which proved invaluable in wartime. However, even this ample pool of shipping was incapable of carrying an army of more than 26,000 men with its equipment and horses across the North Sea. A survey of shipping in the Atlantic ports showed that there were thirty suitable vessels at Le Havre; twenty-four were in southern Normandy; twenty-four at Dieppe and sixteen scattered among the north-eastern harbours from Fécamp to Calais. It was less than half of what was needed. Even these were not easy to equip in the time available.[12]

Edward III's resources were stretched to the limit in 1336. Partly for that reason and partly because the English King's attention was fixed on France, the Scotch campaign of 1336 was conceived as a swift punitive raid on a relatively modest scale. Edward decided not to take the command himself but appointed Henry of Lancaster, the son of the old Earl of Lancaster, in his place. He left for the north in the middle of May 1336 with a small force of about 500 men-at-arms and rather more than 600 infantry, almost all of them mounted men.[13] The Scotch forces were divided. Murray was in the north near the Moray Firth, where he was maintaining a loose siege of the Castle of Lochindorb. The other Scotch leaders had resumed the siege of Cupar in Fife. In southern Scotland the opposition faded away as the English approached. The besiegers of Cupar were put to flight by a raiding party drawn from the garrison of Edinburgh, which secretly crossed the Forth and fell upon them without warning. Henry of Lancaster reached Perth early in June, having encountered very little resistance and waited there for supplies and reinforcements to come up from the south.[14] His objective was almost certainly Aberdeen, which was one of the few ports of eastern Scotland by which supplies could reach Murray's forces. One of Lancaster's retainers, Sir Thomas Rosslyn, was given the task of establishing a secure forward base. Rosslyn sailed in eight ships from King's Lynn to the ruined coastal castle of Dunnotar 15 miles south of Aberdeen with 160 men and horses and a corps of masons and carpenters to rebuild the fortifications. When he landed he encountered fierce resistance. His men were attacked on the beach and he himself was mortally wounded. But the Scots were unable to prevent them from seizing Dunnotar and fortifying it.[15]

News which was reaching Edward III in England was making Aberdeen and the south shore of the Moray Firth more than ever important. Already in the first week of May an English spy sent to Normandy and Flanders had brought back news of unusual activity in the Channel ports. During the first ten days of June 1336, the intelligence became even more alarming. Edward now learned about Philip VI's meeting with the Scots at Lyon and received remarkably detailed information about the French King's plans. According to his reports, Alexander Seton and Walter Twynham, two members of David II's household at Château-Gaillard, had been instructed to proceed to Scotland to take command of the Scotch forces there. The French expeditionary force would land somewhat later, at a place north of the Forth which had yet to be decided. There they would join forces with the Scots and invade the northern counties of England. Edward's informant gave graphic particulars of the preparations. Two thousand sailors and 300 transports were said to have gathered around Harfleur. There were also thirty 'invincible' galleys with copper-sheathed sides to protect them against burning projectiles. In the arsenal at Leure, at the mouth of the Seine, they were making crossbows and pavises, the huge shields which protected the bowman while he rearmed his weapon. Crossbow quarrels were being bought in bulk. There were 14,000 armoured jackets in store. Mercenaries were being hired in Genoa and Brabant. All this was too precise to have been discovered by conventional spying. Edward was either receiving information from someone well place in Philip's service or had rifled the baggage of the Scotch or French diplomatic agent.[16]

This is to some extent confirmed by the fact that Edward's information bore a much closer relation to Philip's plans than to his achievements. The truth was that Philip had succeeded in sending a small advance guard to Scotland under the command of a young knight called Yon de Garencières. But the main force was nowhere near ready. The galleys based in the Mediterranean had not yet arrived. Those which had arrived from other Atlantic ports had not yet been equipped or fitted out. Transports were in short supply. The Count of Eu, who was supposed to be leading the expedition, was having misgivings on account of his lands in England and Ireland and shortly afterwards resigned his command. Other Frenchmen shared this nobleman's ambivalent feelings about Philip's enterprise. Was it not, as one Parisian chronicler thought, a breach of faith for the French King to be fighting against Edward III in his own country for the benefit of mere Scots?[17]

Behind these troubles lay the familiar difficulty of medieval governments in collecting taxes for purposes which were not obviously and directly related to the defence of the communities paying them. The state of Philip's finances in the summer of 1336 was nothing less than disastrous. France had been enjoying several years of low taxation and in many regions no taxation at all. The last general subsidy which Philip had levied from his subjects had been collected in 1328 and 1329 on the occasion of his invasion of Flanders, a war which had been popular, at any rate with the nobility. Evidently Philip did not feel able to ask his subjects to pay another for the invasion of Scotland. This judgement was probably sound. Unfortunately the traditional alternative source of emergency finance, the manipulation of the coinage, was not available in 1336. Philip had carried out an ambitious revaluation in the first year of his reign in an attempt to restore the 'strong money' of St Louis after the repeated and unpopular devaluations of his predecessors. The result had been to aggravate an existing shortage of bullion and finally to force the closure of the royal mints in March 1335 for want of metal. At the beginning of 1336 there was a change of policy for the express purpose of financing the war which Philip expected to have to fight against England. The coinage was devalued once again in the hope of drawing bullion to the mints. The change was expected to make the King unpopular and did so. But it wholly failed to achieve its purpose. The mints remained closed. The French invasion plan was expected by its authors to cost 180,000 *l.t.*, a considerable under-estimate but even so a great deal more than Philip could afford. The government's receipts in 1336 were less than half the average, by far the worst year of the reign. They amounted to little more than 260,000 *l.t.* In desperation Philip turned to the Church, asking the Pope's permission to levy a tenth. Benedict not only refused; he addressed to the King a schoolmasterly lecture upon his fecklessness. The Scotch project had to be financed by scrapings from the barrel: local contributions negotiated with the communities affected, mainly the maritime areas of Normandy; loans from towns, individual noblemen and civil servants; the exiguous and overstretched resources of the royal domain. The French government's use of credit was very primitive by comparison with English financial practice, and their short-term difficulties, essentially difficulties of cash flow, proved to be fatal.[18]

In June and July 1336 the French government was only beginning to understand the scale of what it had undertaken, when Edward III by a bold strategic stroke made its achievement all but impossible. The essential conditions for a successful French landing in Scotland were a friendly coast and adequate harbours where a large number of men could be dis-embarked with their horses and equipment. Moreover, unless the army was to be supplied through the autumn and winter months from Flanders, 700 miles across the North Sea, there would have to be food available for it locally. The only area where these conditions existed was the coastal plain along the south shore of the Moray Firth and between the Moray Firth and the Firth of Tay. Although there is no evidence that Aberdeen had been chosen for the landings, its position and its important harbour made it the obvious choice. Edward III evidently thought so, for Aberdeen and its hinterland were now to be methodically wasted. Edward abandoned a plan to preside over a Great Council of spiritual and temporal lords at Northampton. On 11 June he left in great haste for Newcastle where a small force was scratched together. It consisted of slightly more then 400 men drawn mainly from those of the royal household who happened to be at hand and from the retinue of William Montagu. A few others caught up and joined them at intervals as they marched through the lowlands. The garrisons of Stirling and Perth were astounded at the King's arrival, and even more by the risk which he had taken in passing through hostile territory with so small a force. On 12 July, having added some 400 men to his strength from Henry of Lancaster's troops, he moved north out of Perth.

The speed of his advance surprised the Scots as much as it did the English. Murray's force, which was still in the region of Lochindorb a hundred miles north, narrowly escaped being caught. Inside Lochindorb castle, the Countess of Atholl and her ladies and soldiers were down to their last half quarter of rye when they were relieved. Edward now began the work for which he had come. All the animals which could be found were rounded up and slaughtered, more than 1,000 beasts on the first day alone. On 17 July 1336, the King reached the Moray Firth. The food stores of Kinloss Abbey were emptied. Forres was burned. Elgin's famous church was spared, but nothing was left standing around it. The ripening crops were burned as far inland as Edward's men could penetrate. On the night of the 21st, Edward reached Aberdeen from the north. The whole of the following day was passed in burning the town and demolishing what could not be burned. Edward stayed behind to satisfy himself by personal inspection that nothing remained above the ground. In spite of the modest size of the English force, the Scots offered no resistance. Murray withdrew south of the Forth with as many men as he could gather. The rest 'secreted themselves in the marshes, mountains and woods'.[19]

The Great Council which Edward had summoned before leaving for Scotland assembled at Northampton on 25 June 1336. The threat from

France seems to have been the sole item of business. John Stratford, Archbishop of Canterbury, Henry Burghersh, Bishop of Lincoln, and Edward's brother John of Eltham presided in the King's absence. At this stage the government was asking for advice, not money, and seeking to commit the nobility to a policy which might ultimately prove expensive. Conscious perhaps of this the Council was cautious in its suggestions. They thought that a fresh embassy, the first important one for a year, should be sent to France to discover whether the French King's plans were really as hostile as they appeared to be, and to propose a compromise. It is not clear what this compromise was, but it certainly involved David Bruce, for the Council suggested that the embassy should also be empowered to negotiate directly with him. This was itself a significant shift in English policy.[20]

Both governments had now gone beyond the point at which a change of course could be negotiated. Events were moving too fast, and at distances too great for co-ordination. As the Council dispersed, John of Eltham went north to see to the collection of the levies from the northern counties. At the end of July 1336 he entered Scotland with several thousand men to carry the process of destruction into the south-west of the country. This force ravaged Carrick and the Clyde valley, burning, so the Scots said, whole congregations in the churches were they had fled for safety. In southern England, Edward's diplomats proceeded on their mission of peace. The ambassadors, the bishops of Durham and Winchester and two others, were appointed on 7 July and embarked at Dover on the 24th as soon as their safe conducts had arrived from France. At about the same time, French galleys based in the Mediterranean at last arrived in the harbours of Normandy and Brittany to join the rest of Philip's galley fleet. There were now twenty-six galleys, a creditable force only four short of what had been planned. The English government found out about their arrival in the last week of July, and by mid-August they knew the exact number.[21]

In the Mediterranean, fresh forces were being made ready to join Philip's Channel fleet. The French King's agents acquired several galleys in Genoa, which were in the last stages of fitting out; others were anchored in the ports of Philip's enemy the King of Sicily, protected by the fiction that they were intended for the crusade. The contest between the two northern powers began to spill over into the politics of the Italian states. The English had little diplomatic experience in southern Europe and certainly could not match France's long-standing influence in the Italian peninsula. But they did have good unofficial connections in Genoa. Edward II had given most of his financial business to Genoese bankers, and a significant Genoese community had grown up in London during his reign. Edward III had kept up the connections made by his father. Two London Genoese, the brothers Antonio and Niccolo Usomare, were responsible for the finances of Gascony for more than ten years between 1334 and 1345, and periodically took a hand in the King's dealings with the Genoese republic. The English government's main contacts with Genoa were through the Fieschi, the principal Guelph family of the city, who never in spite of successive revolutions and expulsions entirely lost their influence there. Carlo dei Fieschi, one of the Captains of Genoa, had been an honorary councillor of Edward II, and Francesco dei Fieschi, Count of Lavagna, had accepted the King's livery during a visit to England in 1317. In the 1330s the tradition was continued by Nicolino dei Fieschi, who may have been the latter's brother. This skilful and devious man was employed by the Genoese government in various diplomatic missions to England and France during the early 1330s. In the course of one of them he was taken into Edward's service, and became the principal instrument of English intrigue in Italy and Provence. The first fruits of his work were impressive. Fieschi persuaded the government of his city to arrest and burn the ships that had been hired for Philip's account. The price was high. Edward had to settle all outstanding claims of Genoese merchants against his subjects. This cost him 8,000 marks of silver. By comparison, the obstruction of Philip VI's plans in Sicily was cheap. Fieschi had only to inform Frederick III of Sicily of the true destination of the French King's ships there to procure their confiscation.[22]

During August the bishops of Durham and Winchester had a series of meetings with Philip VI and his Council in Paris and at the royal residence in the Bois de Vincennes. Their discussions were extremely disagreeable. They came to an end on 20 August with the announcement in Paris of the French King's 'final answer'. Philip rejected the ambassadors' proposals in their entirety. He said that he intended to assist the Scots by every means in his power. He had, he explained, recruited a large army both within France and elsewhere and had assembled a fleet of galleys and other ships. With these, he intended to invade both England and Scotland immediately. The ambassadors found Philip's frankness startling, as indeed it was. They did not dare to write down what they had been told in case the paper should fall into the wrong hands. So they sent a clerk, William Tickhill, to warn the royal Council in England by word of mouth. Tickhill left Paris at once with a single squire, reached Dover on 23 August and rode through the night to arrive very late on the 24th at Northampton, where John

Stratford and some senior royal councillors were lodging. Stratford, without waiting to consult the King or even hear the end of Tickhill's message, had writs issued for another Great Council at Nottingham on 23 September, the shortest possible interval. On this occasion, not only the prelates and barons were summoned, but also the representatives of the shires and boroughs. The exhausted Tickhill was then sent post haste to Scotland to report his news to Edward III and to pass on the Council's urgent advice that the King should return straight away to England.[23]

The fighting promised by Philip VI had already begun. On 22 August 1336, four French warships descended on the town of Orford. In Orford roads, they found a large requisitioned merchant ship, the *Caterine*. The few sailors on board were overcome and killed, and the ship carried off to Flanders. On the following day, the same force returned to the Suffolk coast and raided Walton roads, another vanished east-coast harbour now engulfed by the mess of Felixstowe. Here they took the *Paternoster* with a valuable cargo of cloth, dyes and wax. The raiders had letters of commission from Philip VI. They delivered half their spoils to his representative on their return. During the next ten days a much larger French squadron left the harbours of Normandy and Brittany. This force which consisted of both galleys and transports, made for the Isle of Wight, where several of the English King's ships and some loaded merchantmen were anchored. There was no warning of their coming, and very little resistance. The ships were boarded and their crews knifed and drowned. Some were scuttled; others were carried off to Normandy to be sold as prize.[24]

The attackers encountered virtually no resistance at sea. Edward III had appointed admirals to requisition ships in May, when the first rumours of French naval activity had reached the government. A small number had gathered at Portsmouth in June to prevent the very thing that happened. Unfortunately, in the last week of July these vessels had been dispersed to their home ports because of misleading information from the continent suggesting that the alarm was over. They were soon afterwards recalled to their stations, but the disruption occasioned by these orders and counter-orders left the south coast virtually undefended when the French ships arrived. The defensive measures of the English government, orderly at least in their conception, turned to panic after the return of William Tickhill from France and the news of the first attacks. The ships of the western Admiralty were ordered, too late, to collect in the Downs off Sandwich to intercept the enemy. Then, on 6 September, the combined fleets of the two Admiralties were told to attack the retreating French galleys, but by this time they had returned to their bases. It was a cruel mockery of the pretensions of the English King, who had declared less than a week before the French raids began that his forbears had 'ever been sovereigns of the English seas on every side'; therefore, he added, 'it would be a great grief to us and a slight to our royal honour if the defences of our realm against the assaults of the enemy should be weakened in our own day'.[25]

Edward himself was still in Scotland, happily unaware of these events. William Tickhill, having ridden night and day through the Midlands and north of England, arrived at Berwick to find that the eastern lowlands were in turmoil as a result of the depredations of Douglas's guerrilla bands. His bodyguard refused to take him further than Fife. There were no ships available to carry him round the coast. The Council's message did not reach the King until the second week in September. When it did, it was acted upon with dispatch. Edward had been planning a campaign against Douglas in the lowlands. Instead, he hurried south, taking the principal magnates of the army with him but leaving the bulk of his forces behind. The knights and burgesses, and the remaining magnates were already gathering at Nottingham. Edward himself arrived there on 24 September 1336.[26]

The Great Council opened on the following morning and received the sombre news of the outcome of the embassy to France and the raids in Suffolk and the Isle of Wight. As they deliberated, the atmosphere of crisis was heightened by the arrival of gobbets of news about French attacks on English shipping in the Channel and along the sea lanes of the Atlantic coast of France. Southern England was gripped by invasion fever. Since the middle of August, commissioners of array had been selecting men in the coastal towns and villages. Huge bonfires were being built on hill tops for the moment when the French should land. Wild and improbable rumours circulated of clandestine bands of Scots buying up supplies in England for their army, spying out the cities and plotting acts of sabotage. The assembly at Nottingham authorized the recruitment of an enormous defensive army. In every town and county community, up to four commissioners were to be appointed to summon every adult man to appear armed according to his station, with bow and knife, lance, halberd, stave, poleaxe or whatever other weapon he had to hand. From this motley mob they were to choose the best; the others were to contribute at their own expense one large cart from each community and victuals for at least three weeks. By this means it was believed that more than 80,000 men could be raised. No one ventured to suggest further negotiation with France. It was the point at which the English political community accepted that war with France was inevitable.[27]

The English King was filling his war-chests. The assembly at Nottingham granted a tax of one tenth and fifteenth. The clergy conceded a tenth. A special levy on wool was authorized by the merchants. Fresh loans were raised from the Italians, this time not only from the Bardi but from the other great Florentine banking house of Peruzzi, who had not previously made large loans to Edward III. English merchants lent on a generous and, for them, unprecedented, scale. More than £100,000 was borrowed from bankers between the summer of 1336 and September 1337. Most of it was applied straight from hand to mouth in the struggle to keep up with the rapid increase of expenditure. In Bristol the ships requisitioned for defence were immobilized in the harbour because their crews were unpaid and without victuals. In Yorkshire there was a disturbing mutiny, almost certainly for the same reason, among the troops levied for service on the border. Like Philip VI, Edward applied to the Pope for permission to divert the wealth of the Church from the crusade to his own needs; but unlike Philip VI he did not take no for an answer. In October 1336, he seized the treasure which had been accumulated for the crusade in St Mary's Abbey, York. Subsidiary crusade chests were taken from cathedrals throughout England by his officials. Only in the new mood of menace and national solidarity could this outrageous theft have occurred so easily. The clergy almost certainly connived in it.[28]

In France, the King's ministers had already begun to treat English merchants and travellers as enemies. During September they were arrested and their goods seized, certainly in the northern provinces and probably throughout the kingdom. In Flanders, where there was always a large number of English traders and seamen, very many of them were rounded up without warning and thrown in prison. The English, who learned about the arrests in Flanders in October, retaliated in kind.[29]

After the Council of Nottingham had dispersed, Edward III and his friends returned to their uncompleted work in Scotland, now a wearing guerrilla war of sieges and ambushes, of castles in turn taken and repaired by the English, retaken and destroyed by the Scots. Time was short. Winter made movement difficult. On 18 October 1336 the English King marched to Bothwell, the partly dismantled fortress on the Clyde which had been his grandfather's principal stronghold in the lowlands. Repairs were put in hand in harsh conditions. Winter had set in. Food and materials had to be brought under escort from Berwick. The guerrilla bands of William Douglas hovered at the edges of the English encampment attacking supply trains, killing stragglers and foragers. While Edward busied himself on the

Clyde, his work was undone further north. In October, Andrew Murray captured and destroyed the isolated English strongholds of Dunnotar, Kynnef and Lauriston. The Guardian inaugurated a brutal campaign of devastation in his own territories, knowing that he had no other means of making them uninhabitable by English armies. Gowrie, Angus and Mearns were wasted in turn. The tragic consequences for the Scots themselves had to be tolerated:

> In gret distres the comownys ware
> Pynyde to dede in hungyre
> For with his ost as he rade
> Gret wastyng in the land he made.

Many more Scots died of famine and disease in these terrible years than had been killed by English soldiers.[30]

In the south and east of England October 1336 was the high point of the invasion scare. Orders were given for the detention of every single ship in England, from which suitable vessels might be requisitioned with their crews to reinforce those already under the admirals' command. Galleys were summoned to the Channel from Bayonne, and application was made to Genoa for more. Stores of victuals were accumulated near the coast to supply them. Arrows were ordered in thousands. One Nicholas 'the Engineer' was commissioned to make thirty springalds (large ship-mounted catapults). Home guards were recruited in all the maritime counties of southern England.[31]

At sea, the motley collection of requisitioned ships gathered in the Downs. Waiting was bad for discipline. There had already been a mutiny among the pressed crews of the King's ship *Christopher*, a sign of difficulties to come. The men of Great Yarmouth were slipping away to pursue their ancient vendetta against the Cinque Ports, and other ships were reported to be attacking friendly merchantmen in the Channel. In spite of insistent reports that the French were planning another descent on the Solent, the admirals held the remaining ships of their fleet off the mouth of the Thames where they could protect the capital and pursue the enemy in whatever direction they went. It was an intelligent calculation. But nothing happened. Towards the end of October the English decided that the enemy had missed their moment. The larger ships were needed for the annual wine fleet from the Gironde. So on 22 October they disbanded the fleet of the western Admiralty; the northern fleet was dispersed four days later. On 8 November the mass recruitment of men in the coastal areas of England, which had been ordered by the Council of Nottingham, was cancelled.[32]

The French government's intentions defied analysis. Deprived of his reinforcements from the Mediterranean, lacking any suitable port of disembarkation and menaced by the onset of the northern winter, Philip VI at some point in the autumn abandoned his plan to land troops in Scotland. Instead, it was decided to concentrate the admirals' efforts on naval raids on southern England which had originally been devised as mere diversions. In November, there was a destructive but strategically insignificant attack on the Channel Islands. Small groups of French ships and some Spanish privateers flying French ensigns cruised off the coast preying on English and Gascon shipping. The English avoided any serious losses by forming large armed convoys between Gascony and the Solent ports. Towards the end of the year the French campaign at sea faltered and then stopped.[33]

As relations with France soured, the 'Gascon Days' of the Parlement of Paris became busier. By the late summer of 1336 the flurry of litigation was causing serious concern in England. It was becoming difficult to find French advocates capable of standing up to officially inspired pressure, and after a succession of timorous failures serious consideration was being given to disavowing all Edward's standing counsel in Paris. In Gascony itself French royal officers were regularly reported to be entering towns and castles of the duchy to execute the orders of the King's courts. If refused admission they sometimes attempted to take control by force. Behind these legal manoeuvres lay the jockeying for strategic advantage, preliminaries to a war that now seemed inevitable. Since the disintegration of the Anglo-French commission at Langon in 1334, the fortress at Blanquefort outside Bordeaux had been the subject of bitterly contested litigation in the Parlement. Philip deliberately raised the stakes at issue in this arcane testamentary dispute by buying the rights of the Count of Armagnac and then regranting them to one of his most loyal allies in the south-west. This man was promised the support of royal troops in the event of a war with Edward III. It was the most serious case but not an isolated one. On the other side of Bordeaux, the Abbot of La Sauve-Majeure had abstracted himself from Edward's jurisdiction with the blessing of the Parlement and in spite of the protests of Edward's counsel. Saintes, the northernmost of the major towns of the duchy, was the subject of an ancient lawsuit still very much alive. So were Blaye and Saint-Macaire, both important frontier towns. Some of Edward III's principal allies among the Gascon nobility were reported to be failing before the judicial onslaught and on the point of transferring their allegiance to Philip VI.[34]

Inevitably one of these cases would lead to a judgement which Edward would find it politically impossible to comply with. When it happened in July 1336, the occasion was characteristically obscure: an action involving one Garcie Arnaud, lord of Navailles, a troublesome and litigious baron of Béarn who claimed to be owed 30,000 florins by Edward III. Arnaud had been prosecuting his action in Paris without success for years. The Parlement had never decided on the merits because Edward's lawyers had deployed a variety of technical devices for deferring the matter, and their arguments had always prevailed. However, on 11 July 1336 the technical arguments failed and Edward was declared to be in default. A large award of damages was made in Arnaud's favour, which the Parlement ordered to be satisfied by seizures from Edward's assets in Gascony. After a short period of agonizing in England the decision was made to defy the Parlement. It can only have been made by Edward himself. His advisers were in no doubt that it would eventually lead to the forfeiture of the duchy. The French tried to enforce Garcie Arnaud's judgement around the new year. The place chosen was the *bastide* of Puymirol in the Agenais, an enclave of the duchy entirely surrounded by territory in the allegiance of the King of France. The town was badly designed for defence, its keep weakly sited in the shadow of the parish church. But Edward had to hold on to such places if his claim to recover the rest of the Agenais was to be taken seriously, and his officers were ready when the French arrived with their small escort. They were sent away with oaths ringing in their ears.[35]

Preparation for the seizure of the whole duchy had already begun. A contract was made with the Count of Foix. He agreed in return for a lump sum to raise an army of 100 men-at-arms and 500 infantry on the southern march of the duchy by 24 November 1336. The Count's orders were to be ready for a two-month campaign in Gascony as soon as war should break out. On the northern march, in Saintonge, a new seneschal was appointed and given the title of Captain of the King's Wars there.[36] Edward III for his part began to take belated steps to strengthen the defences of his duchy. In the early autumn, the government in Bordeaux set about repairing and victualling, as far as their limited resources allowed, castles which had lain neglected for many years. In England, the first plans for reinforcing Gascony with English troops were drawn up by Edward's ministers.[37]

Early in the new year an attempt by the Pope to mediate was brushed aside without even the usual polite evasions. The quarrel, Philip told Benedict XII, was not between sovereign kings but between sovereign and vassal in a matter than went to the authority of the French Crown. In such circumstances, mediation was an impertinence. At the same time the

French King set about raiding the coffers of the Church. He made no secret of the fact that his object was to finance a campaign in the spring. Benedict reacted with characteristic vigour. He refused to permit Philip to tax ecclesiastical property. In order to forestall any felonious intentions of the French government, he ordered the collectors of the crusading tenth to return the money collected to those who had paid it.[38]

Philip now made a major issue of a grievance which had hitherto been no more than a minor irritant. This was the residence at the English court of his most persistent and venomous domestic enemy, Robert of Artois. Philip later declared the intrigues of this man to have been the main cause of the war, and his version of events, however disingenuous, found general acceptance in France. The truth was not as straightforward.

Robert of Artois, one of the pivotal figures of the opening years of the Hundred Years War, was Philip VI's brother-in-law. He was a clever and personable man of fifty whose life was governed by a single overpowering obsession to which he devoted most of his energies, and which led ulti-mately to his death fighting in a foreign army against his own country. This was the acquisition of the county of Artois which by a quirk of the law of inheritance had passed from his father to his aunt at the end of the thirteenth century instead of to himself. He had prosecuted his claim at different times by litigation, by violence and by intrigue at court but always without success. When Philip VI became king of France Robert saw his opportunity. He became the King's closest friend and adviser, his 'chief and special companion and lover in all of his estates' as Froissart put it; 'and in the space of three years all that was done in the realm of France was done by his advice, and without him nothing was done'.[39] Within a few months, Robert had persuaded the King to take possession of the county in the name of the Crown while his claim was re-examined. The affair aroused extraordinary passions, divided Philip's family and court, and raised a dangerous aristocratic coalition against him. Unfortunately for Robert, the ancient Countess of Artois died in November 1329 and by another quirk of inheritance was eventually succeeded in her rights by the Duchess of Burgundy. The Duke of Burgundy, her husband, as well as being one of the great territorial magnates of the kingdom, was another of Philip VI's brothers-in-law. Robert had been trumped. In December 1330, the dispute abruptly ended. The documents which Robert had tendered in support of his claim were found to have been forged on his instructions. Philip dismissed him from his favour and allowed a criminal prosecution to be brought against him. But Robert declined to meet his judges. He fled to the Low Countries and began an errant life on the marches of France shifting from place to place as his presence brought embarrassment to his friends and hostility from his enemies. In April 1332 he was banished from France and all his possessions there were confiscated.

Philip VI's relentless persecution of Robert of Artois long after the man had become a broken and impoverished exile is revealing of his character. No doubt much of the venom was due to the influence of the Queen (the Duke of Burgundy's sister). Philip himself, although he was not by nature a vindictive man, was an extremely superstitious and unconfident one. He took most seriously the threats which Robert hurled at him from abroad to foment rebellion in France and to strike down his children by sorcery. For more than two years after Robert had left France, Philip sent spies to watch him and thugs to capture him. He had his confessor arrested when he was found in France, imprisoned his wife and family, prosecuted for treason those who spoke warmly of him and constructed warlike coalitions against neighbouring princes who sheltered him.[40]

In the spring of 1334 Robert of Artois arrived heavily disguised in England and asked for asylum at the court of Edward III. He explained that he had been slandered by his enemies in France and intended to return there to justify himself as soon as he could safely do so. On this basis, Edward allowed him to remain. But he refused to give him any help against the French King. This is Edward's own version of the facts prepared several years later when the decision had become controversial. It is almost certainly true, for nothing was heard of Robert for the next two years. The flow of threats and abuse directed at Philip VI and his family ceased, and Philip for his part, although he must have known where Robert was, said nothing about the matter in the course of his long negotiations with the English court. As long as Edward's policy remained the appeasement of France the presence of Robert of Artois can only have been an embarrassment to Edward himself. But as relations with France became cold and then hostile, Robert moved into favour at the English court. In the autumn of 1336 he accompanied Edward III on his expedition to Scotland. He began to receive gifts of money and was allowed to live on a royal manor. Robert was colourful and charming, an excellent horseman and flatterer, the kind of man that Edward liked. However, what really commended him to the English King was the potential which he was thought to have for making trouble for the enemy. Robert of Artois claimed an extensive and useful network of friends in France. He also had relatives among the independent princes of the Low Countries on France's northern border, a region where Edward was already in the autumn of

1336 hoping to construct a great offensive alliance. Robert exaggerated his own usefulness and Edward believed him.[41]

Philip VI was aware of the growing favour which Robert of Artois was enjoying in the English court, although he overstated its significance. At the end of 1336 he began to deliver formal complaints about Robert's presence in England. Angry letters were sent. The Pope was invited to remonstrate with Edward and did so. The English King, Benedict wrote acutely, might care to recall some of the difficulties which foreign favourites had made for some of his predecessors. His messengers would be able to give the King some particulars of Robert's past which it would be indelicate to commit to writing. On 26 December 1336, Philip VI formally demanded Robert's extradition from England. The request was sent, not by diplomatic messenger to Edward himself, but to the English Seneschal in Gascony. The Seneschal was told that he should deal with the Master of the Royal Archers whom Philip was sending to Gascony for the purpose. The French government plainly intended to make this the occasion for the final breach.[42]

Why they should have chosen for their *casus belli* the intrigues of an ageing *émigré* is an interesting question. In Philip's own case, personal rancour may have had something to do with it, but his ministers, who were shrewd and calculating men, are unlikely to have been interested in personal considerations. There were sound political reasons for the decision. In the first place they must have known about the activities of English agents in the Low Countries which had now begun in earnest. They believed, unlike Edward III, that the English King's connection with Robert of Artois would be a liability to him there. Philip VI had treaties with several of the more important princes of the Low Countries which bound them to assist him against Robert of Artois. These treaties had been made some years earlier and in rather different circumstances, but they were still in force and the French government correctly divined that the princes would be reluctant to break them too flagrantly. There were also considerations of domestic policy. To confiscate the duchy of Gascony, Philip needed the political support of the leaders of the French nobility. In strictly legal terms the conduct of Edward III in sheltering Robert of Artois in his own realm where he was a sovereign prince was not a ground for forfeiting his French duchy, but it counted for a great deal before the audience which mattered most. There were plenty of people in France, the dominant party among the nobility, the friends and relations of the Queen, her brother the Duke of Burgundy and their innumerable protégés in the higher reaches of the civil service who would feel threatened by an alliance of Edward III and Robert of Artois. Not all of them would have been eager to dispossess Edward of his duchy for a minor squabble in the Parlement of Paris of a kind which might well one day affect their own possessions.

The Master of the Royal Archers, a Savoyard called Etienne le Galois de la Baume, arrived in the south-west in February 1337. His instructions are not recorded and it is possible that he exceeded them. Shortly after his arrival he tried to take Saint-Macaire by surprise. Saint-Macaire was a small walled town on the north bank of the Garonne about 40 miles from Bordeaux which guarded the main point of entry into Edward III's remaining territories in Aquitaine. Its loss at this point would have been a disaster. But it was not destined to be lost. The citizens closed their gates in time and Le Galois de la Baume had brought no siege equipment. He sent for some to Toulouse, but the arsenal there was empty. The French were obliged to withdraw. To forestall another fiasco of this kind Philip VI began to collect a siege train in readiness for the spring campaigning season. Equipment was taken out of store in the north for 'certain secret purposes' concealed even from his officials.[43]

Notwithstanding the secrecy, Philip's intentions were known, or accurately guessed, in England. The English King left Scotland in the middle of December 1336 and passed Christmas at Hatfield. From the beginning of the new year plans were in hand to defend the south and east coasts of England against the renascent navy of France and to send an expeditionary force across the Bay of Biscay to Gascony in time for the campaigning season.

Both plans called for great numbers of warships. Yet at a time when other western European powers, not only the Italian maritime cities but Aragon, Castile and France, were creating large permanent war fleets of ships built and crewed by the state, the kings of England scarcely possessed a 'Royal Navy'. English efforts had depended for many years on improvisation and luck. The best fighting ships, and the only purpose-built fighting ships of the fourteenth century, were galleys and other large oared vessels. The Mediterranean galley, it is true, had some disadvantages in northern waters. But for offensive operations it was supreme. It was the only completely manoeuvrable ship, capable of very high maximum speeds, able to move regardless of the strength and direction of the wind and to disengage quickly from any fight on unfavourable terms. Its enormous complement (the oarsmen doubled as soldiers) made it extremely effective for mounting raids against undefended towns and villages of the English coast. Unfortunately for the English kings, the economic conditions which enabled the Italian city states to build up large fleets of these vessels did not exist in the Atlantic. In the Mediterranean, galleys had a commercial as well as a military use. For high-value cargoes such as spices and pilgrims calling for speed rather than space they were very profitable. But Atlantic ships depended on bulky cargoes of relatively low value: wool and cloth, salt, fish and wine. In the Atlantic, galleys were dead weight in the state's accounts. Since they were very expensive to build and maintain and required expert handling by large specialist crews the possession of a galley fleet called for prodigious resources. How prodigious can be seen from a memorandum prepared for the King of France in about 1336. This indicated that it cost 800 *l.t.* to build a sixty-oar galley in Rouen which could be expected to last for only three years, an annual cost of 266 *l.t.* per year when depreciated on a straight-line basis. The crewing costs for a single eight-month season were more than ten times this amount: wages of 2,280 *l.t.* plus 180 *l.t.* to bring the men from Provence. When mobilization expenses, oars, cables, sails, armour and consumable stores were added in, the cost was at least 3,555 *l.t.* (about £760) per galley per year not including the considerable cost of maintaining the arsenal at Rouen.[44] Only the French Crown could afford to spend money on this scale, and then only in fat years. English opinion had never tolerated large expenditure on war materials in peacetime, and navies cannot be conjured suddenly into existence at the outbreak of war.

In spite of everything which England's geographical position should have suggested, the onset of war generally found her government unprepared to fight at sea. For a long time this had not mattered very much. In the twelfth century the Angevin kings and their continental allies had controlled the whole of the Atlantic coast of France from the Channel to the Pyrenees. King John, the monarch who was principally responsible for the loss of his dynasty's continental empire, was the first English King since the Norman Conquest to feel the need of a large Royal Navy. At one point he had fifty-two galleys under his control. His son, Henry III, maintained a fleet of galleys in the 1240s at a time when he was nursing large ambitions of continental conquest. But these were short-lived fleets acquired for special purposes. When the immediate need of them had passed they were allowed to rot. In the 1290s, when Philip the Fair created an Atlantic fleet, England faced its first serious challenge at sea since the days of Eustace the Monk, eighty years earlier. There was no naval tradition for the state to fall back on.[45]

Edward I had galleys built in England at great speed to meet the crisis, but galley-construction was a specialized business and English shipwrights were no match for the Italians employed by Philip. Moreover, experienced galley crews were not available in England. These were some of the reasons why Edward I's galleys achieved almost nothing in the 1290s, and specialized warships disappeared from fleets in the early fourteenth century. But a more important reason was the penury of Edward I in his last years and the improvidence of his successors. Edward II, when he needed galleys in 1317, had to hire them from the Genoese or call on a small number of commercial galleys which were available in Bayonne. The Bayonnais were sparing with their assistance. They needed the vessels for trade and for their own defence.[46]

Edward III was in no better position than his father. The permanent fleet of the Crown consisted at this stage almost entirely of round-hulled sailing ships similar to those of his subjects. Even this fleet had been severely run down in the three decades before the beginning of the Hundred Years War. For the Bannockburn campaign of 1314, Edward II had deployed twenty-seven royal ships and a barge. For the next important Scotch campaign, in 1322, there were only eleven. At the end of Edward II's reign, his ships had lain unmaintained and their keepers unpaid for several years. It was one policy of his father's which Edward III did not reverse when he took control of his government. Several vessels were granted away or sold. Others were hired out for long terms to merchants, some of whom allowed them to rot.[47] At the beginning of 1336 Edward III owned three ships: a venerable old ship called the *Christopher* which was famous for its great height; and two cogs, the very large *Cog Edward*, which the King had bought from some merchants for the great sum of £450 in 1335, and a smaller vessel called the *Rodecogge*. These ships were fitted out for fighting. There was also a handful of small ships and barges which were used in carrying troops and supplies. The King's ships usually had permanent masters, but there were no permanent crews. Seamen were pressed for service when they were required. For the many operations which required more seapower than this, Edward depended on the resources of his subjects.[48]

The traditional providers of ships for wartime service were the Cinque Ports, an ancient federation of southern ports, then seven in number. In return for immunities from taxation and military service and a variety of other privileges, these ports were required to provide up to fifty-seven ships when required, for a period of fifteen days at their own charge. At some time in the fourteenth century this was increased to eighty ships for forty days. But the Cinque Ports had difficulty in providing even the original number. The siltation of their harbours had impoverished them.

They were no longer the great maritime power which they had once been. Romney could support only one ship in 1341, and Hythe none at all. The others could produce some ships but not enough to make up their contribution to the service of the federation, and most of these were fishing vessels. Since the last decade of the thirteenth century the Crown had increasingly relied on other maritime towns. By long tradition all of them were liable to have their ships and seamen pressed into the King's service in return for compensation which was conventionally fixed at 3s.4d. per ton per quarter. One, Great Yarmouth, had by 1337 become the greatest naval port of England, far outstripping the Cinque Ports. Great Yarmouth contributed fifty-nine ships to Edward I's Flemish expedition of 1297, only fourteen less than the Cinque Ports: their combined tonnage must have been much greater. For the first great maritime expedition of Edward III's reign, in 1338, the contribution of the Cinque Ports had fallen to thirty-six, half of what they had furnished in 1297. Great Yarmouth by comparison produced sixty-four ships. Many of these were very large vessels, of between 100 and 300 tons carrying capacity, and one or two were monsters comparable to the largest ocean-going carracks of Castile.[49]

The advantage of this system, and the only thing that commended it to the Crown, was that it cost almost nothing in peacetime. It had almost everything else against it. The process of requisitioning ships was so time-consuming and unpredictable that it was rarely possible for England to rise swiftly to any unexpected challenge at sea. The duty of transforming the assorted shipping of the English ports into a fleet of war was shared between two admirals. They were generally professional soldiers or important noblemen holding offices for the duration of a campaign. The Admiral of the north was responsible for all ports north of the Thames estuary, including the major shipping towns of Yarmouth and Lynn. He had not only to provide ships for service against France in the Channel and the North Sea, but also to maintain a continuous ferry service for transporting troops and victuals to the surviving English garrisons in eastern Scotland. The Admiral of the west was responsible for the Kent coast and the whole of southern and western England, an unmanageably large territory which sometimes had to be divided at the Solent and shared with a third admiral. The Cinque Ports organized their own affairs under the nominal supervision of the Warden (always a great nobleman). London, after being disputed for years between the admirals, was eventually placed under the immediate control of the King's household staff. The requisitioning of merchantmen was carried out by royal clerks. They were overworked officials assigned from the Chancery or the Exchequer, who were employed year after year in this work and whose skills improved with experience. No amount of skill, however, could have made the system operate entirely smoothly. Plans for requisitioning ships had to be laid early in the year, in January or February if a fleet was required in the summer. Requisitioning officers had to travel from harbour to harbour when the weather was cold and wet and the going for their horses unspeakable. In each place, it was necessary to find out the names and number of ships, to survey them, to classify them according to their capacity, to arrange for the adaptation of the larger ones for fighting and to pay advances for the expenses of their masters. All this took time. So did the loading of victuals on the ships, the impressment of extra crew members, the discharge of previous cargoes (without docks or cranes), the manufacture of ramps to allow access for horses and hurdles to hold them safely on deck, and the ushering of the ships to their ports of assembly. The ships would be out of harbour when the requisitioning officers arrived, either because the news had got around or in the ordinary course of trading. Ships which had been duly requisitioned, and whose masters had received advances for their expenses, frequently made off before the campaign or on the way to the assembly point. The less crafty ships' masters simply resisted the requisitioning officers by force. It is surprising how often the English government laid plans which depended entirely on perfect timekeeping. It rarely took less than six weeks to requisition a fleet even in optimum conditions, and another two to bring it together at the port of assembly. Six months was quite normal.

The dependence of the English government on requisitioned merchant shipping had other disadvantages inherent in the design of the ships themselves. They were short, tubby vessels, slow and unmanoeuvrable. Because of the shape of their hulls and their use of square sails few of them could tack closer than 80 degrees to the wind. They were therefore peculiarly dependent on the right conditions of wind and sea and could be immobilized for long periods. They had limited deck space and deep holds, ideal for bulk cargoes but less useful for carrying men and horses. They required large crews, doubled for war service, who took up most of the available space: one man for every two and a half tons carrying capacity was the rule of thumb.[50] As fighting ships, their main advantage was their height, an important consideration when the main weapons of marine warfare were bows and arrows, grappling irons and boarding parties. The larger English merchantmen were specially fitted out in time of war to increase this advantage: timber castles were constructed fore and aft and sometimes top-castles on the main masts. Ships large enough for this purpose were rare and greatly prized. One of the perennial naval problems of the English government was the relatively small size of English merchant ships. They were classified according to their carrying capacity (or 'burden') measured in 'tuns', the standard wine barrel of the Gascon trade weighing slightly less than one ton avoirdupois when full. Vessels suitable for fitting out as warships had to be of at least 60 tons burden and preferably more. Most English merchantmen were smaller. They seem to have had a carrying capacity of between 30 and 60 tons. It was only in the upper part of this range that a ship could carry horses or significant numbers of soldiers. The average number of fully equipped soldiers per ship which could be carried overseas was fairly constant over the years. It was about twelve. Only when the horses were left behind were any substantial improvements on this average achieved. An army of 6,000 was small by fourteenth-century standards, but it would have required no less than 500 ships to carry it overseas on one passage.

On 5 January 1337 representatives of the ports of the western and northern Admiralties assembled in London to hear from four of the King's most senior councillors about Edward's ambitious requirements for shipping in the coming year. What he wanted was nothing less than the services of his subjects and their ships for a period of three months without compensation. The ministers waxed eloquent upon the imminent threat to the land represented by the continued existence of a powerful Franco-Scotch fleet on the other side of the Channel. Their eloquence failed. The proposals were greeted with uproar and rejected out of hand. It was some measure of Edward's growing confidence in himself, as well as his fear of imminent disaster in Gascony, that he proceeded at once to extremes. On the following day, 10 January 1337, he obtained the consent of a Council of magnates to the issue of writs requiring free service from the ports with or without the consent of the seamen. All ships of the two Admiralties were to assemble at Portsmouth on 15 March 1337 carrying double crews and stores for three months at own expense. The appointment of Robert Ufford and William Montagu, two of Edward's closest confidants, as admirals followed within a few days.[51] In the small harbours of the east coast of England a campaign of construction was put in hand, belated recognition of the damage done to Edward's military strength by a decade of neglect of his ships. Most of the ships ordered were stout oared barges, transports for troops and horses. A galley was under construction at Lynn of sixty oars 'or more'. At Hull, William Pole was building another. The government brooked no opposition. The Augustinian Prior of Heelaugh, who had refused to supply timber to the shipwrights, was made to watch as six of his largest oaks were felled.[52]

Diligence turned to panic when the English government learned of demand for Robert of Artois' extradition made of the Seneschal of Gascony. During February 1337 the fleet of the northern Admiralty was ordered to assemble a month before the day previously appointed, and to proceed at once to Orwell to await orders. The Admiral's officers travelled up the coast from port to port, ordering out whatever ships they found. In the western Admiralty twenty ships which were already at Southampton were ordered to arm and leave immediately for Bordeaux.[53]

Amid these alarums, Scotland was almost forgotten. At the beginning of February 1337, while Edward struggled to assemble a fleet for the defence of Gascony, Murray took Kinclaven Castle, north of Perth. Then, leaving a covering force to contain the garrison of Perth, he joined up with William Douglas's lowland irregulars and invaded Fife. The English garrisons there had no hope of reinforcements. They were almost certainly low on supplies. The English government knew what was happening, but could do nothing. Edward told Percy and Nevill, his commanders in the north, that threats even graver than Andrew Murray's army were detaining him in the south and ordered them to do the best they could. There is no evidence that they did anything at all. Falkland tower and Leuchars fell to the Scots almost at once. The walls of St Andrews were battered for three weeks by a great siege engine called 'Buster'. On 28 February 1337 it surrendered. In March, Murray attacked Bothwell Castle, which the English had fortified so recently and at such expense. Its garrison surrendered on terms while they were still strong enough to exact any. At all of these strongholds the fortifications were razed to the ground as soon as the Scots had taken possession. The tower of Bothwell was 'scattered from the foundations'. Before the traditional campaigning season had even begun, the Scots had resumed control of almost all Scotland north of the Forth, and undone more than a year of Edward III's work. At the end of March the Scots had marched west across the lowlands and were wasting the lands of Edward Balliol and his supporters in Galloway. As the Scotch chronicler sang:

> 'It wes to Scotland a gud chance
> I hat thai made thaim to werrey in France'[54]

The English Parliament met on 3 March 1337 while Murray's army was approaching Bothwell. Although it had originally been summoned to York, it met in the event at Westminster, a change itself symbolic of Edward's new priorities. It was desirable, Edward explained, to sit closer to the perils which were threatening the realm. Unfortunately there is no record of its proceedings, but it is plain that the coming war against France was the main item of business. The government had to report reverses in Scotland, a menacing assembly of Scotch and French ships in the Channel and an overt threat to Gascony. To deal with the crisis, Edward proposed to recruit two armies, one of which would proceed at once to Gascony, the other at a 'suitable time' to Scotland. While these warlike preparations were in progress, a great embassy was to be sent to the continent. They were also to be provided with a draft treaty, in effect an ultimatum, to be submitted to the King of France. The Lords endorsed these plans in their entirety, and indeed contributed to the drafting of the terms to be presented to Philip VI. A subsidy was voted. It was only a beginning.[55]

Even so, it was a reversal of the traditional suspicions of their class, suspicions of foreign adventures, of the King's Gascon interests and of large expenditure for any purpose. The King himself was conscious of the change and largely responsible for it. The memoranda on foreign policy prepared for him at this time were sprinkled with warnings of the public opposition which had frustrated the continental enterprises of his forbears and with advice on how to prevent history from repeating itself. When Edward had wrested the government from his mother and Mortimer in 1330 he had proclaimed not only that he would govern according to 'justice and reason', a conventional enough sentiment, but that he would do so 'according to the advice of the nobility and in no other way'.[56] He had in fact consulted them in Parliament and in successive Great Councils at every significant stage of the developing crisis with France and had almost always accepted their advice.

Edward worked hard to ensure that he got the advice that he wanted. There was more than one echo in the 1330s of the tradition of war propaganda inaugurated by his grandfather. Englishmen were persuadable. They lived in a relatively small, cohesive country and were susceptible to propaganda and shared emotions which would quickly have faded in the disparate vastness of France. Philip VI had come to seem to many Englishmen the main barrier to the successful occupation of Scotland, and Scotland was a real threat, profoundly hated. The limitations of French power in the 1330s were much less obvious to contemporary Englishmen than they are now. The gravity of England's situation was one point on which the propagandists of Philip VI and those of Edward III could agree. Rumours spread freely in a society with no source of news that even purported to be authoritative. In 1337 it was being said that Englishmen were being massacred in France, that fifth columnists were aiding the Scots in the north of England and that forces of unspeakable strength were gathering for the annihilation of England. In this atmosphere accounts of the burning of fishing villages no doubt grew in the telling, and verisimilitude was given to them by the precautions which sent relays of villagers to the cliff tops to watch over unlit bonfires.

There was not only fear and anger but, among many of the nobility, actual relish at the prospect of fighting. War was heroic and ennobling. From the outset of his reign Edward III had encouraged the jousts and tournaments, ritual celebrations of battle which provided heavy cavalry with the closest substitute for war. They were also public ceremonies, elaborately stage-managed in accordance with conventions of growing formality, watched by large audiences. At the tournament in Cheapside in September 1331, when the King fought with Henry of Lancaster, William Montagu and some dozens more against all comers, the press was so great that the Queen's grandstand collapsed.[57]

Tournaments occupied uneasy ground between reality and pretence, dangerous without being earnest and popular with English noblemen long before war was. By 1337, however, there had been five years' experience of war in Scotland, a war of unglamorous sieges and scorched earth, some major skirmishes and two pitched battles. The Scotch wars of the 1330s completed the military revolution in England which had begun in the time of Edward I half a century before. Edward III's campaigns had been fought by highly mobile armies, composed of a practised elite of heavy cavalry, and of mounted archers and hobelars, moving rapidly through the country on horseback, but fighting on foot. In the army of 1335, the largest which Edward III ever sent into Scotland, more than half the archers were mounted. In the smaller raiding forces, like the one which attacked Aberdeen with such powerful effect in 1336, all the infantry were mounted archers or hobelars. The *chevauchée*, or large-scale mounted raid, which was to be the hallmark of English strategy in France in the 1340s and 1350s, had its origins in Edward's early campaigns in Scotland, just as the classic elements of the battle plan of Crécy could be seen in operation at Dupplin Moor and Halidon Hill.[58]

What was as remarkable as the composition and tactics of Edward's armies in Scotland was the means by which they had been recruited. The feudal summons had been the main method of recruiting cavalry throughout the reigns of Edward's father and grandfather, in spite of the determined attempt of both of them to impose a more rational system, better adapted to a war of prolonged, frequent and aggressive campaigns. No feudal summons was issued by Edward III after 1327. No one told him, as they had told Edward I and Edward II, that their military obligations were limited to the small numbers and short periods prescribed by custom. The whole army was paid wages, from the principal earls downwards. The royal household and the personal retinues of some three dozen noblemen (which they made available by contract to the King) furnished not only the entire cavalry but a good proportion of the mounted archers as well, about half in the army of 1335, rather more in the smaller and more specialized field forces of the following years. This was one reason for the noticeable improvement in the fighting quality of infantry as well as cavalry. These men had some of the strengths of standing armies. They fought together with their friends and neighbours, sometimes year after year in the same retinues. The hobelars and mounted archers of Cheshire, for example, followed Sir John Ward with the King's household troops in three successive campaigns in Scotland and later in Flanders and Brittany as well.[59] The retainers of the nobility were no doubt less diligent, but it is clear that they contributed a great deal to the progressive militarization of English provincial life during the 1330s. War became another field for the elaborate web of interest and obligation which bound their world together.

In spite of the absence of any significant enemy field army, Scotland had had the reputation of a chivalrous battleground and had drawn volunteers from much of northern Europe. Hainaulters from the court of Queen Philippa's father joined most of Edward's armies there, including Walter Mauny, who stayed to become an adoptive Englishman, one of the great captains of the early years of the French war. Germans and Frenchmen arrived in small groups. The Count of Namur crossed the sea in 1335 with more than a hundred men to fight in Scotland. So did a persistent trickle of obscurer Dutchmen and Brabanters.[60] These men cannot have been drawn by booty or high pay, unless they were much deceived. The magnet was Edward's personal reputation and the reputation of his court and army. Edward's own participation in the campaigns, courageous at times to the point of recklessness, had forged bonds of comradeship with his knights and field commanders which explains more perfectly than careful political calculation could do why they supported his aggressive designs against France in 1337. The King, thought Jean le Bel, had 'thrown the English into his campaigns and taught them to fight'. This worldly clergyman from Liège, who had accompanied the disorganized English expedition to Scotland in 1327, could remember the armour of mail and leather in which its leaders had fought. When he next saw the English army, in the Low Countries in 1339, its leading members were resplendent in plate armour.

Good armour was a revealing symbol, an expensive investment, voluntarily made. Henry of Lancaster cannot have been the only one among them who boasted of his equipment and stuck his feet out so that onlookers could admire his stirrups.[61]

How much cupidity contributed to the bellicose mood of 1337 is difficult to say. War could be profitable, particularly for the aggressor. Every battle was followed by the looting of horses, armour and tents from the defeated army, the fall of every town by the wholesale plundering of merchandise, jewellery and money. Ransoms, whose collection and distribution were governed by an increasingly elaborate code, became a major business whose most successful practitioners, such as Walter Mauny, made great fortunes. But, however attractive these prospects were, it is unlikely that at this early stage they were a significant inducement except for professional soldiers of fortune like Mauny. They had to be balanced against the risks, the possibility of defeat and ruin. It was not even clear in 1337 that England would be the aggressor. The invasion of France by the north was a paper project. The strategy of long-distance raids into the French provinces, which proved to be so remunerative in the 1340s and 1350s, was still years away. It was to take experience to whet the appetites of English leaders, and if they went to war for gain in 1337 it was the largesse of the Crown that was expected to supply it.

Characteristically, Edward chose the parliament of March 1337 as the occasion for marking in public the services of friends and servants. He created six new earls. That able and ambitious courtier William Montagu had already earned great rewards by planning the destruction of Mortimer, by his ready advice in a succession of diplomatic crises and by fighting in Scotland where his gallantry had lost him an eye. He now became Earl of Salisbury and was appointed to command the proposed expedition to Gascony. Two other courtiers, William Clinton and Robert Ufford, both of whom had participated with Montagu in the arrest of Mortimer, received earldoms. Henry of Lancaster, who had commanded the Scotch expeditionary force of the previous year, became Earl of Derby. Two earldoms were created for scions of families closely allied with the King's. One of these, William Bohun, although only about twenty-five years old, was a veteran of the *coup d'état* of 1330 and of several Scotch campaigns. He became Earl of Northampton, and would become Constable of England in the following year. Edward's six-year-old heir, the future Black Prince, became Duke of Cornwall, the first occasion on which this peculiarly French title had been conferred in England. Among the lesser men, twenty were knighted by the King in person. The new peers and some of the knights received generous money grants to enable them to maintain their new station. There were a few men, including that hard-bitten soldier Thomas Gray, who thought that Edward would have done better to spend his money on the recruitment and equipment of his army. But his was a minority view, and wrong even as a judgement of Edward's interests. The King was doing what public opinion expected of a king, dispensing largesse to those who were its traditional recipients: his own family, the old aristocracy, and others who had earned their status by performing the services proper to a nobleman. The reversal of his grand-father's guarded attitude to the nobility was quite deliberate. 'We con-sider,' Edward explained in the charter creating the new earls of Huntingdon and Gloucester, 'that it is the chief mark of royalty that by a proper distribution of rank, honour and office it buttresses itself by wise counsel and powerful men. Yet this realm has long suffered a serious decline in names, honours and titles of nobility'. The motive was charac-teristic of him. So was the fact that he announced it.[62]

Parliament closed on 16 March 1337 with the splendid ceremonies at court which properly followed so great a distribution of largesse. Philip VI cut the knot with lesser grandeur. The French King was at his hunting lodge at Saint-Christophe-de-Halate in the second half of March and passed the next month in the forests of the northern Ile de France. At the beginning of May, he came to Paris, where he presided over a meeting of his Great Council enlarged by the attendance of the principal members of the nobility. The ground had been well prepared. It was agreed that the duchy of Aquitaine should be taken into the King's hands on the ground that Edward III in breach of his obligations as a vassal had sheltered the King's 'mortal enemy' Robert of Artois, as well as for 'certain other reasons' on which it was decided not to enlarge. At the end of April, Philip was invited to receive ambassadors bearing the English King's final pro-posals. He refused. The *arrière-ban* was proclaimed throughout the king-dom beginning on 30 April 1337.[63]

CHAPTER VII

Grand Strategy
1337–1338

The triangle of north-west Europe which now comprises Belgium, the Netherlands, Luxembourg and the German Rhineland, consisted in the early fourteenth century of many small principalities divided by economic rivalry and dynastic jealousies, and overshadowed by the enormous presence of Capetian France on their southern flank.

By far the most important of these principalities was the county of Flanders. Flanders was rich, populous and unstable. It was also, alone among the territories of the Low Countries, a province of France. Although it had once enjoyed the same autonomy under its own dynasty as the neighbouring principalities of the German Empire, it had been in the process of absorption into the mainstream of French politics for more than half a century. The battle of Courtrai had proved to be a flash in the pan. By the treaties of Athis-sur-Orge (1305) and Paris (1320) the French Crown had appropriated the three districts ('castleries') of Lille, Douai and Orchies, which included substantially all of Walloon-speaking Flanders, leaving a French dynasty to govern the truncated Flemish-speaking territory which remained. Moreover, although the counts still ruled the richest parts of Flanders, the county was burdened by crushing financial indemnities which the treaties had promised to the French King, and whose payment, stretched over many years, ensured that old wounds did not heal.

Among the Flemings, these events left a legacy of resentment not only against France but against each other. Although the revolutions of the late thirteenth and early fourteenth centuries had loosened the grip of the great merchants over the city governments of the county, the economic foundations of their power survived. Their mansions and towers still rose up from the midst of the squalor and teeming numbers of the cloth-workers. The journeymen were still liable to be buffeted by changes of economic fortune. The economic troubles of the early fourteenth century brought distress which was particularly intense in Flanders, where the balance of population and resources was always delicate. In few other parts of

Europe could the *haut bourgeois* have petitioned the King, as those of Ypres did, to preserve the walls of their city lest the artisans of the suburbs should murder them in their beds at night and loot them of their possessions.[1] Beyond the suburbs, the peasantry and smallholders of the flat country conserved all the rancours against the rich, the rural nobility and the French which had led them to support with so much enthusiasm the revolution of 1302. They had achieved even less for their pains than the townsmen had. The humiliating peace of 1305 was followed by a return of the local nobility who had fled at the revolution, and by a determined assault on the liberties which the peasant communities had arrogated to themselves during their brief and joyful anarchy. In hindsight, it is possible to see that the internal troubles of Flanders foreshadowed similar upheavals which less advanced economies would experience later. At the time, they were peculiar to Flanders, and neighbouring governments including England saw in them an opportunity rather than a warning.

The task of bringing order to this wretched province would have been beyond a much abler ruler than Louis of Nevers, who succeeded his grandfather as Count of Flanders in 1322 at the age of eighteen. He was an unimpressive man, without experience or judgement, who by the deliberate decision of Philip the Fair had been separated from his family at an early age and brought up at the French court. Consequently, he had no knowledge of his principality at his accession and no friends there in an age when friendship was the essential instrument of government. His advisers were Frenchmen, including, as his subjects noted with displeasure, the son of that same Pierre Flote who had been the architect of Philip the Fair's Flemish policy. His stock, already low, was further abased by the enthusiasm which his ministers brought to the collection of the indemnities which the French government had exacted at the peace table. He was, said Froissart, a 'good and faithful Frenchman'. He had occasion, before his reign proceeded much further, to be an even better Frenchman, for within a few months of his arrival in the county all the animosities of the Flemings for their rulers and each other exploded in a civil war of unparalleled savagery. It began, as the revolution of 1302 had begun, with a rebellion of the cloth-workers of Bruges. This was shortly followed by peasant risings throughout western Flanders. From there it spread to Ypres and to much of the rest of the county. Only in Ghent did the patriciate manage to keep control. In rural areas the nobility and the Count's officials were murdered wherever they could be found. By 1328, Louis was an exile in Paris and his government in Flanders had all but disappeared. The job of defeating these 'unreasoning brutes' (Philip VI's phrase) fell to the new King of France, who carried it out with ruthless dispatch in the summer of that year. The Brugeois were defeated at the battle of Cassel on 23 August 1328. The walls of the rebel towns were thrown down. A reign of terror was inaugurated which was still in progress three years later. Louis of Nevers returned to govern his own. But he owed his county to Philip VI and did not forget it. Neither did his subjects.[2]

East of Flanders lay the uncertain boundary of the German Empire, meandering either side of the River Scheldt and leaving untidy enclaves of one county within the territory of another, the seeds of future territorial disputes. With the exception of Brabant, a large duchy with an important cloth industry of its own, the German Low Countries consisted of small agrarian territories much less heavily populated than Flanders and vulnerable to interference from outside. There were few princes of the region who were not in some degree dependent on France. They needed French support against their enemies, or feared French hostility when French power was so close at hand. Many of them held isolated limbs or enclaves of their territory in fee from the French King or owned by marriage, inheritance or purchase estates in the heart of France. Or they were prince–bishops, who owed their election to their sees to the patronage of the kings of France, always closer to the ear of the Pope than a German emperor could hope to be. Or, without any of these overt ties of dependence, they were simply men who felt the attraction of French court culture, married themselves or their kinsmen to French princesses, and maintained mansions in Paris, like that extreme francophile John, Count of Luxembourg, who was also King of Bohemia, the son of one German Emperor and the father of another but by adoption a life-long French courtier who faithfully served Philip VI as a soldier and diplomat until he died fighting for him at Crécy.

All of these princes were vassals of the German Emperor. But the Germany to which they belonged scarcely existed as a political unit. It covered tracts of western and central Europe and Italy too vast and diverse to command loyalty even as an abstract notion. French was spoken in most of Hainault, some of southern Brabant, about half of Luxembourg and in the land of the counts of Namur and the prince–bishops of Liège and Cambrai. Further north and west, it was the adopted language of the higher nobility and of those patricians of the towns who had pretensions to address them on equal terms, Germans who like the sixteenth-century Emperor Charles V spoke German only to their horses. The mass of the population spoke one or other of the local dialects of low German which the French indiscriminately referred to as 'Thiois'. There was no more political than there was linguistic cohesion. Weakened by two centuries of internal dissension and constitutional dispute with the papacy, the German Empire was in an advanced state of political decay. The Low Countries were the extreme western limb of the Empire. They were marginal to the political balance of Germany and their rulers were for all practical purposes sovereign.

If anyone was capable of restoring the Empire it was certainly not Louis of Bavaria, who had occupied the Imperial throne since 1314. For, although he was a man of great ability, he revived and aggravated long-standing differences with the papacy, differences ostensibly about abstractions of canonical theory but which went to the root of the German constitution. The papal theory, dating back at least to the reign of Innocent III in the early thirteenth century, was that the approval of the Pope was required before an elected king of Germany could exercise his sovereign powers. The theory had only recently been redefined in two uncompromising bulls of Pope Clement V. But Louis of Bavaria disregarded it. He performed sovereign acts in Germany and in northern Italy as if election alone was enough. Moreover, as the bitterness of the dispute intensified, he sheltered and patronized some of the most venomous and effective anti-papal pamphleteers who ever wrote, including Marsiglio of Padua. In 1327 and 1328 Louis brought his feud with the Pope to its culminating point by invading Italy, having himself crowned without papal authority in Milan and Rome, and erecting an anti-pope in place of John XXII. John for his part excommunicated Louis and purported to declare the German throne vacant. Such was the condition of the sovereign power beyond France's northern and eastern frontiers when Edward III of England began to meddle there.

At about the time when Edward III was looking for friends among France's neighbours, a number of incidents revealed how vulnerable the princes of the Low Countries were in their ambiguous situation between France and Germany, and how weak a skin the Franco–German border was without any reserve of national power to defend it on the German side. The absorption (which was what it amounted to) of the francophone territories east of the Rhône and Saône rivers into the political orbit of France had been an accomplished fact for more than a century. More recently, in the time of Philip the Fair and his sons, French 'protectorates' had gradually reduced some important Imperial territories on France's north-eastern frontier, such as the Argonne and the bishopric of Verdun, to the same status. Were the Low Countries to be next? There were two concerted attacks on Brabant in the 1330s, one of which was certainly and the other probably engineered by France. Pope Benedict XII, exceptionally well informed and always sensitive to the changing balance of western European sentiment, warned the French King about this as early as May 1336. In April 1337, as the main protagonists were exchanging declarations of war, Benedict told Philip VI plainly that the mood in Germany was one of 'irritation approaching desperation' and that an overt alliance between the Empire and England was likely to follow.[3]

The English King's preferred course would have been an alliance with Flanders. The county, with its long coastline on the North Sea and along the great north European estuaries, and its open border with France, was ideally situated for his purposes. Moreover, as one of his advisers put it, Flanders was to France what Scotland was to England.[4] Unfortunately, relations with Flanders in the winter of 1336–7 were bad. The Scots were being supplied from Flemish ports and Flemish ships were prominent in French attacks on the coast of England. Edward's government demanded redress for these and other incidents, but the raiders had letters of marque from the King of France, and the Count of Flanders was unable to help even had he wished to. Probably, however, he did not wish to. Louis was a loyal servant of his sovereign. Edward proposed a treaty of alliance, which the Count firmly rejected. In October 1336, there was a complete severance of relations between England and Flanders as the result of Philip VI's sanctions against Englishmen and their trade, which Louis dutifully enforced in his own county.[5]

In August 1336 Edward III forbade all exports of wool and leather from the kingdom. This drastic order may not originally have been intended to put pressure on the Flemings. However, what began as financial housekeeping became a political weapon of unforeseen power in the course of the autumn. The Flemish cloth-making industry, and with it the employment of most of the population of the county, depended on English wool. There was virtually no other raw material. The export ban was therefore kept in place, and indeed was extended for a time to embrace wheat and ale and a variety of other items. The economic damage done to England was grave enough, but in Flanders the effect was catastrophic. For a while the Flemings were cushioned by their stocks, but by the end of 1336 the distress was evident. A poor harvest in the previous year added its own contribution. Textile workers were passing through the county begging for bread in roadside villages sometimes as far afield as Tournai and northern France. In the new year, public order began to break down in Ghent and Bruges.[6]

As distress weakened Louis of Nevers' grip on his principality, there was a new crisis in the affairs of France and the German territories further east. The occasion was series of complicated and obscure property transactions in the Cambrésis of a kind which half a century of experience in Aquitaine had made very familiar to the English government. The Cambrésis was a region of great strategic importance lying between the upper valleys of the Sambre and the Scheldt, main highways for any army passing between France and Hainault or Brabant. For several years French noblemen had been buying fiefs in this sensitive region and, although it cannot be proved, the probability is that they had been doing so with the connivance of their government. The Cambrésis was an Imperial territory. Its ruler, the Bishop of Cambrai, was a prince of the Empire. But he was also a suffragan of the Archbishop of Reims and, more often than not, a Frenchmen beholden to the French government for his appointment. The incumbent was a Burgundian, Guillaume d'Auxonne, a protégé of Philip VI's Queen, and the friend and Chancellor of Louis of Nevers, Count of Flanders. A man less likely to defend the interests of the Empire against France can scarely be imagined.

In February 1337, after a short negotiation conducted in the utmost secrecy, Philip bought for his son five castles in the eastern Cambrésis, including Cambrai itself and two places on the vital Scheldt artery. It was an astonishing coup, not unlike the one by which Philip had recently acquired the castles of Blanquefort and Veyrines on the outskirts of Bordeaux. The Emperor's reaction was like Edward III's. Rumours of Philip's intentions had begun to circulate shortly before the transaction was completed, and Louis had protested strongly. He had ordered the Bishop of Cambrai to prevent it on pain of Imperial displeasure. But the Bishop was indifferent to Imperial displeasure. Far from preventing it, in due course he formally conferred the castles in fee on Philip's heir. The French King seems to have been taken aback by the uproar which followed, as well he might be given the passive reception of previous usurpations in Germany. He went to the lengths of preparing a circular, which was sent to the princes and cities of the Rhineland, explaining that there was no intention to trespass on the rights of the Empire. The princes and towns who received it were not persuaded. In the early months of 1337 the idea gained ground that what was needed was a champion to reassert the territorial integrity of the Empire, on which the autonomy of the princes in the last resort depended. It was inconceivable that Louis of Bavaria himself should be that champion. In any event a strong Imperial presence in the Low Countries would probably have been unwelcome to the rulers of the region. So, by a peculiar combination of circumstances, it fell to Edward III to undertake the business on the Emperor's behalf.[7]

It is not clear who sowed in Edward's mind the idea of a great coalition across the northern marches of France on the model of his grandfather's. But the weight of the evidence points to the Count of Hainault, William of Avesnes. William had ruled his county for more than thirty years in 1337, and had acquired a personal stature far greater than Hainault's modest size and resources alone could have warranted. On the face of it, he was a surprising candidate to lead an anti-French coalition. Alliance with France had been the cornerstone of his policy for many years. He had supported the French kings in their struggles against Flanders before 1322 and had brought his contingent to fight at Cassel in 1328. A small part of his territory, the county of Ostrevant on the west bank of the Scheldt, was held by him as a fief of the French Crown. He was married to a sister of Philip VI and in the interregnum of 1328 had vigorously canvassed Philip's claims to the throne. Here was a man deeply enmeshed in the fabric of French politics, and yet a foreign prince with concerns much wider than those of a mere client of France. His court was a famous centre of chivalrous display. He had the Emperor Louis of Bavaria as his son-in-law as well as Edward III, and maintained close relations with both of them, not only at times when this was consistent with French foreign policy. His problem was in one respect that of every prince of the German Low Countries. His position depended on a territorial base which was very vulnerable: Hainault itself, a moderately prosperous agrarian county with a small cloth industry in and around Valenciennes, and the marshy wastes of Holland and Zeeland in the far north.

William was an old man, suffering from gout and stone and racked with pain, still an adroit diplomat but without the infinite patience which might once have enabled him to deal with the hardening attitudes of Philip VI's ministers. French officials were needling at Ostrevant in spite of the King's protestations that he had told them not to. Their thoughts went even further than their deeds. Within the French Chancery much ingenious learning was deployed in proving that the jurisdiction of the King of France included not only Ostrevant but also the Count's capital of Valenciennes on the other side of the Scheldt. Several joint commissions which had been charged with fixing the boundary between the French and German parts of William's territory failed, perhaps deliberately, to complete their work. Uncertainty aided the stronger power. The Count of Hainault's unease turned to outrage when it was learned that Philip VI proposed to buy the five castles of the Cambrésis. The Cambrésis was a region in which he had been carefully building up his own influence for twenty years. Two of the castles in question, Crèvecœur and Arleux, were of particular interest to him. They had once belonged to his family and he had been on the point of acquiring them for his own son when Philip VI snatched them from under his nose.[8]

The princes of the Low Countries belonged to an extended circle of friends and relations on the north and east border of France, men whose ancestors had been allies and clients of King John and Edward I in their time. The English kings had never entirely ceased to cultivate them. The Count of Hainault was Edward III's father-in-law. The Count's brother John, a famous paladin, had fought in Scotland and received a pension of 1,000 marks a year from the English treasury. The Margrave of Juliers, another pensioner and future Earl of Cambridge, had fought in two Scotch campaigns. The Count of Namur had led his contingent into Scotland in 1335. The Count of Guelders was married to Edward's sister. Yet, in spite of the bonds of tradition, trade and marriage, English civil servants of the early fourteenth century knew little about the German Low Countries and less about the main German lands east of them. The gap was filled in some measure by using strangers to the King's service: Englishmen familiar with the Low Countries, such as the York merchant John de Woume, who may have been a Fleming by birth; or the various advisers and clerks whom Edward III or his agents hired on the continent between 1337 and 1340. Edward's main agent on the continent, the shadowy John Thrandeston, may have been a Norfolk man by birth but by adoption he was a German from Cologne.[9]

Thrandeston was sent on his first mission to the counts of Hainault, Juliers and Guelders in the middle of September 1336. He went on the initiative of the King's Council, Edward himself being on campaign in Scotland and out of touch with events. It is therefore unlikely that he took with him any very radical proposals. At the end of October 1336 he passed a fortnight at William of Hainault's court at Valenciennes. This, almost certainly, was when the plans of the next three years were first mooted. During the first three months of the new year there were no less than three separate English embassies at work on Imperial territory. Thrandeston himself visited the Flemish towns and the princely courts of the Low Countries, some of them several times. Another embassy, consisting of one of Edward's household knights and a senior Exchequer clerk, covered a wider territory including the Low Countries and the Rhineland, retaining influential ministers and soldiers. A third agent, a discreet Augustinian friar called Geoffrey Maldon, worked on the princely courts of Châlons, Bourg-en-Bresse and Savoy, Imperial territories on France's eastern march whom it was hoped to recruit for Edward's cause in spite of the traditional attachment of these francophone regions to the French Crown. The expenditure on fees and bribes approached £3,000, a prodigious sum. These men travelled modestly, as the nature of their business dictated. Their instructions were generally given by word of mouth and their work was obscurely referred to in the English records as 'certain secret business of the King'.[10] But so much frenetic diplomatic activity could scarcely remain unnoticed. Philip VI was understandably reticent about his sources of information, but it seems possible that an English diplomatic agent had his baggage rifled in eastern Burgundy, and almost certain that reports were being received from one of William of Hainault's counsellors.[11]

By the spring of 1337, concealment was no longer necessary. William of Hainault announced his intention of convening a great diplomatic conference in his capital at Valenciennes on 4 May 1337. To this conference it was proposed to invite not only Edward's allies and potential allies, but also representatives of Philip VI and those princes of the Low Countries such as the Count of Flanders and the Bishop of Liège who were plainly in Philip VI's camp and unlikely to support an attack on him. William, who was not a naive man, cannot have expected these personnages to appear. His reason for inviting them was to justify his own conduct. If there was to be a war in which Hainault would fight with an English king against France, then it should be made to appear plainly that it was Philip who had rejected peace.[12]

Edward III's own proposals were formulated in the course of April 1337. At the beginning of the month Thrandeston returned from the continent in the company of the agents of the counts of Hainault and Guelders and the Duke of Brabant. They spent some days in London receiving splendid gifts and entertainments while the King deliberated with his Council. On 15 April the composition of the English delegation was announced: Henry Burghersh, Bishop of Lincoln, who was its senior member, and two of the new earls closest to the King, William Montagu, Earl of Salisbury, and William Clinton, Earl of Huntingdon. Burghersh was a significant choice. As a member of the King's Council he had been much concerned with the diplomatic manoeuvres of the past six months, and the days of his greatest influence were now beginning. He was the principal architect of English foreign policy from this point until his premature death at the end of 1340, long enough to witness both the initial triumph of his schemes and their final, catastrophic failure. Like Stratford, whom he disliked and displaced, Burghersh was a worldly ecclesiastical politician, ambitious, devious and unscrupulous. He was not a man whose judgement was to be relied upon in weighing the balance between peace and war, and it says much for Edward III's choice of ministers that while peace with France had remained a possibility, Burghersh's influence on foreign policy had remained small. But as the executant of a war policy once it came to that, Burghersh was supreme. He was, as one contemporary accurately described him, 'an ingenious adviser, audacious and smooth'.

Burghersh's embassy had two functions. He was, in the first place, to deliver to Philip VI or his representatives at an appropriate moment the ultimatum which had been drafted in Parliament. Secondly, he was to equip his master with the continental alliances which would be required in the very probable event that Philip was obdurate or failed to negotiate at all. It was certainly hoped that after suffering an embargo on wool exports for eight months, the Count of Flanders would agree to become one of those allies. The marriage of one of Edward's daughters to the Count's heir was proposed as a possible bait. But Burghersh was to complete the formation of the coalition whether or not Flanders came into it. The means to be employed and the terms to be offered were left to him. He and his fellow ambassadors constituted a branch of the King's Council sitting abroad, able to make their own decisions without referring them back to England, subject only to ratification by the King's own hand when everything was in place. Edward had learned something from the diplomatic misfortunes of the past decade.[13]

Burghersh and his fellow ambassadors left England in the last week of April 1337 and went directly to Valenciennes. No effort or expense was spared to impress the natives of the Low Countries with the power and wealth of the English King. The ambassadors were authorized to draw £2,000 from the Bardi firm on Edward's account, and £1,000 from the Peruzzi. In addition to these enormous sums, the Earl of Salisbury brought with him 5,000 marks (£3,333) of his own in case it should be needed. The arrival of the whole troop in Hainault was celebrated with lavish feasting and display. Valenciennes was a small town and the inhabitants were indeed impressed. 'People came out to watch the show, amazed by such a magnificent spectacle,' Jean le Bel recorded: 'they could not have spent more money if the King in person had been with them.' It was not only the gapers of Valenciennes who were impressed. Before serious negotiation had even begun, the Earl of Salisbury had distributed the whole of his 5,000 marks in gifts and pensions to influential personages.[14]

When the Count of Hainault's conference opened it was found, to nobody's surprise, that only those well disposed to Edward III had appeared. This meant, apart from Count William himself and his brother, the Count of Guelders, the Count of Limburg, the Margrave of Juliers, the counts of Cleves and Alost and a number of lesser princes. The Duke of Brabant, the Count of Namur and the Archbishop of Cologne sent representatives. But the Count and the towns of Flanders were not represented at all. Neither was Philip VI. Nevertheless, those present set about the task of proposing peace before they agreed upon war. An ultimatum was prepared by the counts of Hainault and Guelders for presentation to Philip VI. This contained three demands. First, there was the question of Robert of Artois, who was represented at the conference by a knight of his household. This was a delicate issue. As the French government had predicted when they chose to make an issue of Robert's activities, the princes of the Low Countries did not want to defy Philip VI on a matter on which they would be on such weak ground. One of them, the Count of Guelders, produced for Burghersh's inspection the document by which five years earlier he had sworn to help Philip against his mortal enemy. It was therefore agreed that Philip VI should be invited to grant Robert a safe conduct to return to France and plead his defence before a French court. If the safe conduct was forthcoming and Robert was tried and convicted, then Edward for his part would shelter him in England no longer. The second, more controversial demand was that Philip should abandon the Scots, something which it was hardly conceivable that he would do. Thirdly, the French King was invited to appoint a day when the troublesome litigation between himself and Edward III in the Parlement of Paris might be settled or determined. The two counts offered their services as intermediaries for this purpose.[15] The emissary chosen to carry this message to Philip VI was Jeanne de Valois, Countess of Hainault, the French King's sister and the only participant in this affair whose desire for peace was wholly untinged with hypocrisy. She was a spiritual but still formidable old lady who abhorred the prospect of a war in which all the principal protagonists would be members of her family. So, in the third week of May 1337, she set out for Paris accompanied by the Count's brother John, a personable man who had always got on well with Philip in the past.

When Jeanne and her brother-in-law arrived at the castle of Vincennes they found the French court filled with the bustle of preparation for war. Philip's ministers and courtiers tried not to notice her, and it was only after a great deal of lobbying that she obtained an interview with her brother. It

was a chilly occasion. Jeanne begged him to send representatives to Valenciennes and gave him the written proposals which the princes had drawn
up. Philip dismissed them out of hand. He knew about her husband's role
in assembling a coalition of his enemies over the past six months; more,
probably, than she did. Turning to John of Hainault, Philip accused him of
trying to 'hound me from my kingdom'. They left empty-handed. After
they had gone, the King relented in some small measure. He sent a
messenger after them with a letter which announced that he was, after all,
willing to consider granting a safe conduct to Robert of Artois so that he
could stand trial in France. He would allow him to choose his own counsel
and to object to the presence of any of his enemies among the judges.
Philip had nothing to say about the resolution of disputes in the Parlement.
He proposed to proceed with the confiscation of Aquitaine. As for the
Scots, he said that he was bound by treaty to assist them against England
and intended to do so.[16]

Philip VI had already committed himself to military action on a large
scale. The gathering of the army was fixed for 8 July 1338 at Amiens. A
second army was summoned to meet on the same day at Marmande, a
French fortress–town at the edge of Edward's duchy some 50 miles from
Bordeaux. The Count of Foix, Philip's commander in the south, returned
from a diplomatic mission at the papal court in the middle of May and his
orders were sent to him on the 20th. The Constable of France, Raoul,
Count of Eu, received his on the 23rd. On the following day, 24 May, the
bailli of Amiens was instructed to take over the tiny northern enclave of
Ponthieu. All this happened while Jeanne de Valois was at Vincennes.[17]

Philip's ministers were already co-ordinating their plans with the Scots
and supplying them on a scale which mounted as the English diplomatic
offensive grew more menacing. Not long after the King's uncomfortable
interview with his sister, the *Cogge de Flandre*, one of the largest merchant
ships available, was laden at Calais with armour and jewellery, 30,000
livres of silver and chests of records and correspondence. It sailed for
Scotland with a great number of soldiers on board, and several dignitaries
from the court at Château-Gaillard including the Scotch King's confidant
John Wischart, Bishop of Glasgow. The consignment is known because it
was captured in mid-ocean by ships of Yarmouth. The French put down its
loss to espionage and hanged the man they suspected, but ill-fortune is a
better explanation. In the face of English weakness at sea the consignment
should have got through. Many others did.[18]

The princes waiting at Valenciennes must have expected some such
answer as Philip VI had given them. Nevertheless it took them a long time

to give Edward's ambassadors what they had come for. All of them were agreed on the necessity of a defensive alliance with England, by which they meant an arrangement for the payment of subsidies from the English treasury to themselves in the event that the French should attack first. Most of them were prepared to contemplate a joint attack on French possessions within the boundary of the Empire. But there was a difference of opinion about the prospect of an armed invasion of France, which was what Burghersh and his colleagues wanted. The problem lay in the uncertain attitude of the Duke of Brabant and the Emperor. The Duke of Brabant's support was essential. He was the strongest military power of the German Low Countries. As for the Emperor, although the English ambassadors had high hopes of the military strength which he could bring to bear, his support was needed principally for legal and psychological reasons in order to set the seal of legitimacy on any military enterprise against France. The conference of Valenciennes proved, therefore, to be only the beginning and not the end of the diplomatic campaign. The rest of it taxed Burghersh's negotiating skills to the limit, for it was just at this time that he lost the invaluable assistance of William of Hainault. The old man had been in great pain and only intermittently visible during the conference. On 7 June 1337 he died.[19]

Early in June the English ambassadors led their splendid cavalcade northward across the undulating valleys of northern Hainault to the Duke of Brabant's capital at Brussels. More feasting and enormous bribes. The Duke himself was promised no less than £60,000 for his friendship, payable over the next four years. The prospect of establishing a wool staple in Brabant was held out to him, and export licences were liberally issued to his wool-starved subjects. The ambassadors were full of optimism. In mid-June, they sent report to their master in England that they would be ready to return by the end of the month with the alliances which would allow Edward to mount a major expedition to the continent that very summer. Edward was at Stamford in Lincolnshire, where he passed most of June and July closeted with his Council. Here, from 22 June onwards, a stream of orders was issued for the recruitment of an expeditionary army. It was to be ready to sail from London on 28 July 1337. The inevitable bureaucratic delays and a sense of isolation from the movement of events fed Edward's impatience as he waited at Stamford for further news. But his ambassadors had been too sanguine. As the commissioners of array began their work in the English counties, Burghersh and his companions were travelling east to Frankfurt to confront the Emperor. A fleet of twenty ships of Great Yarmouth arrived at the Dutch port of

Dordrecht at the end of June to carry them back to England, but they were nowhere to be found.[20]

Hitherto the English had had little direct contact with Louis of Bavaria. They had always been conscious that he was a heretic and a pariah. They addressed him by all his titles, but they sought the Pope's absolution for doing so and in the privacy of their own records they still called him 'Duke of Bavaria'.[21] For Louis too it was a matter of some delicacy. For several months now he had also been engaged in desultory negotiations with the French King and the papacy in the hope of bringing an end to his long and damaging vendetta with Avignon. There were signs that Benedict XII was willing to consider a reconciliation. Louis knew that a military alliance with the King of England against France would make that impossible. His difficult choice was swayed by two factors. In the first place, there was the question of the castles of the Cambrésis, which still aroused fear and anger in Germany. Secondly, and perhaps more important for this impecunious ruler, there was the money which the English emissaries were offering, 300,000 gold florins (£45,000). For this sum, Louis was persuaded to agree to furnish 2,000 armed men to fight with Edward's army for two months. Louis hoped, he said, to lead his troops in person. But if he did not, then he promised that Edward III himself would be empowered to act as 'Vicar of the Empire' with all the powers of the Emperor. This seminal idea can only have been Burghersh's. The Emperor's powers, no doubt, were few and little respected, but they undoubtedly included the power to confer public legitimacy on an invasion of France.[22]

Once they had settled matters with Louis of Bavaria, the ambassadors' arrangements with the princes of the Low Countries fell quickly into place. The counts of Hainault and Guelders and the Margrave of Juliers were each promised subsidies of 100,000 florins (£15,000) to furnish troops for the coming campaign. The Duke of Brabant, who had already agreed his fee, made a similar agreement. We cannot know whether in the secrecy of their own counsels these princes had any misgivings about the venture to which they had committed themselves. The Count of Guelders and the Margrave of Juliers certainly had none. They were both men who enjoyed war and their principalities were far from France. They could hope to earn sums which would dwarf their ordinary incomes. But the Duke of Brabant and the Count of Hainault cannot have signed with great enthusiasm. French encroachment in the German Low Countries was a genuine grievance, but a direct assault on France for much wider political objects had dangers at least as menacing. Neither ruler, however, had very much choice. The new Count of Hainault had been made by his father to swear that he would carry the old man's policy through. The Duke of Brabant could not afford to see the cloth industry of his territory brought to a halt by the English embargo and his towns reduced to the chaos which was rapidly overtaking those of Flanders. Even so, the size of his fee, which was larger even than the Emperor's and four times that of the Count of Hainault, is probably a good indication of the reluctance which had to be overcome. None of this, however, troubled the English ambassadors. They had the princes' agreements carried post haste to England and brought to Edward III at Stamford. He ratified them at once.[23]

When lesser princes, hangers-on and soldiers of fortune had made their own agreements in due course, Henry Burghersh and his companions had assembled on paper a contract army almost 7,000 strong:

The Emperor	2,000
The Duke of Brabant	1,200
The Count of Hainault	1,000
The Count of Guelders	1,000
The Margrave of Juliers	1,000
The Count of Loos	200
Rupert, Count Palatine	150
The Count of La Marck	100
The Margrave of Brandenburg	100
The Lord of Falkenburg	100
Others	96
	6,946

The ambassadors had also committed their master, with his grateful consent, to bear a crushing financial burden. The fees exacted by the princes for their alliances exceeded £160,000. In addition, all the treaties provided for the English King to bear the usual expenses of war. He was to pay fixed wages to each purveyor of troops. The usual rate was fifteen florins (£2, 5s.) per man per month. It was normal for two months' wages to be payable in advance at the outset of the campaign. The men were to bring their own horses and equipment, but the King gave the usual undertaking to pay for all horses lost in his service. He also promised to procure the release of any who were taken prisoner, if necessary by paying their ransom.[24]

The agreements bound Edward to a campaign strategy which was not necessarily his best military option. He seems to have had in mind at the outset a landing in Normandy. The princes of the Low Countries would either join his army in England before it embarked or else execute a simultaneous attack on Philip VI from the north. This plan, however, had the grave disadvantage that it exposed the principalities of the Low Countries to an attack by a vastly superior French army while the English were still far away. It was therefore abandoned in the course of the conference at Valenciennes and replaced by a second plan which required Edward III to launch his attack from Hainault. This not only protected his allies against attack. It also gave them some hope that the campaign would achieve their object as well as Edward's. For the Count of Hainault this meant the recovery of Crèvecœur and Arleux and perhaps some other places in the Cambrésis. Louis of Bavaria, so far as he was swayed by policy rather than money, had the same priorities. So Edward's ambassadors promised that the armies of the coalition would meet in the middle of the Cambrésis. The date fixed was 17 September 1337. The Emperor was given a little longer to assemble his contingent: he was to join the allies on about 1 October 1337. The question of how a large English army was to reach the appointed meeting place was left unanswered.[25]

The question must have loomed large in the ambassadors' minds as they waited near Dordrecht to be brought home by the fleet of Great Yarmouth. The French fleet had achieved almost complete command of the sea right up to the beaches on which they were standing. There had been serious losses of English shipping in the Channel and North Sea, and renewed raids on the Channel Islands and the south and east coasts. French galleys lay in wait to intercept them off Holland. From Westminster, Edward railed at his admirals, who by failing to bring the ambassadors home were depriving him of vital information. It was only after a wait of three weeks that the Yarmouth fleet succeeded in embarking the party and escaping under cover of a black storm. Some of them reached England wet and bedraggled on 13 August 1337; the others, who had been driven ashore by the gale, arrived a few days later without their horses and baggage. They landed in a country in which beacons were being built on hill tops, the coasts cleared of foreigners, and a mood of alarm intensified by the continual pounding of war propaganda. The ambassadors reached London in the third week of August to witness the half-organized beginnings of an army: a mass of men from Wales and the West Country milling around the capital without leaders or orders awaiting a campaign of which they knew as yet nothing. The King, who had moved from Stamford to Westminster, could now be apprised in detail of the scale of what he had undertaken. It was exactly a month before it was due to be performed.[26]

*

Edward III was represented in Gascony by some outstanding soldiers and administrators, a striking contrast to the state of affairs which had existed in his father's time in the crisis of Saint-Sardos. The Seneschal was an Englishman, Oliver Ingham, a 'bold and admirable knight' according to the chronicler Knighton. Ingham was a remarkable and ingenious improviser, one of the unsung heroes of the war. He was a Norfolk man with a colourful career in royal service who had taken an active part in the civil wars of Edward II's reign and had first visited Gascony in 1325 during the war of Saint-Sardos. He had been released from Winchester jail by the orders of the Despensers and sent out to serve as one of the counsellors of the incompetent Earl of Kent. After the Earl had departed in disgrace, Ingham held the office of Seneschal for a short period, in which he brought a new spirit of aggressive enterprise to the defence of the duchy. This was in 1326, the year the Despensers fell. The new government recalled him in the interests of peace with France. But Ingham had a talent for ingratiating himself with whomever was in power. In June 1331 he was reappointed seneschal of Gascony. He remained there for substantially the rest of his life. By the standards of contemporary Englishmen he was exceptionally experienced in Gascon affairs and evidently very good at the continuous diplomacy which passed for government among the fickle lords of the region.[27]

Ingham was getting on in years in 1337 (he was about fifty), and his health was not always up to the burden of carrying on a war single-handed. His chief collaborator at the outset of the war was a Gascon nobleman, Bérard d'Albret, who was captain of Blaye and Puynormand on the northern march. Bérard was a cadet of the house of Albret, perhaps the ablest of his ruthless and warlike clan. He had consistently supported the English even in the darkest days of 1324 and 1325 when most of his family were on the other side. The English government rated his military skills highly, and sedulously cultivated his friendship. But his main assets were his influence and his charm, famous in his own day, and a profound knowledge of his own countrymen. 'We have always found him more enthusiastic than anyone else in these parts about the service of the King our master,' an Englishman had written in the time of Edward II, 'and he has drawn more French allies to our side than any other man.'[28]

These men had resources wholly inadequate to their task. There were no English troops in the duchy except for a handful of immigrants and the personal retinues of a few English officials. The government of Gascony depended for its field army on the nobility of the province and their vassals and retainers. The patchy records which survive suggest that in favourable conditions the Gascon nobility could raise between 4,000 and 7,000 men.[29] Even that depended on a high degree of loyalty and enthusiasm. These men were being asked to withdraw their retainers from the defence of their own possessions, to serve on credit, to run the risk of capture and ransom in case of defeat, to abandon what prospect they had of patronage by the French Crown and to forfeit the property which they held in other parts of France. There were not many who felt sufficient confidence in the survival of the English duchy. When Oliver Ingham convened an assembly of the loyal baronage of the duchy in October 1337, a side chapel of the Dominican church in Bordeaux contained them all. There were some notable absences. In spite of the presence of three members of the house of Albret, the head of the family was not there. The lords of Fronsac, Caumont and Duras, whose families were to be stars at the Gascon court of the Black Prince two decades later, were absent. All of them were either firmly on the French side or else (like the lord of Albret) maintaining an attitude of unfriendly neutrality until the course of events should become clear.[30]

The assignment of almost all the available manpower to the garrisons forced the government of the duchy to follow a policy of passive defence against all the personal instincts of its leaders. Other factors born of weakness and poverty pointed in the same direction. The practice of the Bordeaux government was to promise subsidies to local territorial magnates to retain troops for the defence of their own lands and the districts about them. This had the advantage that it was something that the nobility had every interest in doing, if necessary on credit. But the disadvantages were considerable. Some of the recipients of these subsidies became for all practical purposes the military governors of whole regions, exercising an independent political power and strategic discretion uncontrolled from Bordeaux. Pierre de Grailly, for example, and his son John, 'Captal de Buch', were responsible for a substantial block of territory west of Bordeaux, including the fortresses of Benauges and Castillon-sur-Dordogne, the walled town of Libourne and much of Entre-Deux-Mers, as well as another block, less substantial, in the southern Landes near Bayonne. They manned, fortified and provisioned these places as contractors of the King–Duke and levied taxes for their own account.[31] By such methods Ingham was able to make bricks without straw. But the price to be paid was the loss of a considerable measure of control over the deployment of the troops. Only on rare occasions was it possible to concentrate the forces of the duchy at the decisive point. The military organization was static and inflexible, and tended to become more so as the French extended their conquests, as the tenure of the nobility became less secure, as they became more straitened in their circumstances, more defensive and tenacious in their outlook. No significant field army was deployed in Gascony before 1340, and none with any prospect of defeating the French in battle until 1345.

The preservation of the duchy depended on castles, not only strong but numerous, to provide defence in depth: obstructing an invading army at each stage of its march along the river valleys and main roads; harassing the communications of any force large enough to pass them by. Something like this had existed in the reign of Edward I. But his grandson's castles were not numerous. Half a century of grants to much-needed allies within the duchy and two French invasions had reduced them to a fragile line barely following the outer limits of the King–Duke's territory. Nor were they strong. The revenues of the duchy were not large enough to pay for regular reconstruction and repair, and those of England were allocated to more pressing needs. See to it that the castles are kept in good repair, Edward had told his officials four years before, but remember that the Scots have to be fought as well.[32]

The defences of the Gascon duchy were strongest on the southern march, facing the Count of Foix. This region had been little affected by the invasions of Philip the Fair and Charles IV. There was a line of substantial fortress–towns along the Adour valley and its tributaries: Bayonne, Dax, Saint-Sever, Geaune, Aire and Bonnegarde, as well as some isolated strongholds such as the Pyrenean fortress of Mauléon further south. This was not, however, the direction from which the main attack could be expected to come. On the northern march of the duchy the position was much less satisfactory. Saintes, a large town standing across the main medieval road from Paris to Bordeaux, had been sacked by the Count of Alençon during the short war of 1331. He had destroyed the walls of both the town and the castle and had made a start on the demolition of the keep when he was recalled. The agreement which followed included a promise to pay for their restoration. But it was never honoured. At the beginning of the Hundred Years War, Saintes was an open town garrisoned by neither side and probably indefensible. Along the north shore of the Gironde there was a line of insecurely held castles. Talmont, the westernmost of them, occupied a strong position on a rock promontory near the entrance to the estuary, but it was weakly held and succumbed to locally recruited French troops after a siege of two months. Montendre, a few miles off the Saintes road, was strong but out of the way. This left as the sole important English strongholds on the northern approach the twin towns of Bourg, dominating the confluence of the Dordogne and the Garonne, and Blaye, 8 miles downstream. These two places were essential to any scheme for the defence of the duchy. Yet, in spite of their obvious strategic importance, the fortifications of both places were in a sorry state. A year after the outbreak of the war the citizens of Bourg were still struggling to repair their walls at their own expense. At Blaye, a larger town whose fortifications were more extensive, Bérard d'Albret gave Ingham and his officials a dispiriting conducted tour in September 1337. This revealed rotting gateways, crumbling masonry, collapsing roofwork, trenches eroded by goats, moats non-existent or filled up with rubbish. There were unofficial openings pierced in the barbicans; on the north side a new suburb had sprung up whose buildings covered the moat and overlooked the walls; on the south side, by the sea gate and along the strand, there were no fortifications at all. Work was still in progress in a year later. The new suburb was not demolished until early in 1339, when the French were advancing on the town.[33]

The situation was as bad along the other main approach to the duchy by the great artery of the Garonne, navigable in the fourteenth century well beyond Toulouse. Here the problem was not so much the condition of Edward III's castles, which seems to have been acceptable, as their small number and poor situation. The conquests of the French in 1324 had entirely undermined the eastern defences of the duchy. In the Agenais, Penne survived on its great rock overlooking the Lot valley. So did the weak *bastide* of Puymirol to the south. The French had passed them by and occupied the entire valley of the Garonne between the Agenais and Saint-Macaire, including, most disastrously for Edward II and his successor, the enormous fortress of La Réole, which had been built and frequently improved for the very purpose of holding the Garonne valley should the Agenais be lost. Saint-Macaire became the bastion of the duchy and indeed the only important stronghold before Bordeaux.

Even such strongholds as Edward III had, fell to be defended in difficult conditions by men whose loyalties could rarely be counted on absolutely. A close siege tested them to the limit and sometimes beyond the limit. Oliver Ingham, who had been in command at Agen in the war of Saint-Sardos, must have had vivid memories of the way in which its citizens had forced him to surrender rather than face a siege; those of Saint-Macaire would have done the same if they had had the chance. Garrison commanders were men whose own lands were often in the hands of the enemy, whose pay was liable to be in arrears and whose family connections with the besiegers might be closer than any with their own side. Bérard d'Albret, who knew these men well, believed that those places which were lost during the French campaign of 1337 had been betrayed from within. Such allegations were often made and it is difficult to know how often they were justified. There is, however, clear evidence of treachery in some cases. For this reason, there was a policy of appointing Englishmen to important commands when suitable Englishmen were available. Generally, however, they were not available. Edward's territorial interests in Gascony were defended for better or worse by Gascons.[34]

Edward did attempt to reinforce them with Englishmen, but later and in smaller numbers than he had originally intended. Orders went out on 18 March 1337 to raise an army for Gascony which it was intended to shepherd across the Bay of Biscay with the fleet of Bayonne. On the same day Edward III ordered his admirals to requisition all ships in the south- and west-coast ports of England of more than 40 (later 30) tons' capacity. Originally this was to be the main military enterprise of the year, and Edward proposed to command it in person. At the end of March Henry Burghersh was on the point of departing for Bordeaux to take a grip on the affairs of the duchy in preparation for the King's arrival. But as spring turned to summer, the prospect of attacking France by the north grew more enticing. Burghersh was sent to Valenciennes instead. Edward, moreover, encountered mounting opposition to his plans within his own Council, mainly it seems on the ground that it would be impossible to return quickly to England if the realm were menaced by an invasion across the Channel.[35]

Logistical problems and administrative delay gave the King plenty of time for second thoughts. The original timetable envisaged that the army of Gascony would embark at Portsmouth at the end of April 1337, an impossible date which was quickly replaced by others only slightly less unrealistic. Recruiting proved to be slow and erratic, and was hampered throughout the early summer by the competing demands of the army of Scotland, which was being raised at the same time. Finally, after Edward had heaped abuse on his officials and announced no less than three postponements, the sailing date was fixed for 7 July. Only in the middle of June were there signs of Portsmouth of some purpose in all this administrative activity. Stores of victuals accumulated in waterside warehouses. The first galleys of the escort force appeared in the harbour.[36]

It was at this point that Edward III received Burghersh's report of the proceedings at Valenciennes, and finally jettisoned his original plans, announcing his intention of going to the Low Countries instead. Edward III was always over-sanguine about what his small country could achieve, but he was enough of a realist to appreciate that he could not maintain three English armies simultaneously, in Scotland, the Low Countries and Gascony. Once the decision to land in the Low Countries had been made the army of Gascony was progressively downgraded. In July the command was conferred on John of Norwich, a man of minor rank who, like most of Edward's commanders, had learned war in Scotland. The forces made available to him were much reduced. Some of the men summoned to Portsmouth were told to proceed instead to London to embark for the Low Countries; others were told to go no further than Winchester, where they could be directed to either port of embarkation as political developments might require.[37]

Less than a week later, Philip VI and his advisers made a similar decision at Vincennes. The substance of Burghersh's discussions with the Emperor had been reported to them by 28 June 1337, and on that day men who were holding themselves ready to travel to either Amiens or Marmande were directed to the northern army. The French King who, like his rival, had once hoped to take command in the south-west himself, decided that the new threat demanded his presence in the north.[38]

At Libourne Oliver Ingham had already received on 13 June 1337 the precursors of the French army of invasion, two lieutenants of the Seneschal of Périgord, who produced the royal letters declaring the duchy forfeit and called upon him to surrender the towns and castles under his command. Forms were being observed. Ingham temporized. He asked for time to consult his council in Bordeaux, which was permitted grudgingly. He pointed out that Robert of Artois, whose activities were stated to be the reason for the forfeiture, was not in Gascony. He said that he would need several weeks in which to obtain instructions from England. He appealed to the judgement of the peers of France in the Parlement of Paris, invoking the stay of execution which that entailed. None of this was acceptable to the lieutenants. They said that the army charged with enforcing the forfeiture was already on its way.[39]

This was true. Philip of France had settled the main lines of his military strategy closeted with his advisers in Paris in the middle of May 1337. The most important decision made on this occasion was that Gascony would be attacked from the east by the Garonne valley and not (as the English appear to have anticipated) from the north by Saintonge. This suggests that it was intended to bring the campaign to a speedy end by lunging at Bordeaux. The muster date was 8 July 1337, by coincidence the day after the English expeditionary force was due to leave Portsmouth. Philip VI's army, unlike Edward's, arrived on time. It was almost entirely composed of contingents of the southern provinces. The seneschals of Toulouse, Beaucaire and Agen came with the men of Languedoc. The two great southern lords of the French King's obedience, the counts of Armagnac and Foix, provide enormous contingents: nearly 6,000 men in Armagnac's case and about 2,500 in that of Gaston de Foix. The total strength of the army at its peak was probably about 12,000 men, not including garrison troops. These numbers compared poorly with the force of 21,000 which it had been estimated a few years before would be required to conquer Gascony. But given the small strength available to Ingham it was adequate. Its main deficiency was at the level of command, which fell by right of rank to the Constable, Raoul, Count of Eu. He was a man of very limited talent.[40]

His first mistake was to waste time attacking some of the lesser strongholds of the Agenais held for Edward III. He first attacked Villeneuve, which the English seem to have occupied to bar his passage of the Lot. This place was taken on about 10 July 1337. He then made his second mistake, which was to divide his forces, leaving part of his army to besiege other places in the Agenais while he himself marched west. Penne, the strongest English garrison in the Agenais, was left alone, but Puymirol was taken on 17 July, thus avenging the insult given to the Parlement's authority earlier in the year and enabling Garcie Arnaud to satisfy his judgement. It is not clear whether the garrison resisted; the populace certainly did not. They delivered up the lower town to the besiegers in exchange for the privilege of holding an annual fair on St Foy's Day. Why should they endure discomfort and destruction for a distant ruler powerless to relieve them?[41] The real campaign did not begin until the middle of July when the Constable joined forces with Gaston de Foix and the two of them laid siege to Saint-Macaire.

Saint-Macaire had been the scene of the dispiriting failure of March 1337, when the Master of the Royal Archers had attempted to surprise the place and failed for want of equipment. On this occasion there was an elaborate siege train which included in addition to conventional machinery two large stone-throwing mangonels mounted on barges moored in the Garonne. With these he was able to do great damage to the walls of the town and its citadel. We cannot know how long the prosperous citizens of Saint-Macaire would have persisted in the face of the destruction of their houses and the uprooting of their fine suburban vineyards. They were not put to the test. Inexplicably, on 31 July 1337, the Constable abandoned the siege after only a fortnight and divided his forces again into two independent units which he dispatched on raiding expeditions in different

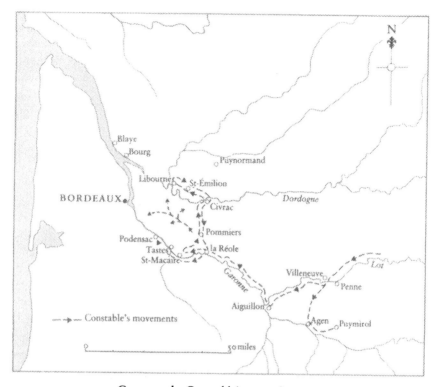

3 Gascony: the Constable's campaign, 1337

parts of the duchy. The object was not so much to take possession of the strategic points of the duchy as to harass partisans of Edward III. The main force, under his own command, burst into the territory east of Bordeaux in the angle of the Garonne and the Dordogne. The big square keep of Tastes near Saint-Croix-du-Mont, the property of one of Edward III's keenest supporters, was taken. At least three weeks more were passed in besieging Pommiers, a large modern seigneurial fortress, one of the few places which had successfully resisted the army of Charles of Valois in 1324. This place fell at the very end of August 1337, whereupon the Constable marched north and pitched his tents before Civrac on the south bank of the Dordogne. Civrac was an old seigneurial castle and probably not in good repair. It capitulated almost at once. These were places of some importance on a provincial level, but they were not the keys to the possession of the duchy. The Constable's other conquests were no more than fortified manor houses.[42]

The second raiding force, which was commanded by Gaston de Foix, marched at speed into the southern part of the duchy and raided the lands of the principal Gascon lords loyal to Edward III in the foothills of the Pyrenees, the valley of the Adour and the hinterland of the great commercial city of Bayonne. There were no great victories. He failed before all the more substantial strongholds, including the great Pyrenean fortress of Mauléon. Gaston lost four of his knights and several good horses on the retreat from this place. He did not even broach the walls of Bayonne or the main ducal garrisons on the Adour at Dax and Saint-Sever. But he occupied many smaller places, and he did considerable damage to crops and buildings, which was probably his main object. On this point Philip VI had expressed his wishes very clearly. 'It is our desire' he wrote, 'that you shall inflict as much damage as you can on the lands of the lord of Tartas and that you shall do so on our behalf and in our name.' The lord of Tartas was probably only slightly exaggerating when he told Edward III after Foix had gone that his loyalty had cost him the whole of his income for many months.[43]

The English adopted the only policy which was open to them. They shut themselves up in their castles and walled towns and waited for reinforcements. The geography of the duchy was an ally: all the main strongholds of the Bordelais were accessible by water from Bordeaux and scarce garrison troops could in case of need be switched from one to another. But in the face of a more determined attack this juggling could not have been sustained for long. The promised reinforcements were kept in their ports in England by political indecision and bureaucratic confusion. During the first ten days of August 1337 it emerged from the babble of conflicting orders that the forces allocated to Gascony were to be yet further reduced. Edward appropriated to the army of the Low Countries all the ships and most of the troops which had been earmarked for it. The levies of the west of England gathered at Winchester trudged along the London road, and sixty-one ships in Portsmouth harbour sailed round the coast to join the mass of shipping which was already clogging the Thames. In their place, John of Norwich was assigned a mixed force of Welsh archers, some Londoners and a handful of men-at-arms. Their port of embarkation was abruptly switched to Bristol. For much of August frenzied efforts were being made to find carts to transport their victuals and equipment from Portsmouth to Bristol. In the end these orders too were countermanded, and in the last days of August John of Norwich finally sailed from London. The exact size of his force can only be guessed, but it was certainly modest. Given the number of ships available to carry it there were probably between 300 and 500 men.[44]

By the time they reached Gascony the momentum of the French campaign had been almost entirely dissipated. The Count of Foix was still engaged in wasting the southern *pays*. As for the main body of the French army, after the fall of Civrac at the end of August, they had been ferried across the Dordogne and had marched on Saint-Émilion and Libourne, the largest towns within easy reach. This was a show of force, not an attack in earnest. Both towns were well defended and Saint-Émilion, indeed, had with rare enthusiasm cleared its suburbs and made its fortifications ready well in advance. Having made their point, the French left. The Constable had left this operation to his subordinates. He passed the whole of September in the safety of La Réole. His behaviour at this juncture is as difficult to explain as anything else in this peculiar campaign. The most probable explanation is that the strength of his army had fallen, not only because part of it had been detached for garrison duty and peripheral raids, but because large contingents had left without being replaced.[45]

The war was still too recent to be taken entirely seriously in the neighbouring provinces of southern France. There had been no obvious threat to the security of the population to provoke a mass out-turn of infantry from the towns and villages, or the payment of compensation in lieu. Money was a perennial problem. The French, like their adversaries, adopted the practice of trying to make the south-western theatre financially self-supporting so far as they could. This meant that every French commander spent a great deal of his time and energy extracting money from the local population. Swingeing taxes had been imposed back in May, a hearth tax and an income tax of 20 per cent on the holders of fiefs. But the collectors had been met by juridical obstruction and in a few places armed rebellion. Most communities paid something in the end but less than had been asked and too late. A few refused absolutely.[46]

There was a spark of hope at La Réole in the middle of September 1337, when Gaston de Foix returned from his destructions bringing no less than 6,000 reinforcements from Béarn. An attack on Bordeaux was mooted. Some preliminary plans were made, and troops were gathered at Podensac 30 miles from the duchy's capital. Part of the French Channel fleet was moved south to La Rochelle to blockade the city from the sea. It would have been a difficult military operation. It was late in the season. The weather was atrocious. And the troops of John of Norwich had now finally reached Bordeaux. However, the decision to call it off was made not by the commanders in the south, but by the government in Paris. They had already decided that the army of Gascony should be disbanded and the Constable recalled. This news reached him on about 20 September and was acted upon at once.[47]

Philip VI and his ministers can hardly have been satisfied with the Constable's achievements, but the reason for his recall was that as the senior military officer of the Crown he was now urgently required in the north. It was one of the abiding strategic difficulties of the French during the early years of the war that although they were operating on internal lines of communication they were hardly ever willing to take the risk of conducting field operations on both the southern and the northern fronts simultaneously. Evidently the French government had the same exaggerated view of England's military capacity as Edward III had.

Between 18 and 26 August 1337 an important meeting of the royal Council was held at Westminster to hear the reports of Bishop Burghersh and the Earl of Salisbury. It was the first comprehensive review of the diplomatic position since early April. It became apparent that there was a division of sentiment between the ambassadors, not all of whom where satisfied with their work. Some of the English King's advisers must have had well in mind the precedent of Edward I, who had paid large subsidies to the Emperor and various German princes only to be abandoned by them at the crucial moment. The Earl of Salisbury, according to one account, was appalled by the cost of the subsidies which the Germans were demanding. He thought that they were being too greedy and that they would not honour their promises even if Edward honoured his, itself a large question. His advice seems to have been that the treaties should be repudiated, even though some of them had already been ratified. Edward rejected this advice. He was well pleased with Burghersh's work and ratified all the remaining treaties on 26 August 1337. To his mind, the problems lay not in the principle but in the performance.[48]

There were two main problems, one military and logistical, the other financial. The military and logistical problem was that Edward III did not have a large enough army to appear with credit in the Cambrésis in the middle of September 1337. Nor did he have the ships to carry them there and defend them against a powerful French fleet cruising off the Flemish coast. There had been a standing army in southern Scotland and the border since April, under the command of the Earl of Warwick. Warwick's forces were too few for their task, but even so they absorbed such manpower as the northern counties could provide, as well as the retinues of many magnates. From the west and south and the Midlands a small army had already been formed to go to Gascony. What was left was very disappointing. Although recruitment had been in progress since March, the best-organized regions were sending only two-thirds of the numbers demanded and the worst none at all. Of the army which should have been ready to embark at London at the end of July 1337 fewer than 2,000 men had assembled a month later. This unimpressive force grew, but by not very much, as stragglers arrived in the following weeks.[49]

The financial problem was even more intractable. The subsidy which Edward III had been voted in Parliament in March was promptly assigned, as such subsidies almost invariably were, to the King's bankers to repay the loans of the past and was not available to finance an expedition to the Low Counties. To pay for that, Edward estimated that he would need £200,000. He proposed to obtain it by a remarkable method. It was intended that almost all the year's wool crop should be compulsorily purchased on behalf of the Crown on credit. It would then be carried to the continent with the army and sold there at the inflated prices which English wool commanded after twelve months in which exports had been embargoed. This scheme had been devised in the course of the summer by a small group of financiers, the chief of whom were William Pole and the London merchant Reginald Conduit. They represented a new breed of war financier, men who were never far removed from the centre of power during the next twenty-five years. Pole, for example, although he was a wool merchant, diversified his business activities as the King's needs required. He was the government's principal banker after the Bardi and the Peruzzi. He had moved into war contracting, building a galley, supplying victuals for the army as well as wax, tenting, metals for siege engines and a variety of other goods.

Pole and Conduit gathered round themselves a large consortium of wool merchants, who met in London on 26 July 1337 and approved both the scheme itself and the details of its operation. The consortium was given a monopoly of the right to export wool. They undertook to buy 30,000 sacks in the English counties, which was about 90 per cent of the quantity usually available for export. The wool was to be acquired at minimum prices fixed by the government, county by county, but in case the growers and local merchants should find them unsatisfactory the consortium would be armed with royal commissions to purvey (that is, compulsorily purchase) wool by prerogative power. As and when they sold it to their customers on the continent, the consortium would pay to Edward III half of their profit and would lend him interest free £200,000. To secure repayment of this large sum Edward would assign his customs revenues to them until they were entirely satisfied. Moreover, until they were entirely satisfied they were to be under no obligation to pay the growers from whom they had bought the wool. If any of these should be bold enough to sue for their price, the courts would be prevented from giving judgement by royal letters of protection. The timetable for wool shipments from England was determined partly by the government's perception of the administrative burden (which they greatly under-estimated), and partly by the date on which the King had promised to pay his allies. There were to be three shipments, each of 10,000 sacks, the first to be made almost at once and the other two in the first half of 1338. It was hoped that this would produce the promised £200,000 in instalments *pro rata* at Christmas 1337 and at Easter and Ascension 1338. It was an elegant device. The merchants' monopoly would guarantee their profit. The growers, although their cash flow would suffer, were protected after a fashion by the minimum prices. The King would receive quickly and cheaply enough money to pay for his expedition. Only the foreigner would suffer. He would be excluded from the export trade and compelled to pay high prices to the English monopolists.[50]

That at least was the principle. The practice was less satisfactory. For in the first place the plan was based on the simple economic fallacy that prices on the continent would remain at the high levels created by the trade embargo even after the very large consignments of the monopolists had begun to arrive on the market. Moreover, like every elaborate scheme concocted by medieval governments without the extensive police powers of the modern state, it depended on a measure of co-operation from those concerned, including many growers and small country traders. They were outraged by the fixed prices and long credit terms which were to be forced on them, and by the monopoly which left them at the mercy of the King's consortium. There was very little that they could do to challenge the main features of the wool scheme, but their resistance was bound to delay its execution and Edward's political commitments on the continent could brook very little delay. Even those who had devised the scheme and were in Edward's innermost counsels could not be relied upon. Pole and Conduit and many of their associates were in varying degrees grasping, unscrupulous and dishonest.

What was plain even in August 1337 was that if everything went according to plan there would still have to be some postponement of the expedition to the Low Countries. For a time, Edward III clung to the idea of landing on the continent in the autumn, albeit later in the season than he had agreed. On 26 August the assembly of the army was put back to 30 September 1337. Even this revised timetable was not expected to be achieved. On the day he announced it, Edward III agreed with Louis of Bavaria to put back the meeting of the English and Imperial armies, which had been fixed for 1 October, by two months. It was now intended to take the field on St Andrew's Day, 30 November 1337, a difficult time at which to find food for an army and march it across the sodden fields of northern Europe. The nobility of the realm and their contingents of men-at-arms, as well as archers and lancers from Wales and southern England, continued to gather slowly in London, at Sandwich and in Orwell.[51]

The troops at Sandwich, some 1,300 of whom had appeared by the end of October, received their orders first. It was decided, probably in order to make the most productive use of scarce shipping, that they should be sent ahead of the main army together with the first large shipments of wool. They were to be landed in Holland, a territory of the Count of Hainault. They were placed under the command of the Admiral of the north, Walter Mauny, and embarked in the Downs in the first few days of November 1337. With them went Bishop Burghersh and three other members of the King's Council to explain their master's perplexing conduct to the allies and pay them something if they insisted.[52]

The rest of the army waited, some of them increasingly hungry and cold on the east coast, the others in their homes on twelve days' notice to arrive at their assembly points. As autumn turned to winter Edward's difficulties accumulated. The Scots began to stage violent diversions in the lowlands and northern England. Carlisle was attacked in mid-October and part of Cumberland wasted. At the beginning of November they laid siege to Edinburgh. Supplies were pouring into Scotland from France through Dunbar and other ports. Edward III began as early as September to divert to the north important noble retinues which had been intended for his continental expedition. In early October he was obliged to send the Earl of Salisbury, one of his principal commanders. Even so, the King did not recognize reality until the second half of November. On 20 November 1337, only ten days remained before he was due to meet the Emperor in the field. The best estimate of the forces available for the Low Countries was then about 1,000 men in addition to those who had already left under the command of Walter Mauny. Louis of Bavaria had not been paid and Edward's coffers were empty. He cancelled the expedition and sent the soldiers home.[53]

Philip VI decided before Edward III did that the English King would be unable to join his allies by the appointed day. Well-disposed individuals in Germany kept him informed of developments, and from the north-eastern march of France spies were sent out to watch for signs of military activity. Their reports were reassuring. The date of the muster at Amiens was reviewed at fortnightly intervals and on each occasion postponed.[54] It was unfortunate that the French government's intelligence, which was so effective in Germany, was able to tell them almost nothing about what was happening in England. Philip had no understanding of the difficulties which Edward III was experiencing in assembling his armies. At the beginning of October, when the muster date next fell for review, it was refixed for 15 November with every sign that the French government was convinced that the crisis was now upon them. The Constable, together with some important southern lords, was summoned from the south and all serious military activity in Gascony was abandoned. During October 1337 arrayers throughout England were being lambasted for their failure to meet the King's demands. The ships, too few in number, were loaded with wool and bottled up by seasonal gales in the mouth of the Thames. But at Vincennes panic had gripped Philip's ministers. Visitors to the French court were pressed by the King with the perils of his situation. Edward III, he told them, would be embarking his army in a matter of days. It was essential that he should be put off before he had embarked, 'extinguishing the spark before it becomes a flame'. Once the King of England had arrived on the continent he would be financially committed to war and governed by greedy and warlike Germans, and there would be no holding him back.[55]

In the middle of the month the French government was convinced that the English intended to land at Boulogne within the next few days. All available troops were placed under the command of the King's brother, the Count of Alençon, and his brother-in-law, Philip of Navarre, and dispatched to the town to meet them.[56] They waited in vain while the blow fell elsewhere. In Gascony, now almost denuded of French troops, the English burst out of their garrison towns and seized almost all the places which the Constable had taken earlier in the year except Puymirol. There seems to have been little or no resistance. The English then crossed the Dordogne in early November and invaded eastern Saintonge. One of the main French garrison towns in these parts, Parcoul on the Dronne, fell without a blow. The commander of the place, a weak-minded man, was bullied into surrender by citizens anxious for a quite life. The English were not grateful. They burned the town and all the villages about it before withdrawing.[57]

At about the same time Walter Mauny's fleet with the advance guard of the army of invasion made another cut-and-run raid on the coast of

Flanders. Mauny was a flamboyant adventurer, a Hainaulter who had come to England as a page of Queen Philippa in 1327 and emerged during the Scotch wars as a man of great personal courage and ostentatious boldness, qualities which endeared him to the English King and ensured that he would be fully employed for the next thirty years. Mauny had eighty-five ships under his command carrying some 1,450 troops and about 2,200 mariners in addition to their cargoes of wool and a crowd of diplomats, clerks and servants. He handled these forces with the utmost recklessness. At the beginning of November 1337 he made an attempt on the port of Sluys but was repulsed. Then turning north he landed his men on 9 November 1337 on the island of Cadzand, a bleak, marshy place of small fishing villages lying at the entrance to the Hondt. The English passed several days there in slaughter and destruction in the hope of drawing out the garrison of Sluys. The garrison rose to the bait. They offered battle and were routed with great bloodshed on both sides. Mauny made no attempt to occupy Cadzand, and his main purpose was probably the capture of valuable prisoners. If so, he was well rewarded for his risks. Among the prisoners taken was the Flemish commander, Guy Bastard of Flanders, the Count's half-brother, whom Mauny later sold to the King for a considerable sum. But the memory of Mauny's butchery returned to haunt Edward III ten years later when his relations with Flanders were closer, and he found it politic to soothe ill feeling by founding a Charterhouse in honour of the dead.[58]

Raids like these, on territory which was won only to be abandoned, achieved no strategic object, but they fed the profound sense of insecurity which had beset Europe's strongest monarchy. Philip VI's mood moved from effortless confidence to craven panic and back again. He acquired an extreme and irrational fear of conspirators and fifth columnists. At the end of the year he was persuaded, on the basis of a confession by a Hospitaller in prison, that the princes of the Low Countries were plotting to poison him and all his family. There began the regular series of executions for treason, hitherto very rare, which were to continue for two decades, attended by the demonstrative ceremonies of drawing, hanging and quartering. The unfortunate garrison commander of Parcoul, who was more incompetent than treacherous, was accused of having marked the weak points of his town with chalk and charcoal to guide the English in. The accusation was fanciful, as the French government later acknowledged, but he was convicted of treason and beheaded in Paris. The King's more perceptive servants knew that indifference was a greater threat than betrayal.[59]

*

As the momentum of warlike operations failed, the thankless task of reconciling England and France fell to two politically inexperienced cardinals who had been appointed as mediators by the Pope in the summer. Bertrand de Montfavence, a cardinal of more than twenty years' standing, was an ecclesiastical lawyer from Provence whose diplomatic experience was limited to a short sojourn in Italy a few years before. Pedro Gomez de Barroso, the Chamberlain of the College of Cardinals, was a learned Castilian with no diplomatic experience at all so far as can be discovered. The efforts of these men to resolve in a few weeks the problems of four generations continued intermittently for almost two years and ended in failure. They were shamelessly used by both sides for temporary political and military ends.

The cardinals were unctuously received in France by Philip VI, then in one of his moods of fear and misgiving, not at all averse to a truce and inclined to feel that they might be turned in his own interest. They arrived in England in late November 1337, equipped as if for a voyage of exploration in a savage land, bringing their own wine cellar and an enormous supply of palatable food. The English government received them with much public joy and private vexation. Indeed, Edward III had at first declined to give them a safe conduct to cross the Channel. He did not change his mind until his hopes of invading France in 1337 were finally abandoned in November. With a characteristic sense of theatre he accorded them his first interview in the famous Painted Chamber of the Palace of Westminster whose walls were decorated with scenes from the wars of the Old Testament. In these unpromising surroundings the cardinals put forward their proposals for a truce.[60]

Edward III's situation was most delicate, and only dimly understood by his visitors. In fact, there was nothing that he wanted more than a truce, now that his immediate military plans had collapsed. However, by the terms of his treaties with the German princes, Edward could not conclude a truce which did not include them. Even to discuss such a thing might suggest a waning enthusiasm for the war, which could create a most unfortunate impression on the continent. He therefore decided to play for time. By the 'admirable customs of England', he told the cardinals, it was impossible to take any irrevocable step without consulting Parliament. Moreover, to defend himself against the aggressive designs of Philip VI he had had to arm himself with allies, and he could not contemplate a truce without their consent, all of which would involve some delay. The cardinals were unsympathetic. They reacted angrily and tactlessly. They told him that Louis of Bavaria's consent was immaterial, he being an excommunicated heretic; as for the other allies, they were only with him for his money and would desert him when it suited them. Indeed, they added untruthfully, the Duke of Brabant and the Count of Hainault had already done so, and sworn secret oaths to Philip VI.

On the following day the cardinals summoned as many English prelates as could be found at short notice to assemble before them in the Convent of the London Carmelites at the eastern edge of the Temple. This was an even more unpleasant occasion. One of the cardinals opened the proceedings with a sermon about peace which was thought to be pro-French, and was loudly heckled by the Archbishop of Canterbury. The cardinals then explained that unless Edward III agreed to the proposed truce the papacy would declare itself openly for Philip VI. They exhibited a panoply of papal letters authorizing them to degrade or deprive ecclesiastics below the rank of bishop who assisted the war effort (this meant almost all the civil service), to dissolve treaties and alliances, to release subjects and vassals from their obligations, to prohibit military expeditions on pain of excommunication and interdict. Edward's ministers took these threats most seriously. It was almost certainly because of them that on Christmas Eve they agreed to a curious hybrid that fell short of a truce but left time for further negotiation and apparently satisfied the cardinals. Edward promised that he would not invade France until at least 1 March 1338, and that unless his own subjects were attacked he would suspend all hostilities at sea and in Gascony until the same date. Meanwhile he would hold a Parliament on 3 February 1338 to consider some more formal arrangement. Writs of summons had already been sent out. Messengers left urgently for the Low Countries to tell Burghersh what had happened and to warn him of the delicate matters which he would now have to broach with the allies.[61]

Bishop Burghersh and his colleagues were already in extreme difficulty. After an uncomfortable sea journey interrupted by the assault on Cadzand, he had landed at Dordrecht in Holland at the end of November 1337. While the wool was being unloaded from the ships, the Bishop made his way through the waterways of Zeeland to Antwerp and overland to the small industrial town of Mechelen in central Brabant, where a gathering of anxious princes of the Low Countries was waiting to have the shifts of English policy explained to them. Events had cast Henry Burghersh in a particularly devious light. He resolved his difficulties in the same way as he had created then, by promising more than his master could give. For the German princes, the moment of danger would come in the spring when

French armies could be expected to appear on their southern borders. Burghersh appears to have persuaded them that Edward III would be with them by then. He certainly promised that a large part of their subsidies, which were already in arrear, would be paid by March. The promise had to be made if the alliance was to hold together, but the resources for meeting it were not there. Burghersh's officials calculated that he would need to raise £276,000.

When Burghersh got back to Holland he called the wool merchants before him at the little port of Gertruidenberg and demanded that they should provide him with £276,000 by 22 March 1338 'or the kingdom of England and all the other lands of the King were in danger of being lost'. Like most aristocrats of the fourteenth century, Burghersh could not conceive that men who lived as splendidly as Pole and Conduit had limited resources. The merchants were aghast. The sum demanded was more than they had agreed to raise for the whole 30,000 sacks of wool, let alone the 11,000 sacks which had been brought from England. They replied that they could not raise such a sum if they sold everything they possessed on the continent. The most that they could do was advance 100,000 marks (£66,666), the first instalment of the promised loan, before the wool had been sold instead of afterwards. Burghersh and his fellow councillors responded brutally. They requisitioned all the wool in store at Dordecht for the King's account. They believed that the merchants were under-estimating the value of it in order to make a greater profit for themselves. It was a grave miscalculation. The officials who now had to sell the wool were not very skilful salesmen. The political pressures on them forced them to dispose of it too quickly and in too small a sector of the market. Merchants from Germany and Brabant offered ready cash for low prices, and Burghersh raised no more than he could have got by accepting the merchants' offer of an advance. When the expenses had been paid there was only £41,679 left, less than a sixth of what was required. Moreover, the result was to destroy the bargain which Edward III had made with the wool merchants in England in the previous summer. Two more shipments of 10,000 sacks each were due to be made, but the merchants would now have nothing to do with them. The bonds which they were given in payment for their wool were dishonoured by the Crown and passed into currency at heavy discounts, a source of scandal and complaint in Parliament for many years.[62]

It was in these trying circumstances that Edward III's agents in the Low Countries learned about the suspension of hostilities which had been forced on him by the cardinals, and of the King's intention to negotiate with Philip VI. They were appalled. Writing from Nijmegen in Guelders, where he had consulted all the leaders of the alliance, Burghersh reported the unanimous opinion of the councillors about him that a truce would be a disaster. England's allies would have to be formally named in it and some of the lesser men among them were most anxious that their identities should not be revealed. If a truce were allowed to delay Edward's continental invasion the allies would become entitled to their subsidies long before they were due to muster their armies. They would then have no motive for honouring their promises. Even the informal cessation of hostilities which had already been declared was received with extreme irritation by the princes when they heard of it. Only the 'beautiful words' which Edward III had addressed to them prevented them from deserting him at once.[63]

Some of them, in spite of Edward's eloquence, had already opened discreet channels of communication with the other side. In particular the Duke of Brabant began to play a game of treachery and bluff which continued intermittently for the next three years. He made Bishop Burghersh sign a renewed undertaking that his treaty with the English King would be revealed to no one. At about the same time he secretly appointed a resident diplomatic agent at the French court, a knight of strong francophile sympathies called Leon of Crainheim. Leon told the King of France that his master had no quarrel with him, in spite of appearances. The Duke, it was said, had done nothing to help Edward's ambassadors except to allow them to lodge in his territory, something which he could hardly refuse since Edward was his kinsman and they paid their own expenses. Leon himself probably believed that this was true.[64]

War without fighting is a strain on morale and 'beautiful words' were becoming necessary in England too. During the autumn there had been a vigorous propaganda campaign in the provinces. The gentry, important local merchants and anyone else who might be thought influential were called to the county towns to hear the justice of the King's cause explained by specially appointed commissioners. For a wider public there were patriotic sermons on Sundays and feast days, and notices in churches listing the concessions which Edward III had made to avoid war and Philip had spurned:

On the very day after I received your instructions [Bishop Grandisson of Exeter wrote to the King in September 1337] . . . I went before the assembled community of the county of Exeter and explained to them personally the document which you sent me. Then I explained it to the common people in English. When I had done that, I interviewed separately the knights, the stewards of the manors, the bailiffs of the hundreds and liberties, and everyone else who was present ... so that at Michaelmas on the occasion of the Sheriff's next tour of the courts and leets of the hundreds the whole matter can in turn be explained to everybody else.'

In the following week the Bishop explained Edward's letter and its enclosed propaganda sheet to the congregation of his cathedral and then to an assembly of the clergy of the diocese attended by the Earl of Devon and a crowd of interested laymen, 'urging and exhorting them as persuasively as I could, illustrating my theme with reasoned argument, scriptural authority and apposite stories'.[65]

The effect of all this persuasion is difficult to gauge. The two cardinals had formed the view almost as soon as they arrived in England that the English people were opposed to the war. But the truth was less straightforward. There was widespread hatred of France and a general disposition to accept that Edward III had been shabbily treated by the French King. The chroniclers faithfully repeated Edward's own self-justifying account of the origins of the war, sometimes in his own words. There was less agreement about the manner in which Edward was prosecuting it. It was irresponsible, the Prior of Canterbury grumbled, to take an army to the continent when the coast of Kent so close to his own church was threatened with invasion. There were many who took the same view, particularly in the north of England, where Scotland was a more potent danger than France. The Scotch raids in northern England in October 1337, which occurred during the sessions of the Parliament, were a shock. It was incidents of this kind as well as the wisdom of hindsight that persuaded the Northumberland knight Thomas Gray that Edward III's continental alliances were an 'enormously expensive and unprofitable' waste of resources which would have been better employed in defending the north and completing the conquest of the Scots. Within the royal administration dissenters had been edged aside when Henry Burghersh and his friends had taken over the day-to-day conduct of English foreign policy, but they were never entirely silenced. William Montagu, Earl of Salisbury, had voiced his misgivings at the Great Council of August 1337. The aged royal cleric Adam Murimuth confided his to the pages of his chronicle. Yet what was impressive, and entirely contrary to the English political tradition, was that these intelligent and articulate representatives of the governing class closed ranks as soon as the decisions had been made. Once it had been decided by the Great Council to ratify the alliances made by Burghersh's embassy, opposition to the war, according to Gray, was regarded as treachery. That was in August 1337. At the end of September Parliament voted the Crown a remarkably generous subsidy of three tenths and fifteenths spread over the next three years. There was no precedent in English Parliamentary history for recurrent taxation on this scale. The essential political and strategic decisions were not challenged as they had been in 1297. Gray and Montagu fought with distinction in France and maintained their intense personal loyalty to Edward III even after events had justified their doubts.[66]

When Parliament next met in London on 3 February 1338, there were complaints about some of the government's marginal devices for raising money, but on the main issue the King received the advice that he wanted. There was to be no truce, only a voluntary abstention from fighting until further notice. The King's continental invasion was to proceed as planned unless Philip VI showed some interest in restoring Edward III's lost territories in France, and a date, 26 April 1338, was fixed for its departure. The wool contract having failed, Parliament authorized the government to get the remaining 20,000 sacks by other means. They were to be raised as a forced loan on the people of England. Up to half of each man's stock might be requisitioned and paid for at a price assessed according to quality, county by county. Payment would be made after two years.[67] As for the cardinals, they did not resort to the arsenal of spiritual weapons that they had exhibited in December. Edward III's ministers humoured them, going through the motions of diplomatic exchange. They drew up proposals for a formal truce, which members of the cardinals' staff took to France in March 1338. These were laid before the French King, but he found them to be 'insincere, hostile and dangerous to our realm' and rejected them out of hand.[68]

Philip made sure that his reasons were explained to his subjects. He was as sensitive as his rival was to the requirements of the home front and the financial consequences of ignoring it. There were masses, processions and prayers in France as in England, reminders of the fearless manner in which Philip VI was exposing his life for the defence of his realm. There were retrospects of recent history, as partial and self-serving as those which had been expounded by Bishop Grandisson to his audiences at Exeter: the King of England's treachery in breaking his oath of homage, his refusal to submit to impartial arbitration, his piratical raids on French shipping and his plans for aggressive warfare in alliance with France's enemies in Germany; all, it was said, borne with marvellous patience by the French King until the provocation had become too great to be overlooked.[69]

*

The English did not wage a war of reconquest in Saintonge in the autumn of 1337 as perhaps they had been expected to do. Instead, Ingham's men recrossed the Dordogne well upstream, raiding the town of Sainte-Foy-la-Grande on the way. They then boldy invaded the Agenais from the north, and crossed the River Lot near Villeneuve. This circuitous route avoided the strong French garrisons which blocked the Garonne valley at La Réole and Marmande. Towards the end of the year they laid siege to Agen, the provincial capital and the seat of the French Seneschal. The story of this siege is very obscure. All that is known about it is that it lasted several weeks and failed. The siege was probably raised by force in late January or early February 1338. The English withdrew eastward away from the enemy and vanished into southern Gascony.[70]

Ingham had conquered no territory, but his enterprise touched on a sensitive nerve. The Agenais was the obvious point of entry for French armies invading the Garonne valley. Possession of it was vital to them. Yet their conquest of it in the 1320s had never been entirely complete. In 1338 they occupied all the significant towns but the English retained allies and influence as well as the incomparable castle at Penne on the Lot. With these advantages they had been able to exercise many of the powers of government side by side with the parallel administration of the French Crown. Edward III granted and regranted land, appointed officers and assigned revenues. Patronage mattered.[71] Even in Agen itself the English had found friends and fifth columnists among prominent citizens, who fought in the army of Oliver Ingham. French officials took firm measures against their property and their families, but reported nervously to their superiors their doubts about the loyalty and security of the place. Here, as in so many provinces of late medieval France, international politics were reduced to the play of local interests, the jostling of rival lords for territory and power, the recurrent feuds of the towns with the barons of the outlying districts. Both French and English armies found themselves fighting the battles of their friends as often as their own.[72]

Philip VI had appointed two 'captains-general' for the south-west to hold his position on the march during the winter: Etienne le Galois de la Baume, the Master of the Royal Archers, who had already had one tour of duty there early in 1337; and a judicial officer of the royal household called Simon d'Arquèry. Their appointment, on 13 November 1337, was probably the government's response to Oliver Ingham's raids. Philip had in mind heavy police work, not a full-scale winter campaign, and most of their time was spent trying to impose order on the shifting loyalties of the Agenais with a mixture of political pressure and military force.[73]

The extent of their problem, which was never perfectly understood in Paris, can be illustrated by the careers of two prominent anglophile lords of this nominally French province. Arnaud de Durfort, lord of Frespech and his son, also called Arnaud, were petty lords of the Lot valley whose ambitions to become greater ones depended largely on the friendship of Edward III. Moreover, they also held valuable properties in the south-west of the duchy around Bayonne, an area firmly under English control. They therefore had abiding reasons to value the English connection. Arnaud *père* had visited England many times and had fought in Scotland. He also had modest business interests in London, dabbling in the grain and wool trades. Edward III showered him with favours which grew more splendid as the onset of war increased his dependence on such men. He granted him a large pension, paid the vast arrears of his war wages extending back through three reigns, and in August 1337 appointed him and his son joint captains of Penne. When the captains-general arrived in the Agenais in February 1338, Arnaud *père* was in England lobbying the King and the Westminster Parliament for very extensive rights, long coveted, over the outlying districts of Penne. Nothing short of the capture of Penne and a permanent military occupation was likely to destroy English influence in the Lot valley while this man flourished.[74] Amanieu du Fossat was probably a more characteristic figure, whose loyalties were more finely calculated and whose outlook was more narrowly limited by the bounds of the province. This unscrupulous and violent hill-baron had briefly been Seneschal of Aquitaine under Edward II, until he was dismissed for repeated criminal violence. He held a well-sited castle at Madaillan, a short distance north of Agen, from which he had for many years conducted a vendetta against the citizens of the town. Amanieu signed a convention with the French captains-general shortly after their arrival, only to repudiate it as soon as the ink was dry. He withstood a siege of six weeks before surrendering for a second time on 16 March 1338. But the French could not offer men like him what they really wanted, in his case the right to bully the citizens of loyal Agen. The persistence of these apparently trivial local vendettas virtually guaranteed that one side or the other would ally itself with the English dynasty. Amanieu was already back in the English camp by July, and the consuls of the town were beseeching Philip VI to finish with him.[75]

The main military operation of the winter was the work of Gaston de Foix on the southern march. During February 1338 he invaded the Tursan, next door to his principality of Béarn, with 6,400 men of his own and a contingent of troops brought by the Seneschal of Toulouse. They

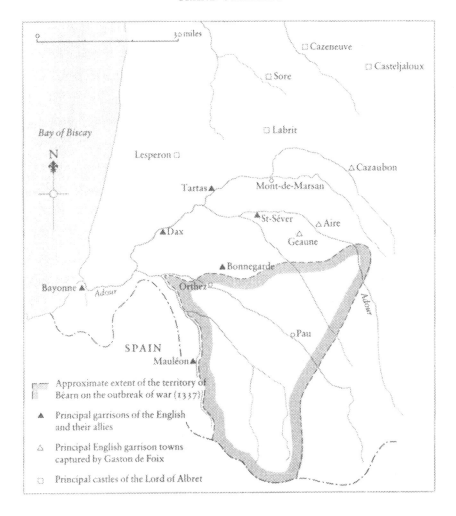

4 Gascony: the southern march, 1337–9

captured the *bastide* of Geaune on 5 February 1338, then marched on the little town of Aire-sur-l'Adour. The Captain of this place was persuaded to surrender for a bribe of 1,000 *livres* and a pension of 50 *livres* per annum. The fortifications were razed. Cazaubon surrendered on 5 March 1338 apparently without a fight. Other places followed.[76] Gaston's campaign illustrated what might have been achieved in the Agenais and the Garonne valley with greater resources of men and money. His conquests paid for themselves, for he was allowed to annex them to his principality in lieu of wages.[77] The conquest of the strategically more important regions further north did not. D'Arquèry and de la Baume were obliged to spend much of their time squeezing money from the inhabitants of Languedoc by methods which were not calculated to make the war popular there: levying forgotten taxes, exacting fines for breaches of the coinage regulations, selling pardons for usury and licences to buy noble fiefs, and settling old scores of the Crown for whatever could be had. They raised enough to keep their army in being and to hold most of what Philip VI already controlled, but that was all.[78]

The French struck their most effective blows against England at sea. In February 1338 Philip VI appointed as Admiral of France one of his financial officials, Nicholas Béhuchet. Béhuchet was a Norman, a short, fat man of low birth whose appointment was not popular at court. But those who said that he knew 'more about book-keeping than naval warfare' seriously under-estimated this brave and intelligent amateur. On 24 March 1338, some six weeks after his appointment, he led a mixed force of galleys and barges from Calais in a bold and successful raid on Portsmouth. His ships arrived without warning flying English flags from their masts. In spite of the importance of Portsmouth as a naval and commercial harbour it had no walls and the French met very little resistance there. Landing parties burned the whole town except for the parish church and a hospital. They then made off with impunity. From Portsmouth Béhuchet made for Jersey, where, on 26 March 1338, his men landed and destroyed crops and buildings over the whole of the eastern part of the island. They almost captured Gorey Castle, the island's principal fortress. These successes were particularly galling for the English government because their excellent intelligence service had given them two months' warning that something of the sort was planned, and had suggested a probable date which was correct to within a week. Attempts to intercept the raid had been made, and failed.[79]

The attack on Portsmouth revealed how vulnerable the English coastline was, with its many small weakly-defended harbours. Béhuchet's fleet, although it was described by the English chroniclers as enormous, must in fact have been quite modest. Such raids (and there were to be more of them) had a strategic value out of all proportion to the physical damage which they inflicted. Because intelligence could not be counted on and the raids occurred at unpredictable times and places, enormous resources of manpower, equipment and money had to be devoted to guarding the whole length of the coast. The main features of the English system of coastal defence dated back to the 1290s. The practice was to designate a strip of land within 6 (sometimes 12) leagues of the coast as 'maritime land'. Men living in this area were exempt from military service away from their homes, and their victuals and property were not to be requisitioned without special instructions. Instead they were required to serve as a coastal militia under the command of local magnates who were appointed as 'keepers of maritime lands' in their counties. For calling them to their duty there were beacons and men permanently manning them not only on the clifftops where great pyramids of wood were a traditional sight in time of war but, from August 1338 onwards, on hills extending inland for a considerable distance. In the inland counties men were expected to hold themselves ready to reinforce the coastal levies quickly at the vital point. Counties were grouped together for this purpose. The men of Berkshire and Wiltshire, for example, were directed to hold themselves ready to come to the aid of Hampshire. Inevitably human failings vitiated this tidy scheme. Panic bred confusion as well as fear. The going on English medieval roads was slow, especially in winter and at night. Militia service was unpopular, expensive and widely evaded. The system failed completely in 1338 and its effectiveness in later years was spasmodic at best.[80]

The mere attempt to make it work greatly reduced the capacity of England to make war on the continent. As the men of Devon and Cornwall explained, because galleys had been seen cruising off every headland, because they had countless harbours, all open and unwalled, and because the land, particularly in Cornwall, was infertile, they had nothing to contribute to the war effort. This was no doubt the worst case. It was nevertheless true that the army which Edward III recruited in 1338 to take to Brabant was much smaller than the army which he had planned, and that one of the main reasons for this was the demands of coastal defence. Recruiting for the continental expedition had to be cancelled in Cornwall and Devon because the men were needed for the coasts. Although every coastal county from the Wash to Land's End was called on to furnish contingents to accompany the King abroad only three, Essex, Kent and Dorset, actually did so.[81]

The French gave serious thought to the strategic purposes of sea power, and it is tempting to suggest that they knew what they were doing. But probably they did not. Nicholas Béhuchet prepared a memorandum for the French royal Council which showed that he perfectly understood the economic effects of maritime warfare. A powerful fleet, he pointed out, could damage the lucrative English trades in wine, fish and salt and by destroying the livelihoods of English seamen could make it difficult for Edward III to man his ships. With control of the sea, the French would also be able to provide more effective assistance to the Scots. But Béhuchet said nothing about missions of destruction against English coastal towns. He probably regarded these as mere morale-boosters and sources of plunder to reward loyal seamen.[82]

In spite of its growing financial embarrassment (civil servants' salaries were stopped for a year in December), the French government had already committed itself to fight at sea on a vastly increased scale in 1338. At the end of October 1337 their representatives entered into a contract to hire a fleet of twenty large Mediterranean galleys from a private syndicate of Genoese shipowners organized by Ayton Doria. Rather later, a similar contract for seventeen galleys was made with another syndicate whose members were Genoese exiles in Monaco brought together by the Grimaldi family. Doria belonged to one of the great Ghibelline families of Genoa. The Grimaldi and their friends were Guelphs. But the pursuit of lucre united them. The galley captains were handsomely paid and were promised a half share of all the booty taken. The contracts called for them to be available in the French Channel ports by the end of May 1338 and to serve for at least three months after that. For service in the Bay of Biscay Philip hired yet another fleet from the Castilians, the major maritime power of the Atlantic seaboard, who contracted to supply a squadron of twenty galleys. In conjunction with Philip's own forces the arrival of all of these ships would have brought the strength of the French navy to about eighty galleys, not to speak of oared barges and sailing ships.[83]

By December 1337 there had been no authorized exports of English wool to Flanders for well over a year. No licences were granted, not even for friendship or ready money. Ships were stopped and searched for contraband at sea. Exporters were required to put up bonds which would be forfeit unless proof were furnished that the wool had found its way to the King's friends. Some wool must have entered the county by circuitous routes, but if so it entered in small quantities and at high prices. Distress mounted as textile workers were laid off in growing numbers and the trades which nourished them withered. In the new year the French Crown finally lost control of Flanders. It is one of the few examples in history of a wholly successful economic blockade.[84]

Bruges, the traditional fomenter of Flemish rebellions, played a passive role. The leadership of the Flemings was assumed by Ghent, the largest of the towns, the most disputatious in defending its autonomy and privileges, and the only one whose walls had not been dismantled by the victorious French in the early part of the century. It is probable that Ghent, which lacked the banking and shipping interests of Bruges, was also the worst affected by the English embargo.

In the early months of 1337 the main Flemish advocate of an accommodation with England was an urban knight called Sohier de Courtrai, a well-known figure in the politics of Ghent who was influential enough to merit a pension from both sides. According to French accounts, which are to some extent corroborated by the English records, he was trying to persuade the men of Ghent and Bruges to declare for Edward's continental coalition and was buying friends with English money. But Sohier was indiscreet. During the early summer of 1337 he had some conversations with English agents at Ghent which were reported to the French government. As a result he was arrested by the Count's officers on 6 July 1337 and charged with treason.[85] The affair of Sohier de Courtrai opened the eyes of the French government to the weakness of their position in Flanders. It also made that position weaker still. For as a citizen of Ghent Sohier was entitled to trial before the courts of the town and ought not to have been arrested on the King's orders. Philip VI's ministers were taken aback by the strength of the reaction. They were well aware of the delicate condition of Flanders and of the importance of placating public opinion there. Although they did not release Sohier de Courtrai they made other concessions which might have had even wider appeal. In August 1337 it was decided that the indemnities for past rebellions, now some two years in arrears, would be reduced. A commission of no less than five senior royal councillors was sent to Bruges to announce this concession. Further reductions followed quickly, and in November 1337, after Walter Mauny's descent on the Scheldt estuary, the Bishop of Thérouanne arrived with fresh messages from the King of France promising that the indemnities would be not only reduced but entirely remitted if he could be satisfied of the Flemings' loyalty.[86]

It was not enough. In the economic catastrophe which was now engulfing the Flemish towns the indemnities could not have been enforced anyway. What was needed was the restoration of the cloth industry, and all that France could offer in that direction was first refusal over her own production of wool, which was small and of low quality. While the French ministers bargained for the friendship of the towns, unidentified, perhaps unofficial, representatives of the Flemings were engaged in secret discussions with the English agent John de Woume at Flushing. These discussions almost certainly concerned the terms on which Edward III would allow wool to be imported into Flanders. The pressure on the Flemings grew stronger in December, with the arrival of half a year's wool crop at

Dordrecht and the overt threat that unless the Flemings submitted the English would establish a staple in Brabant to the lasting detriment of the commerce of Bruges.[87]

At the end of December 1337 there was a revolution in Flanders. The exact course of events is difficult to follow. There was a large armed demonstration in Ghent on 28 December in a meadow by the west wall of the town, outside the Cistercian convent of Biloke. This was followed, on 3 January 1338, by the appointment of an emergency government of the town comprising five 'captains'. Comprehensive controls of food prices were introduced. A curfew was imposed and firm measures taken against disorder. Persons out of sympathy with the movement, many of whom had fled to the churches or to suburban villages, were proscribed. Bruges and Ypres, the other two great towns of Flanders, followed the lead of Ghent.[88]

The leader of the revolution from the outset, and the effective ruler of Flanders for most of the next seven years, was a remarkable patrician demagogue, Jacob van Artevelde. Van Artevelde had not previously played a notable part in the affairs of Flanders, and very little is known about his origins. He was a merchant of Ghent in late middle age. He was rich. He held no public office even in his own town except that he was one of the five captains of the emergency government. Yet no one doubted that he was 'maistre et souverain' (Froissart's phrase). His power rested on his political skills and on the force of his personality, which was felt not only in Ghent but also in the communities of its traditional rivals, Bruges and Ypres. He was a most persuasive speaker who exercised a hypnotic influence over his colleagues and over the mass of craftsmen and journeymen. Moreover, van Artevelde could use more ruthless forms of persuasion when he needed to. He walked the streets with a bodyguard of thugs, suppressed the least signs of opposition and on occasion had the authors of it beaten up or murdered. Jacob van Artevelde has gone down in historical legend as a scion of the common people and a champion of freedom. He was in fact a ruthless autocrat whose rule was made tolerable only by the desperate situation in which Flanders found herself at the outset of the Anglo-French war.

Van Artevelde's policy was summed up in the words attributed to him by a French chronicler. 'Without the goodwill of the King of England,' he is supposed to have said, 'we shall die, for Flanders lives by making cloth and cloth cannot be made without wool. It follows that we must make a friend of England.'[89] This did not necessarily mean an alliance. In these early days, before his ambitions grew, van Artevelde was looking for the line of least resistance. It might be that the neutrality of Flanders would be enough to satisfy Edward III as well as to avert the vengeance of Philip VI.

Both sides reacted rapidly to the news of the Flemish revolution. The King of France, who was in Paris, summoned his army to meet at Amiens by 20 March 1338, the best that could be done in the middle of winter. The Bishop of Cambrai was told to proceed urgently to Flanders to reason with the representatives of Ghent, Bruges and Ypres and if necessary to make concessions to them. But the English King's agents moved faster. Henry Burghersh and the rest of Edward's Council in the Low Countries were at Nijmegen when they heard about the events in Ghent. They travelled south at once and within two weeks were in conference with representatives of the new regime at Louvain in the duchy of Brabant. They had reached an agreement in principle by the end of January which was substantially accepted by all the main towns of Flanders. The towns undertook that they would lend assistance to neither side and would allow neither army rights of passage through their territory. Flemish ports would no longer be used for supplying the Scots or for raiding English shipping, and no attempt would be made to interfere with the passage of the English army up the Scheldt to Antwerp in the summer. In effect Flanders would remain neutral in the coming war in spite of its status as a part of France. In return, the English embargo on the sale of wool to the Flemings was to be lifted. It was a considerable diplomatic and strategic success for Edward III. The first consignments of wool were received from Dordrecht early in March.[90]

Philip VI was outraged. His first reaction was to order the execution of Sohier de Courtrai, who was still being held in prison. This order was carried out on 21 March 1338. On the same day, two French ecclesiastics acting as papal commissioners but on the instructions of the French government pronounced the excommunication of the whole lay population of Ghent. On the 23rd it was announced that the Constable and the Marshal of France had been ordered to see to the demolition of the walls of the town. These foolish outbursts merely advertised Philip's impotence. The call to arms to suppress the Flemings was not popular, least of all in the neighbouring provinces. In Artois, gangs of men toured the county organizing forcible resistance to the impressment of townsmen for the French army. The gathering which was due to take place at Amiens in March had to be abandoned so that the Crown's resources could be conserved to meet the greater threat from Edward III in the summer. As a result, the only forces available to the Constable and the Marshal for enforcing the will of Philip VI on Ghent were the garrisons of Tournai and

Lille and some late reinforcements. The Count of Flanders himself was at Bruges with his own retainers and household men; in addition there was an enthusiastic but small and disorganized army of Flemish noblemen willing to fight for their Count and their King.

Some of these men appeared before Ghent on the eve of Easter (11 April). They were washed away by the opening of the dykes. Others occupied the little town of Biervliet. Van Artevelde and his friends reacted to this threat with the vigour which became characteristic of them. They marched on Biervliet with the militia of Ghent at the end of April and routed the Count's allies with much bloodshed. Van Artevelde's men next entered Bruges, where they joined forces with the townsmen and fought a pitched battle with the Count's men in the streets and markets. Ypres, which had shown some sign of backsliding, was attacked in early May and reduced to obedience. So ended the counter-revolution. To suppress the Flemings now, after the manner of 1328, would have required an enormous French army in addition to the one which was required for the defence of France against Edward III. On 13 June 1338 the French government acknowledged defeat. Philip VI pardoned the townsmen of Flanders for dealing with the King of England and formally recognized their neutrality. He professed to have been moved by the 'great sufferings and hardships of the people of Ghent for want of their trade and livelihood'. The truth was that if Philip had conceded any less the Flemings might well have abandoned their neutrality and joined forces with his enemies.[91]

The negotiation of the treaty of neutrality with the Flemings was the last great service which that ingenious diplomat Henry Burghersh performed for his master before the arrival of the English army on the continent. It remained only to observe the legal conventions. Edward had sworn fealty to Philip VI in 1331 and could not invade his realm without renouncing it. So, at some time in the spring of 1338, probably in May, Burghersh travelled to Paris with his household, carrying the letter of defiance which he had brought with him from England months before. On the afternoon of his arrival the Bishop appeared before Philip VI and his court in the palace on the Island in full episcopal vestments, mitre and crozier and presented the letter to him. Philip handed it to one of his secretaries who read it out. The document, which addressed the King as 'Philip de Valois', declared that he had intruded himself on to the throne of France in 1328 in spite of Edward's own, stronger, claim. 'For which cause', it continued, 'we give you notice that we intend to conquer our inheritance by our own force of arms.' The scene was recalled many years later by one of Philip's household knights who was present. Philip was in good humour, courteous and unperturbed. He turned to the Bishop, smiled and said: 'Bishop, you have performed admirably the task for which you came. Your letters are of such a kind as need no answer. You may go when you wish.' Burghersh went.[92]

The threat might have been mere bombast. During the spring and early summer of 1338 Edward III had to stretch the resources of his small kingdom to fight on four fronts simultaneously: on the south and east coasts of England, in Scotland, in the Low Countries and in Gascony.

Gascony was undoubtedly the theatre which suffered most. The war had damaged its economy more gravely and undermined its institutions more completely than anyone at Westminster can have appreciated. There was a serious shortage of provisions in the towns. The Bordelais and the coastal regions under firm English control produced very little grain and in wartime conditions it was very difficult to import it from further inland. This abiding problem of the defence of Gascony (it had been the same in 1324) was aggravated in 1338 by a long drought which had destroyed much of the previous year's harvest of grain, wine and oil throughout south-western France. From the beginning of 1338 onward it was necessary to ship large quantities of grain from England, a major operation and as time went on an increasingly dangerous one.[93] As the French became bolder in exploiting their superiority at sea, communications between England and Gascony became progressively more difficult. The port of La Rochelle, which the French had begun to develop as a naval base during the previous year, was ideally situated for intercepting English and Gascon shipping as it rounded the island of Oloron. A small French squadron stationed there in August 1337 had been quickly worsted by the men of Bayonne. But at the end of the year it was reinforced and from then until August 1338 a large fleet of French and Castilian galleys was able to cruise with impunity near the mouth of the Gironde. On 23 August 1338, the largest food convoy yet sent to the duchy was attacked by eighteen galleys off Talmont at the entrance to the Gironde. Two of the ships, including one of the largest, were captured and their precious cargoes lost.[94]

The disruption of inland communications was the single most important reason for Oliver Ingham's intensifying financial difficulties. The income of the duchy was derived in large part from tolls and customs levied on the great waterways. Banditry and military campaigns destroyed crops and choked off the movement of goods. The traffic in wine from the *haut pays* through the Gascon ports fell in the first year of fighting to about one-fifth of its peacetime level. The impact on the fortunes of the Bordeaux government was catastrophic. The one surviving set of accounts for this period shows that in the financial year which began on 29 September 1338 only about one-eighth of the wages due to troops could be settled in cash. The rest were paid by debentures or grants in kind. In the previous year the situation is likely to have been even worse. Edward III was in no position to help. In the same financial year the government of the duchy received form England a total of 9,120 pounds of Bordeaux (£1,824) and 196 sacks of wool, a tiny proportion of what Edward was spending in the north. John of Norwich, for example, received no wages for more than six months after he left London. When the King ordered the Exchequer to advance him £200 upon his wages and expenses, they replied that they did not have £200. The money was eventually advanced to him by the Bardi. But John's men were not paid until February 1339, by which time they had been in Gascony for almost a year and a half. The predictable results followed. Morale fell. English troops rioted in Bordeaux. Men slipped away or, worse, sold themselves and their strongholds to the other side. When Gaston de Foix invaded the upper Adour early in 1338 the main reason for the lack of serious resistance was that the defenders were unpaid. The commander of Saint-Sever, the greatest fortress of the region, complained in January 1338 that he had been maintaining 500 men-at-arms and 1,000 infantry at his own expense for many months and was owed the enormous sum of 11,400 pounds of Bordeaux. It is surprising that he remained loyal. Others sold their strongholds and sloped away.[95]

During February and March several prominent Gascons arrived in England in the hope of bending the King's ear. There was a lot of pressure on Edward's resources. He had an army of about 4,000 men in Scotland under the command of the earls of Arundel and Salisbury. They had been besieging Dunbar since the beginning of the year. In order to assemble this force it had been necessary to draw on the retinues of three earls and many lesser magnates and to recruit heavily not only in the northern counties which had traditionally manned the armies of the border and Scotland, but throughout England. Then, on 26 February, orders had been issued for the recruitment of another army for the Low Countries. These envisaged the raising of about 4,500 men in the counties, and probably about the same number from the retinues of the magnates, all of whom were to be ready at Norwich no later than 12 May. All of these men had to be raised south of the Trent. Nevertheless, on 1 March 1338 further writs went out for men to assemble at Portsmouth by 29 April to assist the King's hard-pressed lieges in Gascony. Edward seems to have had in mind a force of about 1,000 men under the command of an important magnate. William

Clinton, Earl of Huntingdon, was suggested. It was not a great army, but it represented a significant additional demand on the resources of the southern and western counties and Wales. The men would have to carry with them their victuals and supplies for a considerable period. The Council calculated that seventy large ships would be required.[96]

In late March 1338 John of Norwich's brother arrived in Bordeaux from England bringing the joyful news with him together with a grandiloquent letter in which the King promised his Gascon lieges that their loyalty would very shortly be rewarded. With stronger cards in his hand than he had held since the outset of the war, Oliver Ingham set about persuading waverers among the Gascon nobility that they could now count on the English King's commitment to his continental dominions. Even the inscrutable Bernard-Aiz, lord of Albret, who had hitherto succeeded in remaining aloof from both sides, gave him to understand that he would declare for Edward III.[97]

It was fortunate for the English that, when the French commanders opened their campaign in the spring, their conduct of it was hesitant and unimpressive. There were to be two thrusts at the duchy; one from the south-east by the Agenais and the Garonne valley; the other the long-planned offensive by Saintonge and the north shore of the Gironde. The captains-general took command of the first. But they were prevented from penetrating beyond the Agenais by the fierce resistance of the great English fortress at Penne. They laid siege to Penne in mid-April 1338. It is entirely unclear why. Its capture could not have been decisive. Of all the English strongholds in the south-west it was likely to be the most difficult to capture quickly. Originally built by that famous castle-builder Richard Cœur-de-Lion and carefully modernized on several occasions since, Penne stood on a rock some 300 feet above the River Lot. Its situation made it impossible to undermine and its walls were beyond the reach of most siege artillery. The French soldiers sat outside the walls for more than ten weeks until, early in July, they abandoned the siege and marched away.[98]

The Saintonge offensive was better conceived, for Philip's ministers had devoted much care to its planning ever since the previous autumn. But it was hardly more successful. The command was shared between two captains: Savary de Vivonne was a rich local knight with a long, undistinguished military career before him; his colleague, Jean ('Mouton') de Blainville was a Norman, a venerable royal official in his sixties. They divided their forces among a number of separate sieges. Their main object was the capture of Blaye at the head of the Gironde, which would have been a great prize. This ambitious venture involved not only investing the town on the landward side but cutting it off by water from its source of reinforcements and supplies in Bordeaux. Several galleys were moved round from La Rochelle and moored in the Gironde off the town.

Oliver Ingham and John of Norwich ignored the doings of the captains-general and concentrated on the closer threat. They gathered a small field army by stripping the garrisons of Bordeaux, Libourne and Saint-Émilion and drawing on the retinues of loyal noblemen of the Bordelais. This improvised force marched on Montlaur, a castle (now vanished) which was probably on the Garonne a short distance upstream of Blaye. Early in July they broke the French siege, suddenly descending on the besiegers in boats and scattering them. The French withdrew northward. In the middle of July they were found besieging Montendre, the last significant English stronghold in the interior of Saintonge, whose Béarnais commander had held out in his isolated position since the beginning of the war. Ingham tried to relieve this place too. But he was either beaten off or abandoned the attempt before reaching it. Montendre surrendered at the beginning of August and was immediately demolished. It was the solitary French success of the campaign.[99]

By now the Earl of Huntingdon's army of relief should have arrived. Its absence must have been a grave embarrassment to the Seneschal. But Edward III's plans had been dogged by misfortune and misjudgement. In April there had been signs of severe strain, the consequence of trying to achieve too much at once. The recruiting officers' returns were very poor, for both quantity and quality. Victuals had proved to be a considerable problem. Men were concealing their stocks and in parts of England forcibly resisted the purveyor's officers. Some of the victuals which they did succeed in collecting for Gascony were stolen by dishonest royal servants. Some of them had to be sold to pay the wages of the seamen. The rest was diverted to Orwell to feed the army of the Low Countries. In early May, neither men nor supplies had reached Portsmouth. Both continental expeditions had to be postponed several times. Although shortage of men and supplies contributed substantially to this outcome, it was the shortage of shipping which was in the end decisive. Edward III had still not learned how difficult and time-consuming it was to requisition ships and impress sailors. At Hartlepool, an officer of the northern Admiral reported, a request for information about ships of 30 tons or more had produced the answer that there were none, 'but I proved that answer false.' At Ravenser, near Hull, the bailiff 'would not comply with the King's orders nor supply the information which I required'. At Hull eight ships were requisitioned but escaped to sea almost at once. At Whitby another eight ships were seized but their crews struck and refused to sail. Explanations of the delay, increasingly awkward, were sent to Edward's embarrassed agents in the Low Countries.[100]

Even worse, the leaders of the army and several thousand men were still, at the end of May, engaged in besieging Dunbar. The garrison, under the command of 'Black Agnes' Randolph, had resisted the efforts of Edward's soldiers and siege engineers for four months, hurling defiance and abuse from the ramparts. Edward had her brother, the Earl of Moray, who was his prisoner, sent north and threatened to have him executed under the walls unless she surrendered. But she was unmoved and Edward did not carry out his threat.[101]

Whitsun in 1338 fell on 31 May. Edward III celebrated the feast at the abbey of Bury St Edmunds, close to his army, which was assembling at Norwich. There were some difficult deliberations with his Council. Dunbar was the only important stronghold which held out for David Bruce south of the Firth of Forth, a dangerous point of entry for goods and men from France, but the siege would have to be abandoned if numbers were to be made up for the crossing to the Low Countries, let alone Gascony. So, on 13 June, the earls of Arundel and Salisbury folded their tents and withdrew. Arundel remained in the north to organize the defence of the border. Salisbury joined the King in East Anglia. The plans for the Gascon expedition were left alone but it was apparent that they had become entirely unrealistic. On 19 June 1338, still short of ships, troops and above all money, Edward cancelled it.[102]

In military terms, the cancellation of Huntingdon's expedition had little impact. By the time the news of it reached Gascony the French campaign in the region had already failed and there was very little time left to them in which to make amends. A general conference of French commanders in the south occurred at La Réole in mid-July 1338. Thereafter, their offensive disintegrated into a number of separate raids in the Agenais and the southern Landes. In the following month all of them, including the two captains-general, the counts of Foix and Armagnac and the men of Languedoc were urgently required in the north. The strength of the French in the south-west was once again reduced to its main garrisons.[103]

Politically, however, it was a severe setback. The barons of the duchy made their calculations and drew the appropriate lessons. Bernard-Aiz of Albret, in spite of his promises earlier in the year, never stirred in the English King's interests. Although Edward III appointed him joint Seneschal of Aquitaine on 1 July 1338 he never assumed any duties and the appointment was allowed to lapse. Philip VI also summoned Bernard-Aiz to join his armies. The lord of Albret's answer is not recorded, but although he carried out some minor raids on Philip's account, he did not fight in the French King's armies. He waited on events. The other lords who had declared themselves for Edward III at the same time did likewise.[104]

CHAPTER VIII

Cambrai and the Thiérache
1338–1339

Edward III's long-prepared armada sailed in the early hours of 16 July 1338, seven weeks late. The King himself and about half the army embarked at Ipswich into ships assembled in the pool of Orwell. The rest embarked at Great Yarmouth. A third fleet bringing late-comers and horses left Great Yarmouth at the end of the month. This great gathering of ships, 350 in all, with nearly 12,000 crew, carried to the continent in the space of about a fortnight a relatively small army. There were about 1,400 men-at-arms, and nearly 3,000 archers together with their horses, equipment and victuals. It was for the most part an army of volunteers. All the men-at-arms served voluntarily and all of them, earls, bannerets, knights and squires, received double the usual wages of war. The archers, whose support for the war mattered less, received the ordinary rates. Rather more than half of them were conscripted men. Most of the others were hired privately to serve in noble retinues. But no less than 445 men from different parts of the country arrived at the ports of embarkation of their own accord and formed themselves into free companies. Edward and his men landed at Antwerp on 22 July 1338, watched from the foreshore by a crowd of onlookers, many of whom had travelled from far away to see such a spectacle.[1]

At about the same time the Archbishop of Canterbury and the Bishop of Durham arrived together with the two cardinals in Amiens to negotiate a truce. It was pure pretence. The English King had not forgotten the shock of the previous winter when the cardinals had threatened to excommunicate him and to annul his treaties with the German princes. Some of these would have been only too pleased to have another excuse for non-performance. Edward could not afford to give the impression that he had lost interest in a peaceful solution. So Stratford and Bury proceeded from Amiens to Paris and were received there by Philip VI at the beginning of August. They had little to say and made it clear to Philip that they did not intend to do anything quickly. They wished to wait until further instructions had been received from Antwerp. Perhaps Philip would appoint a committee of his Council to negotiate with them in some convenient place. How seriously Philip himself took these proposals is not clear, but he did appoint a committee of his Council and directed that the discussions should take place close to the Flemish border at Arras.[2]

The French King had other preoccupations. He had spent the whole summer in his capital receiving regular and on the whole accurate reports of the difficulties of his enemies. He knew that there had been serious problems about supplying the English army: victuals were proving hard to collect both in England and in the Low Countries and forage for horses would not be available in quantity until July or August. Armour was thought to be in short supply in the English army. Friends in Germany had told Philip that all was not well between Edward and his allies. There had apparently been certain difficulties about the payment of subsidies and Louis of Bavaria was threatening to withdraw from the alliance. On 26 July 1338, when Philip learned that the English had finally landed, the muster of the French army was fixed for 8 August. The response was not wholly satisfactory, for except in the frontier provinces of the north the threat was not even now treated seriously by the mass of the French population. There were persistent rumours that Philip was negotiating with his rival and many Frenchmen assumed that a truce would be patched up before the crisis broke. The arrival of Stratford and Bury made these rumours very credible.

Philip could only deny it and dictate letters from the Bois de Vincennes in terms which betrayed his mounting frustration and finally produced some effect. By the last week of August the French were more or less ready on their northern frontier. The Constable, Raoul, Count of Eu, was at Tournai on the march of Flanders and Hainault, about 60 miles from Antwerp. He had with him a strong French garrison, the armed contingents of the town, the Count of Flanders and refugees from van Artevelde's revolution, most of whom were gentlemen trained in arms. Men were working on the walls and gates. Forty miles away at Cambrai the Bishop had been instructed by the Pope (at the prompting of the French government) to defend his city. The main body of the French army assembled on the Somme at Amiens and Saint-Quentin. Philip himself had arrived at Amiens by 24 August 1338 with the Oriflamme, the crimson banner of Saint-Denis which the great Benedictine Abbey invested with mystic significance and ceremonially presented to each French King on the eve of war: 'May the Lord by his Grace and by the intercession of your glorious patron St Denis grant you victory over all your enemies.'[3]

At Arras, Stratford and Bury installed themselves in comfort with a household and diplomatic staff of more than 200. Desultory negotiations had begun by the end of the month, but the two English bishops were distracted by greater events elsewhere. Stratford's household became a busy centre for intelligence-gathering. Runners were sent to Amiens to report on the progress of the French muster and to Paris to listen out for gossip about the intentions of the enemy. Dispatches regularly left for Antwerp with reports of conditions in the French frontier towns, on shipping in the Norman ports and on the state of public opinion in Flanders and Brabant.[4]

The King's sojourn in Antwerp began disastrously. On his first night in the town he narrowly escaped death when the lodgings which had been hired for him were accidentally burned down by his servants.[5] Once he had recovered his composure, Edward set about measuring his resources against his commitments. As a result of the efforts of the Bishop of Lincoln, he could in theory call on his allies to furnish him with a further 7,000 armoured men, in addition to the troops which he had brought with him from England and a steady trickle of soldiers of fortune who arrived during the next three months. But before the allies appeared they were entitled to be paid. Their fees were already greatly in arrears. In addition there were the wages of their men, which had to be paid for two months in advance at the onset of the campaign. The prospects of Edward's continental expedition depended entirely on the forced loan of 20,000 sacks of wool which Parliament had authorized in February. The collection of this wool had been in progress since the end of February and arrangements had been made to store it in the east-coast ports and ship it for the King's account to Antwerp. In order to enable the King to sell it to his best advantage all other exports were forbidden unless licensed, and licenses were granted only to Edward's most favoured creditors and to the subjects of his most important allies. What the King expected to find, therefore, when he reached Antwerp in July were warehouses filled with wool which might, if skilfully sold, be expected to raise between £150,000 and £200,000. In fact the warehouses were almost empty. No wool at all had been shipped until 5 July 1338, less than a fortnight before the embarkation of the English army. Only 1,846 sacks had been shipped by the end of July. Initially it seemed that the explanation was want of shipping, the result of the government's requisitioning of so many ships for use as troop carriers. The ships in which Edward and his army had crossed the North Sea were at once sent back to fetch wool. But the real problem, as it transpired, was that less than 3,000 sacks had been collected. The forced loan had been evaded and resisted with almost complete success. There had been a sudden and unexplained shortage of sacks in which to pack it. The collectors had been dilatory, incompetent and corrupt. There is nothing surprising about these endemic vices of medieval bureaucracy. What is perhaps surprising is that Edward had no inkling of what had happened until he arrived with his army in Brabant. He characteristically blamed his servants. 'I have been badly advised,' he complained bitterly to the Bishop of Lincoln. It was the beginning of the Bishop's fall from favour.[6]

Edward's principal allies, the Duke of Brabant, the Count of Hainault, the Duke of Guelders, the Margrave of Juliers and a host of lesser princes had all come to Antwerp to greet the King and to present their accounts. Edward confronted them empty-handed at a long and painful conference. The Duke of Brabant, as the most powerful prince among them, took the lead. He was not only unpaid but very equivocal about the whole enterprise. So was the young Count of Hainault, a weaker personality than his formidable father and less enthusiastic when it came to the point about the recovery of the castles of the Cambrésis. Edward III pleaded with them to march at once against the French. He had brought his army with him from England and their wages were a crushing burden, mounting daily. The princes were evasive. They said that they had brought only a ceremonial entourage with them, that their men-at-arms had not yet been summoned in due form; that they would have to consult their advisers at home; and that it would be very desirable to put them in funds. Then they withdrew. The next meeting was fixed for 15 August 1338.[7]

While the princes consulted their advisers Edward III scraped the barrel for money. He borrowed more than £70,000 from the Bardi and the Peruzzi on the security of wool not yet shipped. He pressed William Pole for all that Pole could lend. He mortgaged his Great Crown as well as gold and jewellery belonging to rich monasteries in England. His agents scoured the Low Countries and the Rhineland for lenders, Italian, Flemish, Dutch and Jewish without discrimination. Rates of interest of up to 50 per cent per annum were recorded.[8]

Between 26 July and 2 August 1338 Edward's young heir, the Duke of Cornwall, presided over a Great Council at Northampton, which was attended by the prelates and magnates still in England and by representatives of the Commons. An assembly of merchants followed immediately afterwards. Failure in the field had not yet tarnished Edward III's reputation at home, and these men were still prepared to dig deeper into their packets. A new levy of wool was ordered, accompanied this time by ruthless arrangements for its collection. Every community was required to supply wool in proportion to their assessment for Parliamentary taxes. No one might excuse himself on the ground that he did not have any. Those who truly had no wool were to buy some. As a result the new levy was much more successful than the old, but in spite of a relentless flow of hectoring letters from the King in Brabant, it was quite impossible to collect it in time to save the King's plans. In the event hardly any of the wool was to reach Antwerp until the following year.[9] When Edward III next met his allies, near Mechelen on 15 August 1338, he had succeeded in making small interim payments to a few of them but otherwise his position was scarcely better than it had been in July. The princes were unsympathetic. They needed more time, they said. The Emperor, they pointed out, was not present. In so grave a matter as an attack on France they would have to obtain his approval before the campaign could begin. Why, Edward asked them caustically, had they not told him that before?[10]

Although it was some time before the English King recognized the fact, the hesitations of the princes and the King's want of money to pay them put an end to his plans for invading the Cambrésis in 1338. The summer had almost passed. There were perhaps six weeks, at the most ten weeks, of open weather left to him. The Emperor's support, on which the enterprise had now come to depend, was not likely to be obtained quickly or cheaply. Of the 400,000 florins (£60,000) which was owed to Louis of Bavaria, less than a tenth had been paid. Moreover the Emperor, who rarely let an opportunity pass, had begun to invite competing offers from Philip VI. A meeting of ambassadors of France and the Empire was due to take place on 1 September 1338.[11] In these difficult circumstances Edward III acted rapidly. He sent the Margrave of Juliers to Germany to arrange an interview between himself and the Emperor. Then, without waiting for the answer, he set out for Coblenz where Louis was due to hold a Reichstag at the beginning of September. Travelling light across Brabant and Juliers with a handful of advisers and a bodyguard of archers, Edward reached the island of Niederwerth on the Rhine north of Coblenz on 30 August 1338. His household servants and equipment followed laboriously by river barge. A week later John Montgomery arrived, bringing every penny which it had been possible to find in Antwerp: carts and saddle packs laden with 50,000 florins (£7,500) in specie, and bags of jewellery to be pawned to the merchants of the Rhine cities. Edward needed to impress. At Niederwerth he entertained magnificently as if the money had fallen like ripe fruit into his hands instead of being borrowed on ruinous terms from usurers. Louis of Bavaria's relatives and advisers were plied with cash. One important Imperial councillor received 4,000 florins (£600); the

Empress received 2,400 florins (£360) and her secretary 60 florins (£9). For Louis himself there was nearly £6,000, which brought the total of payments to him to a fifth of what was due. The rest was promised in two instalments in January and March 1339. The Emperor was mollified. On 5 September 1338 he sent the Imperial barge to bring the English King into Coblenz. Here, at a splendid public session, the electors of the Empire gave their approval to Edward's appointment as Imperial Vicar and invested him with all the powers of the Emperor himself. The English King received absolute property of this office until such time as he should have conquered France 'or a substantial part of it.' Edward's wars were pronounced to be wars in defence of the integrity of the Empire against the usurpations of France, and disobedience to him tantamount to treason. The Emperor sat enthroned with orb and sceptre, a naked sword held aloft behind him. Beneath the throne Edward III watched the proceedings seated, robed in scarlet between the Margraves of Meissen and Juliers and surrounded by a great crowd of knights and princes of Germany.[12]

Edward set about putting these grandiose declarations into effect as soon as he returned to Antwerp. On 18 September 1338 he summoned his allies to attend him on pain of forfeiture of their fiefs to hear the decrees of Coblenz recited and to receive his commands. The meeting took place on 12 October 1338 in the covered market of the little town of Herk in Loon because it was near at hand yet not in the dominions of the Duke of Brabant. The Duke was still trying to avoid proclaiming too openly his hostility to France. Indeed he declined to attend in person at all, sending representatives instead. Edward set up his throne on a butcher's counter to receive the plaudits and loyal oaths of the assembled princes and knights and to announce his plans for the coming year. At Coblenz the opening of the campaign in the Cambrésis had been provisionally fixed for May 1339; now it was thought prudent to put it back a little further until July. In order to force the legal point the Bishop of Cambrai was summoned to attend upon Edward sitting as Imperial Vicar at Mechelen on 26 October 1338 on pain of deprivation. So were those other firm allies of France, the Bishop of Liège and the Count of Flanders. There was some grumbling. The Duke of Brabant's bluff had been called; his representatives declared that further consultation would be required. The Count of Hainault added that although he would be glad to fight in the Cambrésis, where he would benefit by any conquests, he doubted whether he could properly cross into France. But when the princes reassembled at Mechelen at the end of the month and the Bishop of Cambrai with other francophiles predictably failed to appear, the doubts and equivocations were temporarily silenced.

Edward's allies were still unpaid and some of them still uncertain, but they kept their counsels to themselves.[13]

Edward III withdrew his household to Antwerp at the beginning of November and remained there for most of the winter. The Queen joined him from England. There were friends to gamble and hunt with him. There were pennies to be counted and pounds to be spent on the steady drain of wages, subsidies and household bills. The troops, which had now been in the Low Countries for more than three months without seeing any action, were dispersed in small groups among the towns of Brabant, Hainault and Flanders. Many of them deserted and tried to make their way home to England, 'for want of food to eat' as Edward admitted to his Council. The rest drank heavily, strained their welcome by pilfering and violence and waited for the spring.[14] At Arras the plenipotentiaries of the two sides went through the motions of diplomacy under the chairmanship of the two cardinals. Four prelates of the French royal Council attended, including the two principal experts on relations with England, Pierre-Roger, Archbishop of Rouen, and Jean de Marigny, Bishop of Beauvais. On the English side Archbishop Stratford and Richard Bury, Bishop of Durham, represented Edward III. Others, including Henry Burghersh and William Montagu, Earl of Salisbury, came and went. For a short while in December 1338 and January 1339, the discussions were removed to Paris. The circumstances were not propitious. The cardinals put forward a series of proposals. The French or the English or both rejected them. Their minds were on other things.[15]

The French stood warily on their frontiers. Although most of their troops were released on 15 September 1338 they were told to hold themselves equipped and ready to return at short notice. One thousand mounted troops and 5,000 infantry were retained at reduced wages for garrison service during the winter. These men were eventually, in November 1338, disposed in four military commands along the border. Godemar du Fay, an able full-time soldier, was appointed Governor of Tournai and placed in command of the left bank of the Scheldt and the western sector of the march of Hainault. He was given a strong garrison of Picards and Normans at Tournai itself and subsidiary forces at Mortagne, Douai and Arleux. The Cambrésis was the responsibility of the Count of Auxerre. Further west, the march of Flanders and the coast from Calais to Boulogne were guarded by more than a dozen garrisons extending well to the rear. Smaller garrisons were distributed through those parts of Normandy and Brittany which were regarded as vulnerable to English coastal raids. It was a scheme of defence in depth which stands out principally for the contrast with the arrangements which the English had made in rather similar circumstances in the south-west in 1337. None of the garrisons except perhaps those of Tournai and Cambrai could have held out for long against a determined assault, but they were strong enough to delay an invading army until the main French army could be reassembled and brought forward to relieve them.[16] Philip VI was much criticized at the time for keeping his troops on a defensive footing throughout the summer of 1338 and during the following winter without attempting so much as a show of force against the territories of Edward's allies. But these criticisms did not allow for the delicacy of his diplomatic situation in the face of a coalition which seemed likely to disintegrate under its own internal strains, and with whose principal members he was covertly in contact. These were not matters which could easily be explained to those who led contingents in his army, men whose limited outlook historians have sometimes been content to adopt.

Philip did not get much credit from his countrymen for the great French success of the autumn of 1338, the aggressive campaign at sea which began at the moment when the danger was passing on the landward front. During the summer the French had been greatly hampered by the failure of their contract fleet of Italian galleys to arrive from the Mediterranean. The ships had not reached the Channel until August, some three months overdue and too late to prevent the English army from leaving England. They were not too late, however, to cut the shipping lanes between England and Gascony and to threaten Edward III's long and poorly defended lines of communication across the North Sea. Edward was receiving by sea not only money and wool desperately needed to pay his allies, but a large proportion of the army's victuals and stores. The English were concerned about the threat to their supplies and went to great lengths to obtain advance warning of the movements of enemy ships. A spy was sent from Bordeaux to Genoa to watch the galleys of the contract fleet being fitted out. The Bardi bank maintained agents in the Channel ports to report on warlike activities there. From Arras John Stratford sent runners at regular intervals to Dieppe, Rouen and Le Havre to observe the galley fleet once it had assembled.[17]

Nevertheless the English were caught unawares at the beginning of September when the galleys of Monaco descended on the Channel Islands with a raiding force under the command of one of the Marshals of France, Robert Bertrand. The islands were an obvious target. They were close to the coast of the Cotentin, an important staging post for the trade of southern England, Gascony and the Norman and Breton ports, as well as a springboard for raids on France. Sark, which was wholly undefended, had already been raided in April 1337 by a combined Norman and Scotch squadron. A year later, in March 1338, Nicholas Béhuchet had made his destructive descent on Jersey when he had tried and failed to take Gorey Castle. As a result of these incidents the islands had been reinforced, but unfortunately for the English their troops there were heavily concentrated in Jersey. On Guernsey there were only sixty-five men at Castle Cornet when the place was surprised and taken by assault on 8 September 1338. All of them were killed. Jerburgh, the only other castle on Guernsey, was defended by just twelve archers and fell on the same day. The local seamen put up some resistance. There was a fight in the course of which the Italians lost two of their galleys. But in spite of their efforts the French were able to occupy the whole island and they were to remain in possession of it for several years.[18]

The messengers who had tried to reach England from Guernsey to find help were caught in mid-Channel and their ship burned. It took almost a week for the news of the loss of the island to reach the Council.[19] By this time the galley fleet had turned north in search of other prey. They collected Genoese and French reinforcements at Harfleur and Dieppe and made for the estuary of the Scheldt. There were now about forty galleys and some Norman barges in the fleet, under the overall command of the two French admirals, Nicholas Béhuchet and Hugh Quiéret. A spy noted the arrival of the galleys off Cadzand. But his warning came too late. Off the island of Walcheren there were five English ships laden with wool and victuals waiting to discharge. They included two of Edward III's largest and finest ships, the *Cog Edward* and the *Christopher*. They were caught unprepared on 21 September 1338 with their sails packed, their masters away in Antwerp conferring with the King and part of their crews ashore. The men still on board were heavily outnumbered. After a ferocious fight, which lasted all day, they were overpowered and surrendered. A force of English household archers which tried to reach the ships by barge from Antwerp arrived after the fight had ended. The French dealt ruthlessly with their prisoners. They were all put to death on Quiéret's personal instructions. As for the ships, they were taken to Normandy and commissioned into French service.[20]

The news of this reverse caused great distress to Edward III. On 27 September 1338 the Council in England ordered the ships of both Admiralties to put to sea to search out and destroy the enemy. The order was lackadaisically carried out by shipmasters weary of the constant requisitioning of their ships.[21] On 5 October 1338 the French fleet entered the Solent and landed an armed force several thousand strong near Southampton. Once again the English received some warning, probably from gossip in the French Channel ports. Hugh Quiéret, who was in command, had been offering a prize of 100 *livres* to the first man to breach the defences of Southampton. Nevertheless, resistance was patchy and disorganized. The ships of the western Admiralty which had been detailed to guard the entrances of the Solent never appeared. The Hampshire levies had not yet been arrayed. The men of Berkshire and Wiltshire who should have come to their assistance never left their counties. Church bells which rang out the alarm were thought to be calling for divine service. Southampton itself was only partly walled. On the seaward side the only defences consisted in a large but vulnerable wooden barbican and the stone gates closing off the ends of streets which led to the waterfront. It was not therefore surprising that few of the townsmen made any attempt to defend their homes. Instead, when they heard about the French landings, they fled in panic into the surrounding countryside together with the officials who had been charged with their defence. A few men of stouter heart and the small permanent garrison of the castle remained behind to fight the invaders. They succeeded in containing the first assault, which was led by Normans of the Admiral's retinue. But the next wave, 200 crewmen of Ayton Doria's galley, forced them back. The French and Italians poured into the town. Once inside they had the place to themselves for the whole night and were able to remove to the galleys a great deal of wool, wine and other stores as well as the scales which were used to weigh out merchandise at the Custom House. It was not until early the next day that the first signs of armed resistance appeared outside. Disorganized bands of angry villagers congregated along the roads leading to the gates. The invaders decided to withdraw, starting fires in five separate places as they did so and leaving much of the town in flames behind them. Returning townsmen and Hampshire rustics completed the disorder by running riot through the streets looting what the invaders had left behind. The damage done was appalling. The whole southern part of the town comprising the parishes of St John, St Michael and Holy Rood was destroyed. Southampton's commerce ceased almost entirely for a year. The great trading houses, including the Bardi and the Peruzzi who traditionally shipped their wool at Southampton, all withdrew. Many of those who fled never returned, or returned briefly only to migrate elsewhere.[22]

The French admirals had originally intended to resume their raids on the south coast as soon as they had revictualled their ships and discharged their booty. In the event the weather deteriorated and they were unable to do so. The ships were laid up for the winter early in November 1338. In a short period, however, they had succeeded in creating panic in southern England and demoralization on both sides of the North Sea. Reports came in rapid succession of French plans to attack the Isle of Sheppey, the Kent coast, London and the Medway ports, and wool stores as far north as Hull. In London, it was believed that the French raids presaged an invasion in force in which 'the whole realm of England would be seized and slaughtered'. The city government took emergency measures to prevent landings on the strands of the Thames, driving wooden piles into the river bed. Stores of weapons including artillery were collected at the Guildhall and elsewhere, and watches organized at the gates.[23]

It was not at all clear what could be done to prevent such catastrophes. The government's explanation, when these matters were discussed in Parliament in 1340, was that England had been worsted 'pur defaute d'une navie sur mer'. Edward III had made some attempts, after the first naval encounters, to acquire a galley fleet of his own. In 1336 he had built at great expense a galley called the *Philippa* which was based at King's Lynn. Another was built for him at Winchelsea a year later. The Poles, those diligent war contractors, had two galleys built for the royal service. One, belonging to William Pole, accompanied the King on the crossing of the North Sea in the summer of 1338. His brother Richard, who held the office of King's Butler, operated a galley called *Le Botiller*, which saw service in Scotland in 1337. None of these vessels, however, played a very notable part in the warlike operations of the following years. They were rather small and the probability is that like earlier galleys built in England they were unseaworthy.[24] The only galleys regularly in English service were those of Bayonne, and they rarely served north of the Bay of Biscay. The solution, no doubt, was to take a leaf out of Philip VI's book and to hire galleys complete with their crews in the Mediterranean. Nicolino Fieschi had succeeded in hiring for him in Marseille just two Italian galleys, which served in the North Sea for most of the year 1338. During the summer a less reliable and possibly dishonest Italian agent called Sarzana was soliciting galley masters on Edward III's behalf in the ports of Provence. He had no success at all. He was provided with funds which were quite inadequate and even these were impounded by the Count of Provence.[25] Three days after the loss of the *Christopher* and the *Cog Edward* Fieschi was sent on a fresh mission, ostensibly to the papal court at Avignon, in fact to retrieve what he could of the money given to Sarzana and to try to achieve better results himself. The clumsiness of these early intrigues explains their failure quite as much as Edward III's lack of ready cash does. On the one occasion (it was in 1339) when Edward's agents did succeed in hiring a significant number of galleys in Aigues-Mortes and Nice, the agents of the French Crown arrived from Paris with bulging purses and bought them off.[26]

Whether it would have made any difference to the security of the coast if the English fleet had been stronger is another question. Even if the ships had existed, it would have been impossible without a superbly accurate intelligence service to intercept them at sea or to ensure that they were in the right place when the French chose to attack. Even with a superbly accurate intelligence service it was difficult enough, as the sack of Portsmouth had demonstrated earlier in the year. Once the invaders landed it is unlikely that any system of coastal defence could have been wholly successful in repelling them. Forty galleys as large as those operated by the Genoese contained more than 8,000 men. To concentrate a force capable of engaging them in pitched battle would have taken a long time. The only effective protection was the possession of a sufficient number of fortified refuges into which men could be brought in time of danger with their families, animals and goods. The problem in England, as in France, was that many years were required to plan, finance and build any significant defensive works. Hardly any attention had been paid to the fortifications of the coastal areas of England until 1335, when the French had devised their first seaborne raids. In that year surveys had been made of the fabric of several royal castles, including the Tower of London, Canterbury, Porchester and Carisbrooke on the Isle of Wight. These surveys had sometimes led to proper repairs, but more often they had not. The defences of the Tower of London were extended along the riverside between 1336 and 1338, an important improvement. Large sums were expended at Carisbrooke. Some work, but rather less than was required, was undertaken at Dover, Pevensey and Porchester. Elsewhere almost nothing was done. At Canterbury for example, where the bridge had collapsed into the moat and the towers and walls were crumbling, just two pounds was spent during the following half-century. At least in the case of the royal castles, the responsibility for maintenance was clear. In the boroughs, where responsibility was uncertainly divided between the Crown and the townsmen, the condition of the defences was almost always worse. At Winchester the ancient walls had collapsed in several places. Long sections of the town walls of Dover were ruinous. The walls of Chichester were said to be indefensible on account of the gaps in them. The citizens complained that they could not afford the cost of repairs. In the immediate aftermath of the Southampton raid there was a brief flurry of enthusiasm for wall building. The men of Winchester, who must have felt that they had had a narrow escape, began work at once. But the impetus was quickly lost. Portsmouth, the first large town to be sacked by the French, remained unfortified until the end of the fourteenth century. Southampton, which had suffered terribly for its unreadiness in October 1338, was an even more remarkable case. The royal Council gave explicit instructions that a stone wall was to be built along the western and southern strands and even provided money for the purpose. But the citizens were fond of their gardens and liked to have direct access to their ships. They were not at all enthusiastic about doing garrison duty. When the Earl of Warwick inspected the defences of the town in July 1339 he found the garrison grossly deficient in both quantity and quality and the fixed defences in lamentable state. He considered that 200 men-at-arms could have forced the town at any point. No systematic scheme of fortification was attempted at Southampton until after 1376.[27]

Morale in England sank very low in the winter of 1338-9, a mood to which the immobility of the war on the continent and the successes of the French fleet contributed much unease and misgiving. The second winter of the war was exceptionally severe. It rained incessantly until December and then froze so hard that over much of England the grain and fruit crops were lost. The remarkable three-year subsidy granted by Parliament in September 1337 was still being collected year upon year. The wool prize authorized by the Council of Northampton in July 1338 had proved so troublesome to enforce that collection was still in progress a year later. These burdens were heavier than any which the English people were called upon to bear during the fourteenth century. Moreover, their incidence was often arbitrary and uneven. Since Parliamentary taxes were levied on movables, rents (the nobility's main source of revenue) were not touched. The taxes were paid mainly by tenant farmers and peasants, and by urban householders. The richest and strongest often refused, even if they were not exempt, to contribute to the assessments of their communities, and defied the rest to make them. The Hertfordshire knight Sir Stephen Bassingbourne thrashed the collectors with the flat of his sword until they fled.[28]

To these misfortunes were now added the effects of purveyance on an unprecedented scale to satisfy the army and the fleet, voracious acquisitions of beef, mutton and pork, grain, malt and fish, and prizes of barges, carts and horses. Not only had the scale of compulsory purchase increased, but the manner of its enforcement had become more brutal. Instead of being carried out by the sheriffs and local officials, the practice since the beginning of 1336 had been to appoint merchants or royal clerks with roving commissions extending over several counties and draconian powers to enforce their will. As the King's demands became more pressing, some of these purveyors got completely out of hand, entering houses by force, ordering the arrest and imprisonment of whole villages who obstructed them and appointing large numbers of deputies with powers as extensive as their own and even less restraint in using them. They frequently failed to pay, or paid with debentures or tallies. In the worst cases they took the year's seed-corn or broke up plough teams, inflicting distress which was felt for years. The effects were particularly severe in certain regions, chiefly East Anglia and the East Midlands, which included the main grain-growing counties and were closest to the North Sea ports by which Edward's army was being embarked and supplied.[29]

There was a squeeze on agricultural incomes and a severe deflation, exacerbated by the general European shortage of coin and the export of huge quantities of it to pay the wages of troops and the subsidies of princes. The evidence is anecdotal, but it is almost entirely consistent. There was 'great plenty of goods and great scarcity of money', empty markets, low prices and destitution in the face of insistent tax collectors. During the early years of the war cultivated land went out of cultivation at an accelerating rate, and while there were many reasons for this pheno-menon, surveys carried out for the Exchequer in 1341 suggested that war taxation, purveyance and military service were prominent among them. As depression set in and the government's grip was seen to loosen after Edward III's departure, there was a noticeable breakdown of public order, with outbreaks of rioting and gang warfare reminiscent of the last years of Edward II.[30]

These difficulties were not likely to be surmounted by the men whom Edward had left to govern in his absence. The nominal Guardian of the realm was Edward, Duke of Cornwall, the future Black Prince, who was then eight years old. The King had with him in Brabant all his most experienced lay and ecclesiastical advisers and almost all his adminis-trators of any proven ability. Instructions were issued in the young Prince's name by a group of royal councillors who were no more than moderately competent and had the minimum of discretion. Because this was well known they had very little personal authority. Officials on whom they tried to impose their will found it all too easy to appeal to the protection of powerful individuals in Brabant and to justify themselves by malicious gossip about those in charge in England. Edward III, who never understood how heavy his ministers' burdens were, was very ready to believe it. In December 1338 he summarily dismissed the Treasurer Robert Woodhouse. 'May God be pleased that I shall never again serve a master who has so little interest in my efforts and so little concern with the burdens that I carry for him,' Woodhouse confided to a friend. It was only one incident in what became in the following year an open war between the King and his home officials, marked by ignorance and venom on Edward's side, fatalism and passivity on the other. In September 1338 Edward even announced that as a measure of economy he proposed to stop the salaries of the civil service except in cases of proven hardship. This extraordinary order was ignored. In the following May, when Edward repeated it, he was told that were he to insist his servants would resign in a body. They kept their salaries, but they had few enough reasons to serve the King well.[31]

The weakness of the home administration was one reason why there appeared in England earlier than in France a large class of profiteers and embezzlers who found their opportunity in the urgency of the King's needs and the growing bureaucracy which was necessary to satisfy them. William Dunstable, Edward's chief purveyor, was charged with trafficking in goods purveyed for the army, together with his brother and several of his staff. Chief Justice Willoughby was accused a little later of having 'sold the laws like cows or oxen'. Public opinion held these men guilty and believed that their crimes were only a trickle in an ocean of dishonesty. There is not much doubt that they were right.[32]

Overt opposition to the war was still rare. But the rumblings of future discontent were heard in the Parliament of February 1339, which met to consider measures for the defence of the realm but was largely taken up with an 'immense clamour' about purveyance. These were complaints about means, but there were others willing to challenge the ends. At about the time that Parliament was sitting, a remarkable anonymous poet railed bitterly against the government and the great of the land who voted taxes to sustain their improvident schemes. 'He who takes money from the needy without just cause is a sinner,' this man declared. Edward III's continental ambitions were not a just cause but a dereliction of duty to which the nation had never truly consented. The Parliamentary subsidy of 1337 was an iniquity. The peasantry, the poet wrote, were now selling their cows, their tools and even their clothes to pay for Edward's war, but the time would come when there would be nothing for them to do but rise in rebellion. It is difficult to say how widespread these opinions were. But they must have been more than the isolated eccentricity of their author, for the government found it necessary to answer them in its propaganda. In the spring of 1339, when the Council was trying to enforce an onerous scheme of compulsory military service for the defence of the realm, commissioners were sent out to harangue provincial communities about the menace of the French and to soothe their discontents. A broadsheet was drawn up in Parliament suggesting what line they might adopt. 'It is not the intention of the King and his Council to make the communities serve at their own expense,' this document said, 'but at the expense of the rich and powerful who can afford it.' It is probable that once Edward III had abandoned the campaign of 1338 the poet's views were held in a more respectful form by very many people. The return from so much expense seemed too meagre. The Northumberland knight Thomas Gray cannot have been the only one who thought that the King in Brabant was 'only jousting and having a jolly time'.[33]

Between November 1338 and July 1339, while Edward tried to scrape together the resources to press his invasion of France, the French very nearly succeeded in doing away with the English presence in the southwest. The decisions were made at Vincennes early in November 1338 and revealed some limited readiness to learn from past mistakes. In the first place it was proposed to devote adequate resources to the task. This meant sending large forces from other parts of France instead of relying exclusively on unenthusiastic local levies and the princes of the south-west like the Count of Foix whose strategic notions were dictated by their own territorial ambitions. Secondly, although it was intended to finance this campaign, like previous ones, from local sources, the French did not repeat the mistake of asking their generals to act as administrators and tax-collectors. Political direction of the campaign and absolute civil power in the south-west was entrusted to John of Luxembourg, King of Bohemia, quixotic knight-errant and adoptive Frenchman who had become one of Philip VI's closest confidants in his time of trouble. Moreover, the French were not on this occasion going to dissipate their forces in razzias about the long Gascon march, but were going to concentrate them against the principal strongholds of the English, the first of which was to be Penne d'Agenais. The Count of Foix was loaded with favours, paid in land all his vast arrears for past services and sent to invest the place at once. With him went Le Galois de la Baume (one of the captains-general of the summer) and another Savoyard, Pierre de la Palu.[34]

It was probably these decisions of the French government which were discovered by a group of four spies whom John Stratford had sent to mingle among the crowd of gossiping suitors and courtiers at Vincennes. What is certain is that on 20 November 1338, a few days after they had been made, Edward III attempted a diversion in the north. Although he had agreed that the campaign in the Cambrésis would be postponed until the following summer, he suddenly issued orders in the name of the Emperor commanding all his allies to assemble in Hainault between Mons and Binche on 18 December 1338 whence, he declared, they would march at once and in force against the enemy. A few days later Edward commanded the Bishop of Cambrai to appear before him to answer serious charges of treason against the Empire on pain of forfeiture, the prescribed prelude to an armed attack on his principality. There was a brief alarm in France. The main French garrison in the north, at Tournai, was reinforced by troops commanded by Philip's cousin the King of Navarre. The Duke of Normandy, Philip's heir, mustered another force at Péronne on the Somme. In about the middle of December 1338 William, Count of Hainault, crossed his frontier into the principality of Cambrai and wasted a tract of territory north of the episcopal city. Several of the Bishop's granges and windmills were destroyed and two castles in the Scheldt valley within a mile of the city of Cambrai were taken by surprise. The Count left garrisons there to await the main campaign expected in the summer. Then he withdrew. Nothing else happened. Edward's other allies refused to move and his orders eventually had to be cancelled. On 19 December 1338 the French army was once again reduced to garrison strength. The incident failed to achieve even a short respite for Gascony. Philip VI continued to give instructions for the southern campaign even while he was on his way north to meet the new threat. The King of Bohemia left Philip's presence for the Garonne valley at the beginning of December 1338 as if nothing was amiss.[35]

Gaston de Foix and the two Savoyard captains arrived in the south-west in mid-November 1338 and set up their headquarters at Marmande. John of Bohemia arrived in the province about a month later. Their combined forces laid siege to Penne and the subsidiary tower of Castelgaillard, which stood over the approach to it. The besieging army was not large. There were the modest personal retinues of the commanders, some 1,200 men recruited in Rouergue by the Count of Armagnac and a siege train directed by a small group of German specialists, part of the great diaspora of German sappers and miners of the middle ages. Penne normally had a garrison of 250 and was certainly well manned in 1339. Yet in less than a fortnight the town surrendered, leaving the castle above them to hold out alone. The reason was plain. There was no prospect of relief from

Bordeaux. Without relief the likelihood was that sooner or later the town, whose defences were weaker than those of the castle, would be assaulted, and its inhabitants would lose their property and many of them their lives. The citizens sent several despairing messages to Oliver Ingham pointing out the weakness of their position and asking what they should do. Eventually their leader, a lawyer, went out to bargain with the Count of Foix.

There were more than 100 soldiers of the garrison in the lower town. Their commander, a mercenary from Béarn called Fortanier d'Esguarre-paque, was persuaded to deliver both town and castle to the French. He received an enormous bribe, more than 14,000 *livres*, for distribution among the garrison. In the event the plan went awry. The town opened its gates at about Christmas time. But it seems that most of Fortanier's men refused to join him. Instead they went to reinforce the garrison of the castle, whose gates remained firmly shut. By the time the French discovered the deception Fortanier had made off with the money. He did not enjoy it for long. On 26 December Oliver Ingham's officers found him near Bordeaux and shut him up in the gatehouse of the Château de l'Ombrière.[36]

In January 1339 the French built up their strength in the south. At the beginning of the month they had 5,700 men under arms, a figure which steadily increased until it exceeded 12,000 at the end of April. Not all of them were used in field operations. In the meticulous way which characterized their military method the French applied themselves diligently to basic facilities. A heavily fortified wooden bridge had been built in 1337 at Sainte-Foy, the point at which most supplies and reinforcements crossed the Dordogne. At the end of 1338 two bridges were constructed on floating pontoons over the Garonne at La Réole and Marmande and a third, slightly later, at Le Mas d'Agenais, enabling troops and supplies to be moved rapidly across as well as along the great river valleys. A fleet of forty-two barges was assembled on the river, some of which were equipped with siege engines and high machicolated superstructures. At the same time the main routes were denied to the English. Fords were guarded or made impassable to horses by driving sharp stakes into the river beds. The region was sprinkled with garrisons ranging from the four or five troopers stationed in a hill village to stiffen the locals, to the 700 men who defended the army's northern flank on the Dordogne at Sainte-Foy. In the first four months of the year, forty-five new French garrisons were established, of which more than half were concentrated in the Garonne and Dordogne valleys and the territory in between. These garrisons not only held territory

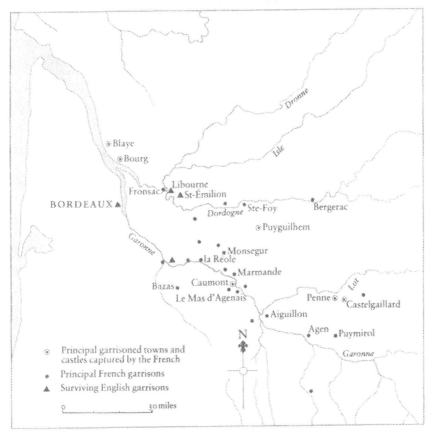

5 The French offensive in the Garonne, November 1338–July 1339

and lines of communication, but formed a reserve from which reinforcements could be drawn, a protection against unexpected counter-attack, and a shield behind which towns and castles could be invested by relatively modest forces without fear of relieving armies. The administrative burden of these arrangements and their enormous cost (about 45,000 *livres* per month at the height of the campaign) was the responsibility of a growing military bureaucracy lodged in the castle of Marmande and at a branch of the Chambre des Comptes established at Agen.[37]

After the fall of the town of Penne a small force consisting for the most part of Le Galois de la Baume's Savoyards was left to blockade the castle for however long it should take to surrender. The main body of the French army worked their way towards Bordeaux. They descended with a siege train and armed barges on Caumont, an isolated English garrison on the

Garonne, the only one left above Saint-Macaire. The defenders of this place resisted fiercely but without success. It was in French hands by the end of February 1339. Next it was the turn of Puyguilhem, the great rectangular keep on the confines of the Agenais and Périgord. Here, the resistance lasted longer. In the course of March 1339 it was necessary to bring up powerful reinforcements as well as additional siege engines and a corps of sappers to undermine the walls. The siege is the earliest recorded instance of the use of cannon in the Hundred Years War. On 6 April 1339 the captain of Puyguilhem gave up hope of relief and surrendered his damaged fortress to the French.[38]

The middle of April 1339 was a time of triumph for French arms in the south-west. Their army was now approaching its maximum strength. At Penne and the outlying tower of Castelgaillard the beleaguered garrisons had exhausted their supplies and their strength. On 10 April the commander of Castelgaillard sold himself to the enemy and delivered the place up. The citadel of Penne accepted terms a week later. The French were now able to plant on its ramparts the royal banner which they had prematurely ordered in December. Their greatest successes, however, occurred further west in the Gironde. On 20 April 1339 a force of galleys from La Rochelle under the command of the Admiral of France and the Seneschal of Saintonge attacked Blaye. On the river side the town was only lightly fortified and the attack came without warning. Both the town and its citadel were taken swiftly and with only the lightest casualties. It was clear that the defenders had not even had time to arm and assemble. Blaye was delivered over to be pillaged and burned by the soldiers. Almost immediately afterwards Bourg was captured in the same way. For the English these events, following one upon the other within a single week, were a disaster of the first order. Penne perhaps had become little more than a symbol now that the territory west of it was so securely occupied and garrisoned by the French. But the loss of Bourg and Blaye meant that the whole north shore of the Gironde was in French hands and Bordeaux liable to be cut off from its markets and source of reinforcements in England. In addition Edward III had lost one of his ablest and most loyal commanders in Bérard d'Albret, who was captured with some twenty-five other important prisoners and carried off to the Temple in Paris. There was a brief and strange epilogue of which unfortunately almost nothing is known. Shortly after its capture and before the French had properly garrisoned it, Blaye was recaptured by the English Seneschal's troops, probably from the river. But they were unable to hold it and were soon expelled. Philip VI commemorated his victory by delivering Blaye to the family of Melun, who had unsuccessfully fought for it through many years of litigation in the Parlement of Paris and had personally taken part in its capture. As for Bourg it was placed in the King's hands and guarded by an enormous garrison.[39]

It was the beginning of the most difficult period which the ducal government experienced in the first part of the Hundred Years War. The defeat of the English in 1339 began a vicious circle from which there was no escape except by the dispatch of money and troops on a large scale from England. Men who held lands after the fashion of the Gascon nobility scattered through the province now had fine calculations to make if they were to decide whether they would rather lose their estates in French-held territory by remaining loyal to the English or their lands in English districts by deserting to the French. Every loss of territory caused a failure of loyalties which led directly to the next one. Those who did, in spite of everything, remain loyal to the English dynasty brought their own problems, for they had to be rewarded and compensated for their losses. Yet with each contraction of its territory the resources of the Bordeaux government dwindled and with them the means of preserving friendships for a better day. They turned to ingenious expedients, unusual taxes and devaluations of the Bordeaux pound, putting up with the mounting inflation which followed. The pressure on the Seneschal remained, and in the course of 1339 and 1340 increased. Refugees who had served Edward III in towns and castles now lost to the enemy eked out an indigent existence in Bordeaux hoping to be succoured by a grateful government, men like William Gordon, who had lost everything in the fall of Bourg and petitioned Edward III for a pension to save himself and his wife and son from starvation. For them and a few others in their position there was outdoor relief on a modest scale. For those whose state had been greater it was necessary to begin the practice of making grants of lands and revenues at places in the possession of the French to take effect when, if ever, they were reconquered. A very high proportion of royal grants were of this kind from the middle of 1339 onwards. A year after the fall of Bourg Oliver Ingham addressed to Edward III an anguished plea for some of the petitioners. One had served the King with more than 600 men without being paid for their wages, and with no better reward than the loss of much of his land to the French. Another, who had served Edward's father before him, had brought his wife and children and his entire household to Bordeaux when the French had occupied every acre he owned. He was now living in humiliating penury in Libourne. Theirs was a loyalty of sentiment, not calculation, rare in Gascony. 'He has a good heart utterly and unstintingly devoted to your service.' Yet Ingham could not reward it. He had made assignments, he explained, from the customs of Bordeaux which French conquests had now made almost worthless. The whole of the lands and revenues of the duchy had been granted to others, and there was not a penny left at his disposal.[40]

The Normans and Genoese returned to their ships, in spite of the bitterly cold weather, in February 1339, and were ready to put to sea in early March. The English government (according to the report which its representatives gave to Parliament) had 'reliable information from several sources' which suggested that the French were planning a descent on the coast of East Anglia. This may at one stage have been true. But by March the French government's designs had become more ambitious.[41]

The ships under their command were divided into two independent fleets. One of them was to raid the harbours of East Anglia in the manner of 1338. The other was sent to attack the Channel Islands again, and then proceed to Gascony to assist the flourishing campaign in the Garonne valley. The Channel Islands expedition, which was the larger of the two, left the mouth of the Seine between 9 and 11 March 1339. It consisted initially of seventeen Italian galleys of Carlo Grimaldi, about thirty-five Norman barges and a cog, none other than Edward III's great ship *Christopher* captured off Walcheran in the previous year and now serving under French colours. Another five galleys joined them later. About 8,000 soldiers and seamen were embarked on this armada under the command of the Marshal, Robert Bertrand. Bertrand had been granted the lordship of the Channel Islands after his last descent, and was bent on expanding his demesne. On 12 March 1339, he landed on Jersey near Gorey Castle on the east side of the island. An ultimatum was delivered to the garrison. The garrison was at full strength, some 260 Englishmen and about 40 local men. They replied, by their own account, that the castle would 'not be given up as long as there were ten men alive in it'. Bertrand's summons had been largely bluff. He did not have the use of the fleet for more than a short time: it was urgently required in Gascony. So, after reconnoitring the defences of the castle he attempted an assault which failed. On 16 March, the fleet sailed on to Guernsey, where the French were already in occupation. Bertrand and some of his men remained there to reinforce the island. The rest sailed for La Rochelle in company with a large commercial convoy. It was this fleet which captured Blaye and Bourg in April.[42]

The other fleet, consisting of eighteen Genoese galleys commanded by Ayton Doria, was ordered north to Sluys, which in spite of its proximity to

Bruges had remained effectively under French control and was being used as a base from which to attack English shipping carrying wool, supplies and reinforcements into the Scheldt. On their way there, a detachment broke off to attack the East Anglian ports where these much needed commodities were being loaded. On 24 March 1339 the French ships arrived off Harwich, an unwalled fishing town at the entrance to the harbour of Orwell. It was the anniversary of the first French landing in strength at Portsmouth in 1338. On this occasion local resistance was stronger. Although the French could not be prevented from landing they were fiercely resisted at the edge of the town. They lit fires at three points, but the wind blew them away from the buildings until they went out. Shortly, the invaders re-embarked and sailed away.[43]

Since the beginning of the year Philip VI's ministers had been negotiating with the communities of Normandy upon a vaster scheme of naval war. This envisaged not simply raiding England's coasts but landing an army of conquest. The Normans were proposing to furnish the Crown with an army of 24,000 men including 4,000 cavalry and 5,000 archers, together with ships to carry them across the Channel. This force, which was to be placed under the command of the King's heir, the Duke of Normandy, was thought to be large enough to achieve the conquest of the whole of England in ten to twelve weeks. The Normans were promised valuable juridical privileges in return for their services, but the main inducement was a share of the spoils. They were to receive for distribution among themselves the entire landed wealth of England except for the royal domain, which was reserved for the Duke of Normandy; the property of the papacy, which would remain undisturbed; and lands to the value of £20,000 per annum, which would be permitted the English Church for its upkeep. This extraordinary scheme was approved by most of the leading Normans at a meeting in the castle of Vincennes on 23 March 1339, about the time when the galley fleet was approaching Harwich. The Estates of Normandy ratified it a month later. How seriously it was taken by either party is difficult to say. The agreement envisaged that the invasion would take place that very year. However, it also envisaged that it might have to be postponed if Edward III invaded France, which was expected to happen in June. This did not leave very much time for even a short campaign of conquest.[44]

Nevertheless the French made practical preparations with every sign of earnestness. They drew up detailed articles for the conduct of the expedition, which dealt with such matters as the custody and distribution of booty, signalling between ships of the fleet, the order of battle at sea and on land, the manner of landing, and the fighting of a rearguard action in case it should be necessary to retreat to the ships. Steps were also taken to join up the dispersed squadrons of the French and Italian fleets from the Bay of Biscay and the North Sea.[45]

The English Council took the plan extremely seriously when they heard about it, as they inevitably did given the public manner in which it had been resolved upon. The custody of the coast was placed in the hands of the principal noblemen still in England. The Earl of Huntingdon, who was Constable of Dover Castle, took command in Kent; the old Earl of Surrey in Sussex; and the Earl of Arundel in Hampshire. The Earl of Oxford was made responsible for the defence of London and the Essex coast. Inland, the council found as powerful a reserve army as it could, and placed it under the nominal command of the young Prince Edward. Almost from the outset the government decided that the French were likely to attempt their landing in Hampshire, and it was there that they concentrated their strongest forces. Southampton received an enormous garrison. The garrisons of Portsmouth and Porchester were almost as large. Troops and supplies were rushed to the Isle of Wight. Stocks of food were taken into Winchester, which was probably the safest walled city of the county for all its defects. Specially valuable items such as the King's horses were moved out of the county altogether.[46]

What the French admirals really intended is far from clear, and no doubt changed from time to time. The Norman army of conquest, if it was still part of their plans in May, was evidently not ready. The transports and barges remained in the ports of Normandy and Picardy. The southern squadron revictualled in the Seine ports and sailed north in mid-May to harry the south coast of England, hit-and-run raids of the traditional kind.[47] As the English Council had predicted, and perhaps known, the galleys first made for the Solent. On about 15 May 1339 they arrived off Southampton and tried to find a suitable place to land. But the strands of the town were defended by temporary works, and the county levies could be seen drawn up in strength all along Southampton Water. The Isle of Wight seemed equally unassailable. The French commanders became concerned about the danger of being bottled up in the waterway if the English fleet should appear. They left quickly and headed west, where the defence would perhaps be less well prepared. Their instinct was sound. There was no army drawn up on the long indented coast of Devon and Cornwall. No English fleet opposed them. They cruised with impunity around Land's End and into the Bristol Channel, picking off and plundering merchant vessels as they found them and killing their crews.

On 20 May 1339 they arrived off Plymouth. Plymouth in the early fourteenth century was a mediocre place, comprising four scattered villages on the eastern side of the Sound and the Benedictine priory of Plympton. But there chanced to be several ships in the Sound taking refuge from the raiders, including seven merchantmen of Bristol. These were seized and burned. The French and Italians then landed their men on the shore. The commander of the Devon levies was the Earl of Devon, Hugh Courtenay, a vain and rebarbative old man in his sixty-fourth year but lacking nothing for vigour. He marched on Plymouth when the news of the raid reached him and arrived just as the French were beginning to set fire to the houses. There was a sharp, indecisive skirmish in which both sides suffered heavy casualties. The French then withdrew to their ships pursued by angry West Countrymen who drowned many of them at the water's edge.

As they passed back along the south coast towards their bases, the galleys left behind them a trail of burning fishing boats. On 24 May 1339 they landed briefly on the Isle of Wight but were chased off. During the following week they made several attempts to land on the Kent and Sussex coasts, but at Dover, Folkestone and the Isle of Thanet they found powerful forces arrayed behind the beaches and were obliged to withdraw. Only at Hastings did they succeed in getting ashore any significant number of men. Hastings, once the chief of the Cinque Ports, was a small fishing town whose days of prosperity had passed just as those of Plymouth were about to begin. The town was unwalled. The castle, which belonged to the collegiate church of St Mary, was ungarrisoned, unrepaired and at its southern end falling into the sea. On 27 May 1339 the French and Genoese administered the *coup de grâce* to Hastings, from which there was no recovery until the holidaymakers arrived at the end of the eighteenth century. Their galleys came right into the harbour and landed, apparently unopposed, on the quays and strands. They burned much of the town, including the three parish churches. They invaded the castle and plundered the canons of their ornaments and plate. The townsmen had fled. At the beginning of June 1339 the Monégasques of Carlo Grimaldi, who had played the leading role in this raid, were back in Calais parading through the streets and exhibiting the naked and mutilated bodies of English fishermen as their trophies.

England's coastal defences had succeeded tolerably well. Her naval forces had not. On 16 February 1339, while the Westminster Parliament was still sitting, the Council had called for service at sea from a large number of ports of southern and eastern England. This should, by their reckoning, have produced by 15 March 1339 an eastern fleet of 31 ships at Orwell and a southern fleet of 111 ships in two squadrons at Portsmouth and Winchelsea, all fully manned and victualled for three months' service. In fact nothing of the kind occurred. Neither fleet was ready in time to resist the French raiders. The southern fleet seems never to have materialized except for the service of the Cinque Ports.[48]

In the North Sea the fleet of the other Admiralty had gathered by early April, but its performance was very mixed. Robert Morley, a Norfolk knight who had recently been appointed Admiral of the north, proved to be one of Edward III's more energetic and able commanders. Lack of seagoing experience was never considered a defect in a fourteenth-century admiral, and Morley's was made good by his assistants. John Crabbe, a colourful and disreputable figure, was by origin a Flemish pirate who had been noticed by Robert Bruce in the 1320s and hired as a naval commander and military engineer. Walter Mauny had captured him in a skirmish in the lowlands and sold him to Edward III for 1,000 marks. He did not care for whom he worked. These two men put to sea in early April 1339 with a convoy of sixty-three ships carrying money, wool and reinforcements for the continent. Off the Flemish coast they fell upon a merchant convoy of the enemy, escorted by some Genoese galleys. They pursued them north up the coast and right into the harbour of Sluys where a bloody battle took place. In the confined space of the harbour the galleys were unable to make use of their superior manoeuvrability and speed and stood by helplessly. The English took many of the convoyed ships as prizes. They also boarded other vessels which they found at anchor in the harbour. Unfortunately they plundered not only French ships but also those of Flanders and Spain, neutrals whom they had been strictly enjoined to leave alone. These included a huge Spanish carrack, which was in the course of loading a cargo from lighters. One of the English King's household knights, who was carrying money for Edward's treasury, had to flee for his life and take refuge with the money in a monastery in Bruges. These acts of indiscipline caused grave diplomatic embarrassment to Edward III and cost him some £23,000 in compensation, a misfortune far outweighing the damage done to the Genoese galleys. The sequel was almost as discouraging. When the English had returned to Orwell with their booty they quarrelled over its division, as a result of which part of the fleet mutinied and sailed away.[49]

In July 1339 the French admirals collected all their strength for a great raid on the Cinque Ports, which they may have supposed, in common with romantic historians of the nineteenth century, were the principal pillar of

England's maritime strength. The entire galley fleet in the North Sea, consisting of Ayton Doria's Genoese squadron at Sluys and a small number of French galleys, was withdrawn to Boulogne. Twenty Norman barges were fitted out in the Channel and Seine ports. Carlo Grimaldi's squadron, now rested from its exertions, joined them. The combined fleet of sixty-seven vessels included thirty-two galleys. They sailed shortly after 20 July 1339 under Béhuchet's command. The venture was a disaster. The first objective was Sandwich but when they arrived in the Downs they found the Kent levies waiting for them in force along the coast. They therefore turned south to Rye, where they were able to land some of their men and do a great deal of damage. But before they had finished their work their ships were surprised in Rye Bay by Robert Morley with the combined fleets of the northern Admiralty and the Cinque Ports. Panic spread among the French and Italian seamen. They seemed to have thought themselves in the presence of 400 English ships, at least three times the real number. They re-embarked and raced for the French coast. Morley's ships pursued them. The two fleets confronted each other off Wissant, but there was no battle. The French forces escaped safely into their harbours.[50]

At this point the French campaign at sea was brought to a sudden end by a crisis in the affairs of the Genoese. They had now been in northern Europe since August 1338, much longer than they had originally intended. They were private contractors in business for profit and set-piece battles such as the one which might have occurred in Rye Bay or off Wissant were much less to their taste than plundering the ports of southern England. Many of them were unwilling to go on. Moreover, they had begun to quarrel among themselves. It seems that while the French government had punctiliously paid Doria, he had not been paying his crews, or had done so only after making large and unwarranted deductions. When Ayton Doria's squadron returned to Boulogne the oarsmen mutinied for their pay. They elected a spokesman, who went with fifteen companions to enlist the sympathy of Philip VI. But Philip was not sympathetic. He had them arrested and thrown into prison. This was a mistake. When the news reached the other oarsmen in Boulogne they took over their galleys by force and sailed for Genoa. Two of Grimaldi's galleys deserted at the same time. At a stroke Philip VI had lost nearly two-thirds of his battle fleet. There remained only his own galleys, most of which were now laid up; the remnant of Doria's squadron, probably four galleys, which had remained loyal to him; and the Monaco squadron of Carlo Grimaldi, now reduced by losses and desertions from seventeen galleys to twelve. Grimaldi remained in French service for another two months, but they were idle months for which the French government got little value.

By the end of the year all the Italian oarsmen who had not mutinied appear to have been sent home, for although their vessels remained in France they were beached in the mouth of the Orne below Caen, and only two of them took any part in the great events of the following year. Relations with Grimaldi remained amicable enough, but Doria became increasingly embittered. Two years after the mutiny he was still owed 30,000 florins by his own reckoning and was intriguing with Edward III's ministers in Gascony, offering to change sides, burn his galleys and surrender all the strongholds under his control.[51]

Faced with no real opposition at sea, Robert Morley's fleet passed July and August in raiding the French coast. The Englishmen cruised down the coast of Picardy and Normandy, burning ships and villages much as the French and Italians had done in southern England earlier in the year. They sacked the town of Ault and destroyed the harbour. At Le Tréport they put a large landing party ashore under the noses of the inhabitants, who thought that they had to do with a convoy of Spanish merchantmen and put up no resistance. The English burned the harbour and much of the town, and devastated the country about. Then they marched up the coast and sacked the harbour village of Mers before re-embarking. The Countess of Eu, wife of the Constable of France, who was staying only 2 miles away, was very nearly captured. The militia of Eu did not arrive on the scene until after the invaders had left. It was a mirror image, on a smaller scale, of the English fiasco at Southampton in 1338. The fleet continued down the French coast, rounding the Breton peninsula and attacking harbours in northern Poitou. Where the English had begun, the Flemings enthusiastically followed. Shortly after Morley had returned to England a Flemish fleet raided Dieppe, the principal commercial port of Normandy, which appears to have been undefended. They burned much of the built-up area before they were driven off.[52]

How much had either side achieved? In terms of physical damage the honours were about equal. But in spite of the miserable end of their campaign the French had used their fleet to their decisive strategic advantage. Within England they had caused the usual panic and disruption. In Hampshire, although the French were repulsed, the alarm provoked by their second appearance within a year caused a widespread flight of men away from the coast. Many of them took all their goods with them and refused to come back in spite of adamant royal commands. Edward III's attempt to supply and reinforce his army in the Low Countries was persistently hampered by the strain which was inflicted on the resources of England. Some of his reinforcements had to be diverted to do garrison duty on the south coast. Others were bottled up in the pool of Orwell by shortage of shipping and the dangers of the crossing. English ships carrying wool and stores had to proceed in heavily defended convoys across the North Sea from Orwell or London. The ships of the northern Admiralty were responsible for the safety of the Orwell convoys; the London ones were escorted from Gravesend by ships of the Cinque Ports. These measures were reasonably effective in protecting cargoes from attack, but they involved a considerable diversion of ships and men which England could not easily spare. They also caused delay and meant that vessels which might have carried troops and cargoes had to be filled instead with fighting crews. Some shipmasters, impatient to return to profitable trading, defied the admirals' orders and attempted to make the passage unaccompanied. They were usually captured.[53]

The most serious consequence of the raids for the English war effort was financial. In Antwerp Edward III had to spend money which he did not have on buying supplies which never reached him. In England his Council was obliged to spend very large sums on coastal defence, fortification and shipping which Edward was counting on for his own purposes and in some cases had already assigned to his creditors. At one point Edward became so incensed at the amount which his officials were spending in England that he forbade them to spend any money whatever except on maintaining his castles in Scotland and satisfying the Bardi and the Peruzzi. It was useless. Are we, the Council inquired by way of reply, to ignore:

the defence of the Isle of Wight and Jersey, the garrison of Southampton, the royal castles in England, the wages of the crews of the King's ships, the victualling and supply of fleets of the Northern and Southern Admiralties, the wages and fees of the Admirals and their officials, the subvention of Gascony, the defence of the towns and strongholds of Scotland, the subsidies of the Scottish King [sc. Edward Balliol], the huge cost of bagging, carrying and storing the King's wool and all the other expenses which become more numerous and urgent every day and which can only come from the domain revenues and taxes of England?

Edward did not, doubtless could not, answer.[54]

By comparison the threat and occasional reality of English seaborne raids on France caused much less disruption there. The attack on Le Tréport in August 1339 was the first significant raid on the French coast since the start of the war. Other more destructive raids on more important places were to follow. But the French government retained its composure.

It never allowed itself to be forced into the kind of costly diversion of resources to coastal defence which persistently addled the English war effort. Why not? It was partly because maritime trade was relatively less important to France. It was partly because they were defending a shorter coastline, about 430 miles between Calais and Mont-Saint-Michel. They had a different order of priorities.

The French system of coastal defence had its origins (like the English one) in the wars of the 1290s. When relations with England were formally severed in 1337 one of the French government's first acts was to dust off the records and undertake a careful review of it. It was not particularly effective either before or after the review. There was a number of fixed garrisons and a mobile reinforcement in each area commanded by a local 'Captain of the Sea Frontier'. There were usually three captains in the north of France. One of them was responsible for the coast from the Flemish border to the Somme, and was generally an officer of the Count of Artois; a second commanded the coast immediately north of the Seine estuary and a third the Cotentin peninsula south of it. Captains were also periodically appointed for the sea frontiers of Poitou and Saintonge between the Loire and the Gironde. Except in moments of extreme panic the forces at the disposal of the captains were small, probably no more than a few hundred, including the fixed garrisons. There was a somewhat ill-defined right to call for assistance on major local lords and on towns immediately inland. The lords of Estouteville in Normandy, for example, whose lands were close to the sea, regularly supplied soldiers for the defence of the coast. The citizens of Arras were expected to reinforce the garrison of Calais whenever an English landing should occur. Those of Eu should have gone to the aid of Le Tréport in August 1339. In general the assistance given by inland towns was limited and late. It was a much less ambitious scheme than the English one and it never succeeded in preventing a landing or even in defending the major ports against a determined attack. It is difficult to say which was the sounder policy. In due course the French would pay a heavy price for their lack of an effective scheme of coastal defence.[55]

That Edward should have ordered his ministers to stop spending money in England and apparently expected them to obey him is some indication of how desperate his financial position had become.[56] He had now been in the Low Countries since July 1338. He had already borrowed in the first three months after his arrival everything that he could induce his creditors to lend in the forlorn and unsuccessful endeavour to mount his invasion of

France within the year. By the beginning of 1339 some of these debts were falling due and fresh instalments of his allies' subsidies were accruing all the time. The Duke of Brabant should have received £33,333 by Christmas 1338 and, since he was the most important and least enthusiastic of Edward's allies, had been paid as much as three-quarters by 1 January 1339. Another £30,000 fell due to the Emperor Louis of Bavaria on 6 January 1339, none of which was paid. Enormous sums promised in the previous year to the Archbishop of Trier remained unpaid. He was promised punctual payment of £16,650 between March and June 1339. On 27 February the Great Crown of England was redeemed from pawn in Bruges and pledged to him as security. These were only the largest and most pressing of the English King's creditors, men who were better able to enforce their demands than the mass of minor princes, retained knights and miscellaneous contractors who pressed with growing insistence for their money. Edward's financial officials presumably told them the story which they recorded in their accounts. 'Nothing has reached us from England for a long time,' they said; '... and we can find no one to lend us any more money.' This was in January 1339. 'The King has nothing left with which to make these payments, nothing to pay his own men and support his court ... for nothing has come from England for so long and we have all exhausted our credit,' another, later, entry ran. In his winter quarters in Antwerp the English King surrounded himself with a small band of intimate advisers: Bishop Burghersh, the former Chief Justice Geoffrey Scrope, William Montagu, Earl of Salisbury, the Margrave of Juliers, and his powerful private secretary William Kilsby. All these men, except perhaps the Earl of Salisbury, were wholly devoted to the continental strategy conceived in 1337. As the financial and administrative difficulties continued to frustrate it their opinions and advice increasingly shielded the King from reality.

Edward plainly believed that there were infinite resources in his kingdom which were kept from him only by the incompetence or sabotage of his subordinates there. 'Although time after time we have sent them letters and messengers impressing on them our penniless condition and begging them to send us at once some wool, money and whatever supplies they could raise,' he wrote in May 1339, 'we have received none of the subsidies which were voted to us, none of our ordinary revenues, nothing at all.'[57] The truth was that Edward had spent it. The taxes and revenues had been assigned long before to repay loans which he had spent. The same was true of the new wool levy which was to have been the salvation of Edward's enterprise. The orders for its collection, issued in early August

1338, envisaged that all 20,000 sacks would be collected within a month, an absurd and impossible forecast. In fact rather less than three-quarters of the quantity voted was collected, the result, as the Council nervously explained, of the adamant refusal of clergy to contribute and of various miscalculations of what was available.[58] Most of the wool which was collected never reached the Low Countries because Edward directly assigned it to his bankers to pay for loans contracted in the previous autumn. More than 9,000 sacks were assigned in this way, mostly to the Bardi and the Peruzzi. The rest were shipped to the Low Countries in small consignments between November 1338 and July 1339 and much of that went straight to the continental creditors. The King himself received a mere 2,300 sacks with which to pay his allies. Moreover, Edward was beginning to suffer the natural economic consequence of this unusual mode of public finance. A glut developed in the markets of Bruges and Antwerp, and English wool, which had fetched £9 a sack in the autumn was selling at £7 in the summer. At one point Edward was trying to tempt potential lenders with promises of repayment in non-existent wool at £5 per sack.

Edward's principal creditors, the Bardi and Peruzzi of Florence, would probably have thrown good money after bad if they had been able. But the great loans of the previous year had exhausted their resources and provoked disquieting rumours about their own solvency. They had also led to the arrest of their agents and the confiscation of their assets in France.[59] The Peruzzi were so gravely affected by the troubles of Edward III that the senior partner of the firm travelled to the Low Countries from Italy in July 1338 and remained there for fifteen months. News of Edward III's fortunes was sent by special messenger to Peruzzi branches as far away as Rhodes in order to forestall a run on deposits. As for the Bardi, they began in the last weeks of 1338 to default on some of their obligations, early signs of the crash which came five years later. The two firms continued to provide a money-transfer service and to make some generally modest loans. But they could do no more than that.

They were succeeded as the principal creditors of the Crown by the tenacious William Pole. Pole was greedy, but social ambition was his strongest motive. He wanted to acquire the great royal manor of Holderness in the hinterland of his native Hull and to raise his family to the level of the foremost barons of the land. He thought that the King could be pressed to part with it for much less than it was worth. The Italians had found themselves imperceptibly enmeshed in Edward's web, but Pole flew straight into it. He found very large sums from his own resources and borrowed even larger sums on his credit, which was better than Edward's. By October 1339 he had lent the King at least £111,000. The great merchant was already well on his way to achieving his vulnerable eminence.

For the rest Edward was obliged to turn to less vulnerable lenders who could drive harder bargains. He borrowed money at exorbitant rates of interest from merchant syndicates in Brussels, Louvain and Mechelen. He bought wool on credit at interest and sold it at a loss for cash. He mortgaged his warhorses. He allowed his principal advisers, the Bishop of Lincoln and the earls of Salisbury and Derby, to be held as hostages by his creditors. The King's financial officials were told that they were to borrow regardless of the cost, provided that money was obtained at once. Edward was a man profoundly conscious of his dignity. He found the means by which he fought off bankruptcy 'dangerous and humiliating' (his own words),[60] tolerable only in order to avoid the worse humilation of returning to his own country without having taken the field. He paid his allies just enough to put off until the muster the moment when his coalition should collapse.

Uncertainty about what Edward III would or could do posed its own difficulties to the French government. Their admittedly larger budget was much strained by the scale of their operations in 1339 and nice judgement was required to allocate resources between four fronts: Gascony, the north, Scotland and the sea. There had been a general review of these resources early in March 1339. At that time it was expected that the King of England would be ready to invade from the north in June. Until then the main effort on land was to be concentrated in the Garonne valley where 2,000 men-at-arms and 10,000 infantry would be deployed. From mid-May the plan was to run down the southern army and build up the northern one until, by 1 June 1339, there would be 10,000 men-at-arms and 40,000 infantry along the Somme in addition to the household troops of the King and the Duke of Normandy. The northern army alone was expected to have four times the combined strength of Edward III and all his allies. In addition the fleet was to operate at full strength throughout the summer. The cost of these plans was prodigious. The Chambre des Comptes calculated that between June and September 1339 military expenditure would be running at 252,000 *l.t.* (about £50,000) per month, which was nearly four times the anticipated receipts of the treasury even when extraordinary taxes were included. This balance sheet was prepared on 4 March 1339. Between that date and the beginning of June, there was a determined attempt to make good the deficit by summoning provincial assemblies to vote fresh extraordinary taxes and sending commissioners to visit bishops, monasteries and rich men with promises of future favours in return for immediate loans and contributions. Four provincial assemblies were planned, at least one of which (covering the frontier *baillages* of Vermandois, Amiens and Senlis) certainly took place and produced moderately satisfactory promises of help. There were also substantial contributions in cash or kind from the representatives of Normandy and Paris. The *arrière-ban* was proclaimed and large sums exacted in lieu of service. Past mistrust was appeased in some parts of France by offers to place the money in the hands of stakeholders appointed by the local communities, to be released only when it was confirmed that the King himself, or his eldest son, was marching against the enemy. These measures were relatively successful. The French Crown's receipts from extraordinary taxation in 1339 were as large as and possibly slightly larger than they were in any other year of the reign.[61]

The gathering of an army was a simpler process in France than it was in England and usually took about two months. About a month was required to transfer a contingent of any size between the Garonne and the Somme. Nevertheless, no date was fixed for the assembly of the northern army until 21 May 1339, when the nobility of the realm was summoned to be at Compiègne by 22 July. Even this date was regarded as provisional. Edward III was known to be in extreme financial and diplomatic embarrassment. Indeed he was reputed to be contemplating returning empty-handed to England. Philip VI felt that he had time to press his advantages in the other theatres of the war which the English King had stripped of resources to supply his ill-starred venture in the Low Countries. In both Gascony and Scotland the English came under intolerable pressure.[62]

In Gascony Philip ordered a halt to the run-down of the southern army. This decision was taken in the spring although it took some time to put into effect. A senior royal councillor, Jean de Marigny, Bishop of Beauvais, was appointed as the King's lieutenant at the end of March. Marigny, who was the half-brother of Philip the Fair's famous Chamberlain, was a less chivalrous but more effective lieutenant than his predecessor John of Bohemia. He was not only a highly competent administrator, but an intelligent diplomat and politician and a fair strategist who was to spend many years representing the King's interests in Languedoc and the march of Gascony. He arrived on 23 April 1339 just after the capture of Bourg and Blaye, when the French effort was beginning to flag for want of any significant prizes which could be captured before the dispersal of the army northward. The Bishop at once injected renewed vigour into it. He took command of all the royal forces in the region at the end of May 1339. At about the same time he announced his intention of attacking Bordeaux. Large reinforcements were necessary for this purpose. It was decided, notwithstanding the threats to the northern frontier, to provide them. They included some prominent noblemen whose presence so far from the Somme valley suggested supreme self-confidence on the government's part: Pierre de Bourbon, Philip's kinsman Louis of Spain, Count of La Cerda, and the Constable's brother Walter of Brienne, titular Duke of Athens, were among them.[63]

The French government's plans for Scotland involved a smaller expenditure of resources but they revealed the same boldness of conception. William Douglas was in France in the first half of 1339. With his arrival the quality of French intelligence on the state of the country markedly improved. Douglas's guerrillas had achieved a large measure of control over the lowlands. North of the Firth of Forth, territory nominally ruled by Edward Balliol, the English and their friends were now confined to the garrisons of Perth, Stirling and Cupar in Fife, which were becoming increasingly difficult to supply across tracts of desolate and hostile country. By now they were receiving almost all their victuals and reinforcements by sea from Hull and King's Lynn. In April the Scots renounced the truces and began to attack this long vulnerable line of supply with a small fleet of oared barges hired in France. The cost of these vessels must have been met by the French government. In May 1339 the Scots laid siege to Perth, the northernmost of the surviving English garrisons. In June William Douglas sailed from France with five oared barges commanded by a French privateer by the name of Hugh Hautpoul. With him went not only a force of exiled Scots recruited at the court of Château-Gaillard but several French knights and their retinues. They were the first French troops to fight the English in Scotland.[64]

In Antwerp Edward III was impotent to protect either of the extremities of his far-flung dominions. All that he could do was give a more serious impression of hostile intent than he had done hitherto in the hope of drawing French troops to northern France. On 20 June 1339 Edward left Antwerp with the English army and marched on to Vilvoorde, a small cloth-making town a few miles south of Brussels. There they camped by the River Senne and waited for their allies. Money continued to pass in packets into the coffers of the Duke of Brabant: a little at the end of March, a little more on 9 April, a few hundred florins on 2 May and again on 23 and 27 May. Another £3,300 was found by the Peruzzi branch in

Bruges and carried overland to the Count of Hainault. The small size and great frequency of these payments was eloquent evidence of the difficulty with which they were made. But effort alone did not impress the allies. They made a concerted demand for a minimum sum which was much more than they had yet received. 'Otherwise', they said, 'there is nothing that we can do for your war.' Edward's embarrassment could not be concealed. 'No money, no men,' the courtiers of Philip VI sang gleefully among themselves.[65]

The Emperor's case was particularly delicate. Louis of Bavaria could not decide whether his political interests would be best served by invading France with the King of England or by seeking a reconciliation with the papacy. Benedict XII made it very clear that he could not do both. In Germany the possibility was canvassed of accepting all of Edward's money and doing nothing. It was perhaps because these rumours had reached Edward's ears that careful arrangements were made for matching payment to performance. Louis of Bavaria was due to receive 200,000 florins (£30,000) by 9 May, whereupon he would march towards Cologne with his army. When he had set out but before he had reached Frankfurt, another 100,000 florins (£15,000) were to be deposited with the Templars of Cologne as stakeholders. When this sum had been paid to him he would leave Cologne for the assembly point in Hainault. Louis, however, was never called upon to perform this elaborate ritual, for apart from 5,000 florins (£750) collected with the utmost difficulty at Antwerp and sent to him in April 1339 none of these sums was paid. The most that Louis could be persuaded to do was to send five ambassadors of modest rank to the camp at Vilvoorde, there to announce publicly that the Emperor and his Vicar were still linked by indissoluble bonds of treaty and affection and that gossip which suggested otherwise was false.[66]

Edward III's allies would have been even more reluctant if they had known that he had plans after the Cambrésis had been overrun to invade Artois for the benefit of Robert of Artois. Robert had lain low in England for two years and his movements had been restricted for at least part of that period. In February 1339, however, he was smuggled by royal officials into the Low Countries and passed the early summer in Brabant concealed in the house of a citizen of Brussels. Edward seems to have believed that Robert had a sizeable following in the county of Artois, although he had never governed it (except for a few months in 1316) and his claim to it was a creature of legal analysis. The English plotted on his behalf with conspirators in Arras who were said to be well disposed towards him. This was probably how the secret escaped. In June 1339 rumours of it had even reached the papal court at Avignon. The allies were outraged. They had pointed out to Edward's ambassadors in 1337 that they could have nothing to do with Robert of Artois and had received Bishop Burghersh's promise that the King would distance himself from the man. In July 1339 Edward was forced to repeat these promises in person and to send Robert away to the court of his sister, the Countess of Namur. He remained there until November 1339 when he was surreptitiously returned to England. His moment would come. Philip VI followed these events from Conflans on the Seine where he had now established his headquarters. On 11 July 1339 he deferred the assembly of the northern army until 15 August. He was 'reliably informed', he said, that Edward would not be ready before that date.[67]

The Bishop of Beauvais launched his attack on Bordeaux at the beginning of July 1339. It came very close to success. Between 12,000 and 15,000 men, the largest field army which the French had yet assembled in the south-west, converged on the city from two directions. The main army under the command of the Bishop and the Count of Foix gathered at La Réole and approached up the Garonne valley, arriving outside the city walls on 6 July. A subsidiary force raised in Périgord and Saintonge crossed the river at Bourg and invested the city from the north on the same day. Bordeaux was filled with refugees from captured strongholds of the hinterland. Morale was low. The French troops assaulted the walls at once. With the aid of some traitors they had already planted some of their men inside the city before the siege began. A gate was opened as they approached. The French royal banner appeared briefly on a tower. Panic and confusion followed. The citizens on guard concluded that all was lost, laid down their arms and fled to their houses. Oliver Ingham, who was in the citadel, collected the garrison and as many armed citizens as he could find and set upon the French, fighting them through the streets of the city until they were forced to withdraw. In spite of their successful infiltration of the city's defences the French attack had not been well planned and reinforcements had not been available quickly enough to consolidate the gains made at the gate. The planning of the siege which followed was worse. The French commanders had not anticipated a prolonged investment of Bordeaux. They had little if any heavy siege equipment. They had not accumulated stocks to feed their great host, and were short of barges, carts and pack animals to bring in supplies from elsewhere. Within a week the besieging army was starving and some of it had to be sent away. On 19 July 1339 the siege was abandoned.[68]

The other diversionary attack, on the English garrisons in central

Scotland, fared rather better. At the beginning of July 1339 William Douglas and Hugh Hautpoul were able with their small fleet of barges to close the Firth of Tay. This sealed the fate of Perth and Cupar, both of which were low on victuals and had no other line of communication with England. Cupar Castle was surrendered by its commander William Bullock, who took a bribe and did homage to David II. The change of allegiance of this sharp, ambitious and experienced clergyman who had been Balliol's chamberlain for six years, showed which way the tide of Scotch affairs was moving. In the northern counties of England a determined attempt was made to prevent the same fate from befalling Perth. A force of some 1,300 troops was raised quite quickly and entered Scotland in June. But it hovered ineffectually about the siege, attempting little and achieving nothing. The Scots succeeded in draining the moat of Perth and began to undermine the walls. Inside, the garrison was starving. Their commander, Sir Thomas Oughtred, surrendered on terms on 17 August 1339. He and his men received a safe conduct and left. The Scots destroyed the walls. Oughtred was arraigned before the next Parliament to answer for his conduct, but he defended himself with vigour. He had, he said, resisted as long as his impossible situation permitted. The lords of Parliament agreed with him. Edward Balliol's client kingdom had all but disappeared at the moment that Edward III launched his scheme of continental conquest.[69]

In Arras the two cardinals made their final heroic effort to make peace between the belligerents after almost a year of fruitless discussion in the city. The Pope had long before given up the job as hopeless. Archbishop Stratford had no proposals to make and there is no evidence that Philip VI's ministers were any more accommodating. In June 1339 Stratford finally left Arras to rejoin Edward III in Brabant and deliver his report. A list was prepared of five preliminary conditions on which Edward III would consent to enter into further negotiations. They were carried back to Arras in July by two Chancery clerks and were found on examination to be bleakly uncompromising. They included the immediate cessation of French assistance to the Scots and a withdrawal from all territory which Philip's generals had conquered in Gascony in the past year. As the Pope observed, these looked more like the outcome of negotiations than their preliminaries. Philip VI rejected them. The long conference of Arras then came formally to an end.[70]

The King of England spent the whole of the second half of August in Brussels pleading with his allies. The Duke of Brabant, the Count of Hainault and his uncle John of Hainault, the princes of Guelders and

Juliers were all there, but their men were not. Edward's bold front in dealing with the cardinals belied the real weakness of his position. The last shipments of wool from England had been sold at wretched prices in July and the proceeds hurried to Edward. The Bardi and the Peruzzi lent 15,000 florins (£2,400) to redeem some jewellery from pawn in Bruges which was sent off at once under armed guard to be pawned again in Germany. Loans were raised for short terms at high rates of interest from moneylenders in Mechelen and Antwerp. Pole found an extra £7,500 to advance to the princes of Guelders and Juliers. For the rest of what was due Edward persuaded his allies to accept his bonds for payment by September 1339, failing which he acknowledged that they should be discharged of all their obligations to him. These bonds were issued on 14 August 1339. Within a week, however, Edward was forced to admit that there was no prospect that they would be honoured. 'Our resources are so stretched by the cost of our own men that we cannot take the field against the enemy,' he told the Margrave of Juliers on the 19th. In this extremity Edward played his final card. He told the princes that he would lead his own army into France without them and confront the French alone, and if he should be killed then he would at least have died honourably. The princes grudgingly replied that they would follow him. They accepted for their wages and fees new and yet more stringent bonds by which Edward not only promised to remain in the Low Countries with all the greatest men of his court until his creditors should be fully satisfied but offered six distinguished knights of his retinue as hostages, and four earls, six barons and three bishops as guarantors to the full extent of their fortunes. To protect his allies against further unpleasant surprises, such as the scheme of restoring Robert of Artois to his county, one of the princes, the Margrave of Juliers, was at once to be sworn to Edward's Council. On these terms the allies were willing to receive their payments in deferred instalments at the end of the year and through the next. The terms are apt to seem humiliating, but they represented in reality a considerable diplomatic triumph. The King had put off for a little longer what had seemed only a few days earlier to be the certain collapse of all his schemes. The Margrave was duly admitted to the royal Council, and later became Earl of Cambridge.[71]

The princes, with one exception, sent messages to Philip VI renouncing their fiefs in France, or promised that they would do so as soon as the expedition was under way. The exception was the Duke of Brabant, but even he could not avoid the issue for much longer. He began with painful deliberateness to assemble his contingent. It was agreed that the allied armies would gather outside Mons in Hainault on 15 September 1339 and march at once on Cambrai.[72] The question whether they would follow Edward III from the Cambrésis into France was perhaps not posed and certainly not answered. Philip VI put back the assembly of his own army to 8 September, a week before his enemy was due to move. On the 11th, he received the Oriflamme from the Abbot of Saint-Denis.[73]

Edward III left Brussels in the second week of September 1339 and arrived with his army at Mons on the 13th, his creditors snapping at his heels.[74] There he installed himself in a Cistercian nunnery a short distance from the town and waited for his allies. Some of them came. Others did not. The Duke of Brabant was still corresponding with Philip VI. His intentions were so uncertain that many French knights assumed that he would not appear, and dispensed themselves from the muster at Compiègne. To Edward III the Duke protested that he was not yet ready. He had an enormous statement of account drawn up showing what further sums had fallen due to him since Edward had last composed with his creditors in Brussels a month before. The lesser allies and foreign retainers pressed for their two months' wages in advance. Edward's own army was clamouring for its pay, which had to be found if there were not to be an embarrassing mutiny on the territory of a friendly prince. The war treasury was completely empty. More bonds were issued; more hostages offered and more onerous promises made. But there were many who would accept nothing less than cash and their demands threatened to bring the whole expedition even now to a halt. In this new crisis Edward was saved by William Pole, whose supreme efforts to scrape together enough to pay the more insistent troops were said by Edward himself to have saved him from the abyss of sudden collapse. It is not known how much Pole found or where, but for his services he was promoted to the rank of banneret, the first occasion on which this had happened to a mere merchant. Edward's army struggled on slowly to Valenciennes. He arrived there on 18 September 1339.[75]

The first attack on French territory was made while Edward was gathering his strength at Valenciennes. Fifty men impatient for action moved north under the command of Walter Mauny to attack towns in eastern Hainault and the county of Ostrevant, where the French government had infiltrated its garrisons. They arrived at dawn one morning outside the walls of Mortagne and finding the gates open burst in and started to pillage and set fire to the houses before they were driven off. Much damage was done and several citizens were killed in this act of pointless and ostentatious daring. The real campaign began on 20 September when

Edward III marched out of Valenciennes accompanied by all his allies (except the Emperor and the Duke of Brabant), by the leading members of the English nobility and by Henry Burghersh, for whom this moment was the consummation of two years of diplomatic labour. They marched southward along the Scheldt into the Cambrésis.

The Bishop of Cambrai had been formally summoned in the name of the Emperor to allow the passage of the army through his territory. But he had refused to do so and intended to resist, which he was well placed to do. The French government had repaired the walls and ditches of his city and had thrown a large garrison into the place commanded by some of its most experienced military officers. Cambrai was invested on the northern side on the first day of the invasion. The ground on this side consisted in the fourteenth century of a dismal expanse of marshland guarded by three castles. Two of these, at Escaudœuvres and Relenghes, within a mile of the walls, had been in the possession of the Count of Hainault since the short raids into the Cambrésis in December of the previous year. The third, guarding the road and river approaches a little further away, was the old twelfth-century fortress of Thun-l'Évêque. Thun-l'Évêque was captured almost at once. The garrison commander was a Fleming with no love for his French masters. Just as Walter Mauny's men were about to assault the walls he accepted a bribe and abandoned the place. The main body of Edward III's army passed round the east side of the city and encamped between the walls and the city's source of relief and supplies in France. The English and their King pitched their tents in the fields by the Scheldt near the village of Marcoing 'within the march of France' as Edward grandly wrote to his subjects at home.

The first news that Philip VI received of the attack on Cambrai came after a French troop escorting a consignment of money for the garrison rode straight into the English army and was captured together with the money. This was followed within a day by the arrival of a messenger from within the city demanding to know why the French army was not already on its way. The French army was in fact at its assembly point at Compiègne, 65 miles further south. Its strength cannot be exactly known but the most plausible contemporary estimates suggest that Philip VI had about 25,000 men, more than twice the number available to Edward III. Nevertheless he decided not to relieve Cambrai but to remain on his frontiers, the first of a succession of decisions which was to earn him a reputation for timidity. There were, nevertheless, good reasons for his caution. One was that the relief of the city would have involved entering Imperial territory and antagonizing Edward III's German allies while there

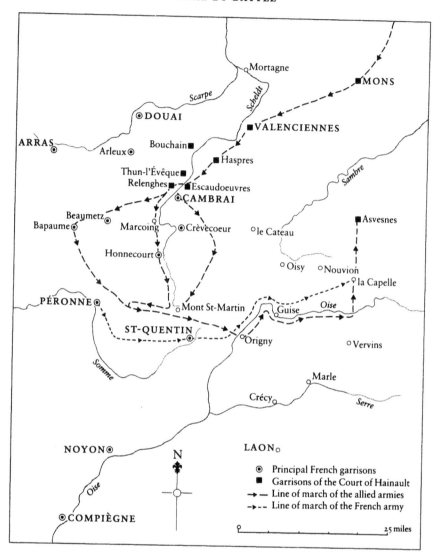

6 The Cambrésis and the Thiérache: Edward III's campaign,
September–October 1339

was still some prospect of their deserting him. The Pope, now a staunch advocate of French interests, urged him not to do so and he probably received the same advice from others closer to his counsels.[76] Philip knew that Edward III could not sustain a war for more than a short period. Before long, winter and penury and the fickleness of his mercenary allies would defeat him as surely as any reverse in battle. It was Edward III who needed a battle and had to fear a stalemate which would leave nothing decided before his army fell apart. The French army advanced to Noyon and then to Péronne, where the Paris road crossed the Somme 22 miles from Cambrai.

Edward III was dismayed by his enemy's inactivity. In the last days of September 1339 the siege was pressed forward with vigour in the hope of drawing a relief army which he could confront in battle. Raiding parties were detached from the main army and sent to lay waste the property of the Bishop and castles held by Philip's subjects and friends. 'On the Monday, the Eve of the Feast of Saint Matthew,' Edward wrote to his son, 'the troops began to burn in the Cambrésis and they burned there for the whole of the following week so that the whole territory was laid waste and quite stripped of corn, cattle and everything else.' The devastation was so great that four years later the rich ecclesiastical estates of the region were lying uncultivated and abandoned.[77] Against defended places the results were less consistent. The Earl of Suffolk captured Beaumetz with great bloodshed and burned it. But the Hainaulters failed before Oisy.[78] At about the end of September there was a determined and almost successful attempt to take Cambrai by storm. By the Scheldt at the northernmost point of the city there was a fortified gate known as the Château de Celles (which, rebuilt by Vauban, still exists). Its captain, another Fleming, was bribed to lower the drawbridge and admit the enemy. But before enough of them had penetrated into the streets the cathedral bells rang out the alarm and the gate was recaptured. As the French had discovered at Bordeaux in July it was remarkably difficult for an army to fight its way through the narrow streets of a defended town.

By the beginning of October 1339 it was clear that Edward was achieving nothing. He was not bringing the French King to battle. He was not subduing Cambrai, a city for which he had little use in any case. It is probable that there was also a shortage of victuals, in spite of the enormous stores of provender which had been looted in the Cambrésis. Medieval armies usually needed to keep moving in order to eat and Edward's army, small as it was by comparison with Philip's, was nevertheless as large as the population of a substantial city. Edward estimated that he had about 15,000 men before Cambrai, although there is reliable evidence that the true figure at this stage was about 10,000, of whom rather less than half were Englishmen.[79] On 30 September 1339 the Duke of Brabant at last arrived with another 1,200 men-at-arms. The Emperor's son, the Margrave of Brandenburg, arrived three days later with a prestigious name and further reinforcements.

It was a time for reassessment. Edward pressed his allies to carry the war into France and provoked a new crisis among them. The Rhineland princes, whose territory was far away from the French government's vengeance, were glad enough of the prospect of pillage and ransoms. But the Duke of Brabant still had his permanent agent in Philip VI's entourage offering reassurances which became daily more incredible. The Duke asked to be allowed to send an ultimatum to Philip VI first.[80] On that condition he was persuaded to take the momentous step of renouncing his homage for his French lands. The French lands of the Count of Hainault, however, were more extensive than those of anyone present except Edward III. The Count had a real territorial interest in capturing the castles of the Cambrésis but none at all in invading France, as 'aucuns sages' pointed out to him. William II of Hainault was an impressionable young man without the firmness of purpose of his father. He was torn between the 'sages', cautious lawyers, bureaucrats and ecclesiastics of his council, and the greater part of the nobility of Hainault, whose spokesman was John of Hainault, the Count's belligerent uncle. In Count William's tents the wise men prevailed. William said that he would not only withdraw his forces from Edward's service but would bring them over to the French side. It was, he said, his duty as a vassal of France to defend it against invasion. It was a courageous gesture, but an almost empty one. William left to join the French army, but John continued to serve as Marshal of Edward's army, and most of the nobility of Hainault stayed with him.

The allied army marched south on 9 October 1339, crossing into France that evening. Their marching order was devised so as to enable them to live as far as possible off the land and to spread destruction over the widest possible area. The men were disposed across the whole of the western Cambrésis and advanced along a front about 20 miles wide, destroying everything in their path which they did not pillage for their own use. The eastern wing of the army followed the road leading south-east from Cambrai (corresponding to the modern D 960). Only two places put up any significant resistance and compelled them to pass by. In the centre Edward III and Henry of Lancaster, Earl of Derby, followed the main road along the valley of the upper Scheldt. The only resistance which they encountered came from a troop of French soldiers under the command of the Constable who were making for Cambrai to reinforce the garrison there. They took refuge in the nearby castle of Honnecourt, which the French had repaired and fitted out as an advance post only a month before.[81] A ferocious attack was made on the walls which lasted for the whole of 10 October and was beaten off with so many casualties that the English King became concerned about the dissipation of his strength before the decisive battle to come. The pattern was the same elsewhere: an effortless ride through undefended villages spreading fire and death, followed by repulse at castles which they had neither time nor equipment to capture. On the western wing of the army the Earl of Warwick narrowly failed to take Bapaume, the great border fortress guarding the cloth road from Flanders to Paris. Its commander had been bought over but by the time the English arrived to take delivery he had been discovered. They found his mulitated body displayed from the battlements and the gates closed and guarded. They then swept south into eastern Picardy, systematically wasting the land to within 2 miles of the town of Péronne, where most of the French army was. Villagers and local ruffians completed the tale of chaos and destruction by joining in the pillaging on their own account. A year later two papal officials followed in the footsteps of the allied army distributing alms, recording the fate of the inhabitants in their accounts with a sobriety far more powerful than the excited descriptions of the chroniclers. Fifty-five villages of the diocese of Noyon had been largely or entirely destroyed: here a village 'burned', 'devastated', 'abandoned'; here a market town populated only by beggars; here a priest knocked senseless while saying mass. Many of those who had fled to safety in the main walled towns like Saint-Quentin found that they had nothing to go back to. They were still begging in the streets there in the autumn of 1340.

On his first evening in France, the King of England established his headquarters in the nunnery of Mont-Saint-Martin, which was about 10 miles north of Saint-Quentin and only a little more from Péronne. Here he was found out on 10 October 1339 by the cardinals. They had made their way under safe conduct from Arras in a final attempt to turn Edward back. It was a brave but naive and useless gesture. When it failed they tried to delay the King with advice on strategy. At least Edward should wait until his army received further reinforcements from Germany, they said. 'The Kingdom of France', they told him, 'is surrounded by a thread of silk which not even the whole strength of England will break.' One of them,

Bertrand de Montfavence, was taken by the old Chief Justice Scrope to the top of the convent tower. The sky glowed in the night and the countryside could be seen burning for 15 miles around. 'Do you not think', Scrope asked, 'that this thread of silk about France is already broken?' The Cardinal fainted.

Philip VI left Noyon on 10 October 1339 to join the main body of his army at Péronne. He was accompanied by the King of Bohemia and six dukes together with their household troops. By the time the King reached Nesle they could see the smoke of burning villages ahead. Péronne itself was crowded with soldiers and refugees and unwelcome messengers from princes serving in the allied army. The Duke of Brabant's defiance was read out in the presence of his diplomatic agent at the French court. This man was so mortified by the deception of which he had been the unconscious agent that he abandoned his master and accepted a pension from Philip VI. William of Hainault was there in person to offer explanations of the past and promises for the future. Philip asked him whether he had come to betray him. Had he not allowed the English passage through his territory and assisted them to ravage the Cambrésis? One of Philip's friends, the Count of Évreux, took the King aside to remonstrate with him. Philip was unmoved. He told the wretched Count that he would reconsider his position in due course. William took his place in the French army with 400 or 500 men and followed it for the rest of the campaign. But the King treated him as a pariah and addressed not another word to him.[82]

The invaders drew their scattered forces together in the plain east of Péronne. Edward himself left Mont-Saint-Martin on 14 October to join them. His movements in the next few days lacked his usual decisive manner. On the evening of the 14th the two armies came within a mile of each other close to Péronne. In the French camp the leaders of the army decided that they would attack the enemy on the following morning. Edward might have had his battle. But he was not ready. He was probably concerned about his line of retreat in the event of disaster and did not want to be caught so far west between the main French army and the strong French garrisons of Cambrai, Tournai and Lille. When the French decision was reported to him by spies, as it was almost immediately, he decamped by night and withdrew rapidly eastward past the walls of Saint-Quentin towards the River Oise. The English were first across the river. They burst into the town of Origny and burned the whole place including the nunnery and the Benedictine abbey.[83] Edward installed himself among the ruins. This was on 16 October. Philip VI, hearing that his prey had gone, delivered an angry tirade against the indiscretion of his servants and courtiers, the raw material of every hostile spy. 'Can I not speak quietly in my private room without the King of England listening? Must he always sit invariably by my side?' Then he moved his troops out of Péronne to Saint-Quentin and waited.

In Edward III's army conditions were becoming difficult. There had been fresh dissensions among the allies on the march from Péronne. There was a growing crisis about victuals. The English had organized their supplies very thoroughly. They had many beasts of burden and a large wagon train loaded with plundered victuals. But the allies had nothing of the kind. Edward had had to buy carts and teams for the Margrave of Brandenburg, who had arrived in the Cambrésis with no transport at all.[84] The others appear to have had some transport but not enough. They had expected to fight the decisive battle as soon as they entered France and, the battle having been deferred, they had nothing to eat. From Origny the English and the Hainaulters launched raids deep into French territory in search of loot and supplies. The earls of Derby, Salisbury and Northampton and John of Hainault took a troop of 500 mounted men on a long ride up the valley of the Serre. They burned Crécy-en-Laonnais, the suburbs of Marle and at least fifteen other villages and towns. The convent of La Paix-Notre-Dame near Marle was so completely wrecked that the sisters were still begging in the streets of Laon a year later. At Sains the inhabitants took refuge with all their possessions in the castle, where they perished in a huge conflagration after the place had been taken by assault. The rest of the army sat by the Oise consuming its stores and complaining. On 17 October the allies came before the King and told him that they intended to withdraw before they starved. Edward offered to supply them from his own stores. He suggested that they should mount their infantry on his cart-horses and move rapidly on to new territory which had not yet been stripped of all foodstuffs. They grumbled among themselves and said that they could see no point in going on.

These discordant voices were silenced by a sudden reminder of the closeness of the French. The leaders of the French army sent Edward a formal challenge to battle on the following Thursday or Friday, 21 and 22 October, at a 'convenient place uncramped by rivers, walls or earthworks', a fight on even ground and a fair appeal to God's judgement. The message reached the allied camp in the form of a letter from Le Galois de la Baume to a kinsman of his, another Savoyard soldier of fortune who was serving in the English army. After a long period of deliberation he replied on behalf of Edward III and all the allies accepting the challenge.

Origny was not the place to fight the battle. The allied army was spread out in a broad bend of the River Oise which cut off its line of retreat to the north. It was decided to withdraw into the Thiérache, towards the border of Hainault. There were high hopes of taking Guise, which offered a bridge over the Oise towards Hainault. The place belonged to John of Hainault's son-in-law and was occupied by his daughter. The captains of Edward III's army were already in touch with the garrison commander who had sold them victuals and weapons.[85] But when John of Hainault arrived with his men outside the walls, the place resisted. So he burned the suburbs and passed by. The army followed the Oise eastward, burning every village as they came to it. The villagers of Monceau-le-Vieil told the papal almoners that the soldiers had emptied their houses of the contents and made a great bonfire of them, then burned the village itself to the ground. It was not an unusual story. In most places the inhabitants fled until the storm had passed. The French army followed through the charred fields and hamlets about half a day behind.

On the evening of 21 October 1339 Edward III called a halt between the small town of La Capelle and the village of La Flamengrie, where the forest of Nouvion opens out into cultivated fields. The French stopped on the 22nd at Buirenfosse, a hamlet at the edge of the forest about 4 miles from the English encampment. It was in the early evening that three French spies found reconnoitring the allied positions gave the first certain intelligence of the French King's presence. They were taken away and questioned separately. All of them agreed that the French were intending to attack on the following day, 23 October 1339.

Edward had chosen his battlefield with great skill. The ground sloped gently away from La Flamengrie towards the French positions. The forest prevented any outflanking movement to the west and the allies securely held the road junction of La Capelle, blocking any eastward movement of the enemy. From Edward's encampment the Roman road ran north to Avesnes in Hainault, 10 miles away, his line of retreat. The dispositions of his army were fixed by the King with his commanders on the evening of the 22nd and completed shortly after daybreak on the following morning. Edward dismounted all his troops, sending the horses to the rear. He placed his archers on each of his flanks. Between them, slightly set back, the rest of the army was arrayed in three lines behind a deep trench guarded by Welsh lancers. Edward himself took command in the centre of the first line with Burghersh and Scrope and the troops of the royal household. Henry of Lancaster, Earl of Derby, and the Earl of Suffolk held the right of the line, while the earls of Salisbury, Northampton and Pembroke held the left. The Germans, including the Margrave of

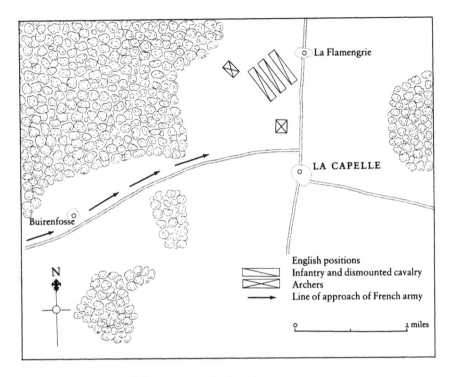

7 English positions at La Capelle, 23 October 1339

Brandenburg, the Margrave of Juliers and John of Hainault, were placed in the second line. The Duke of Brabant formed the rearguard. It was in fact the battle plan of Dupplin Moor and Halidon Hill, and of Crécy seven years later. The Germans had never seen anything like it, 'but seeing that it was a strong position, cunningly laid out, and that the King was content, they were satisfied. They took up their positions ready to live or die.' The Duke of Brabant promised 1,000 florins to whomever should first bring him a piece of the Oriflamme even if it were no more than the size of a man's palm. There was a special distribution of wine. Very large numbers of squires received knighthoods at the hands of the King himself, some of whom, like Sir John Chandos,[86] were destined to make famous careers.

The French army passed the night in battle order. They slept very little. Walter Mauny and other bold spirits of the allied army repeatedly penetrated their defences in small groups, killing sentries and falling upon isolated bodies of men. In the early morning the French vanguard advanced a short distance from the encampment and waited for their orders. None came. In the King's tent a venomous dispute had broken out about whether to give battle at all. The classic English battle plan depended on the enemy throwing his cavalry into the centre of the English line so that it could be impaled on planted lances and massacred by longbowmen firing from the flanks. The French leaders must have been aware of this. The size and depth of the trench in front of the English lines had been reported by scouts on the previous afternoon and the exact dispositions of all the allied troops were described early on 23 October by some captured German knights. Might not mere delay defeat the English King just as effectively as a frontal attack? There were other considerations. The French army had been marching for several days through territory wasted by Edward III and they were hungry and thirsty. The contrary arguments owed more to emotion than military calculation. 'The King will look like a fool and a knave if he refuses battle when the enemy has burned and wasted the kingdom under his nose and his army has come so close.' Philip decided towards the middle of the day that he would not attack but would wait for the allies to do so. The vanguard of the French army was ordered to retreat and dig in. It was not a popular decision. A purely defensive war brought no ransoms, no booty, no glory and a deal of contempt for Philip personally. French noblemen accused the King's advisers of 'foxiness' ('renardie') and disported themselves in fox-fur hats and skins hooting abuse. On strictly military grounds, however, it was probably the right decision. Had it not been made La Capelle might have been as famous a name as Crécy, remembered for something more than the site of the Armistice of 1918.

From the English lines the retreat of the French vanguard was noticed at once. Soon afterwards the French were seen to be digging trenches and drawing large tree trunks in front of their position. Edward did not laugh at his enemy's inconstancy. He knew that it marked the failure of his campaign. The princes and the leaders of the army conferred. An attack on a much larger army in prepared defensive positions was unthinkable. To keep the allied troops drawn up and waiting was impossible. They too were short of food and water. The princes became restive. They declared that Edward's army had won a moral victory, for they had destroyed large tracts of northern France with impunity; they had dared the French King to do his worst and he had done nothing. Towards five o'clock, as it was growing dark, the allies mounted their horses. There was a brief stir in the French camp as it was thought that they were about to attack. But instead the allies turned north and marched away along the Roman road to Avesnes. The only fighting was between the English and some of the Germans who quarrelled about the division of booty. After the allies had left Philip VI departed hurriedly for Saint-Quentin. His army passed the night at Buirenfosse and in the morning went out to examine the position in which the allies had stood. From close at hand it seemed less formidable, the trench less broad and deep than they had expected. Then they returned to Saint-Quentin and were paid off.

Oliver Ingham, who had arranged to mount a diversion in the south-west, coinciding with Edward's invasion of the north, began late and achieved no more than his master had. The French had withdrawn large numbers of their troops in July to meet the threat in the north, including almost all the higher nobility of the region. But there were still formidable French forces there, some 3,200 men-at-arms and 12,000 footsoldiers levied locally and spread among the thickly clustered garrisons of the Garonne and Dordogne valleys and the south-east march of the duchy. Ingham's intentions shifted. On 12 October 1339 he marched out of Bordeaux and up the Garonne valley with his modest army. They first tried to surprise Langon, which lay on the south bank of the Garonne opposite Saint-Macaire at the edge of English-held territory. But when they arrived there, on 13 October, they found the place defended by a garrison of 340 soldiers, a large force for a small and well-walled town. The attackers failed to take it. Within a few days the French had begun to concentrate against Ingham's army and by the end of the month he had been forced to retire southwards into the Bazadais. At one point his small force lunged briefly towards the great city of Toulouse, the city's first encounter with the military reality of the war. Ingham seems to have found some substantial support among the nobles of the Toulousain. But with the harvest in and the city securely held there was little real damage that he could do. By the beginning of December 1339 he had returned empty-handed to Bordeaux.[87]

Parliament opened in Westminster Hall on 13 October 1339, a despondent assembly whose tone was set by demoralized civil servants and the rump of the aristocracy which was not on campaign with the King.[88] The grain harvest had been poor. Wool prices were low, the result in large measure of the quantities which Edward III and his magnates had precipitately dumped on the north European market. The north and especially Cumberland and Northumberland had resumed its secular decline to barren waste, the outcome of almost continuous guerrilla warfare and semi-official banditry. But the burden of taxation and purveyance was as great as ever.

Edward III had been warned by his councillors that it would be a difficult meeting and had sent three men, Archbishop Stratford, Richard

Bury, Bishop of Durham, and William Pole from his camp with concessions to meet some obvious grievances. Stratford made a long speech at the opening of the session. He explained how the King had been compelled by financial hardship and inadequate supplies from England to postpone the opening of his campaign for more than a year, and how he had invaded the Cambrésis in the middle of September. He read out newsletters from the Earl of Huntingdon and the agents of the Peruzzi bank recording how Edward had entered France and reached the neighbourhood of Saint-Quentin. All this, he said, had been possible only because the King had borrowed enormous sums of money on ruinous terms, money which he could not hope to repay without generous parliamentary taxes. The audience was probably not told how ruinous the terms of the loans were, but they were told the amount of them. Edward's debts, Stratford revealed, now exceeded £300,000, a sum which represented the equivalent of some ten years of ordinary revenue or more than seven Parliamentary subsidies.

Stratford nearly got what he wanted. Both houses of Parliament agreed that the King stood in need of 'une tres grante somme' and the Lords, who had been skilfully worked upon, proposed a tax in kind of a tenth of one year's yield of corn, wool and lambs. But the Commons were preoccupied by their campaign against purveyance. They demanded concessions. In particular they wanted a statute that in future all royal purveyors should pay cash or be liable to arrest. The Council retreated. The current chief purveyor was arrested and consigned to the Fleet prison on the Commons' petition. At about the same time all outstanding warrants of purveyance had to be cancelled. As for taxation, the Commons deliberated for a long time among themselves before concluding that their constituents would probably repudiate their authority if they agreed. The sum required was very large, they said. They would have to consult their communities at home. Perhaps the matter might be raised again at the next Parliament. But they hoped that God would continue to honour the King with victory. The Commons dispersed on 28 October 1339, too early to have heard about events at La Capelle. On the same day Edward III arrived in Brussels to begin a week of jousting with his friends and allies and to reconstruct their plans. 'Always bear in mind', the Pope wrote to him a few weeks after this, 'how many of your subjects have been ruined already by the burdens of this war, how much heavier those burdens will grow as it continues, and how uncertain is the outcome of all wars.'[89]

CHAPTER IX

The Flemish Alliance and the Campaigns on the Scheldt
1339–1340

When Edward III was proclaimed King of France on 26 January 1340 the event came as a surprise to the rest of Europe. At Avignon Pope Benedict XII declared himself to be 'astounded, stupefied' by the news, although his representatives had been about the English court for more than two years. The Florentine community in Bruges, which had followed Edward's doings with close concern ever since he had become the major debtor of the Florentine banks, were quite as much taken aback. 'Imagine', they wrote back to the Republic, 'what news we have to tell you.' It was a remarkable *coup de théâtre* whose consequences were felt for another 120 years of French and English history. Yet Edward III's most spectacular political act had its origins in political calculation at once cynical and mundane, and when the decision was made it was made with hesitation and misgiving. The mere fact that it was made so late, after three years of war, is some indication of this.[1]

In 1329 the English Parliament, in spite of the strong views of Edward's mother, had advised that Edward's claim was a nonsense and ought to be forgotten. And so it was, for almost a decade. Nothing at all was heard of a Plantagenet claim to the French crown between 1329 and 1337. Moreover, a number of things happened in that period which made the claim even more far-fetched than it had been at the outset. Edward III had done homage to Philip VI in Amiens cathedral in 1329. Two years later in 1331 he had agreed that he should be treated as having done liege homage, the closest bond of feudal dependence known to the middle ages. It was true that he had been a minor in 1329, but the agreements of 1331 were his own, made several months after he had seized power in England. There could not have been a more complete acknowledgement of Philip VI's kingship or a more perfect renunciation of his own claims, such as they were. There was, moreover, another difficulty. In May 1332 Joan of Navarre gave birth to a son Charles, who, as 'Charles the Bad', was to play such a destructive role in the French civil wars of the 1350s. Joan was the daughter of Philip the Fair's eldest son, Louis X. It followed that if (as

Edward's lawyers asserted) a woman could transmit a claim to the French crown then it was neither Edward III nor Philip VI but the infant Charles who had the better claim. This point was not lost on contemporaries who thought about the matter. But the truth was that very few of them did think about it. The possibility that anyone other than Philip VI might be rightful king of France was not taken seriously even in England until 1337 and it was not considered elsewhere until 1339.

At a very early stage the credit for reviving the claim was given to that king of intriguers Robert of Artois. Robert's activities in England between 1336 and his death in 1342 received scarcely any attention from the English chroniclers. On the continent, however, his hand was discerned in almost everything that Edward III did, an obsession which almost certainly had its origins in French official propaganda. Within a very few months of Edward III's formal assumption of the French crown somebody wrote a celebrated verse legend, *The Vow of the Heron*, which in one form or another circulated widely in northern France and the Low Countries. According to the poet, Robert had shamed the English King into asserting his claim at a banquet in London. Entering Edward's 'marble hall' in the midst of the revelry he had presented Edward with a platter bearing a roast heron, 'the most timid of birds for the most cowardly of kings, deprived of his inheritance in noble France which is rightfully his, but for his cowardice, destined to be deprived of it until he dies'. It was true, Edward was supposed to have replied, that he had done homage to Philip VI. 'I was young of years so it is not worth two ears of corn.' But now he will swear to carry fire and death into France and make no truce or peace until the crown is in his possession. The others present, a gathering of almost all the military heroes of the next twenty years, swore similar oaths. 'Now I have my way,' Robert said, 'since through this heron I caught today a great war will begin.' From versifiers and pamphleteers, the deeds of Robert of Artois passed into historical orthodoxy. Writing in the early 1350s the great Liège chronicler Jean le Bel, who was by no means anti-English, gave it as a fact that Robert insinuated himself into Edward's favour in the winter of 1336-7, and inflamed the English King's ambitions by persuading him that he had a better claim by inheritance than Philip did and that the judgement of the princes of the blood in 1328 (to which Robert had been a party) was vitiated by their failure to give a proper hearing to Edward III's proctors. Half a century later the final version of Froissart's chronicle has Robert of Artois seated in the Parliament of March 1337 while an unnamed prelate delivers a learned and passionate address in support of Edward's hereditary rights which Robert had written for him beforehand.[2]

The true reasons for asserting a claim to the crown of France were less colourful. There was, in the first place, a serious legal difficulty about waging open war on Philip VI in France if Philip were to be regarded as the king of France. For if Philip were king of France then Edward was undoubtedly his vassal for the duchy of Aquitaine and the county of Ponthieu. These properties had been declared forfeit, and if Edward wished to challenge the forfeiture it seemed that he would have to do so in Philip's courts. A subject could not wage aggressive war. Even the right of a subject to defend himself against his sovereign by force was very doubtful and certainly did not extend to invading France from the north with an army of Englishmen and Germans.[3] Moreover, if Edward were to wage war on Philip, feudal practice absolutely required that he should first renounce the personal bond of homage and 'defy' his former lord. But in doing so Edward would be renouncing the sole legal basis on which he could continue to hold his French dominions. There was no escape from this legal conundrum unless it was that Philip was not truly king of France at all, and therefore never Edward's sovereign. One should not under-estimate the attachment of medieval men to legal forms, and particularly the attachment of such a man as Edward III. He presided over a bureau-cratic government filled with lawyers, and was served by diplomats who always saw international relations in legal terms. Edward III shared their outlook even if he did not have their learning.

The same considerations applied to those of Edward's allies (the majority) who were Frenchmen or held fiefs in France for which they were as much vassals of the French Crown as Edward was. Edward did not need Robert of Artois to tell him how valuable a weapon of war propaganda were the doubts which might be raised against Philip's right to rule France. The threat was sufficiently obvious to have become a talking point in both kingdoms as early as the autumn of 1337.[4] Edward III had a genius for turning other men's quarrels to his own account and recruiting traitors and malcontents to his cause. Like the invaders of any age he probably entertained exaggerated notions about the support which they could bring him. Robert of Artois was only the first of them. At the opposite end of the country, a Burgundian lord like Jean de Faucogney, who had married a cousin of Philip VI and was engaged in a bitter property dispute with other members of the royal family, found it natural to correspond through trusted servants with the King of England. Edward's support in Flanders was certainly not confined to the revolutionary governments of the three great towns but included some influential noblemen. Henry of Flanders, the Count's uncle, did homage to Edward III in February 1339. Guy of Flanders, his illegitimate half-brother who was captured at Cadzand in 1337, reappeared as a supporter of Edward III in 1340. Edward had bought him from his captor for £8,000, some indication of the value which he attached to such support. It would be interesting to know how many others were included among the 'various magnates of France' to whom Edward III was writing three weeks before his assumption of the crown. The only occasions (and they were rare) when Edward III called himself King of France before January 1340 were occasions on which he was negotiating with such men as these. For them, the assertion that Edward III was really king of France made the difference, important to their followers as well as to themselves, between rebellion and civil war, between politics and treason.[5]

Within the English government opinion fluctuated. It is quite possible that the usefulness of a claim to the crown of France was discussed in the Parliament of March 1337 which sanctioned the first campaign of the war. One English chronicler in addition to the inventive Froissart says so.[6] But if it was, the outcome cannot have been encouraging, for the embassy which Edward sent to the continent on Parliament's advice took with it powers to negotiate with 'the most excellent prince, the lord Philip, illustrious King of France'. Indeed, in the propaganda broadsheet which Edward issued at the end of August 1337 to justify the war to his subjects not only was there no reference to a possible claim to the French crown but Philip VI was referred to throughout by his correct title. The habit of calling him 'self-styled King of France' originated not in Edward III's Chancery but in that of the German Emperor, Louis of Bavaria. Louis perceived the propaganda advantages of publicly doubting his adversary's kingship before Edward did. Pope Benedict XII noted this affectation with displeasure and declined to answer Louis's letters when they referred to Philip in that way.[7]

The disparaging phrase was at first adopted by Edward only when corresponding with the German Emperor. But a noticeable change occurred in October 1337 during the sessions of the second Parliament of that year. It was probably the result of the King's deliberations with the Lords. At this stage Edward was still expecting to invade France within a matter of weeks. Troops were asembling in the east-coast ports. Bishop Burghersh and other important members of the royal Council were about to depart for Holland with the advance guard of the army. It was now necessary to send a formal defiance to Philip VI and to resolve the difficult legal problem of renouncing a homage without renouncing the territory for which the homage was due. A view had therefore to be taken on whether

Philip VI was or was not king of France, and the only view consistent with Edward III's continued possession of Gascony was that he was not. So the territory which Edward still held he kept, and the territory which he had lost to 'Philip de Valois' he renounced 'not to you but to the safe-keeping of God'. The letter of defiance was dated 19 October 1337 and was carried by Burghersh to the continent in the following month. At the same time Burghersh was furnished with a variety of diplomatic procurations, not always consistent with each other, for use as the occasion might arise. One of these was a power issued in Edward's name as King of England and Duke of Aquitaine to 'negotiate with the most excellent prince, the lord Philip illustrious King of France or his designated representatives upon the question of the right to the kingdom of France and whether it ought to belong to him or to us'. Diplomatic tact could hardly be carried further. Bishop Burghersh, however, was also supplied with some less coyly phrased documents. These boldly announced Edward III as 'Edward by the Grace of God King of England and France'. They declared that the crown of France had by hereditary descent devolved upon him and that now, after years in which he had remained ignorant of his royal rights, he intended to take up the duties of his office. Several royal lieutenants, including the Duke of Brabant, the Count of Hainault and the Margrave of Juliers, were appointed to act for him within France, explaining the King's just rights to prelates and noblemen there and inviting their support. These documents were obviously intended for use in confidential negotiations with the enemies of Philip VI within his own realm, and in particular with the Flemings. But as it happened they were overtaken by events. Within six weeks of their being drawn up the invasion of France was postponed and Edward was made by the cardinals to declare a temporary cessation of hostilities. The letter of defiance was therefore placed in abeyance. It was not presented until well into the following year. As for the documents authorizing royal lieutenants to explain Edward's rights in France, the probability is that they never left the satchels of Burghersh's clerks. The decisions made in October 1337, however, were not a dead letter. After that date the line consistently followed by the English government in its public documents was that Philip was 'self-styled' or 'de facto' king of France. The question who ought to be king of France if Philip was not was discreetly ignored. Evidently the policy was to preserve the right to make a claim in case of need and to do nothing meanwhile which might be thought to acknowledge Philip's title. For the time being, Edward was willing to wound but afraid to strike.[8]

The English government maintained this equivocal position throughout

1338 and for much of 1339. During the long and unproductive diplomatic conferences at Arras, which lasted from late August 1338 until July 1339, the English Chancery engaged in elaborate documentary contortions designed to avoid calling Philip king of France without driving him from the conference table by overtly denying his title. The English ambassadors' powers were prepared while the King was waiting at Walton for his passage to the continent. They were all drawn up in duplicate, one set referring to the King of France by his proper title and the other by the ambiguous phrase 'our cousin of France'. When Edward arrived at Antwerp nearly a month later, one of his first acts was to cancel the one which addressed Philip as king. It is difficult not to see in this change the hand of Henry Burghersh, who was present on the second occasion but probably not on the first. When the procurations were renewed in November 1338 the alternatives were 'our cousin of France' and 'self-styled King of France'. On each occasion the ambassadors were enjoined to do nothing which might prejudice a future claim by Edward III to Philip's crown. The interesting question is: which set of procurations was in fact used? It seems that it was always the more respectful version. The Pope, whose agents presided over the conference and fed him with a constant stream of news, was quite unaware of any challenge to Philip's kingship during the winter of 1338–9. As he saw it Edward was not disputing that he ought to be Philip's vassal; the problem lay in defining the terms of his dependence. Benedict was right. At this stage Edward was not interested in his claim to France except as a legal device and a weapon to be kept polished in the background in case another occasion required its use, as it shortly did. Only at the very end of the Arras conferences, when negotiations were about to collapse amid the clash of arms, did the English representatives formally place their master's claim to France on the agenda. It was, they explained, the only course left to them in view of the obstinate refusal of the French negotiators to concede anything. Even now they might think again if a reasonable offer were forthcoming. This must have happened in about June 1339. In July the English suggested that the quarrel should be submitted to the mediation of the Pope in person. They prepared for this purpose submissions of great length and learning in which Edward III's claim to the throne of France was justified by reference to scripture, custom and law. But the French declined to take any part in this exercise, and all the ingenuity and persuasive skill lavished on the document was wasted.[9]

There is little doubt that Edward III was finally persuaded to declare himself king of France by the Flemings who insisted on it as a condition of their making a military alliance with him. The Flemings, whose neutrality had been recognized by both sides, had at first watched the events on their southern and eastern borders with the detachment of men only marginally involved. The main harbour of Flanders, at Sluys, was used as a base by French and Italian warships in spite of the treaties of neutrality, and had been the scene of a minor battle (already described) in May 1339. Otherwise, reminders of the war were few and undramatic: a constant run of messengers, spies waiting by the foreshore on the Hondt, escorted convoys of pack animals carrying money from the Peruzzi bank in Bruges to Antwerp, Brussels and Valenciennes. Edward III did his best to insulate the Flemings from the war, paying generous and surprisingly prompt compensation to the victims of drunken soldiers and undisciplined shipmasters.[10] He never abandoned his earlier hopes, frustrated in 1338, of making the Flemings his allies instead of neutral spectators. His interest in the shifts of public opinion in the county was remarkable. He corresponded regularly with the leaders of the three towns and flattered them with pensions and gracious answers to their petitions. He paid an itinerant Dominican to preach his cause in the county and sent a chaplain on horseback 'nearly all the length and breadth of Flanders' to discover what its people thought about him.[11]

Sentiment in Flanders was moving in Edward's favour throughout 1339 and continued to do so even after his enterprise was checked at La Capelle in October. The war brought ancient resentments to the surface. Philip VI endeavoured to appease the anti-French feeling which he knew existed in Flanders, but his concessions were not enough for Jacob van Artevelde. Van Artevelde conceived in the course of 1339 the ambition of recovering for Flanders the three castleries of Lille, Douai and Orchies, which had been severed by Philip the Fair and annexed to the royal domain. It was a remarkable ambition. The three castleries were separated from the rest of Flanders not only by the River Lys, an important natural frontier, but by their language, which was French, and by their commercial interests, which were entirely inimical to those of Ghent, Bruges and Ypres.[12]

Van Artevelde's personal motives can only be guessed. The security of his own position must have been one of them. He belonged to a government of usurpers exercising power by their own decision but in the Count's name. The Count himself, who was ineffective and unpopular but had the aura of legitimacy, struggled to conserve his freedom of action, veering, like Louis XVI during the French Revolution, from impotent assent to all that was required of him to overt, impetuous defiance. In September 1338 he was to be seen in the uniform of the magistracy of

Ghent walking in the procession of Our Lady of Tournai. Three months later he attempted to lead a rebellion in western Flanders and failed. He fled, half-dressed, in the middle of the night to Artois and for most of the rest of the year was resident at the court of Philip VI, leaving the county to be governed on no very clear constitutional basis by the committees of the towns. To the Flemings van Artevelde was the man who had restored the flow of English wool to Flanders, 'like God descended from Heaven to save them' as a chronicler put it. His power in Ghent was for the time being unassailable. His friends, relatives and allies filled the magistracy. His standing among the crowds was extraordinarily high. Bruges and Ypres, the other two great towns of Flanders, were allies weaker than Ghent and falling steadily into dependence. Outside the three great industrial towns, however, van Artevelde and his shadowy friends in Bruges and Ypres depended on an uneasy mixture of persuasion and force. The lesser towns had captains and special commissioners attached to their governments, generally appointed by Ghent. Their function was to enforce compliance with the treaties of neutrality with France and England. But they used their powers in the political and commercial interests of Ghent. The regulations which suppressed competition against the industries of the three towns were enforced with unwelcome vigour and in a few places resistance was put down with considerable violence. Among the rural nobility, particularly in western Flanders, the burghers of Ghent, Bruges and Ypres had few friends. Over the border at Saint-Omer in neighbouring Artois, there was a growing band of exiled and embittered Flemish noblemen waiting for the opportunity to return. Hostility to France had great political value in the hands of a skilful Flemish politician like van Artevelde.[13]

Edward III sedulously encouraged the territorial ambitions of the Flemings and inflamed their grievances against France. In the winter 1338–9 he was offering a variety of benefits to tempt them into a military alliance. They included everything that the Flemings had vainly sought from the kings of France for many years: the complete revocation of the penal clauses of the treaties that they had made with Philip the Fair, the recovery of the 'lost' castleries of Walloon Flanders and the restoration of all the ancient privileges of the Flemish towns. Plainly, only a King of France could give them all this. Edward's offers were therefore made as King of France and expressed to be contingent on God according him possession of the throne. 'The Count and his subjects', Edward said, 'have been despoiled by the Crown of France of what was once theirs ... The King is now ready to make amends for the wrongs that have been done to

Flanders in depriving it of so much of its territory. Its inhabitants will be guaranteed their privileges and showered with benefits which they and their descendants will remember for ever.'[14]

For the time being these proposals failed to draw the Flemings into the English King's camp. They fell into abeyance in the constitutional confusion and internal disorder which followed Louis of Nevers' flight from Flanders in January 1339. The rulers of the towns continued to negotiate with both sides, diffidently with the Count and the King of France, who hated them, and conspiratorially with Edward III. As the English design against France's northern frontier grew more menacing they began to make their own plans to exploit Philip VI's difficulties. During the summer of 1339, Flemish forces began to collect in the Lys valley ready to seize Lille, the northernmost of the three castleries. At the end of July unpleasant reports of these movements were circulating in Paris. French troops were diverted to Lille from Tournai and elsewhere. The Flemings assured Philip VI that they had no aggressive plans. But there is no doubt that they had, and very little doubt that their plans were made in collusion with the English King. In early September 1339, during Edward III's march to Mons, he had a series of secret meetings with Jacob van Artevelde's brother John. At the end of September, Edward was outside Cambrai and planning to march south; Philip was at Compiègne and the bulk of his army at Péronne; the Flemish troops on the north bank of the Lys were still being reinforced. Philip was seriously alarmed. He decided to send Louis of Nevers back to Flanders to restore some semblance of control. But Philip had misjudged the Flemings and their leaders. Although Louis loyally returned and was splendidly received in Ghent, he became at once a prisoner of van Artevelde and exercised no influence at all on his plans. Edward III entered France on the evening of 9 October 1339. On the 21st, a deputation left Ghent with the unhappy Count Louis to present an ultimatum to Philip VI. Unless the French King agreed at once to return the three castleries they would cross the Lys, they said, and attack Lille.

They were too late. By the time they reached the French court, Edward's army had withdrawn from La Capelle. The pressure on Philip had suddenly eased. He rejected the Flemish demands. The Flemings were now in an impossible position. They had broken with Philip VI but were unable to carry out their threat. Indeed unless they joined the Anglo-German alliance they would be helpless in the face of Philip VI's revenge.[15]

All this had befallen the Flemings at a most opportune time for Edward III, who had been obliged to reconstruct his plans for defeating France in the aftermath of the failure of his autumn campaign. More than ever

Edward needed the support of Flanders with its great resources of man-power. On 28 October 1339, the day on which he returned to Brussels, he invited representatives of the three great towns to a conference of his allies. The conference took place at Antwerp on 12 November 1339. What transpired is extremely obscure, although the results are plain enough. On the day after the Antwerp conference had ended the Duke of Brabant and six English royal councillors were instructed to negotiate the terms of a treaty of alliance with the Flemings. They were to promise the Flemings 'all the ancient privileges, liberties and immunities which they have enjoyed in our time and in that of our ancestors the kings of France and England'. They were also to offer to restore Flanders to its ancient frontiers, making whatever territorial concessions were necessary. Louis of Nevers had not been bidden to the conference, but there was no reason to suppose that he would make trouble. Louis was alone in Flanders, without his friends and retainers, and his movements were carefully controlled by the city govern-ment of Ghent. His public acts were dictated by a body called the Council of Flanders, whose membership was entirely drawn from the friends and allies of Jacob van Artevelde. He was a cypher.[16]

The negotiations were conducted on Edward's behalf by the Duke of Brabant. On 3 December 1339 he attended a crowded congress of repre-sentatives of the towns of Flanders and Brabant and of those Flemish noblemen who were known to support the new regime. An offensive and defensive alliance between Flanders and Brabant was concluded. It was generally perceived to be the preliminary to a more radical accommoda-tion with the King of England. The traditional exception of their sovereign the King of France from those whom the Flemings were prepared to fight was pointedly omitted. The negotiations which followed were mainly concerned with the practical consequences of an English connection.[17]

These were very significant. The documents by which the communities of Flanders had ratified the treaty of Athis-sur-Orge had provided that in the event that they were ever to act in breach of it the Flemings would submit to a papal interdict. 1309 Pope Clement V had with some reluc-tance become party to an arrangement by which the King of France was enabled to procure the interdict to be laid on Flanders and lifted again at will. There were, moreover, large sums of money deposited by the towns of Flanders in the papal treasury which were liable to be forfeited in the event of their rebellion. These were the reasons, in addition to the need for some legal authority to redraw the boundaries of Flanders and the terms of the treaties, why the Flemings insisted that Edward III should proclaim himself king of France. There would then, as they reasoned, be no legal basis for an interdict or for forfeiting their funds at Avignon. The Flemings formulated their terms by the end of December 1339 and Edward accepted them early in the New Year. The English King's acceptance was certainly not a foregone conclusion. He was under no illusions about the radical nature of the step that was being suggested to him and the difficulties which it would place in the way of a satisfactory accommodation with France. He 'took good counsel and advice' said Jean le Bel,

knowing what a serious thing it was to take the arms and title of a kingdom which he had not yet conquered and might never conquer; yet on the other hand he could not do without the assistance of the Flemings who were in a better position to further his enterprise than any men living. And so, having thought carefully and weighed every consideration, the advantages against the disadvantages, he took the arms of France quartered with those of England, called himself King of France and England and did what the Flemings asked of him.

Jean le Bel's account substantially accords with every other well-informed contemporary assessment of the circumstances in which Edward decided to assume the crown of France. It was, as he correctly anticipated, an act whose consequences were to be much more persistent than its causes.[18]

The Count of Flanders foresaw the way that the negotiations would go. He feigned unctuous acquiescence in all that was being done in his name. He put his seal to the treaty with Brabant. He even concurred with apparent enthusiasm in the plan to recognize Edward III as king of France. But he was determined not to be party to any treaty with the English King. So he secretly arranged for his wife, who was staying in France, to write to him saying that she was dying and needed him by her side. Louis read out the letter before the Council of Flanders and obtained their leave of absence for a short period. Then he left quickly and rode hard until he reached Paris. He did not return.[19]

The King of England remained in Antwerp for the first three weeks of the New Year while the details of the new treaty were worked out. They were comprehensive in their concessions to the Flemings. Edward ceded to them not only the three castleries but Artois (which had been severed from Flanders for more than a century) and the Tournaisis (which had never belonged to Flanders). The right of the King of France to procure an interdict on the county he solemnly renounced, together with all the penal provisions of the treaties and accrued debts in perpetuity. In his capacity as king of England, Edward promised the Flemings that he would declare Bruges to be a compulsory staple town for the export of all English wool for a period of at least fifteen years and that Flemish merchants would have perfect liberty to ply their trade in England free of duties and free of such irksome restrictions as, for example, those which the Londoners inflicted on foreign merchants for their own protection. The military clauses were elaborate. The sea-lanes between the Low Countries and England were to be defended against the French by a combined fleet furnished in equal proportions by England, Brabant and Flanders but paid for entirely by England. On land, the nature of the operations to be undertaken was not spelled out in the treaty. But it was informally agreed that the armies of the alliance would gather at the end of June 1340 and would begin with an attack on Tournai. The Flemings agreed to contribute 80,000 troops for this adventure, for which they would be paid a subsidy of £140,000. On no account, Edward promised, would he make a peace or truce without them or even enter into negotiations with Philip VI unless they consented.[20]

On 22 January 1340 Edward III took delivery at Antwerp of new banners displaying the arms of France quartered with those of England. Then he set out for Ghent with his queen who was in the last stages of pregnancy, accompanied by his entire household and the dukes of Brabant and Guelders. The ceremony took place on the day of his arrival, 26 January 1340, in the Friday Market of Ghent, the largest open space within the walls. Edward stood on a platform decked with the new banners. Around him were the principal dignitaries of his court and the magistrates of the three great towns of Flanders, including Jacob van Artevelde. Much of the population of Ghent had crowded into the square. Edward asked them in a loud voice whether they acknowledged him as king of England and France and whether they would swear to obey him as they had obeyed previous kings of France. The magistrates of the towns swore that they would. Those who held fiefs of the French Crown did homage to him, beginning with Guy of Flanders, the Count's half-brother. Edward swore on the Gospels that he would respect the liberties of his people, and the main articles of the treaties with their valuable commercial concessions were read out to the crowd. The rest of the day was given over to celebration and jousting. A Florentine merchant who was present asked some Flemings what they thought. The better sort among them, he reported, thought that it was 'puerile'.[21]

To the French not only in Flanders but throughout the kingdom Edward announced the event in a series of proclamations issued from Ghent in the early days of February 1340. He told them that he would restore the good laws and customs of 'our predecessor Saint Louis'. There would be an end of the devaluations of the coinage by which successive French kings since Philip the Fair had exploited their subjects. His own government would be bound by the advice and consent of the nobility and the leaders of the Church.[22] Edward knew his adversary's weaknesses. So, perhaps, did Philip himself. He had gone to great lengths to prevent the defection of Flanders. He had procured menacing letters from the Pope. He had threatened to embargo their supplies of grain. He had made generous offers including, according to one report, two of the three castleries of Walloon Flanders.[23] When Edward's proclamations were published, the loyal magistrates of Saint-Omer received copies and sent them to the King at Vincennes. There was much curiosity at Philip's court about the seal, which showed Edward enthroned with a sceptre in one hand and the lily of France in the other, and the arms of both kingdoms on the obverse side. On 24 February 1340 Philip ordered his officials to have it proclaimed that anyone found carrying a copy of Edward's proclamations would be arrested and punished as a traitor. They were to check every church door and public square to ensure that copies had not been posted there. Any that they found should be torn down and burned. The French government spread alarm among its officers in the frontier provinces. Emergency measures were taken for the defence of the march of Flanders. Troops were drafted into Calais from neighbouring towns. At Aire-sur-la-Lys, a border town with a large number of Flemings among the population, the local *bailli* took hostages for their loyalty. Philip VI felt suspicious, mistrustful and insecure.[24]

The Flemings themselves were beyond forgiveness. Stringent economic sanctions were imposed on them within a few days of the ceremony at Ghent. All movement of goods across the border in either direction had been stopped by the end of January. Debts owed to the merchants of Flanders and Brabant were frozen and Frenchmen ordered not to pay them. On 5 April 1340, as the Flemish leaders had feared, the whole of the errant county was laid under an interdict on the instructions of Pope Benedict XII and most of the churches were closed. Ghent remained impressive in its solidarity. But elsewhere there was anxiety and unrest and occasionally disorder. Not all the lesser towns who had been required to swear oaths of loyalty to the English connection did so willingly. The French King appealed directly to the loyalty or conservatism of individuals and to their desire for self-preservation. Handsome indemnities were offered to those who were prepared to leave their property behind them and rally to his cause. Among the gentry and nobility of Flanders many did so, and served in Philip's army against their fellow countrymen throughout 1340.[25]

*

The news that Edward III had made himself king of France was received rather coolly in England. It revived memories of John, Henry III and Edward I and other kings who were suspected of looking to the continent for their own fortunes and not England's. Edward knew this and he was defensive about it. It was no part of his intention, he said, to prejudice the traditions and liberties of England and Englishmen; he had had to assume the crown of France for 'various pressing reasons' which he would explain to Parliament in due course. His claim hardly ever featured in the propaganda which he addressed to his own countrymen.[26]

During Edward's long absence on the continent he had lost touch with public opinion in England, which he had once been so adept at managing. His petulant and demanding letters home had only added to the resentment created by the burden of taxation and purveyance. When Parliament had met on 19 January 1340 the King was still in Antwerp preparing himself for fresh dignities, and it was Archbishop Stratford who opened the proceedings. Money, the business left unfinished in October 1339, was the foremost item on the agenda. But the Commons were in no mood for generosity. They said that they would need time to think about the government's demands, and deferred their answer to 19 February. On that day there was an acrimonious session of the Lords and Commons. Edward was still absent. The Lords granted a tax for their own estates of a tenth of their corn, wool and lambs. But the Commons produced instead a comprehensive list of grievances. They said that they were willing in principle to grant a tax in kind of 30,000 sacks of wool, but only if certain conditions were satisfied. These were very radical. Not only did the Commons want an inquiry into the embezzlement of past taxes, but in order to prevent the recurrence of such scandals in future they wanted a committee to be appointed from among the peers to supervise the expenditure of tax revenues. 'And if the conditions are not observed then the taxes shall not be paid.' There was consternation among the ministers present. They had no authority to agree to such a thing. All that they could do was to send the unwelcome document to Edward III on the continent. At the insistence of the Lords, who pointed out that without an immediate infusion of money it would be impossible to raise a fleet to defend the coasts, the Commons grudgingly voted 2,500 sacks of wool. That was all. The session then broke up in indecision and confusion.[27]

Edward's need of money at this point was more acute than it had ever been. He had counted on the Parliament of October 1339 to vote him the money which he had promised to his allies in August. They had not done so and the instalments were falling due. On 22 November 1339 a review of his finances had suggested an immediate need of £40,000. Commissioners were appointed to borrow this sum from wherever they could find it. But the King's credit was not good. It was impossible to come by more than part of what was needed. The financial crisis was reaching its height as Edward proclaimed himself king of France. The archers who escorted him to Ghent had no wages or food. After his arrival, splendid celebrations alternated with humiliating pleas for cash addressed to creditors old and new.[28]

The bonds which the English King had issued to his more important creditors in the previous year promised that he would not return to England until he had seen them paid. Yet without returning to England it now seemed unlikely that he would receive the Parliamentary subsidies from which alone they could be satisfied. Edward did in the end succeed in extricating himself from the Low Countries, but only on the most humiliating terms. He was obliged to leave behind him as hostages his wife and younger son and the earls of Salisbury and Suffolk. The strictest promises were required by his allies that he would return with money as well as an army not later than 1 July 1340. The English King took ship at Sluys on 21 February 1340 and landed at Harwich on the same day. For the next four months Edward bent the whole policy of his government to performing his promises.[29]

On the day he landed in England a new Parliament was summoned to meet at Westminster on 29 March 1340. Twelve commissioners, all influential councillors, were appointed to raise loans on his behalf and lists of rich men were supplied to them for the purpose. Edward browbeat the principal lenders in person. There is a graphic account of one of these occasions, involving the corporation of London, whose members were summoned before the council to be told that their offer of 5,000 marks was inadequate and ordered to supply a list of rich Londoners on whom a forced loan of £20,000 could be assessed. The parties compromised at £5,000. Part of this sum was ordered to be delivered forthwith to van Artevelde's agent. Parliament, when it met at the end of March 1340, required a more compliant approach. Edward painted a black picture of what would happen to him if no grant were made. He would be forever dishonoured; his duchy and his kingdom would be threatened with extinction; his allies would be lost; and he himself would have to return to Brussels to submit to imprisonment by his creditors until all his debts should be paid. 'But if a tax should be granted, all of these terrible perils will vanish and the enterprise on which he has embarked will be brought with God's help to a fitting conclusion, to peace and contentment for all.'

Edward certainly believed in this vision. When the Commons delivered their conditions again he was uninterested in their constitutional implications. He wanted the money, and he submitted without arguing the principle. On 3 April 1340 they voted a subsidy of a ninth of all grain, wool and lambs and a ninth of every townsman's moveable property.[30]

Edward had achieved some improvement in the public relations of his government since the nadir of the previous autumn, and his hearers may have been persuaded that one more push would achieve the objects of the war. Until the time of the great English victories, still far into the future, 1340 was the year in which England seemed most united and energetic in the pursuit of a common goal. Yet there remained uncertainty and equivocation about what that goal was and some disagreement about what it ought to be. Edward III solemnly acceded to the petition of the Lords and Commons that they should never be called upon to obey him in his capacity of king of France and that England should never be absorbed into Edward's other kingdom. There were those who thought this to be the most notable event of an eventful Parliament.[31]

The French war effort called for expenditure on a scale vastly greater than Edward III's in a country not as used to heavy taxation. In the northern provinces, where alone the threat to France's security was taken seriously by tax-payers, the subsidies voted in the previous year began to come in in February 1340. Fresh grants were made by the nobility and no less than thirty-two towns imposed sales taxes for the support of the war. Paris offered a subsidy of more than 20,000 l.t. Substantial funds were being collected from the clergy with the consent of the Pope to fight a coalition whose leader was the Vicar of an excommunicated heretic. Philip abandoned the reticence of earlier years about raiding the treasure accumulated for the crusade. The French clergy, intimately involved in the business of government, abetted him as those of England had abetted Edward III. The steady devaluation of the French coinage, a hidden tax, continued. In the provinces of France rich bourgeois and monastic houses received personal visits from insistent commissioners deploying much the same mixture of threats and promises as Edward III's agents were using in England at the same moment.[32]

The year 1340 proved, like 1339, to be a good one for Philip's finances. Even so the war treasurers lived from hand to mouth. The French government lacked its rival's ingenious way with financial improvisation and its skill in manipulating credit. Revenue arrived in unpredictable spurts from taxation decreed long before, vitiating financial planning and therefore much military planning as well. In January 1340 the important garrison of Tournai was threatening 'from day to day' to desert for want of pay in spite of Philip's personal assurances that he would shortly be in funds. French troops received a reasonable wage and knights a generous one, which began to accrue as soon as they left home and continued until they returned. They too were by tradition entitled to an advance of two months' wages at the beginning of their service, and while there was some elasticity about the settlement of final accounts the men expected and normally obtained punctilious payment of the advance. In May 1340 the men of Douai were refusing to fight because their pay was overdue and the field treasurers had run out of money. In July the *bailli* of Macon, who had brought his men from Burgundy to Paris, announced that he would go no further until he was paid. The war treasurers, poor men, expressed amazement at how fast their resources were being consumed.[33]

Philip VI had two strategic ends in view. In the first place he wanted to be revenged on the Count of Hainault for what he conceived to be the treachery of the previous year. The Count had not earned Philip's gratitude by changing sides at the crucial moment of the autumn campaign but only his greater contempt. Hainault was a useful lesson for other members of Edward III's coalition, vulnerable because bordering on France and politically divided. Moreover it was the gateway to Brabant, Philip's second objective. Brabant was the most powerful state of the coalition after England herself, and politically the key to its coherence, as Philip knew. He did not intend to repeat the demoralizing strategy of the previous year by waiting until Edward's return before taking the offensive. The object, at least initially, was to knock Brabant out of the war before Edward III could land.

The key to Philip's offensive plans in the north was the city of Cambrai on the Scheldt, less than an hour's ride from Count William's territory and still almost encircled by the chain of castles which William's soldiers had occupied in 1338 and 1339: Bouchain, Thun-l'Évêque, Relenghes, Escaudœuvres and Haspres. The city was maintained on a war footing throughout the winter of 1339–40. In November the French government formalized an old understanding with its citizens, nominally subjects of the German Empire. A French force of 600 men was stationed there. Philip VI assumed responsibility for the maintenance of the city's fortifications and provided a large quantity of field artillery including ten cannon. Volunteers were recruited from among the inhabitants and in the outlying districts, men who turned naturally to soldiering after the destruction of their homes and livelihoods by the scorched-earth campaign of Edward III.

They needed no encouragement to visit a ferocious revenge upon the enemy. On 11 November 1339 Walter Mauny's brother, who had been taken in an ambush near the city, was lynched by a mob as he was being brought through the northern gate. This was to be the regular pattern of a war in which few men distinguished between soldiers and civilians.[34]

Needling raids on William of Hainault's possessions began early. In December 1339 the Cambrai garrison, reinforced by some citizens and armed with siege equipment, carried out a succession of raids in strength against the ring of castles about them. Early in the month they attacked Escaudœuvres and, although the old marshland fortress could not be taken, they entirely destroyed the town. Relenghes, a fortified manor house on the opposite side of the Scheldt, was attacked immediately afterwards. The garrison of this place, eighteen archers commanded by an illegitimate son of John of Hainault, resisted until they were exhausted. Then they set fire to it in the middle of the night and slipped away across the marsh. In the week before Christmas there was a particularly savage raid on Cimay, some 50 miles away, which was where the principal lands of John of Hainault were. Although Cimay itself was not taken the French destroyed five smaller towns around it. Count William failed to read the signs. He professed to regard the raids as spontaneous banditry and asked Philip VI to restrain his troops. He suggested a meeting at Senlis where the two men could discuss any differences they had. But Philip did not restrain his men. He commended them, and although he was willing to attend a meeting his acts made serious peacemaking impossible. In March 1340 there was another foray by the men of Cambrai, this time to the south-east of the city. On the 26th the French completely destroyed the town of Haspres, where Edward III had established his headquarters for a few days in the previous September. Adding insult to injury they brought out criminals from Cambrai and executed them before the walls of Escaudœuvres, a symbol of possession and authority and a calculated offence to the Count of Hainault.[35]

These acts had a purpose beyond mere offence and destruction. The object was to clear hostile forces from the Scheldt valley between Cambrai and Valenciennes, and to open the route of the French army of invasion. The French had been planning this stroke for most of the winter. In the second half of March the chivalry of the northern and eastern provinces was summoned to be at Amiens and Compiègne (later changed to Saint-Quentin) by 18 May 1340, six weeks before Edward III was due to return to the continent.[36]

The discovery of these plans terrified the leaders of the coalition.

England's interests in the Low Countries in the spring of 1340 were represented by the Earl of Salisbury, William Montagu, serving many roles as ambassador, military commander and hostage for his master's debts. He was accompanied by the Earl of Suffolk. It was already clear to them within a fortnight of Edward's departure that the crisis would break before the English army could return. Their own forces, which were stationed in southern Flanders close to the large French garrison of Tournai, were very meagre. They comprised some retained knights and cavalry from Brabant and other parts of Germany, a handful of renegade French knights from Flanders and Artois and militiamen provided by the town of Ypres, not more than 200 men in all. In England plans were hurriedly made to meet Salisbury's urgent call for reinforcements. A fleet of fifteen ships was ordered into being to carry some 200 soldiers to the continent under the command of the earls of Oxford and Warwick. In spite of the urgent tone of these orders the earls did not arrive until April and then brought barely two dozen men. Salisbury had to make do with what he had.[37]

There was an anxious conference in the royal lodgings at Ghent. The Queen of England was recovering from childbirth. The leaders of her husband's coalition gathered about her to debate their plans: the earls of Salisbury and Suffolk, Jacob van Artevelde, the Duke of Brabant, the Margrave of Juliers and a very frightened Count of Hainault. The Count came as a suppliant, the deserter of the previous autumn but for whom, as van Artevelde roughly declared, the present menace would not have arisen. The decision made was that the assault on Tournai, which had been planned as the principal military operation of the summer, would be brought forward in the hope of drawing the French army away from Hainault. It was proposed that the allies should converge on Tournai from three directions. Jacob van Artevelde would approach the city from the north with the men of Ghent and the Flemish towns. The princes, including the Count of Hainault, were assembling their forces in Hainault. They were to cross the Scheldt and invest Tournai from the south. Meanwhile the English earls were to launch a noisy diversion. Their plan was to approach Tournai from the west through Walloon Flanders making a feint against Lille on their way. It was not a bad plan. But it called for the careful co-ordination of three independently commanded armies, which proved to be its undoing.[38]

On 2 April 1340 William of Hainault issued his formal defiance of the French Crown from Mons. However, instead of marching at once on Tournai, as he had been expected to do, he allowed himself to be persuaded by his uncle John to proceed in the opposite direction and invade

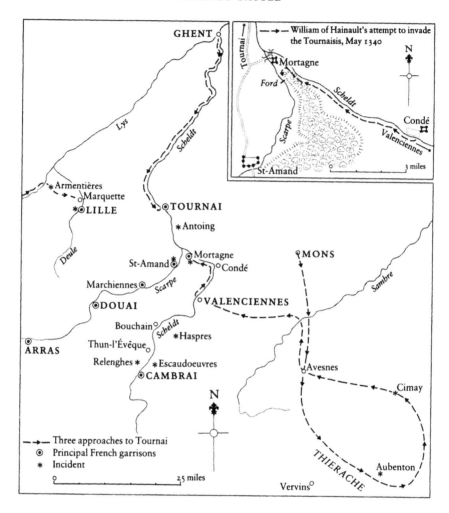

8 Fighting in the Low Countries, December 1339–May 1340

the Thiérache, the scene of the stalemate of the previous year. The reason
for this remarkable decision was that a large number of French troops was
believed to be assembling in the Thiérache which John of Hainault conceived to be a threat to his own extensive lands in eastern Hainault, as
well, he suggested, as a vulnerable force whose defeat in the field would
have a great impact on French plans. But the truth was that there was no
benefit in this sideshow nor, as it turned out, any victory in the field. It was
true that there was a force of French garrison troops in the Thiérache but it
was not particularly large and Walter of Brienne (titular Duke of Athens)

who was the commander of this sector of the frontier was away conferring with the French King at Vincennes. William and John of Hainault arrived with their troops in the border area on about 20 April 1340. The other princes followed in their path. The French, however, seeing that they were greatly outnumbered, simply retreated into the walled town of Vervins a few miles south of the border and waited for reinforcements. The Duke of Athens was ordered on 24 April 1340 to return urgently to his command and must have arrived a few days later. Baulked of their prey the Hainaulters turned to revenge and destruction, and then retreated back into Hainault. Some forty villages were reduced to ashes.

The main victims were the unfortunate citizens of Aubenton, a prosperous walled town a little too far to the east to have been sacked by Edward III in the previous autumn. This place was almost undefended. Most of its garrison was in Vervins with the rest of the French border force and the others had fled. There was only a group of about thirty men-at-arms who happened to be passing through the town on their way to somewhere else. They put up a gallant resistance assisted by the citizens. But they were overwhelmed and those of them who were not killed were taken for ransom. The town was pillaged and then destroyed with ruthless deliberation. A large part of the population, which had taken refuge in one of the parish churches, was burned alive in it. It was the most savage incident of its kind in the early years of the war. The survivors were found living indigently among the ruins of their homes when the papal almoners visited Aubenton later in the year. No less then 370 heads of households had been reduced to beggary. John of Hainault was said to have been satisfied with the result of this sortie, but it is unlikely that anyone else was.[39]

In the meantime disaster struck the English-led force in Walloon Flanders. The earls of Salisbury and Suffolk crossed the Lys punctually at the beginning of April 1340 at the head of a few hundred men-at-arms and perhaps 2,000 archers and infantry, most of whom were raw levies from Ypres. Armentières on the Lys, weakly defended by a contingent of hired Genoese crossbowmen, was captured on 6 April 1340 and sacked. The earls then led their men eastward. These movements had the desired effect on the French. Their commander in this part of the march was Godemar du Fay, an experienced civil servant who had always felt more comfortable on horseback than in the office: a 'good soldier but no judge', said the order which dismissed him from his *baillage* some years before. He was in his element now. Godemar assumed, reasonably enough, that Lille was the main target. Van Artevelde's desire to annex it was well known. One of its citizens had only recently been executed after being detected corresponding with him. The town was placed at once on a siege footing. The suburbs were demolished and the population brought within the walls. All inward and outward movement through the gates was forbidden. Some hundreds of men were summoned from other places, including Tournai.

In fact the earls' line of march would have taken them well north of Lille. On 11 April 1340, however, in a moment of 'audacious folly' (the chronicler Adam Murimuth's phrase) they decided to reconnoitre the defences of the place and to engage in a little plundering. Leaving their army encamped on the banks of the River Deule they rode towards the town accompanied by Guy of Flanders, a renegade French knight from Artois called Perceval d'Aubrequin, some thirty cavalry and a small number of mounted archers. After they had passed through the suburban village of Marquette their movements were observed and reported to Godemar's lieutenant in command of the Lille garrison. He organized a sortie from the northern side of the town. The earls and their party were cut off and were eventually trapped between their assailants and the town moat. They dismounted and fought a valiant but hopeless pitched battle against vastly superior numbers until by nightfall they were overwhelmed. The two earls and five of their companions were captured. Guy of Flanders managed to escape on horseback. All the others were killed. The leaderless army of Ypres townsmen broke up and returned home. As for the prisoners, they were bundled into a cart and sent under armed guard to Paris where Philip VI received them with extreme satisfaction. The traitor Perceval d'Aubrequin was summarily executed. According to reliable sources, Philip threatened the earls with the same fate. He was only dissuaded by John of Bohemia, who knew the conventions of war and pointed out that they might be needed for exchange with prisoners of the English. So they were locked up in the Châtelet. The news, which was brought to Edward III in the middle of a tournament at Windsor, was a severe blow. Salisbury had been one of Edward's closest confidants among the English nobility and for three years had been the loyal and efficient instrument of a war policy in which he had little confidence.[40]

Of the three armies which had agreed to meet under the walls of Tournai only van Artevelde's arrived. His troops, some 2,000 men of Ghent and an unknown number of soldiers contributed by the other towns of Flanders, reached the flat plain north of Tournai between 7 and 11 April 1340 and camped on the banks of the Scheldt. Within the city the cathedral bells rang out the alarm and the citizens manned the walls according to a practised drill. Men were sent out into the suburbs to burn the buildings on both sides of the river. For the Flemings the prospect of a siege was unattractive. It was bitterly, unseasonably cold. The princes of the coalition with much the largest of the contingents were more than 60 miles away, uselessly engaged in plundering the Thiérache. Then on 12 April 1340 a servant of the Earl of Salisbury brought the news of the disaster which had overtaken his master. Van Artevelde summoned Tournai to surrender. He received in reply a robust declaration of loyalty to Philip VI. Then he marched his army away.[41]

The French seized their strategic advantage as soon as van Artevelde and his men had gone. Four miles downstream from Tournai lay the village of Antoing, an important river crossing dominated by the imposing twelfth-century castle which still exists behind the romantic encrustations of the nineteenth century. It was the only gap in the string of French strongholds which held the line of the Scheldt and the Scarpe at Tournai, Mortagne, Saint-Amand and Marchiennes, barring every main route from Hainault. It was held against the French by an old and blind half-uncle of the Count of Hainault. On about 30 April 1340 the garrisons of Tournai and Lille led by the Duke of Burgundy, the Constable and the Marshals of France rushed the place, captured it and marched into the lands of Hainault on both sides of the river, destroying everything within reach, thirty-two towns according to official report.

The rulers of Hainault had paid dearly for their diversion into the other extremity of the theatre. They tried to restore the position. A large force of men, mostly Hainaulters but with some Brabanters and Germans, came up the valley from Valenciennes and attacked the most important of the French fortified river crossings at Mortagne. Under cover of the assault another force tried to seize an unfortified ford some 3 miles downstream. Both endeavours failed. At Mortagne the small French garrison was commanded by a Burgundian knight, Jean de Vienne, who was later to win fame for his courageous defence of Calais against the English. The assault continued for four hours under Count William's personal direction until the Hainaulters flagged and fell back. At the ford an even more remarkable feat of arms occurred. Ten French soldiers obstructed the river with obstacles improvised from old building timbers and fought off the enemy for two hours until they were reinforced. This was a shock for Count William. He had counted on finding the ford in friendly hands if he had to withdraw from Mortagne. Instead he found the triumphant ten, now supported by hundreds of well-entrenched French troops from Saint-Amand and the surrounding region. There was a sharp battle quickly broken off after the Hainaulters and their allies had begun to suffer heavy casualties. In the evening they returned empty-handed towards Valenciennes.[42]

The long-awaited French spring offensive[43] against Hainault and Brabant began punctually on 18 May 1340. The commander was Philip VI's eldest son John, Duke of Normandy, an unconfident and unhealthy young man of twenty-one, the apple of his father's eye, who was exercising his first military command. With him went the King's most influential councillor, Mile de Noyers, and a large body of experienced soldiers, including the counts of Alençon and Foix. They started from St Quentin. On 20 May 1340 they had reached Cateau-Cambrésis where they were joined by the Duke of Burgundy and the Constable and Marshals leading the border forces from Tournai. Except for a disagreeable episode near Cateau-Cambrésis, in which a group of Hainaulters attacked a French billet and killed some dozens of soldiers as they slept off their drink, the French army encountered no resistance at all as they passed north. The Count of Hainault behaved as if he had not expected the French offensive. His army was in the field but did nothing to oppose the invaders. He himself fled to the Duke of Brabant in Brussels to plead for help. An anxious meeting of the leaders of the coalition gathered there on 20 May 1340 to consider what was to be done in this calamity.[44] On the 22nd, four days after leaving Saint-Quentin, the advance guard of the French army crossed into Hainault and arrived outside Valenciennes.

Here, however, their difficulties began. Such had been the speed of John's advance that he had outrun his supplies. His lines of communication ran by road and river along the Scheldt valley, a long and vulnerable route which was interrupted between Cambrai and Valenciennes by three strong castles still in enemy hands: Escaudœuvres, Thun-l'Évêque and Bouchain. John's army was about 10,000 strong, large enough to make heavy demands on limited local supplies and on the available carts and barges. Few of these supplies were getting through, and French troops had already begun to feel the pinch of hunger when they arrived outside Valenciennes. Unfortunately Valenciennes was not an easy place to take quickly. It was a compact, well-walled town on the east bank of the Scheldt with access by two fortified bridges to the west bank and by river to an extensive hinterland. The Hainaulters had learned from prisoners of war that Valenciennes was to be attacked[45] and had had time to prepare their defence. The place was commanded by the Count's lieutenant, Henri d'Antoing, an able and determined francophobe. He was assisted by Edward III's representatives in the Low Countries, the earls of Warwick and Northampton.

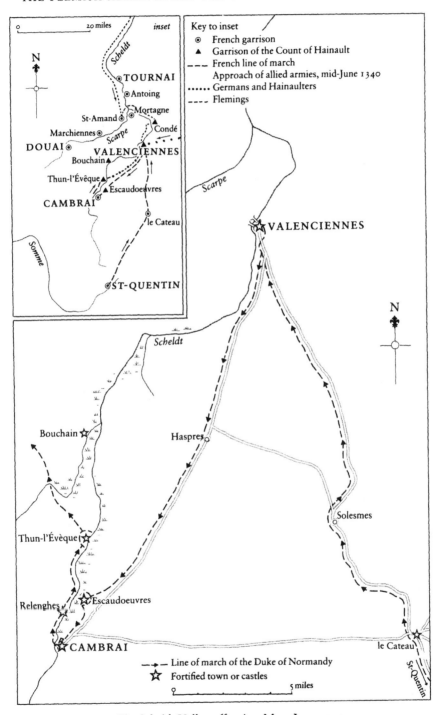

9 The Scheldt Valley offensive, May–June 1340

The French army began the routine of waste and destruction in the deserted suburbs and outlying villages on the day of their arrival. Everything within 2 miles of the walls was reduced to ashes, including most of the convent buildings of Fontenelles, of which John of Normandy's aunt was the abbess. John probably intended an assault on the following morning, 23 May 1340, for new knights were made in the French host that evening.[46] If so, he was pre-empted by the enemy. Early on the 23rd, to the sound of clattering bells within the town, the garrison issued forth from the gates with a horde of armed citizens and, catching the French unprepared, drove them in disordered flight down the Cambrai road. John's army lost a great quantity of equipment and many casualties killed and captured. John himself learned his first lesson in the art of war: a large army cannot be kept in the field unless its lines of communication are secure or it remains constantly on the move. He withdrew to the northern Cambrésis and set about reducing the castles from which the Hainaulters were blocking the upper Scheldt. On 24 May 1340[47] he laid siege to Escaudœuvres.

Both sides strained their resources to the limit to raise an armed force which would tip the balance quickly. The Count of Hainault clucked and flapped between Brussels, Ghent, Bruges, Ypres, Dendermonde and Mons pleading with his allies and vassals, as an army of relief came into being with appalling slowness. In Germany Louis of Bavaria fidgeted on the eastern frontier of France talking of an invasion through Burgundy in the hope of drawing off French troops. Philip VI sought to meet both threats, stripping his frontier garrisons and summoning more men-at-arms from the northern provinces.[48]

Escaudœuvres was quickly taken. With a garrison of only 23 men and an army of 10,000 spread out across the marshes outside, the commander Gérard de Sassigny can be forgiven for his nervousness. Godemar du Fay, an old comrade in arms, persuaded him on the third day of the siege to surrender the castle if help had not come from the Count of Hainault within a week. The French agreed to let Gérard go in person to the Count at Mons to appeal for relief but the time allowed was absurdly short and William's preparations were not complete. On 3 June 1340 he returned to Escaudœuvres and surrendered it. For this service the French paid him 10,000 florins and the value of the great hoard of provisions had been accumulated for a long siege. But Gérard never enjoyed his fortune. He was seized by his own soldiers as soon as they were clear of the French encampment and delivered up to the Count of Hainault. William had him broken on the wheel.

The French demolished Escaudœuvres and marched 4 miles down the Scheldt to their next objective at Thun-l'Évêque. The morale of the defenders was higher there. They were a larger garrison defending a stronger fortress and relief was known to be on the way. On 6 June 1340 the French began to batter the walls day and night with heavy siege machinery. They made several breaches. Both sides were bringing up reinforcements. French troops withdrawn from the garrisons of the Meuse provinces, the Thiérache and the Laonnais arrived on 7 June 1340. The King of France himself came into the French camp on about 15 June with a large cavalry force and placed himself under his son's command. There were now some 18,000 French troops in the field. The relief force of the Anglo-German coalition approached Thun-l'Évêque from two directions. The princes, who had assembled their forces, predominantly Brabanters, around Valenciennes, were making their way up the east bank of the Scheldt. A very large force of Flemings[49] commanded by Jacob van Artevelde was marching through the Tournaisis to approach from the west.

The castle of Thun-l'Évêque was situated on the west side of the Scheldt a short distance from the river. The French were encamped around it. Close by, and firmly guarded, was a number of pontoon bridges which the French had built to bring in supplies. The plans of the allies depended, unfortunately, on their two forces meeting the French army from opposite sides, the Flemings attacking from the west, the Germans forcing a crossing of the Scheldt and coming on them from the east. But that did not happen. The princes arrived opposite Thun-l'Évêque on about 20 June. They tried to rush the pontoon bridges but were repelled in vigorous hand-to-hand fighting. They challenged the French to an arranged battle, but the French held the river and refused. They were therefore compelled to stand impotently on the river bank watching the enemy on the other side. Everything depended on the Flemings. But the Flemish troops, although numerous, were inexperienced and undisciplined. They were unable to reach Thun-l'Évêque. The crossings of the River Scarpe were held against them by a detachment of 500 men from the garrison of Tournai. The Flemings tried to take the long way round by Condé and Valenciennes. But they were still far away when William of Hainault decided to give up the fight. The garrison of Thun-l'Évêque, which was now defending improvised barricades amid the rubble of the castle walls, concluded that further resistance was useless. On the night of 23 June 1340 flames were seen rising from the castle buildings. The French rushed to arms and stormed the outer circuit of walls in order to prevent the defenders from escaping. They found the place empty. The garrison had left by an unguarded opening and made their way across the river to join the allied army. An hour before dawn the princes of the coalition withdrew northward, leaving the enemy in possession of the ruins of Thun-l'Évêque and the whole Scheldt valley south of the border of Hainault. The next objective of the French army would have been Bouchain, the last important fortification south of Valenciennes.

Bouchain was saved by events elsewhere. As Philip VI and his son were leaving Thun-l'Évêque the news arrived that Edward III and his army had sailed from the port of Orwell on 22 June and that the English fleet was lying off the Flemish coast.

CHAPTER X

Sluys and Tournai:
The War of the Albrets
1340

The main lines of English naval strategy in 1340 were laid down on 23 January at Westminster at a meeting between the royal Council and shipmasters from the main English ports. Unusually for an operational matter, they were approved by Parliament, which was then in session. Two, perhaps questionable, assumptions seem to have been made: first, that the French would spend their energy in raids on the English coast rather than try to contest the army's passage of the North Sea; second, that because France no longer had the use of the Flemish ports only the south coast was really threatened. The ports of the West Country agreed to provide seventy large ships of 100 tons or more, contributing to the cost only what they could afford, which was unlikely to be much. The Cinque Ports agreed to provide twenty ships of the same size and London another nine, the cost of which would be shared equally between the local communities and the King. Except perhaps for the Londoners all the maritime communities had promised more large ships than they had. But the government took their promises seriously. On 12 February 1340 it ordered all of these vessels to assemble at Dartmouth and Winchelsea by 26 March 1340. Later, in April, both fleets were ordered to wait in Rye Bay, ready to intercept any armada coming from the French Channel ports. This left at Edward's disposal for the crossing of the North Sea all the ocean-going ships, large or small, of the northern Admiralty and the smaller ships from the other parts of England. Orders were issued to requisition these on 6 March 1340. Most of them were only fit for service as transports. For fighting ships Edward counted on Yarmouth and on a small contingent furnished by the Flemings.[1]

The English government made a determined attempt, yet again, to hire galleys in the Mediterranean. There was an application to the Venetian Republic for forty of them, the hire to be paid in bullion in advance. The Venetians returned an evasive answer. Nicolino Fieschi, now in semi-permanent residence as Edward's agent at the papal court in Avignon, was largely concerned with the hiring of warships in southern France and the obstruction of Philip VI's attempts to do the same. Precisely what he achieved is not known but he was diligent enough to cause serious concern to French officials. They decided to baulk his plans by a bold and illegal move. One night in April some of them kidnapped him from his house in Avignon and dragged him half-dressed to Fort Saint-André, the huge castle at Villeneuve-lès-Avignon on the French side of the Rhône, a violation of his diplomatic immunity which resulted in a brief but serious rift between the papacy and the French government. The ambassador was released early in June, by which time it was too late to hire Mediterranean galleys for a summer campaign.[2]

There was, however, a consolation prize of immeasurable value. For in the first few months of the year 1340 the English succeeded by a succession of *coups de main* in depriving Philip VI of most of his own galley fleet.

In September 1339 there was a popular revolution in Genoa. The great patrician families, both Guelph and Ghibelline, were dislodged, and power fell into the hands of a skilful plebeian demagogue, Simon Boccanegra. It was an event of unexpected significance for the French government. The prime movers had been the disgruntled mariners of Ayton Doria's galleys who had returned home after the mutiny at Boulogne. The new regime therefore had no reason to favour the French government or help them to replace the seamen that they had lost. The English moved quickly to exploit the rift. During the winter both governments had agents in Genoa intriguing on their behalf. The French agents succeeded in hiring some crossbowmen and a small number of galleys. But the shipmasters were bought off by the English, who paid them a total of 1,100 marks to do nothing. The money was obtained at short notice from the Bardi bank in Florence. This remarkable (and inexpensive) coup seems to have been the work of Niccolo Usomare, Edward's Genoese Constable of Bordeaux, who passed many months in the city at this time, engaged in what the English government darkly called 'great dangers, labours and expenses'.[3]

The French-built galley fleet at the beginning of 1340 numbered twenty-two vessels. They would usually have been laid up for the winter in the arsenal at Rouen. However, because they were required to escort a convoy to La Rochelle as soon as the weather permitted, they had been kept beached and ready for use.[4] Early in January 1340 some English seamen of the Cinque Ports captured at sea a ship of Boulogne and took for ransom four merchants whom they found on board. When these men were interrogated in England they revealed that there were eighteen unmanned galleys beached in Boulogne harbour guarded by just six watchmen. On about 14 January 1340 the English raided Boulogne. A fleet of small vessels of the

Cinque Ports approached the place under cover of a heavy mist. They were not seen by the guards until they were actually within the harbour. Complete surprise was achieved. The English took over the lower town while they destroyed the ships within the harbour and the buildings around. It took several hours for the French in the upper town to collect their forces and attack the raiders. After fierce fighting the English were expelled with heavy casualties. But by this time they had burned all eighteen galleys together with their entire equipment of oars, sails and weapons which had been stored in a warehouse nearby. Twenty-four merchantmen were also destroyed.[5]

The loss of these powerful ships and the impossibility of finding either ships or crews in Italy was a grave setback for the French. It left them with just four of their own galleys, which had been at Leure in the mouth of the Seine instead of at Boulogne. There were enough Italian oarsmen still in Philip's service to crew two Genoese galleys. They were placed under the command of one of Doria's captains, a colourful Mediterranean corsair called Pietro Barbavera whom the French commanders never entirely trusted. In addition there were twenty-two capacious but rather less powerful oared barges. Most of these were kept at Abbeville and Dieppe.[6] This fleet was not negligible but it was not a fleet for offensive operations on a large scale. The direct result of the Boulogne raid was that the French lost the initiative in the Channel and North Sea for the first time since the outbreak of the war at sea in 1336. The English were able to mount cross-Channel raids with growing confidence. Dieppe was attacked at the end of January 1340. Le Tréport and Mers were raided (again) in May.[7] Much more significant was the decision, which was forced on the French by the loss of the galleys, to fight a purely defensive battle against Edward III's invasion fleet. Instead of seeking to blockade it in its home ports or attack it in mid-ocean it was resolved simply to obstruct its access to the mouths of the great rivers north of Flanders. Mobility was less important for this purpose. It could be done with armed merchantmen, the same kind of vessels as the English had been using as improvised warships for many years.

This decision, which led to the disaster at Sluys in June, appears to have been made in late January or early February 1340 and was put into effect with characteristic determination and bureaucratic competence. Philip decreed into being a Great Army of the Sea. It was to consist of 200 of the largest ships which could be found from his own resources or requisitioned in the ports of Picardy and Normandy. Unlike the English government the French paid prompt and reasonably generous compensation for requisitioning ships, including a month's hire and wages in advance. The cost, which would be prodigious, was to be met by levying a heavy tax on the province of Normandy. It is some indication of the burden falling on a single region of France that the Crown expected to receive no less than 300,000 *l.t.* from this source in addition to the ships and crews (nearly three-quarters of the total) which the Norman maritime communities were contributing and the payments which many Norman towns and districts had had to make in lieu of military service in the land army. Nevertheless the Normans agreed. Collection began on 12 February 1340.[8]

Edward III was informed more or less accurately of the extent of the damage inflicted at Boulogne. But he failed to draw the conclusion that a powerful French descent on the south coast was now much less likely to occur. Moreover, although spies (generally Flemings) continued to be sent into France their reports were for some reason less informative in 1340 than they had been hitherto, and it was not until a surprisingly late stage that Edward realized what the French were planning to do. Consequently the arrangements made in January and February 1340, which involved the use of many of his largest vessels for the defence of the south coast, were left unchanged.

The transports to carry the army and its supplies were expected to be ready by Palm Sunday, 9 April 1340. Embarkation was to take place at two points, in the Pool of Orwell and in the Downs off Sandwich. Although Edward III was now for the first time imposing timetables which allowed for some slippage, the usual difficulties and delays were intensely frustrating against a background of rapid military movement on the continent. In early May 1340 the French softening-up raids on Hainault had begun and urgent appeals for help were arriving in England. One of the Count of Hainault's knights had arrived to report on events. He entered upon a scene of depressing disorganization and unreadiness. The recruitment of troops was going badly. The Welsh arrived in London, to find no ships or victuals, and had to be sent home. Except for the fleets of Yarmouth and the Cinque Ports no ships had arrived at either of the two embarkation points. Embarkation was postponed on 4 May and again two days later. On 16 May 1340, just before the punctual departure of the Duke of Normandy's army from Saint-Quentin, the English royal Council met in a mood of foreboding and gloom in the Carmelite convent of London to consider a further and longer postponement. By this time the formal deadline for the gathering of the ships had been put back to 12 June 1340, which would indicate a sailing date of about the 20th. Delay seemed inevitable but postponement was rejected.[9]

The pace of France's naval preparations was dictated by the collection of money from the Normans. Their tax payments were delivered in specie by the provincial treasurers in Rouen and loaded directly on to pack animals for carriage to the ports. In the space of seven weeks, from 1 April to 20 May 1340, 61,000 *l.t.* were received and laid out in advances to shipmasters. The whole of the Norman fleet was crewed, equipped and paid by the last week of May 1340. On the 26th it sailed from Harfleur. The ships of Picardy waited in their ports and joined the Normans as they sailed past. It was an impressive feat of administration. There were 6 galleys, 22 oared barges, 7 royal sailing ships and 167 requisitioned merchantmen, making a total of 202 vessels. The fleet carried more than 19,000 men of the maritime towns. But there were very few experienced soldiers, less than 500 crossbowmen and about 150 men-at-arms.[10]

On 4 June 1340 the King of England met his Council again, this time at Ipswich, to review their progress. The delays of April and May were not being made up. It was now clear that the only way of keeping to the timetable which he had set for himself was to cross the sea with a small entourage, his household troops and the principal noblemen and their retinues in those ships which were ready, leaving the others to follow as soon as might be. There were forty ships in the Pool on which up to 600 men and their horses and equipment might be embarked. This was what they decided to do. They did not yet know about the scale of French naval preparations nor about the movements of the French fleet, which had just passed Calais.[11]

The Great Army of the Sea appeared in the Hondt on 8 June 1340. They swiftly and brutally occupied the island of Cadzand and anchored in the mouth of the River Zwin opposite the harbour of Sluys. The news passed rapidly through the Low Countries, spreading panic in coastal towns and drawing a great crowd of gapers to the foreshore to watch the denouement. The news reached the English government on 10 June 1340 when Archbishop Stratford received at Ipswich a messenger of the Duke of Guelders. In Edward's quarters there was a succession of acerbic exchanges between the King and his advisers. Archbishop Stratford insisted that the size and strength of the French fleet at Sluys made it impossible to proceed with the expedition. However grave the consequences of abandoning the coalition (whose army was just then gathering to march on Thun-l'Évêque) they were not as grave as the capture or death of the King. Edward replied that it was out of the question to cancel the expedition. Stratford then walked out of the meeting. Robert Morley and John Crabbe, the two men in charge of the shipping arrangements, were summoned. They expressed the same view as Stratford had. Edward, in a vile temper, accused them of settling their advice in advance with the Archbishop and announced that the expedition would sail as planned. 'Those who are afraid can stay at home.' The most that Edward could be persuaded to do was to postpone his departure for a few days to enable additional ships to be found and arrangements to be made for transforming a fleet of transports into a battle fleet. The horses, which had already been embarked, were taken off in order to make room for more fighting men. Biting messages were sent to every port which could be reached in time demanding the provision at once of every ship of over 40 tons' burden. The King's officers were ordered to brook no argument. Edward personally confronted the mariners of Great Yarmouth, who had so far provided less than half the ships which they had found for his service in 1338. Robert Ufford, the Earl of Suffolk's son, put to sea at once with a small squadron and 100 men-at-arms to reconnoitre the Flemish coast.[12]

The result of all this activity was truly remarkable. The nearby harbours were emptied of shipping. The ships assembling in the Downs and the fleet of the Cinque Ports were brought up to the Pool of Orwell. The large ships of the western Admiralty joined them. They were no longer needed for coastal defence now that the French fleet had passed into the North Sea. An invasion fleet had been assembled by 20 June 1340 whose size cannot be precisely known but which seems from contemporary estimates to have comprised between 120 and 160 ships complete with victuals, equipment and crews. Edward set up his quarters in the *Cog Thomas*. Archbishop Stratford havered and then resigned.[13]

The English fleet passed the point of Harwich at dawn on 22 June 1340, blown by a strong north-westerly breeze.[14] Late on the afternoon of the 23rd they stood off the Flemish coast, west of the opening of the Zwin estuary. Within the estuary the mass of the French fleet could just be seen, their sides built up and their bows, poops and masts fortified with timberworks 'like a row of castles'. Including allies (some Flemish ships loyal to the Crown and some Spanish auxiliaries) their strength now stood at 213 vessels. On board one of them the French commanders gathered in council. Barbavera, the most experienced sailor among them, was becoming concerned by the confined anchorage in which the French fleet was moored. There was not enough room in the estuary for such a huge fleet to manoeuvre. The wind was blowing into the mouth of the river. He insisted that the admirals, Hugh Quiéret and Nicholas Béhuchet, should take their fleet out into the open sea that evening and attack the English from the windward quarter when they tried to land their men. But Quiéret and Béhuchet were no more inclined to listen to old seadogs than Edward III was. They were concerned that if they left for the open sea the English might slip past them and land their army in Flanders before they could intervene. So they drew up the ships in three lines across the mouth of the estuary like an army on land. In the first line they placed nineteen of their largest vessels including the captured *Christopher*, which stood out like a monument from the surrounding mass of shipping. Each line was chained together to form an impassable barrier to the enemy.

The English held their council of war a little later than the French. Reginald Cobham and two knights had been put ashore at Blankenberg to spy out the Sluys anchorage. They presented a full report of the battle order of the French fleet. From their account the English could see for themselves the weakness of the French position of which Barbavera had warned his superiors. They decided to hold back until the following day when they could attack with both wind and tide behind them.

The estuary of the Zwin silted up at the end of the fifteenth century and today the site of England's greatest medieval naval battle is covered by reclaimed agricultural land and sand dunes. In 1340 the estuary was a stretch of shallow water about 3 miles wide at the entrance and penetrating some 10 miles inland towards the city of Bruges. It was enclosed on the north-eastern side by the low-lying island of Cadzand and on the west by a long dyke on which a huge crowd of armed Flemings stood watching. Along the west side lay the out-harbours of Bruges: Sluys, Termuiden and Damme. Like the French the English drew up their fleet in three battle lines. In the early afternoon of 24 June 1340 they began to bear down from the north on the entrance to the Zwin.

Among the French ships all was not well. They had been too long at their battle stations and the chained lines of vessels, which originally extended across the breadth of the bay, had drifted eastward piling the ships up against each other on the Cadzand shore and reducing their searoom still further. The chains were useless in these conditions. The admirals in a moment of belated wisdom ordered them to be cast off. The French fleet then tried to edge back towards the west. A detached vessel of their front line, the *Riche de Leure*, got entangled with the first of the English ships. These two ships grappled together at the edge of the scene while the English front line crunched into the French one.

The two front lines included the largest ships on each side: on the English side the ships of Yarmouth and the larger vessels of the Cinque Ports, including Edward III's flagship the *Cog Thomas*; on the French side the captured *Christopher*, the *St Denis*, a monster carrying 200 seamen, and other large cogs of the royal fleet and the Seine ports. The technique

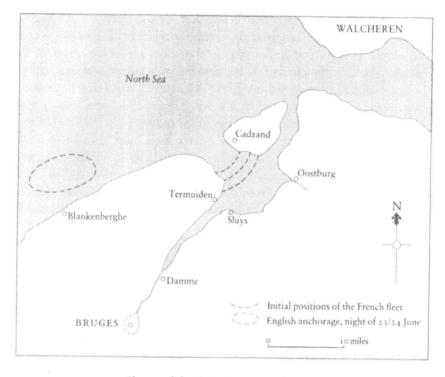

WALCHEREN

North Sea

Cadzand

Oostburg

Termuiden

Blankenberghe

Sluys

N

Damme

BRUGES

Initial positions of the French fleet

English anchorage, night of 23/24 June

0   10 miles

10 Sluys and the Zwin Estuary, 24 June 1340

was for each ship to moor itself inseparably to an enemy with hooks and grappling irons, to shower arrows at the enemy's decks from the endcastles and masts and then to board and cut down the survivors. Both sides also used small but cumbersome stone-throwers and giant crossbows known as 'springalds', but the role of these machines was more dramatic than useful. The decisive advantage of the English ships lay in their much larger complement of non-mariners, experienced and well-equipped men-at-arms and archers. The longbow once again proved to be greatly superior to the crossbow used by the French and their Italian auxiliaries. It was more accurate. It had a longer range. Above all it could be fired at a very rapid rate, the arrows falling down on the French crews 'like hail in winter', as a Londoner described it; whereas crossbows had to be lowered and steadied at the stirrup while the wire was strenuously levered back between every firing. As the day wore on the French bowmen suffered the added discomfort of having to aim into the blinding sun.

The front lines were locked in battle from about three o'clock in the afternoon. By about seven o'clock it was clear to the French ships in the rear lines that there had been a terrible massacre of their fellows in the front. They were unable to join in the fight, for their own front line lay between themselves and the English and they lacked the searoom to tack round by the west. Their own turn came in the evening when the English, penetrating through the remnants of the French front line, fell upon them. Because the smaller French ships had been placed in the second line the English now had the additional advantage of greater height from which to fire their weapons. Seeing how the battle was going, the Flemings now poured out of Sluys and the other Zwin harbours in their own ships and joined in the fighting, attacking the French from behind as the English did so from the front. As night began to fall the third French line, which consisted of Norman merchantmen led by the ships of Dieppe and the King's oared barges, tried to escape from the cul de sac. The battle opened out into a series of skirmishes as the English tried to block their path. At about ten o'clock at night the fighting died down. Two ships fought on throughout the night. The *Saint-Jame*, the largest of the ships of Dieppe, and a ship of Sandwich belonging to the Prior of Christchurch were unable to disentangle themselves: when the English finally boarded the *Saint-Jame* at dawn on the following day they counted 400 bodies of the enemy.

The French had suffered a naval catastrophe on a scale unequalled until modern times. Of the 213 French ships present at the battle the English captured 190, including the *Christopher* and the *Cog Edward* taken from them in 1338, and several other ships of the same size. The six galleys under Barbavera's command made use of their speed and manoeuvrability to flee as soon as it became clear that the French front line was failing. Four of the six oared barges based at Dieppe also got away.[15] Thirteen others made good their escape in the early hours of 25 June 1340, pursued without success by John Crabbe with the Yarmouth fleet. The crews and troops on board the ships which did not escape were killed almost to a man. No quarter was given once a ship was boarded, and those who threw themselves into the sea, as many did, were picked up by the Flemings on the foreshore and clubbed to death. Even Froissart, that romantic poet of battles, recoiled from this 'ferocious and horrible' encounter. 'On the sea,' he wrote, 'there is no retreat and no flight, and no survival but by fighting and abiding the judgement of fortune.'[16] Edward reported with satisfaction to his son that every tide deposited more corpses on the Flanders coast. Between 16,000 and 18,000 Frenchmen lost their lives, including both admirals. Quiéret was killed when his ship was boarded. Béhuchet was recognized and taken for ransom. But the conventions of aristocratic warfare were not thought to apply to the ravager of the English south coast. Edward III had him hanged from the mast of the ship which he had commanded.

The effect on the morale of the French was very serious. The captains of the 'sea frontier', who usually had pitifully small forces at their disposal, were suddenly reinforced to meet the danger of a subsidiary landing on the coast of Normandy. Thirteen hundred extra troops were sent to the Cotentin peninsula alone and one of the Marshals was placed in command of them.[17] Philip's court fell to bickering and recrimination. Barbavera, whose flight at the height of the battle was bitterly recalled by the Normans who survived, was ordered to be arrested for treason. He was not reconciled with the government until the following year when balanced reflection on the disaster suggested that the Normans would have done better to listen to his advice. Béhuchet was posthumously reviled for his low birth and accused of deliberately excluding men-at-arms from his ships in order to save money. Thus began the tendency of the French nobility, which grew more noticeable as the wretched 1340s continued, to blame all their misfortunes on the crudeness and cowardice of the lower orders: the school of thought which declared after the battle that France was better off without the unruly pirates of the Norman ports and that the saving of their wages was an uncovenanted boon to emerge from the carnage. Philip VI at least did not think so. He was profoundly affected by the fate of the communities of the Norman coast who had lost almost all of their merchant ships and many of their menfolk. Among the survivors, a few of whom continued to find their way home during the months of July and August 1340, there were many who were so mutilated by their injuries that they would never work again. In 1342 an institution was founded at Leure for some of these men, a flash of sympathy in an age which rarely thought about the welfare of soldiers and hardly ever about the welfare of defeated men who would never fight again.[18]

The reaction of the English was predictable:

> This was the bataile that fell in the Swin
> Where many Normands made mekill din;
> Wale war thay armed up to the chin
> But God and Sir Edward gert thair boste blin.

Even before Edward III's victory dispatches reached London on 28 June the capital was filled with rumours about a great victory. It meant more than the satisfaction of national assertiveness and francophobe instincts. The prevailing opinion that it meant an end of the French threat to the south and east coasts, although it was wrong, made much of the hardship of the past two years seem bearable. It became, after the failures which followed, the only bright memory of these years, the occasion commemorated on Edward III's famous gold florin minted in dismal circumstances three years later: 'IHC TRANSIENS PER MEDIUM ILLORUM IBAT': 'Jesus passing through the midst of them went his way' (Luke 4:30).[19]

The French defeat at Sluys coincided with unwelcome news from an unexpected direction. In the final stages of the preparation of the French campaign in the Scheldt valley, alarming reports had begun to arrive from the south-west. A quiet time there had been one of the premises of French strategic planning. But the reports became worse. For a few weeks between April and July the French position appeared to be collapsing not only in the areas which they had conquered since the outbreak of the war but further afield in places which they had securely held for many years.

The origin of these events lay in a radical shift in the alliances of the three great noble houses of the south-west, Armagnac, Albret and Foix. At the outset of the fighting in 1337 all three families had with varying degrees of firmness been allies of France. The counts of Armagnac and Foix had supplied a high proportion of the troops which had fought with the Constable in the campaign of 1337 and a smaller, but still significant part of the armies which had been deployed in the south-west in subsequent years.

The counts of Armagnac and Foix did not get on well with each other. Their families had competed for influence and territory for many years, and had fought periodic private wars since the middle of the thirteenth century. The war between England and France had embittered and intensified the competition. The main reason lay in the personality and ambitions of Gaston II, Count of Foix, a ruthless and self-serving warlord and an able commander whose domains could produce large bands of warriors at short notice. He had conducted a succession of independent campaigns on the southern march of the duchy, and in the process had extended his own power a long way north of its traditional base in Béarn. By the end of 1339 Gaston de Foix's vassals and garrisons controlled land extending in speckles on the map right up to the Adour valley and beyond. In parts of this region, such as the upper Adour and the southern Landes around Mont-de-Marsan the speckles were coalescing into formidable territorial blocks. The territory of the Count of Armagnac was concentrated in two regions, in Quercy, Rouergue and Gévaudan, well east of the English duchy; and in the swathe of land immediately north of the upper Adour which included the county of Armagnac itself. It was in this second region that he came up against the voracious and expansive Gaston de Foix. There was a succession of abrasive incidents. As early as the winter of 1338-9, when both noblemen were fighting in the French royal armies, the Count of Armagnac was making plans and alliances for the day when the cessation of hostilities between England and France would enable him to commence them against the Count of Foix. In the event he did not even wait that long. At the end of 1339, shortly after his return from the campaign in the north, Armagnac attacked Miramont, a small town to which he laid claim but which was situated south of the Adour in territory dominated by Gaston's soldiers. 'Enormous excesses' were committed in this short, violent private war. The place had to be taken into royal custody in order to separate the two combatants.[20]

At almost the same time Oliver Ingham achieved the political coup which had been his ambition since 1337 by recruiting Bernard-Aiz, lord of Albret, to his master's cause. Albret had so far played an extremely equivocal role in the war. He had been an ally of the French Crown ever since the war of Saint-Sardos, the result of a succession of bitter disputes with Edward II of England and some judicious patronage by Charles IV and Philip VI of France. But geography made of him a natural ally of the English, for his most important domains lay in the heart of the territory which they still controlled: in the Landes and in the lower valley of the Adour around Bayonne. Edward III and Oliver Ingham had mended many of Edward II's quarrels in the course of the 1330s, and most of Albret's family had rallied to the English Crown. His sister Mathe was an active ally of Edward III. At least two of his brothers had fought in Ingham's armies and one of them had been captured defending Blaye against the troops of Philip VI. Bernard-Aiz himself resolved his difficult dilemma by taking almost no part in the war on either side, a remarkable feat which only a man of his influence and power could have achieved. When, in 1338, a powerful relief army had been expected to arrive from England, Ingham had felt strong enough to threaten Albret with the forcible occupation of his domains in the Landes if he did not commit himself. All of this came to nothing when the relief force was cancelled, but Albret was still visibly havering in the following year. In March and April 1339 an emissary of Philip VI made two journeys to the south to plead with him. He was promised the restoration of everything that he might lose to the English by holding to the French King's cause. Potentates of the French King's court wrote personal letters to win him over. 'We know', the Duke of Normandy wrote in his, 'that you have it in your power to do more damage to our interests than any other man in those parts.'[21]

These entreaties, combined with the triumphs of French arms, kept Albret loyal for a few months longer, but in the autumn of 1339 he finally threw in his lot with Oliver Ingham. On the face of it the timing of the decision was odd. He made it at one of the lowest points of Ingham's fortunes. Why? Some of his motives were very similar to those of the Count of Armagnac. Albret's interests were also concentrated in the southern part of the duchy, and Gaston de Foix had been no more mindful of them than he had been of Armagnac's. Bernard-Aiz was already spoken of as an ally of the Count of Armagnac in 1338. The two men were closely related by marriage and interest. At some point (which cannot be exactly known) they sealed a treaty of alliance which was expressly directed against Gaston. There is some evidence that in August 1339 the Count of Foix's men occupied Tartas, a town of the Landes which although held by troops of the duchy (and therefore a fair target) belonged to Bernard-Aiz. This may have been the last straw. Evidently Albret would gain nothing if the English duchy disappeared only to be replaced in this sensitive region by a vastly extended principality of Foix-Béarn.[22]

There was, however, another factor in Bernard-Aiz's decision. He and his brothers, although they were on different sides of the conflict of England and France, had pursued for many years a single-minded endeavour to acquire a valuable group of lordships around Bergerac in southern Périgord, rich lands at a focal point of the road and river communications of south-western France. They had belonged to the ancient Rudel dynasty, the last of whom, a feckless simpleton, had died in 1334 leaving his inheritance to be disputed between two women, his widow and his sister. The sister was married to the Count of Périgord; the widow was Mathe d'Albret. Thus began the most venomous phase of another long-standing vendetta of the south-west, between the Albrets and the counts of Périgord, men who even a decade earlier had been called 'capital enemies'. The matter was litigated at great length before the Parlement of Paris, but, long before that body had pronounced, both parties had taken the law into their own hands. The Count of Périgord had occupied Bergerac by force, holding a sword to the throat of the royal official who was guarding it. The Albrets had seized two important subsidiary castles at Montcuq and Montignac as well as some lesser places. They killed the Count in battle and continued to wage open war against his successor. When the war broke out between England and France, Bergerac and its region assumed great strategic importance. Philip VI evidently regarded the counts of Périgord as the more dependable friends and increasingly took their part. The Count justified Philip's support.

Unlike Bernard-Aiz he led his troops in French armies, and never tried to improve his position by manoeuvring between the two powers.

In May 1338 Mathe d'Albret, who had always been inclined to support the English side, sold her claims to most of the Rudel inheritance including Bergerac to Edward III, reserving to herself only the fragments of it which she was actually occupying. This act made the remaining proceedings of the Parlement almost irrelevant. In September 1338 Mathe died. Her rights over the fragments which she was holding passed to Bernard-Aiz. The lord of Albret and the King of England suddenly had a common interest. Philip VI responded swiftly. At the end of 1338 and during the first few months of 1339 his officers cited Bernard-Aiz to deliver up what he had of the Rudel inheritance. The ultimate object of royal policy was reasonably clear. It became clearer still at the beginning of the following year when Philip VI first recognized the claims of the Count of Périgord and then purchased them for himself. Bernard-Aiz found himself compelled to make the hard choice which he had so far successfully avoided. Sentiment was probably worth something in his calculations, but the chequer-board of his family's landed interests in the south-west counted for much more.[23]

The outcome was that Gaston de Foix was henceforth preoccupied with the defence of his own gains and ceased to make any very substantial contribution to the French war effort in the south. The Count of Armagnac became for all practical purposes a neutral in the southern war. In May 1340 both of them left Languedoc for the northern front, each no doubt reassured by the presence of the other far from home. Both of them periodically made overtures to Edward III's representatives during the next five years.[24] As for Albret, he abandoned his former neutrality entirely, carrying over to the English side a formidable network of alliances, a personal retinue of some two or three hundred vassals who could produce an armed force of at least ten times that number, and a fortune from which he was more than once to save the delicate financial balance of the duchy in its dark hours. When Oliver Ingham marched into the south of the duchy and raided the Toulousain in the autumn of 1339, the lord of Albret marched with him.[25]

The significance of these events was better understood at Antwerp than it was at Vincennes. The English King broke off at a delicate point of his discussions with the Flemings to receive the emissaries of Ingham and Albret. On 3 January 1340 (the day before he agreed to assume the Crown of France) Edward appointed two lieutenants to exercise in his name all his powers in the duchy. One of them was Albret himself. The other was Hugh of Geneva, a great Savoyard nobleman and soldier of fortune who had been retained for Edward's service since 1337 and had fought with distinction in the campaign in the Thiérache. Like so many of the nobility of Savoy and the western Alps who embroiled themselves in the Hundred Years War he was a man of fierce courage whose most basic loyalty was to his reputation and to his pay. His kinsmen, the counts of Geneva and Savoy, fought for Philip VI.[26]

The campaign of 1340 in Gascony was the most ambitious which the English had yet fought there, an achievement made possible for a bankrupt government only by Albret's deep purse. He expended no less than 45,779 pounds of Bordeaux (£9,156) in cash, rather more than half of which was advanced to the Constable of Bordeaux, the rest paid out in wages and subsidies to his allies and retainers fighting in the army. This was about three-quarters of the ducal government's receipts in a good year from all other sources combined. Albret also contributed his many friends and allies: the lord of Pons and Ribérac, one of the principal barons of Saintonge; the lord of Mussidan in Périgord; the Caumonts of Sainte-Bazeille and much of their extensive clan. These prominent and influential southern nobleman all had connections of their own to bring to Edward II's cause. Indeed, Bernard-Aiz almost achieved the coup of capturing for the English King the allegiance of the Count of Armagnac. When Armagnac went to join Philip VI's northern army in May 1340 he left Bernard-Aiz with the terms on which he would be willing to do homage to Edward II as King of France and serve Edward's government in Gascony with 600 men-at-arms and 2,000 infantry. Bernard-Aiz sent the documents to London and had them sealed in Edward III's name.[27]

Hugh of Geneva arrived in Gascony at the beginning of March 1340. He took the field on the 27th with an army composed almost entirely of Gascons. At the same time there was a swift and well co-ordinated uprising of Albret's friends and allies in the Garonne and Lot valleys. Villages and small towns, most of them ungarrisoned, silently followed the shift of their lords' allegiances, denying entry to French officers and laying hands on French money and stores. In the larger garrisoned towns French troops had to keep within the walls for safety. In some cases they were hemmed in to the keep. The region principally affected was the western Agenais and the swathe of territory which extended from Sainte-Foy in the north, across the line of the Garonne and down into the Bazadais and the Condomois. This area included the two principal French garrisons in the south-west at Marmande and La Réole. It was crucial to the French network of road and river communications on which they depended for

11 Gascony: the war of the Albrets, March–August 1340

their ability to concentrate their dispersed forces in time of need. Albret's
interests were strong here but the dominant figure was one of his allies,
Guillaume-Raymond, lord of Caumont, whose family were seigneurs or
co-seigneurs of several important towns of the region: Sainte-Foy,
Villeneuve-Sur-Lot, Sainte-Bazeille, La Réole, Bazas and Condom. His
kinsman Alexander de Caumont was one of the commanders of Hugh of
Geneva's army, which now burst into the middle Garonne valley in support
of the uprising. On 4 April 1340 it fell on Sainte-Bazeille, a small town on
the Garonne mid-way between La Réole and Marmande. Sainte-Bazeille
was defended by a Provençal knight with a small garrison. They fought and
lost a pitched battle in front of the gates. There was a short siege. Then the
place was stormed and taken with much destruction and bloodshed. Groups
of Gascon soldiers spread out to overrun the western Agenais north of the
river, mopping up compliant communities in their path.[28]

The French were caught on the wrong foot. The senior French officer in the region was another Savoyard, Pierre de la Palu. He was a man of modest rank and ability who had been appointed seneschal of Toulouse in the previous year and left to conduct a holding operation while the decisive events occurred in the north. At the beginning of April 1340 he had some 7,000 men at his disposal, most of them garrison troops scattered in penny packets across the vast area of his command. Reinforcing and concentrating these forces quickly was an almost impossible task. The occupation of large parts of the Agenais by rebels and enemies had completely dislocated his communications. The roads between the middle Garonne and the Dordogne valleys were impassable except to large bodies of armed men. Traffic between the mint at Domme and the war treasury at Agen was having to be rerouted to the east via Cahors and long delays were occurring. To add to La Palu's misfortunes the spring rains had gorged the Garonne, making the fords impassable and washing away the three bridges of boats which had secured the crossings at La Réole, Marmande and Le Mas d'Agenais since the first campaigns of the war. Panic seized the French garrisons. At Agen influential men of the town were known to be sloping off to join the enemy. Citizens passing in and out of the gates were made to identify themselves; hostages were taken from the families of suspected traitors and locked up in the keep; in the candle-lit gloom of the Dominican church men filed past Pierre de la Palu's commissioners to swear oaths of loyalty to the Crown. Yet Agen had a strong tradition of loyalty to the Crown. Conditions can hardly have been better in other places.[29]

June 1340 was the most dangerous moment for the French. The rebellion began to spread beyond the Garonne valley. At the beginning of the month there was a powerful English offensive south of the Agenais in the Condomois and Gabardan. They were infertile, unpopulous regions of little strategic importance. The attack on them was probably connected with the covert negotiations which were in progress between the representatives of Edward III and the Count of Armagnac. He was not willing to declare for the King of England unless he was assured of substantial compensation for the territories which he would lose in France. The main compensation which he required was the delivery of Montréal, Mézin and Condom, the principal towns in the region between the Garonne and his own county of Fezensac. All of them were in territory held for the King of France. Montréal was the first to be attacked, probably early in June. The place was ungarrisoned. The inhabitants resisted with ferocity. But their town was captured.[30]

Confronted with this new crisis Pierre de la Palu reacted with rather greater vigour than heretofore. By stripping the nearby garrisons to dangerously low levels and bringing in reinforcements from outside the province he was able to recapture Montréal, it seems in the second week of July.[31] This briefly restored the position south of the Garonne but no sooner had it happened than the foundations of French power began to fail further north. Most of the troops with which La Palu had recaptured Montréal had been raised in Périgord, hitherto a province conspicuously loyal to the Crown. While their backs were turned there was a concerted series of rebellions there in the valleys of the Isle and the Dronne.

The leading light of the rising in Périgord was Raimond de Montaut, lord of Mussidan. At the time of the war of Saint-Sardos this man had been described to the King of England as 'one of the worst enemies that you have in all your duchy'. Only the year before he had brought his retinue to the French army. But he was also Albret's principal ally and protégé in the province, a venomous enemy of the Count of Périgord and a man with many disappointed claims. Albret promised him handsome territorial gains and compensation out of his own lands in Gascony for whatever he should lose by joining the rebellion. He was appointed joint captain of Périgord for Edward III. By the beginning of July 1340 southern Périgord was impassable to French officials. In August Raimond de Montaut's bands were advancing along the River Isle. Saint-Astier was captured on 21 August with the assistance of its inhabitants. Early in September they had reached the suburbs of Périgueux.[32]

La Palu marched north and recrossed the Garonne in the middle of July to attend to the new threat. As soon as he had done so the English struck again in the Condomois at Mézin, a small market town, the second of the places which it was hoped to deliver to the Count of Armagnac. Mézin was taken by storm on 23 July 1340. A week later the English appeared before Condom, the third of the places Armagnac coveted and the main market town of the region. The siege of Condom proved to be the principal military operation of the year on the southern front and the one which broke the enterprise of the ducal government after its promising beginning. The French had withdrawn their garrison from Condom in May for service elsewhere. But the English dawdled after their capture of Mézin and missed their opportunity. Bertrand de l'Isle, who was proving himself to be much the most energetic commander on the French side, put more than fifty men into the town on his own initiative on 30 July 1340 and assumed command of the defence. The English arrived on 1 or 2 August but not in sufficient strength to storm the place nor to invest it completely.

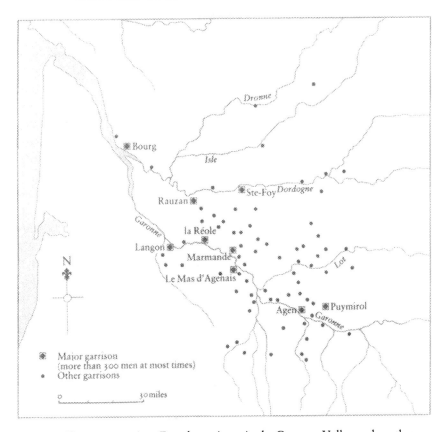

12 A military occupation: French garrisons in the Garonne Valley and southern
Périgord, August–September 1340

Pierre de la Palu, who was at Agen, learned of the English attack on the
3rd and began to concentrate his troops from every part of Languedoc.
The first reinforcements reached Bertrand de l'Isle in Condom on 9
August, penetrating the English lines, and thereafter men arrived daily. By
23 August there were no less than 1,365 French troops in Condom, in
addition to many volunteers drawn from the population of the town. A
larger relief force was on its way. The English recognized defeat and
marched away.[33]

The French had by now recovered their balance and enormously
increased their strength. The rebellions were methodically put down town
by town in the course of August and September. But not every place
occupied by the English was recovered. They retained Mézin in the Condomois. In Périgord, although Raimond de Montaut's offensive faltered

337

during September and most of his prizes were lost, the English remained in possession of Saint-Astier. Both sides had lost heavily. The English had demonstrated once again that they could achieve nothing permanent without a major infusion of manpower and money from England. The Count of Armagnac never in the event came into their camp and eventually obtained from Philip VI some of the benefits that he had been impotently offered by the English. For the French the suppression of the rebellion involved a prodigious expenditure of effort and money. They created more than seventy new garrisons in the course of the summer. The number of troops on their payroll rose to a peak of more than 20,000 at the end of September (including garrison troops). It was some indication of the gravity of the threat to their position that this was the largest number which they had yet deployed in the southern theatre, exceeding even the number which had taken part in the great offensive of 1338–9. It was not far short of the force which Philip VI was deploying at the same time to meet a much more dangerous threat to his security in the north. This substantial diversion of resources was the more serious because it was unexpected and unprovided for. Troops from Languedoc which had been intended to reinforce the northern army had to be reassigned by a succession of confused counter-orders to largely defensive operations in the Garonne valley. Raoul, Count of Eu, the most senior military officer of the French Crown, and Louis of Spain, one of its ablest captains, had to hurry south to Saintonge to hold the northern shore of the Gironde. They were still there when Edward III was landing his army in Flanders. An intolerable additional burden was thrown on to the stretched resources of the French Crown at a delicate point of the war. The correspondence of the war treasurers at Agen speaks for itself: anguished, frequently repeated demands for coin addressed to the principal mints at Domme and Saint-Pourcain; protests coming back that there was no bullion from which to make it; urgent appeals to the collectors and receivers of revenue; warnings to La Palu and the garrison commanders that their men's advances could not be paid; calls on the resources of the treasury in Paris; silence in response.[34]

Edward III, who had been wounded by an arrow in the thigh, remained on the *Cog Thomas* for two weeks after the battle of Sluys and conducted his councils in the aftercastle. Jacob van Artevelde and the leading men of Ghent came out by boat on 30 June and the main lines of the coming campaign were worked out between the English and the Flemings. Reliable figures do not exist for the size of the army at their disposal. The best estimate that can be made is that Edward had no more than about 2,000 English troops with him, of whom about two-thirds were archers. Horses, equipment and victuals were all in short supply and had to be ferried across the sea during the next few weeks. Some reinforcements arrived with them. The English King was counting on his allies. He expected to have at his disposal no less than 150,000 Flemings in addition to the armies of England and the princely states. These figures were a gross over-estimate, but their is no doubt that Edward did have a very large force under his command even if the bulk of it was hastily recruited in the streets of the industrial towns of Flanders, untrained, inexperienced and unmounted.

The main danger, as it seemed to the men gathered in the *Cog Thomas*, was that while they fought their way into France from town to town through the Scheldt valley the French army would come round their flank and overrun Flanders. Substance was given to this fear by the news that within a few days of the battle of Sluys very large French forces had begun to concentrate in Artois. It was therefore decided to divide the allied forces into two independent armies. The larger one under Edward's personal command would march into the Scheldt valley and besiege Tournai in accordance with the plans laid in January. The second army would gather in southern Flanders and attack Saint-Omer at the western extremity of Artois. It is possible that this army if it had triumphed was intended to go on and capture Calais, a long-standing ambition of the Flemings and an obvious target for the English. As its commander Edward appointed Robert of Artois, a decision made at the last moment and unexpected even by Robert himself, who had left most of his horses, equipment and retainers behind in England. The reasons for the appointment were political. Edward was still persuaded that Robert had a large following in Artois which would rally to his cause. Nevertheless, it was an unfortunate decision. The truth was that Robert had no following at all in Artois. He was an old man, his mind filled with memories and illusions. As a military commander he was brave but incompetent. He was to have with him most of the English archers, all the contingents of the princes and 50,000 men from southern Flanders including the contingents of Bruges and Ypres. Edward himself prepared to enter the Tournaisis with the English men-at-arms, about 1,000 strong, and 100,000 men of Ghent and northern Flanders. On the northern as on the southern front, the English King had become the leading actor in French civil war.[35]

Philip VI's plan of campaign was intelligently conceived but poorly executed. As soon as he learned the outcome of the battle of Sluys he detached 4,000 men to cover the Cambrésis and continue the harassment of southern Hainault. The rest of the French army marched west into Artois. The *arrière-ban* was proclaimed throughout northern France on 4 July 1340. Every French community was called to send its men of fighting age to Arras by the end of the month or money in their place. On the 6th Philip himself entered Arras and set up his headquarters there. Arras was the hub of the road system of the north-west, from which the whole 80-mile stretch between Calais and Cambrai could be watched. The French defensive arrangements were formidable. Their field army, which had been fighting in Hainault and the Cambrésis since May, was already in being, encamped in the plain north of Arras along the Lens road under Vimy Ridge on what became one of the great battlefields of the First World War. Reinforcements increased its numbers to about 24,000 men in the course of July. Seven-eighths of these men were mounted men-at-arms, a remarkably high proportion which gave the French the advantage of mobility and training over their adversaries but made them a vulnerable and unbalanced force for the battlefield. Along the marches of Flanders and western Hainault strong garrisons were placed at Aire, Saint-Venant, Lille, Douai, Mortagne, Saint-Amand and Cambrai. In addition the Duke of Burgundy in his capacity as ruler of Artois maintained garrisons of his own in the western and coastal sector of the frontier.[36]

The French had not expected an attack on Saint-Omer. But the lumbering progress of Edward III's preparations gave them plenty of warning of what was afoot. On about 15 July the Duke of Burgundy entered the town with several thousand men-at-arms and began the work of demolishing the suburbs.[37] Robert of Artois was still 15 miles away at Cassel haggling with his own troops. There were not enough of them: perhaps 1,000 English archers commanded by Sir Thomas Oughtred and between 10,000 and 15,000 Flemings, less than a third of what had been expected. Their morale was low and their discipline poor. Most of them came from the smaller towns of southern Flanders and had no reason to share the political ambitions of Ghent and van Artevelde. They were more worried about the safety of their homes and not at all convinced that attack was the best form of defence. Robert cajoled them forward. He had friends, he said, who had sent him written promises of support. They would open the gates on his appearance. It would all be over very quickly. On about 16 July 1340 Robert's army reached the muddy ditch between the Lys and the Aa which marked the border and crossed in ramshackle order into the county of Artois. Some pressed forward in small groups only to be cut off and killed by the French. Others dallied behind to loot and burn. The best part of a day was spent destroying the town of Arques while barely a mile away the Count of Armagnac led fresh troops into Saint-Omer to reinforce the Duke of Burgundy. During the next few days the Anglo-Flemish army spread itself out on the eastern side of Saint-Omer. The main body of Philip VI's army began to move slowly up behind them from the south-east.

On 26 July 1340 Robert of Artois realized that he was in danger of being crushed between the French forces in Saint-Omer and the vastly superior army commanded by Philip VI. He offered battle to the garrison. In the early morning he carefully drew up his men in the open ground between Saint-Omer and the ruins of Arques. He placed the cream of his troops in the front line: the English men-at-arms and archers and the troops of Bruges. Behind them in three battalions stood the men of Ypres on the left, the men of Furnes and Berghes in the centre and on the right the contingent of the outlying territory of Bruges. The other Flemings remained at the rear to serve as a reserve and guard the camp. Across the front of the army and along its left flank Robert had constructed lines of ditches and outworks defended by anti-cavalry obstacles carefully camouflaged. Thus protected he waited for the enemy.

With a large French army on its way up the Arras road the Duke of Burgundy's obvious course was to ignore Robert's challenge and sit tight behind his walls. That was what the King had ordered him to do, but his subordinates took the decision out of his hands. At about mid-day, when Robert's men had been standing at their stations for four hours, some hotheads burst out of the south-east gate of Saint-Omer leading most of the Duke's retinue and a large body of local levies after them, and threw themselves against the defended outworks on the left flank of the Anglo-Flemish army. They were repulsed. Foolishly, however, the men of Ypres who were defending the barrier leaped over it and rushed into the open country in pursuit of their adversaries. They were followed by the whole of the rest of the second line. Seeing that the Flemings no longer had the protection of their outworks the French turned about and counter-attacked. A vicious fight began which continued for most of the afternoon. The Duke of Burgundy, who could see all this from the walls, could bear it no longer. He and the Count of Armagnac led their retinues, about 850 men, out of the town gates. This happened at the end of the afternoon. The Count of Armagnac and his men galloped round to the southern edge of the battlefield to join the mêlée which had been in progress since mid-day. The arrival of this force, which included 300 heavy cavalry, was decisive. The men of Ypres and the other Flemings who had once formed the second

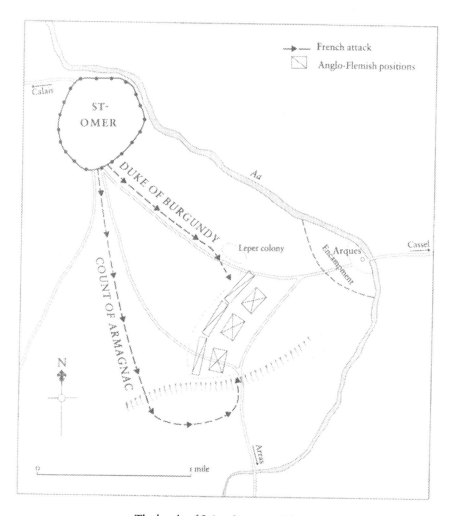

13 The battle of Saint-Omer, 26 July 1340

line of Robert of Artois' army were driven back with heavy losses and
eventually took to their heels. Fleeing through the open encampment of the
Anglo-Flemish army they spread panic among the rearguard who were
waiting there. The French crashed into the encampment after them and,
trapping the fleeing Flemings in the bend of the River Aa, slaughtered
many thousands of them.

While all this was happening an entirely independent battle was in
progress elsewhere. The Duke of Burgundy did not accompany the Count
of Armagnac to the battle on the southern flank. Instead he rode straight

342

down the Arques road towards the front line of the Anglo-Flemish army. Here Robert of Artois with the English and Brugeois had stood all afternoon immobile behind their fieldworks. All of them were dismounted. When they saw the Duke of Burgundy's banners approaching them they charged. The Duke's horsemen were unprepared and were overwhelmed by the weight of numbers. They fell back into the south-eastern suburbs of Saint-Omer, where they found themselves jammed into narrow streets unable to escape and unable to retreat through their own closed gates. One of the most difficult operations of a medieval garrison was to hold open a gate for long enough to readmit a returning sortie party and then to close it against the pursuing enemy behind. The archers on the walls concentrated their fire against the pursuers while the Duke of Burgundy and his men slowly squeezed their way into the city and forced the gates closed behind them. In the falling light the Duke was welcomed through the streets with torches and cheers. But he had suffered heavy casualties and a humiliating tactical defeat.

Neither the Duke of Burgundy nor indeed Robert of Artois realized that a mile and a half away the bulk of the Anglo-Flemish army had been destroyed by the Count of Armagnac. There was a surreal encounter on the Arques road. Robert of Artois' victorious troops marching east towards their camp came upon the Count of Armagnac's victorious troops marching west towards Saint-Omer. Until they were a lance's length away neither side recognized the other in the darkness. They passed each other by with only a few desultory and disorganized fights. Both parties were exhausted. Only when Robert reached the site of his encampment did he discover to his horror what had happened to the rest of his army. The camp was deserted, the tents empty and the horses unattended at their tethers. When dawn broke on 29 July the bodies of some 8,000 Flemings could be seen scattered across the country for several miles along the Cassel road. The Flemings with Robert did not wait for the French to return. They fled to Cassel and Ypres. Robert himself, after a moment's hesitation, followed them. The French captured the Anglo-Flemish camp intact, taking many warhorses, 600 carts, all the tents, huge quantities of stores and most of the Flemish standards.

Edward III's campaign of 1340 had begun badly. The loss of several thousand Flemings was bearable. The survivors, including almost all the precious English archers, did eventually rejoin him at Tournai. But the defeat had more serious strategic consequences. It exposed southern Flanders to the revenge of Philip VI. It enabled the French to concentrate their forces against the main army of the coalition in the Tournaisis. It dented the prestige of the coalition and undermined its cohesion. Within a few days of the the battle representatives of Ypres and Bruges and of van Artevelde's enemies in Ghent made contact with the French court to find out on what terms they could be readmitted to the French King's peace.[38]

As Edward III's first army marched to its defeat he struggled to bring together the second and larger force which was to attack Tournai. The English King disembarked from the *Cog Thomas* on 8 July 1340 and arrived in Ghent on the evening of the 10th. There he met for the first time in six months the princes of the coalition. The proceedings of this conference were not harmonious.[39] Edward's decision to attack Saint-Omer was presented to them as a *fait accompli*. Their views about it can be inferred from the fact that none of them took up their appointed roles at Robert's side. The Duke of Brabant had actually disbanded the army which he had assembled for the relief of Thun-l'Evêque three weeks before. His enthusiasm for the war had visibly diminished as Edward III had drawn closer to the Flemings. He disliked Jacob van Artevelde personally and cannot have thought highly of the communal governments of Flanders. His subjects were jealous of the economic strength of Flanders and resentful of the transfer of the English wool staple from Antwerp to Bruges. There was an unbridgeable gulf between those such as van Artevelde and (now) the Count of Hainault who had powerful political motives for prosecuting the campaign and the others, like the Duke of Brabant and some of the Germans, who needed to keep faith with their partners and preserve themselves from Philip's wrath but no longer had anything to gain except money. Unless Edward III paid them they would not even have money.

Edward's financial position at this stage was difficult and deteriorating. The collection of the Parliamentary subsidy had begun in April 1340. But it was to be assessed according to entirely new principles. A ninth of all grain, wool and lambs was to be collected in the counties, and a ninth of all movables in the towns. It was collected in kind and then sold for the government's account. This unusual form of taxation was modelled on ecclesiastical tithes. It had been suggested to the government in Parliament (in place of the traditional tenths and fifteenths in cash) because of the severe agricultural depression which made goods hard to sell and cash hard to find. But for the same reason its yield was small and slow in coming in. Only £15,000 had been raised by November 1340. The government's position would not have been much better even if the tax had fulfilled its hopes. They were expecting to raise £100,000 by 1 November

1340 and another £100,000 the following year. But in the six weeks before the King's departure from England the whole of the first instalment and substantially all the second had had to be assigned to his principal bankers and the leaders of the English army in part payment of debts contracted in 1339. The result was that Edward arrived in the Low Countries quite penniless. He could not even pay the daily expenses of his household except by the indulgence of his creditors. On 24 July 1340 the earls of Northampton, Derby and Warwick, who had guaranteed some of the King's past debts, were arrested in Brussels and taken to a debtors' prison at Mechelen. They were only released to join the campaign in exchange for four knights apiece and firm promises to return to captivity later. Edward issued strident calls for money to his officials. He had a fixed conviction that money would somehow be found in England and put on the next ship. This was presumably what he told the princes at Ghent. But it was an illusion.[40]

On 12 July 1340 while the princes were still in session in Ghent, Parliament assembled yet again in the Painted Chamber of the Palace of Westminster. There was a familiar tone in the Chancellor's opening speech and the earnest entreaties which followed. Two earls and a knight of Edward's household arrived on 15 July from Flanders to fan the assembly's enthusiasm. They brought with them an official account of the battle of Sluys and a letter from Edward III explaining his military strategy for the summer campaign. They expounded the King's case in what seemed at least to the King's ministers who were present to be a most persuasive style. They dwelt upon the terrible dangers which the King was facing in Flanders and northern France and on the anguish which he was feeling together with his Queen and the noblemen of his army. But all this would go for nothing unless he could find some way of anticipating the collection of the last Parliamentary subsidy. Unless his allies were paid they would make a separate peace with Philip VI and Edward would be left at the mercy of his enemies. 'I and my country, my children, the nobility and my whole people will be undone.' What the government wanted was a forced loan in kind which would be repaid during 1341 from the second instalment of the subsidy. The Commons were not greatly impressed. It was only on 24 July 1340 after particularly long discussions that they agreed to a forced loan of 20,000 sacks of wool. Even then stringent terms were imposed designed to ensure that the money did not pass into the hands of the war financiers who had made off with the earlier levies. Reporting to the King, his ministers explained that it would be necessary to make elaborate administrative arrangements to collect the loan and that discussions with the wool merchants were in hand. The government did not intend themselves to set up as wool merchants as they had done with such disastrous results in the winter of 1337–8. Instead they dealt with a number of merchant syndicates who agreed to buy the wool and pay the money directly to Edward III's war treasurer at Bruges. On 13 August 1340 the Council told the King that they expected very soon to be able to send him substantial sums. Edward took this promise seriously.[41]

Every day it became more difficult for ministers at Westminster to fulfil it. The first shock came in late July with a revival of French seapower which perhaps should have been anticipated. In spite of the victory of Sluys it was found that the French were still able to launch piratical raids on lone merchantmen in the North Sea, and even to ferry fresh men and supplies to Scotland. Occasional captures and shipwrecks on the east coast of England gave Edward's ministers some idea of what was happening. Spies began to report renewed activity in the French Channel ports within ten days of the battle. The French government appointed Robert Houdetot, an energetic Norman knight, as admiral, to replace the ill-fated Quiéret and Béhuchet. He proceeded at once to the Seine ports and began to requisition ships and equipment. In the last week of July Houdetot was at sea with a small squadron: three galleys and seven armed barges, most of them survivors of Sluys; and an important contingent of armed Spanish merchantmen hired in the Biscay ports.[42]

This happened at a delicate moment for the English government's schemes. Believing that they had entirely eliminated the naval threat from France the English had stood down most of the ships of the western Admiralty to whom the task of coastal defence had previously been assigned. Shipments of victuals and equipment were passing unconvoyed across the North Sea as well as convoyed cargoes of wool belonging to the King's bankers and the magnates of his army. In the Channel an important military enterprise had been on foot since the beginning of July when Sir Thomas Ferrers had embarked at Southampton for the reconquest of Guernsey, Alderney and Sark. Ferrers landed on Guernsey on 12 July 1340 and established control over all the undefended parts of the island. On the 17th he laid siege to Castle Cornet with a force of 330 men. The capture of the castle, without which the conquest of the rest of the island would be useless, required a steady flow of reinforcements and supplies from the south-coast ports.[43]

Robert Houdetot irrupted into this scene on 26 July 1340. His squadron surprised an English convoy in the Channel and captured thirty merchantmen laden with wool. Their crews were slaughtered. Then turning westward he made for the Solent and landed his men on the Isle of Wight on about 1 August 1340. They were eventually driven back to their ships by the local militia but not before they had inflicted great damage on the island and heavy casualties on its defenders, including the commander Sir Theobald Russell, who was killed. Their next target was the Isle of Portland, which was wasted on the following day. Teignmouth was attacked without warning and burned. They tried to do the same at Plymouth, a day's passage further west, but by this time they had lost the advantage of surprise. They burned a manor house and took some prisoners but failed to get into the town. By 5 August 1340 they were back in their bases revictualling and making plans for another descent on the Solent.[44]

The English had been caught off balance. The fleet of the western Admiralty had to be called back into being by a fresh round of requisitions. The ships of London, Yarmouth and the Cinque Ports were hurriedly congregated in the Downs. Robert Morley was sent with other ships of the northern Admiralty to the Channel Islands to prevent the French from relieving Castle Cornet by sea. The coastguard militia was mobilized all along the south coast and the convoy system reintroduced for all outbound ships. These energetic but belated measures were enough to parry the threat from Houdetot's small squadron. His second cruise, which began on 29 August, was a failure. By the time he left the Seine the English fleet had assembled in strength and was standing off Winchelsea. In September Morley's fleet was able to take the offensive, cruising off the mouth of the Seine and the Channel Islands and mounting a devastating raid on Brest (a neutral port), where many laden merchantmen were sheltering from the rival fleets. The spoils included six merchant galleys from Genoa with their cargoes worth more than £10,000.[45]

The renewed war at sea, although its outcome was reasonably satisfactory for the English, was expensive and disruptive and it coincided with other demands on the English government's resources. In the lowlands of Scotland guerrillas had taken control of the open country and were making war 'right up to the gates of the town' according to the warden of Berwick. They were launching cattle-rustling raids deep into Northumberland. In mid-August 1340 the leaders of the Scots decided to undertake an autumn campaign against Stirling, now the northernmost outpost of English strength. This made it necessary for the Council to order the recruitment of a fresh army in the northern counties and to spend money in carrying victuals and reinforcements by sea to their isolated garrisons in central Scotland.[46]

When the English government began to collect the forced loan of 20,000 sacks of wool in its discontented and insecure island, it encountered furious resistance. Quotas were assigned to each county at the end of July and values fixed according to the Nottingham scheme of 1337. County commissioners were appointed everywhere. But by 20 August 1340, when large quantities should have been in hand, they had collected almost nothing. On the 21st the wool merchants appeared before the Council in London to make arrangements for the purchase and disposal of the produce, but there was nothing for them to buy. Of the 20,000 sacks required, a mere 854 had been placed at the government's disposal, two-thirds of which had been raised in London. Elsewhere the levy was a complete failure. The Council, who were receiving frequent and increasingly hysterical letters from the King at Tournai, thrashed about. They called the county officials to Westminster to account for themselves. They replaced some and threatened others with worse. The officials turned on the population. There were sporadic outbreaks of violence. In Lincolnshire wool was being removed into fortified stores to be defended from the collectors by main force. In Essex there was armed and organized resistance. In Somerset the collectors were assaulted and left for dead. The Council was losing control. They believed that these black incidents would coalesce into a general rebellion. Less than a month after they had told the King that he would soon be in funds, they were sending him the most alarming reports. 'We dare not do more than we have,' they said, 'for we shall have a civil war on our hands; the population will fight us rather than give us their wool.'[47]

The date appointed for the attack on Tournai was 29 July 1340. Edward himself left Ghent in good time on the 18th and proceeded slowly up the Scheldt valley accompanied by his own men-at-arms and by the Flemings under the command of van Artevelde. On 23 July they halted at Chin, a small village 3 miles north of Tournai where there was a bridge over the river. The Hainaulters and most of the Germans joined them in the course of the next week. Of the Duke of Brabant, who was contributing the major part of the cavalry, there was still no sign. On 26 July, without waiting for further reinforcements, Edward committed his reputation to the capture of the city. He issued a bombastic challenge proclaiming himself rightful king of France and offering 'Philip de Valois' trial by single combat or, if that were unfair to his corpulent and middle-aged adversary, a staged battle between 100 selected champions on each side. Otherwise, he said, he would recover his inheritance by overwhelming force. The French King returned a curt answer. He had, he said, seen a letter addressed to one 'Philip de Valois' but since it was evidently not intended for him he had given it no consideration. In due course he would throw Edward and his allies out of his kingdom. This message reached Edward III on 31 July 1340. On the same day the English King moved his host downstream from the bridge of Chin and invested Tournai.[48]

Tournai was not a place of any particular strategic importance to Edward III.[49] Its capture would have extended the boundaries of Flanders but would not have opened up the gateway to France. Nevertheless its loss would have been a severe blow to Philip VI's prestige. It was an important ecclesiastical and industrial city standing on both sides of the Scheldt in the angle of Flanders and Hainault. It controlled a rich entrepôt trade between France and the Low Countries as well as a modest cloth-making industry. It was famous throughout Europe for the production of marble carvings and metal armour. Although it was far from being in the same class as Paris or Ghent, its population was probably about 20,000 in 1340, which made it one of the larger provincial cities of France. Its walls, which in a few places still stand, were formidable. They were modern (begun in 1295) and complete. Their circuit, which roughly corresponded to the inner ring of boulevards around the modern city, was about 3 miles long and was defended by seventy-four towers.[50] In addition to the permanent garrison commanded by Godemar du Fay, the Constable and both Marshals of France were at Tournai with their contingents. On 23 July 1340, the day of Edward III's arrival at Chin, the Count of Foix, who had been detached by Philip VI from the main body of his army outside Arras, entered the city with more than 3,000 soldiers. There were now almost 5,800 French troops in Tournai, two-thirds of them men-at-arms and the rest Pyrenean infantry of famous ferocity. The nominal commanders were the Constable of France by right of precedence and the captain of the town. But the directing mind was that of the Count of Foix. His powerful personality brooked no opposition. He was the ablest soldier there and most of the garrison were his men.

The King of England set up his tents by the western sector of the city walls. His own army consisted of the retinues of the English magnates and the bedraggled English and Flemish survivors of the battle of Saint-Omer, who had rejoined him at the end of July. They were spread out to cover the Lille and Douai roads by which any relieving army could be expected to come. On the other side of the river, against the northern sector of the walls, there was a vast open meadow known as the Pré-aux-Nonnains after a small convent church which lay in the middle of it. Jacob van

349

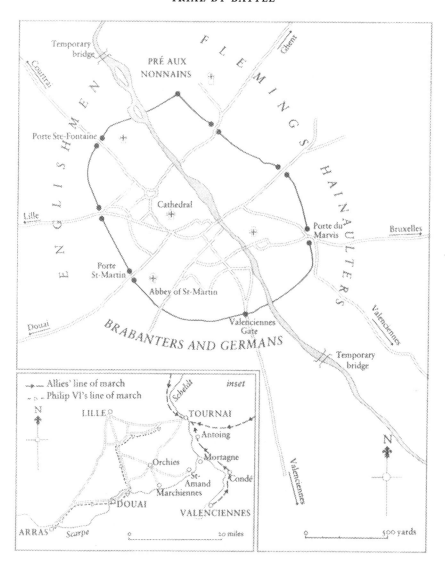

14   The siege of Tournai, July–September 1340

Artevelde and the rest of the Flemings set up their headquarters here. From the belfry of the church they could observe the comings and goings of the garrison. The Count of Hainault and (when at last he arrived) the Duke of Brabant covered the south-eastern sector, including the Valenciennes gate. The rest of the walls on the right were invested by the German princes. To maintain communications between the allied camps and to seal off the approach by river into the town, wooden pontoon bridges were built over the Scheldt north and south of the city.

Where the ground rose away from the walls the allies sited their siege engines, immense mechanical slings mounted on wooden frames and assembled on site by specialist carpenters. Experiments conducted with reconstructed machines in the nineteenth century suggested that these devices could hurl a 25-pound stone stone ball nearly 200 yards to destroy the top work of walls and towers. Their noisy operations were good for the besiegers' morale but otherwise achieved nothing. The walls of Tournai had been built to withstand them. From beginning to end of the siege they killed only six defenders, less than one for each machine. The Count of Hainault experimented with more elaborate devices which could hurl explosive bombs into the city, but he was even less successful. The engineer who was commissioned to construct the bombs made off with his advance and was never seen again.

Given the size of the garrison an assault on the walls would have been a costly and hazardous operation. Until the fourth week of the siege the allies did not attempt it. Instead they waited for Tournai to fall into their hands by treachery or famine or for their missiles to bring down a large enough section of the wall. They tried to draw the main French army to battle by the traditional method of wasting the territory around. They filled their camps with spoil and struck out around them settling scores for the Count of Hainault. The first victim of this brutal process was the town of Orchies, 12 miles down the Douai road. This place was attacked on 1 August 1340. The leading men of Orchies came out to parley but while the talks continued the army assaulted and sacked it. Great quantities of booty were found here, and the richest citizens were taken for ransom. Before dawn on 3 August the Count of Hainault led his men against Saint-Amand, 10 miles south on the border of his own dominions. An expedition from Valenciennes attacked simultaneously on the other side. Saint-Amand had a strong French garrison. They fought a protracted battle against their assailants outside the town, and when they were driven back they fought on from the walls. But they were overwhelmed. Many of them were killed and the rest captured. The Count utterly destroyed

Saint-Amand. He threw down the walls and demolished the famous monastery, carrying off for ransom those citizens who had taken sanctuary inside it. The booty included a large quantity of gold and cattle and seventeen bells.[51] Ten days later a detachment of the besieging army destroyed the great Benedictine abbey near Marchiennes and the small town around it. Fire took hold very quickly in the cramped alleyways and wooden buildings of which medieval towns and villages were made. For 15 miles about the walls of Tournai nothing was left standing. To the south-west the torch-bearers came within sight of the gates of Douai.

The garrison and citizens of Tournai conducted a spirited defence. From monastery gardens under the walls their own stone-throwers fired continuously but more or less at random into the enemy camps outside. They achieved rather more than the equipment of the allies did. One of their missiles destroyed the bell tower of the convent in the Pré-aux-Nonnains, thereby depriving the Flemings of their observation post. Another destroyed a Flemish siege engine within a few yards of Jacob van Artevelde's tent. A third struck the Count of Hainault's chief engineer and took his head off. The defence of the walls and gates was in the hands of the citizens, who distributed watches and stations among themselves. The garrison were kept in reserve for fighting off assaults and launching sorties from the gates. Small parties of volunteers crept out from the walls to fall upon isolated groups of the besiegers, to seize valuable commodities, and to capture cartloads of provisions. In one daring sortie a group of men led by a squire of Godemar du Fay succeeded in capturing part of the booty which the Count of Hainault was bringing back from his sack of Saint-Amand. Another sortie by sixty horsemen invaded the English camp and penetrated the tent of Bishop Burghersh while the Bishop was eating his dinner. A French knight set at him with his lance. He was saved only by the devotion of a squire who threw himself in the way of the assailant and took the blow himself. These adventures, although good for the spirits of the city, were very costly in men and horses and achieved nothing of real military significance. There was also a serious danger that the pursuing enemy would force their way through the gates as they opened to readmit the sortie party. This very nearly happened after the attack of Bishop Burghersh's tent. Because of incidents like this the city authorities took firm measures to curtail unauthorized sorties. At one point they were confiscating the keys of over-enthusiastic gate crews.

The main danger facing the town was that they would run out of food. There had been no time to accumulate great stores, as the French had done at Cambrai in 1339. The defenders were already in difficulties at the outset of the siege. It was a hot airless summer. Food could not be preserved. Pasturage within the walls was quickly exhausted and cattle put out to graze at night were seized by the enemy and eaten. Grain was plentiful but there was a dire shortage of flour because the millers of Tournai were dependent on windmills in the suburbs which were in the hands of the enemy. The very size of the garrison, equal to a quarter of the population and accompanied by several thousand horses, added to the problems. At an early stage of the siege old men, women and children and the poor and weak, all 'useless mouths', were expelled. The price of food rose to astronomical heights. Curiously there was no attempt to create a 'siege economy'. The garrison troops had to buy their provisions from the citizens out of their own pay at whatever was the going rate. In early September they were in the peculiar situation of having to arrange for groups of men-at-arms to bring supplies of money through the besieger's lines at night at great danger to themselves in order to prevent their companions from starving.[52] The Count of Foix, who at one point had sat down with his entire household to dine on one loaf and one fish, threatened to abandon the town and fight his way out through the lines if something was not done. He succeeded in obtaining from the city authorities an old and disused portable mill which his men repaired and set up in the buildings of St Martin's Abbey. This brought some relief. But it was not until the very last days of the siege that the city fathers instituted strict controls over stocks and prices. The French garrison commanders must often have been tempted to take ruthless measures against the self-interested citizens whom they were supposed to be defending. They never did so. A city the size of Tournai could so easily be delivered up to the enemy by a handful of disaffected burghers, however large the garrison.

The besiegers had no difficulty in supplying themselves. Around them lay some of the most fertile agricultural regions of northern Europe. Barges laden with produce arrived regularly by river. But the armies of the coalition had other difficulties. A long siege is boring and demoralizing and subject to diminishing returns of plunder. In the third week of August there were signs of impatience and a change of policy among the besiegers. Instead of gradually starving the city into surrender, it was decided to assault it by force of arms. The first important attempt occurred on 26 August 1340. An assault force of 2,000 Flemings and an unknown number of Englishmen tried to scale the walls by the Porte Sainte-Fontaine at the northern extremity of the city. But they were repulsed with heavy losses. On 2 September 1340 another attempt was made at the same place. Great quantities of brushwood were sent against the wooden gates and lit. As the gates burned the siege engines battered at them. The assault, when it came, lasted most of the day before it faltered and was broken off. For their gallantry the defenders of the Porte Sainte-Fontaine received a barrel of burgundy.

These attempts exacerbated the strains in the allied councils not only because they failed but also because it was only the English and Flemings who took part in them. The Hainaulters had done great deeds of their own at the other end of the town but the Germans and Brabanters had done nothing. This did not pass unnoticed. The Flemings openly accused the Brabanters of treachery. There was an ugly incident after a piper from the army of Brabant was caught in the English sector of the walls engaged in conversation with one of the defenders. Van Artevelde had him tortured to the point of death to make him say that he had been acting on the orders of his superiors.[53] A little later van Artevelde delivered a tirade against the cowardice and inactivity of the Duke of Brabant at a conference of the allied leaders in the King of England's tent. One of the Duke's knights told him to go back and brew beer in Ghent. Van Artevelde ran this man through with his sword. All of Edward's diplomatic skills were required to prevent the Duke from leaving the army forthwith.

The Brabanters and the German princes had no reason to bring any enthusiasm to the fighting. The mercenaries would be worthy of their hire when they received it. Edward excused himself and pointed to the strenuous measures which his ministers were taking in England. But his thoughts were not as optimistic as his words. In the middle of August when the siege had been in progress for only two weeks he had already made the first tentative approaches to the French court. As September came and no money arrived from England, Edward had to pay 20 per cent interest to usurers for money to feed himself and his troops.[54] By the end of the first week of September 1340 it had become apparent that if negotiations failed there would be little time left in which to capture Tournai or force his adversaries to battle before his own army abandoned him.

Philip VI had as good an opportunity as he would ever have to destroy the English King's pretensions in the summer of 1340. He had a large army under his command. The enemy's forces, although more numerous than his own, included very few of the feared English archers and an unduly large proportion of raw Flemish townsmen. Philip's indecisive manner and hesitant movements seemed incomprehensible. His army had remained encamped under Vimy Ridge until 22 or 23 July when it began to shuffle slowly off in the direction of Saint-Omer, arriving too late to take part in the battle. Philip himself followed in its tracks. On the evening of 29 July 1340 he came to Aire-sur-la-Lys on the Flemish border. A force of about 2,000 men was detached here, placed under the command of the Duke of Athens and sent off in pursuit of the remnant of Robert of Artois' army. While this force failed to take Cassell and engaged in some desultory destruction in the Flemish borderlands, the rest of the army waited for its orders.

In St Andrew's Priory outside Aire the French royal Council met. They had before them two Franciscan friars from Tournai who had made their way through the lines of the besiegers with letters from the garrison commander. He reported the complete investiture of the city and the grave shortages which existed within the walls. Two possible courses were discussed: the army could invade and sack Flanders, toppling van Artevelde's regime and perhaps drawing off the Flemings from Tournai; or it could march to relieve Tournai. The decisive voice was that of the Count of Flanders. Louis of Nevers passionately opposed an invasion of his county, knowing that its destruction by a French army would ruin perhaps forever his chances of a reconciliation with his subjects. It was therefore decided to march on Tournai instead.

The two Franciscans hurried back with the news. Yet it took Philip no less than five weeks to reach Tournai. The delay was only partly explained by disorganization. At Béthune there were prolonged discussions with representatives of van Artevelde's enemies from the three great towns of Flanders. This was too promising a sign of disintegration in the enemy camp to be spurned. But the discussions came to nothing and delayed Philip by a week. At Douai, where Philip arrived in the third week of August, there were other messages of peace, perhaps disingenuous, this time from Edward III himself. The French court seemed remarkably anxious to avoid the decisive battle. They remained for nearly two weeks in Douai. Within the walls of Tournai the slow progress of the French army added to the distress of the inhabitants and the garrison. On the night of 10 August 1340 two messengers were secreted out of the city to lay before the French King the state of their defences and supplies. He received them with ill-concealed irritation. Their function, he said, was to hold out. He would see to it that they were rewarded after the campaign.

The French army at last entered the Tournaisis on 7 September 1340 and pitched its tents at Bouvines, some 10 miles west of the city. Bouvines was an evocative place, the site of the great battle of 1214 in which Philip Augustus had defeated King John and his German allies, putting the seal on the destruction of the Angevin Empire. It was a tiny hamlet beside a

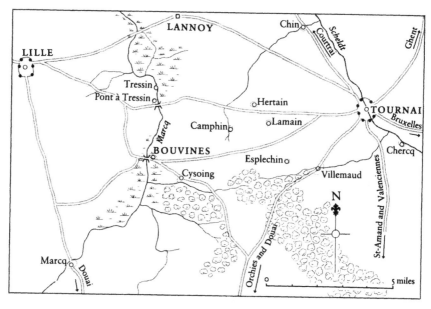

15 Bouvines, September 1340

narrow stone bridge over the River Marcq. The old Roman road from
Tournai to Estaires stretched east and west. On either side the river
broadened out into impassable marsh. Behind this natural barrier the
French army waited. A few volunteers made their way across the marshes
to the city walls, bringing bags of cheese, meat and other delicacies. Within
the city the garrison was preparing itself for a great sortie at the decisive
point of the forthcoming battle. The commanders sat down with the
leading burgesses in the city hall. They wanted volunteers from among the
citizens. The burgesses wanted undertakings that the sortie parties would
pay their bills before they left and return to defend the town after the battle
had ended. At nightfall criers passed through the streets calling men to
arms.

Edward III redisposed his forces about the city. Leaving only small
covering forces by the gates, all the princely armies and most of the
Flemings crossed to the western side of the Scheldt to stand between the
city walls and the enemy. The Duke of Brabant held the southern flank in
front of the village of Chercq; the Count of Hainault and his uncle stood to
the north; Edward himself raised his standard in the centre. In front of
them lay the great expanse of open, level ground into which the French
army was expected to issue.

There was no battle. The French defended their positions, but they did not come out into the open fields where the enemy was waiting for them. Needling attacks on their flanks failed to draw them. Early on 8 September 1340 the Hainaulters and some volunteers from other contingents of the allied army carried out a reconnaissance in force towards the French encampment under the guidance of a local bandit who knew the ground. They collided in the dawn mist with a large foraging party from the contingent of the Prince–Bishop of Liège, who was fighting with the French army. There was a bloody skirmish along marshland paths south of the bridge before they were beaten off. A little later on the same day the Hainaulters tried to make their way round the north side of the French positions by the bridge over the Marcq at Tressin. Here there was another short, fierce fight in which the Hainaulters were worsted. It was a poor return for all their efforts.

Once the tension provoked by Philip VI's arrival broke, the leaders of the allies fell to quarrelling noisily in their tents, and their army began to fall apart. The imminence of battle concentrated men's minds on the absence of their pay. What were they to die for? The first murmurs of mutiny came not from the princes but from their men. In the army of the Duke of Brabant the lead was taken by the levies of Brussels, Louvain and Antwerp, which included most of the Duke's infantry. They threatened to withdraw from the army 'with or without leave'. There were influential men in the army of Hainault who were of the same mind. Within a few days of the arrival of the French at Bouvines exploratory talks were in progress between Edward's allies and those of Philip VI. Edward was told about these discussions and permitted them. But he took no part. The point was not lost on the French negotiators. They reported to Philip that the enemy's nerve was failing. Large concessions could probably be extracted.[55]

The French King was changeable and irrational. He took the view, as he had done before La Capelle in the previous year, that a battle should be avoided. But he had a strong sense of personal grievance against Edward III, whom he regarded as a bumptious vassal, and he was reluctant to conduct formal negotiations on French territory with the representatives of the man who had invaded it. Nor would he countenance any dealings with the rebellious and excommunicated Flemings. It was not until 22 September 1340, by which time Philip had been at Bouvines for a fortnight, that he was persuaded to relent by his brother the Count of Alençon and his sister Jeanne de Valois, Abbess of Fontenelle and dowager Countess of Hainault. This forthright and censorious lady then crossed the marshes with a small escort at night and presented herself in the tent of her son-in-law, the King of England. She found Edward unmoved by her appeal to his finer moral sense, but interested in an accommodation with his enemy for more calculating reasons. He intensely desired to capture Tournai and save his honour, and he believed that the city was on the verge of surrender. Henry of Lancaster had captured a messenger passing between the walls and the French camp. This man had told his interrogators what he thought they wanted to hear, that the garrison was down to 200 men and had less than a fortnight's food left. But Edward did not have a fortnight. He knew that most of his army would not fight and that his campaign was lost. He wanted only a dignified way out. The leaders of the coalition were called to his tent. Robert of Artois and Jacob van Artevelde were opposed to any suggestion of negotiation. Van Artevelde invoked the treaties of the coalition and the oaths of the men present. The Duke of Brabant spoke strongly in favour of compromise and the mood of the meeting was undoubtedly with him. Without the men of Brabant the prospects in a battle were not good. Van Artevelde reluctantly assented.

About halfway between the two armies, outside the hamlet of Esplechin, there was a small chapel. The plenipotentiaries met here on 23 September 1340: on the French side, John of Bohemia and the Bishop of Liège, the King's brother the Count of Alençon, and the counts of Flanders and Armagnac; on the English side, Henry Burghersh and the four principal allies of England, the Duke of Brabant, John of Hainault, the Duke of Guelders and the Margrave of Juliers. The French had a strong hand and as the negotiations proceeded it became stronger. Everyone in the allied camp knew what was happening. It was difficult to maintain any enthusiasm for the prosecution of the siege which was now all but over. The Brabançon troops around Tournai faded away in the face of sorties from the town. The Flemings, who were afraid for their own future, were arriving in droves in the French camp to throw themselves humbly before Philip VI and beseech his pardon.[56] The French skilfully exploited the divisions among their enemies. By the end of 24 September 1340 agreement had been reached.

There was to be a truce of nine months until 24 June 1341 not only in northern France but in Scotland, in Gascony, at sea and in the Channel Islands. All parties were to hold their existing positions, however gained. All prisoners of war were to be released on parole, to return to captivity if hostilities were resumed. All of this was highly satisfactory to the allied princes. The truce would protect them from the vengeance of the French

King for long enough to contrive a permanent agreement with him. Those who had made conquests (in practice only the Count of Hainault) could hold on to them for the time being. There were significant concessions for the Flemings. Philip undertook that for the duration of the truce he would prevent the return of the exiles who had fled from van Artevelde's regime. He promised that he would arrange for the ecclesiastical penalties against Flanders to be lifted and that he would make no further use of the notorious papal privilege by which the kings of France were able to call down excommunication and interdict on the province. As for Edward III, it would not be right to say that he gained nothing from the truce of Esplechin. The huge army which Pierre de la Palu and Bertrand de l'Isle had now gathered in the south-west, which was poised to conquer what was left of the English positions in the Garonne valley, was halted and dispersed. The Scots cancelled their plans to attack Stirling, which they would probably have captured. But Edward's eyes were fixed on the northern march of France, and his failure there was complete. All that he gained was a liberty to withdraw gracefully. On the following morning, 25 September 1340, the truce was formally sealed and the cessation of hostilities was proclaimed by the heralds in both camps.[57] The Brabanters had already gone. The princely armies vanished. The English and the Flemings spent two days packing up their belongings and then marched off northward.

Edward III was greatly embittered. He believed that he had been on the verge of a great victory when the ground was taken from under him. He did not blame his allies, as many of his followers and most of the chroniclers did. He was too embarrassed about his own broken promises to do that. He blamed his ministers in England, idle, incompetent, treacherous or disloyal, who had failed to send him money in his hour of need. 'Truly,' he wrote to them in October, 'if we had had but a pittance at the right moment we could have accomplished our great enterprise and achieved renown above all other princes.'[58] This was unrealistic and absurd. Edward owed his allies so much that no amount of money which his ministers might have provided would have made them keen to continue a war from which they wanted only a safe and honourable escape. The garrison of Tournai was certainly in severe straits, but their position was not as hopeless as the exaggerated tales of the captured messenger suggested. Morale in the city was high and some of the problems of food distribution were being overcome. They could probably have held out for some weeks. And what if they had fallen? The city would have passed at least temporarily to Flanders and Edward would have been left to retreat northward or deploy unenthusiastic allies against a powerful French army. He would probably have been defeated. The question, however, was never put to the test, for Philip VI was safe behind the line of the Marcq and had no intention of risking in a battle what he could certainly have without one. It was an inglorious policy and a missed opportunity. But it achieved the essential object: the English coalition broke up and the English King departed.

Edward III arrived in Ghent on 28 September 1340 ostensibly as king of France, in fact as the hostage for his enormous debts. He jousted and feasted with the princes of the coalition and with the Count of Flanders, and exchanged splendid gifts with them while from all over the Low Countries and the German Rhineland his creditors gathered round to press their demands. The Council in England travailed with growing desperation and fear to satisfy them. At Westminster on 2 October 1340 there appeared before them in response to a peremptory summons a host of sheriffs, mayors, bailiffs and collectors to explain why no wool had been raised. They could only offer 'frivolous excuses', such as that all the wool had been secreted out of the county before the loan commissioners had arrived. This grim news was promptly brought to Edward in Flanders. He was unable to pay his daily living expenses in Ghent let alone his debts accumulated in the course of his campaigns. On his arrival there he had been able to borrow £100 to pay for his archers' meals. Thereafter no tradesmen would extend him any credit at all. He could not even buy fodder for his horses and had to send most of them home to eat in England. His evident distress must have made it difficult to bluff his creditors. They were very insistent. The banking syndicates of Mechelen and Louvain were holding three earls as hostages. The Bardi and the Peruzzi bound themselves to pay off these debts not later than 12 November 1340 in return for an assignment of wool. But when no wool came the Italians defaulted. The Great Crown of England was in the mercenary hands of the Archbishop of Trier, who was threatening to break it up. This fate was averted by another syndicate of bankers who took over the pledge. But they too proposed to break it up if they were not paid within a year. Edward's unpaid allies were angry and in some cases rude. The lord of Falkenburg wrote a 'most acidic' letter (Edward's phrase). Impotence and frustration fed this German prince's anger. Others were in a much stronger position. In August 1339 Edward had promised some of them including the Duke of Brabant that neither he nor the great men of his court would leave the Low Countries until such time as their debts had been entirely satisfied. At the end of October 1340 the English King confronted his princely creditors at a painful conference. He offered them in part payment 12,000 sacks of wool in two instalments, the equivalent of about £100,000 in a good market. But they insisted on cash.[59]

From England there came no money but only news of bureaucratic inertia and incipient rebellion. At about this time Edward received an unidentified official from England who brought with him the most lurid account of conditions there. The Council, he said, far from suppressing opposition to the collection of the wool levy, were conniving with the opposition and contributing to the agitation by blaming Edward for the burdens of the nation. According to this source they were wilfully disregarding Edward's instructions and taking the direction of policy into their own hands. It was pure malice. But it had a powerful effect on the English King and the small group of officials and commanders who were about him. Frustration turned to fear and anger. 'I believe', the King wrote to the Pope, 'that the Archbishop wanted me for lack of money to be betrayed and killed.' Some of Edward's courtiers openly contemplated Stratford's execution for treason.

During the first fortnight of November 1340 Edward succeeded by extraordinary efforts in borrowing about £9,000. He got £2,100 from Henry of Lancaster, who pawned his jewels; and 44,000 florins (£6,600) until the following April from a usurer who received personal guarantees from the Earl of Northampton, the Duke of Guelders and the Bardi and Peruzzi banks and took four knights and a partner of each bank as hostages. This was thought sufficient to secure repayment even from a bankrupt king. It enabled Edward to negotiate from the Duke of Brabant permission to return to England, where alone he could raise enough money to pay his debts. Even then leave was given grudgingly and on terms that hostages would have to be sent back in his place.[60] No such arrangement was made with the men of Ghent, in whose power Edward was. But early on the morning of 28 November 1340, Edward wrote them an apologetic letter, and then pretended to go riding in the suburbs of the city. He took with him eight companions, including the Earl of Northampton, Walter Mauny and his private secretary William Kilsby. When they were out of Ghent they bolted for Sluys and embarked on a small boat for one of the Zeeland islands. There a ship was found to take them to England.

The royal party arrived in the Thames on 30 November 1340 and reached the water gate of the Tower of London at midnight. There had been no warning of his coming. The Constable of the Tower was out of town. The fortress was pitch dark. The King had to grope his way through the unguarded gate. His arrival was like a stroke of thunder. The Sub-Constable greeted him on his knees. Rooms were lit at once for his use. The Mayor of London, the principal war financiers and the councillors and higher officials of the government were summoned from their beds. The Chancellor (John Stratford's brother Robert) and the Treasurer came at dawn. They were summarily dismissed. The others were detained as they arrived and shut up in separate rooms to be interrogated apart. In France the sensation caused by these events provided the first firm intelligence that Edward III had indeed left the continent. On 14 December 1340 a messenger arrived in Paris from Amiens with the news gleaned from a traveller that Edward was in London and had imprisoned most of his ministers. This was true. Almost all the principal home ministers and officials (except bishops), the financiers William and Richard Pole and John Pulteney, the Chief Justice and four puisne judges were incarcerated. Two of the judges had been seized while they were presiding at Cambridge assizes. The senior home officer of the chamber had broken jail and become an outlaw. John Stratford had taken sanctuary in his cathedral like a common criminal.[61]

On 2 December 1340 there died in Ghent, probably of dysentery contracted at Tournai, the two men who had been most closely associated with Edward III's schemes in the Low Countries: Sir Geoffrey Scrope and Henry Burghersh, Bishop of Lincoln.[62] Their plans had failed completely. They had failed, moreover, not by military defeat but by weaknesses of conception and entirely foreseeable weaknesses of execution. The disintegration of the coalition after November 1340 followed as a matter of course. From the Imperial alliance Edward III had gained nothing except legal sanction for his acts, a modest number of troops in 1339 and a decorated ceremonial chariot in 1340 which was captured by the French. The Emperor, who had never received all of his subsidy and had found in the alliance another obstacle to his reconciliation with Avignon, began to withdraw from it early in 1341. He patched up his quarrel with the King of France in March. In June 1341 he announced that Edward III's powers as imperial Vicar were revoked. This was followed by the desertion of most of the German princes of the Rhineland.[63] In the Low Countries the English alliance continued to enjoy a faint life, acknowledged but not invoked for any practical purposes of war until the princes fell away between 1343 and 1347. Only Flanders remained. But although Flanders was a valuable thorn in the French flank, no significant English army was to fight there again until the 1380s.

Edward III's three-year preoccupation with the Low Countries had caused him catastrophic territorial losses in every other theatre of war. Of his possessions in France he had lost the county of Ponthieu and much of the remnant of the duchy of Aquitaine which he had held in 1337. The whole of the duchy north of the Gironde had gone, leaving the northward route through Saintonge open to the enemy and Bordeaux a frontier city. The last strategic footholds in the Agenais had fallen. Almost everything south of the Adour was either wasted or in the tenacious hands of the Count of Foix. In the Channel Islands, Guernsey had been lost and although much of the island was reconquered by the English in 1340 the siege of Castle Cornet had to be abandoned on the news of the truce. Edward's most serious losses, however, were in Scotland, where the work of the years 1333–6 was largely undone. At the beginning of the French war the English had controlled the whole of lowland Scotland south of the Forth together with Fife north of it. By the end of 1340 they held the border fortresses of Berwick, Roxburgh, Jedburgh and Lochmaben, and beyond the border only Stirling and Edinburgh. Neither was destined to remain very long in English hands. The guerrillas of William Douglas surprised Edinburgh in April 1341 and captured it. Early in June 1341 David II landed with his court and some French advisers at Inverbervie, bringing an end to a seven-year exile in Normandy.[64]

The possibilities of recovery were limited by the English King's bankruptcy. He had exhausted his credit and the financial capacity of his subjects. Edward's two-year expedition to the Low Countries was by far the most costly military enterprise undertaken by any medieval English King. It had cost £386,546 up to the end of May 1340 (when the surviving accounts end) and probably approaching £500,000 altogether.[65] This was of course only part of the cost of government, as Edward's officials in England had so often reminded him. In three years the King had borrowed some £400,000 and levied taxation on a scale so great as to bring parts of the country to the edge of rebellion. The financial history of the following years was a story of disorderly repayments to those of the creditors who were secured or too powerful to offend. The earls of Derby and Warwick remained in captivity at Mechelen until May 1341. The Great Crown of England was not redeemed until 1345. Some of Edward's continental creditors, such as the Bartolomei bank in Lucca, were still being repaid in the 1360s. William Pole was never entirely repaid. As for the Bardi and the Peruzzi, who lent more to Edward III than anyone had, their debts after some initial hesitation were repudiated. The Peruzzi bank failed in 1343, the Bardi in 1346, the result, Giovanni Villani thought, of their 'great greed and folly'. It was the end of the first great age of Florentine banking, and of an intimate association between the English Crown and Italian financiers which had lasted for seventy years.[66]

Edward added self-inflicted wounds to his difficulties. He allowed his frustration and rage at the débâcle of Tournai to get the better of his political judgement, and provoked a brief but dangerous constitutional crisis which all but paralysed his government during the first four months of 1341. He was not content to purge the central administration of scapegoats. He took all the reins of government into his own hands and those of a small clique of advisers who had been with him on the continent in 1340 and had shared the worst of his humiliations there. Instructions were given to collect all the unpaid arrears of the ninth of 1340, and to impose it illegally on the clergy, who had granted their own distinct subsidy and in many cases paid it. A vindictive and indiscriminate campaign of retribution was begun against provincial officials, down to the humblest local bailiffs, customs officers, arrayers and foresters, and even their clerks and servants. Commissioners of 'trailbaston' toured the counties inflicting summary trials and large fines not only on errant officials for their laxness, but on the population at large for ancient breaches of the peace and trivial peccadilloes. A sober chronicler reported that no one brought before the tribunals escaped unpunished, however impeccable his conduct; all had to pay stiff fines to stay out of prison. There was 'grand duresse' throughout England, said another. In London there were riots on Tower Hill. Archbishop Stratford, whom Edward and his friends had singled out as the object of their special vengeance, took advantage of the intensifying discontent to launch a sustained assault on the government from the sanctuary of Canterbury cathedral. As God had punished Henry II for his persecution of Becket by depriving him of most of his continental dominions, Stratford said, so would Edward III suffer the loss of the rest of them unless he mended his ways. The Archbishop poured forth sermons and pamphlets whose barbs against arbitrary power, excessive taxation and royal favourites were carefully calculated to arouse all the emotions which had set the English political community against the Crown during the crises of the last three reigns. Although Edward retained the loyalty of most of the aristocracy, Stratford's radicalism provoked a strong enough response to show how close those emotions still were to the surface of English political life fifteen years after the deposition of Edward II. Earl Warenne dismissed Stratford's enemies on the royal Council, men like William Kilsby and the King's Chamberlain Sir John Darcy, as stooges: 'those who should be foremost among them are shut out,' he told

Edward III to his face, 'while such men as these fill the seats which belong by right to the lords of the land who alone can sustain you in your great enterprise.'[67]

The situation of the French Crown was not much better, although its weaknesses were less obvious and its quarrels less public. Philip VI was not bankrupt. He had repelled the invasion in the north. He had gained territory in the south-west. By rights his government should have looked confidently forward. It did not.

The major loss was Flanders, which had in effect seceded from the French kingdom. The concessions which he made to the Flemings at Esplechin left the city governments in effective control of the province and promised the lifting of the papal interdict. The future political allegiance of Flanders was not mentioned. Philip probably thought that he would be able to restore his influence in the aftermath of Edward III's defeat. This tactful compromise, however, was frustrated by the obstinacy of Benedict XII. The Pope was irritated by the overtly political use which was being made of ecclesiastical censures, and when the delegates of the Flemings presented themselves at Avignon to discuss their reconciliation they were told that they would have to swear to remain faithful subjects of the Count and the King. Since they would not, the censures remained in force. Philip VI protested loudly. At a stroke Benedict had removed his one bargaining counter, alienated the Flemings from the Crown and made him appear to dishonour his promises. In the Flemish towns Philip's enemies, shaken by the failure of the Tournai campaign, recovered their balance and their grip on the territory. The Count, Louis of Nevers, remained in exile until his death at Crécy in 1346 and Flanders remained in the political orbit of England until the 1360s. This meant the loss of France's richest province and a considerable added burden on French defences. Large garrisons now had to be kept in readiness on the north-western border even when the English threat lay elsewhere.[68]

Internally France was as much strained by the first four years of the war as England was. Defensive warfare is costly. Only the aggressor can choose his time and place. The French government had laid out much more in resisting Edward III than Edward had in attacking them. They had maintained armies and fleets several times as large as Edward's for longer periods. The burden of taxation was heavier in 1339 and 1340 than in any other year of Philip VI's reign. In 1340 the northern provinces of France were simultaneously paying large lump sums for commuting the *arrière-ban*, a sales tax of four pennies in the pound, a levy of 2 per cent on the assets of the nobility and an income tax of a tenth on the domains of the Church. In addition to these overt taxes there were the covert ones: the forced loans, the arbitrary requisitioning of supplies and the manipulation of the coinage. The silver coinage was devalued in February 1337 and December 1338 and three times in 1340, representing a total reduction of 60 per cent of its nominal value. The *monnayage* (the proportion of the silver value which was taken by the King as a coinage fee) rose to 25 per cent in the spring of 1340.[69]

Requisitions, it is true, were not carried out in France with the same regularity nor on the same scale as they were in England, and payment was usually made more promptly and generously. They did not therefore arouse the same generalized and ferocious resistance. But when the army was in the field the effect could be devastating in the districts through which it passed. Enormous numbers of carts were required, traditionally one for every fifty soldiers; wheels, tools and beasts of burden, the means of earning their owners' living, could be peremptorily removed in exchange for an IOU; barns and stores were stripped of fodder and victuals. The Cluniac Prior of Elincourt and his party were dragged from their horses while travelling on the road to Paris in order to supply the retinue of the Count of Alençon. He embarked on a campaign of litigation. Not everyone was as well placed to complain.[70]

The burden of the French King's demands fell unevenly on different provinces and with crushing intensity on some. The war, a source of terror in the north and parts of the south-west, was still a matter of relative indifference in the east and centre. Its onset exaggerated the fissiparous tendencies of France and the inward-looking habits of provinces remote from the clash of arms. The invasion was not the unifying experience for the French which the coastal raids had been for the English, none of whom lived very far from the sea. The provinces worst affected were Normandy, which supported the 'Great Army of the Sea' with men and money; the large and populous royal bailiwicks of Amiens, Vermandois and Senlis and the duchy of Artois, comprising the belt of northern France which lay across the invasion routes and paid proportionately the largest share of taxation. The same provinces bore the brunt of war damage and requisitioning, and of the huge expenditure on war works, principally fortification.

It was these provinces which contained the 'silken thread' of fortified towns which the cardinals had told Edward III in 1339 could not be broken. They were much less strong than the cardinals implied. The region had not been threatened by an invader since the Flemish crisis of the

1290s, which was the last occasion on which systematic attention had been given to its defences. Events followed much the same course at the start of the war as they did in England, although the scale was magnified. A general survey of French fortresses was undertaken in 1335 and proceeded rather slowly. The results were not encouraging, but very little was done about them until the crisis broke. Philip VI was appalled when passing through Noyon during the campaign of 1339 to observe the lamentable condition of the walls and ditches. Saint-Quentin and Reims were both open to the country at one side, the result of the premature abandonment of work undertaken in the thirteenth century. The arrival of Edward III at Antwerp in 1338 had had the same catalytic effect as the sack of Southampton had in England. There was a panic-stricken programme of works, not well co-ordinated, not well executed and still incomplete in almost every case when the truce of Esplechin brought another excuse for relaxation. In the province of Artois alone major works were undertaken in at least seven towns and castles between 1337 and 1340. Some of them were very extensive. The burden of these works fell heavily and suddenly on those who had to pay for them, generally the lord of the town (if there was one), the bishop, the citizens and the outlying villages in proportions which were uncertainly prescribed by tradition and productive of bitter dispute and litigation. The works at Reims between 1337 and 1340, unsatisfactory as they were, cost 10,000 *l.t.* Arras in the same period carried out heavy repairs at seven gates, recut the town ditch and built fortified outworks on one side at a total cost of 1,900 *l.t.* Expenditure on this scale represented an enormous public investment. What it meant at Arras can be seen from the fact that a tax of 25 per cent on income from property raised little more than half of what was required to pay the bills. The rest had to be raised by a variety of financial expedients such as the sale of annuities, which burdened the inhabitants for a generation. Some towns were financially crippled. The walls of Saint-Quentin, which were largely financed by annuities, brought such 'grands oppressions de dettes' upon its citizens that the central government's taxes could not be collected from them for four years in the mid-1340s.[71]

On top of this came the direct damage done by troops. The horrifying wastage of the Thiérache by Edward III in the autumn of 1339 and by John of Hainault in the following spring had a profound impact. The scale and system of these destructive expeditions was relatively new to western European warfare. In the summer of 1340 the province of Artois lost two border towns, Aire and Arques, both razed to the ground by Flemish armies. Three substantial towns of the Tournaisis were wiped out during the seven-week siege of Tournai, one of them (Saint-Amand) for a recognizable political object, the others for loot and entertainment. These places were at the epicentre of the earthquake. Lesser tremors spread outward over long distances: from the carnage of Sluys to Dieppe and other Norman towns which lost many of their adult menfolk: from Aubenton, which was destroyed by the Hainaulters in April 1340, to Reims and other northern cities where the news of the event brought panic, disorder and flight; from La Capelle, burned by the English in 1339, to the accounts office of the Abbey of Saint-Denis which owned it. Not all of the destruction was the work of the enemy. Towns like Saint-Omer, Aire and Lille had to destroy their own suburbs on the approach of the enemy. They were often the newest and richest districts. When the King of England landed at Antwerp in 1338 orders went out to all French officials to break every river bridge and causeway in the frontier provinces by which the invaders might pass.[72]

In the mood provoked by these events Philip VI's policy of avoiding battle, however sound strategically, was a grave political error. It seriously diminished his prestige, which was the main political asset of any French king and the one unifying factor among the diverse provinces of France. Moreover, it made royal taxation and the purposes for which it was raised seem irrelevant, a wasteful diversion of resources from the defence of every man's own community. When the royal army, the only national instrument of defence, appeared to be doing nothing, why should men not think in local terms? To the knights and noblemen who marched with the army the King's inactivity was a betrayal of instincts which made the pitched battle the highest form of warfare and its avoidance tantamount to defeat. Each of these men took back to his home his own kind of camp-fire dissidence and gossip. We cannot know how many men agreed with the squire from the Orléanais who had joined the army in every year from 1337 and told his friends that Philip had been too frightened to attack Edward III at Tournai. Edward may have suffered a strategic reverse but to this man he was 'the most valiant of Christian kings'. Edward's boldness won him other admirers whose help was more effective. The French castellan of Estambourc not only surrendered the place to the English on their march to Tournai but joined Edward III's army. These were minor figures, although their outspokenness is revealing. There is no doubt that some greater but more discreet men took the same view. John, Count of Armagnac, one of the plenipotentiaries who concluded the truce of Esplechin on Philip's behalf, had secretly offered his homage to Edward III only four months earlier. The Countess of Hainault told Philip VI in his tents at Bouvines that there were many princes of his court who would cheerfully betray him to the King of England. Many? No doubt the statement was hyperbole. But Philip, whose fear of treachery was obsessive, took it seriously enough to lose his temper.

> Ne croi pas tout ce qu'on te dit
> Partout a fraude et tricherie

a versifier had once written to the French King. He did not feel like a victor.[73]

CHAPTER XI

Brittany
1341–1343

John III, Duke of Brittany, a gentle vacillating man who had peacefully governed his duchy for almost thirty years, fell ill at Caen on his way back from the siege of Tournai and died there on 30 April 1341. The 'Good Duke John' had been a better friend of Philip VI than most of his predecessors. He had fought with his vassals, at his own expense, in the French armies which invaded Flanders in 1314 and 1328, and in spite of his close connections with England he had fought in those which faced the Anglo-German coalition of 1339 and 1340. He had conserved the independence of his principality, without the abrasiveness which characterized the affairs of Flanders and Aquitaine. But he was guilty of the ultimate offence against his own dynasty: he died childless and with no obvious heir. 'And so we come to the epic of Brittany,' Froissart wrote, 'to the great adventures and fine feats of arms which happened there and will light up the pages of my book.'[1]

The origins of this savage civil war which lasted for nearly a quarter of a century and ruined Brittany for a generation longer lay in the obscurity of Breton successorial law and the rancours of a family quarrel. John III was survived by a niece, Jeanne de Penthièvre, and by a half-brother, John de Montfort, the issue of the previous Duke's second marriage. Which of them had the better right was a nice question. Jeanne's partisans asserted that since her father Guy was a full brother of the dead Duke he would have had an indisputable right to succeed him had he still been living. They also asserted, although perhaps with less conviction, that by the customary law of Brittany Jeanne, as her father's sole heiress, had the same right as he would have done. Unfortunately, the customary law of Brittany had never previously had to answer such a question and its effect was a great deal less clear than the submissions of Jeanne's lawyers. Brittany, moreover, was one of the peerages of France and the better view was that its devolution was not governed by Breton customary law at all but by the same law which governed the succession to the crown of France. By the law of the crown women were excluded. John de Montfort's case was very simple: he was the closest blood relation of the last Duke and the only male candidate. He was probably right.[2]

Although a great deal of legal analysis was applied to the dispute the outcome was determined by political manoeuvre. The late Duke had had no affection for his father's other family. He believed that the financial provision made for them had been altogether too generous, and he had once passed many years in an undignified and unsuccessful attempt to have his father's second marriage retrospectively annulled and its issue bastardized. For most of his reign he was determined that John de Montfort should not succeed him. He even proposed, in 1334, to disinherit both candidates and sell the succession to Philip VI. This remarkable plan, which would have extinguished permanently the independence of the duchy, had almost been agreed when it foundered on the opposition of the Breton nobility, adroitly stirred up by John de Montfort himself. The result of its failure was that Jeanne de Penthièvre became the only available means of preventing a Montfortist succession. The Duke knew that a woman was vulnerable in the harsh political climate of Brittany and so, in 1337, he married her to Charles of Blois, a younger son of the house of Châtillon, a notable military family which had great possessions in northeastern France, and was closely connected with the house of Valois. His mother, Marguerite de Valois, was the King's sister. Charles was an unusual man, then eighteen years old. He was austere, intensely pious, but at the same time a fine horseman and a brave and intelligent soldier who was always able to command strong personal loyalty from those around him. A better guarantee of Jeanne's succession could hardly have been found. There is little doubt that that was John III's object. Although the marriage contract said nothing about the succession to the duchy, it seems that shortly after the nuptials Charles of Blois was received as the heir of Brittany at a solemn session of John's court. He was made to swear that on the Duke's death he would bear the arms of Brittany and honour its customs.[3]

Early in 1340 Duke John seems for some obscure reason to have been reconciled to his half-brother and to have undergone a change of heart about the succession. He made a new will after prolonged deliberation with his closest advisers in which, to the great surprise of everyone who knew about it, he declared John de Montfort to be his heir after all. On his deathbed his last words on the subject were true to his havering spirit: 'For God's sake leave me alone and do not trouble my spirit with such things.'[4]

It hardly mattered. Charles of Blois' position was too strongly entrenched by John's past acts. John de Montfort claimed the support of the

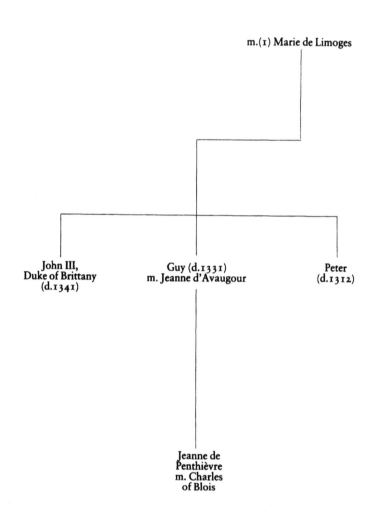

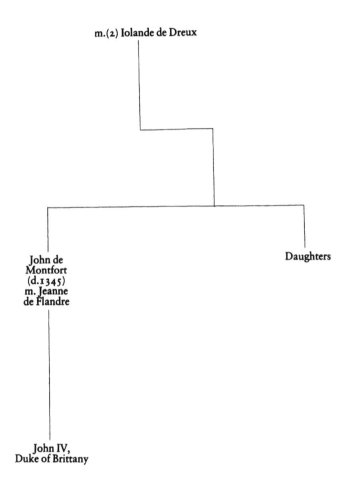

Arthur II, Duke of Brittany
(d.1312)

m.(2) Iolande de Dreux

John de
Montfort
(d.1345)
m. Jeanne
de Flandre

Daughters

John IV,
Duke of Brittany

common people and the towns, but there was no doubt that those who counted in Brittany took it for granted that Charles of Blois would succeed. Shortly after the death of John III an assembly of Breton notables met. The bishops accepted Charles's claim by a majority of seven to two; the nobility were overwhelmingly in his favour. This was not in the least surprising. It simply illustrated how a French principality could be practically autonomous but nevertheless part of the larger community. The clergy of Brittany belonged to the archdiocese of Tours; they were wedded like the rest of the French Church to law and to a notion which made the French Crown the ultimate source of political legitimacy; the more educated of them had studied at Angers (there was no university in Brittany); and the more ambitious looked to the French civil service for their prospect of advancement. As for the higher nobility, their marriages, their more distant possessions, their language, their chivalry and their ambitions all marked them out as members of the French aristocracy. However loyal these men may have been to the duchy and its rulers, it was natural for them to look to the French political community to fill a void. Charles of Blois was the official candidate.[5]

By comparison with his rival John de Montfort was an outsider in Brittany. He possessed the lordship of Guérande at the mouth of the Loire, which included some of the richest salt beds in Europe.[6] But otherwise his lands were concentrated in the Ile de France, in the Loire valley and in Artois. Since he had been elbowed away from power throughout the reign of his half-brother there had been little opportunity to build alliances in the duchy. We cannot know how well he would have used his opportunities if he had had better ones. His actions suggest an enterprising and quick-witted man. But he was a political incompetent who misjudged both the fickleness of his friends and the ruthlessness of his enemies. The dominant personality in his camp was not his own but his wife's. She had 'the spirit of a man and the heart of a lion', according to Froissart. Jeanne de Flandre, Countess of Montfort, was a tough, rich and ambitious woman, a sister of the Count of Flanders and the owner of great properties in the counties of Artois and Nevers. She was a complete stranger to Brittany, but in her brief career as a war leader she inspired the same extravagant loyalty from her followers as Charles of Blois could do on his side. There is no reason to doubt the assertion of a well-informed chronicler that she was the principal author of her husband's plans in the summer of 1341.[7]

The old Duke was buried in the Carmelite monastery of Ploermel early in May 1341.[8] As the Breton nobility dispersed to their homes John de

Montfort arrived outside Nantes with 200 men and bloodlessly took possession of it. Nantes was the principal city of Brittany, an important administrative and economic centre living well on the trade in salt and wine and on the tolls of the Loire. Its citizens did not know what to do. John de Montfort was the only claimant to the duchy who appeared to be asserting his rights; Charles of Blois had not yet stirred. So they did homage to him but with reservations. They would fight for him, they said, unless Charles of Blois should be pronounced Duke of Brittany by the King. They too saw the Crown of France as the source of all legitimate power. The couple installed themselves in the ducal castle of Nantes, which was the main seat of the Breton government, and summoned the whole baronage of Brittany and representatives of the town to come before them to do homage. Three days of festivities were arranged. While they waited for the response of the Bretons, John and his wife laid hands on as much as they could find of the treasury of John III. Part of it was seized from the cathedral sacristy of Nantes, where it had been placed for safekeeping. Most of the rest was kept at Limoges, an outlying possession of the dukes of Brittany some 200 miles into the heart of France. At some time in the middle of May John launched a bold raid on Limoges with a handful of armed men. The citizens of Limoges were as confused and compliant as those of Nantes. They took their new seigneur at his face value, accepted his largesse and delivered up the treasury.

The first signs of resistance did not appear until after John had returned, loaded with cash, from Limoges to Nantes. This was probably towards the end of May 1341. When the appointed day came for the baronage and towns of the duchy to do homage almost everyone of any consequence stayed away. The only important Breton feudatory who was willing to throw in his lot with John de Montfort was Hervé de Léon, the head of the principal noble house of Finistère, a self-serving schemer who had concluded that John was the man of the future. This view was wrong and Hervé did not hold it for very long, but his alliance, however brief, was valuable. Hervé had the local connections which John de Montfort lacked and he was a shrewd political adviser. As the men of Nantes and the gentry of south-eastern Brittany ate the banquet laid out for the great, John suppressed his disappointment and devised a bold show of force. The object was to take possession of as much territory as possible before any serious opposition materialized.

Brittany is a broad peninsula extending about 160 miles into the Atlantic from the march of France to the western extremity of Finistère. In spite of the unifying hand of the ducal government it was a fragmented society, revealing marked local contrasts. Eastern Brittany, roughly corresponding to the modern *départements* of Ille-et-Vilaine and Loire-Atlantique was a fertile and densely populated plain given over mainly to vineyards and to cattle farming and possessing in Nantes and Rennes the only truly important commercial towns of Brittany. This was Gallo-Brittany, speaking French and belonging to France as recognizably as the neighbouring provinces of Maine, Anjou and Poitou, which it physically resembled. West of this region lay the massif of lower Brittany, 'Bretagne Bretonnante', demonstrably different and overwhelmingly Breton-speaking. The main geographical feature of lower Brittany is a chain of granite and sandstone hills running east–west from the Menez to the Arrée mountains, not particularly high but covered by a thick impenetrable mantle of forest. The insatiable naval dockyards of the seventeenth and eighteenth centuries had not yet stripped it bare and created the bleak void that exists today. Western Brittany in the fourteenth century consisted of an inhospitable central region of high, cold and almost uncultivable ground surrounded by a narrow fringe of coastal land, marginally cultivable, where most of the population eked out a living by keeping pigs and goats, by growing vegetables (even then), by fishing and salt production, and by piracy.

There were obvious reasons why eastern Brittany should fall naturally to any candidate supported by France. It was a francophone region, wide open to invasion from Normandy or the Loire provinces. But the converse was not true of 'Breton' Brittany, whose allegiances were determined by complicated patterns of geography and feudal dependence. In the extreme west and the coastal plain of the south Vannes was the only large town, and the house of Léon the only significant aristocratic power. Lorient did not yet exist. Brest was a small village. It was a region of little harbours and minor seigneuries without cohesion or obvious natural loyalties. The rest of western Brittany was dominated by powerful local dynasties firmly opposed to John de Montfort's ambitions. On the south face of the central massif there were the viscounts of Rohan. The main centres of their power were the fortified towns of Rohan, Pontivy and La Chèze. They were by far the most powerful noble house of all Brittany as well as the most consistently francophile. On the north face of the massif as far as the sea lay the great lordships of Tréguier and Penthièvre, which covered most of the territory comprised within the modern *départment* of the Côtes-du-Nord. This was the personal domain of Charles of Blois' wife, the appanage which had made her father the most considerable man in Brittany after the Duke. These were not regions which John de Montfort could hope to capture except by deploying the kind of overwhelming strength which he did not have.

What he could hope to do was to take possession of the eastern plain and the approaches from France, the three principal cities of Nantes, Rennes and Vannes and the bulk of the ducal domain in the south and west from which the day-to-day government of the duchy was financed. At about the beginning of June 1341, John de Montfort marched out of Nantes with the banner of Brittany borne before him. His first objective was Champtoceaux, which was a large castle belonging to the dukes situated on a spur of land on the left bank of the Loire guarding the approach to Nantes by the river valley. Once he had garrisoned this place and secured the main approach to his capital, John marched on Rennes, the second city of Brittany.

The inhabitants of Rennes fell to violent discord on his approach. The town was protected by a strong garrison and a large circuit of walls, but the mass of the population was minded to open the gates. The more prominent citizens urged resistance. The garrison commander havered until he was captured during a sortie. The town put up a half-hearted resistance and then surrendered. The effect on John's cause was magical. Saint-Aubin du Cormier, the great circular keep built by the dukes at the end of the thirteenth century to guard the road from Paris to Rennes, fell apparently without a blow. Dinan opened its gates. John now held every major stronghold of eastern Brittany except for Vitré and Fougères, strong modern fortresses held by hostile noblemen which were wisely left alone. In early July he was back in Nantes.

The south and west coasts appear to have been taken in the course of July and August. With the exception of Vannes and Hennebont, both of which had powerful defences, the towns and harbours were protected only by ditches and palisades or at best by antique seigneurial towers dating from the twelfth century. These places were guarded by men without orders, confused by events and uncertain of their loyalty. None of them resisted except for La Roche-Périou (which was passed by) and Brest (which was stormed). By the middle of August John de Montfort was in possession of the greater part of his duchy and in spite of his lack of support in the Breton establishment was beginning to look like the stronger claimant.

Philip VI reacted passively to these events. The development of his thoughts is not easy to follow. He had certainly assumed like everyone else that Brittany would fall to Charles of Blois, but it was not a foregone conclusion that he would support his nephew once John de Montfort had taken possession. John had hitherto been a loyal subject of the Crown. He had a strong claim in point of law. The prospect of dislodging him by force cannot have been attractive. For more than three months after the death of John III Philip did nothing. Charles's first appeals for help were received, according to report, with cold embarrassment.[9] At some stage which cannot be determined but was probably early in the summer of 1341, the contested succession was referred to the Parlement of Paris, whose deliberate procedures could be expected to last a long time. Philip's motives are a matter for conjecture but the delicate state of relations with England must have been the main one. At the time when John de Montfort was occupying most of Brittany, the truces were already breaking down on the march of Gascony and there was every prospect of a fresh English invasion of the Low Countries.

Two events occurred in the south-west which advertised the fragility of the peace there and the insecurity of the government's position. The first arose from an apparently petty row between Philip VI and James II, King of Majorca. This impetuous Aragonese prince ruled a number of territories on the Mediterranean coast of France. In some he was an autonomous monarch but in others, including the great Mediterranean lordship of Montpellier, he was a vassal of the French Crown. He was therefore in much the same position in Montpellier as Edward III was in Gascony, and he had it in mind that the English King might help him shake off the sovereignty of France. How much encouragement he received is unclear. He certainly received some. His agents visited Edward III in Ghent in the autumn of 1340 and arrangements were made for English officials in Bordeaux to engage in some discreet negotiations early in the following year. In March 1341 James conducted a tournament before a great crowd of onlookers in defiance of a royal ordinance and the express commands of the royal lieutenants of Languedoc. One of James's squires dressed his horse in the arms of England and shouted 'Guyenne!', the war-cry of the English duchy, as he rode into the lists. Very soon afterwards James repudiated the sovereignty of France. At this point Philip's lieutenants in the south were the Bishop of Beauvais, Jean de Marigny, and Louis of Poitiers, Count of Valentinois. They began drawing troops to Toulouse during April 1341, and in June they occupied Montpellier by force.[10]

While their backs were turned the English recaptured Bourg, thus making good the most serious of their losses in the years between 1337 and 1340. This coup appears to have been a private enterprise of three members of the La Motte family, a large divided clan whose members were to be found on both sides of the war. In the first week of June 1341 the La Mottes recruited a band of about sixty men, less than half the size of the garrison. They arrived under the river wall in barges a little before sunrise. Two accomplices let them into the town through a window of the abbey buildings of St Vincent, which were built into the defences in the weakest part of the town. Once inside they raised the townsmen and rushed the citadel. The garrison, which was completely surprised, was found distributed between the town walls and the citadel. The men in the town were overcome. Those in the citadel had time to close the gates and arm themselves. They fought off their assailants and held out for another three weeks before they too were obliged to surrender. The garrison commander was accused by the King of treason, but he could hardly have done more. It was a serious breach of the truce, which must have happened with the connivance of the ducal government. Oliver Ingham certainly condoned it. The castellany of the town was eventually conferred on Amanieu de la Motte, and the leading actors received handsome rewards.[11]

What the incident illustrated was the virtual impossibility of enforcing the truce when public war was only lightly superimposed on so many private wars. Local noblemen, particularly on the English side, had lost too much to resist the temptation of a swift *coup de main*: a handful of men gathered at dawn, a cart jammed under the portcullis, an unwarned, undermanned garrison half asleep quickly overcome, and the possessions of one's ancestors recovered from the ancient rival or useful parvenu to whom the Bishop of Beauvais had recently granted them. And not only the possessions of one's ancestors. The English practice of making grants from territory yet to be conquered was an invitation to violate the truce which was very often accepted. The fall of Bourg was the signal for an explosion of unofficial warfare across the marches of Gascony. Bands of dispossessed Anglo-Gascons poured across the Gironde to loot and burn in Saintonge. There was serious fighting in the Agenais, in the Dordogne valley around Bergerac and further north, right up to the walls of Périgueux. By the end of June 1341 the guerrillas had been joined by government forces on both sides. Ingham hastily retained men and took the field on the 29th. The French royal lieutenants proclaimed the *arrière-ban* in all the southern provinces. 'The truce counts for nothing down here,' one of them wrote to Philip VI.[12]

In England Edward III's government was slowly emerging from the paralysis of a savage administrative purge and a constitutional crisis. Parliament began to assemble on 23 April 1341 and sat until the last week of May. The King adeptly retreated before the storm of protest against his conduct during the past four months. He abandoned the judicial commissions. He renounced the attempt to collect the ninth of 1340 from the clergy. He submitted to statutes providing for the enforcement of Magna Carta against his ministers and the appointment of officers of state and of members of his household who should be answerable to Parliament. He agreed to an audit of his government's use of tax receipts going back to the beginning of the war. In return he obtained a fresh Parliamentary grant in kind, 30,000 sacks of wool, which relieved some of the more severe pressures on his budget. Edward read the signs more skilfully than his father or grandfather would have done at such moments. He broadened the circle of his advisers and mended his quarrel with Stratford, allowing the charges against him to be quietly forgotten and restoring him to most of his old influence. Stratford for his part forgot the radicalism of his pamphlets and became as royalist as he had ever been. Within a few months of the dispersal of Parliament, the King had sufficiently recovered his authority to annul its more unwelcome statutes by royal warrant. They were 'contrary to law and reason' and had been imposed upon him by duress. Never again, until the years of his senility and decline, did he misjudge the political mood of England so completely as he had in 1340. Edward's retreat from the abrasive manner of the previous year enabled him to contemplate however distantly the resumption of the war when eventually the truce of Esplechin expired.[13]

It was due to expire on 24 June 1341. The terms envisaged that there would be negotiations for a permanent peace, but Edward III showed no interest in serious negotiations with the French government. His defeat and bankruptcy in 1340 had served only to sharpen his determination. 'My power has not been laid so low and the hand of God is not yet so weak', he had written to Simon Boccanegra in April, 'that I cannot by His grace prevail over my enemy.' In the same month he had told Parliament that the war could now be expected to last for many years and had obtained the consent of the Lords for another seaborne expedition to the continent. Preparations for this expedition, which had been in hand since February, were expected to be complete by the end of May. They were conceived on an ambitious scale. An army of about 13,500 was planned. Nearly two-thirds of them were to be archers.[14] It was only when the King's preparations suffered the inevitable obstruction and delay that the English showed any interest in resuming diplomatic contact with the French, and then only for the purpose of securing short extensions of the truce for what were manifestly strategic rather than diplomatic reasons. On 9 June 1341, a fortnight before the truce was due to expire, three princes of the French royal Council met the leaders of the Anglo-German coalition in Flanders and agreed to extend it until 29 August, ostensibly in order to enable serious negotiations to begin. A peace conference was called into being at Antoing, a castle overlooking the Scheldt on the borders of Flanders and Hainault. But the small time allowed for it hardly augured well for the outcome. It was due to convene on 1 August 1341. In England, Edward ordered the ships of the invasion fleet to be ready at the embarkation ports by 15 August and the troops a week later.[15]

In retrospect it is possible to see that the King of England's plans were doomed to failure by the reluctance of his allies and the weakness of his financial position. But Philip VI and his advisers took them as seriously as their author did, and they had their hands full with warlike preparations. From April to November 1341 a strong fleet, including twenty-one galleys, mostly French but with some Spanish and Portuguese auxiliaries, cruised between La Rochelle and the Biscay ports of Castile in case the English should attempt to land their army in Gascony. All merchant ships between Calais and the Gironde were surveyed for war service. Relations with the Genoese were patched up well enough to enable rowers and crossbowmen to be hired for the surviving vessels of Doria and Grimaldi. There were plans for reinforcing the garrisons of the northern frontier, which were at low strength. A general summons was issued in May for the assembly of the army at Arras a week before the expiry of the truce.

In the south-west men were already being deployed in increasing numbers in response to English violations of the truce. At the end of June 1341 the French royal lieutenants in Languedoc had 4,500 men under arms; a month later there were just under 6,000; 7,000 at the end of August; 12,500 at the end of September.[16] Most of these men were employed in the most cautious possible way, on garrison duties. But there were significant field operations towards the end of the summer. During August 1341 the Count of Valentinois moved west along the north bank of the Dordogne into Saintonge. On the 25th he even succeeded in re-occupying Bourg, although probably only the town not the citadel. His success at any rate was short-lived. The Anglo-Gascon forces, commanded by Hugh of Geneva, crossed the Dordogne at Libourne. On 26 August 1341 he surprised the French under the walls of the old Benedictine abbey of Guitres and pursued them for several miles to the north. The two armies were probably both very small. Hugh had no more than 1,200 men, the enemy rather fewer. The encounter was indecisive but the French withdrew up the Dordogne valley and their men in Bourg, whose position had now become untenable, decamped a week later. Although the French

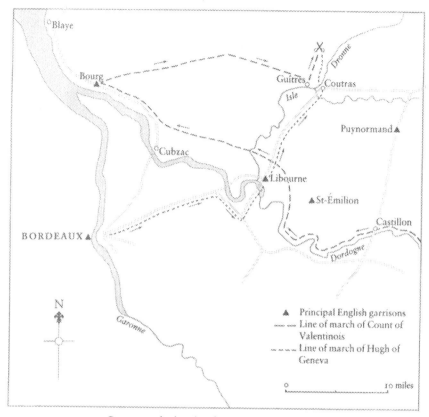

17 Gascony: the battle of Guîtres, 26 August 1341

greatly increased their field army in the course of September they dissipated
it in a succession of minor sieges in southern Périgord, police work on a large
scale directed against anglophiles and bandits who had entrenched themselves in isolated towns and castles. In the border regions men regarded
these events as a significant setback for French arms. A number of towns
threw out their French garrisons and received English ones.[17]

The effort that lay behind all this activity not only mesmerized the
French King and his advisers but consumed the whole of their financial
resources. French tax-payers were notoriously reluctant to pay up in time
of truce, when the apparent danger had passed, and they were not
impressed by the cost of repaying past borrowings or preparing to fight
future battles. In most of France the government's receipts from taxation
dried up in 1341. Philip pressed the ingenuity of his officials for raising
money. The profit margin exacted from the issue of coins rose to

unprecedented levels. The *gabelle du sel* or salt tax made its first, short-lived, appearance in parts of the realm, provoking furious opposition wherever attempts were made to enforce it. Officers of the Chambre des Comptes were sent on tours of the provinces, cajoling wealthy noblemen and ecclesiastics into submitting to a tax on the revenues of their domains. The results of so much effort were very poor. Treasury receipts fell by almost half.[18]

In the face of this concatenation of problems the last thing that Philip VI desired was a civil war in Brittany and if events had taken a different turn John de Montfort might have been left in undisturbed possession. Early in August 1341, however, there were persistent rumours that John was about to make common cause with the English. Philip believed that John was preparing to do homage to Edward III and he may even have heard wilder reports that it had already happened. The prospect of a descent on Brittany by the fleets now gathering at Winchelsea and Orwell was horrifying. The precise moment when this possibility dawned on Philip VI cannot be determined, but it was probably in the middle of August 1341, when the first military measures were taken to prevent it. On the 13th, orders were given to proclaim the *arrière-ban* throughout France. The sixteen remaining galleys of Doria and Grimaldi were taken out of lay-up and sent to lie off the Breton coast. At about the same time plans were laid to invade Brittany from the east and dislodge John de Montfort by force. The French government's attitude to the Breton succession was transformed.[19]

At Antoing the peace conference proceeded with a painful slowness which appeared to confirm the worst suspicions of the French. The English delegation, led by the Earl of Huntingdon, did not arrive until 6 August 1341, almost a week after it had opened. On the 10th they agreed to extend the truce by just two weeks from 29 August to 14 September 1341. Discussions about a further extension continued, but on 19 August the Earl of Huntingdon abruptly left to seek further instructions in England and in his absence the conference was suspended. The news that the truce had been extended until mid-September reached England on about 18 August 1341 and resulted in orders that the army should be ready to embark on the day after its expiry. There were now between 200 and 250 vessels in the south- and west coast ports of England waiting for orders to proceed to the assembly point at Winchelsea; a rather smaller number were gathered at Orwell; thirty huge ships, including ten galleys, were due to arrive in England from Bayonne. In Paris Philip VI had already set in train the procedure for dispossessing John de Montfort. The proceedings in the Parlement were accelerated. In Nantes John was served with a citation by a royal officer. On 20 August 1341 he left hurriedly for Paris.[20]

In the Parlement the decision fell to be made not by the ordinary tribunal but by the peers of France assisted by the opinions of professional lawyers and by the report of a commission which was instructed to examine the evidence. The proceedings advanced at speed once the urgency of the King's political needs became clear. Long written memoranda were submitted by both sides. On 27 August the commission, consisting of two bishops, began to hear witnesses. John de Montfort arrived in Paris to find the city tense with preparations for war. John was received by Philip VI at a chilly audience in the royal palace which left no one in any doubt about the King's sympathies. Philip directly confronted him with the rumours of his treasonable dealings with the English, which he denied. At the end of the interview he was peremptorily ordered not to leave Paris until after the Parlement had pronounced judgement. The implication was plain. When the duchy had been awarded to his rival, John would be held as a hostage for its peaceful delivery. At the beginning of September 1341, John secretly left Paris and fled to Nantes. All his garrisons in Brittany were put on a war footing.

When his flight was discovered the proceedings were initially suspended in confusion, then rapidly brought to an end and adjourned for judgement. On 7 September 1341 the Parlement gathered at Conflans, a royal castle outside Paris, and pronounced judgement in favour of Charles of Blois. There were no proceedings against John for treason, and it may be that the King had decided to suspend disbelief on this point. He did, however, order the immediate sequestration of John's county of Montfort l'Amuary in the Ile de France until the facts should become clearer. The courtiers dispersed to gather their retinues. The army had been summoned to assemble at Angers on 26 September 1341.[21]

The disputed succession of Brittany was naturally of great interest to the English government. It seems surprising that Philip VI's advisers should have taken so long to realize it. A hostile power controlling Brittany could sever communications between England and Gascony, ruin the wine trade of the Gironde and make the Channel Islands untenable. A friendly power in Brittany would not only secure England's maritime communications but give her a bridgehead into northern and central France. Even before the death of John III, in 1336, Edward III had tried to obtain the hand of Jeanne de Penthièvre (whom he called the 'heiress' of Brittany) for his younger brother. After the war with France had begun Brittany continued to be treated with the utmost circumspection by the English. Bretons were not treated as Frenchmen when it came to applying the laws against enemy aliens. Moreover John III almost alone among French noblemen was allowed to retain possession of his valuable estates in England. When the news of his death reached England in May 1341 immediate steps were taken to discover what could be expected of his successor.[22]

The rumours which Philip VI heard in August 1341 were true. John de Montfort had not finally committed himself to Edward III but he had certainly had exchanges with him of a kind which were inconsistent with his status as a vassal of the French Crown. The initiative was Edward's. At the beginning of June 1341 he sent one of his household knights, Gavin Corder, to Brittany to make contact with the pretender. Corder was unfortunately delayed in England for a long time by contrary winds. He finally sailed from Dartmouth on 1 July 1341 accompanied by a Chancery clerk and an armed escort and landed at the little harbour of Guérande in south-eastern Brittany on the 7th. On 10 July he found John de Montfort in Nantes. John saw the English agents in private. The tenor of their discussions has to be inferred from oblique references and later events. It seems that John was very forthcoming. He said that he thought that Philip VI was bound to try sooner or later to expel him from Brittany and expressed interest in an alliance of some kind with Edward III. The impression which he gave was that if Edward was prepared to help him he would consider recognizing him as King of France. What he would not do was commit himself formally while there was still some prospect of obtaining Brittany without such dangerous assistance. He therefore kept the English agents waiting for six weeks upon his formal answer. They had still not received it when John was abruptly called away to Paris. So, on 21 August 1341, the day after John's departure, the Englishmen left. They reported to Edward III in London on 12 September.[23] Almost immediately afterwards the news arrived of John's flight from Paris, the edict of Conflans and the sequestration of the county of Montfort l'Amaury.

When John de Montfort arrived back in Nantes one of his first acts was to send two of his confidants to England with his formal proposals. These broadly reflected the conversations with Gavin Corder. He wanted military support against Philip VI urgently; when he got it, but not before, he was willing to do homage to Edward III for Brittany.[24] John's messengers, however, arrived too late. In the last week of August 1341 the Earl of Huntingdon had returned from Antoing to report that Edward's allies and in particular the Duke of Brabant would not support another campaign in France launched from their territories. They insisted on an extension of the truce. With no news from Brittany and unfavourable news from the Low

Countries there had been nothing that Edward could do except authorize his agents at Antoing to extend the truce of Esplechin into the following year. The decision had been taken at an enlarged meeting of the English royal Council on about 2 September 1341. The ships under requisition along the south coast had been released; the Bayonne galleys had been stood down; the troops had been sent home. On 12 September 1341, even as Corder was delivering his report to Edward III, the plenipotentiaries at Antoing extended the truce to 24 June 1342. To assist the Bretons now it would be necessary to rewind the spring and to repudiate their deed.[25]

Edward III did make some attempt to do this. The homage of Brittany was a great prize and something had to be done to impress John de Montfort's representatives. Probably at the beginning of October 1341 the English King sealed a treaty of military alliance with the two Breton agents. £10,000 was earmarked from the proceeds of the wool subsidy to pay wages of war. On 3 October orders went out to requisition all merchant shipping in ports between London and Bristol and assemble them at Portsmouth. The first ships were to be ready to carry the advance guard to Brittany by the end of October or the beginning of November 1341; the main body of the fleet was to be assembled by 18 November. The command of the ships was given to Robert Morley, Admiral of the north, and of the troops to those ready adventurers Walter Mauny and Robert of Artois. Once the orders had been given the two Bretons returned home.[26]

Edward's enterprise was conceived on a modest scale. The numbers were small and most of them were drawn from the personal retinues of the participants. There was no attempt to conscript troops in the counties. Even so, it was a hopeless endeavour. No one had ever previously succeeded in assembling a fleet of any size from requisitioned ships in less than four months. Most of the ships of southern England had only just been released from requisition for the abortive Brabant expedition. It was the season of the great Gascon wine fleets. Many of them had left their harbours to trade. Others fiercely resisted the admirals' officers. By the middle of November 1341, eighty-seven ships had been requisitioned along the south coast of England to carry the advance guard to Brittany and some of them had arrived at Portsmouth. Shortly after this, the expedition was cancelled. It had been overtaken by events in Brittany.[27]

The French army gathered in the last days of September 1341 at Angers on the Loire about 50 miles upstream of the Breton border.[28] It consisted, according to the least unreliable contemporary estimate, of about 5,000

Frenchmen and some Genoese, probably about 2,000 strong, drawn from the crews of the galleys. There was a powerful train of siege artillery. The command of the army was given to John, Duke of Normandy, but he was straitly supervised by the King's closest confidants, the minister Mile de Noyers and Philip's brother-in-law the Duke of Burgundy. Philip's instructions to his son were profoundly revealing of this cautious, troubled man. He did not like the hazards of war, and John was told that he was on no account to take risks. In particular he was not to attack any town unless reconnaissance had shown that it could be swiftly captured. If the opportunity arose of avoiding war by compromise it was to be taken. Philip was prepared to see John de Montfort generously compensated with land in other parts of France and even to guarantee him the succession to the duchy if Jeanne de Penthièvre should die without heirs. The main point was to keep the English out of Brittany. Philip was to be informed as soon as they had landed at whatever time of night or day it happened. There was an interesting additional instruction. When the Prince wrote to his wife at court he should on no account omit to say how large was his own army and how feeble the enemy's: 'she has heard things about the King of England . . . which terrify her.'

The original plan was to march immediately on Vannes, which was the closest port of any importance to Nantes and an obvious landing place for an English army. This idea was quickly abandoned. It would have involved penetrating deep into Brittany, leaving John de Montfort's garrisons in Nantes and Rennes to harass the French army's lines of communication. The Duke of Normandy had learned the unwisdom of that strategy in the Hainault campaign of the previous year. In the event most of the fighting took place around Champtoceaux, which was the first obstacle to be met by any army entering Brittany through the Loire valley and had been garrisoned by John de Montfort with mercenaries under the command of some Germans from Lorraine. Charles of Blois left Angers with the advance guard of the French army at the beginning of October 1341 and laid siege to this place on about the 10th. The Duke of Normandy followed him on the 14th with the main body of the army and most of the dignitaries: his minder Mile de Noyers, the dukes of Burgundy and Bourbon, Philip VI's brother the Count of Alençon, the Constable, the Marshals of the army and the Admiral of the French fleet, Louis of Spain. It was an imposing demonstration. John de Montfort made a bold attempt to relieve Champtoceaux with wholly inadequate forces. He led them out of Nantes and following the south bank of the river arrived at a fortified farmhouse called L'Humeau about 3 miles from the siege. He expected to find this place held by his own men. In fact, he found Charles of Blois there and came very close to capturing him. But after two days of fighting around the tower of the farmhouse the Montfortists were driven off by the Duke of Normandy with much bloodshed. Champtoceaux fell on about 26 October 1341.[29]

It proved to be the turning point of the campaign. John de Montfort returned in headlong flight to Nantes. The army of the Duke of Normandy arrived outside the city a few days after him at the end of October. Nantes should have resisted for a long time. It was well supplied by river and its walls on the landward side were too long to be completely invested by the French. But the citizens had no enthusiasm for its defence. They knew about the defeat of the Montfortists at L'Humeau. The French overwhelmed the outlying castles of the Nantais with the utmost ferocity and beheaded their prisoners in front of the city walls. The townsmen reminded John de Montfort of the reservations which they had made when they had done homage to him and refused to fight. They were eventually persuaded to support him, but only on terms that if relief had not arrived after a month the pretender should leave the city and chance his fate outside. Short of time and without news from England, John organized a succession of desperate and costly sorties, some of which he led in person with great courage. The last of these sorties, which was designed to seize a victuals train, ended in the precipitate flight of John's mercenaries and the massacre of a large number of townsmen. It also provoked a bitter quarrel between John and Hervé de Léon, who had led the flight. The men of Nantes had had enough. They called a great assembly and in spite of their recent agreement with John they decided that unless he opened negotiations at once with the besiegers they would do so themselves. John had no option but to agree. He went into the Duke of Normandy's camp and agreed to surrender Nantes to his rival. This probably happened on 2 November 1341.[30] The siege had lasted for less than a week. Immediately afterwards Charles of Blois entered his capital, which received him with the same festivities as they had put on for John de Montfort six months before.

There remained the difficult question of John's personal position. He had not been prepared to surrender Nantes without some assurances for himself, for all the weakness of his hand. So the Duke of Normandy offered him the prospect of negotiations with the King and presumably some hope of a compromise. In return he was required to surrender all his garrisons in Brittany into Philip's hands to abide by the further consideration of his claim. For this purpose John was given a safe conduct to Paris and back again. For a few weeks he remained in Nantes with his enemies. Then, at the end of December 1341, he accompanied the Duke of Normandy to Paris. When he arrived at the Royal court some negotiations did indeed occur. John was invited to sign a treaty with his rival renouncing in return for a pension and a grant of land in France his entire claim to the duchy and everything that he possessed there. He refused. Philip then repudiated his safe conduct and ordered him to be imprisoned in the Louvre.[31] In Brittany John's erstwhile supporters had already begun to desert him. Hervé de Léon led the way. He became one of Charles of Blois' principal counsellors very soon after the fall of Nantes and began to write to his friends and connections urging them to submit. The enormous fortress of Saint-Aubin du Cormier on the north-eastern march surrendered at once. Many of John's most important captains submitted during January 1342 and received pardons from the King. By February 1342 Charles of Blois controlled all of the French-speaking regions of eastern Brittany except for Rennes.[32]

When Nantes fell the Countess of Montfort was at Rennes some 70 miles away to the north. She had with her the greater part of the ducal treasury, still the main asset of the Montfortist cause, and a force of garrison troops. Her husband's military strength seemed unlikely to survive his capture for very long. But it still existed, for the moment, intact. The main body of the army had not been with John at Nantes but was encamped at Saint-Renan in Finistère waiting for the arrival of the English. There were garrisons installed for the same reason along the western coast, in particular at Le Conquet and Brest. These forces were commanded by a group of minor Breton lords, the principal of whom were Tanneguy du Châtel, the captain of Brest castle, and Geoffrey de Malestroit, who appears to have been in command of the field army. These men were under strong conflicting pressures. Several of them had land in territory now controlled by Charles of Blois and their families had made their peace with him. The Crown was offering them free pardons for their loyalty, and they were wavering.[33]

The Countess made a number of acute decisions. The first was to dispatch her treasury to safety at Brest. The second was to leave Rennes, a strong city but a place of divided loyalties, inland and far away from help. At the end of the year she joined forces with Geoffrey de Malestroit. Leaving enough men at Rennes to hold it she fought her way south, captured the town of Redon by storm and occupied the Guérande peninsula at the mouth of the Loire. From there she marched west and established her headquarters at Hennebont. Hennebont was a small walled town at the head of the estuary of the River Blavet on the Morbihan coast of Brittany. It had stout walls built at the end of the previous century. It was probably more easily defended than any other place in western Brittany. From here, Jeanne asserted her authority over all the surviving field and garrison forces of her husband. Their two-year-old son was proclaimed as the nominal head of their party and the heir apparent should John be put to death in Paris.[34] As his guardian the Countess appointed the ablest and most prominent of her advisers, Amaury de Clisson, a member of the great Breton family whose elder brother Olivier was even then fighting for Charles of Blois.

In February 1342 Amaury de Clisson arrived in England with the widest powers to commit the Countess's party, and chests loaded with cash from the ducal treasury. The English King had passed the winter in a barren show of force in the lowlands of Scotland which achieved nothing and ended early. On 11 and 12 February 1342 he was engaged in a most spectacular and expensive tournament at Dunstable, fighting in the lists as a simple knight with almost all the noble youth of England. Serious consideration of the renewed civil war in France did not begin until some days later. During the third week of February the nobility gathered in London to lay plans for the prosecution of the war. Edward responded to the Countess's invitation with enthusiasm. The treaty which he had made with the Breton agents in the previous October was renewed. Plans were prepared for intervention in Brittany which amounted to nothing less than the immediate assumption of control by the English government over the Montfortists' territory there in the name of the Countess and her young son. All the towns, harbours and castles of the coast of Montfortist Brittany would be taken over by the English. The command of them was committed to Walter Mauny, who was to take a sufficient company of men to the duchy early in March. A much larger force, of 1,000 men-at-arms and 1,000 archers, was to sail in April 1342 under the command of the Earl of Northampton and Robert of Artois. In order to maintain the pretence that the truces were being observed these men were probably intended to fight under John de Montfort's colours. But when the truces expired in June Edward intended to come over to the duchy in person to 'support the Duke and recover his own right in the crown of France'. To finance this venture, Amaury de Clisson promised to make over the whole ducal treasury to the English King by way of loan. Edward was paid at once the equivalent of £1,000 in gold, silver and jewellery from the chests which Amaury had with him. This was intended to meet the initial expenses of Mauny's force. A further 68,000 *l.t.* (£13,600) was to be advanced after Northampton and Robert of Artois had arrived. The remaining contents of the ducal treasury would be advanced when Edward himself landed in the summer. Edward appointed an English civil servant to return to Brittany with Amaury to take custody of the coffers lodged at Brest and a team of craftsmen to coin their contents into money. These arrangements were more or less complete on 21 February 1342 when the Bretons put their seal to the treaty.[35]

The following eight months were a story of persistent struggle in the face of administrative and diplomatic obstacles to bring help to Jeanne de Montfort before she succumbed to the overwhelming military strength of France. She manoeuvred skilfully for time. At some point in February 1342 Jeanne moved from Hennebont to Brest. On the 24th she was found there by an emissary from Philip VI, Henry de Malestroit. Henry, a senior judicial officer of the royal household, was a Breton, the brother of the Countess's military commander. He was to undergo agonies of divided loyalty. His instructions were to require submission from the Countess's partisans, including his brother and Tanneguy du Châtel, and to demand the surrender of Brest into the King's hands in accordance with the arrangements made between John de Montfort and the Duke of Normandy on the fall of Nantes. The first instinct of the Countess's friends was to resist. Tanneguy answered that he had taken up the cause of the true line of Brittany and would defend himself to the death. But wiser counsels prevailed. The French were asking for nothing more than a formal surrender which would leave the Countess and her friends in actual possession. Was it not better in a time of weakness to avoid provoking them? The Countess conceded the point. Five days later on 1 March 1342 she negotiated a truce with Henry which froze the military position until 15 April and left her in effective control of the west. This was approximately the date on which the Earl of Northampton was expected to arrive from England.[36]

Help came from England with appalling slowness. The first, unofficial and rather ineffective assistance came in the form of shipmasters from the Cinque Ports, the West Country and Bayonne who received letters of marque to prey on French shipping in return for a third of the spoil. They were recruited by an Englishman, Oliver Stretford, who was installed in the Countess's administration in Hennebont Castle and was styled the 'Duke's lieutenant'. These privateers were very active in the early spring of 1342 but indiscriminate in their choice of victims and not overscrupulous about accounting for their takings.[37]

The advance guard of the expeditionary force, which was due to sail under the command of Walter Mauny to secure the landing places, gathered punctually in Portsmouth in March 1342 but was delayed by the usual difficulty in requisitioning ships. Of the sixty medium-sized vessels which had been called for, only forty-four had been found by the requisitioning officers by the end of the month. Some of these arrived laden with cargo and had to be laboriously discharged; most arrived late; one group of shipmasters anchored in the roads and refused to enter the harbour until they had been paid; seventeen failed to appear at all. Mauny fumed impatiently. He was not a man to understand bureaucratic limitations.[38]

The delays to the main army of Northampton and Robert of Artois do not seem to have been due to the officials, who on this occasion surpassed themselves. One hundred large vessels were available at Yarmouth by the end of the first week of April; in the harbours between Portsmouth and Bristol, where requisitioning did not begin until 1 April 1342, 117 ships had been found within the month. It was an impressive achievement by the standards of the past five years.[39] But the assembly of the army which was to fill them was deliberately delayed. The main reasons seem to have been political. Edward III had made ambitious promises to the Bretons very hastily, too hastily to consult his allies. The main point in the treaty which he had sealed with Amaury de Clisson was the dispatch of an army to a province of France two months before the expiry of the current truce. The reactions of his allies in the Low Countries when they were told are not recorded but they can be guessed. These men were parties to the truce which Edward proposed to violate, and they were potential victims of a French counter-attack. They had no interest at all in Brittany. England's alliances with the princes of the Low Countries were strained by now and had become more than anything a memory of past stalemate and uncollected debts. But Edward could not ignore these men. He still had cause to value their capacity to hold down large French forces on the great open frontier of the north. The deliberations of the English government are obscure. All that is known is that at the end of March Edward was persuaded at short notice to appoint representatives to attend yet another peace conference between the French ministers and the princes of the Low Countries which was due to open at Condé in Brabant on 14 April 1342. In Paris, too, attention was fixed upon the Low Countries. Philip was slow to recognize that for the first time in half a century it had ceased to be the decisive theatre. On 11 April 1342 he summoned his army to meet at Arras on 24 June, the day on which the truce was due to expire.[40]

In southern and western England troops had been told to be ready by early May to proceed to their ports of embarkation for Brittany.[41] The

French did not wait. As soon as the local ceasefire between the Countess of Montfort and the French Crown expired on 15 April they attacked the easternmost outpost of the Montfortist party at Rennes. On this occasion the command was taken by Charles of Blois himself. His chief lieutenants were his older brother Louis, Count of Blois, and Louis of Spain. The latter was the kind of princely adventurer who had always thrived at the courts of Capetian France, a man who might have been king of Castile but for the *coup d'état* which had elbowed his father from the throne many years before, just as John of Bohemia might have reigned in Germany and Walter of Brienne in Greece or Florence. Because Philip VI was still anxious to preserve the truce, Charles of Blois and his companions had had to raise their own troops, and for that reason the number of men-at-arms available to them was probably small, consisting of their own retainers and Breton lords from the regions which were loyal to him. The mass of the army was made up of Italian and Spanish seamen. Ayton Doria was certainly in Charles's service by this time, and probably Carlo Grimaldi as well. They left their ships laid up in Normandy and used the two or three thousand crewmen as archers and infantrymen. The Spaniards were drawn from the crews of a squadron of galleys hired by Louis of Spain in Castile. These men had established a base to beach their ships in a small harbour of Beauvoir-sur-Mer at the southern end of the Bay of Bourgneuf in the Vendée. They were present in force in Charles's army from May onward.[42]

Charles had no difficulty in taking Rennes, which was too far from the heartlands of the Montfortists to be relieved and too large to be effectively defended by its garrison. The citizens decided at the beginning of May that resistance was hopeless. They called on the garrison commander to surrender. When he refused they arrested him and opened their gates. This event was followed by the submission of almost all the remaining partisans of John de Montfort in the francophone regions of eastern Brittany.[43]

Shortly after Charles of Blois entered Rennes, Walter Mauny at last arrived with the English advance guard at Brest at the opposite extremity of Brittany. His force was pitifully small, 34 men-at-arms and 200 mounted archers, and its function was limited. It was required for securing the coastal towns, principally Brest itself. Mauny may have been told not to attack troops of the French Crown while the truce remained in force. At any rate, for whatever reason, he did not do so. Instead he turned the occasion to his own advantage by a brief plundering raid against the turncoat Hervé de Léon, Charles of Blois' only significant supporter in the far west. Not long after their arrival the Englishmen fell on the fortified manor house at Tregarantec in northern Finistère where Hervé was staying. They attacked at dawn, burned down the doorway and captured the surprised occupants almost without bloodshed. The prisoners included not only Hervé himself but six other ransomable noblemen and a large number of lesser men who were no doubt worth something to Mauny's followers. The chronicles are full of stories of Mauny's fabulous deeds and audacious attacks on the French army in the summer of 1342, but they were fishermen's tales drawn from the faulty recollections of his old age. The truth was that neither he nor the Montfortists had the strength to attack Charles of Blois in the field and for most of May and June 1342 they did nothing. Charles of Blois ignored Mauny's presence in his duchy. He sent his brother to invest Vannes. He himself together with the greater part of his army marched on Hennebont, where the Countess was.[44]

Edward III was still struggling with his allies and reconciling himself to the existence of the truce with France. There was therefore a pause in England at the high point of the French campaign in Brittany. Edward splendidly entertained the Count of Hainault at Eltham and saw him wounded in a tournament. He sent the Bishop of London and the Earl of Warwick to explain matters to the other German princes at another grand conference of the coalition at Mechelen. The troops did not receive their orders until 20 May, the shipmasters five days later.[45]

The army of Charles of Blois arrived before the walls of Hennebont in late May 1342 and encountered the most ferocious resistance. The castle and the town were stuffed with victuals and defended by a garrison entirely devoted to the Countess's cause. Almost as soon as they arrived the French suffered a humiliating reverse. A number of their Genoese and Spanish troops rushed forward without orders and milled about the gates and walls engaging in undisciplined tourneys with groups of the defenders. In order to extricate them it was necessary to mount a full-scale assault on the town before the army was ready. The result was a massacre followed by a disorganized retreat. Charles of Blois' camp was overwhelmed by the Montfortists and most of the tents were burned. According to Jean de Bel (whose account of this campaign is unfortunately very erratic) the Countess was to be seen riding through the streets and suburbs of Hennebont haranguing her men from a charger. The French made a number of other attempts to take the town by storm but all of them were costly failures. They therefore settled down, probably in early June, to starve the place out. In the second half of the month the momentum of their reconquest had been largely dissipated and their army split up in penny packets along the Morbihan coast. Louis of Spain and the Viscount of Rohan remained at Hennebont with a small force consisting mainly of Spaniards. They steadily battered the walls with siege artillery until, probably in late June, they gave up and raised the siege. Charles of Blois himself moved to Auray and sat outside the town with the main body of his army. Further east, Vannes still held out. Small detachments spread out along the roads of the inland hills, killing and looting. It was the beginning of the most wretched period in the history of medieval Brittany.[46]

Charles of Blois was lavish in his promises to those who might abandon the Countess's cause for his own. But the imprisonment of John de Montfort had made a profound impression here. Philip VI and his friends and protégés were distrusted, and were resisted by men whose interests might have brought them to submission long ago. How long their resistance would last was another question. Walter Mauny, not a man to shy away from a difficult undertaking, was so pessimistic about the Montfortists' prospects of survival that when the main English expeditionary force failed to arrive at the end of June he proposed a truce to Charles of Blois until 1 November 1342, in effect for the whole of the campaigning season of that year. On about 8 July Mauny arrived back in England to lodge his prisoners in safety and to press this idea on Edward III. But Edward was not interested and promptly repudiated him.[47]

On the continent the political balance was shifting fast in the French government's favour. Pope Benedict XII, that austere and independent man, had died on 25 April 1342. He had had little sympathy for either protagonist in the war and his relations with Philip VI had become particularly cool as a result of the French King's rapprochement with the outcast Louis of Bavaria. On 7 May, to Philip's unconcealed delight, the conclave of cardinals elected as his successor Pierre Roger, formerly Archbishop of Rouen and one of Philip's principal ministers and advisers during the 1330s.

Pierre Roger was the ablest but perhaps the least edifying of the Avignon popes before the Great Schism. He was a native of the Corrèze, by birth therefore a subject of Edward I. But his real origins were in the Benedictine abbey of La Chaise-Dieu in eastern Auvergne, where he had been professed as a monk at the age of ten. Its magnificent buildings are, together with the grandest parts of the papal palace at Avignon, his principal surviving monument. They are also revealing of his personality. He was a man of princely tastes and worldly outlook, an ecclesiastical politician of the great style. He was also wedded to the interests of France. This is not to say that he was a creature of Philip VI. However, he had spent the prime of his life in the secular employment of the French government and although he was not among the anglophobes of Philip's circle he had the views of an urbane and intelligent French courtier. He truly believed that France's interests were the interests of Christendom and of peace, and that Edward III was a rebel and an aggressor. It was a tenable view. Pierre Roger took the title Clement VI. He was crowned on 19 May 1342 in the vast church of the Franciscans of Avignon in the presence of a crowd of French notables including the dukes of Normandy, Burgundy and Bourbon, whose vassals were at that moment marching with Charles of Blois against Hennebont. To the Duke of Normandy fell the honour of holding the reins of the Pope's horse and sitting at his right hand at dinner. Observers were not slow to notice it.[48]

Clement began to interest himself in the war at once. Within a fortnight of his coronation he had appointed two cardinals to mediate between Philip VI and his rival. Edward III received news of this appointment in the middle of June 1342. He regarded it as a transparent attempt to delay his expedition to Brittany until the Countess of Montfort had been defeated and he declined to co-operate. The cardinals were in France throughout June and July 1342 and were well received at Philip VI's court. But when they asked for leave to cross the Channel for discussions with the King of England they received a caustic reply. Edward said that since he was about to visit 'our Kingdom of France' they might save themselves some trouble by attending upon him there.[49]

Clement meanwhile assiduously set about widening the gap between the King of England and his allies in the Low Countries. On 12 June 1342 he conceded to Philip VI what Benedict XII had persistently denied him. He agreed to lift the interdict on the county of Flanders which had been the source of so much ill-feeling between the Flemings and the French government. Another emissary was sent north from Avignon to discuss terms with the Flemings. The terms on offer have not survived but they certainly included a requirement that the Flemings should abstain from any active part in the war. The Flemings must have been tempted. They wanted to be absolved from the excommunication and to see the interdict lifted, but they wanted even more to maintain their supplies of English wool and to recover the large sums which the English government still owed them. Their response was ambivalent. In the event they made no formal agreement with France. But they listened to the Pope's proposals and in the meantime they took no steps to stir up the war on their southern frontier. The Duke of Brabant and the Count of Hainault went further. They met the cardinals at Antoing in the third week of August 1342 and concluded what amounted to an independent truce. They undertook that unless Philip VI invaded Flanders they would not make war on him without giving him at least one month's notice. It was for practical purposes the end of the Anglo-German coalition.[50]

The effect on the military fortunes of the French was striking. They were able to maintain and even expand their forces in the south-west, which they would otherwise have withdrawn by mid-summer, and to concentrate troops in Brittany which might have been idly guarding their vulnerable northern frontier.

On the marches of Gascony a large French army, recruited locally, reoccupied enclaves of English strength north of the Gironde, in Saintonge and in the Agenais which had been lodged there in the previous year.[51] In the Garonne valley the Bishop of Beauvais and his brother Robert de Marigny set about retaking the towns which had thrown out their French garrisons. They mopped up almost all the isolated outposts of the Anglo-Gascons in the western Agenais and the Bazadais one after the other. Most of them surrendered after a nominal siege. Damazan, an important *bastide* on the left bank of the Garonne opposite Aiguillon, achieved more than most places by holding out for three weeks. On 21 August 1342 the *arrière-ban* was proclaimed in Languedoc and the strength of the Bishop's army gradually rose to some 10,000 men. It was fortunate for the Anglo-Gascons that he was so cautious in the use of them. They passed the rest of the campaigning season encamped outside Sainte-Bazeille, which had expelled its garrison earlier in the year. Sainte-Bazeille resisted with ferocity but was finally captured at the beginning of October 1342, the fourth occasion in the past two years when this important garrison town on the Garonne had changed hands. It was not until the end of that month that the Bishop began to wind down the scale of his operations and prepare for his own return to the north.[52]

The army which had been summoned to meet at Arras on 24 June 1342 duly assembled there, and although the surviving records do not enable us to assess its strength a list of the principal participants suggests a host of at least 10,000 men and probably more. A covering force was left in the north, the command of which was eventually assumed by the Count of Eu and the Duke of Bourbon. By far the greater part of the French army was redirected to Brittany to reinforce Charles of Blois. There was a surge of fresh activity at sea. In the last few days of June, as the northern army was being transferred to Brittany, the Genoese were withdrawn and sent to relaunch their ships. The two Genoese captains now had fourteen seaworthy galleys between them. They were taken round the tip of Ushant during July to support the land army. In addition to these the French had twenty-one of their own less efficient galleys and oared barges. They were relaunched at Leure in the Seine and ordered to cruise off the south coast of England with a view to blockading the English expeditionary force in its ports of embarkation.[53]

Charles of Blois' reinforcements arrived in Brittany in the first half of July 1342 and found no serious opposition. Of Edward III's promised armies the Countess of Montfort had so far seen only 230 or so men left in Brittany by Walter Mauny. In the course of July 1342 the Montfortists were driven relentlessly back to their fastnesses in the west of the peninsula. The garrison of Auray, which had been reduced to eating its horses, abandoned the place, slipping through the French lines at night to take refuge in the inland forests. Vannes surrendered on terms after some of the principal gates had been stormed. At Guémenée-sur-Scorff, an important fortified village on the main road west, the commander was forced to surrender by the inhabitants. The Countess of Montfort fled from Hennebont and took refuge in Brest. Here in mid-August 1342 she found herself besieged by an enormous French army on the landward side and blockaded by the Genoese galleys from the sea.[54]

The logistical difficulties of the English government in mounting a seaborne invasion of Brittany were much more formidable than those of 1338 and 1340. Although the Breton campaign was conceived on a smaller scale England had less to expect on this occasion from its allies. The demands made on the country's manpower and shipping were the most exacting of the war so far. About 5,500 English troops fought in Brittany in 1342 in addition to about 1,400 reinforcements who were assembled in England but never reached the continent. This was probably fewer than Edward III had originally envisaged. Even so, at least 440 ships were employed, most of which performed more than one passage.

The English had learned something from their past experience of confused, congested ports and interminable delays while fleets of transports were drawn together from their far-flung home harbours and bored, hungry and thieving soldiers rampaged through the countryside. On this occasion it was proposed to embark a number of independent forces each under its own commander from half-a-dozen ports between Kent and Devon. In their final form the plans called for three main armies followed by smaller contingents for reinforcement. The first army was to sail from the Solent ports, Southampton and Portsmouth. William Bohun, Earl of Northampton, the companion of Edward III's *coup d'état* of 1330 and of many campaigns in Scotland and the Low Countries, a bold spirit now about thirty years of age, was given the command of this army and was appointed as the King's lieutenant in Brittany and France with extensive power to carry on the war in his name. The ships which carried his men to Brittany were then to return to Sandwich and Winchelsea to join forces with freshly requisitioned vessels and embark another army commanded by the King and the Earl of Warwick. In the autumn a third army recruited in Wales and the West Country and led by the earls of Gloucester and Pembroke would leave on newly requisitioned ships from Dartmouth and Plymouth. The later reinforcement drafts would leave in packets from the harbours of the West Country.[55]

While these elaborate movements were being carried out, it was proposed to launch a spoiling operation in Gascony to draw as many French troops as possible away from Brittany. Oliver Ingham was in England during the summer of 1342. A small force of English archers and men-at-arms, some six dozen men in all, was placed at his disposal under the command of Hugh Despenser, the son of Edward II's fallen favourite. A subsidy was promised. The more pressing arrears of war wages owed to the Gascon nobility were paid. Ingham and Despenser sailed from Dartmouth in the second half of July 1342. However, when their ships put in at Saint-Mathieu at the south-west tip of Brittany, the traditional port of call on the route to Bordeaux, they were so alarmed by the weakness of the Countess's position in Brest that Despenser agreed to stay behind to reinforce her garrison. Ingham had to proceed to Gascony on his own.[56]

Northampton's army was seriously delayed. By 8 July 1342, the date which had eventually been fixed for his departure, there were no ships in Portsmouth, and only forty-five ships had arrived there a week later. Then, when the fleet was ready it was held up by adverse winds. Northampton's force was not only late but small: only 1,350 men, roughly equally divided between archers and men-at-arms, embarked on 140 transports. With the converted merchant ships of Yarmouth and the northern Admiralty and some galleys of Bayonne, the fleet numbered 260 vessels.[57]

Nevertheless the Earl was immediately and spectacularly successful. The French galleys and barges which had been sent to intercept him arrived too late to stop him leaving the Solent. They had the satisfaction of burning Portsmouth for the second time in five years and of lying off Southampton for several days while terror gripped the inhabitants of Hampshire. But that was all. The English fleet sailed on 14 and 15 August 1342. On the 18th, after three days at sea, they entered the roads of Brest. The magnificent roadstead of Brest is like an inland lake connected to the Atlantic at its western end by a narrow channel little more than a mile wide and divided in two by the mass of the Plougastel peninsula jutting in from the east. Brest itself lies on the northern shore just inside the entrance channel. In the 1340s it was a fishing harbour overshadowed by an old stone castle. The River Penfeld, which passed under the castle walls, was no more than a narrow shallow stream tapering into marsh just north of the village. The fourteen galleys of the Genoese were anchored within sight of the town off the mouth of the Penfeld. They were taken by surprise and were almost immediately enveloped by the slow and unmanoeuvrable but much more numerous ships of the English. The only means of escape into the open sea was blocked. At at Sluys, the French were deploying galleys in a way which deprived them of their mobility, their principal natural advantage. Only three of them were able to make off up the estuary of the River Elorn. The other eleven retreated into the mouth of the Penfeld, where they grounded in the mud between the forces of the invader and the garrison of the castle. Their crews scrambled ashore and abandoned their ships to be burned by the English. Thus perished the last remnant of the great Genoese galley fleet which had fought under French colours since 1338. The reaction of the French army encamped around Brest was extraordinary. They cannot have realized what a small army a fleet of 260 sailing ships carried. They abruptly lifted the siege and withdrew. Charles of Blois retreated with the main body of his army and Grimaldi's Genoese seamen towards his wife's territory in northern Brittany . Louis of Spain and Ayton Doria led their Spanish and Genoese auxiliaries in rapid retreat across southern Brittany towards the Spanish ships beached in the Bay of Bourgneuf. For the time being western Brittany was left to the English and their friends.[58]

Within a few days of the battle Northampton's army was reinforced by the arrival of Robert of Artois with about 800 men. They had been delayed in Southampton by a shortage of weapons and of ramps and hurdles for embarking horses, and had not sailed until later.[59] With these men and the handful of Englishmen who had been in Brittany since the spring Northampton had at his disposal about 2,400 Englishmen and an unknown number of Bretons. Once he had secured Brest his main object was to capture a harbour on the north coast of Brittany. This was to be an abiding preoccupation of English commanders in Brittany for years. The Montfortists did not securely hold any territory on the north coast, and until they did it would be necessary for ships carrying supplies and reinforcements from England to make the perilous passage through the reefs off Finistère and Ushant. Northampton was advised to march on Morlaix, a small walled town with a good natural harbour about 30 miles north-east of Brest. Unfortunately he does not appear to have begun this enterprise until the beginning of September and by then the defenders of Morlaix were ready for him. On 3 September 1342 the Anglo-Breton army delivered an assault on the place which was repulsed with heavy casualties. The English sat down to a tedious and time-consuming siege.[60]

The fleet which had carried Northampton to Brest left Brittany immediately after disembarking the army, and if all had gone well it would have brought Edward III and Warwick to Brittany in the first half of September 1342. All did not go well. The shipmasters, some of whose vessels had been under requisition for three months, were in a rebellious mood. They had already lost some of the best trading weather of the year and were about to miss the autumn wine fleet from Gascony. So when the main body of Northampton's fleet reached England on 22 August it was found that many of them had deserted. They included no less than forty-five ships of Dartmouth and the whole fleet of Hull. The second army of Brittany was due to sail on 1 September 1342. By the middle of September there were about 840 men-at-arms and just under 2,200 archers waiting for their passage by the Kent and Sussex coasts. Less than half the number of ships required was available and some of those were deserting day by day. Requisitioning officers were racing from port to port to scrape the barrel for more. Even smacks of twenty tons were considered. Important contingents from Wales had to be diverted to Plymouth to join the army of the Earl of Gloucester because there was no hope of finding shipping space for them in the south-east.[61]

Ironically the immobilization of Edward III's army in south-eastern England was almost as beneficial to the Earl of Northampton as its arrival in Brittany would have been. The reason was that the French government's intelligence-gathering had improved immeasurably since 1337 and the scale of the preparations at Sandwich and Winchelsea was reported to them, probably with some dramatic exaggeration, in the course of September. The south-eastern ports seemed unlikely places from which to sail to Brittany. The distance and the prevailing winds would be against them. Philip VI and his advisers therefore concluded that Edward's real intention must be to land in the Pas-de-Calais while the best of the French army was engaged in Brittany. Ominous movements of the Flemings north of the Aa pointed in the same direction. Consequently large numbers of troops were withdrawn from Brittany at the very time when they were most needed there. They were concentrated instead around Boulogne and Calais and along the northern frontier. Charles of Blois was left with a much reduced field army, the main elements of which were some 3,000 cavalry, 1,500

Genoese survivors of the galleys of Brest and a motley force of Breton infantry. These figures are derived from English scouts and erred, if at all, on the high side.[62] By the time the French government realized their mistake Charles had suffered a minor but humiliating and morale-denting defeat.

He moved out of his headquarters at Guingamp in the last week of September 1342 with the evident intention of relieving Morlaix. On the afternoon of 29 September he had reached the vicinity of Lanmeur, about 7 miles north-east of the town, when his presence was detected and reported to the Earl of Northampton. In order to avoid being caught between the sorties of the garrison of Morlaix and the main body of the French army he withdrew most of his men from the siege at nightfall and marched them through the darkness towards the enemy. The break of day on 30 September found the English dismounted and dug in across the French line of advance about 2 or 3 miles from Lanmeur. Their positions were covered by a thick wood on one side and by trenches and pit-traps concealed with greenery. The French attacked them. They approached across the open land west of Lanmeur in three successive lines. The front line was composed mainly of Franco-Breton cavalry commanded by Geoffrey de Charny, a famous Burgundian paladin. Geoffrey's line charged the English positions and was thrown back. The second French line after a moment's hesitation followed by a route which took them straight into the pit-traps. There were appalling casualties. The French losses of knights alone were some 50 killed and 150 captured, including Geoffrey de Charny himself. They made the classic French tactical error to be repeated in almost every pitched battle of the decade including Crécy: dashing their cavalry against dismounted men in prepared positions and making virtually no use of their infantry. How much the English had to fear from skilfully deployed infantry was apparent from the confused sequel of the battle. Rather than face the great horde of unmounted French troops who were still in their starting positions, Northampton's men withdrew into the forest with their prisoners, where they were besieged for several days and suffered great privations. The battle of Morlaix therefore ended with a whimper. It was, moreover, strategically insignificant. The town, it is true, was not relieved, but neither was it taken.[63]

Oliver Ingham's spoiling operation began in October. Unfortunately, it was poorly provided, and the Seneschal was unable to take any of the major garrison towns from the French. Instead he crossed the Gironde and invaded Saintonge. His initial purpose seems to have been the capture of

Blaye, whose inhabitants had laid plans to expel their French garrison as soon as he should appear. It would have been a great prize. But the plot failed. There were too many in the secret. It was betrayed to the garrison commander and the ringleaders were arrested. The Anglo-Gascon force passed on towards Angoulême doing much damage but capturing little of value. Their only known prize was Blanzac, a castle on the edge of Saintonge and Angoumois which was taken by storm and garrisoned.[64]

The most significant gains of the autumn campaign were in the Agenais and they were achieved (as most things there were) by political machination rather than military force. The *bastide* of Damazan expelled its new French garrison soon after the Bishop of Beauvais had departed, and received an English one instead. Casseneuil, a fortress dominating one of the crossings of the Lot, invited in the English at the end of November. Curiously, the French ignored the loss of Damazan although they had passed three weeks of the summer in besieging it and in spite of its situation by the confluence of the Lot and the Garonne, the two major rivers of the south-west. Casseneuil, on the other hand, was bitterly fought over. Ingham's deputies succeeded in putting 60 cavalry and 500 infantry into the place before the French could gather their forces, a considerable achievement since it was more than 80 miles from Bordeaux. During the next month the ducal government was able at some risk to its position to supply fresh reinforcements by stripping troops from the garrison of Bordeaux and the march of Béarn. A French army some 5,000 strong was engaged in the siege of Casseneuil by the beginning of the New Year. All of these troops, however, were recruited in the south and would probably not have fought in Brittany anyway. Ingham's diversion did not even succeed in retaining the Bishop of Beauvais on the march of Gascony.[65]

Edward III boarded his flagship, the *George*, off Sandwich on 4 October 1342 and after three weeks of gales and extreme discomfort reached Brittany on the 26th.[66] After the landing, the English King went straight to Brest, where he met the leaders of the Montfortists and the commanders of the English forces already in the duchy. It was resolved at this stage that the main object of the campaign should be the recapture of Vannes. Vannes, Edward wrote to his son, was 'the finest city of Brittany after Nantes and the best place from which to reduce the land to our obedience; for the advice which we have received is that if we had tried to penetrate beyond Vannes without taking it we would have lost all our conquests'. It was sound advice. Vannes was a walled town lying across the main routes between the Loire estuary and the coastal plain of southern Brittany, where the Montforists' strength was concentrated. There was also a good sheltered harbour by which it could be supplied and reinforced if necessary from England. So, while Edward III enjoyed himself hunting in the forests of Cornouaille for deer, boar, foxes, bears, monkeys and other beasts 'plentiful beyond measure', Walter Mauny and two other knights were given the task of exploring the walls of Vannes. They reported towards the end of the first week of November that there were weaknesses which should enable it to be taken by assault. The army began to move out of its encampments around Brest on 7 November 1342. The fleet was ordered to follow along the coast.

The fleet had the more eventful journey. It began with a mutiny. The reasons might have been foreseen: want of pay, despair at the prospect of an indefinite period of service to the state, in many cases a real fear that after several months of service under requisition the ships were in poor shape and liable to founder in the winter gales. When the time came to leave Brest it was found that half the fleet, 186 ships, had defied the admirals and sailed away. The rest were placed under the command of Robert of Artois. He probably took with him the troops which he had led from England, about 800 men. It was an unfortunate choice. Robert had lost none of the recklessness which he had shown at Saint-Omer in 1340 and had learned no generalship. He made good speed along the coast and at some stage in the second week of November he arrived in the Bay of Bourgneuf. He resolved to attack the Castilian galley squadron at Beauvoir. It was probably his own decision. But he was soundly beaten. The Spanish and Genoese were present in force. They not only prevented Robert from landing near the town but succeeded in boarding their own vessels in time to attack him first. The English lost some large ships and suffered heavy casualties.

Undeterred, Robert led the survivors back along the coast into the Gulf of Morbihan. Without waiting for the main army he tried to take Vannes by a *coup de main* with the troops he had with him. He very nearly succeeded. The garrison unwisely came out to attack him on the open ground outside the town walls. As they did so the English adroitly turned their flank and seized the gate by which the French had left. Unfortunately, Robert's men lacked the strength with which to follow up their gains. On the following day they were dislodged by a mixed force of garrison troops and citizens, including a mob of furious women. In the course of the fighting Robert himself was wounded. The wound was not fatal, but the cure was. Robert was laid up in his camp, where he contracted dysentery and died. His body was carried back to England and buried in the

Blackfriars church of London. Thus ended the life of the great plotter, characteristically leading a foreign army. 'Don't pray for him,' wrote the chronicler of Saint-Denis.[67]

The Anglo-Breton army under the English King's personal command swept through southern Brittany meeting no significant resistance. The only important garrison of Charles of Blois in western Brittany, which was at Roche-Periou, surrendered apparently without a blow. All the main towns of the south opened up their gates. But at Vannes their fortunes changed. The bungled attack of Robert of Artois had removed any possibility of surprise. The French had reinforced the garrison, bringing its strength up to about 300 men, and had placed it under the command of Louis of Poitiers, Count of Valentinois, a plodding man but loyal and experienced. In the Gulf of Morbihan the English fleet lay leaderless and mutinous at anchor. Another twenty-nine vessels sailed away. There was no siege train. The English had been compelled by shortage of shipping space to leave it behind. As a result on 22 November 1342 Edward III had to call a halt at Grand-Champ, 12 miles north of Vannes, while new engines were specially made.[68] This took a whole week, an unfortunate and costly delay. On 29 November 1342, the English and their Breton allies finally arrived outside the walls of Vannes and delivered their assault. It failed. Edward was obliged to sit down outside the city, a significant strategic setback.

The English King made as much use of idle time as he could, and did so to some effect. Large raiding parties were formed from the besieging army and sent to reduce as much as possible of eastern Brittany to Edward's obedience before the resistance of the French hardened. At the end of November the English captured three strong towns on the inland road, Rédon, Malestroit and Ploermel. The last two places resisted, but in vain. They had to pay protection money to spare themselves the horrors of a sack.[69] Further west the Earl of Northampton invaded the territory of the Viscount of Rohan, who had fought for Charles of Blois from the outset. Pontivy was taken and Rohan itself burned to the ground. At the beginning of December 1342 Northampton set out with the Earl of Warwick, Hugh Despenser and 400 men-at-arms to attack Nantes. They broke the Loire bridge, invested the city on the northern side and spread terror through the Nantais. In mid-December, yet another flying column commanded by the Earl of Salisbury appeared in the far north-east corner of Brittany, where neither the English nor even the Montfortists had yet penetrated. Here they burned the suburbs of Dinan and the villages around Dol and briefly threatened Pontorson and Mont-Saint-Michel. Not all of these raids achieved anything of strategic significance, but the effect on the morale of the French was shattering. There was a steady stream of desertions of Breton notables to the Montfortist cause.

The main weakness of the English was the small size of their army. Edward had at this stage less than 5,000 English troops. Some of the Welsh forces under his command had agreed to serve for fixed periods. Four hundred of them withdrew on 17 December 1342. There was a contingent of Breton lords, said by French spies to be large, but of uncertain quality. The shortage of infantry and archers, which could only come from England, was acute, and once the French entered the field, which they had so far conspicuously failed to do, the deficiency would be sorely felt. A fresh army, commanded by the earls of Gloucester and Pembroke, had been due to leave England for some weeks from Plymouth and Dartmouth but had failed to arrive. The reasons were the usual ones. By 3 November, the date finally fixed for their departure, only fifty-six ships had been found for them, enough to take only 600 men to Brittany. Even they got no further than the Scilly Isles. They were driven ashore there by Atlantic gales and in December had to be brought back to Falmouth and Lostwithiel to wait for another passage. The rest, some 800 strong, waited at Plymouth until February, when they were sent home. Only the two earls and their personal retinues reached Brittany. On 14 December 1342 those magnates who remained in England gathered in a sombre mood in London and resolved that it was impractical to send any further reinforcements overseas in mid-winter. Instead the earls of Arundel and Huntingdon undertook to sail with a new army of 6,000 men, four-fifths of them Welshmen, on the earliest realistic date, which they fixed, perhaps too optimistically, for 1 March 1343. That was likely to be too late.[70]

The French were operating on internal lines and overland, but their logistical difficulties should not be under-estimated. Winter mud is a formidable enemy to the movement of armies and feeding them required organization on an enormous scale. Uncertainty about Edward III's destination and perhaps a lingering hope that he would give up altogether made advance preparations difficult. A fresh army had to be mustered from scratch when the news of Edward's landing reached the French court at the beginning of November 1342. Its supplies had to be collected at a forward base at Angers. In spite of the catastrophes which were occurring in Brittany it proved impossible for the French army to march before 14 December 1342. The command as on previous occasions was given to the Duke of Normandy. The size of the force at his disposal cannot even be guessed but it was undoubtedly much stronger than the Anglo-Breton army.[71]

The campaign was short and unglamorous and it ended in a sudden compromise. John of Normandy entered Nantes around Christmas just in time to prevent a faction of the citizens from surrendering it to the Earl of Warwick. Eighteen men of Nantes were arrested and summarily put to death to teach constancy to a city which wanted above all to be left alone. Warwick's men were forced to make off rapidly towards the main army around Vannes. In January 1343 the French marched up the inland road recapturing successively Rédon, Malestroit and Ploermel. At Ploermel they stopped. About 18 miles of woodland and marsh now separated the two armies. But for the third time in just over three years they avoided battle.

The two cardinals whom Edward III had rebuffed in the summer had been watching events from Avranches, the cathedral city on the march of Brittany and Normandy. The English King sensed the weakness of his position well enough to find time for them now. They were allowed to enter the duchy and to approach as close to Edward's army as Malestroit. They were probably there when the French retook the place from the English some time after 10 January 1343. During the second and third weeks of January their staff carried proposals and counter-proposals between the French and English armies and the court of Philip VI which was installed at Rédon. Edward was careful to hide his weaknesses. The papal officials, whom he suspected of being on the side of the French, were never allowed to come within sight of his army. On the 19th a truce was concluded in the priory church of St Mary Magdalene at Malestroit. The terms were astonishingly favourable to the King of England. They did not give him Vannes. That was placed in the hands of the papacy as stake-holder for the duration of the truce. Moreover, it was agreed that the cardinals would deliver the place to Philip's officers when the truce expired. But the rest of Brittany was to remain in the hands of its present possessors. In most of the south and west, this meant Edward III and his friends. Not only the English King's territorial gains but the allegiances which he had found among Philip VI's subjects were to be left untouched. John de Montfort himself was to be released from the Louvre, where he was still languishing. In Flanders, Gascony and Scotland the two kings were to hold their present positions.[72] At Casseneuil on the Lot, the great French host which had gathered to recapture the place turned away and dispersed.

The truce was intended to last until 29 September 1346. Its avowed object was to enable both governments to send their plenipotentiaries to

Avignon to negotiate a permanent peace under the auspices of the Pope. There was a measure of unreality about this. Edward III did not intend to make any permanent peace except perhaps on terms which the French government did not intend to offer him. The truce was an expedient judged by both sides on its immediate advantages. In public both of them expressed entire satisfaction. Writing to the King of Aragon two days after it was signed, Philip VI announced that the English had retreated wherever a French army had approached. Edward had 'gone away, to our infinite credit, without conquering anything of ours'. For his part, Edward described it as 'an honourable truce creditable to himself and his allies'. It is, on the face of it, easier to understand Edward's attitude than Philip's.[73]

Edward III's main losses were in Scotland. Ever since David Bruce had returned to his kingdom in June 1341, he had been anxious to prove himself as a king, and to prove the value of his alliance to the French. He had mounted a savage raid on Northumberland in February 1342 while Edward was negotiating with Amaury de Clisson. Roxburgh, one of the principal border fortresses of the English, was captured at the end of March 1342 by a band of soldiers who set their ladders against the wall at dawn and fell on the garrison without warning. Stirling, the last English stronghold north of the march, surrendered a few days later after a long siege, as the English government struggled to collect the men and ships to invade Brittany. In the interests of the main object Edward had to allow these losses to pass, and the truce consolidated them. Edward was bored with Scotland, 'half in a melancholy', as Sir Thomas Gray had described him when he had wintered in the north the year before.[74]

The losses of Philip VI were much more serious. In the first place the truce confirmed that Flanders was to remain, as it had effectively been for three years, a province outside the French political community, recognizing a sovereign who was France's principal enemy. At the end of November 1342, at the height of the Breton campaign, the Flemings had assembled at Damme to make a solemn reaffirmation of their alliance with the English King.[75] The loyalty of van Artevelde and his friends was rewarded by the terms of the truce, which acknowledged their practical control of the province. The Count of Flanders was not to return there without the leave of his subjects. His supporters among the exiled Flemish noblemen in France were not to return at all.

Brittany was now added to the regions of France where Edward III could claim to be king, but with the important difference that whereas he had never exercised direct administrative control in Flanders he did so in those parts of Brittany which the Montfortists occupied: the far west, the south coast to the outskirts of Vannes, and the Guérande peninsula west of Nantes. John de Montfort, in spite of the French King's promise at Malestroit, remained in prison in the Louvre. The Countess of Montfort, whose courage had kept her husband's cause alive, returned to England with Edward III. Shortly afterwards she went mad. In October 1343 she was taken with all her personal possessions to the grim Norman castle of Tickhill in southern Yorkshire. She survived for more than thirty years, but took no further part in events. Her infant children were lodged in the Tower of London, where a small household was created for them under the charge of a royal clerk.[76] In Brittany a hybrid administration gradually took shape in the course of 1343, which was controlled partly by English officials and partly by a changing group of Breton noblemen. The Earl of Northampton, Edward's lieutenant in the duchy, left for England in the spring of 1343 not long after his master. He was replaced by the first of a series of resident lieutenants, John Hardeshull, an elderly English knight who, like others after him, held office jointly with one or sometimes two Breton noblemen. Hardeshull disposed of a small force of English garrison troops which was regularly supplied and occasionally reinforced with fresh drafts of contract soldiers from England. There was also, at least during the first two years, a small naval squadron of four ships furnished by the city of Bayonne and stationed more or less continuously off the south coast of the duchy. In the extreme west of the duchy, strategically much the most important region for their purposes, the English created a separate military governorship for the Captain of Brest. This officer was virtually independent of the King's lieutenant in the duchy and administered his territory as an appendage of England with no pretence of doing so for the Duke's account. The first Captain, John Gatesden, was appointed in December 1343 and exercised direct authority over Brest and Saint-Mathieu and the whole viscounty of Léon together with the offshore islands. Brest grew under the impact of England's Atlantic strategy from a minor fishing port into a great fortress town with a substantial population, the last redoubt of the English in Brittany which remained in their possession for more than thirty years after the Breton civil war had ended.[77]

The cost of all this was met as far as it could be from the resources of Brittany. The English brought over a royal clerk by the name of Coupegorge, who may have been a Breton by origin. Duke John III had previously employed him to run his estates in England. This man was appointed receiver-general of Brittany. He conducted the financial operations of the Breton administration in the Duke's name but on instructions which came to him from England. The lucrative sale of *brefs de la mer*, which exempted the holder from the Duke's right to seize wrecks washed up on his shores, was taken over by the English King's officials. Purveyance was taken in Breton towns and forced loans collected there. Taxation was imposed fairly summarily on movable property. The money raised was minted into coins which revealed their origins by designs borrowed from England and Gascony.[78]

Men like Hardeshull and Gatesden held difficult and responsible offices which were nevertheless too minor for the great noblemen who traditionally commanded armies. They represented a new kind of soldier: a career professional, generally of modest origin, serving for long terms for pay and the profits of war, and sometimes for fame. They behaved for reasons of cupidity as well as policy very much as the twentieth century would expect the soldiers of an army of occupation to behave, and their government was frequently characterized by 'outrageous theft and extortion, maladministration and greed': the words belonged to one of Edward III's later lieutenants.[79] As the war became more complicated, more permanent, and more widely dispersed across the provinces of France its conduct fell increasingly to their like.

CHAPTER XII

The Truce of Malestroit
1343–1345

Philip VI and his ministers had not anticipated the permanence of the English occupation of south and west Brittany, nor the high degree of organization which would be brought to bear on the business of maintaining it. They believed (as Philip once said to the King of Aragon) that once Edward III was prevented from carrying on the fight he would simply go away with all his men, as he had done in 1340, leaving the fate of Brittany to be determined by political manoeuvre. That was a contest in which the French Crown, close at hand and armed with great resources of force and patronage, could hardly fail. It was a grave misjudgement. Another, equally serious, was connected with it. When Philip told the Aragonese King that Edward had conquered nothing of 'ours', he seemed to be looking upon the Breton duchy as if it were an island unconnected with his kingdom. In fact, it proved quite impossible to contain the turmoil of the Breton civil war within the confines of the duchy. The French King's advisers did not appreciate how many Bretons had come into Edward III's allegiance during his victorious sweep through the duchy even in regions which he did not conquer by force of arms. They did not know how influential some of them were outside Brittany. They were quite ignorant of how costly it would be in political terms to give these men an amnesty for the duration of the truce.

The most significant of the defectors was Olivier de Clisson, a man who certainly belonged as much to France as to Brittany. He was the head of the principal noble house of north-western Poitou. The enormous castles at Clisson and Montaigu, which still stand over the road from Poitiers to Nantes, are visible evidence of his family's wealth and strength. His income, drawn not only from his Breton barony but from estates throughout western France from the iron mines of southern Normandy to the outskirts of La Rochelle, was estimated at 20,000 *l.t.* per annum, a very substantial fortune. Olivier de Clisson's motives for deserting the French royal house are difficult to divine. A man with stronger connections with the court could hardly have been found in Brittany. He had fought with

Philip VI in Italy before his accession and received knighthood at his hands when both of them were much younger. He had fought for Philip in Gascony. Indeed, although other members of his family, particularly his younger brother Amaury, were prominent Montfortists, he had fought in the King's army in Brittany in the winter of 1341–2.[1]

Nevertheless, in November 1342 when Edward III was outside Vannes, Olivier made a secret alliance with him which seems to have included an acknowledgement of his title to the crown of France. He brought with him into Edward's allegiance most of his great network of clients, protégés and friends. Substantially the whole baronage of north-western Poitou joined him, including Girard Chabot, lord of Retz, and his kinsman Girard de Machecoul, lord of La Bénaste. These two young men possessed most of the territory south of the Loire and west of Nantes, including a line of castles along the march of France and southern Brittany. They too were men belonging as much to the kingdom as to the duchy. The lord of Retz was a son-in-law of one of Philip's Marshals. Yet when the earls of Northampton and Warwick launched their exploratory raid on the Nantes region in December 1342 all of these lords and their numerous vassals crossed the Loire and joined forces with them. As far away as La Rochelle the garrison commander, who was a client of Olivier's, tried to deliver up his town to the English before he was discovered. Olivier de Clisson's wife, another of the formidable warlike women of this period of the war, conducted an independent campaign of banditry in Poitou and off the coast. The strategic importance of these events was not lost on Edward III. As he pointed out to his son, Poitou joined Brittany with Aquitaine.[2]

Godfrey of Harcourt was a traitor of smaller substance but with a longer and more destructive future. He was the lord of Saint-Sauveur-le-Vicomte, a lordship of middling importance in the Cotentin peninsula of southern Normandy, who embarked upon a brief and unsuccessful war against the French Crown at the beginning of 1343.[3] It was his own war, not Edward III's, born of his own rancours and ambitions, in that sense quite different from that of Olivier de Clisson. But it showed how easily the King of England, once he had occupied part of France, could be perceived as an alternative government, a stimulus to rebellion and, after rebellion, to continued obduracy. The immediate reason for Godfrey's rebellion was characteristically personal: a dispute with Robert Bertrand, lord of Bricquebec, about the marriage of a local heiress. The quarrel had reached such a pitch of venom by 1341 that both men were summoning their retainers to do battle, 'a thing neither honourable nor proper at a time when we are ourselves at war', as Philip said in forbidding them to fight each other. In September 1342, when they met at court, swords were drawn in the King's presence. This offence against the royal dignity resulted in both brawlers being summoned before the Parlement. Godfrey refused to appear. Instead, he began to make warlike preparations in his domains in southern Normandy. During the winter campaign in Brittany spies set to watch the castle of Saint-Sauveur reported the accumulation of weapons and the gathering of allies. Not all of the allies were Godfrey's retainers and dependants: some of them were influential members of the Norman nobility with their own resentments and ambitions.

Shortly after the truce of Malestroit, too late to combine his movements with those of Edward III, Godfrey of Harcourt gathered his supporters in a forest near Mortain and led them out on a campaign of destruction against the property of the Bishop of Bayeux. The Bishop was Robert Bertrand's brother. Two of his manors were attacked. One of them was demolished. The government reacted with vigour. The castle of Saint-Sauveur, which was defended in Godfrey's name by one of his confederates, was besieged and when it was taken was razed to the ground. The rebellion was completely suppressed in the course of March 1343. Godfrey himself fled to Brabant.

The treasons of 1343 were startling signs of the internal divisions of western France and the declining prestige of the Crown there. Philip VI, always sensitive to the threat of betrayal, reacted savagely. In July Olivier de Clisson was unwise enough to attend a tournament in Paris. He cannot possibly have imagined that the King was ignorant of his doings; he must have been relying on the amnesty promised at Malestroit. However, he was arrested and charged with his dealings with Edward III. He admitted them, and on 2 August 1343 was executed in Paris. The government went to great lengths to make a spectacle of his death. He was drawn on a hurdle to Les Halles and beheaded in the market place. His head was sent to Nantes to be impaled above the main gate. His wife, who had been summoned to answer for her own offences, absconded and was sentenced in her absence to be banished from the realm. Clisson's great wealth was confiscated by the King.[4]

The government's attitude to the activities of Godfrey of Harcourt was initially rather mild. The incident was treated as a police operation on a large scale but no more sinister conclusions were drawn from it. Godfrey himself was convicted in his absence of lèse-majesté and was banished with the loss of all his property. Most of his followers were quite quickly released from custody and some of them even recovered their lands. However, the affair acquired a more portentous significance in Philip's mind in the autumn of 1343 and the early part of 1344 as the result of persistent rumours that Godfrey had concerted his rebellion with the English. According to reports he had recognized Edward III as King of France in return for a promise that he would become duke of Normandy in place of Philip's eldest son. The reports were probably untrue. But they appeared to be confirmed when early in 1344 three Normans who had been confederates of Godfrey's were captured fighting for the English in Brittany. These men received no mercy. They were condemned by royal warrant in April 1344 and were beheaded at Les Halles as soon as the warrant reached Paris. Their bodies were hung on the gibbet of Mont-faucon and their heads taken back to the Cotentin to be displayed in the market place of Saint-Lô.[5]

The rebels of the Cotentin were not great lords in the mould of Olivier de Clisson, but some of them were men of substance on a provincial scale. The King, it was reported,

was greatly disturbed by the revelation of so much treason about him, the treasons of so many men, so widely spread about the provinces of his kingdom. The duchies of Brittany and Normandy seemed to him to be seething with rebels, led by the very noblemen who had promised to serve him till his dying day. He was shocked and puzzled. He even summoned an assembly of the nobility of the realm to consider what could be done about the evil, and how the rancours dividing his kingdom could be calmed.

Whatever advice this assembly may have given has not been recorded, but the fact that Philip decided to consult a wider body of opinion is sufficiently revealing. Moreover, after the assembly had dispersed he took some cautious steps towards a more open style of government, abandoning for example the use of his secret seal to authenticate acts of state. But Philip's circle of trusted advisers remained very narrow, a fact which others noticed and resented. Even from his isolated position Philip must have known what people were saying. Ever since the middle of the 1330s power had been unduly concentrated in the hands of a few relatives and officials, the principal of whom were Mile de Noyers, an exceedingly tough old man; the King's brother-in-law Odo, Duke of Burgundy; Jean de Marigny, Bishop of Beauvais, Philip's able and long-standing representative in the south-west; and the princes of the blood, the Duke of Bourbon (until his death in February 1342), the King of Navarre and the heir to the throne, John, Duke of Normandy. 'The King's secret council' is a phrase which appears for the first time in 1342, and it is apt. There was also the lame and venomous Queen, who was particularly close to her husband

and whose severe views were believed to carry much weight. 'A vindictive woman, laden with hatred', Froissart called her. The King's circle was not popular.[6]

Two things counted more than anything else against these men in the eyes of the French nobility. The first was their conduct of the war, which was thought to be pusillanimous and discreditable. This was unfair to men who thought carefully and intelligently about strategy and had countered Edward III's diplomatic offensives with some skill. But their achievements were less evident than the fact that the King had faced his adversary three times across a battlefield and fought no battle. The second grievance was a more complicated matter, the mounting financial difficulties of the aristocracy, originating in the agricultural depression and aggravated by factors which could fairly be laid at the government's door. Noblemen did not entirely escape taxation even if they fought as well. They suffered more than anyone from the manipulation of the coinage. They paid sales taxes like everyone else. In 1340 they had been assessed in many parts of France to a capital levy of 2 per cent. The war wages earned by French knights, although generous by European standards, would have done no more than cover their out-of-pocket expenses even if they had been paid promptly and in full, which inevitably they were not. Thrift was not an aristocratic virtue in war any more than it was in peace. It may be that Raoul de Brienne, Count of Eu and Constable of France, did not need to spend a fortune on cutting a fine figure at the wedding of Philip's Chancellor, but given the scale of the war and the office and rank of the man, most of his prodigious expenditure in the 1330s and 1340s was unavoidable: the payment of a great retinue, the maintenance of a huge stable of warhorses, the heavy cost of constant travelling with his entire household, for much of which he was reimbursed very late or not at all. In spite of handsome stipends, gifts and allowances from the Crown his debts swamped his assets and he died bankrupt in 1344. The Count of Eu was an extreme case but his problems were experienced on a smaller scale by almost all the military aristocracy. They sold large parts of their land, which was generally broken up into small parcels or passed to ecclesiastical corporations or lawyers and civil servants whose prosperity seemed undiminished. They mortgaged what was left to secure loans contracted from usurers at ruinous rates of interest well above the legal maximum of 21 per cent. The scale on which the nobility was selling land in the early 1340s was so great that buyers were troubled by the possibility that they might be made to restore their purchases after the peace. The King's private secretary, who was a busy purchaser of land and knew Philip's mind if anyone did, took the precaution of obtaining royal letters against the day when 'the King or his successors may graciously permit the nobles of his realm to recover their heritages and possessions sold to commoners on account of the burden of our wars, paying nothing more than the purchase money they received'.[7]

These two grievances were intimately connected. The lacklustre performance of French commanders and the defensive instincts of the King deprived the troops of most of the traditional means of making war profitable. Louis of Spain, when he was serving as admiral off the Breton coast in 1342, exacted large sums in protection money from merchant shipping. Somebody (it is not clear who) must have done well by the capture of the earls of Salisbury and Suffolk. The Constable did extremely well out of the spoil of Bourg and Blaye. But these were rare opportunities. The war was fought on French soil which could not be plundered. Apart from Bourg and Blaye, no significant towns were stormed by French troops. Without battles there were few opportunities to take prisoners for ransom.[8]

Thirty years before, the chronicler Godfrey of Paris had described the disappointment and anger of noblemen who had mortgaged their land to buy warhorses for the Flemish campaign of 1314 and had then been turned back by a shabby peace:

> Gentils homs deceuz en furent
> Qui chièrement les chevaux eurent
> Dont lor terre orent engagé.[9]

The King of France cannot have forgotten that it was the same combination of economic sacrifice and avoidance of battle which had provoked the nobility of his father's generation to the most dangerous rebellion of recent times.

In these conditions the patronage of the government assumed growing importance as the means of buying loyalty and bridging the gap between the mounting expenditure of the aristocracy and their shrinking incomes. Philip was sensitive to this. He made generous grants to his friends and followers. The citations which explained them in his charters speak for themselves: to this man a pension to enable him to maintain his noble status; to that one a contribution to his ransom; to the other a gift to help him replace his captured equipment. The Crown, however, did not have the resources to relieve all of them of financial pressures, which its own treasury was experiencing also. Its largesse inevitably seemed capricious to outsiders, the contrast between those who had the King's ear and those who did not unforgivable. The consequences of this state of affairs were felt far beyond the court. A grant of conquered or confiscated property, a profitable public office, permission to hold a market or charge tolls, a valuable wardship, an exemption from this or that species of taxation or from encroachment on a seigneurial jurisdiction: all these boons could make the difference between prosperity and relative penury. Competition for them was intense, and in the provincial communities of France the hazards of royal favour mattered very much.

In the Cotentin the Bertrand family had once competed on more or less equal terms with the Harcourts and the Taissons for influence and wealth. By the beginning of the 1340s a respectable but not particularly distinguished career in royal service had enabled Robert Bertrand to eclipse his rivals altogether. They enjoyed incomes in 1343 estimated at 3,000 *l.t.* per annum apiece, a reasonable sum but certainly not equal to their pretensions. Robert's income from royal grants alone must have substantially exceeded it. There were generous stipends, valuable markets at Honfleur and Magneville, extremely lucrative privileges in the heavily protected timber forests and, perhaps, an heiress for his second son, all the fruits of royal favour. In addition to the grants which brought him income there was the patronage of his office, the capacity to procure privileges for his friends, and the status derived from his captaincy of the nearby coasts and the lordship of the newly conquered Channel Islands. If Bertrand had not been a Marshal, it is unlikely that his brother would have become bishop of Bayeux, one of the richest sees of Normandy, in 1338. The sudden distortion of the local balance of power was probably the main cause of Godfrey of Harcourt's rebellion and the reason why the Bertrand family was its principal target. The head of the house of Taisson joined him. Yet Robert Bertrand was very far from being the most favoured of Philip's servants.[10]

Normandy also illustrated in an extreme degree the political problems of high taxation which must have mattered even more to Godfrey's followers than the rise of an upstart Marshal. Like other provinces of France Normandy had enjoyed a tax holiday for several years before the outbreak of the war, which made heavy taxation the more intolerable now. Norman opinion of the next generation regarded Harcourt's civil war as a rebellion against tax and devaluation. Yet this was a rich agricultural province. It was also an autonomous duchy belonging to the King's heir, with a strong representative assembly and formidable charters of privilege. Other provinces, particularly those in the north and centre, fared worse.[11]

The benefit to the Crown was increasingly disappointing. The government's receipts from taxes touched a peak in 1340 before declining steadily in the face of growing resistance. It was just possible, in 1341 and 1342, to generate a sense of national peril which brought in some money, but as the news of the truce of Malestroit spread through the country the flow almost entirely ceased. The sales tax of four pennies in the pound became difficult and in some places impossible to collect. Philip's commissioners tried hard to persuade individual magnates to go on paying it in their domains, but only those closest to the royal family agreed. Many of the grants which had been painfully negotiated with the local communities had to be formally cancelled; others were simply not paid. The process of piecemeal negotiation of taxes was proving disastrously inappropriate in wartime conditions. Alternative schemes, less affected by local particularism, could have been imposed only by a stronger government enjoying greater prestige than Philip's did. It was another unfortunate consequence of the stalemates on the battlefields. Some attempts were made. But they increased the government's unpopularity out of all proportion to the gain in revenue.[12]

In August 1343 the Estates-General of the whole kingdom met in Paris to consider what had by then become a grave financial crisis. The proposal which was put to them was politically shrewd. It involved a promise to abandon the policy of devaluations, which was now bringing little benefit to the Crown, and to restore the legendary coinage of St Louis. In return the government was to be permitted to continue levying the sales taxes of 1340 and 1342 notwithstanding that the war had given way to truce, an important concession of principle and a departure from past prejudices. The government was also permitted to extend these useful taxes to the south, which had traditionally preferred hearth taxes. All this was agreed subject to the confirmation of each local community. The confirmation was almost everywhere obtained. It was a considerable political achievement.[13] Yet the actual results were wretched. The revaluation of the coinage involved a reduction of the nominal value of silver by three-quarters and a very severe deflation. It was carried out all at once in October 1343. Prices fell, but not as far or as fast as they should have done. In spite of the notional appeal of the coinage of St Louis, the revaluations of 1343 proved to be as unpopular as the devaluations of earlier years had been. The government could do nothing right. As for the sales taxes, their effect on the royal finances seems to have been short-lived. The harvest was bad in 1343. Individual tax-payers proved more resistant than their representatives. The revaluation made them feel poor as well as resentful. In 1343 the Crown was once more resorting to a miscellany of sharp financial expedients to raise meagre sums of money.[14]

Although the financial crisis led to anxious reviews of garrison strengths and naval establishments,[15] its impact on the defence of the country was for some time masked by the fact that the same symptoms of exhaustion affected England. Chronic devaluation of the coinage was not, admittedly, a failing of English royal policy, but the overvaluation of the English coinage and the manipulation of the wool trade had been almost as damaging and the burden of taxation relatively greater. England needed time for recovery as much for political as for financial reasons. The Parliamentary wool subsidies voted in 1340 and 1341 continued to be collected until 1342, but there followed a two-year period during which the King avoided asking for any conventional war taxation. This was realism, not largesse. What was available went to pay off those of the King's debts which it was impolitic to repudiate. The Italian bankers recovered a small proportion of their loans; Pole, because he was indispensable, rather more over the years; for diplomatic reasons the German and Flemish bankers and the more important princes of the Low Countries enjoyed priority and received most of what was due to them in the course of 1344 and 1345. Symbolic moments marked the stages of this long process. The Hanse bankers surrendered control of the customs in June 1343; the Great Crown, pawned for an improvident loan in 1339, returned to England in 1344 and was finally redeemed in the following year. None of this, however, restored the King's credit to the point where he could contract fresh bank loans; and it left very little over for fresh war-making. The Breton campaign of 1342 had been relatively short and cheap, the first of the rapid spoiling raids in force which were to become a hallmark of English strategy. It had cost less than £40,000, which was excellent value by comparison with the prodigiously costly and unsuccessful campaigns of 1339 and 1340. But even so it was the equivalent of more than a standard Parliamentary subsidy and in the end it had to be found from the English treasury rather than the Breton duchy. No provision had been made for it. Some of the nobility who brought their retinues to the army had been paid by assignments from the wool subsidies. Others were obliged to serve on long-term credit. For the time being, further adventures of this kind were out of the question.[16]

Exhaustion, therefore, rather than goodwill, preserved a semblance of peace between January 1343 and June 1345, two and a half years in which no major campaign took place. But it was a tense, unstable peace. There were periodic alarms about real or imagined threats of invasion, more often, now, in France than in England. Reports that Edward III's personal standard had been seen flying from a vessel lying off Calais could still produce panic at the French King's court and a scramble to find soldiers to guard the coast.[17] The south-west lapsed into banditry almost as destructive as public war. In Brittany, in spite of the truce, fighting continued between the partisans of Montfort and Blois almost without interruption, warfare on a miniature scale but persistent enough to keep political hatreds alive.

Gascony had problems peculiar to itself. Distance and ignorance, and the absence of any source of objective advice, were serious obstacles in the way of the English government's efforts to understand them. Ever since the King's return from the continent at the end of 1340 he had been deluged with petitions from damaged towns, dispossessed landowners, unpaid soldiers and disappointed men with grudges and unfulfilled ambitions. Some of them arrived in England to bend his ear in person. The King's great tournament at Langley in February 1341, the first after his return, had been crowded out with Gascon noblemen, many of whom had large unpaid arrears of war wages, demands for favours and projects for the renascence of English power in the south-west. Privately Edward's councillors found these men very tiresome. Nevertheless, the jaundiced opinions of Gascons at the English court were probably the government's main source of information and advice about the duchy's affairs.[18]

Oliver Ingham was old and ill and increasingly difficult to deal with. He had refused to come to England at the beginning of 1341, when the Council wanted to carry out a general review of the affairs of the duchy. The lord of Albret, who was still Edward's lieutenant there, came to England a few months later and stayed for more than a year. But he was regarded, quite correctly, as an ambitious self-seeker. The government did not trust him. At a Council meeting devoted to Gascon affairs in December 1341 Bernard-Aiz painted a sombre picture of the state of the duchy and promised to do great things if he was paid enough. But the Council declined to endorse his plans. Their main conclusion was that it was essential to bring Ingham to England as soon as possible.[19] Ingham paid a short visit to England in 1342, but at a difficult moment when the Breton crisis was at its height and the King's attention and resources were engaged on other matters. Some kind of stocktaking evidently did occur. But the results were poor, and whatever resolutions were made had not, in the opinion of the Council, been carried out a year later. The result was that Edward III finally parted company with his long-standing Seneschal. In

April 1343 Ingham received an extremely peremptory summons to return to England. He sent the Constable, Niccolo Usomare, in his place with the familiar story: the whole income of the duchy had been assigned to past creditors or spent on wages of war, and the coffers were empty. The Council was incredulous. Weston, the treasurer of the Gascon army, was called from Bordeaux to explain himself. When he arrived, early in July 1343, he brought with him one of Ingham's clerks, bearing another gloomy report and asking for instructions. On 20 July Ingham was removed from office. He was dead within six months. At Ingham Priory in Norfolk, the remains can still be seen of the stone tomb and effigy of this great but unremembered servant of the English monarchy whose work made possible the more famous deeds of Henry of Lancaster and the Black Prince.[20]

It was time for Ingham to go, but the reasons for his going suggest that the English government had still not grasped that the problem was insufficiency of resources rather than maladministration. It was a remarkable fact that although the duchy had been attacked by French armies up to 20,000 strong, hardly any English troops had yet served there except for the small number brought by John of Norwich in 1337. The proposed expedition of 1338 had been diverted to the Low Countries. The proposed expedition of 1342 had been diverted to Brittany.

The English government was only marginally more generous with financial assistance to its penurious officials in Bordeaux. Bernard-Aiz of Albret, whose services were indispensable and who may have threatened to withdraw them, presented claims amounting to £21,725 8s. 1d. sterling and 600 écus. He received huge sums in 1341 and 1342: an assignment worth more than £8,000 from the English Parliamentary subsidy and a promise of the rest from the English treasury in due course. The effect of these transactions was that in spite of the parlous state of the English revenues they were used to pay most if not all of the cost of the campaign of 1340 in Gascony, which Bernard-Aiz had financed in the first instance out of his own pocket. This was still regarded in England as an unavoidable exception to the policy of making Gascony sustain its own war effort. But it became less exceptional. In June 1344 another large sum, 100,000 pounds of Bordeaux (£20,000), had to be found to pay arrears of war wages, some of which dated back to 1336. The money was borrowed from an Italian banking firm on the security of the profits of the English mint. In addition to these payments, which were usually the result of one of the periodic crises in the government's relations with the Gascon nobility, there were more frequent deliveries of smaller sums for special purposes which the King could not bear to see neglected by his agents in Bordeaux: a subsidy for Ingham's campaign of autumn 1342; another for the defence of Bourg when it became apparent that the Constable of Bordeaux could not afford properly to garrison or victual the place.[21]

The removal of the Seneschal in July 1343 was followed within a few weeks by the death of the Constable, an opportunity to remake the administration in Bordeaux which was largely wasted. The new Seneschal was Nicholas Beche, a household official of the Prince of Wales. John Walwain, an ancient Exchequer official who had briefly been Treasurer of England under Edward II, became Constable. John Shoreditch, who had been the government's principal legal and diplomatic adviser on the affairs of Gascony during the 1330s, was called out of retirement to become the senior judge of appeals. None of these men, except possibly the last, was outstanding or knew much about Gascony; none of them had a status or reputation which commanded loyalty; none of them was in the King's inner confidence. The appointments had a provisional look about them. It may have been intended that the role of royal lieutenant would be resumed by Hugh of Geneva, but even he was no more than an august mercenary.[22]

Beche was at least astute enough to perceive some of the main administrative problems, although not to make any very significant contribution to solving them. His proposals included a general investigation of grant-holders and the revocation of those grants which had not obviously been earned; the cancellation of all royal letters requiring the payment of privileged debtors in undevalued coin; the suppression of the countless petty frauds by which men boosted their war wages or obtained excessive compensation for property conquered by the French. His most radical suggestion was an ambitious scheme to levy a sales tax in all the major market towns of the duchy at the very high rate of a shilling in the pound, which was three times the rate paid in the towns of northern France. The Council agreed to all of this. Presumably some attempt was made to put it into effect, but if so it failed. Most of the administrative vices which Beche had diagnosed remained as problems for his successors. There is no trace of any systematic re-examination of past grants. The sales tax seems at some stage to have been quietly abandoned.[23]

Beche entirely failed to restore civil peace to the duchy. Private war, a long-standing privilege of the Gascon nobility, continued to destroy whole regions and to divide and weaken Edward III's allies. It seems likely that Guilhem-Raymond, lord of Caumont, who had been one of the leading lights of the English campaign of 1340 but defected to the French two years later, did so as a result of becoming involved in a private war with the Albrets. He was never reconciled to Edward III. The English government's correspondence with its officials in Gascony during this period is filled with complaints of civil disputes between noblemen and injunctions to reconcile the rivals before one of them deserted to the enemy. In the southern extremity of the Landes and the Bayonnais the last vestiges of central control had disappeared in the early 1340s. Arnaud de Durfort, who had been granted the lordship of Labourde for its better defence against the French and Navarrese, conducted a private feud against the Albret clan here throughout this period, and both groups waged a persistent guerrilla war against the citizens of Bayonne. Edward III initially sent the Chief Justice of the Gascon court of appeals (Shoreditch's predecessor) to restore order and then attempted to enforce his will by confiscating Labourde. These measures were entirely ineffective. Arnaud reoccupied his lands with 'slaughter, mayhem and destruction'. The merchants of Bayonne continued to be attacked and plundered on the roads and waterways about the city. Stone towers appeared throughout the area and robbers made their camps around them. In the two years ending September 1343 the ducal revenues of the Bayonnais yielded nothing. On account of the anarchy prevailing there, the clerk recorded in his ledger, it was 'quasi tota destructa'. It was an extreme but not a unique case. Nicholas Beche went about in these days with an escort of forty men-at-arms, which was twice the number that his predecessor had required. There was no point in blaming him for these difficulties. His job called for greater authority than any mere administrator could possess.[24]

Beche's most significant contribution to the well-being of the duchy was to enforce the truce of Malestroit a great deal more effectively than his more bellicose and conspiratorial predecessor had enforced the truce of Esplechin. There was a good deal of semi-official banditry on the march of Gascony in Beche's time but no campaign was fought there between February 1343 and June 1345. This respite of nearly two and a half years from major war expenditure had become essential to the recovery of the duchy's administration and must have enabled at least a part of the arrears of war wages to be cleared. No one, however, can have imagined that the truce had long to run or that the war, when it was resumed, could be fought again as the English had fought it before. When the curtain of defensive fortresses was so thin, a policy of static local defence was bound to fail at some point. The walls of Gascon towns and castles needed a programme of repairs extending over longer than the English were likely to be given, at a cost far greater than they could afford. Attack was now the only means of defence, and conquest was the only means of paying for it. The loyalty of the Gascon nobility was being bought by large grants of territory yet to be reconquered from Philip VI. These promises could not be indefinitely postponed. By 1345 a great offensive in the south-west led by the King or someone who could convincingly represent him had become a condition of the duchy's survival.

The English were naturally better acquainted with their own problems than with those of Philip VI. It became apparent, however, that the difficulties of the French government in the south-west were even greater. The performance of French armies there in the early 1340s had been most unimpressive in spite of their superiority of numbers. Neither the Count of Valentinois' campaign of 1341 nor the Bishop of Beauvais' in 1342 had done more than recapture a few of the places which the English had snatched in breach of the truce. The financial crisis of the French Crown bore particularly heavily on the administration in the south. The sales tax, which was still being fitfully collected in the main towns of the north, did not exist in Languedoc, and the refusal of the southern tax-payers to go on paying hearth taxes in time of truce was absolute. The Bishop of Beauvais, who resumed his functions as the King's lieutenant about a month after the truce of Malestroit, was faced almost at once with widespread and some-times violent resistance to his commissioners, which he had no means of suppressing. Between March and May 1343 the Bishop was obliged to cancel the collection of taxes in one district after another. Apart from the taxes agreed by the Estates-General of August 1343, the Crown levied no taxes in the south in the years 1343, 1344 and 1345.[25]

The symptoms of a crisis of loyalty and a grave breakdown of public order became very noticeable from the end of 1342 as economic distress intensified and demobilized soldiers began to pour across Languedoc. In some cases the source of the disorder was the old phenomenon of private war, but fought on a larger scale and with more venomous persistence. The men who laid waste the Albigeois in 1345 did so with banners unfurled, trumpets blowing and 400 cavalry. In the march of Gascony private war had actually been legalized by the French Crown in time of peace or truce on the basis that these regions had once formed part of the duchy of Aquitaine where custom sanctioned it. The appearance of the first self-governing companies of *routiers* was a more sinister event: large gangs of armed men, organized like military units with a formal structure of command, emblems and names. The Société de la Folie, so called, terrorized the district of Nîmes for some eighteen months until its leader was taken and hanged in June 1344. Like most of his kind he was a member of the minor nobility of the province, the group which had suffered most from the economic troubles of the period. Incidents like these, and there were many of them, dented the prestige of the Crown and diminished its capacity to demand taxes as well as the capacity of the inhabitants to pay them. Moreover, they encouraged the communities of the south-west to think in terms of local not collective defence. Perhaps there was little choice. Agen obtained letters of privilege in 1341 limiting its military obligations to the provision of 200 sergeants for forty days and then only for the defence of the march of Gascony in time of war. Condom negotiated a very similar arrangement. Both towns lay in regions distressed by brigandage and private war.[26]

The collapse of civil order gradually merged with the war. It was too easy for rebellious local lords to transform brigandage into politics and to make their private causes the causes of Edward III in the hope of obtaining his support. Edward's officials had no reason to be selective. In the Agenais this was a problem of long standing. With its rash of seigneurial castles and its continual private wars the province had a tradition of civil violence older than the war and had harboured anglophiles of sentiment or convenience for a long time. The appearance of the same conditions in other provinces where the recollection of English administration was fainter was a more recent development with more serious implications for the future course of the war. Périgord was the province most seriously affected, but it was also a grave problem in the Angoumois and Quercy.

In Périgord the change of sentiment was very striking. Except in the Dordogne valley the English had not enjoyed much influence there even in the heyday of their administration. In the first campaigns of the Hundred Years War the nobility of Périgord had fought almost to a man in the armies of Philip VI. Within the province, however, quarrels of growing intensity divided the nobility in a way which was bound, sooner or later, to offer an opening to the English King's agents. The Talleyrands, counts of Périgord, although still the dominant family of the region, were a declining power. The Rudels, lords of Bergerac and principal potentates of the Dordogne valley, had died out in 1334 in a welter of fighting and private war. Their place was being filled by aggressive and covetous rivals from the neighbouring regions of Aquitaine, pre-eminently the lords of Albret and Caumont, and by a host of turbulent petty lords very similar in their outlook and ambitions to the hill-barons of the Agenais. The Count of Périgord, who was a firm ally of France, was a natural focus for their opposition. The rebellion of some of these men in 1340, which had been largely brought about by the machinations of the Albrets, was a watershed in the province's history, introducing a long period of anarchy and civil

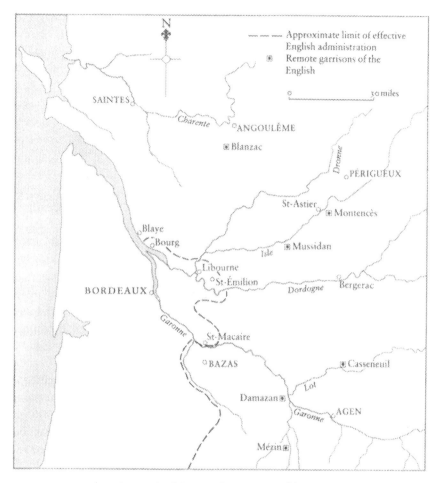

18 The march of Gascony, January 1343–May 1345

war of which the Bordeaux government took full advantage. In August
1340 the English had lodged a garrison at Saint-Astier in the Isle valley
which remained there for a year until the place was taken by storm in the
autumn of 1341. The 'rebels and enemies' who had occupied Montencès in
the name of Edward III at the same time, withstood a siege of more than
six months in the following year and were not dislodged until 1342. Fresh
sores were continually opened. At about the time that the Bishop of
Beauvais was demolishing the towers of Montencès, the English planted
another garrison at Mussidan, with the assistance of its lord, and began to
reconstruct the town's defences. This place remained in English hands for

more than five years. The boundary between banditry and war was never exactly drawn. The French government, however, referred to the provincial capital of Périgueux as a frontier town.[27]

To all these intruders the documentary records and the local population indiscriminately applied the name 'English', a convention followed in this book although almost all of them were in fact Gascons or Béarnais or mercenaries in English pay who came from beyond the Rhône or the Pyrenees. Long terms of garrison service interrupted by guerrilla warfare, armed robbery and cattle-rustling under minor commanders was not a life for the impressed townsmen and minor landowners who traditionally made up the numbers of medieval armies. Instead the fighting fell to volunteers drawn from a growing military underworld of disparaged gentry, refugees and drifters, malcontents and petty criminals. The court records and letters of pardon of the period are filled with the stories of their lives. The tale of Arnaud Foucaud could stand for many of them. He came from the small village of Clion in Saintonge. His family seem to have been rich peasants. He had learned how to fight on horseback and could handle a lance. When Foucaud was about fourteen or fifteen years old he got involved in a village feud and killed one of his antagonists in a fight. This was in 1337, the first year of the war, as the French were overrunning English-occupied Saintonge. When the Seneschal's officers came to arrest him he fled to the nearest 'English' garrison, which was at Montendre, an enclave of the duchy about 15 miles from his home. The commander there, a louche petty nobleman from Béarn, hired him as a soldier. His life at Montendre consisted in keeping watch and periodically pillaging and burning villages. When the castle was captured by the French in July 1338, Foucaud received a safe conduct as part of the terms of capitulation and returned home. In 1340, after two relatively uneventful years, he went to Jonzac, the nearest market town, and met two relatives of the man whom he had killed. There was a fight. Foucaud himself was badly wounded, but both his antagonists were killed. Five weeks after this incident, as he was still nursing his wounds, he was arrested. But he never stood trial. The Seneschal only wanted to be rid of him. So he allowed him to go free on condition that he leave the province for good. Foucaud went to Bordeaux. Here, he took service in the household of Jean Colom, a rich urban knight who employed him as a cavalryman and took him on several expeditions with the army of Oliver Ingham. In June 1341 another soldier in Colom's pay persuaded him to join a small armed band which was being formed for some private purpose of the La Motte family. This turned out to be the daring capture of Bourg, by far the most brazen of the Bordeaux government's breaches of the truce of Esplechin. Foucaud fought gallantly in this enterprise and served in the garrison of the town after it had fallen. But his reward was meagre. His wages were unpaid and his share of the spoils amounted to no more than ten *livres*' worth of equipment. Moreover, he quarrelled with the garrison commander, who suspected him of being a French sympathizer, and tried to extract a confession by torturing him. By 1342 he was back in Bordeaux hiring out his services as a jobbing trooper. He joined a band of 100 men recruited by the lord of Pommiers to carry out long-range raids in Saintonge, but the pillage of this enterprise was worth only fifty *livres* to be divided between all of them. He fought with Ingham's army in the campaign of Saintonge and Angoumois in the autumn of 1342, taking part in the capture of Blanzac, and gaining ten *livres* in cash as his share of the spoil. At some stage during 1343 he seems to have obtained a pardon from the French royal lieutenant in the south, the Bishop of Beauvais. But by the autumn of 1344 he was back in Bordeaux. According to evidence which he gave under torture (and which he tried to retract) he was next hired in Bordeaux by a Béarnais nobleman to take part with twenty-five others in a raid on a small priory not far from the city. He and six men stood guard outside, while the rest went in, tied up the Prior and his servants and stripped the place of gold and silver, horses and everything of value. But the captain of the troop took most of the spoil for himself. Foucaud's share was only twenty florins. This incident was his undoing, for it was not covered by his pardon. It is not clear how he fell into French hands. He probably tried to go home. In May 1345 he was taken to Paris and held in the prison of the Châtelet to answer charges of treason, robbery and murder. He was convicted on the 27th and beheaded in Les Halles on the following day. Foucaud was twenty-three years old when he died. Booty was an incidental bonus for men like him, but it was not booty that drew them to warfare and most of them got very little of it. They were drop-outs, desperados.[28]

Even a small number of these licensed bandits posted as garrison troops in the middle of French-held territory had a catalytic effect in accelerating the breakdown of public order, inciting local men who knew that help was at hand to carry their point from resentment to rebellion. They stole and killed over an extending radius, creating islands of uncultivatable territory and roads too dangerous to pass. No one has described for us what life was like in the neighbourhood of Mussidan after 1342, but it is not hard to imagine. In the spring of 1343 the visitors of the Order of Cluny, touring the provinces of the Order in western France, were able to see very little in the southern parts of Saintonge and Angoumois. Most of the priories there were inaccessible, abandoned or incapable of feeding their occupants. 'They have enough to eat today,' the visitors reported about one of these places, 'but they have no idea whether they will eat tomorrow. The troops and mercenaries stationed hereabouts are eating up the whole wealth of the house.' This was at Montbrun, 15 miles east of Angoulême and some distance from the march of Gascony. The garrison of Blanzac had reduced everything within marching distance to desert. This had been French-occupied territory for more than half a century, but the reputation of the French Crown here must have been low. Populations numbered by fatalism and impotent in the face of successive disasters became indifferent to the political purposes of either side.[29]

At Blanzac, as at Mussidan, the Bordeaux government was directly involved. What was striking, and became even more so as the war continued, was that men were willing to challenge the French Crown in Edward III's name even in provinces which had never even nominally been part of the continental possessions of the English house and were too far from Gascony for there to be any possibility of military assistance. Perhaps they were too optimistic, these barons of a few villages. More probably, like the King of Majorca's squire and like his many imitators in the later years of the fourteenth century, they sensed the value of Edward's arms and war-cries as party labels, less a political statement than a common bond with men of like mind. 'Guyenne! Guyenne!' the hoodlums cried as they invaded the property of their enemies in furtherance of their private vendettas. It would be interesting to know who were the men of the Toulousain, 'noblemen and commoners alike', who spontaneously came to the assistance of Edward's armies in the autumn of 1339; who were the large body of men of 'the English party' who in June 1341 occupied the castle of Belcayre in the heart of the Rouergue 150 miles from Bordeaux; or what lay behind the case of Mende, a small town of the Gévaudan 200 miles from Bordeaux which had to be stormed by French troops in the autumn of the same year. We have only fleeting and incidental references in the fragmentary surviving records of the French provincial administrations to tell us that anything at all happened in places like these.[30]

In the border country closest to Bordeaux, where the war damaged was greatest, and the castles, freebooters and ex-soldiers thickest on the ground, the French Crown was peculiarly dependent upon the uncertain loyalties and mobile self-interest of the inhabitants. There had been plenty of support here in the 1330s when a swift French victory had seemed likely and surrender was the way of peace. Perceptions were different now, in the 1340s, that the French appeared to have lost their opportunities. What

French royal government meant in wartime was described in the catalogue of grievances presented to the Crown by the Estates of Languedoc in 1346: a stream of special commissioners and sergeants charging non-nobles found to be in possession of fiefs; assessing villages for the repair of roads and bridges; enforcing long-forgotten debts; making unrealistic demands for military service; rejecting the men proffered for reasons frivolous or groundless and then levying fines instead. Very similar complaints had been made in the time of Philip the Fair. None of it was new. But it was new to the conquered regions of the march severed from the English duchy since 1324. In two years of French rule between 1339 and 1341 Bourg had had to support a French garrison which was never less than 100 strong and sometimes as large as 500. The suburbs and outlying villages had been so completely plundered that the abbey of St Vincent and many of the citizens of the town had been reduced to indigence. This was presumably why the canons let in La Motte's band in 1341 and why the citizens rose spontaneously in their support. When Sainte-Bazeille defected to the English later in the same year the townsmen assessed the damage which they had suffered under French occupation at 24,000 *l.t.* After the first campaigns of the 1330s the English never, even at the most parlous moments of their fortunes, lacked friends in the French-held towns of the march ready to open the gates at night or sound the alarm in the wrong direction.[31]

These men may well have been right in supposing that life would be more agreeable as an English frontier town. Edward III's claim to be King of France is unlikely to have excited much emotional sympathy but his government had perforce ruled with a lighter hand than the Bishop of Beauvais', and its servants belonged to a gentler administrative tradition. Edward III's officials were very conscious of their need of friends. Moreover the French government was more obviously foreign. The sergeants, officials and immigrants who followed every French advance received grants from the French royal lieutenants at the expense of denizens whose loyalty was more doubtful. Even at a relatively humble level the French Crown's representatives in the south-west included a remarkably high proportion of immigrants from other provinces of the south as well as northerners, Provençals and Savoyards. By comparison the local administration of the dukes of Aquitaine had traditionally been a Gascon affair. Arnaud Foucaud told his interrogators in the cells of the Châtelet prison that the King of France would suffer for the arrogance of his officials in the south. Edward III had only to send a man of his own blood to represent him in Gascony for the castles and towns of the march to throw open their gates to him. Foucaud was executed only a few weeks before his prophecy was vindicated.[32]

In March 1343 Philip VI granted to his son John, Duke of Normandy, all the territory which had been conquered from the English in the south-west since 1322, the latest of a succession of grants by which Philip had ceded income and status to build up this frail, unconfident twenty-four-year old. John now added 'Lord of the Conquests' to his official titles. Philip VI, who never entirely released his son from the leading reins, reserved to himself the administration of most of these territories, including the 'conquests', which continued to be governed by the Bishop of Beauvais and other officials of the Crown as before. But the Prince's appointment was not a purely symbolic gesture. Philip could see that his government was in difficulty in the south-west even if he did not appreciate the full extent of the difficulty. He was as much in need as Edward III was of a viceroy who could embody the Crown more completely than any holder of official letters patent of appointment. But John lacked judgement as well as experience and his lack of independent authority must have been plain for all to see. Moreover he did not reside in the south-west as Derby was to do for much of the late 1340s and the Black Prince during the 1350s and 1360s. In September 1344 he paid a brief visit to Agen in the course of a three-month tour of the southern provinces of France, and received the oaths of allegiance of his new subjects in the great hall of the Dominicans. After the ceremony the Duke, who had been very ill in the course of his tour, removed himself hastily to the shrine of Rocamadour. It was the last that the march provinces saw of him until the catastrophic events of 1345.[33]

In Brittany the signature of the truce made little difference. The chroniclers are almost entirely silent about the brutal, unglamorous fighting there in which few men and no great ones were engaged. Small bands of garrison troops, rarely more than a few dozen strong, laid ambushes for each other on minor roads or fell suddenly on merchant convoys of carts and pack-animals; coastal villages were attacked without warning from the sea by men who disappeared within hours with their plunder or were caught and butchered with unexampled savagery by local men; inland villages were burned by the troops of both sides for want of protection money; farm-houses attacked at dawn to seize some local nobleman in his nightshirt and hold him for his ransom. The administrative correspondence of the period only occasionally casts a flash of light on disconnected incidents like these. The main line of events is, however, clear. The English held on to their coastal strongholds like winkles on rocks. Charles of Blois' partisans never succeeded in dislodging them and were rarely strong enough to try. They did, however, succeed in destroying the Montfortist party by a well-judged mixture of force and political pressure until the moment came when the English could no longer maintain the pretence of being supporters of the ducal government: they became more and more obviously a force of occupation.

The main problem of the Montfortists was the absence of any Breton leader to serve as a focus for their loyalty. For more than six months after the truce of Malestroit John de Montfort remained, in spite of the French King's promises, a prisoner in the Louvre, a breach of faith about which Edward III protested loudly. But when eventually he was released, on 1 September 1343, the event did nothing for his cause. The French government exacted stringent terms. John was made to promise that he would not go back to Brittany but would live peacefully on his estates in France and would attend at court at once whenever he was summoned. He also had to find sureties for his good behaviour, including a bond put up by his cousin for the enormous sum of 60,000 *l.p.* These terms were scrupulously observed until 1345. The fact that John was free but declined to help the Bretons who were fighting in his name was far more demoralizing than his imprisonment had ever been.[34] There was no one else. The Countess remained in England, her insanity a well-kept secret and her absence inexplicable. Their children were too young even for use as symbols. The political leadership of the Montfortists remained in the hands of a small number of Breton noblemen who had been the closest counsellors of John and his wife in the summer of 1341: Geoffrey de Malestroit and his kinsman Tanneguy du Châtel, and Amaury de Clisson. Some of these men were tied to the cause only by the fear of what would happen to them if they fell into Philip VI's hands.

Even with more effective leadership it would have been difficult to maintain the loyalty and morale of the Montfortists. A sizeable minority of them owned land in the rich areas of eastern Brittany occupied by Charles of Blois, which they could not recover without either violating the truce or submitting to him. In the event they did first the one and then the other. In the autumn of 1343 there was a succession of violent incidents in south-eastern Brittany. The most important of them was a rising in Vannes by a well-organized group of partisans within the town. The place was in the custody of the papacy and it was virtually undefended. The papal governor and his small garrison were seized and expelled. It was a golden prize. The nearby city of Rédon was brought over to the English side at about the same time, probably by the same methods. Very shortly afterwards a small force of Bretons attempted to build on their success by capturing Charles of Blois himself. They ambushed him on the road from Nantes to Angers. But Charles moved about in these days with a bodyguard of eighty men, and the attackers were beaten off with heavy losses. The French government was outraged. They delivered a furious protest to the Pope as the creator and guardian of the truce. Twelve prisoners captured in the attack on Charles of Blois were brought to Paris to be executed with the usual theatrical display. The victims included Geoffrey de Malestroit and his son, two of the most courageous of John de Montfort's partisans.[35]

Neither the English government nor its commanders on the spot appear to have been consulted in advance about these enterprises, and although Edward III congratulated those responsible he may not have been wholly delighted. The English garrisons in Brittany were at low strength. The coffers were empty. Communications between England and Brittany in December were difficult. A French counter-attack at that moment would have been irresistible. A few days before Christmas, Amaury de Clisson arrived in alarm in England to plead for reinforcements and supplies. The English King saw him at Westminster and issued orders at once, but compliance was a different matter. The time allowed was absurdly short. The Admiral of the west was told to have twenty-four ships at Southampton and Dartmouth within a fortnight. Gavin Corder and two other knights were sent to find a force of some 250 men to fill them. His men were not ready before the middle of March 1344 and there were only 190 of them. Corder's small army and some shiploads of victuals were the only assistance which reached Brittany from England. Preparations were put in hand for a much larger expedition to follow in the summer, but the possibility of paying for it seemed remote.[36]

If Edward III was afraid of a French counter-attack on the scale of the operations of 1341 and 1342 his fears were unfounded. Like Philip VI he over-estimated his enemy's resources. Philip, moreover, was genuinely anxious to preserve the truce, at least in the north, and took very seriously the Pope's long-standing plans to call a peace conference at Avignon. The French government's public position was that it would not support Charles of Blois in time of truce with either money or troops. Indeed Philip offered at one point to write 'harsh and threatening letters' to still the warlike activities of his nephew.[37]

If Philip wrote them, Charles certainly did not comply. The truce bound only the King of France and his 'adherents'. Charles of Blois constantly denied being an 'adherent': he said that he was fighting his own war and not Philip's. Perhaps he was right. He made competent use of what he had. Early in March 1344 he marched through most of the length of Mont-fortist Brittany and laid siege to Quimper. Quimper was the main town of the Cornouaille region of south-western Brittany. Its importance lay in its position across the main lines of communication overland from Brest to Vannes. But its walls were weak, and probably in poor condition. The English fared badly. Edward's lieutenant in the duchy, John Hardeshull, was captured in a skirmish outside the walls together with several of his principal Breton officers. The English archers suffered heavy casualties. In spite of the ferocity of the defence, Quimper was assaulted from the river on 1 May 1344 and captured. In the massacre which followed it was estimated that 1,400 townsmen died. As for the prisoners, the English ones were held for ransom but the Bretons and Normans were taken to Paris and tried for treason. They did not deny that they had given their allegiance to John de Montfort and Edward III. They claimed the benefit of the truce. But John de Montfort disavowed them and they were executed. Philip's special venom was reserved for Henry de Malestroit, a former officer of his own household. He had deserted in 1342 and then reap-peared as the English King's lieutenant in Vannes. Henry could not be executed because he was in holy orders. But he was sentenced to life imprisonment by an ecclesiastical court at a public ceremony in front of Notre-Dame cathedral, and arrangements were made for him to be lyn-ched by a mob immediately afterwards.[38]

The English government was not entirely passive in the face of these losses, but there was nothing that it could do quickly. A general requisition of all ships of over 30 tons' burden was ordered on 25 March 1344. Plans were laid to embark an army from Plymouth at Whitsun under the King's personal command. But the money to pay for this army did not exist. The nobility and the bishops met at Westminster in April 1344 but could do nothing without Parliament. Parliament could not be assembled before June. Although the Parliament which met then was sympathetic and very generous, its subsidies were voted too late to finance a campaign in that year. The first instalment was not payable until November 1344. The days were over when the English government could call on the resources of the German and Italian banking communities to anticipate its taxes. The result was that the King's orders were a dead letter. The harassing stream of instructions, reminders and threats which habitually issued from Edward's Chancery on the eve of a great expedition petered out uncertainly in August 1344, and the plans were formally cancelled in early October.[39]

By then the English King's plans had become irrelevant. During the summer of 1344 the leaderless and decimated English forces in Brittany fell apart, dividing into small roving bands which passed through the duchy looting, burning and exacting protection money, making themselves even more hated than the soldiers of Charles of Blois. The leaderless Montfortists submitted to Charles of Blois in large numbers, making the best terms they could. Charles, for all his paucity of men, was able to mop up many of the smaller places of southern Brittany with comparative ease. In September 1344, the surviving core of the Montfortist party in Brittany made a final plea for help from England. They sent a distinguished Breton nobleman and two Dominican friars to find Edward on the marches of Wales and explain to him that their cause was all but ruined. From the wreckage of his expeditionary army Edward was able to assemble a force of just 250 men. Amaury de Clisson, who had spent the whole of the spring and summer at the English court waiting for an expedition which never materialized, was put in command of them. These men arrived in Vannes in October 1344 and were probably responsible for preserving that town as an English outpost. But by this time there was nothing else to be done. In November Tanneguy du Châtel, one of the three lieutenants of the King of England in Brittany and the only Breton among them, submitted to Charles of Blois in return for a royal pardon. He was followed by most of the leading Bretons of the west, including almost all the heroes of 1341 and 1342 who had not been killed in battle or executed in Paris. Finally, at the end of December 1344, within a few weeks of his landing in the duchy at the head of a force of English troops, Amaury de Clisson himself made his peace with the French. Deprived of substantially all their political support in the duchy the English retreated to the few strong walled towns by the sea which they could defend with their limited manpower: Brest, Hennebont, Vannes and a few other places. They knew the limits of their strength, as Charles of Blois did of his.[40]

John de Monfort had watched these events from the distance of the Ile de France and had not stirred. If he hoped to earn his passage back to royal favour he was to be disappointed. Once his party had disintegrated the Crown set about completing the business of dispossessing him. In January 1345 the viscounty of Limoges, which had not been dealt with by the edict of Conflans in 1341, was awarded to Charles of Blois by the Parlement. At about the same time John appears to have been placed under some form of house imprisonment. On 25 March 1345 he escaped and fled to England. He was no more than a figurehead now, without friends, money or political resources: another Edward Balliol. Philip VI forfeited the bonds that had been lodged for his good behaviour and procured his convictions for treason.[41]

The diplomatic conference which was the ostensible reason for the truce opened in the autumn of 1344, sixteen months late, in the papal palace at Avignon. The delay had been almost entirely due to English obstruction, a succession of procedural devices which revealed the English King's view of the negotiations as eloquently as any rude rejection could have done. He appointed no ambassadors until May 1343. He then appointed a most distinguished embassy under the nominal leadership of the Earl of Derby but declined to send any but its most junior members, with the result that the Duke of Bourbon, the Dauphin of Vienne and 'other prelates and personages of high authority' found themselves in August 1343 sitting opposite a Chancery clerk. Then, when Edward III was prevailed upon to send out a nobleman of royal blood with whom the princes of the French delegation could be expected to negotiate, he lighted upon John Grey of Ruthin, an obscure baron distantly related to the royal house who reached the papal city in September 1343 but whose instructions did not extend beyond pressing his master's claim to the crown of France. Grey sent home for further instructions, and when none came by the end of the year he withdrew.[42]

It seemed likely at first that the same thing would happen in 1344. The opening of the conference was put off until March 1344, then June. Neither date was effective. On the first occasion there were only two English emissaries, both of low rank, who announced that their master was outraged by the French King's violations of the truce and was reconsidering his position. The second occasion was even more absurd.[1] The English government had announced to the Pope on 12 May 1344 that their delegation would be ready at Avignon in June. When the time came the Earl of Derby duly appeared but only, he said, in his private capacity and for 'devotional reasons'. The dukes of Normandy and Burgendy and the Chancellor of France, Guillaume Flote, who were there in their public capacities, had to listen as lesser English functionaries explained that they were without instructions. After a while, the two dukes left. Flote stayed until early August when he too left.

Derby's visit was not, however, a complete waste of time, for he had a number of lengthy and apparently productive private discussions with the Pope. In the course of these Clement offered both inducements and threats to bring the English to the conference table. Exactly what he said has not been recorded, but it was sufficiently compelling to persuade the English

King's Council in July 1344 that it was necessary to go through the motions of participating in the conference. A new embassy was appointed at the beginning of August and its members left at once. The senior member and spokesman was William Bateman, an exceedingly intelligent and effective lawyer who had passed most of his career in the papal service at Avignon and had recently become bishop of Norwich. He deserves to be remembered as the founder of Trinity Hall, Cambridge. In reality, the most important of the English ambassadors was not Bateman but the King's private secretary John Offord, the only one of them who was privy to Edward's inner counsels. With then went Offord's younger brother Andrew (a Chancery clerk), the conspiratorial Nicolino Fieschi, and a knight called Hugh Neville. The Pope regarded it as an inadequate team for the occasion, which it was. The French King's representation was much more impressive. The Bishop of Clermont acted as their nominal president and spokesman. There were also Louis of Spain and Louis of Poitiers, Count of Valentinois, two of Philip's principal generals; Simon Bucy, First President of the Parlement, a man closely associated with the French King's persecution of traitors; and another powerful permanent official, Pierre de Cugnières, President of the Chambre des Comptes.[44]

Distrust of the papacy was the main reason for the English government's behaviour. The terms of the truce of Malestroit provided for the Pope to act 'as mutual friend not as judge'. But as Philip VI remarked soon after these words were written, the Pope was 'my own friend, you know'. Edward III's complaints about French breaches of the truce may have smacked of hypocrisy given his own flagrant breaches; even so it was galling for the English to find that on such difficult matters as Philip VI's right to hold John de Montfort in prison until he had found sureties for his good behaviour, or the summary execution of Edward's allies who fell into French hands, or Charles of Blois' refusal to be bound by the truce, Clement was generally content to accept the official French explanation however disingenuous. The English believed that the Pope could be relied upon to protect French interests in any matter that was fundamental to them. The College of Cardinals, which in the fourteenth century served as a permanent council of the Pope's advisers, had a large majority of Frenchmen and was overwhelmingly favourable to Philip VI. The result of this imbalance could be seen not only in a predisposition to regard Edward III as an aggressive outsider with absurd pretensions, but in some revealing decisions of principle. Clement never, for example, gave the dispensation which was necessary to enable Edward III's heir to marry the daughter of the Duke of Brabant. The dispensation was necessary because the betrothed were within the prohibited degrees of affinity, as almost all the ruling houses of Europe were at a time when it was unlawful for persons to marry who had a common ancestor within seven generations. It would ordinarily have been a formality, but the marriage mattered too much politically and the Pope had given private assurances to the French court that he would not allow it.[45]

For their part the English, in whom hostility to the papacy was an old tradition, grew progressively more offensive in the expression of it. It was very widely believed in England that fees and taxes charged by Clement VI on the English clergy went to swell the war treasury of Philip VI and that the Pope's power of appointing to vacant ecclesiastical benefices in England was being used to provide a comfortable income for anglophobe functionaries and cardinals in Avignon. In May 1343 the Commons in Parliament had petitioned for a complete prohibition on the importation of certain papal letters to England. Edward III took up their cause in letters to the Pope so blunt that the agent who delivered them fled from Avignon immediately after the audience. This man's fears were not absurd. Had not Nicolino Fieschi been captured and assaulted by French roughs in Avignon only four years earlier? The reports of other English diplomatic agents leave little doubt that the papal city with its unruly mobs and crowded streets, its militantly clerical atmosphere, packs of hangers-on attached to the enormous households of the French cardinals and the looming shape of Philip VI's great fortress at Villeneuve was a profoundly uneasy place for a Englishman to be in the 1340s. Clement VI himself was a smooth diplomat, but it was not easy for him to present himself as an impartial arbiter to a government which he was denouncing as the worst oppressor of the Church since the days of Thomas Becket.[46]

The proceedings[47] opened on 22 October 1344 with the pleasantries that were customary on such occasions: a 'most pleasing' speech from the Pope, who had lost none of his rhetorical powers; another, gracious and conciliatory, from Bishop Bateman, who assured Clement that King Edward had always wanted a just and durable peace and that he and his fellow ambassadors were 'simple men and lovers of concord' who would be found entirely open in their dealings. As for the French, the Pope said that he had spoken privately to them and was satisfied that they had come with the genuine intention of agreeing a treaty and the fullest powers for the purpose. None of this meant very much. Both sides had come with confidential instructions which doomed the conference to failure before it began. The French ambassadors were empowered to make limited concessions of territory on the margins of Gascony, including the provinces conquered in the war of Saint-Sardos, but only if they had to and then on the strict understanding that the duchy was to be held as a fief of the French Crown. The Pope was shown their instructions on this point and confirmed for himself that they were absolute. Not surprisingly they were equally absolute on the subject of Edward III's claim to the throne of France. Philip's representatives were not even to discuss it.

Unfortunately, it was the only subject which Bateman's team were empowered to discuss, apart from the English King's complaints about breaches of the truce. They were not allowed to make any concessions at all. They did not even have the limited freedom of manoeuvre that their adversaries had. This was not because Edward regarded his claim to the throne as the only thing worth discussing, or because he was uninterested in territorial concessions in Gascony. It was because he did not want to make peace at all at a stage when he had so few cards in his hand and so many plans for getting more. Apart from the ports of western and southern Brittany, which were not directly ruled by Philip VI anyway, Edward's claim to the throne was really only a bargaining counter, and as his ambassadors admitted in a moment of candour it was a difficult one to use. Edward, they pointed out, had proclaimed himself to be at war with Philip VI for the possession of the whole kingdom of France and had publicly assumed the arms of France. There could surely be no question of his entering into negotiations which overtly contemplated the possibility of acknowledging Philip as his sovereign in Gascony. It would be tantamount to acknowledging that he 'had set out to recover a kingdom which was not his, and launched himself upon an unjust war'. This was the abiding problem of the English at every stage of the Hundred Years War. Except occasionally in the mood of hubris generated by their greatest victories the English kings were realistic enough to regard their claim to be kings of France as something to be surrendered as part of a satisfactory settlement. But authority was conferred by God, not men. They could not bargain about such a surrender without conceding the mundaneness of the claim, destroying much of its value and undermining the many alliances that they had made which were based on it. Almost a century later the English were confronting the same difficulty and described it in language very similar to Bateman's. If the King were to trade his claim for territory, wrote one of Henry VI's ablest servants, 'it might be said, noised and deemed in all Christian lands that not [Henry] the King nor his noble progenitors had nor have no right in the Crown of France, and that all their wars and conquest hath been but usurpation and tyranny'.[48]

The Pope's method of mediation was to keep the two delegations as much as possible apart. Except on one or two occasions when for some special reason it was necessary to address both delegations together, he bargained with each side on its own while the other waited its turn in a nearby room. The object was to persuade each of them to confide to the Pope 'as if under the seal of the confessional' the irreducible minimum which it must have in order to make peace. He had no idea how limited Bateman's discretion was, and when the Bishop protested that he had come to discuss nothing but the throne of France he assumed that this was only an opening position. 'Holy Father,' the Englishmen said, 'the only proposals which we can discuss are those which have some prospect of being found acceptable to our lord the King, who has, as you know, put forward as his own claim the crown of France.' After four frustrating sessions with the English delegation, during which the Pope had made no progress and had found it increasingly difficult to suppress his exasperation, Clement withdrew from the conference, leaving the negotiations to be carried on by a commission of two cardinals.

They fared no better than the Pope had, and their patience was thinner. It seemed to them, the cardinals began, that since the war had its whole origin in the duchy of Aquitaine there was much to be said for starting from the point where things had gone wrong, in 1325. The English were persuaded to talk about Gascony, but not to treat the truce of 1325 as their starting point and certainly not to deal with the duchy in isolation. Their starting point was their master's claim to the whole of France. At this, the cardinals became irritable. In that case, they asked, why had Edward III done homage to Philip VI and sworn to observe that very truce? The English answered that he had done it without prejudice to his hereditary rights. They declined absolutely to negotiate about the duchy *qua* duchy since their case was that it was a province of Edward III's kingdom. What would the English say, the cardinals inquired, to a proposal which restored the duchy to its extent on the eve of the war of Saint-Sardos? It was the first glimpse of what the papacy had in mind as an acceptable compromise. The English returned to their well-worn theme. They would consider no proposal which involved treating Gascony as part of a duchy subordinate to Philip VI. They might, however (and here came the first glimpse of what they believed Edward would accept), consider settling the territorial dispute in Gascony on the basis that it would be treated as 'allod', free of any feudal subordination to the French Crown and in effect severed from the kingdom. The cardinals agreed that while the feudal bond subsisted no peace was likely to survive very long. They cited the interesting analogy of Scotland. But they had obviously raised this question with the French delegation already, and been rebuffed. They said that they could see no prospect of Philip VI agreeing to the dismemberment of his kingdom, and thought that the Gascons would probably object also. If the two kings agreed to it, the English responded, the Gascons would like it well enough.

At this point the cardinals produced three proposals of their own (or perhaps they were the Pope's) all of which were designed to sever the feudal bond in Gascony by removing the English monarch from France altogether in exchange for compensation of various more or less unrealistic kinds. The first proposal may have been the one which Clement had suggested in confidence to the Earl of Derby in June. Edward, it was suggested, should renounce Gascony in exchange for the grant of all the lands of the Hospitallers in England together with possessions of the foreign priories there. The English said they thought that Edward would find this a very inadequate return for so much effort and sacrifice and that it would dishonour him personally. 'What would you say,' the cardinals asked, producing their next proposal, 'if the King of France were willing to bring pressure to bear on the King of Scotland to surrender his kingdom to your King, receiving instead compensation on the continent?' The ambassadors did not think that that would be acceptable. Scotland belonged as of right to Edward III anyway. In that case, the cardinals said, how would Edward III react to the offer of a very large sum of money? The English replied that their master was not a shopkeeper, and considered the crown of France to be beyond price. The English were invited to return three days later on 7 November with a more considered answer, but when they did so the answer was the same.

On 8 November 1344, a fortnight after the conference had opened, the cardinals produced another proposal. Perhaps, they said, Edward might consider acknowledging Gascony to be a fief of France but devolving it upon one of his sons. The feudal bond would survive but at one remove from the King himself. It was the last constructive suggestion which they made. The English rejected it.

The sessions degenerated into sterile exchanges about the merits of the English King's claim to the French throne. 'The war broke out over Gascony', the cardinals said, 'long before your master ever mentioned his claim to the crown of France'; and they produced some recent letters of Edward III dated 1344 'in the fifth year of our reign of France'. The English said, 'May it please your lordships, it is true that the war began long before our lord the King assumed the title of King of France, but it began on account of the King's right to be called King of France, which right existed before the war began.' There followed a short historical excursus concerning the claims made on the young Edward's behalf by his mother in 1328. The cardinals then said, 'Did your King not do homage to the King of France for Aquitaine and Ponthieu? And did he not subsequently promise by letters patent under his great seal that his homage should be treated as liege homage, there being not a word in these letters of any pretended right to the crown of France?' It was a difficult question, which the English evaded: 'That is one of the arguments of the French, and when it suits his Holiness the Pope to hear us on the point, we shall answer it.' The cardinals agreed, for different reasons: 'Our lord the Pope also considers it preferable to leave that issue out of the negotiations, and in any event the French ambassadors will not agree to make their master's sovereignty a matter for debate at these meetings. They will no more broach that issue than a poison chalice.'

Two days later, on 10 November 1344, the English returned to confirm that they would not consider accepting compensation for the loss of Gascony outside France. The cardinals for their part reported that they could not prevail on the French to agree that the duchy of Aquitaine should be severed from the kingdom and held free of feudal obligations. In that case, the English replied, the conference had evidently reached an impasse. Unless the French position shifted, they could not see themselves usefully employed in Avignon any longer and thought that Edward would probably recall them.

The English ambassadors were profoundly embarrassed by the obdurate position which they were compelled to adopt. Long before the formal business of the conference had begun, while the Englishmen were waiting for the French delegation to arrive, Offord had concluded that a valuable opportunity might be missed unless Edward III could be persuaded to take the conference more seriously. Clement had skilfully lulled their suspicions, according them long, friendly audiences, entertaining them at his dinner table and professing to sympathize with some of their grievances. During the sessions of the conference he even hinted that he thought their master's claim to the French throne was 'not wholly without factual or legal foundation'. In their inner counsels, he said, the French government thought so too. Offord wanted the King to abandon his plans to send troops to Britanny during the winter, and hoped that he would enlarge his ambassadors' powers. 'It seems to me, my lord,' he wrote, 'that the Holy Father is at last taking your interests to heart.' As the proceedings continued the English ambassadors' reports to their government became increasingly insistent. They reminded Edward of their earlier advice. 'We are amazed', they said, 'that nothing has yet reached us here.'

Edward had in fact received Offord's request for further instructions and had considered it at length with John Stratford and a handful of close advisers. But he had reached no decision. He told Offord that he would do nothing without calling a full meeting of his Council. Fresh agents would then be sent with up-to-date news of his position. The full Council did not meet until late in October. They resolved to send yet further embassies to Avignon: the first, rather low-grade embassy would leave at once with the news that Edward had renounced all his plans to invade Britanny for the winter, and bringing full powers to discuss the enforcement of the truce. Another more impressive embassy, including the earls of Derby and Northampton, would appear at Avignon after Christmas with powers as yet undefined and, no doubt, dependent in practice on the advice of Bateman and Offord.[49]

They, however, were growing daily more pessimistic and more concerned for their own safety. News was reaching Avignon of fresh outrages in England against the privileges of the papacy in the matter of provision to English benefices. They included copies of a writ of prohibition addressed in the most disrespectful terms to one of the cardinals, as well as broadsheets against the Pope which had apparently been nailed to the doors of St Paul's Cathedral and Westminster Abbey. The Pope was planning to send two legates to England with an armoury of spiritual powers. Voices had been raised in the College of Cardinals to suggest that, if any harm befell them, reprisals could be visited against Edward's agents in Avignon. The French, on the other hand, stood in high favour. On 15 November 1344 the English had to sit among the banqueters to celebrate the investiture by the Pope of one of the French ambassadors, Louis of Spain, with the nominal dignity of Prince of the Canary Islands.

On 20 and 21 November 1344 the English were received in audience by the Pope. He tried to persuade them that all was not lost. Perhaps Edward III might appoint some prince of the royal blood to represent him at further sessions of the conference. Philip would then be obliged to increase the stature of his own ambassadors, and that might be the occasion for giving them fresh instructions. Neither Bateman nor Offord thought much of this proposal. They wanted to be recalled. Money was running short. The Bardi office in Avignon was declining to pay the expenses of their couriers without personal guarantees. The atmosphere in the city was intensely hostile. 'I stand in grave peril here,' Bateman wrote home to the King, 'without accomplishing anything at all for your purposes.'

Hugh Neville left Avignon in the last week of November 1344 and reached England just after Christmas. Bishop Bateman followed shortly after him. Fieschi departed for Italy on other diplomatic business. The Pope would not release John Offord. He remained in the papal city so that Clement could pretend that his conference was still in being. None of the Englishmen believed that anything would come of the projected embassy of Derby and Northampton. In February 1345, after a good deal of havering, it was cancelled. When this news was announced in Avignon in March, Offord abruptly left the city without leave and fled as fast as he could for England.[50]

Resolving the dispute was by now much more than a diplomatic problem. Although the war had lasted only eight years, less than the war of Edward I and Philip the Fair, which had had similar origins, it had more completely antagonized the two nations than any previous crisis of their affairs. The chivalry of England and France retained some shared values which may even have intensified among those on both sides who found in war a pleasure and a challenge. But this was not the view of the mass of the population. The scale of the effort required, and the variety of people affected, not only by the operations themselves, which were sporadic, but by the tremendous financial and bureaucratic preliminaries, were of a different order now than in any previous war, and were growing year by year. Both governments did what they could to feed the suspicions of their subjects with propaganda, and to distance them from the enemy.

The first symptoms had been the sequestration of the assets of enemy aliens. At the outset of the war, the English government had taken into the King's hands the possession of all Frenchmen, with a few favoured exceptions: the Gascons, the Bretons and after 1338 the Flemings. The main victims were French monasteries, particularly the great Burgundian abbey of Cluny and the Benedictine houses of Normandy, which had been large landowners in England ever since the time of the Norman kings. A few of them, such as the abbey of Saint-Pierre de Dives in southern Normandy, were so heavily dependent on their English revenues that they were ruined by Edward III's confiscations well before his armies engulfed them. In the case of ecclesiastical land the English government stopped short of outright confiscation. They simply administered the property, taking the income for themselves and making a minimal provision for the living expenses of the occupants if there were any. The relatively small number of French nobleman who held estates in England and Ireland were at first dealt with in the same way. But in their case the government progressed from sequestration to confiscation quite quickly. The Constable of France,

Raoul, Count of Eu, may initially have hoped to recover his enormous estates in Ireland when the crisis had blown over, and he continued to maintain agents there who co-operated with the English King's custodian. But by the early 1340s Edward was granting out his lands to others. By January 1343 the Count had written them off and received compensation from the French treasury. The severance of ancient connections with England among some influential French noblemen and ecclesiastics was a misfortune in the long term. The Count of Eu and the present Pope (when he had been abbot of Fécamp) were only two of the Frenchmen whose possessions in England had offered occasions for less formal and more sympathetic contacts with Edward III's court than any diplomatic exchange.[51]

The French government seems to have been more cautious in its sanctions against English landowers in France, although the evidence is so fragmentary that it is difficult to be sure. The cathedral priory of Canterbury, one of the few English churches which possessed assets there, was able to resume possession of them in 1344, during a time of truce. Some other ecclesiastics were not so lucky. The property in France of the more prominent laymen residing in England was confiscated and granted by the French Crown to others. Very few people were affected. The main victims of the French government's measures against aliens were expatriate Englishmen living in France, who were surprisingly numerous. Some of them had been there for many years. They were in a difficult position, belonging fully to neither one country nor the other. In 1338 they were required to declare their assets on oath and to submit to a one-off tax of one-third of their capital value net of debts. The response of many of them was to apply to be naturalized as Frenchmen.[52]

Trading with the enemy became illegal in both countries, although the law was not consistently enforced in either. The seepage of enemy goods around the frontiers continued. Notions of economic warfare were primitive. The governments of both countries were much more interested in preventing exports to their enemy than imports from them, the reverse of modern economic prejudice. Moreover, in neither country were the motives of the government exclusively strategic. Concern about shortages at home, particularly of foodstuffs, was at least as important; and in England the control of trade was designed more to raise money than to injure the French. The effect, however, was the same: the loosening of old connections between Englishmen and Frenchmen, the severance of the few remaining ties of interdependence. At the outset of the war the French government pursued a comprehensive prohibition of all commercial dealings with the subjects of Edward III whether in Gascony or England, and the penalties of treason were prescribed for breach of it. Not only the importation but even the use of English wool was forbidden unless a special licence was obtained.[53] The English began with a more selective approach. Their embargo on wool exports, which brought Flanders to its knees between 1336 and 1338, was among the more ruthlessly enforced and politically successful trade wars of the middle ages. But after 1338, when its objects had been achieved, the government relaxed its efforts. English wool had to be sold in order to raise money for the Crown and, the market being weak, it was impossible to be too choosy about who was buying it. It was freely bought in Calais at the height of the campaigns of 1339 and 1340. In the course of the 1340s economic warfare became a more consistent feature of English policy even in time of truce. In 1343 a most comprehensive scheme of export controls was instituted for a mixture of reasons: protectionism, financial manipulation and foreign policy all contributed. The scheme drew on practices which had been devised but only intermittently employed during the previous six years. The export of grain was permitted only at certain ports and only to specified destinations, excluding France. The shipmasters were made to swear an oath before the mayor or bailiff of the port of shipment that they would carry the cargoes only to the permitted destinations. A bond was required as security for the exporter's good behaviour, which was released (in theory) only upon the production of a landing certificate from the authorities at the port of discharge. Very similar rules were applied to the export of wool, hides and pelts. These were England's principal exports. Periodically, however, other goods were added to the list of controlled exports, usually because they were thought to be of use as war materials. Ships, timber and horses were controlled at various times. It is unlikely that these measures achieved very much.[54]

Oddly enough, there was very little official interference with the freedom of movement of individuals. In both countries a somewhat haphazard distinction was made between aliens temporarily present in the realm, such as merchants, seamen and other travellers, and aliens with some fixed place of abode. Those in the former category were almost invariably arrested when they were found, in France as early as September 1336, in England rather later. Resident aliens on the other hand were by and large left alone, except where they were conceived to be a direct threat to the security of the realm. Philip VI's government did not at first repeat Charles IV's order of 1326 to arrest all Englishmen resident in France. But it did, in August 1338, order a search to be made of their homes and it confiscated their weapons. The French government also from time to time incarcerated Englishmen who were found living in frontier areas. Two Englishmen, for example, who were found operating a brewery at Compiègne in 1340 were locked up in the town belfry during the siege of Tournai. The French government's fears were by no means absurd. Englishmen living in France did occasionally act as spies and guides. The man who guided Edward III across the marshes of the Somme in August 1346 and enabled him to avoid being trapped was a local resident who appears to have hailed from Yorkshire.[55] The English policy was very similar to the French. During the first few years of the war Frenchmen were forbidden to reside on or go near the coasts. Men of French origin were the victims of periodic moods of panic about espionage and fifth columnists. During Edward III's invasion of Brittany in 1342, suspected French spies and couriers were detained and searched at the ports and any document found on them sent to London to be scrutinized. A substantial number of suspicious persons, most of whom were probably entirely innocent, was incarcerated in Newgate prison.[56] But there was no consistency of policy and no general internment of aliens in either realm. It seems surprising to find a young Englishman living *au pair* with a family in Amiens in the early 1340s in order to improve his command of French. Anomalies of this kind were quite common in England. A Picard could live quietly at Salisbury between 1341 and 1345 learning English, and another from Amiens who arrived in 1340 could still be found plying his trade there five years later.[57]

On both sides of the Channel the year 1345 was a time of intensifying hostility against enemy aliens. After the English government repudiated the truce of Malestroit all French merchants recently come into the realm were presumed to be agents of the enemy and in September 1345 orders were given for their arrest. The French government went further, ordering the arrest and imprisonment of every Englishman living in France and the confiscation of his property. When Charles IV had done this at the time of the war of Saint-Sardos he had been much criticized. But in 1345 the government was almost certainly acting under the pressure of public opinion. In the Paris area men did not wait for the King's authority. Englishmen were spontaneously attacked and imprisoned wihout any legal warrant as soon as the news of the fighting arrived.[58]

In both countries the measures taken against nationals of the other encouraged the persecuting instinct which war brings out in most societies. Jean Tête-Noir, one of Philip VI's household servants, had been born in England of an English mother and a French father and had spent almost all his life in France. But he was repeatedly pressed for payment of the tax on enemy aliens, and eventually had to apply for formal letters of exemption. He must have felt rather like Peter Hughes, a Frenchman settled in Cirencester for more than twenty years with an English wife and children, who was obliged in the first few weeks of the war to apply for royal letters recognizing him as a denizen. English officials had the utmost difficulty with Bretons and Flemings, who although Frenchmen were exempted from the government's sanctions; with francophone Savoyards, who were subjects of the Empire but many of whom fought in French armies; with francophone Gascons and Channel Islanders, who were subjects of Edward III; with francophone Englishmen, who were more numerous than they realized; with the French-born wives and widows of Englishmen; with Burgundians from the duchy of Burgundy who were Frenchmen and Burgundians from the county of Burgundy who were Frenchmen in practice but not in law. How were they to classify William of Cusance, who came from the county of Burgundy but had valuable properties in Paris and had been one of the principal financial officials of the English royal household for more than thirty years? For a short time at the beginning of the war this man found himself treated as an enemy alien in both countries. Men had to declare their loyalties. In a country whose connections with the language and civilization of France were as ancient and as intimate as England's, this meant for many people severing themselves from their own past. The French had fewer difficulties. Englishmen were more readily identifiable by their language (even when speaking French). Englishness was not built into the fabric of any French past. Even the French, however, had to learn to recognize Scots, many of whom had settled in France over the years or arrived there more recently in the service of David II. William Scot, a tailor of Noyon born at Berwick on Tweed, cannot have enjoyed his nickname 'the Englishman'. It cost him his liberty for a short time in 1326 and caused him to be harassed by tax collectors and officials after 1337. But he was more fortunate than the four Scots living near Amiens who were killed by a group of soldiers. Their assailants protested in their defence that they thought that their victims were English. When they explained their mistake they were pardoned.[59]

Feelings like these explain the ready audience which propagandists found for their lies and exaggerations in both countries. The French government and its semi-official chroniclers lost no opportunity of associating Edward III with Robert of Artois, the bogeyman of French official mythology, or of blackening him with tales like the much repeated but fictitious story that he raped the Countess of Salisbury while her husband was a prisoner of war. Edward III for his part accused the French

King of trying to stamp out the English language, just as Edward I had done forty years earlier. Men's fears and hatreds were inflamed by official rumours, such as the bizarre story circulating in 1346 that Philip VI had filled his Italian galleys with Turks to inflict untold horrors on the coastal villages of England. The truth was usually just as effective. The atrocities of the Calais seamen were given the widest possible publicity. Captured documents revealing Philip VI's plans to invade England were read out in public places and laid before Parliament. The Franciscan and Augustinian friars, the greatest public preachers of their day, were commended to 'fire the hearts of our faithful subjects' with the justice of the King's cause and to trumpet his victories when they occurred. The francophobia already latent in the English mind was sedulously encouraged and intensified. Some contemporary English writers, like the poet Lawrence Minot and the Oxfordshire clerk and chronicler Geoffrey Baker, brought their hatred of Philip VI and his subjects to a pitch of ferocity which makes parts of their work unreadable.[60]

Translating grudges and xenophobia into support for the King's wars and the heavy fiscal burdens that went with them was an exercise in which Edward III succeeded better than his rival. It must have come as a shock to him, after his return from the continent in November 1340, to discover how close his realm had come to rebellion on account of the crushing taxation of the past four years. The burden was certainly lightened during the 1340s. There were fewer Parliamentary subsidies. Purveyance was milder. A determined effort was made to prevent abuses by minor officials and to punish those reponsible. Military service was the only burden which significantly increased, and there is no doubt that it was unpopular. Arrayers and sometimes even the men whom they had arrayed were liable to be abused and physically attacked.[61] But military service was a burden which was too occasional and fell too capriciously to provoke general discontent. Even the great army of 1347, the largest Edward ever raised, represented a very small proportion of England's adult males. For the man whose lot was drawn in the village assembly and who had no one else to sow his seed or harvest his crop, service in the army might be a personal disaster. For the generality of men it cannot have made much difference. Some probably relished the chance of wages and plunder.

It was in the maritime communities of the south and east coasts that the war took its worst toll on the livelihoods of men. Coastguard service required the deployment of much larger numbers than ever fought in the King's continental armies, and at intervals which were less easily predicted. In Hampshire, the worst-affected county, there must have been many villages like Eling, whose men were so often called away to guard the coast at sowing and harvesting time that cultivation had been abandoned in large areas of the parish by the early 1340s. In the ports and harbours, the interruption of trade with France and the manipulation of wool exports inflicted great hardship. War service at sea was more persistently required and more onerous to perform than any other kind of military service. The extreme case was Great Yarmouth, whose ships, because of their number and their size, had contributed more to Edward's wars than any other port. They served against the Scots or the French in every year (except one) from 1333 to 1347. At the beginning of this period the town had possessed, in addition to its important fleet of fishing vessels, no less than ninety 'great ships' capable of carrying between 100 and 300 tons. At the end of it there were only twenty-four. The rest had been captured, destroyed by the enemy, wrecked, or put out of service by wear and damage. The trading profits of Great Yarmouth's shipowners had fallen so far that lost vessels could not be replaced and damaged ones were rotting on the beaches for want of money to repair them. Essential harbour works were not being carried out, and the siltation of the harbour mouth was forcing larger vessels to discharge their cargoes into lighters in the roads. The town, which was surrounded by worthless land, had no other livelihood. Not long afterwards, six substantial businessmen of the town were reported to have lost almost all their fortunes and several hundred seamen were unemployed. The troubles of Great Yarmouth differed only in degree from those of other ports of southern and eastern England. There must have been plenty of men who agreed with the rowdies of Chichester who attacked the Bishop's servants in the streets and tore up the letters which they carried calling for prayers for the King's wars.[62]

After the ports, it was probably in Wales that the burden of the war had been felt most intensely. The Welsh had made a disproportionate contribution to the war effort, supplying very large contingents of spearmen and archers to the army throughout the 1330s and 1340s in addition to meeting the heavy cost of royal purveyances and Parliamentary subsidies. In May 1343 Edward III had made his eldest son Prince of Wales and invested him with all the lands and rights of the Crown there, including the coasts and mountains of the west.[63] The young Prince played an increasingly important role in his father's wars from the mid-1340s onward, and as his military activities became more strenuous the demands made on the Welsh intensified. Welshmen belonged to a society in which violence was never far below the surface of daily life, even two generations after the Edwardian conquest had brought an end to the ancient pattern of border warfare. Their units in Edward III's armies, recruited in the western hills and coastlands and at the gates of castles the length of the old border, had a roughness and *esprit de corps* peculiar to themselves. English-speaking migrants living in Wales were rigorously excluded from their ranks. They were among the first soldiers on either side to wear full uniform: the green and white of the Black Prince's men from the north, the red and white of the Earl of Arundel's men from Chirkland, and the men of the southern lordships in their own distinctive colours. They marched with their local leaders, every hundred men behind their own standard, following the army on foot and encountering extremes of exhaustion over long marching days unknown to most of the English infantry, who were mounted. Alone among the units recruited for English armies of this period, they brought their own chaplains and physicians with them, as well their own interpreters and criers.[64] So much solidarity was easily turned against their English masters, and signs of overt resistance were appearing by 1345. In January and February there was a number of particularly serious outbreaks of violence against English officials in Wales. The Prince of Wales's attorney in North Wales was murdered while travelling about his duties and the sheriff cut down in his court room. In some districts the roads became impassable. Much of the unrest arose from grievances older and deeper than anything connected with the war. But the pressures of continual recruitment and the tightfistedness and dishonesty of those charged with paying wages were at least partly responsible. In the following weeks there was to be an embarrassing succession of disorders and mutinies among Welshmen assembled to join Edward's armies, some of whom refused to march or would do so only on their own terms.[65]

Higher up the social scale, however, there was now widespread acceptance of the war by Englishmen as inevitable and just, and for a growing number, glamorous. Almost all of the nobility of military age volunteered to take part in offensive campaigns, even in places like Scotland and Brittany where there was little prospect of profit. Henry of Lancaster, Earl of Derby, for example, had had a difficult and frustrating war, including a spell in a debtors' prison at Mechelen, but he was still professing his 'love of the soldier's life'. There were very many like him, even if the nearest they came to a soldier's life was a tournament. Edward III's tournaments were packed with participants and onlookers. The Dunstable tournament of 1342, which was interrupted by the arrival of the ambassadors of Brittany with the news of the fall of Nantes, was attended by 'all the noble youth of England'. The 'beautiful' tournament held at Smithfield market in London at mid-summer 1343 was followed by imitations throughout the country. In January 1344 the traditional participants in these chivalrous extravagances were joined by much of the citizenry of London and a 'measureless crowd' of others at Windsor Castle for a week of jousting and eating, the occasion when Edward III announced his plan to found a new Round Table after King Arthur's model with 300 knights. The King had his own reasons for promoting these showy events. He wanted to 'trumpet the reputation of the soldiers, to celebrate the profession of arms and to strengthen the Crown by gathering together a vast number of experienced warriors'.[66]

There is plenty of evidence that he succeeded. The King's relations with the aristocracy were close, in marked contrast with the situation in France. The nobility were indispensible, the leaders of his campaigns, in large measure his financiers, the only group which might have conducted a sustained and coherent opposition to his policies. But the events of 1297 were not repeated in the 1330s and 1340s. Edward scrupulously observed the forms of Parliamentary consultation. Support for the government was carefully rehearsed. Councils of the nobility met on occasions when a summons of Parliament was not appropriate and an increasing number of magnates were called to them. The bruising constitutional quarrels of 1341 which had followed Edward's return from the siege of Tournai and had almost lost Edward control of his own government had been appeased. The unity of purpose which had been seen at the outset of the war appeared to be returning.

In April 1343, shortly after the truce of Malestroit had been sealed, Parliament had given the King an undertaking that if he could not obtain an honourable peace they would 'aid him in his cause with all their strength'. For the time being Edward had done with attempts to monopolize the wool trade, which had proved unpopular and unremunerative. Instead he freed the trade and charged duties. Parliament was persuaded to vote him a 'maltolt' or supplementary duty on exports of wool of £2 per sack (on top of the 'ancient custom' of 6s. 8d.) for the next three and a half years. This surprising degree of support for the resumption of the fighting was due in part to their appreciation of the great cost and danger of an armed truce which left the political initiative to the enemy. A successful campaign soon might in the long run be cheaper. It seemed to the next Parliament, meeting rather more than a year later in June 1344, that:

the end of this present war and an honourable treaty of peace will never be had without bringing powerful forces to bear on the enemy. Wherefore let the King so soon as he is ready pass over the sea to take what God may bestow upon him and to press on with his enterprise until he has brought it to an end, all messages and protests of the Pope notwithstanding.

They granted a subsidy for each of the next two years, the second year's grant being conditional on the King leading his army abroad in person. The clergy, meeting in convocation at St Paul's at the same time, voted a tenth of their income for three years. For the first time in several years Edward's finances were equal to the strain of a major campaign.[67]

He had resolved well before the breakdown of the conferences at Avignon that he would repudiate the truce of Malestroit in the summer of 1345, a year before its time. His strategic position on the continent, in Gascony, Brittany and Flanders, had been so weakened that he could not have delayed the decision any longer even if his respect for agreements had been greater than it was. The first detailed plans for a renewed invasion of France were prepared in February 1345 just as it was becoming clear in Avignon that the peace conference had failed. The original proposal was to send two armies to the continent early in the summer. The King himself intended to lead one of them to an unspecified (and possibly undecided) destination in northern France. The men and ships assigned to this army were expected to be ready for embarkation on a date which, after several postponements, was finally fixed for 5 June 1345. A somewhat smaller army was destined to leave for Gascony under the command of the Earl of Derby, Henry of Lancaster.[68]

It was impossible to keep planning on this scale secret, and perhaps not even desirable to do so. The news of Edward's doings encouraged every malcontent in France who hoped to build a political position on the humiliation of the French state. John de Montfort reached England on 1 April. Godfrey of Harcourt, whose exile in Brabant was becoming progressively more uncomfortable as the Duke of Brabant moved closer to Philip VI, arrived in England about six weeks after him in May, bringing several of his Norman cronies. Edward's agents were busy on the continent trying to suborn other French noblemen.

Edward had, as usual, extravagant hopes about the help which men like these could bring to him, and the exiles sedulously nourished his optimism. On 20 May 1345 there was a small ceremony in the Archbishop of Canterbury's palace at Lambeth in which John de Montfort acknowledged Edward III as King of France and did liege homage to him for the duchy of Brittany. Godfrey of Harcourt performed a similar act of homage a little later. Both men were pressed into Edward's service at once and troops were found for them to fight with. In the course of April and May 1345 a third army was carved out of the resources assigned to Edward's own expeditionary force. The Earl of Northampton was reappointed as Edward III's lieutenant in Brittany. About 500 men were placed at his disposal, plus a small additional force under the command of Sir Thomas Ferrers which was destined for the reoccupation of the Channel Islands. It was agreed that John de Montfort would accompany the Earl of Northampton back to his duchy. Godfrey of Harcourt would accompany Ferrers: the Channel Islands were a good base from which to resume contact with real or imagined friends in the Cotentin.[69]

On 14 and 15 June 1345 Edward formally renounced the truces, 'compelled by necessity', he told the English, 'for the defence of our English kingdom and for the recovery of our lawful rights'. At the same he issued for the attention of the Pope and his continental allies a verbose denunciation of Philip's aggressions which Clement VI was to describe with some justification as an act of undiluted hypocrisy. The first of Edward's continental armies had in fact already left. Northampton and Ferrers sailed from Portsmouth in the first few days of June. The Earl of Derby's fleet had been ready since the end of May and needed only a favourable wind. The King's own army was ready in the last week of June.[70]

CHAPTER XIII

Bergerac and Auberoche
1345–1346

'Now let us speak first of the Earl of Derby,' Froissart wrote, 'for he bore the heaviest burden and enjoyed the best adventures.'[1] Henry of Lancaster, Earl of Derby, was the ideal choice for Edward III's purpose. He was the King's cousin, and for all practical purposes (since his father was old and blind) the head of the house of Lancaster, a man who for rank and reputation exactly fulfilled the freebooter Arnaud Foucaud's requirements for a successful military commander in Gascony. But Derby was not a mere dignitary like Edmund of Kent, who had presided over the disaster of Saint-Sardos twenty years before. He was a diplomat and military strategist of conspicuous intelligence. Moreover, his personality was calculated to make him many friends among the Gascony nobility: flamboyant and showy, generous, fond of women and good living. The terms of Derby's contract with the King stipulated that he would spend eighteen months in the duchy. He was to enjoy viceregal powers there and the title of King's lieutenant. But his military objectives were left entirely to his discretion. He was to do 'whatever could be done' with the strength he had: 500 men-at-arms, 500 Welsh infantry and 1,000 archers who would accompany him from England, together with whatever forces could be raised in Gascony itself. His companions included a distinguished band of captains, among them the Earl of Pembroke and those reckless heroes Sir Walter Mauny and Sir James Audley.

Edward III and Derby made their plans in February 1345. The Seneschal, Nicholas Beche, was recalled. He had not been a success and his health was failing, the fate of many Englishmen sent out to the marshy environment of medieval Bordeaux. He was replaced by Ralph, Lord Stafford, a much more august figure who was sent out to Bordeaux with a small advance guard to prepare the ground as soon as shipping could be found for him. Derby himself expected to follow in May.[2]

All the military disasters of the French in 1345 sprang from the decision which they made in the opening months of the year to avoid offensive warfare in the south-west and to conduct a mere holding operation there while the main effort was made elsewhere. It was not that the French ministers were ignorant of Edward III's plans for the south-western theatre. They knew the general thrust of them with surprising exactness by mid-March 1345 at the latest.[3] But they were desperately short of money. Apart from the ecclesiastical tenths and the uncertain contribution of the *gabelle du sel*, the only significant tax revenues which were being collected came from the sales taxes of four pence in the pound which was still being paid by certain towns of the northern and central provinces. Nothing was being collected in the south. The government's efforts to improve the position did not begin until March 1345, when the breakdown of the Avignon conference made the war seem serious again to some, if not all, tax-payers. But they did so then by the time-honoured method of conducting piecemeal negotiations through commissioners with one community after another. The Parisians granted a generous subsidy at the beginning of April, equal to the cost of maintaining 500 troops for six months. The rest of France was urged to follow their example, but the results were extremely patchy and especially disappointing in the south. Moreover, most of those who agreed to pay a subsidy did so on terms that its collection would begin in September, an extraordinary delay in the political conditions of 1345.[4]

Philip's ministers formed the view that the main threat would come in the north. In a sense they were right about this. It is where the main threat would have come if Edward had not been thwarted by events. For this reason, and because the defence of the north was always a more sensitive matter politically, the whole military resources of northern and central France were concentrated there. The *arrière-ban* was proclaimed on 29 April 1345. The assembly of the army was fixed, not long afterwards, for 22 July at Arras. Not only were no reinforcements sent to the southern theatre from other parts of France, but troops recruited in Languedoc were directed to the north. For reinforcing their men on the Gascon march the French appear, astonishingly, to have counted on the governments of Castile, Aragon and Portugal, with whom very slow-moving negotiations were then in progress. As a result, Philip VI's forces were seriously over-stretched throughout the summer, and particularly in the early part of it. A small coastguard watched the shores of Saintonge and Poitou. The entire council of La Rochelle was engaged in preparing the defences of their town, which was the major Atlantic port south of the Loire. But there was no war fleet there to intercept Derby's ships. The few ships which had been mobilized, some galleys from the Rouen arsenal and sailing ships requisitioned in the Channel ports, were all in the north. Inland, garrisons absorbed most of the available manpower. There was a small number of troops in Saintonge, along the northern shore of the Gironde, commanded by Louis of Poitiers, Count of Valentinois, who had been sent specially from Paris. Another force was collected in his own area by the Seneschal of Agen, Robert Houdetot. He was appointed royal lieutenant in Languedoc. Containment was the only policy open to these men. The population of the south was exhorted to increase its efforts and subjected to a torrent of royal propaganda dwelling upon the horrors which the English were about to visit upon their homes. But the truce of Malestroit was still in force. The appeals were received with deadening apathy. Most communities found some reason for evading the royal commissioner's pleas for funds and men; some, such as Carcassonne, refused point-blank.[5]

Henry of Lancaster's army was ready at Southampton by 22 May 1345, within a week of its appointed time, a masterpiece of careful preparation nullified by the vagaries of the weather. Strong south-west winds held his fleet of more than 150 ships for several weeks in the Solent.[6] In Gascony men excited by the prospect of recovering their lost lands could not wait. Small bands of armed men had already begun to infiltrate themselves into French-occupied Saintonge during May. At some time between 4 and 6 June 1345, the Gascons attacked Montravel, an enormous moated castle near Castillon on the north bank of the Dordogne. They came without warning and captured it. Montravel was the kind of place which must have been under-manned by the French in the conditions of 1345. Monbreton, a short distance upstream, was taken a few days later. These were the first acts of open war, the repudiation of the truce which all France had been told to expect daily. At Agen the Seneschal called for reinforcements to be sent urgently from Toulouse. Across the neighbour-ing provinces the nobility were called to arms in one district after another as the news percolated through to officials during the next few days.[7]

The formal campaign was opened by the English Seneschal, Ralph Stafford, in the second half of June 1345. He laid siege to Blaye and then, leaving a strong covering force there, to Langon. They were the closest significant French garrison towns to Bordeaux, obvious targets for an English offensive, therefore well prepared and garrisoned. Neither showed any sign of surrendering quickly. While the main forces of the duchy sat patiently outside Blaye and Langon, a war of movement was fought by irregular bands of freebooters and adventurers, small groups who made their way into French territory and fell without warning on vulnerable places. This bewildering succession of widely dispersed attacks was

extraordinarily difficult for the thinly spread forces of the French commanders to deal with, and caused disruption out of all proportion to the
importance of the gains. Moreover, not all the gains were unimportant. In
Périgord, which was the worst-affected region, Gascon raiders joined
forces with rebellious local noblemen throughout the length of the province and not only in the southern parts which had risen with the Albrets
in 1340. In the extreme north of Périgord, on the march of Limousin, a
disaffected bastard of the Count's family roamed about with a mixed band
of Gascons and local men. Nontron, a hill town which was one of the main
markets of the region and was defended by a royal garrison, fell to him in
July. Ans, just east of Périgueux, followed in August. Périgueux itself
might have fallen to a well-organized conspiracy between a group of
citizens and a local nobleman in English service. If their plan had not been
betrayed, they would have seized a gate of the Puy Saint-Front and
occupied the Bourg with the aid of sixty men-at-arms and a contingent
from the Anglo-Gascon garrison at Mussidan.[8]

The French defence was as uncoordinated as the assaults of the Anglo-
Gascons. By the beginning of August 1345, French forces in Saintonge
were tied down in beating off raids and defending Blaye. The small army
which Robert Houdetot had collected in the Agenais, perceiving that the
threat was still far away, was engaged in the siege of Casseneuil, the only
English garrison in their immediate neighbourhood. Some 40 miles away
an independent force which the Count of Armagnac had assembled was
besieging an insignificant Anglo-Gascon garrison at Monchamp just outside Condom. The largest concentration of French troops in the south-
west had been assembled in the course of July by Bertrand de l'Isle and the
Count of Périgord. They laid siege at about this time to Montcuq, a castle
occupied by the lord of Albret's men which stood over the road south from
Bergerac, a short distance away from the town. This decision appears to
have had no better strategic justification than the fact that the Count
claimed Montcuq for his own. In northern Périgord and in the march of
the Bazadais around Langon, there were no significant French forces at all.
The Bishop of Beauvais was with Louis of Poitiers in Saintonge. But he was
not a military man and whatever efforts he made wholly failed to impose
strategic order on this chaos.[9]

Philip VI and his ministers were mesmerized by the dangers which had
yet to materialize in the north. The first English troops to reach France
landed in Brittany (probably at Brest) with John de Montfort and the Earl
of Northampton during the second week of June 1345. Within a week a
flying column commanded by one of Northampton's lieutenants, Sir

Thomas Dagworth, had penetrated into central Brittany. Dagworth, a rising star among the lesser English captains, found Charles of Blois in the marsh of Cadoret near Josselin and inflicted a humiliating defeat on him. The Governor of the Channel Islands, Sir Thomas Ferrers, landed on Guernsey at about the same time with a mixed band of Englishmen and seamen of Bayonne. They laid siege to the French garrison of Castle Cornet on 2 July 1345. The numbers involved in these adventures were still small, about 500 in Brittany, not much more than 100 on Guernsey.[10]

In England, the ships of the army of Gascony were still tacking along the west coast into stiff south-westerly winds while Henry of Lancaster and his men followed on land. The army of Edward III himself, which included the Prince of Wales and most of the higher nobility of England, was embarking at Sandwich in the last days of June. The probability is that Edward intended to land in southern Normandy. But his plans were so completely shrouded in secrecy that not a trace of them can be discovered in the sources or had reached the ears of the French. Large garrisons and coast-guard forces therefore had to be stationed along the march of Flanders and the whole length of the coast from Picardy to the Cotentin to account for every possibility. Philip VI had left Paris at the end of May 1345. He passed the whole of June and July in the lower valley of the Loire, close to the Breton front and equidistant from Gascony and Flanders.[11]

Edward III's plans for his own army, whatever they had been, were briskly put aside as a result of a sudden crisis of events in the Low Countries at the end of June 1345. The Low Countries were no longer central to the English King's thinking as they had been five years earlier. He had finally lost the alliance of the Count of Hainault, who had been reconciled to Philip VI in April 1343. That veteran soldier John of Hainault, once among Edward III's closest mentors, had lost interest in his cause and was soon to make his peace with the King of France and fight in a French army. The Duke of Guelders, Edward's closest friend and counsellor among the German princes, was dead. The Duke of Brabant had remained friendly for just long enough to see his dues more or less paid and then relapsed into an increasingly unfriendly neutrality. Many of the lesser princes had still not been paid. They were openly hostile.[12] Flanders was the only important ally surviving from the grand coalition of 1340. The events of 1340 had taught Edward III not to look on Flanders as a source of great contract armies or even as a landing ground for English ones, but the county remained an invaluable strategic asset, the only province of France apart from Gascony and the occupied parts of Brittany which recognized

Edward III as king, a thorn in France's northern flank which tied down large French forces in the border garrisons of the Lys and Aa valleys, forcing Philip VI to divert energy and money far away from the main point.

Flanders mattered enough for 'sudden news' about its fate to make Edward put back his expedition. The 'sudden news' has not been recorded but it can be guessed. Edward's position in Flanders depended entirely on the governments of the three great towns, and in particular on Ghent, the richest and most populous of them. Their rule was not entirely secure. In the rural areas and the smaller towns it was a government of force. Moreover, it was ruthlessly exercised in the economic interest of the great towns, which suppressed the municipal autonomy of their rivals and crabbed their competing textile industries with onerous regulations and controls. Periodic outbreaks of rebellion in towns like Dendermonde, Poperinghe and Aalst had always in the past been efficiently put down. But the system was inherently unstable and it depended on unity of purpose among the three towns, which could not be taken for granted.

Ghent in particular had grave internal problems. Jacob van Artevelde was a declining power there, insensitive and isolated behind the walls of liveried bodyguards who surrounded him, his reputation dented by the military fiasco of 1340, even his value as an orator and demagogue undermined by growing remoteness and by the widening divisions within his own town. In January 1343 van Artevelde's enemies had taken to the streets and very nearly succeeded in deposing him. He was saved not so much by his own supporters in Ghent as by the militiamen of Bruges and Ypres. An even more serious incident had occurred much more recently in May 1345 as a result of a long and bitter industrial dispute between the weavers of Ghent and the fullers. The quarrel was about wages, not politics, but it divided the oligarchy of the town, most of whose members were publicly identified by trade or sympathy with one side or the other. On 2 May 1345 in the Friday Market, the scene of Edward III's first proclamation as King of France five years earlier, the members of the two guilds fought a pitched battle in which several hundred men were killed.[13]

Louis of Nevers and the exiled nobility of Flanders who were with him in France grasped their opportunity. In May 1345 the town of Dendermonde in north-eastern Flanders declared itself for the Count and threw off the government of Bruges. It is almost certain that Louis' intrigues lay behind this incident as well as the outbreaks of violence which occurred at Aalst, Grammont and Oudenarde at about the same time. For a while, he was prevented from re-entering his county and completing the chaos only by the terms of the truce of Malestroit. The repudiation of the truce in the south released him.[14] In the last week of June 1345 Edward III was told that he was likely to lose Flanders very quickly. The embarkation of his army had already begun. On 29 June, he abruptly changed his orders. The fleet, some 300 ships carrying more than 2,000 troops with all their stores, equipment and horses on board, was ordered to sail first to the Hondt. The ships sailed from England on the evening of 3 July 1345. On the morning of the 5th they lay off Sluys.

Edward's intention was to sort out his affairs in Flanders as quickly as he could before proceeding with his original plans. Unfortunately, his negotiations took longer than he had expected. The ships remained at their anchorage with the men and horses cooped up on board for two and a half weeks, from 5 to 22 July 1345.

On 7 July van Artevelde arrived from Ghent, a frightened man, more like a refugee seeking asylum than the representative of his town, and obviously dependent upon the protection of the troops provided for him by Bruges and Ypres. Other delegations came and went. Edward received them on board his ship. No record of their discussions has survived. It seems clear, however, that the King wanted to force Louis of Nevers to make a choice. The fiction that the Count's government continued in his absence while Louis did his best to upset it from beyond the borders of the county had a gravely unsettling effect on Flemish politics. Louis should return to Flanders and govern his county as Edward's vassal, or be permanently deprived of it. There may have been some truth in the rumour that Edward wanted to appoint his son, the Prince of Wales, in Louis' place if he should choose the second alternative. But if this proposal was ever made it was certainly not acceptable to the Flemings. They preferred a legal fiction to an illegal one. Bruges and Ypres seem to have favoured the status quo, uncomfortable as it was. The problem was Ghent, whose desires emerged only in the course of a covert power struggle within the municipality while the conferences at Sluys were in progress. Only the outcome of this struggle is known. The sizeable minority within the town which questioned the whole notion of an alliance with England was defeated. It was decided to continue the policy of van Artevelde. But the man himself was dispensed with. He was thought to be too ambitious and too ready to use his intimacy with Edward III to buttress his personal position. The magistrates of Ghent peremptorily commanded him to return. On 17 July 1345, after a great deal of hesitation, he went. In the evening a mob was whipped up by a rival demagogue, a weaver called Gérard Denis, the rising star among van Artevelde's enemies. They collected around his house. 'Come out and tell us the news about the King of England,' Denis cried, according to the most reliable account of what happened. Van Artevelde replied that it was late. He would give a full report tomorrow. 'Break it down, men!' the mob cried. 'Kill him!' Van Artevelde tried to get out through a stable wing and make for sanctuary in the Franciscan church a short distance away. But he was caught and battered to death. The municipality which he had governed for many years confiscated his property and banished his family.

Edward III had always regarded van Artevelde as the principal pillar of the Anglo-Flemish alliance. He was profoundly affected by his death. For some years afterwards van Artevelde's family lived under his protection in England on pensions paid from his treasury. But the truth was that van Artevelde had become a marginal factor in the politics of Flanders by July 1345, as Edward must have realized in the course of his visit. How marginal was apparent from the fact that his death made almost no difference to the course of Edward's relations with the Flemings. It may even have made them smoother. During the third week of July, Louis of Nevers was presented with the joint decision of the three great towns that they would not permit him to return unless he recognized Edward III as his sovereign. Louis refused. No attempt was made to depose him, but on 19 July, two days after the murder of van Artevelde, the English King sealed an agreement with each of the great towns by which they undertook not to allow the Count to resume the government of Flanders while he remained loyal to Philip VI of France. In the meantime public business would continue to be conducted on his behalf by the oligarchies of Ghent, Bruges and Ypres. Edward promised to give them what help they needed in putting down any internal opposition. He declared himself satisfied, and probably he was. Louis of Nevers made no progress thereafter in reoc-cupying the county and his supporters, who had immured themselves in Dendermonde, were in due course expelled.

The English King's visit to Flanders was a considerable diplomatic success. But it put his military plans for the year into disarray. When his ships sailed from Sluys on 22 July 1345 for their secret destination they were hit by a violent summer storm which drove them north for two days and then back on to the English coast. At dawn on 26 July 1345 the leading vessels arrived in the Downs. The rest were scattered across the North Sea and found their way home over the next few days. The men could not be confined to the ships any longer. They had to be disembarked, itself a time-consuming business, and once it was completed even more time would be required to rest and re-embark them. Meanwhile not only the soldiers but several thousand seamen would have to be kept by the Kent coast under the orders of the Marshals and Admirals. Edward travelled to Westminster to deliberate with his Council on what should be done next. The argument lasted eight days. The outcome was the cancellation of the expedition. So the army was dispersed. The ships were allowed to return to their ports. Fresh arrangements were made for two new and much smaller armies to be collected between August and October to reinforce the troops already sent to Brittany and Gascony. It was probably not the decision that Edward himself would have made. Although the Council meeting had been held in the utmost secrecy the result could hardly be concealed. Within a very few days after it had broken up, Philip VI felt safe enough in the north to begin switching money and troops to Brittany and the south-west. On 8 August 1345 he appointed the Duke of Bourbon as his lieutenant on the south-west march.[15]

Henry of Lancaster completed the disembarkation of his army in Bordeaux on 9 August 1345, the day after the Duke of Bourbon's appointment.[16] He made his presence felt immediately. Ralph Stafford's cautious policy of pushing the boundaries of the duchy outward from the centre by a succession of methodical sieges was briskly repudiated. Derby had arrived late and intended to achieve the maximum political impact in the shortest possible time. He had no desire to lose the initiative by becoming involved in a succession of interminable sieges, and no desire to give the French time to concentrate their dispersed forces. A local truce was therefore made with the French castellan of Blaye. The Anglo-Gascon troops besieging the place were recalled. The Earl then marched up the Garonne valley from Bordeaux to join forces with the rest of the army of the duchy encamped with Stafford himself outside Langon. The two men did not get on well. Derby rebuked Stafford for wasting effort on the siege of so insignificant a place. There was a meeting of the commanders of the army. It was decided to abandon the siege, and instead attack Bergerac.

The main author of this scheme appears to have been the lord of Albret. He had his own reasons for wishing to see English arms triumph in the Dordogne valley. Of the many pockets of French troops carrying out miscellaneous operations in the south-west, the largest was engaged in the siege of his own castle at Montcuq. Foremost among the besiegers was Albret's most persistent enemy, the Count of Périgord. There were, however, sounder reasons for the decision. Bergerac was the major French garrison town of southern Périgord. The great stone bridge was the principal crossing of the Dordogne in Périgord. It was a superb forward base

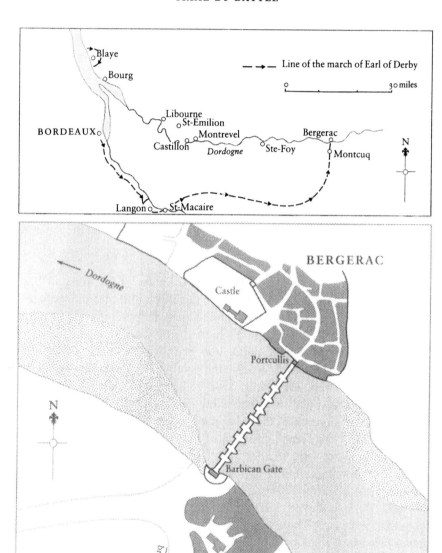

19 The Bergerac campaign, August 1345

from which to raid deep into French-held territory to the north and east. There were good communications by river with Bordeaux and Libourne. At the same time the town was weak, situated on low-lying ground and defended by old and inadequate fortifications: a castle dating from the eleventh century, a ditch and a wall which was still made up of the joined façades of houses at the edge of the town.

The Earl of Derby's army marched day and night from Langon and arrived at Montcuq before the news of its coming. In the French camp, there was consternation, then panic. Abandoning their equipment, the besiegers fled towards Bergerac, pursued by the mounted contingents of the Anglo-Gascon army. The pursuit extended across 3 miles of flat marshland, ending in the small village on the south bank of the Dordogne opposite Bergerac known as La Madeleine. The bridge of Bergerac crossed the river between village and town, a narrow causeway some 200 yards long which was guarded at its southern end by a powerful moated barbican, but at the northern end by nothing more than a portcullis. In the middle of the bridge the causeway was partially obstructed by a small chapel. The Anglo-Gascons reached the south end of the bridge in the early evening while the rearguard of the French army was still struggling through the barbican and along the causeway into the town encumbered with horses and equipment. The troops within the town attempted to sortie from the portcullis at the northern end of the bridge. The Anglo-Gascons simultaneously launched an assault on the barbican and forced their way on to the bridge at the southern end. In the confusion the refugees from Montcuq were crammed between the two. They were killed in great numbers by archers shooting from the sound banks in the river. As the massacre ended, dismounted men-at-arms of the English army rushed the entrance of the town. A frightened horse jammed the portcullis and prevented the defenders from bringing it down. The attackers were able to carry their pursuit into the streets and by the end of the day they were masters of Bergerac. Like any place taken by storm, Bergerac was given over to the plunderers. The booty of the town was immense: that of the defeated army possibly greater: tents, horses and equipment for several hundred men-at-arms. The haul of prisoners was the largest yet taken by either side in the course of the war. It included the Seneschal of Périgord, ten prominent French noblemen and a host of lesser persons.

The military organization of the French in the south-west was now in complete disarray. The survivors of the army of Montcuq and Bergerac had been split in two by the fighting. Those who had escaped southward were reconstituted as an army of sorts by Bertrand de l'Isle and withdrawn

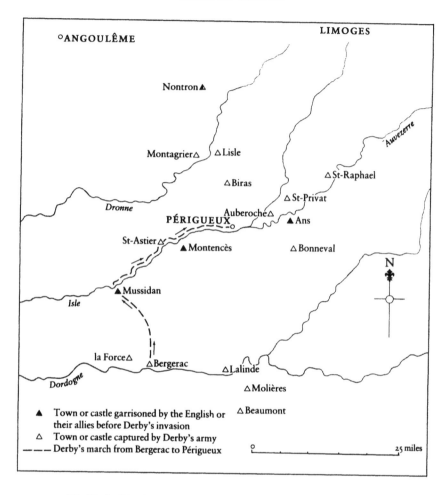

°ANGOULÊME

LIMOGES

Nontron▲

Montagrier△ △Lisle

Auvezerre

△St-Raphael

△Biras

△St-Privat

Dronne

Auberoche△

PÉRIGUEUX—° ▲Ans

St-Astier△ ▲Montencès △Bonneval

N

▲Mussidan

Isle

la Force△ ▲Bergerac

△Lalinde

Dordogne △Molières

▲ Town or castle garrisoned by the English or
     their allies before Derby's invasion △Beaumont
△ Town or castle captured by Derby's army
— — — Derby's march from Bergerac to Périgueux

25 miles

20 The Earl of Derby's invasion of Périgord, September–October 1345

to La Réole, the strongest of the Garonne fortresses. Another force, of
which the Count of Armagnac took command, was collected from the
remnants who had found their way out of Bergerac by the north. They
withdrew towards Périgueux and shut themselves up there.[17]

The shock felt at the French court when the news reached them can be
imagined. Gascony was now given priority over every other front. Within
ten days of the battle a fresh army was being formed. The Duke of
Bourbon arrived to take up his lieutenancy in Languedoc in September. He
threw himself into a campaign of recruitment extending over the whole of
that month and the next. All the soldiers who could be found in the

seneschalsies of Beaucaire, Carcassonne and Toulouse were assembled at mustering points in the north of the province. A headquarters was set up at Angoulême. Most of the men recruited in Languedoc were directed there from their mustering points. They joined forces in the fields outside the walls with the army which had been operating in Saintonge under Louis of Poitiers, with the survivors of Bergerac commanded by Bertrand de l'Isle and with fresh men raised in more distant provinces of France, mainly Burgundy and Auvergne. The overall direction of affairs was placed in the hesitant hands of the young Duke of Normandy.[18]

Derby remained at Bergerac for just over two weeks after the battle, resting, distributing the spoils and mopping up the fortified places within easy reach. These included most of the castles and *bastides* of southern Périgord. The inhabitants, according to a French official, were paralysed with fear. No one resisted. On 10 September 1345 the Earl divided his forces, leaving 1,500 men to hold Bergerac under the command of the Albret brothers, Bernard-Aiz and Bérard. The rest, consisting of 2,100 men-at-arms, with perhaps 4,000 to 6,000 footsoldiers and mounted archers, marched north under Derby's own command to the town of Mussidan, where the Anglo-Gascons had maintained an isolated garrison for more than three years. From Mussidan, the Earl turned east along the valley of the Isle towards the provincial capital, Périgueux.[19]

The defences at Périgueux were in an even worse state than those of Bergerac. Like a number of towns of central and southern France, Périgueux was a double city with two entirely independent systems of fortification. The Cité to the west had its origin in the old Roman town. It was a geometrical grid of streets around the church of St Étienne (then the cathedral), the castle of the counts of Périgord and the remains of an old amphitheatre, defended by low crumbling Roman walls of the third century with only a few modern improvements; the much larger, more densely populated Puy Saint-Front to the east was an organic growth around the great monastic church which now serves as the cathedral, protected by walls dating from the twelfth and thirteenth centuries. Between them lay the open suburbs of Entre-Deux-Villes. Only the accident that the Count of Armagnac had fled there with some of the survivors of Bergerac enabled this great expanse of walls to be defended, and indeed turned to the town's advantage. Derby cannot have had enough men to invest such a large conglomeration entirely. He maintained a loose siege, prowling with large raiding parties around the roads into the city, plundering the land about, and attacking those nearby castles and towns which had kept their gates closed. By the middle of October 1345 the English had taken control of a tight ring of fortified places around the northern and eastern sides of Périgueux and had more or less cut off the city from its sources of supply.[20]

The fall of Périgueux would have been a misfortune for the French as great as that of Bergerac, but it was a long time before they made any serious attempt to prevent it. The Duke of Normandy arrived in Angoulême in the first half of September 1345 and marched his men in a wide arc around the north of Derby's theatre of operations, eventually establishing his headquarters at the safe distance of Limoges. By October he had about him (according to a reliable contemporary estimate) some 8,000 men-at-arms and 'innumerable' footsoldiers.[21] At the beginning of October he decided to detach 3,000 men-at-arms and a large number of footsoldiers to go to the aid of Périgueux. The command of this force was given to Louis of Poitiers, but it also included Bertrand de l'Isle and many of those who had fought with him at Bergerac. John of Normandy himself followed by an uncertain route with the rest of his army.

The precise sequence of events is obscure. What appears to have happened is that Louis of Poitiers successfully relieved Périgueux, forced the main body of the Anglo-Gascon army to withdraw, and then, in accordance with the established French military practice, began the slow, methodical reconquest of the surrounding strongholds. Derby had left garrisons in all the more important of them in order to maintain pressure on Périgueux and delay the progress of the French army. In about the middle of October 1345 the French laid siege to one of these places, the castle of Auberoche. Today Auberoche is a small hamlet on the north bank of the river Auvezère 10 miles east of Périgueux. In the fourteenth century it was the site of a large seigneurial fortress belonging to one of the many petty lords of Périgord who had (in the French Chancery's phrase) 'turned English'. He had surrendered it as soon as the English army had arrived. Derby placed its defence in the hands of Alexander de Caumont, a fearless old man, one of the principal Gascon lords of the English army.

The besiegers sat outside the castle of Auberoche for a time. Then, on the morning of 21 October 1345, they were attacked suddenly and in force by the Earl of Derby. He had approached them by night with the main body of his army. The French suffered heavy casualties from arrow wounds before they had even come within fighting distance of their enemy. Although they had the advantage of numbers and at one point seemed to be prevailing, by mid-day they had begun to waiver and fall back. As their lines broke, the garrison sortied from the castle. The men-at-arms of Derby's army remounted their horses. The combined force pursued the separated groups of fleeing French soldiers, inflicting upon them the appalling carnage always reserved for the defeated in battle. Louis of Poitiers was taken after a savage fight but died of his wounds, the end of an uninspired general but a courageous and loyal servant of the French Crown who had fought in every significant campaign since 1338. Bertrand de l'Isle, an abler but more self-serving man, was also captured. He could not bring himself to utter the words of surrender when he was overpowered, but being too valuable to kill was dragged away to captivity. The other prisoners included one count, seven viscounts, three barons, the seneschals of Toulouse and Clermont, twelve other bannerets, a nephew of Pope Clement VI and more knights than anyone counted. The ransoms exceeded even those taken at Bergerac.

By a convention which persisted well beyond the end of the middle ages prisoners were not the state's affair but the private property of their captors. They might sell or mortgage them, detain them at pleasure or make what terms with them they could extract within the very broad limits fixed by the customs of war and the law of contract. So much so that prisoners released on parole to find their ransoms could expect to find their bargains enforced against them in their own country by the code of honour of their class and even by the courts of the sovereign in whose service they had been captured. Prisoners were by far the most valuable prizes of war, pursued in many cases with greater energy and courage than more important military objectives and occasionally at the expense of them. The egregious Walter Mauny, who was the most successful collector of prisoners of his age, had already captured the engineer John Crabbe in the Scotch wars and sold him to the King of England for 1,000 marks; between 1337 and 1340 he took a further £11,000 worth of prisoners in Flanders and northern France, including Guy Bastard of Flanders; in 1342 there were seven Breton noblemen, allies of Charles of Blois captured in the course of an otherwise useless enterprise in Finistère. Mauny had made a substantial personal fortune out of prisoners. But in spite of his example the English had so far taken relatively few of them. There had been too few victories. It was the battles of Bergerac and Auberoche which opened the eyes of both sides to the financial rewards of victory in the field and the catastrophic consequences for the defeated.[22]

There was an uncertain principle that ransoms should be reasonable. But the only limit recognized in practice was the amount which the prisoner could afford, with the aid of his friends, relations and tenants if need be. The inhabitants of Montricoux, a village in the valley of the Aveyron whose lord was captured at Auberoche, had to find the large sum of 200 *l.t.* to contribute to his ransom, 'not wishing to see him destitute'. Some, who had exhausted their own resources and connections, turned to the Crown. Half a century later, Froissart recorded the recollections of some of the prisoners of Auberoche about the way they had been treated in Paris: squatting on the ground outside the offices of household officials day after day, hoping for an audience of the King as their purses were drained by greedy Parisian innkeepers. 'Come back tomorrow or, better still, the day after.' It has the authentic ring of officialdom, but it is hardly fair to Philip VI, who was at his wits' end to find money to defend his realm and made generous grants in hard cases: 2,000 *l.t.* (£400) in one case, 2,000 gold *écus* (£375) in another, many smaller sums to knights and squires who, having paid their ransoms, could no longer afford to arm or mount themselves. The ransoms of Bergerac and Auberoche were thought to be particularly steep. The Pope's nephew, according to his indulgent uncle, was made to pay Alexander de Caumont a sum so large that he would have to sell a large part of his estates. Indeed, some ransoms were never paid. The prisoners languished in jail for years or, like Jean de Galard, lord of Limeuil, took service with the English in lieu of payment and found themselves accused of treason by their erstwhile companions in arms. For Derby's army the profits were immense. The Earl himself was reliably reported to have made enough money from the prizes of Bergerac to cover the entire cost, 52,000 marks (£17,333), of rebuilding the Savoy Palace in the Strand, and to have made another £50,000 from the ransoms of Auberoche.[23]

The battle of Auberoche marked the end of the French campaign of 1345 in the south-west. Although the Duke of Normandy was only about 25 miles away when the battle was fought, and commanded a fresh army larger than the one which had been defeated, he abandoned the effort as soon as he heard the news. His troops returned to Angoulême and were disbanded there on 4 November 1345. The Duke himself led his entourage north to lay plans for the following year in the austere castle of Châtillon-sur-Indre. It may be that shortage of money left him no alternative. Some of his troops were certainly in a very bad way. The Seneschal of Beaucaire had been complaining in September that not only were his men unpaid but they did not have the wherewithal to feed themselves and their horses. Some had already sold their equipment and deserted. The position is unlikely to have been better at the end of October, and was probably worse. Even so, the Duke's decision to withdraw from the field was remarkable, and it had serious consequences for the French war effort in the south-west. There was no one to oppose the Earl of Derby in the field between November 1345 and March 1346.[24]

In spite of its promising beginnings the English expedition to Brittany ended in disappointment. On Guernsey, Castle Cornet had been stormed by the seamen of Bayonne on 24 August 1345 and the entire French garrison killed. This event completed the English reoccupation of the Channel Islands and removed the most serious threat to England's communications with Brittany and Gascony.[25] But then progress faltered. There were several reasons. Northampton's army was of high quality but it was only a few hundred strong. Moreover, control of its operations was shared with John de Montfort, who had to be allowed to cut a good figure in his own duchy but proved to be a thoroughly inadequate commander. After Dagworth's flying raid into central Brittany in June there was a long delay before the real campaign began at the end of July. It is not clear why this delay occurred, but its results were unfortunate. In June and July 1345, Charles of Blois was weak. In August, the French government, realizing that Edward III's threatened invasion had been abandoned, began to transfer to Brittany troops previously reserved for the defence of the north. Many of these troops had been deployed in Normandy. Their transfer was therefore achieved much more speedily than the other great movement of men to Périgord and Languedoc which was planned at the same time. Charles of Blois had already received substantial reinforcement by 9 August.[26]

It was John de Montfort who conducted the main military operation of the summer. In the last few days of July he laid siege to Quimper, now the only significant town which his rival held on the south coast of the peninsula. The siege was a terrible failure. When John tried to storm the flimsy defences on 11 August he was driven back with heavy losses. Charles of Blois arrived a few days later with his newly enlarged army and brought the siege to an abrupt end. John, who appears to have received no warning of his coming, withdrew in disorder. He himself was surrounded in a fortified house nearby and escaped only by corrupting a sentry in the middle of the night. Not long afterwards he withdrew to his castle at Hennebont where he fell gravely ill. On 26 September he died. He had been a hesitant politician and an uninspired soldier, always the tool of other men's ambitions. But however unsatisfactory John had been while he was alive, his death created worse problems than it solved. The English once again had to remake the Montfortist party around a new symbol. The Earl of Northampton received the homage of the surviving Montfortists in October 1345 in the joint names of Edward III and the dead man's son, also called John. But the new Duke was only a child. He was about five years old and was being brought up in England. The outlook seemed more than ever uncertain.[27]

On 16 October 1345 the English King's Council assembled at Westminster for what must have been a rather sombre review of events. The news of Derby's capture of Bergerac, which arrived in the middle of the proceedings, was the only bright note. At this stage it was still proposed to send fresh armies to Gascony and Brittany to reinforce the men already fighting there. They were due, in theory, to leave the Solent ports in a matter of days. This proposal had never had much to recommend it. It was the compromise which had emerged from the lengthy debates in the Council in July after Edward had been obliged to cancel his project of invading northern France. Reality had crept in by now. Even if the timetable could be kept (which it could not) it would have been folly to spend scarce money on dispatching penny packets of troops to the continent at the very end of the campaigning season. The government announced the cancellation of both expeditions on 22 October 1345. A new expedition to the continent was to be undertaken as early as possible in the new year. The shipmasters, whose vessels had in most cases been under requisition since the spring, were not released. They were simply licensed to trade on putting up bonds to secure their reappearance at Portsmouth by 17 February 1346. The embarkation of the new army was fixed for 1 March 1346.[28]

It is unlikely that any firm decision had yet been made about its destination. The most likely place at this stage was Brittany. In October 1345 the Earl of Northampton embarked on a long winter campaign in the north of the Breton peninsula, the object of which appears fairly clearly to have been the capture of harbours more accessible from southern England than Brest or Vannes. Northampton's difficulties were particularly acute in this part of Brittany, where the family of Jeanne de Penthièvre (Charles of Blois' wife) had been the dominant power for decades and natural loyalties were as strong as anywhere in the duchy. It was all very well to inflict a sharp defeat on Charles of Blois on open ground, as Northampton succeeded in doing at the outset of the winter campaign. Charles always withdrew in good order. Northampton was unable to capture his strongholds. He failed to take Carhaix, an important road junction on his way north. He failed to take Guingamp, Charles of Blois' headquarters, which had been heavily fortified since 1343. Northampton's siege engines made no impression at all on its walls. At Lannion there was another embarrassing failure at the end of November. The Earl succeeded only in capturing a large consignment of Spanish wine which was being stored outside the walls. By the end of the year he had established a tenuous hold over the long inlet of the River Jaudy on the Tréguier peninsula. But it was almost useless to him. Tréguier, the principal harbour, was unfortified save for the tower of the cathedral, which had to be demolished in order to prevent it from being used by the French. The only place where the English could establish a permanent garrison was the small town of La Roche-Derrien, 3 miles upstream, which was captured in the face of ferocious resistance by its citizens after a series of assaults extending over several days. La Roche-Derrien was to be the focal point of the Breton war for the next two years and its retention, so far away from the main centres of English strength, proved to be a costly business. A large garrison was left there and one of Northampton's principal captains, Richard Totesham, was put in command of it. But the harbour could take no vessels larger than 60 tons' burden and these only at the top of the tide. It never could be, certainly never was, used as a landing place for large bodies of troops.[29]

At Westminster the English King received a papal ambassador at a disagreeable audience. The ambassador, Niccolo Canali, Archbishop of Ravenna, was the harbinger of another pair of peacemaking cardinals. He had come to obtain a safe conduct for them and to draw the King's attention to the fact that the truce of Malestroit still had nine months to run. Edward's answer, which was delivered by one of his household officers, was a litany of abuse against the King of France. Edward would appoint 'neither place nor date' to discuss a permanent peace. On the contrary he intended, he said, to claim his rights by armed force and then, if the Pope was pleased to send him cardinals with reasonable proposals, they might be graciously received. The Archbishop inquired where those cardinals would go. When the King of England comes, was the answer, all Christendom will know of it, and the Pope will have no doubt where to send his messages. The interview ended on this grandiloquent note. Edward could be confident now that English opinion would support him in any quarrel with the Pope even in the face of excommunication and interdict. Clement probably thought so too. He did not dare to resort to these extremes. The ambassador stayed at court for a while 'because it was Christmas', wrote the acerbic Adam Murimuth, 'and because his expense allowance was fifteen florins a day.' When the cardinals renewed their application for a safe conduct, in February 1346, their messenger was thrown in prison.[30]

The Earl of Derby changed the direction of his campaign after the battle of Auberoche. Instead of pressing the siege of Périgueux, he left a group of garrisons close by to watch their opportunities and then marched south towards the Garonne valley to begin the recovery of territory on the eastern march of the duchy in more favourable conditions than any which an English army had yet enjoyed there. The *bastide* of Pellegrue surrendered on terms; Monségur, another *bastide*, resisted and was stormed and sacked. Early in November 1345 the Earl arrived outside La Réole.[31]

The defences of La Réole were very powerful and were manned by a large French garrison, but, as Henry of Lancaster once observed, no fortress was strong enough to resist the enemy within. The citizens of La Réole had no stomach for a siege and no natural loyalty to the King of France. Before its capture in the war of Saint-Sardos the town had enjoyed a more prominent place in the English duchy than it could ever hope to have in a French province. It had also had privileged access to the sea for its wines and a greater degree of municipal autonomy than any French seneschal was likely to tolerate. The leading citizens discussed among themselves what they should do, and agreed to deliver up the town to the Earl. On 8 November 1345 a feint was arranged at one side of the town. The men on watch summoned help from the garrison while others opened a gate at the opposite side and allowed the English in. The garrison were lucky to avoid being trapped on the town wall. They saw what was happening in time to reach the citadel, grabbing a troop of pigs in the street as they went, to sustain them for a siege.

The citadel stood at the western edge of the town on a promontory overlooking the river. It was a great square fort with broad corner towers built by the engineers of Edward I. The English bombarded it with stone-throwers without effect and launched assaults over the walls which were driven back. But the citadel was vulnerable to undermining from within the town. After three weeks of burrowing (the Earl worked in the tunnels himself) the garrison commander struck a deal with the besiegers. He had resisted long enough to save his honour before the court of France. So he agreed to observe a truce of five weeks and to surrender if a relieving army had not appeared by the end of that time. Conditional surrenders of this kind were quite common and, provided that the garrison was recognizing reality, not colluding with the enemy, the custom of war sanctioned them. The garrison commander sent notice of the treaty which he had made to the Duke of Normandy and called on him to relieve the town. But the Duke was far away at his winter quarters on the Indre. He did nothing. Bourbon, who was closer at hand, had proclaimed the *arrière-ban* in Languedoc and the march provinces as soon as the English had arrived at La Réole. But the response to his summons was poor. He had squeezed the

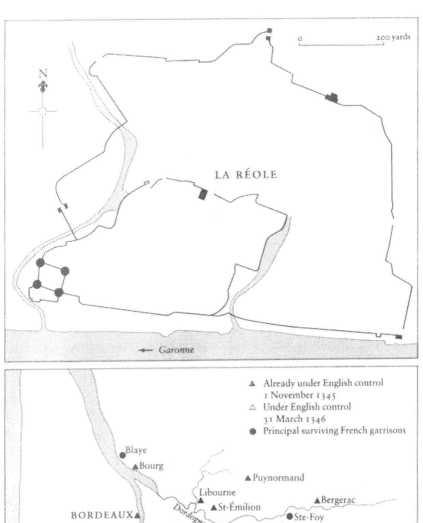

21 English occupation of the Bordelais, winter 1345–6

lemon dry to swell the army which John of Normandy had just disbanded. These men were still trudging back across southern France to their homes. In December the Count of Armagnac was trying to recruit men for Bourbon in his domains in the Rouergue, but if anything came of this it was too little or too late. Early in January 1346 the garrison of La Réole marched away and the English took possession of the citadel. The townsmen were generously treated for their pains.[32]

The Earl of Lancaster (as he had now become, on his father's death in September) remained in winter quarters at La Réole until March 1346 and most of his army was dispersed. The Gascon lords and their retainers returned to their homes until the spring. Some of the principal retinues which had come with the Earl from England went back there, including those of the Earl of Pembroke and Sir James Audley.[33] Those who remained occupied themselves in raiding ill-defended towns and castles of the enemy. Small detachments overran the Garonne valley between La Réole and Saint-Macaire and carried out attacks deep into French territory north of the river. The most spectacular case was the seizure of Angoulême by a small force commanded by the Englishman John of Norwich, which occurred at the end of 1345. Angoulême, which was quite unprepared for an attack, appears to have surrendered after the most perfunctory resistance. John did not hold it for very long. He was compelled to withdraw in February 1346 and it might be supposed that he had gained nothing except spoil. In fact, adventures of this sort hamstrung the French government's conduct of the war. They made men divert effort and money into local defence. No doubt it made sense for Toulouse to begin a great campaign of fortification in December 1345 and for Limoges not only to start rebuilding its defences but to man them day and night during the winter. In most such cases there was a direct cost to the state. The towns sought and almost always obtained the privilege of diverting the state's local tax revenues at source to pay for their work. It became difficult or impossible to recruit men to serve away from home. The tendency of provincial societies to turn in upon themselves in the face of danger was never more clearly expressed than by Gilbert of Cantobre, Bishop of Rodez, writing some eighteen months after these events, in April 1347. The fighting had by then taken a more serious turn, but it had still hardly touched his own diocese. Yet this nervous cleric proposed a scheme of local defence which treated the Rouergue as if it were an independent republic, not a province of the French kingdom. There was to be conscription and taxation organized by local captains, district by district. There was to be a captain-general for the whole province. Elaborate arrangements were proposed for mutual assistance between neighbouring towns and districts. But the captains were on no account to take their men beyond the boundaries of the seneschalsy, and they were not to be obeyed if they tried to. No levies were to be paid to support any military operations outside Rouergue 'but only to pay for the defence of our homeland here in this province'. As for the taxes collected by the Crown, they were to be entirely abolished, and Philip VI invited graciously to content himself with his ordinary revenues.[34]

These places were far from the seat of the fire. Fear, which inspired their inhabitants to urgent effort, paralysed those who lived at the edge of the Bordelais, where the English conquest proceeded swiftly. Froissart relates a conversation between a garrison commander and a deputation of townsmen which was invented but must in fact have occurred in many towns of the south-west. 'Think of us,' the townsmen said; 'if the English capture the town we shall all be killed and our homes overrun.' 'And what do you expect us to do about that?' the captain's attendants asked. 'We want you to stop the assaults of the English by parleying with them, so that we can be left alone in peace, for otherwise we shall not be safe whatever happens. But if you are not prepared to do that, then why not at least withdraw into the citadel to carry on your war, for we have had enough of ours.' This man did as he was asked. A less percipient commander might have rejected their petition out of hand.

Sir Hugh was very harsh [Froissart wrote about one such man]; he told them that the place was strong and well supplied and could hold out for a good six months. They were making a fuss about nothing. When they heard this, they did not argue the point but left him most respectfully. Then, at vespers time, they seized him and threw him into a cell, shouting that he would not be allowed out until he had agreed to do their bidding. 'And what may I ask is that?' 'It is that you shall use your authority to go out and treat with the Earl of Derby and the English, so that we can live in peace.'

In a few places an energetic local commander with a large garrison was able to uphold the cause of Philip VI with élan. The captain of Sainte-Foy-la-Grande, which was now the main obstacle to free communication by river between Bordeaux and Bergerac, beat off a strong attack on his town, one of the few reverses which the English suffered. At Bazas, the French captain returned a defiant answer to Henry of Lancaster's summons to surrender, and managed to hold the townsmen's loyalty for another year. These men were not typical. Langon, which had successfully resisted in the summer, surrendered in the winter. Sainte-Bazeille was recovered for the

477

third time. Marmande was now the only significant French garrison on the Garonne between Bordeaux and Aiguillon.[35]

In the Agenais every hill-baron was assessing the impact of the English victories. In November 1345 the Durforts of Duras, the major noble house of the northern Agenais and the richest branch of the great dispersed clan of Durforts, switched their allegiance to the King of England. Their sudden change of loyalties illustrated the snowball effect of victory in the field. Aimeric de Durfort had been one of the many lords of the south-west forced to make hard choices on the outbreak of war eight years before. He had consistently supported the French Crown, and forfeited valuable estates of his family in the Bordelais in consequence; but he had retained much more extensive possessions in the Agenais and southern Périgord which Philip VI would otherwise have confiscated, and had received periodic grants of territory conquered from supporters of the Bordeaux government. When Aimeric died in 1345, probably at the battle of Auberoche, the situation was very different. The English were now in possession of most of southern Périgord and poised to reconquer the Agenais. Aimeric's calculation did not seem as sound to his brother Gaillard, who succeeded him. Gaillard, who was to become one of the pivotal politicians of the south-west in the next decade, was a shrewd and cynical ex-priest who had once been a professor of canon law at Toulouse University and among the most successful accumulators of ecclesiastical benefices in France. Only the political difficulties of his family induced him to abandon a clerical income of 3,000 *l.t.* per year in middle age in order to marry, take knighthood and throw himself into a dynastic war and the many vendettas of his tribe. He accounted for the allegiance of his three brothers, a large military retinue, major fortresses at Puyguilhem and Duras and, with his allies, 'towns, places, castles, lords, all restored to the obedience of our lord the King'. Lancaster made sure that they were well rewarded.[36]

It was the first sign of the way the wind was blowing in the Agenais. Except in places which were directly garrisoned by the French Crown (as opposed to local lords for the Crown's account) Philip VI's officials rapidly lost all control there during the winter. According to a complaint which the main garrison towns addressed to the King, the region was reduced to anarchy by the end of November and defections were occurring 'daily'. The English opened their campaign at the beginning of the following month. They seized Aiguillon, the town which commanded the confluence of the Lot and the Garonne. As soon as Ralph Stafford appeared before the town the inhabitants fell upon the garrison, killing some and imprisoning others. Then they opened their gates. At which, said Jean le Bel, the Earl of

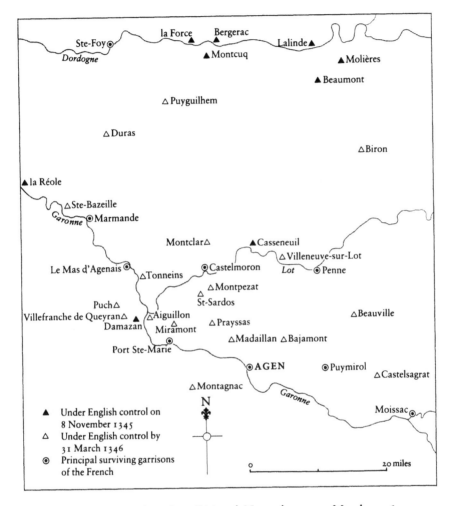

la Force
Bergerac
Ste-Foy◉
Lalinde▲
Dordogne
▲Montcuq
▲Molières
▲Beaumont

△ Puyguilhem

△Duras
△Biron

▲la Réole
△Ste-Bazeille
Garonne ◉Marmande
Montclar△
▲Casseneuil
△Villeneuve-sur-Lot
Le Mas d'Agenais◉
◉Castelmoron
Lot
◉Penne
△Tonneins
△Montpezat
△
St-Sardos
Puch△
△Beauville
Villefranche de Queyran△ ▲ △Aiguillon
△Prayssas
Damazan
△
Miramont
◉
△Madaillan △Bajamont
Port Ste-Marie
◉AGEN
◉Puymirol
△Castelsagrat
△Montagnac
N
Garonne
▲ Under English control on
    8 November 1345
△ Under English control by
    31 March 1346
◉ Principal surviving garrisons
    of the French
Moissac◉
0
20 miles

22 Agenais and southern Périgord, November 1345–March 1346

Lancaster was 'as pleased as if the King of England had suddenly become £100,000 richer'. Judging by the flow of gifts to the coseigneurs of Aiguillon, the coup had been arranged with them in advance. Before they captured Aiguillon the English had no garrisons in the Agenais except at Casseneuil on the Lot. During the next three months they took possession of substantially the whole region, mainly by defection rather than conquest. In some places the local inhabitants joined in the plundering of their neighbours. The only sustained resistance which is recorded occurred at Montpezat, which had a royal garrison. They defended the place with courage until the inhabitants rose up and killed them. By March 1346, the French were reduced to their major strongholds: Port-Sainte-Marie, Agen and Moissac on the Garonne, and Castelmoron on the Lot.[37]

The Duke of Bourbon kept his quarters throughout the winter at Agen, the provincial capital. There was already a siege atmosphere there. All the roads out were cut off one after the other in the first three months of 1346. River traffic downstream beyond Port-Sainte-Marie was closed off by the English capture of Aiguillon. In the fourteenth century, before the fruit trees took over, the men of Agen made some of the most famous wines of the south-west on the hillsides behind the town, which were now speckled with enemy garrisons. Bajamont, the closest, had been recovered by the Durforts, those persistent enemies of the town, a base from which to resume the harassment of the citizens suspended on their family's expulsion years before. The inhabitants of the suburbs were pressing into the town, carrying all their possessions with them. The cathedral canons moved their wine from the sheds in the vineyards where it was made, to stores within the walls. Weapons were distributed to the citizens from the common stocks. Tremendous works were in progress on the walls, which had never completely enclosed the town. A new wall appeared on the northern side, where previously a ditch and a canal had been thought enough. Two towers which had been allowed to collapse were rebuilt. The cluster of buildings between the east gate and the river was being demolished, and a new tower was rising at the head of the Garonne bridge. Great gaps had appeared in the market place where once had stood the mansions of prominent citizens, now disgraced for defecting to the English King. The tension generated a sense of common purpose, but also venomous antagonisms: between the citizens and the refugees; between both groups and the soldiers of the Duke of Bourbon. The refugees, if they were not penniless and thrown on to the grudging charity of their hosts, were suspected of staying alive by selling their possessions in competition with local traders. The troops, bored, unruly and possibly unpaid, helped themselves to what they needed. The situation deteriorated sharply in February and March 1346 when fresh contingents began to gather for the forthcoming campaign, including several hundred Genoese and Tuscan mercenaries. There were some ugly incidents. Several Italians were lynched after one of these. Agen refused point-blank to supply any contingent of its own to the army in spite of its wealth and size: their men, the citizens said were needed to guard their hearths.[38]

*

The extent of the French government's financial problem in the south is graphically revealed by the tone in which the Seneschal of Périgord and Quercy was addressing his subordinates in December 1345.

We have heard that the proceeds of the ecclesiastical tenths are on deposit with certain persons at Sarlat [this man told his officers there]. The King's needs are plain. He must have everything that he can get if he is to prevail over the enemy. There is plenty of money in Sarlat. Go and find it and bring it to me wherever I may be on pain of a fine of twenty silver marks. If anyone makes a fuss, seize all his goods.[39]

This approach, which had already generated unrest in other part of Périgord, was unproductive. Sensible men recognized that overbearing methods of collection were also politically unwise at a time when the Earl of Lancaster appeared to be invincible and was offering attractive terms to defectors.

At the end of the year the French government, chastened by the continuing flow of bad news from the south, resolved upon a radical reform of the tax system, a difficult enough enterprise at any time let alone at a time of grave political disaffection and impending military crisis. The Estates-General was summoned to meet in two great assemblies, the representatives of the north and centre in Paris, and those of Languedoc in Toulouse. The tone of the summonses betrayed the King's misgivings. They were very defensive. The King had heard, he said, that his subjects considered themselves grievously oppressed by the burden of taxation which they had been asked to bear, as well as by the harsh methods of the numberless provosts, sergeants, commissioners and tax farmers which he had loosed upon them, 'for which evils we are truly sorry and sore of heart'.

The Paris assembly opened first, in the great hall of the Augustinian friars on the left bank of the Seine. The proceedings lasted for about a week, and although no account of them has survived it is reasonably clear what happened. The government was aware that there was a widespread fear that the sales tax and the *gabelle du sel*, both of which had begun as temporary expedients, were becoming permanent taxes. They offered to abolish both of them and replace them with a uniform tax directly related to the Crown's military needs. Each community would be assessed to furnish the cost of a fixed number of men-at-arms for up to six months in the year for the duration of the war. The formula which the government had in mind was: one man-at-arms for each 200 hearths, or 300 hearths in the poorest communities. In addition Philip's ministers promised a number of administrative reforms. They proposed to abolish the farming of taxes, to restrain the more notorious excesses of their financial officials and to limit the requisitioning of carts and foodstuffs, a prerogative which was no more popular in France than it was in England. These were intelligent and attractive proposals which appear to have been welcomed by the three estates. The problem was that there had been no preliminary discussion of them before the assembly opened. They seem to have been devised either in the course of the assembly's deliberations or immediately beforehand. It was therefore necessary for the representatives to return home to consult their constituents. No final answer could be given until a further round of assemblies had met, province by province, during the spring and early summer of 1346. Thereafter, there was bound to be more delay while the assessments were prepared and collection was organized. There was simply not time to do all this across the whole of northern and central France. In the meantime it was understood that the *gabelle* and the sales taxes would continue, however inadequate their yield or difficult their collection.[40]

Languedoc, with its long tradition of obstruction and rebellion against taxes, was more cautious. The Estates opened at Toulouse on 17 February 1346 under the presidency of the Bishop of Beauvais and agreed to grant a hearth tax of ten *sous* per hearth. Since by the Crown's reckoning it needed to raise the equivalent of twenty-seven *sous* per hearth throughout the kingdom in order to finance an army of between 20,000 and 30,000 men the representatives of Languedoc were conceding little more than a third of what was required of them. Moreover, it was payable in instalments in April, May and June, well after the date fixed for the opening of the campaign. The long-term proposals which the government had presented to the Paris assembly did not arrive in the south until some time after the representatives had departed. Another assembly had to be summoned to consider them in May. But there was little enthusiasm for them even then. Another ten *sous* per hearth was granted, payable in July. Further discussion of the tax was put off until yet another assembly, which, in the event, never met.[41]

These taxes narrowed, even if they did not close, the gap between income and expenditure in the Crown's accounts. The main difficulty which they did not solve was the heavy concentration of military expenditure in the weeks before the campaign and at its opening, when equipment and stores had to be bought and advances paid to the troops. The burden was particularly heavy in 1346. This French government's plans were ambitious and they had to be laid well in advance.

Ships and archers were perceived to be the main deficiencies in the

French defences. The French evidently distrusted the quality of their own galleys and oared barges, and they were probably not as seaworthy as the vessels of the Genoese. The problem of the great English superiority in archers must have been apparent to the French ministers for many years. Morlaix, the first significant pitched battle of the war, was a sombre warning. Auberoche was another. Less than a month after it was fought Philip VI was trying to recruit crossbowmen in Aragon. An intense campaign of recruitment was begun in Italy, the main source both of skilled crossbowmen and of fighting galleys. Pietro Barbavera, the scapegoat of Sluys, left Paris for Genoa at the beginning of December 1345. Marquis Scatisse, the King's Lucchese financier, followed him three weeks later accompanied by the Admiral of France, Floton de Revel, and Jean de Boucicaut, the future Marshal. They were busy in Nice, Monaco and Genoa in the new year.

Philip's emissaries hired no less than thirty-two galleys, all but two of which were full-sized vessels of sixty oars. Their crews (most of them carried more than 200 men) would provide a valuable reserve of infantry and crossbowmen to fight on land as well as at sea. The chief entrepreneur responsible for assembling this great fleet was that veteran of past naval campaigns, Carlo Grimaldi of Monaco. A large number of the galley commanders were members of his own family. Most of the others were his friends and dependants. The crossbowmen who fought on board these vessels had to be recruited separately. During March, the French officers passed under review a disorderly mass of Provençal and Genoese marine soldiers in the gardens of the Carmelites of Nice.[42]

In the early part of 1346 the financing of these projects fell chiefly on the war treasurers of the south and the tax-payers of Languedoc. The Bishop of Beauvais, who was in charge of the collection of the hearth tax, struggled to anticipate as much of it as he could. He allowed some communities to pay lump sums at a discount. Italian moneylenders were mulcted (again) for forced loans. The King borrowed heavily from his relatives. The Queen borrowed on her husband's account from divers Paris moneylenders. John of Bohemia somehow found 1,000 l.t. for Philip's coffers. But the government's largest creditor by far was the Pope. Clement had always gone as far as he could to relieve the financial distress of the King. He had allowed Philip to go on levying a tenth of ecclesiastical incomes year upon year. In June 1344 he had dispensed Philip from the duty to repay the money previously collected for the cost of the abortive crusade, something which his predecessor had always refused to do. But, apart from one recorded loan of 50,000 florins (£7,500) in 1343, Clement had stopped short of lending money to the French King. It might be thought inconsistent with his role as a peacemaker. In the aftermath of the battles of Bergerac and Auberoche, and the capture of his nephew by one of Lancaster's commanders, Clement's scruples disappeared. In the utmost secrecy Philip's conspiratorial private secretary, Robert de Lorris, made three visits to Avignon between November 1345 and March 1346, in the course of which he arranged loans amounting to 330,000 florins (£49,500) from Clement himself and 42,000 florins (£6,300) from principals and bankers at the papal court. These were enormous sums. Almost half of them went to swell the Duke of Normandy's war-chest either directly as payments to him or as advances paid to his Genoese mercenaries in the ports of Provence. Clement also lent money to some of Philip VI's friends and commanders, including Charles of Blois and the Duke of Bourbon.[43]

Even so, there were acute shortages of cash at awkward moments. In April 1346, the Duke of Normandy was obliged to issue commissions to three of his financial officials to seize rebel property, sell letters of pardon and letters of nobility and legitimacy, assume jurisdiction in every species of civil or criminal dispute in which fines could be levied and do almost all the things about which the King had written so apologetically in summoning the Estates-General. 'Amass all the money that you can extract for the support of our wars. Take it from each and every person you can, and see to it that every penny is transmitted directly to our Treasurer.' Few documents are more evocative of the hand-to-mouth existence of a fourteenth-century government.[44]

Serious as the financial problems of the French Government were, it was not by want of money that they were defeated in 1346. The army which John of Normandy commanded in the south-west was the largest which they had ever deployed there. Not since the campaigns of 1339 had so many northern noblemen fought in Gascony. They included the Duke of Burgundy and his son, as well as the Count of Boulogne, Walter of Brienne Duke of Athens, a host of knights from the north and centre and all the military officers of the royal household: the Constable, Raoul II, Count of Eu, both Marshals and the Master of the Royal Archers. These men marched south from the Loire valley in February. The Duke of Bourbon and the Bishop of Beauvais formed a second army in Toulouse drawn from all the southern seneschalsies. They collected a train of siege equipment which included five cannon. The two armies joined forces in Quercy in March 1346 and began to move slowly down the valley of the Garonne. Fresh groups of men joined them throughout the spring and summer. By comparing the known strength of earlier armies with what is known about the recruitment of this one, it is possible to guess that John of Normandy had between 15,000 and 20,000 men under his command at the height of his campaign, including 1,400 Genoese mercenaries. The first English-held town on the army's line of march was Aiguillon. The van of the French army arrived before its walls on about 1 April 1346. On 2 April the *arrière-ban* was proclaimed in the south. In the middle of April the Duke himself arrived with the rearguard and the great noblemen and principal officers of the army.[45]

Aiguillon, which had fallen in a matter of hours to Ralph Stafford, was besieged by the Duke of Normandy throughout the summer of 1346.[46] Indeed, at one disheartening moment of his fortunes there, he swore an oath that he would never withdraw from it until it had fallen. The Duke was much criticized for his obstinacy. The real object of his campaign, as he had publicly announced, was the recapture of La Réole, the loss of which in the previous year had been a grave setback for the French position in the Garonne valley.[47] But John of Normandy, although a poor soldier for his own part, was not short of expert advice. The truth was that Aiguillon was vital. It commanded the confluence of the Lot and the Garonne upstream of La Réole, and its possession by the English denied the French the use of both rivers. These rivers were the routes by which any French army encamped around La Réole would have to be supplied. There was no practical alternative. The condition of the roads in the south-west was appalling, and they ran through country which was in a state of anarchy and in places occupied by the English and their allies. John of Normandy had some personal experience of these matters. His first campaign on the Scheldt in 1340 had failed chiefly because he had attempted to capture towns without securing the river communications in his rear. There were, however, considerations of a more intangible kind also. The Duke of Normandy was the first man of the realm after the King. Once he had delivered his formal demand for the surrender of the town his dignity was committed to a successful outcome. One of those present at the siege was that famous paladin and authority on matters of chivalry, Geoffrey de Charny. Was it, he asked some years afterwards, even more dishonourable for a man who had laid claim to a town to march away without winning it than to refuse a relieving army's challenge to battle?[48]

One of the first things which the French army did was to dig trenches and earthworks behind their positions, to guard against surprise from behind, and to preserve themselves from the fate which had befallen the army of Auberoche. But the Earl of Lancaster had no intention of being drawn into battle against forces so enormously superior to his own. He withdrew to Bordeaux a few days before the siege began to reconstitute his forces and muster those of the Gascon nobility. Reinforcements, mainly archers, had also been promised him from England. Some of them arrived during May and June.[49]

Aiguillon was left to be defended by Ralph Stafford and the captain of the town, a Leicestershire knight called Hugh Menil. They commanded a strong garrison, plausibly estimated by Jean le Bel at 600 archers and 300 men-at-arms, including two of the more famous captains on the English side, the Hainaulter Walter Mauny and the Gascon Alexander de Caumont. They had to make up by courage and numbers for the inadequacy of the fixed defences. Aiguillon was a small town consisting of two *bourgs* which had gradually coalesced. Lunac d'Aiguillon was an ancient Gallo-Roman town on a square plan with crumbling brick walls, the remains of a low keep at its western end, and the castle of its seigneurs rising out of the river at the north-east corner. Le Fossat d'Aiguillon was the castle of another local family lying just south of Lunac around which a small village had grown. A modern rectangular perimeter wall about 270 by 170 yards around both *bourgs* had been begun but never finished. The gaps in it had to be filled with wine barrels packed with stones. On the north side there was a delapidated fortified bridge over the Lot ending in a barbican gate on the far bank.[50]

It took a very long time for the French to invest Aiguillon entirely. At first they encamped in the plain east of the confluence of the two rivers, leaving free access between the town and La Réole by river and across the Lot bridge to the open country north of it. Lancaster had left strong garrisons in Damazan and Tonneins to hold the ground west and north of Aiguillon. To occupy this territory without splitting the besieging army into three parts and exposing them to defeat in detail, it was necessary for the French to take possession of the nearest bridge over the Lot at Clairac, 5 miles upstream, which was accomplished without difficulty; and to build a wooden bridge across the Garonne a short distance downstream of the town, a more formidable undertaking which occupied some 300 carpenters and journeymen working for several weeks under the protection of an enormous escort of Genoese crossbowmen. In the early weeks of the siege the garrison made two or three sorties a day in the attempt to destroy these works. Eventually they took to attacking them from barges. The Garonne bridge was broken up twice before it was finally completed towards the end of May 1346. Having occupied the ground beyond the rivers, the French stretched chain across the Garonne to stop supplies or reinforcements reaching the garrison from the west.[51]

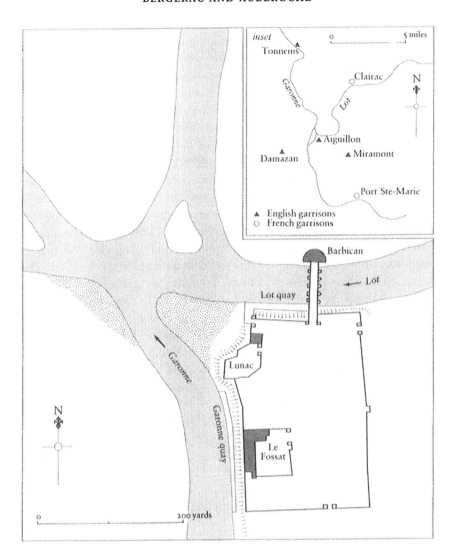

23 Defences of Aiguillon

On 16 June 1346 the French tried to bring two huge barges laden with supplies from Toulouse past the town into the lower reach of the Garonne. The defenders launched two hazardous sorties against these barges. One sortie party attacked in small boats from beneath the west walls of Lunac; the other, about 100 men-at-arms commanded by Alexander de Caumont, sallied over the Lot bridge, through the French encampment on the far side and along the north bank of the river. The barges were captured and brought into the town under the noses of the besiegers. It was a remarkable feat of arms, but it was achieved at great cost. For the French soldiers north of the bridge launched a furious assault, supported by stone-throwing artillery, against the barbican gate on their side, just as Alexander de Caumont's force was trying to retreat back through it. After several hours of fighting, during which both sides were heavily reinforced from behind, the French succeeded in capturing the barbican gate and fought their way on to the bridge. In order to prevent them from getting into the town itself, it was necessary to bring down the portcullis at the southern gate. As a result the sortie party was cut off. Many of them were killed and others, including Alexander de Caumont himself, were taken prisoner. He had to redeem himself for an enormous ransom, most of which was advanced by the Earl of Lancaster. This transaction was completed almost at once and Alexander was back in the thick of the fighting within a few days of his capture. Perhaps a more intelligent calculation of French interests would have kept him in prison for longer, but prisoners were above all a marketable commodity.[52] The battle of the bridge of Aiguillon boosted the moral of the besiegers as well as making money for a few of them. Thereafter nothing went their way.

CHAPTER XIV

Aiguillon and Crécy
1346

At the beginning of February 1346 a Great Council of all the lay and ecclesiastical magnates of England met at Westminster to contemplate the coming campaign. Representatives of Edward III's only remaining continental allies, the Flemings and the Bretons, were also there.[1] But Edward had learned the limits of his allies' usefulness in 1340. It was always clear in 1346 that the enterprise was to be undertaken primarily by English troops and not by subsidized Flemings, Germans or Bretons over whom the King could exercise control only indirectly and sometimes not at all. This meant recruiting troops in the English provinces on a scale hitherto unheard of for a continental expedition. It meant shipping the whole of the army and not just a modest English contingent across the Channel, in requisitioned fleets much larger than those which Edward had needed in 1338 and 1342. It meant purveying victuals and other stores throughout the country to supply the enlarged army and fleet for several weeks while the men waited to embark on the south coast of England or marched through territory in France which its inhabitants had scorched or emptied of all usable supplies.

Of the two-year subsidy voted by Parliament in 1344 the first year's instalment had been spent and the second year's was still coming in. Edward needed, like Philip VI, to resort to heavy borrowing, necessarily from his own subjects. The year 1346 saw the final collapse of the Bardi Bank in Florence, a dreadful warning to any foreign financier who might have thought of lending money to the English government without security. The King began with the Church. Ninety rich ecclesiastics were assessed in February 1346 for forced loans amounting to nearly £15,000. The towns were also assessed for loans by a process of haggling case by case. Edward proceeded more brutally against others. Foreign clergymen beneficed in England, hardly any of whom resided there, were an unpopular and vulnerable group, in England as in France. Their agents and receivers were summoned before the Council early in March and invited to contribute a whole year's income to the English war effort.

When they refused, Edward told them that he would take it anyway. The proceeds were farmed out for ready money to a syndicate of financiers controlled by John Wesenham, a wholesale grocer from Lynn who had also been for some time the farmer of the customs. Men of his kind were unpopular, but they were enjoying growing influence and power in Edward's realm as the King's ambitions and needs expanded. In May, another syndicate of equally shadowy men, led by two London merchants, Walter Chiriton and Thomas Swanland, began to lend money to the government on an even larger scale than Wesenham in return for a promise that they should be allowed to take the Customs over from him in the autumn. They raised the necessary funds from businessmen in London, York and other towns, an expanding network of financial dealings reaching into the English provinces and swelling, like the efforts of the purveyor, the tax collector and the recruiting officer, the numbers drawn into the support of Edward's campaigns.[2]

Money was only part of Edward's problem and not even the greater part. It was in fact cheaper for him to fight with his own subjects than to pay the Duke of Brabant and his like to fight with theirs, provided that the formidable administrative difficulties could be overcome. The English King seems to have envisaged an invasion force of between 15,000 and 20,000 men. This was not only four or five times the number which had crossed to the Low Countries in 1338. It was more than Edward III had previously recruited even for service against the Scots. To raise them he embarked on a controversial experiment in compulsory military service which had been in preparation for some time. During the previous year the government had had a census of lay landowners carried out. They were classified by income from £5 a year upwards. A £5 man was assessed to serve as a mounted archer, a £10 man as a hobelar, a £25 man as a man-at-arms, a £1,000 man as the leader of forty men-at-arms and so on. The ostensible purpose of this exercise had been to update the ancient and rusty system of recruiting troops for the defence of the realm against invasion. But in February 1346 the government went a step further, as perhaps they had always intended. They demanded service in accordance with the assessment not only in the defence of the realm against invasion but in the army overseas. Those who would not, or for their age or infirmity could not, go abroad were made to find substitutes or pay a fine in lieu. It was a radical break with past practice. Compulsion had hitherto had only a limited place in the manning of Edward's armies and among the men-at-arms none at all, one of the reasons why opposition to the war had been restrained and brief.[3]

The compulsory purchase of stores during the winter of 1345–6 was the largest exercise of its kind that the English government had carried out. Some thousands of new, white-painted bows and tens of thousands of sheaves of arrows were requisitioned by the sheriffs' agents and collected at central stores in the Tower of London, Greenwich and elsewhere. Quivers, nails, rope and chain, loading ramps and horse pens were all required in quantity. The major enterprise, however, was the collection of victuals: meat, poultry, grain, vegetables and fodder. The accounts, which survive only in part, reveal something of its scale. In Yorkshire alone ten mounted men were engaged in assessing, buying and collecting victuals, delivering debentures or occasionally cash in payment. There were seven collection points at which the goods were taken off carts to be packed into barrels and loaded into barges for carriage by river to Hull. Outside Hull, two mills continuously ground the corn into flour. Warehouses were hired. Clerks prepared inventories and receipts. Stevedores laboured to fill up coasters hired by the Admiral of the north. Hull handled the output of only four counties: Yorkshire, Derbyshire, Nottinghamshire and Lincolnshire. Similar operations were taking place in almost every other county of central and southern England. From Boston, Lynn, Maldon, London, Sandwich and Bristol small vessels ferried supplies round the coast to the embarkation port of the army at Portsmouth. The whole operation was completed with remarkable speed and success. Indeed, more food was supplied than the army could eat before it soured or rotted. Some of it had to be brought back from France and sold off as surplus later in the year.[4]

In spite of the burden which the English were being asked to bear resistance was muted. There was a barrage of propaganda. From January 1346 onwards Englishmen were warned in proclamations and officially inspired sermons about the French King's determination to reject every offer that might be made to him, about his incitement of the Scots, and about his aggressive designs against the language and life of the English nation. The news of Philip VI's naval plans was broadcast across the realm as soon as it was received.[5] Whether this was taken at face value it is difficult to say. Probably by most people it was, and without doubt it softened the impact of fresh burdens and hardships by persuading Englishmen to look upon the war as part of the ordinary condition of life, something which most Frenchmen could still not bring themselves to do even in 1346. Adequate harvests during the mid-1340s made the government's task easier. Parliament, which was the natural focus of resistance, did not meet in 1346 until September. By then victory had to some extent disarmed criticism. It is unlikely that Edward would have got away with so much if the military tide had not turned in his favour.

Neither the target for recruitment nor the King's ambitious timetable was achieved. The ships requisitioned in the previous year were supposed to be at Portsmouth by the middle of February 1346. Few of them were. Great storms lashed the south coast of England. The vessels that were on their way were scattered. Others were imprisoned in their ports. But even if they had all arrived there would not have been enough. To transport in one crossing the enlarged army which was now envisaged would have required at least 1,500 ships, which was probably more than the entire English merchant marine could furnish. There was a fresh round of requisitions in March. The traditional limitation to vessels over 30 or 40 tons' burden had to be abandoned. The requisitioning officers were told that anything better than a fishing smack would do, even if it carried only 10 tons. The date of sailing was put off from 1 March to 1 May 1346, then to 15 May.[6]

The army which was to fill these ships took even longer to raise. Some of the troops, particularly the Welsh archers and spearmen who were recruited in larger numbers than ever before, refused to move from their homes until they had been paid their advances. A significant number of those who were recruited according to the new census of landed income turned out to be infirm, unfit or inadequately armed. They had to be sent home to find substitutes.[7] In March and April the recruiting programme was severely disrupted by fresh threats to the security of England, from the Scots and from French naval activity. Neither of these appears to have been taken into account when the plans were laid. In the case of the Scots it was decided at a fairly early stage to run risks. The counties north of the Humber were left to defend themselves in the ordinary way with their own manpower and with only limited financial assistance from the royal treasury. The border lords, Lucy, Neville, Percy, Segrave, Mowbray and others agreed to expand their military retinues. Plans were made to raise the county levies at short notice. On 27 March 1346 the clergy and nobility of the north gathered at York to hear the King's representatives expound his plans and promise a small contribution to their cost, half the proceeds of the Parliamentary subsidy in the northern counties. Even that had to be found out of a budget already committed to operations elsewhere. The threat to the coast of southern England, although it was much exaggerated, was taken more seriously. Beacons appeared once more on hill tops. Commanders were appointed in every coastal district. All those living within 15 miles of the coast were placed at their disposal, instead of being available for the expedition to France. These measures alone must have deprived Edward III of several thousand men. From one cause or another he raised only about half of the army that he conceived was needed, and only just enough ships to carry even those, late, across the Channel.[8]

The King went to great lengths to hide his plans from the French. There had been a general arrest of French traders in England in the autumn of 1345. The ports were watched. Newgate prison was once again packed with aliens who had aroused suspicion for one reason or another. But effective concealment was out of the question. The scale of the King's preparations made them impossible to hide, and his timetable was known all over England, where in every county purveyors and recruiting officers were struggling to keep to it. Moreover, Edward's plans had to some extent to be shared with the Flemings, whose role was to launch diversionary attacks from the north. Flanders was full of French spies. Some of them penetrated into England, passing themselves off as Flemings and picking up valuable gossip in London. In the middle of February 1346 the French government received a 'vivid' report of the proceedings at Edward's Great Council at Westminster on the 3rd and the state of preparations at Portsmouth.[9]

What they did not learn until a very late stage was the destination of Edward's great expedition. Edward himself changed his mind more than once, and if he talked about it to his friends and lieutenants, he did so discreetly. Not only did the King avoid announcing his plans (as he had usually done in previous years) but judging by the silence of the administrative records he said nothing to those who were to execute them until the last moment. The probability is that he originally intended to land in Brittany. But this idea must have been abandoned at an early stage. Edward was losing interest in Brittany, partly because the political possibilities appeared to have been exhausted there, partly because the Earl of Northampton had failed to capture any significant place along the north coast during the winter. In January 1346, the Earl was recalled to England to attend to greater things. For some time the King appears to have kept all his options before deciding in about April or May 1346 that he would proceed to Gascony. This decision was probably made in the short-lived mood of alarm in Bordeaux and Westminster which followed the arrival of the Duke of Normandy's legions in the Garonne valley. Edward had obligations to the Earl of Lancaster. He had promised that if the Earl were 'attacked by so great an army that he cannot survive without help from the King, then the King shall rescue him in one way or another if he can'.[10]

The French government seems to have assumed that Edward would land somewhere in Brittany or Gascony, where he already had secure bases, although whether this was knowledge or guesswork is hard to say. Their assessment of the position was reflected in the disposition of their troops. They kept most of the men that they had mustered and all their most experienced commanders on the southern front. They left the defence of Brittany to Charles of Blois. But he was allowed to recruit heavily among the French nobility; he was also spending large sums of money in hiring mercenaries beyond France's frontiers, much of which is likely to have come from the royal treasury. In May, Philip VI went further and sent him some powerful infantry contingents form the seneschalsies of Béziers and Carcassonne which had been withdrawn from the army of the Duke of Normandy.[11]

North of the Breton peninsula the only troops available were coast-guards thinly stretched from Mont-Saint-Michel to Calais, and garrison troops in the major towns by the coast and along the Flemish border. They were stiffened by large numbers of Genoese crossbowmen who began to arrive in April and May. There were some crude attempts to fortify the coast. The entrances to the main harbours were obstructed with wooden piles. But the French could hardly construct an Atlantic Wall. If the English tried to land in the north-east of France it would be up to the French war fleet to stop them.

Philip VI had an altogether exaggerated idea of what armed ships could achieve against a seaborne invasion. He might perhaps have learned from his own successes against the south coast of England in the late 1330s that the very limited techniques of reconnaissance and navigation available to his seamen made it virtually impossible to intercept a hostile fleet at sea. One needed to blockade it in its ports of embarkation or to have precise information about its destination. Nevertheless, an attempt was made. A census of merchant shipping in the French Channel ports was begun at the end of March 1346. The larger ships were requisitioned and elaborately fitted out with castellated wooden superstructures. At least seventy-eight ships were made ready in Lower Normandy alone. In Upper Normandy and Picardy, which were more important shipping centres, there must have been more. In the event they were never used. The reason was that the French plan of defence called for them to serve as auxiliaries of Grimaldi's galleys, with Genoese officers and crossbowmen on board. But the galley fleet of 1346, like that of 1338, arrived too late. These low-freeboard vessels could not cross the Bay of Biscay until May, and they were not due to reach Boulogne according to their contracts until the 20th. In the event

Grimaldi did not leave Nice until 6 May and the other galley masters were later still. Thereafter every possible delay befell them. They paused to plunder shipping off Majorca. They were scattered by Atlantic storms. They took refuge in the mouth of the Tagus. They were still there in the first week of July.[12]

During the weeks in which the French waited for the invasion, things began to go badly wrong on both of the principal fronts on which their troops were operating.

In Brittany a succession of defeats encouraged the myth of English invincibility. There were some incidents in the Tréguier peninsula, the work of Richard Totesham and his garrison at La Roche-Derrien. They raided and sacked the town of Lannion by night, carrying off valuable stores and prisoners. The event was famous for the heroic defence of a single French knight, Geoffrey de Pont-Blanc, who awoke to find the enemy already inside the gates and blocked a narrow street, fighting them off with his sword and lance, and then with his bare hands until they shot him with an arrow and clubbed him to death on the ground. One of Charles of Blois' lieutenants attempted to intercept Totesham's men as they returned to La Roche-Derrien. But his force, although it was much larger than Totesham's, was ambushed in the marshland south of the town and driven off with heavy losses.[13]

It was shortly after these catfights that Charles Blois began his major offensive of the summer. According to English sources (which may have exaggerated his strength), Charles now had a substantial army under his command. It included his vassals among the nobility of northern and eastern Brittany with their retainers, and a large number of mercenaries from the Imperial territories of Frisia, Burgundy and Savoy, as well as the Genoese crossbowmen of Ayton Doria and the infantry contingents which had recently arrived from Languedoc. With some of these forces he proceeded to lay siege to three of the principal English garrisons, at Brest, Lesneven and La Roche-Derrien. Then, gathering the main body of his army around him, he conducted a sweep across the north coast. The English garrisons in Brittany had received no significant reinforcements for some time and their total strength probably amounted to no more than a few hundred men. There were disturbing indications that some of their Breton allies were reading the signs and preparing to abandon them, setting up as independent captains or selling their loyalty and their strongholds to Charles of Blois. It was the most serious threat to the English position in the duchy since 1342.

It came to an abrupt and unexpected end. The English deputy lieutenant in Brittany, Sir Thomas Dagworth, had decided to leave the beleaguered towns to be defended by their commanders while he made a rapid tour of the other English strongholds in the peninsula and saw to their security. He had with him no more than a strong escort: eighty men-at-arms and a hundred archers. On 9 June 1346, shortly after dawn, he was suddenly confronted by Charles of Blois and his army in northern Finistère, near Saint-Pol de Léon. His men were trapped and forced to fight it out against an overwhelmingly superior force. They dug themselves in on the summit of a hill and, although surrounded on three sides, fought off their assailants until nightfall. The French attacked them on foot with dismounted men-at-arms, crossbowmen and some of the men of Languedoc, a tribute to the influence of English battle tactics which Charles of Blois learned to imitate long before any other French commander. The last and strongest assault on the English lines, which was led by Charles himself, came in the early evening and failed. He was forced to retreat as darkness fell, leaving many of his men dead or wounded on the hillside. The Picard knight Guillaume ('Le Galois') de la Heuse, who led the first attack, was said to have promised to bring Dagworth trussed up into the French camp. He was disabled and captured. After the battle a roll-call showed that all the English men-at-arms had survived. But almost every one of them was wounded, some seriously. 'I commend my troops to you,' Dagworth wrote in his report to the King; 'you will not find better men in all your realm.'[14]

At Aiguillon there was no progress at all. In spite of their numbers and their great field works and river barriers, the Duke of Normandy's men could not even seal off the town. Small groups of English and Gascon men-at-arms got in by stealth, bringing supplies with them. One intrepid Gascon made several round trips. In July a detachment of the Earl of Lancaster's army fought its way through the French lines with victuals for the garrison. Evidently there was concern about its ability to hold out, or desperate enterprises like these would not have been attempted. But their situation was, as it turned out, rather better than that of the besiegers. The Duke of Normandy had to feed at least ten times the numbers of the garrison and townsmen of Aiguillon combined, probably more when camp followers were included. As the Bishop of Beauvais had discovered in 1339, when he had tried to take Bordeaux, a large besieging army is rooted to the spot and cannot live off the land for more than a short time. The circle round the French army from which supplies had to be drawn expanded steadily as they exhausted those which could be had close at hand. To the north and west, foraging was made difficult by the tight ring of English-held castles in southern Périgord and the lower Garonne valley.

French purveyors were requisitioning herds of cattle in the Aubrac hills of southern Auvergne, some 200 miles away by road, and in the Pyrenean foothills of Béarn, one of the sparsest regions of France. The whole of the seneschalsy of Toulouse was stripped, according to its disgruntled inhabitants, of grain, wine and foodstuffs for the use of the army. Even so, the besiegers began to suffer from hunger and from that other great scourge of medieval military encampments, dysentery. The Earl of Lancaster moved from Bordeaux to La Réole with his army, harassing the enemy's lines of communication, killing foragers and messengers, seizing cart-trains and falling on detached groups of French soldiers.

The besiegers switched the main thrust of their attack from the southern side of the town to the older and lower north wall by the Lot. A scheme was devised for assaulting the northern citadel from three specially constructed wooden towers mounted on barges. It was a failure. On the day fixed for the attack one of the towers was struck by a stone from a trebuchet as it was being manoeuvred across the river. It capsized, drowning all its occupants. The others were withdrawn.[15]

Edward III had been at Porchester since 1 June 1346. He could now look out from the old twelfth-century keep across the enclosed water of Portsmouth harbour, where his fleet was assembling, more than a month late. The army was encamped about the harbour and along the Winchester and London roads. By the end of the month there were about 750 ships in the harbour according to the most reliable estimate, ranging from coastal barges to cogs of 200 tons. The combined carrying capacity of these ships suggests an army of between 7,000 and 10,000 men. Judging by the King's orders to his recruiting officers, archers accounted for more than half of them. There were specialists and camp followers: miners from the Forest of Dean to work as sappers, masons, smiths and farriers, engineers, carpenters and tent-makers, surgeons, several dozen officials, clerks and household servants. The men were paid up to date and for another fortnight in advance. The ships were victualled for two weeks, the length of the passage to Gascony.[16]

They were not destined to go to Gascony. The King changed his mind and decided instead to land in northern France. It was generally believed at the time that this decision was made at the last moment, when the army was already embarked and on the point of going to sea. But the probability is that it was in fact made earlier, at a secret meeting of the King's closest military advisers on about 20 June. Edward III's new plan was to invade the Cotentin peninsula of southern Normandy. Jean le Bel and Froissart after him attributed the decision to the influence of Godfrey of Harcourt, who was certainly with the King at Porchester.

The country of Normandy is one of the most plenteous countries of the world [Froissart has the old traitor say]; Sire, in jeopardy of my head if you will land there there is none that shall resist you. The people of Normandy have so far had no experience of war, and all the chivalry of France is gathered outside Aiguillon with the Duke. And Sire, there you shall find great towns without walls where your men shall have riches to last them twenty years.

The thought, if Godfrey ever uttered it, can hardly have come as a revelation to the English King. An invasion of Normandy had been discussed as one of a number of possibilities ever since the outbreak of the war. It had been Edward's preferred point of entry into France in 1337, before he was drawn by his allies into the scheme for invading by the Scheldt valley from Brabant. He had made occasional attempts to stir up trouble in Normandy long before he met Godfrey of Harcourt. The main reasons for choosing the Cotentin in 1346 were probably that it was the closest landfall to Portsmouth and that the winds were blowing from the west. Edward must have remembered the long delays which the weather had forced on him in 1342 when he invaded Brittany and the even longer ones which had held up the Earl of Lancaster in 1345. But Godfrey may well have had something to do with the new plan even if he did not devise it. It was true that the region was virtually undefended, something which he is likely to have known. It was his home country and he spoke for some significant men there. Godfrey no doubt exaggerated their numbers.[17]

In order to increase the impact of the invasion and divide the forces of the French it was proposed to stage a noisy diversion on France's northern frontier. Hugh Hastings, an enterprising and ambitious Norfolk knight who had recently returned from Gascony, was appointed as Edward's lieutenant and commander in Flanders on 20 June 1346. He was assigned as assistants John Montgomery and John Moleyns, old hands in the affairs of Flanders, and a devious adventurer called John Mautravers who was believed to have been one of those responsible for the murder of Edward II and who had for some years unofficially represented Edward III's interests in Ghent. These men were provided with eighteen barges, 250 archers and a handful of men-at-arms and told to leave for the Low Countries at once. Edward had been working on the Flemings. The representatives of the three great towns deliberated, first at Bruges then at Ghent. On 24 June, while Hastings was in the midst of his preparations, they agreed to give the English King all the help he needed.[18]

Edward III made no secret of Hugh Hastings' destination, but his own was still wrapped in secrecy. His Chancery was informed only that the King would go where God's grace and the caprice of the winds might take him. The masters of his ships were given sealed orders to be opened only if the fleet was scattered by the winds. Until then they were to follow the admirals. Instructions were given early in July 1346 to close the port of London, which was believed to be full of French spies, as well as those of Dover, Winchelsea and Sandwich. No one of whatever rank or status was to be allowed to leave the country until a week after the sailing of the fleet except Hugh Hastings, and he was to have his men searched in case they were carrying indiscreet papers about them.[19]

How much information reached the French government cannot be known. But they certainly learned something in the last ten days of June 1346, for at about that time there was a sudden panic about the security of the north. Towards the end of the month the Constable was recalled from Aiguillon with part of the army of the Duke of Normandy. He was put in command of Harfleur at the mouth of the Seine. The Count of Flanders was sent to join him there. The Marshals seem to have been recalled from the south at the same time. Artillery and equipment were delivered to the garrisons of Leure, Étretat and Chef-de-Caux. All this suggested that they were expecting a descent in northern Normandy. But they took precautions everywhere along the coast. All the local men of military age were called to arms. At about the same time summonses were issued for the recruitment of a fresh army for the defence of the north.[20]

In these straits, Philip VI turned to Scotland. 'In Scotland,' the English Chancellor had told Parliament two years before, 'they are saying quite openly that they will break the truces as soon as our adversary [of France] desires, and will march against England doing all the damage in their power.' The Scots did not break the truces. But they began to mass by the border as soon as they learned that Edward had broken them. The English believed that they were deliberately acting in concert with the French government and they were probably right. Fighting against the English was one of the few unifying factors in Scotch politics. For David II it was a source of plunder to restore his impoverished treasury, a chance to shine before friends and rivals older and more experienced than himself, as well as a long-standing obligation owed by treaty to France. Nevertheless, the raids of the Scots, however damaging to the three northern counties, had so far achieved no significant diversion of resources from Edward's continental adventures. David's invasion of the north in October 1345 had lasted only six days before his men exhausted the more accessible sources of loot and returned home.[21] It is almost certain that Philip VI had been pressing for a more sustained campaign in the north. In June 1346 the French King's pleas took on a note of desperation as English troops gathered around Portsmouth and hints of their destination began to escape: 'I beg you, I implore you with all the force I can, to remember the bonds of blood and friendship between us. Do for me what I would willingly do for you in such a crisis, and do it as quickly and thoroughly as with God's help you are able.'[22]

As at similar moments in 1340 and 1342 Philip brooded on real or imaginary betrayals. The *cause célèbre* of these months was the case of a rich citizen of Compiègne, Simon Pouillet, denounced by a relative for declaring at his dinner table that it was 'better to be well governed by an Englishman than badly by a Frenchman'. Pouillet was dismembered with a meat axe in Les Halles in Paris. The event marked a new degree of savagery in the official treatment of traitors, even if they offended only by word of mouth and in private. 'Of such shameful death', a loyal Frenchman wrote about it, 'all France might say as our Lord did: "now begins the time of our sufferings".'[23]

Edward III boarded his own ship and sailed out of Portsmouth on 28 June 1346. For several days the wind impeded every movement of his fleet. He made his way west along the coast of the Isle of Wight until he reached Yarmouth. Here it was necessary to stop and wait for the other ships to tack through the channel and catch up. Then, when they had all arrived, the wind changed. The whole mass of shipping made its way back along the Solent and reassembled between Portsmouth and the Forland. Two weeks were lost. It was not until 11 July 1346 that they sailed south for Normandy in perfect conditions of wind and tide. The Genoese fleet was still several days' passage south of La Rochelle. The merchantmen which the French government had armed lay beached in their harbours. Before dawn on 12 July 1346 the English fleet anchored off the great open beach south of Saint-Vaast-la-Hougue (next to 'Utah Beach' of 1944).[24]

If there had been any serious resistance on the beaches it would probably have been impossible to land. But there was none. The main French forces in Normandy were north of the Seine. The senior representatives of the King in southern Normandy were the Marshal, Robert Bertrand, who was captain of the 'sea frontier' there, and various officials of the *baillages* of Cotentin and Caen.[25] They had only very limited forces at their disposal. A troop of Genoese crossbowmen which had been stationed at La Hougue since the end of April had deserted for want of pay only three days earlier. Bertrand had summoned all local men of military age to present their arms and equipment district by district. By coincidence the inspection of the district of La Hougue was to take place on the very day that the English arrived. It had to be abandoned. The local inhabitants had vanished into the woods and marshes as soon as they saw the English fleet stretched out across the bay. As the news spread towns, villages and manors were abandoned for 20 miles around. La Hougue itself was completely deserted. Eleven ships, including eight which had been armed for its defence, were lying unattended on the beach. The English burned them. Robert Bertrand hovered all day behind the town, struggling to find able-bodied men to resist. During the morning he managed to gather some 300 men about him and made a brief attack on the beach. But the English must have had several thousand men ashore, including seamen, by this time and Bertrand's men were driven off. Most of them deserted him soon afterwards.

At about mid-day Edward III landed with his attendants and climbed a hill by the shore. There he knighted many of the young noblemen of this army. They included his sixteen-year-old son, the Prince of Wales; William Montagu, Earl of Salisbury, the son of the man who had planned his *coup d'état* of 1330; and Roger Mortimer, the grandson of its main victim. Godfrey of Harcourt did homage to the King for his possessions in Normandy. Robert Bertrand, his long-standing rival, retreated southward towards Carentan with the handful of men, about thirty, who remained at his side.

On the first day of the invasion, Edward issued a proclamation 'out of compassion for the wretched fate of . . . his people of France' commanding that no one should molest any old man, woman or child, or rob any church or shrine, or burn any building on pain of death or mutilation. A reward of forty shillings was offered to anyone who found men disregarding these orders and brought them before the King's officers. It was a dead letter from the beginning. The Constable and the Marshal of the army were responsible for discipline, and they maintained deputies and drumhead courts for dealing with looters, brawlers and insubordinates.[26] But without any clear chain of command it was quite impossible for them to control the formless mass of men about them. From a hill overlooking La Hougue the King could see for himself the bursts of flame spreading outward across the country, slowly coalescing into a radiant red ring round the horizon and lighting up men's faces at night. On 13 July, La Hougue itself was burned. The King was forced to abandon his quarters there and move to an inn at the nearby village of Morsalines. On the 14th the first English raiding parties reached Barfleur, the main harbour of the district, from which the invasion fleet of William the Conqueror had set out three centuries before. They found only a few men there, whom they took for ransom, and more armed ships abandoned by the shore, which they burned. The mobs of seamen which followed on their heels looted the place so thoroughly that ships' boys were reported to be turning their noses up at fur coats. Then they reduced the whole town to ashes. In the country around there was only isolated and uncoordinated resistance. The Earl of Warwick and his men were ambushed as they took over an inn by a group of local men who had hidden in the woods nearby. Occasionally some villagers came out of hiding to resist the plunderers. Most of them were killed. Within a day of two all those who were capable of carrying arms had withdrawn to the nearest walled towns. Refugees filled the roads south.

It took five days to rest the army, disembark the horses and discharge the enormous quantity of stores from the ships. On 17 July the King's Council drew up a plan of campaign. They intended to march along the coast towards Rouen, then to invade the Ile de France by the valley of the Seine. Three divisions were formed. The Prince of Wales took command of the van with the earls of Northampton and Warwick to guide him. The command of the rear was given to the Bishop of Durham, the magnificent and worldly Thomas Hatfield ('I should promote a jackass if the King nominated one,' Clement VI was supposed to have said when appointing him). Edward himself took command of the centre. 200 ships of the fleet, presumably the larger ones, were chosen to pace the army along the coast. The rest were sent back to England.

The fleet began by sailing north around the Cape of Barfleur, passing from village to village, landing their crews and destroying everything within 5 miles of the coast. At Cherbourg the garrison of the castle held out, the only one in the Cotentin which stayed at its post. But the town was destroyed. The abbey of Notre-Dame du Voeu, a foundation of Henry I's daughter Matilda, was burned by Englishmen for the third time in half a century.[27]

The army moved out of its encampment on 18 July 1346 and marched toward Valognes, a market town 10 miles inland across a windy expanse of coastal marshland. Valognes was an open town, its walls unmanned, its castle ungarrisoned and its gates open. The population came out to meet the King on the road. They asked for nothing more than their lives. Edward reissued his proclamation safeguarding the lives and property of the Normans, and took possession of the town, installing himself in a manor house of the Duke of Normandy. But the army helped themselves to what they wanted, and on the following morning, when they marched south by the Rouen road, they left the town in flames.

Philip VI had no army to challenge the English in pitched battle but only scattered coastguards and garrisons. The Duke of Normandy's troops were still in the south, clinging to their dwindling chances of capturing Aiguillon. The government's military summonses of June could not possibly produce an army of any size before the beginning of August. The great nightmare which had justified the premature termination of every campaign in Gascony since 1337 had finally come about. In the second half of July all the efforts of the French were bent towards delaying the progress of the invaders while a force was collected which was strong enough to confront them. The plan was to stop the English at Caen, which was the largest walled town west of Rouen. The River Orne, on which the town stood, was probably the best natural line of defence before the Seine. This decision appears to have been taken on his own initiative by the Constable, Raoul II, Count of Eu, who commanded the largest concentration of troops in Normandy. He transferred his entire force by boat from Harfleur to Caen as soon as the news of the English landings reached him. The Chamberlain, Jean de Melun, lord of Tancarville, joined him. The royal Council endorsed the decision later. During the next fortnight every available man was sent to reinforce them and great stores of victuals were accumulated in the castle.[28] The Orne from Caen to Ouistrehan was clogged with ships and barges carrying supplies and reinforcements. Robert Bertrand struggled to gain time for these preparations to be completed. He did not have enough troops to defend every place in the English King's path. But garrisons were left in some of the citadels, and Robert himself retreated steadily before the English army with his small force of locally recruited troops, harassing them where he could and breaking every bridge after he had crossed it.

Hugh Hastings and his men arrived in Flanders on about 21 July 1346. The purpose of his mission was already known to the French ministers, and spies set to watch for his landing dispatched the news post-haste to France.[29] Part of the French army was instructed to assemble at Amiens to hold the line of the Somme against the Flemings and their English auxiliaries. The rest was directed to Rouen. Philip VI himself went to Saint-Denis, where he received the Oriflamme on 22 July 1346. He set out with his entourage on a slow progress down the Seine valley. Small groups of confused troops arrived daily to swell his numbers. Philip wrote his second letter to David II of Scotland in little more than a month. 'The English

King', he said, 'has landed in the Cotentin ... He has most of his army with him there, another division in Gascony and yet others in Flanders and Brittany.' From these menaces, Philip took refuge in fantasy. In England, he told David, there was a 'defenceless void'. If the Scots invaded the north of England, surely Edward III would abandon his campaign and return with all his men across the Channel. When that happened, Philip declared, he would embark his own army in the French Channel ports and lead them into England behind the retreating King. 'I implore you to remember our friendship and our treaties and to strike as hard at England as you can.'[30]

The Scots hardly needed Philip VI's lessons on strategy. The defence of the northern march of England was in disarray, as anyone could see. The guardians of the march had very few troops. The government's promises to assign tax revenue in their favour had not been honoured. The garrison of Berwick and many of the retained men stationed on the border were threatening to desert. There was a gloomy and acrimonious meeting between representatives of the government and the leading barons of the north on 17 July 1346. One of them pointed to the terms of his indenture and said 'curtly' that he would march away at once if he was not paid in accordance with its terms. The Scots had already begun to mass on the border at the end of June, and in July they started to raid Cumberland. But they were not yet ready for the major invasion of England which Philip required and their leaders were rent by private feuds. Percy and Neville attacked the raiders and pursued them into lowland Scotland. At the end of July a brief truce was agreed until 29 September.[31]

Robert Bertrand's strategic retreat from the Cotentin went badly from the beginning. The English army reached Saint-Côme-du-Mont by the River Douve on the evening of 19 July. Beyond Saint-Côme lay a vast marsh which, until the drainage works of the eighteenth century, extended as far as Carentan (2 miles away) and beyond Carentan for 5 or 6 miles towards Bayeux to the east and Saint-Lo to the south-east. The bridge had been broken, but the carpenters rebuilt it during the night and the whole of the army passed unimpeded across the river on the following day. Beyond the river the soldiers had to pick their way in single file along a narrow path with water on both sides. No attempt was made to defend the approaches of the town or to challenge the vulnerable files of English soldiers. When they reached the castle it was promptly surrendered by two Norman knights of the garrison, protégés of Godfrey of Harcourt who had been in the pay of the English for a long time.[32] Edward III was unable to restrain his raw troops. Much of the great store of food which was found there was

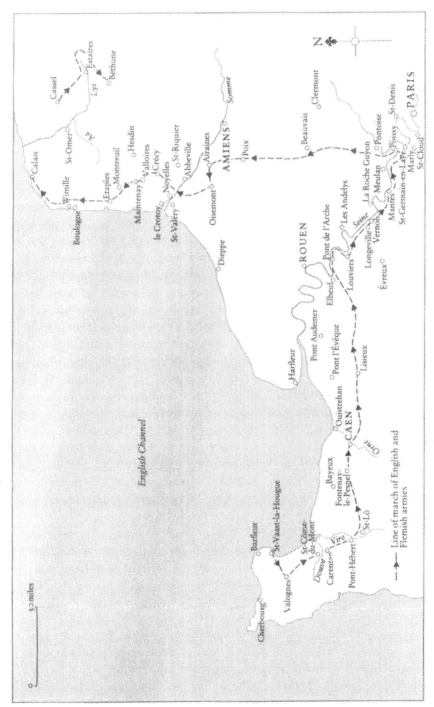

24 The English army in northern France, July–September 1346

pillaged. Even more of it was wantonly destroyed. In spite of the King's express orders the town was burned as the soldiers left it. 'Not a man or woman of substance dared to wait in the towns and castles or in the country around,' Bartholomew Burghersh wrote back to England; 'wherever our army appeared they fled away.' Only the common people stayed behind. Most of them were cut down in the streets and houses.

From Carentan the English did not proceed eastward towards Bayeux and Caen, as perhaps they had been expected to. They followed the narrow causeway which passed south through the marsh towards Saint-Lô. The bridges were intact here until they reached the River Vire at Pont-Hébert, about 4 miles before Saint-Lô. At first Robert Bertrand intended to make a stand on the Vire. He broke the bridge at Pont-Hébert and put all his men into Saint-Lô. The citizens co-operated with enthusiasm, manning the walls and filling the breaches left by more than a century of peace. Unfortunately, no attempt was made to defend the crossing of the river. The Prince of Wales, who reached Pont-Hébert first on 21 July, had the bridge repaired and crossed it with his men on the following day. Once the English had established themselves on the east bank of the river Bertrand changed his mind and gave up the defence of Saint-Lô as hopeless. He retreated along the Caen road as the English took possession of the town without striking a blow. Over the main gate they found the skulls of the three Norman knights who had been captured fighting for Edward III in Brittany in 1343 and executed for treason, the source of one of Edward's bitterest complaints against the French King. Saint-Lô was a rich town, the major market of the Cotentin and an important cloth-making centre. There was an orgy of theft and destruction. Great quantities of food, cloth and money, and several hundred barrels of wine were looted. Robert Bertrand's sudden failure of nerve had left the inhabitants no time to escape. The richest were taken for ransom. The others were killed.

Between Saint-Lô and Caen, a distance of about 40 miles on the ground, the English passed through some of the richest country in France, difficult country for an army on the march, with its warrens of narrow, sunken paths, but dense with signs of Normandy's agricultural wealth: farms, orchards, cattle and horses. The soldiers spread out, burning a swathe of land between 12 and 15 miles wide. What Edward's soldiers did to the Cotentin and the southern Bessin regardless of his orders, the seamen of his fleet did to the villages of the coast by deliberate policy. Their object was to do as much damage as possible to the communities which sustained French seapower in the Channel. One of Edward's clerks, Michael

Northburgh, estimated that everything had been destroyed or carried off within 5 miles of the sea from Cherbourg to the mouth of the Orne at Ouistrehan. They burned more than a hundred ships, including sixty-one which the French had fortified for war service. So much spoil was taken into the holds of the English ships that many of them could carry no more. The masters began to desert in large numbers, making their way back to England to land their prizes at home.[33]

On 25 July 1346 the English army was encamped about 10 miles west of Caen around the small Cistercian priory of Fontenay-le-Pesnel. Inside Caen there were high feelings among the soldiers and officials. They knew about the devastation which the enemy had left behind them and could see for themselves from their quarters in the castle the mass of refugees crammed with their carts and animals in the streets and spaces below. In the evening an English friar arrived with letters of Edward III summoning the town to surrender. The citizens were promised their lives, their goods and their homes. But the council of the garrison rejected Edward's demands out of hand. The Bishop of Bayeux, who was presiding, tore up the letters and had the messenger thrown in prison.

Caen was the largest town of Normandy after Rouen, with a population in normal times of between 8,000 and 10,000 people. It was set on low, marshy ground among the branches of the Orne and Odon rivers, which separated and coalesced in a lacework pattern of islands as they approached the sea. The huge mass of William the Conqueror's castle occupied a position of great natural strength. But the old town beneath it was weak. Its fixed defences consisted of low walls of the eleventh century, incomplete, unmaintained and in places crumbling away. The modern Boulevard du Maréchal Leclerc follows the dried-out course of the River Odon which in 1346 flowed by the south wall of the town. South of the Odon, unwalled but entirely enclosed by water, lay the Ile Saint-Jean, the richest and most populous suburb of Caen, which extended from the church of St Pierre to the River Orne along the axis of the rue Exmoisine (now the rue Saint-Jean). The suburb was connected to the town by a large fortified bridge over the River Odon. The two great foundations of the Conquerer, the Abbaye aux Hommes and the Abbaye aux Dames, both lay outside the town, surrounded by their own walls. Those of the Abbaye aux Hommes had been constructed very recently, a rare display of foresight by one of the richest churches of western France. But it was wasted, for there were not enough men to defend it.[34] Both foundations had to be abandoned to the enemy. Inside Caen the Count of Eu and the lord of Tancarville had between 1,000 and 1,500 men, including several hundred

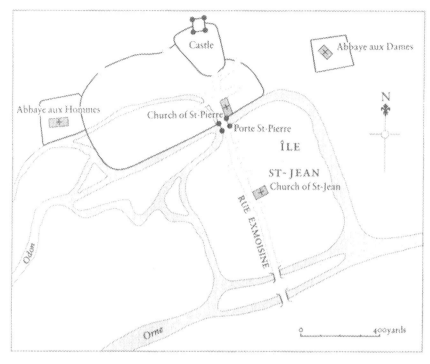

25 Caen

Genoese crossbowmen. The inhabitants armed themselves as best they could. The garrison had passed some days in strengthening the walls on the north and west sides with trenches and palisades. The south wall had been reinforced by mooring thirty ships and barges along the banks of the Odon and posting archers on their decks.

On the following morning, 26 July 1346, the English army appeared over the brow of the low ridge surrounding the town, a crowded mass of lances and standards. It was about nine o'clock. They had marched since before dawn, spread out across a front several miles wide and preceded by their camp followers to make them seem more numerous than they really were. Their arrival, although it had been expected for several days, caused a great commotion in the town and an abrupt change in the arrangements for its defence. Instead of fighting at the walls and gates of the old town the Count of Eu and the lord of Tancarville now decided to abandon it and instead to defend the suburb on the Ile Saint-Jean. There may have been sound military reasons for this remarkable change of mind, but it is more likely to have been forced on the commanders by the townsmen. Their assistance was essential. Most of them had their homes and wealth on the island. So about 200 men-at-arms and 100 Genoese crossbowmen were left in the castle under the command of the Bishop of Bayeux. The commanders then withdrew across the Pont-Saint-Pierre onto the island, bringing with them the remainder of the garrison and the population of the old town. The island was very weak. Its only fixed defences were the line of ships and barges along the Odon, and the Pont-Saint-Pierre, which was fortified on the wrong side. An improvised barricade was thrown out to hold the unfortified north side of the gate against the enemy. On the south and east, the suburb was protected only by the branches of the rivers. Unfortunately, it had been a dry summer and the water level was low.

The attack began earlier than either side had expected. The Prince of Wales led his men round the north of the town and encamped by the deserted buildings of the Abbaye aux Dames. Suddenly, some of them seized one of the western gates of the old town. The Earl of Warwick rushed through the gate into the empty streets with a few men-at-arms and a troop of archers. He was followed by the Earl of Northampton and Richard Talbot, leading a disorderly mob of men. When they reached the church of St Peter and the bridge beyond, some of them began to fire the houses about while others rushed to the barricades in front of the bridge and engaged the French troops in hand-to-hand fighting. Within a short time almost all the French garrison were crammed into the small space behind the bridge, supported by townsmen armed with building timbers and any other weapons that they could find, while more and more English and Welsh joined in the fighting on the other side. Edward III, who had encamped with the greater part of the army at the opposite end of the town, was alarmed to see an assault developing before he had had time to concentrate his men. He ordered the Earl of Warwick, who was the Marshal of the host, to sound the retreat. But the signal was ignored. Warwick, unable to break off the fight, threw himself into the thick of it instead. The battle spread from the bridge along the line of the river. The archers and Welsh lancers tried to wade across in the face of concentrated fire from the crossbowmen on the boats. When they reached the line of boats they set fire to two of them and clambered on board the others, fighting their way over the top of the vessels and on to the river bank on the far side. The French line of defence along the river failed at several points. As the defenders fell back the troops at the bridge, who were still holding, found themselves outflanked and attacked from behind. They included most of the men-at-arms of the garrison and all the commanders. A few, including Robert Bertrand, managed to flee into the old town and found sanctuary in the castle. The Constable and the Chamberlain and some of their men escaped into the upper storeys of the bridge tower. Below them the archers and the spearmen, 'gens de petite conscience' Froissart called them,[35] were killing every man they encountered. Only the men-at-arms of the English army paused to take prisoners whose fine armour and coats of arms revealed their wealth and value. The French knights looked out for men of rank to take their surrender and grant them their protection, a point of honour as well as self-preservation. The Constable recognized Sir Thomas Holland, with whom he had fought in the Baltic crusades of the 1330s,[36] and yielded up his sword to him. The Chamberlain surrendered his to Sir Thomas Daniel, a retainer of the Prince of Wales. About 100 knights, more than 120 squires and a very large number of the richer citizens were taken alive. They were fortunate. When the English had completed their rampage through the Ile Saint-Jean, more than 2,500 bodies were counted in the streets, houses and gardens. This figure did not include those who were cut down as they fled into the fields outside. One eyewitness estimated the total French casualties at about 5,000. The bodies of 500 Frenchmen, stripped of their clothes and of every mark of rank were collected together to be buried in a great communal grave in the churchyard of St Jean on the island.[37] Nobody recorded the casualties of the English. Only one man-at-arms died, but there must have been heavy losses among the infantry and archers who had led the assault against the better judgement of their superiors and whose reckless courage had won Edward the day.

The English stayed for five days at Caen. They tried and failed to take the castle. They completed the plundering of the town. They rested in their encampments and treated their wounds. A few, including Michael Northburgh, inspected the Abbaye aux Hommes and the tomb of William the Conqueror. Edward occupied himself with the forthcoming march into the Seine Valley. The King planned to cross the river between Paris and Rouen, and then to make for the Somme 60 miles north of it. He needed reinforcements, particularly of archers. Orders were given to raise 1,200 archers in those parts of England, principally East Anglia and the southeast, which had not already been emptied of them in the spring. There were warrants to purvey 2,450 bows and 6,300 sheaves of arrows. One hundred large ships were to be requisitioned to replace the ones which had deserted the fleet and to convoy men and supplies from Winchelsea to the continent. Edward wanted all these arrangements completed by 20 August. To receive them, it would be necessary to capture a port. Edward told his Council to send the fleet to him off Le Crotoy, a small harbour on the north shore of the estuary of the Somme a few miles from Abbeville.[38]

About 300 captives were loaded on to the ships at Ouistrehan at the mouth of the Orne a few days after the fall of Caen and taken back to England in the charge of the Earl of Huntingdon. They were distributed among a number of castles about the country. Some of the lesser prisoners redeemed themselves quite quickly. But the greater ones were destined to spend several years in captivity. Edward III learned earlier than the French did the danger of releasing prisoners to rejoin the armies of his enemy. The Count of Eu was kept by Sir Thomas Holland until the following year, when the King bought him for 80,000 florins (£12,000). It was three years before he was to return to France and then only on parole to raise his ransom. Since he was executed not long after his return it is possible that the ransom was never paid. The Chamberlain, the lord of Tancarville, was claimed by the Prince of Wales because his captor, Sir Thomas Daniel, was a knight of his retinue. Unlike Holland, Daniel received only a tip for his pains, 1,000 marks (£666) and a pension of 40 marks (£26 13s. 4d.) per annum. The Chamberlain's brother, who had been captured at the same time, was allowed to return to France on parole in March 1347 to find ransoms for both of them. But Tancarville himself was closely confined in Wallingford Castle until the end of 1348. His ransom was paid by a complicated arrangement by which the prisoner mortgaged several estates to a Norman abbey, which surrendered £6,000 worth of land in England to Edward III, who in turn reimbursed the Prince of Wales. It was not as rich a haul as Henry of Lancaster's at Bergerac and Auberoche, but these were men much closer to the French King. The political impact of their capture and ruin was far greater.[39]

The arrival of the prisoners at the beginning of August 1346 was not the first or the only sign of the events happening in France to strike public opinion in England. Shipmasters had been returning with their spoils throughout the second half of July. John Stratford, who presided over the royal Council in England in the King's absence, received several letters from friends with the army which were copied and widely circulated. The King himself wrote to both archbishops a week after the fall of Caen with instructions to organize prayers daily and processions twice a week, and sent an account of his deeds to be published throughout England. In the records of the municipality of Caen, Edward's clerks found a copy of the agreement made in March 1338 between Philip VI and the communities of Normandy, which contained detailed stipulations for the invasion and despoiling of England. This document was shipped to England and read out by Stratford to a great crowd of Londoners in St Paul's churchyard. The King, Stratford said, was wasting Normandy for the better security of England.[40]

The English army moved out of its camp at Caen on 31 July 1346. Edward left a small force behind him to continue the siege of the citadel and then moved slowly east towards Rouen, covering an average of only 5 or 6 miles a day. His men burned everything in front of them. Philip VI could do nothing to stop them. The two cardinals, who had left Arras as soon as they had received the news of the landing at La Hougue, made their way from the Seine valley towards the English army in a courageous attempt to halt its progress which their master in Avignon had already written off as hopeless.[41]

At the end of July the French King was at Vernon when a spy reported that the second invasion of France, from Flanders, was about to begin. The King's arrangements for the defence of the march of Flanders were hardly more satisfactory than those which had failed him in the Cotentin. The army of the north was not yet in existence. There was a barely adequate garrison in Calais. The war treasurers made available some materials for making gunpowder 'but nothing more is to be done for them'. East of the Calais marshes, in Artois, some troops had been deployed by the Duke of Burgundy's officials and every town was recruiting for its own defence, but there were no royal garrisons. The invaders set out on 2 August 1346, a tiny band of English archers and men-at-arms, some crossbowmen supplied by the three great towns, and a large, undisciplined crowd of Flemings. The nominal commander, Henry of Flanders, was the uncle of the Count of Flanders. But he was virtually a prisoner of Ghent. It was Hugh Hastings who was in control. When they reached the boundary at Estaires on the River Lys, they were stopped by troops holding the bridge. A large number of Flemings with more enthusiasm than sense were cut down or drowned in the attempt to force a passage. Hastings withdrew downstream. On 4 August the French commanders in the north-west sent out orders to find garrisons for all the principal castles of Artois. On the 10th Hastings, having outpaced them to the east, entered the French King's territory.[42]

At the opposite extremity of the kingdom the original strategic purpose of besieging Aiguillon was receding into the background as its capture became an object in itself. The Duke of Normandy insisted on saving his face before marching north to meet the main threat, a point on which he quarrelled with his military advisers and probably also (the facts are obscure) with his father.[43] Everything went wrong. The pressure on his lines of supply intensified. From the castle of Bajamont above Agen the 'Archdeacon' Gaillard de Durfort made frequent descents on the suburbs of the town and the vital French river corridor between Aiguillon and Moissac. Robert Houdetot, the Seneschal of the Agenais, had deployed several hundred men against the garrison of Bajamont without success. On 18 July 1346 the Duke's council decided to detach a much larger force to go to Houdetot's aid. Their instructions were extraordinarily cautious. They were to contain the Archdeacon's men with field works and starve them into submission. The citizens of Agen levied a man from every household to reinforce them. But the result was a dismaying humilation. The French force, which must have been at least 2,000 strong, was attacked and defeated by the garrison of Bajamont before they could build their field works. Many of them lost their lives. Houdetot himself was captured. It was the last significant action in which the Duke's army was engaged.[44]

Beset with problems and threatened from three directions at once Philip VI does not appear to have had any coherent plan of campaign. On 29 July he ordered the *arrière-ban* to be proclaimed and called every available man of military age to Rouen. Quite a large number of soldiers had already gathered there, but they were disorganized and badly equipped, and too many of them were raw local levies. Within a few days they were reinforced by the Genoese who, having arrived too late to do useful work at sea, were ordered to beach their galleys in the Seine and fight with the army on foot. Of the rest of the French King's forces in the north, some were on the march of Flanders, some were assembling in Paris or at Amiens, some were still on their way from their homes.[45]

Philip's intentions changed daily. At first he proposed to meet the English south of the Seine. He reached Rouen on about 31 July, and crossed the river at the beginning of August, moving hesitantly west. Then, on about 3 or 4 August 1346 there was a major shift of strategy. The news of Hastings' manoeuvres on the march of Flanders was almost certainly the reason. Instead of meeting the English King in his path the French army withdrew again to Rouen, breaking the Seine bridge as soon as they had crossed it. The new plan was to hold the enemy at the river. South of the Seine the population was to be left to its fate. They sheltered in the towns and prepared to defend themselves as best they could. At Pont-l'Évêque the *vicomte* emptied the prisons to find men for the walls.[46]

The King of England received the cardinals at Lisieux on 3 August 1346. But they had nothing to offer him. They exhorted him to stop. They complained about the Welsh, who had stolen their horses. Edward's answer was frigid. He told them that he would have to receive serious proposals before he would contemplate calling off his campaign. He called for their letters of authority empowering them to make such proposals on the French King's behalf, and when it turned out that they had none he dismissed them.[47] On the following day the English army quickened its pace through the fertile basin of the lower Seine. On 7 August it reached the river at Elbeuf. Runners spread across the countryside lighting fires right up to the deserted south-bank suburbs of Rouen. Sir Thomas Holland, the captor of the Constable, rode up to the end of the broken bridge with a handful of other exhibitionists, killing two Frenchmen in their path and shouting 'St George for Edward!' across the water. Philip was being pressed by the cardinals to produce the 'serious proposals' which Edward had demanded. He sent them back, accompanied by a French archbishop, to meet the English King on the road, bearing the first formal concessions that he had yet offered. He was willing, he said, to restore Ponthieu and the lost provinces of Aquitaine. But they were to be held as Edward's father and grandfather had held them, as fiefs of the French Crown. This was always to be the sticking point. Philip also proposed a marriage alliance. The cardinals delivered their message to Edward III, but they could not conceal their pessimism. They did not think that Philip would yield anything else of importance and they said so. Edward was not interested. He told them, that he would respond to the French King's proposal at some future date, but meanwhile he did not intend to lose a single day's march in discussion of them.

Philip now began to concentrate all his resources on stopping the English army at the Seine. The troops assembling at Amiens were diverted in all haste southward and the march of Flanders left to be defended by a few small detachments of men against Hastings' army. The wishes of the Duke of Normandy were finally overruled. Orders went out peremptorily recalling the army of Aiguillon to the north.

There were four principal bridges over the Seine between Rouen and the Paris area, at Pont de l'Arche, Vernon, Mantes and Meulan. All of these places except the last were walled towns on the south bank of the river which were open to unlimited reinforcement and supply for as long as the French held the north bank. When the English tried to rush the walls of Pont de l'Arche (the nearest of the four bridge towns) they were held off by the *vicomte* of the town for long enough to enable the main army to arrive from Rouen.[48] So the English had to continue their march upstream, shadowed by the French from the opposite bank. They began by burning the rich cloth town of Louviers. It had probably been evacuated. Then they spread out, wasting everything in a 20-mile band south of the river as they moved slowly eastward towards Paris. The English stormed the great fortress of Longeville outside Vernon and massacred the entire garrison. But the town itself was found to be impregnable. They got no further than the suburbs. At Mantes, the next bridge town, there were several thousand French troops drawn up in prepared positions under the walls. They were left alone. On 11 August the English army passed close to Meulan, the one town that lay north of its bridge. The earls of Warwick and Northampton approached to investigate the possibility of forcing a crossing. But they found that the bridge had been broken by the north bank and was guarded at its southern end by a heavily fortified barbican whose defenders yelled abuse at them as they rode up. The English were stung into attempting a disorganized assault, but they were driven back ignominiously and several of the leading men-at-arms received serious wounds from crossbow bolts. Upstream of Meulan, French soldiers stood at the edge of the water laughing and baring their backsides to the enemy. The only notable feat of arms on the march was the courageous and profitable but useless enterprise of a Staffordshire knight, Sir Robert Ferrers, who crossed the river with some companions in a rowing boat and fought his way into the outer bailey of the fortress of La Roche-Guyon on the north bank. The garrison commander thought that he was under attack by the whole English army, and instead of withdrawing to the keep, surrendered the whole fortress together with all the men under his command. Ferrers took their parole to pay ransoms in due course and then scuttled back across the river.

> Quand le Châtel de Guyon est pris,
> Donc fletra le fleur de Lys,

ran a popular song: 'When La Roche-Guyon falls then shall the Fleur de Lys wither.'

On 12 August the King of England came within 20 miles of Paris. From high ground near the road he could see the walls and towers of the city across the five great bends of the Seine, enclosing the huntsman's landscape in which the kings of France scattered their lodges and palaces from the twelfth century to the eighteenth: Marly, Poissy, Saint-Cloud, Saint-Germain-en-Laye, 'the principal residences and recreations of the King', complained the chronicler of Saint-Denis; 'for which reason [he added] it was not only discreditable but plain treason that all the nobility of France could not boot out the King of England but instead left him to take his ease in the palaces of the King of France, drinking his wine and smashing his property as he pleased'. Paris was in a state of great alarm and excitement.

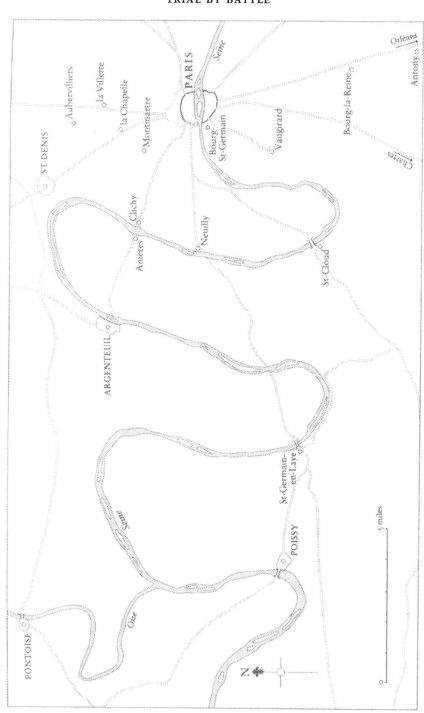

26 Western approaches to Paris

Public order was beginning to break down. The government was obliged to deploy 500 men-at-arms of John of Bohemia and his son about the city in order to keep control. In the quarters close to the gates men were building barricades at street corners and accumulating stores of stones and other missiles at upper windows. Outside in the spreading suburbs preparations were being made to demolish whole districts.

There was a renewed crisis of Philip's counsels, intensified by the pressures of opinion in his capital. The King's army, although more than equal to Edward III's, was small by comparison with the huge hosts of 1339 and 1340. Most of the unsatisfactory infantry force which had been scratched together at Rouen had been disbanded at the start of the march up the Seine. The Genoese seamen had been dispersed to serve as garrison troops in ports and towns from the Loire to the Somme, relieving the specialized Italian infantrymen and bowmen already there, who now joined the main French army.[49] According to well-informed contemporary estimates Philip had about 8,000 men-at-arms, about 6,000 Genoese and a large body of infantry of uncertain number and quality.

The deployment of these men was a difficult matter. The Seine, which had hitherto been Edward's main problem, now became Philip's. He could not defend Paris both north and south of it without dividing his army into two perilously small units. He could not defend both of the two principal bridges west of Paris, at Poissy and Saint-Cloud, without running the same danger, for they were separated by the bends of the river: more than 40 miles for the French army by the north bank, but only 12 for the English army by the south. A bold spirit might have crossed the river and confronted the enemy before he could reach either place. But Philip VI was not a bold spirit. On 12 August he decided to break the bridge of Poissy, evacuated the population of the town to Paris and abandoned it to the enemy. A small force of infantry was left to guard the stumps of the bridge from the north bank. Philip established his headquarters in the abbey buildings of Saint-Denis. His army marched round the north-west suburbs of Paris and encamped on the right bank by the bridge of Saint-Cloud.

The English occupied Poissy and Saint-Germain-en-Laye without resistance on the following morning, 13 August. They wandered astonished among the empty buildings: the famous priory of Dominican nuns; the brand new mansion of the King next door to it, where Edward III installed himself; the old palace nearby, which the Prince of Wales occupied; the fine churches with their beautiful stained-glass windows and treasures of painting and jewellery which in their haste the inhabitants had had to leave behind them.

The King of France and the principal officers of his court were still at Saint-Denis, preparing to celebrate the feast of the Assumption, when they learned that the English had begun to rebuild the bridge of Poissy. The paroled prisoner of war who brought them this news was received with incredulity and, at first, derision. When Philip was finally persuaded that it was true, he tried to find troops to stop them. There was a contingent of men on its way south from Amiens. The men were met on the road and diverted to Poissy. But by the time they reached the river bank opposite the town the English carpenters had already thrown a 60-foot tree across the gap and several dozen soldiers had made their way across it on to the northern side. There was a sharp encounter on the strand. The French, most of whom were ill-trained infantry levies, were driven back in confusion. The more quick-witted among them unharnessed the horses from their supply train and fled, three to each animal. The rest, at least 200 of them, were cut down as they ran. By the following morning, 14 August 1346, a temporary timber bridge was in place fit to drive carts over. The foundation of Philip VI's campaign strategy had been destroyed.

When the French King learned that the English were installed on both banks of the Seine he broke the bridge of Saint-Cloud, where his army had been encamped, and withdrew them northward to the plain between Paris and Saint-Denis. The English stayed south of the river. Paris was in uproar. From the southern quarters of the city the towns of Saint-Cloud and Saint-Germain-en-Laye could be seen in flames. Smoke rose from the villages and hamlets along the Chartres road and spread slowly round to the south of the city as groups of raiders detached from the English army took courage from the immobility of their enemy. The Parisians were contemplating abandoning all of the left-bank quarters of the city and breaking the Petit Pont which joined them to the Ile de la Cité.

From Saint-Denis, Philip issued a public challenge to Edward III to meet him in battle on chosen ground, the kind of challenge which was so often made and so rarely accepted in the course of the war. Philip suggested a date between 17 and 22 August and a site south-east of the Augustan wall of Paris in the great open meadows between the Bourg Saint-Germain and the village of Vaugirard, the area now covered by the VIIe *arrondissement* which was then the traditional battleground of the students of the university and the louts of the city. An alternative venue was suggested in the plain west of Pontoise.[50] This invitation was issued on 14 August and carried to the English King by the Bishop of Meaux. What, if any, answer Edward gave him was a controversial question. There was no reason why he should help Philip to resolve his strategic quandary. On the other hand there were good reasons why he should try to draw Philip's army south of the Seine. French sources are insistent that even if Edward deferred his formal reply he gave Philip to understand that the challenge would be accepted. This version of events is entirely consistent with Philip's movements during the next few days. It is probably what happened.

On 15 August Philip VI moved his entire army through the streets of the capital to the southern wall by the abbey of St Germain. Here the marshals and their deputies conducted their muster, counting numbers, sorting troops by skill and status, recording the condition of horses and weapons, and the pay to which every man was entitled. Philip had his men assembled in battle order. Then he marched them some 4 miles south of the city wall and drew them up on rising ground among the vineyards of Bourg-la-Reine and Antony, rich suburban villages now engulfed by the industrial outskirts of Paris. The chosen battleground stretched out below them.

Away from Paris the French position deteriorated daily. Hugh Hastings and Henry of Flanders, having burned a track across Walloon Flanders since 10 August, arrived outside the town of Béthune on the night of the 14th and laid siege to it on the day Philip VI crossed Paris. They began to destroy the outlying villages and a widening circle of territory around them. The region had been almost denuded of troops. Just 180 men had been spared for the defence of Béthune itself. Many of these were Genoese crossbowmen who, like their countrymen in Normandy, were unpaid and mutinous.[51]

Henry of Lancaster received a deputation from the Duke of Normandy in his quarters at Bergerac on the same day. The Duke, who had now received his father's orders, had no choice but to abandon his campaign and take his army away to shore up the French position in the north. He only wanted to save what he could of his dignity. His emissaries offered to 'suspend' the siege of Aiguillon if Henry would agree to a local truce. But Henry intended to take the maximum advantage of his opponent's discomfiture. He was well informed about the course of events in the north. He had summoned all the nobility of Gascony who were not already in arms and had stripped his garrisons to the limit to strengthen his field army. He rejected the Duke of Normandy's proposal out of hand. So, on 20 August, the French abandoned the siege of Aiguillon in which they had invested five months of effort and suffering. The decision was so suddenly made and swiftly executed that there was no time to draw up the army in marching order. Some of the men were pushed into the river and drowned as they struggled across the wooden bridge over the Garonne. The whole of their camp with its valuable tents, horses and equipment was left behind in the charge of some of the locally recruited men. They were quickly dispersed by the garrison of Aiguillon and the spoil carried in triumph into the town. That arch-spoliator Walter Mauny took the lead. As for the Duke and the men still with him, they marched east up the Garonne to Agen and Moissac, travelling as fast as they could, with Lancaster's men snapping at their heels.[52]

On 16 August 1346, as soon as the march of the French army across Paris presented him with his opportunity, Edward III bolted northwards, leaving Poissy in flames and breaking the bridge again behind him. Once he had travelled a safe distance he wrote a disingenuous letter by way of formal answer to Philip VI's challenge.[53] It was probably prepared chiefly for consumption in his own army, among which copies were immediately circulated. Philip, he said, could have had his battle at any time during the three days which the English army had passed at Poissy. But since the French King had done nothing he had resolved to continue his march so as to help his allies and punish 'those rebels whom you call your subjects'. If Philip still wanted it, Edward would be ready for battle wherever Philip might find him.

At this point Edward was to be found at Auteuil, a short distance south of the great cathedral city of Beauvais. The King of France reacted to Edward's flight with unaccustomed speed and decisiveness. He recrossed Paris with his army, loudly proclaiming to the emotional crowds gathered in the rue Saint-Denis that he had been tricked. He led his men in a succession of forced marches covering up to 25 miles a day across the northern French plain towards the Somme, which was now the principal natural barrier between the English army and the Flemish border. There was already a French army on the Somme, but it was still in the process of assembling and, although its strength cannot be precisely known, it was certainly smaller than the army about the King.[54] Edward knew the importance of reaching the river first. He abandoned as much as possible of his wagon train and mounted his footsoldiers on the great number of captured horses which had been taken in Normandy and the Seine valley. But he could not move with the speed of the French. They had emptied the countryside of supplies, forcing the English to forage over great distances from their line of march in order to feed themselves. A great deal of time was also lost in the quest for plunder and ransom. The Prince of Wales division was principally at fault. These troops wasted a day attacking the insignificant village of Vessencourt. They were stopped as they were on the point of assaulting Beauvais, but could not be prevented from burning the suburbs and most of the outlying churches, villages and farms. According to Froissart, the King had twenty men summarily hanged whom he found burning a monastery.[55] But the King and his marshals could not be everywhere. The walls of Poix-en-Beauvaisis were undermined and assaulted with artillery and scaling ladders in defiance of Edward's express instructions and threats of retribution. The result was that the French army overtook them. On 18 August, the day on which the English passed west of Beauvais, Philip reached Clermont-sur-Oise due east of it. On the 20th, he arrived at the Somme with the advance guard of his army. On the following day, when the English were still some 25 miles south of the river, they came briefly into contact with troops of the French rearguard commanded by John of Bohemia. The inhabitants of the plain of Picardy took courage. They began to gather in armed bands to pick off isolated groups of English troops, the first time that Edward's army had encountered any popular resistance on a significant scale.

The English King stopped on the evening of 21 August in the small town of Airaines. From here he sent out detachments of troops to test the defences of the Somme. The river was found to be everywhere impassable. The French had broken every bridge except those of Amiens and Abbeville, which were enclosed by walled cities, and a handful of other places which were heavily guarded. There were French troops stationed everywhere between Amiens and the sea where the river was low enough to be forded. On 22 August the Earl of Warwick tried to force a passage by the village of Hangest, but he was driven back. At Pont-Rémy the bridge was found to be defended by a powerful force of cavalry, archers and local men commanded by John of Bohemia and Edward III's erstwhile friend and ally John of Hainault, now in French service. Warwick suffered heavy casualties here and failed to capture the bridge. At Fontaine-sur-Somme the English made their way across marsh tracks towards the river but they were defeated in front of the bridge of Long. At Longpré, nearby, it was the same story. Edward III was in his own territory, the county of Ponthieu which he had possessed until the outbreak of the war, like his father and grandfather before him. But by all appearances he was trapped there, boxed in between the river, the main body of the French army to the east and the sea at his back. His troops were beginning to suffer from their month of marching. They were completely out of bread and were rapidly exhausting their other supplies. Many of them had gone through their shoes.

On the 23rd the French moved west out of Amiens along the south bank of the Somme towards the English army. Edward might now have had his

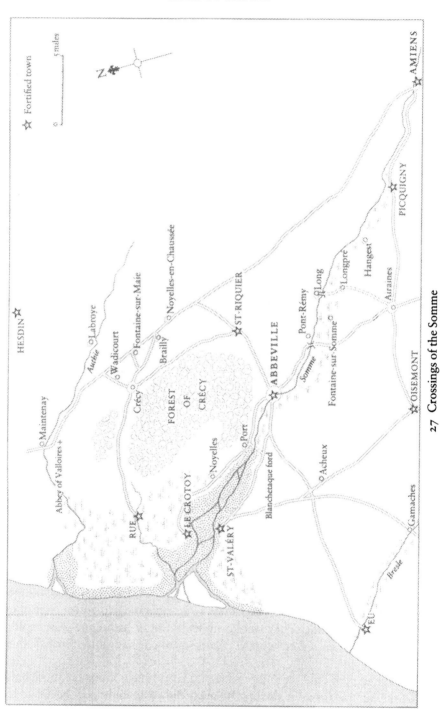

27 Crossings of the Somme

battle. But he hurriedly left Airaines and retreated towards the coast. Philip VI's officers ate the meal which had been laid out for him. Then they spread their troops out to close off Edward's corner. Behind the English army, at Oisemont, the chief market town of the district, all the local men of military age were gathering to block his path.

The English reached Oisemont late in the morning of 23 August. The scratch army, which had been drawn up in front of the gates, was dispersed with a single cavalry charge. Most of its members were butchered as they fled. Edward's troops wasted some time in burning and pillaging this place before turning north towards the mouth of the Somme. When night fell they had reached Acheux, a small village about 6 miles from the river. The French were still keeping their distance. Philip VI himself fixed his quarters in the town of Abbeville.

About five miles downstream of Abbeville there was a ford known as Blanchetaque. Here, long before the construction of the Abbeville canal, the Somme broadened out into a great tidal marsh about 2 miles wide, a desolate landscape of reeds and dunes which could just be crossed at low tide by men wading in water up to their knees. The French commanders had anticipated that Edward III might make for this place. But Edward himself seems to have been unaware of its existence until the last moment. Either a prisoner of war in his camp or a Yorkshireman living in the district (there are conflicting accounts) offered to show him where it was and to guide him across. On 24 August, shortly after midnight, the English army rose and picked their way in darkness across the marsh.

When they reached the main stream of the river they saw that the opposite bank was heavily defended. One of Philip VI's more experienced commanders, Godemar du Fay, had been stationed there with about 500 men-at-arms and 3,000 infantry. Moreover, the tide was still too high to cross, so the English were obliged to sit down in full view of the enemy as the sun rose and Godemar drew up his men at leisure in three lines along the water's edge. At about 8 a.m., 100 men-at-arms and about the same number of archers began to wade into the river, led by the Earl of Northampton and Reginald Cobham, a veteran whose fifty years had done nothing to dull his energy. When the archers arrived within range of the French troops on the opposite bank, they loosed a rain of arrows down upon them. Under cover of the archers' fire the men-at-arms pressed on to the north bank of the river and held a beach-head there while others crossed behind them. As the beach-head expanded Godemar's men, who had fought ferociously at the water's edge, were slowly pushed back before breaking and fleeing towards Abbeville, pursued by the exultant English up to the gates.[56] Within an hour and a half the whole English army together with its carts and equipment had crossed to the north bank. It was a remarkable feat of arms.

Philip VI was no longer in Abbeville. He had left the town by the south at dawn hoping to catch the English army in the angle of the river and the sea. He followed in their tracks as far as the southern end of the Blanchetaque ford. But by the time he arrived there the last English soldier had escaped. The tide was coming in. Pursuit was impossible.

The French commanders assumed that Edward III would now make a dash for the north and try to join forces with the Flemings outside Béthune. The main garrisons north of the Somme were reinforced at once as heavily as resources would allow. Hesdin, which was the most significant town on the road from Abbeville to Béthune, received nearly 300 men.[57]

On the very day that the English army forced the Somme, the Flemings unexpectedly abandoned their campaign and dispersed. They had been held up outside Béthune since 14 August by the enterprising captain of the town, Godfrey d'Annequin. His main asset was the enthusiasm of the townsmen. They settled the arrears of the Genoese garrison (who had been threatening to desert). They burned their suburbs (the richest quarters of the town).[58] They ambushed the Flemings as they arrived in disorderly groups at the beginning of the siege, inflicting heavy casualties on them. On 16 August 1346 they beat back an assault which lasted from dawn to vespers, wounding Henry of Flanders among others. It was the day on which Edward III began his march from Poissy to the Somme. On the 22nd, when Edward was still 60 miles away at Airaines, Godfrey led a sortie from the town into the main camp of the besiegers and destroyed a large part of it. The Flemings were disheartened. They fell to quarrelling among themselves. Fights broke out between the men of Bruges and the men of the western provinces. The decision to call off the siege was probably made at this time. The exact chronology is obscure. On 24 August the Flemings burned their siege engines and marched away. Edward III had remained in fairly regular contact with Hugh Hastings by runners ever since he had landed in Normandy.[59] His actions suggest that he learned of the Flemings' decision on 24 or 25 August, at about the same time as it was being executed. Philip VI may not have learned until later.

Once the English King had escaped from the pocket south of the Somme, his most pressing need was to replenish his stores. They were now so low as to imperil the fitness of his men. Part of his army was therefore detached under the command of Hugh Despenser and sent on a major foraging raid along the coast. Despenser carried out his orders with the utmost violence and efficiency. He sacked Noyelles-sur-Mer in the afternoon of 24 August and burnt Le Crotoy in the evening in spite of the efforts of its Genoese garrison. Le Crotoy, an important harbour and victualling station, yielded a rich haul of cattle and provisions. But of the reinforcements and supplies from England which should have been waiting off the shore, there was still no sign. The ships were not yet loaded. The men were still gathering in Kent.[60]

The main armies of England and France stood watching each other across the flow and ebb of the Somme estuary, the French deliberating whether to fight their way across, the English drawing up their battle lines. Philip allowed two tides to pass without crossing. Then, on the morning of 25 August, he returned to Abbeville where he spent the rest of the day. His army followed on behind.

It was not until the early morning of Saturday 26 August that Philip left Abbeville on the Hesdin road to try to cut off Edward by the north. He rode ahead with the principal commanders, the vanguard of the army and the troops of his household, followed at disorderly intervals throughout the day by the rest of the French cavalry, the Genoese and the slow-moving crowds of infantry. In the fourteenth century the great forest of Crécy, part of the domain of the counts of Ponthieu, covered most of the territory between the banks of the Somme below Abbeville to the valley of the River Authie some 14 miles north. Philip's men rode round the eastern edge of it by Saint-Riquier and Noyelles-en-Chaussée towards the Roman road from Amiens to Montreuil. A short distance north of Saint-Riquier Philip was met by a group of scouts who had been sent ahead to reconnoitre. They reported that the English had passed through the forest and that they had crossed the River Maye and halted beyond the village of Crécy.

Crécy lay north-west of Philip's position, about 10 miles away by road. The King sent another scouting party forward, five knights led by a French-speaking Swiss, Henri le Moine, to obtain more detailed intelligence of the English army's position. They found the English drawn up waiting for them in battle order between the villages of Crécy and Wadicourt. By the time they had completed their reconnaissance the first standard-bearers of the French army were scarcely 3 miles from the English lines. Le Moine halted the French column. Philip and his commanders conferred by the roadside. It was by now late morning. Most of those who were with the King were against advancing any further. The greater

part of the French cavalry and the Genoese crossbowmen and their auxiliaries were close behind. But they were tired, having been several hours
on the road. And the rest of the army, including most of the infantry and
almost all the baggage train, was spread out along the road back to
Abbeville. Some important contingents had not even reached Abbeville
yet. Philip's advisers, even bold spirits like John of Hainault, wanted him
to march round to the north of the English position and encamp for the
night at Labroye on the River Authie. Once they had cut off the English
King's line of advance, they reasoned, there would be time to collect their
forces and rest their men. But others took a different view. They remembered the humiliations of Buirenfosse in 1339, of Bouvines in 1340 and
Ploermel in 1342, when powerful French armies had come within sight of
the English line and failed to engage them. Philip was of their opinion. By
1346 his reputation could not bear a stalemate any more than a defeat. So
the trumpeters called to arms everyone who was within earshot. The first
units moved forward into open ground beyond the village of Fontaine-sur-
Maye.

Philip arranged his army in three battalions, one behind the other. In the
first he placed the Genoese crossbowmen. With them were John of
Bohemia and his son Charles and about 300 cavalry, including their own
German and Czech retainers. In the second battalion stood the elite of the
French cavalry, including many of the greatest noblemen of the realm.
They were commanded by the Count of Alençon, the King's impetuous
younger brother. The third division, which the King commanded in person, included the rest of the cavalry. It is probable that the infantry (or
such of them as arrived in time) were placed in their own formations on
the wings of each of the three main battalions.[61] Reinforcements continued to swell the ranks of the French army during the afternoon. The
number who were present at the battle is a matter of conjecture. There
were about 12,000 men-at-arms according to reliable contemporary
estimates. There were the 6,000 Genoese who had marched north from
Paris with the King. But as for the rest of the infantry, said by the
chroniclers to have been 'innumerable', most of them were left behind on
the road. Philip VI may have had between 20,000 and 25,000 men under
his command.

At the far end of an expanse of gently rising ground the English could be
seen waiting in their lines with the forest of Crécy-Grange behind them.
Edward III had deployed his troops in person, laughing with them according to Jean le Bel and urging every one of them to do his duty, 'making
even cowards into heroes'. They were stretched out across the hillside, the

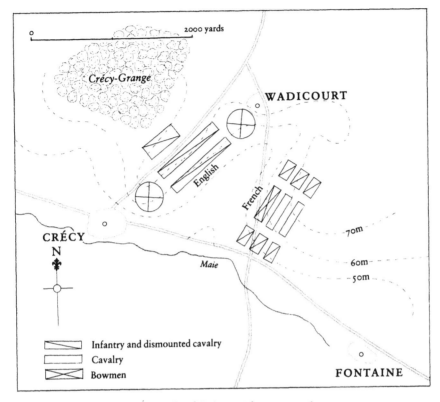

2000 yards

Crécy-Grange

WADICOURT

English

French

CRÉCY

N

Maie

70m

60m

50m

FONTAINE

Infantry and dismounted cavalry

Cavalry

Bowmen

28 Battle of Crécy, 26 August 1346

Prince of Wales in the front line with the earls of Warwick and Northampton and the cream of the English nobility. The English King commanded the reserve at the rear. The archers, who made up about half of his army's numbers, were placed at the wings, forward of the main lines of soldiers after the fashion of Dupplin Moor and Halidon Hill. To protect them from the enemy's cavalry a circle of baggage carts was drawn up around them. In front, a large number of shallow pit-traps had been dug across the approaches to the English lines. Behind the English positions another circle of carts enclosed the horses. All the English men-at-arms fought dismounted.

Underneath the carts which Edward had placed around the archers at the wings of his army was a number of gunpowder cannon. The English had experimented with these weapons in their campaigns against the Scots, and had probably used them in the siege of Berwick in 1333. The French had certainly employed them for some years in defending and attacking fortified towns, although not on a large scale. Neither side, so far as is known, had ever used them on the battlefield, where they were likely to be most effective. Gunpowder artillery of the early fourteenth century was light, short-ranged and inaccurate. There were no machines capable of firing heavy projectiles and replacing the stone-throwing trebuchets and mechanical slings which in more or less refined forms had been standard siege equipment for centuries. But they caused noise, confusion and fear. Most of the English machines were 'ribalds', which were ideal for these purposes, extremely primitive field pieces consisting of clusters of barrels bound together and mounted on small carts about the size of wheelbarrows from which bolts were fired rather like those out of crossbows. There were about 100 of these. There was also a smaller number of rather heavier pieces which fired metal pellets like grapeshot.[62]

Towards the end of the afternoon the sky clouded over and it began to rain. At this point (it was about five o'clock) the French attacked. The desultory shouts of abuse suddenly gave way to a deafening noise of trumpets and kettledrums. The crossbowmen advanced against the English lines from the south-east, shooting their bolts as they came. From the right wing of the English army the longbowmen began to loose volleys of arrows into the air towards the advancing Genoese. It was an unequal contest. The longbowmen caused carnage among the Italians while the bolts of the crossbows fell well short. The great protective shields which the Italians usually had carried before them into battle by their 'paviseurs', were still on the road from Abbeville. So was most of their spare ammunition. The rain got into their machines and slackened the cords. When the English saw that the crossbowmen were wilting they intensified their fire and began to fire their cannon. The Genoese fell back, then broke into headlong flight towards the shelter of their own lines.

Few of the French army had any experience of massed longbowmen. They did not understand what was happening to the Genoese. A murmur spread around the ranks of horsemen that the crossbowmen were cowards and traitors in the pay of the enemy. Without warning and apparently without orders the Count of Alençon suddenly charged forward with the second French battalion, running down the fleeing Italians, trampling them under the feet of their horses and cleaving them with their swords. 'Kill this riff-raff! Kill them all!', Philip is supposed to have shouted from the rear; 'they are doing nothing but getting in our way.'[63] After a moment of hesitation, much of the French cavalry careered pell mell after them. They charged in a dense mass across the English lines towards the centre where the Prince of Wales was. As they came within range of the archers men began to fall from their horses into the path of those behind. Others lost control as their animals turned in terror away from the arrows and cannon fire, dragging their masters after them. When the survivors reached the first line of the English army, there was a savage fight around the Prince of Wales. These formless mêlées were murderous affairs at a time when few men wore uniform or recognizable liveries, and the yelling of war-cries was the main means of identification: 'Saint George!' for England, 'Montjoie Saint Denis!' for France.[64] The sixteen-year-old Prince, who had never been in action before, stood out from the ranks by his great height and his standard carried beside him. He 'ran through horses, cut down their riders, crushed their helmets, split their lances, all the time shouting encouragement at his troops'. Men advanced from the lines behind to fill the gaps left by the wounded and the dead. At one point the Prince's standard was seen to fall. It was Sir Thomas Daniel, one of the heroes of Caen, who forced his way into the thick of the fight to raise it up again.[65] Many years later the chronicler Froissart told the famous, perhaps apocryphal, story of the knight who was sent out from the dense mass of men around the Prince to summon help from the reserve gathered about the King:

Then the King said, is my son dead or hurt, or on the earth felled? No sir, quoth the knight, but he is hardly matched, wherefore he hath need of your aid. Well, said the King, return to him and to them that sent you hither, and say to them that they send no more to me for any adventure that falleth as long as my son is alive; and also say to them that they suffer him this day to win his spurs; for if God be pleased I will this journey be his and the honour thereof, and to them that be about him.[66]

It was not until the end of the battle that Edward committed part of his reserve to his son's assistance.

By then it was clear that the English had triumphed. The French cavalry repeatedly wheeled, rallied and charged. But as darkness fell, and the mounds of dead men and horses accumulated across the battlefield, the attacks tailed off. When the blind King of Bohemia was told what was happening he ordered his men to lead him directly into the English line nearest Edward III. It was the incident by which the battle was most often remembered by both sides, the great example of that reckless valour that made a knight into the *preux chevalier* of contemporary poets. They galloped into the centre of the field shouting John's war-cry 'Prague!' until, surrounded by Englishmen, the King was dragged from his horse and killed.[67] From behind the English lines the horses were brought forward and the English men-at-arms remounted, charging the surviving groups of French horsemen on the field and the infantry still standing in their lines behind. All around them the French were fleeing into the darkening night. The bulk of the infantry escaped as soon as they saw the English cavalry coming towards them. Philip VI was left with no one around him except for a handful of companions, his personal bodyguard and some infantry levies from the city of Orléans. He was briefly caught up in a ferocious soldiers' battle. His standard-bearer was killed beside him. He himself had two horses killed under him and received an arrow wound in the face before he was extricated by John of Hainault. John, who had lost much of his own retinue and had had at least one horse killed under him, led the King off the field under cover of darkness, and took him to a village a few miles away where there was a fortified house. The royal standard and the Oriflamme of Saint-Denis were abandoned on the ground behind them.[68]

On the following morning, 27 August, at dawn, at least 2,000 French infantrymen, escorted by a detachment of men-at-arms under the command of the Duke of Lorraine, stumbled on to the battlefield. They were part of the army for which Philip VI had refused to wait. They had passed the night sleeping in ditches and under hedges along the Abbeville road. They knew nothing of the fate of their fellows. They thought that the English horsemen who suddenly appeared out of the morning mist were friends. The earls of Northampton, Suffolk and Warwick and their men scattered them with a single charge and pursued the fleeing survivors across the countryside, killing as many as they could catch and running down dazed groups of men-at-arms who had escaped from the slaughter of the previous night.

It was not until late in the morning that the English knew the full extent of their victory. Their own casualties were light. A roll-call showed forty men-at-arms missing. The number of dead and wounded among the infantry and archers must have been higher. But the losses of the French were catastrophic. Edward III had been determined not to allow the main point to be lost in the scramble for plunder. He had given orders that there was to be no pillaging of the dead and no quarter for the living, orders which he steadfastly refused to revoke until the battle was over. In the course of the 27th, the heralds passed through the field identifying the dead by their arms. The bodies of 1,542 French knights and squires were counted close to where the Prince of Wales's line had stood. Some hundreds more lay in the fields around where they had been cut down in the pursuit at the end of the battle or on the Sunday morning. No one troubled to count the infantrymen who had died. Their equipment was not worth looting. The heralds had not yet mastered their arcane science and their lists of French casualties were full of errors. But there was no doubt about the more famous of them. The bodies of John of Bohemia and his companions were found where they had fallen. Eight other princes of the blood were identified. They included the Count of Alençon, who had contributed more than any one man to the disaster; Philip VI's nephew Louis, Count of Blois, brother of the claimant of Brittany; John, Count of Harcourt, head of the clan whose most famous member was fighting in the English army; the Duke of Lorraine, who was married to Philip's niece; and Louis of Nevers, Count of Flanders. Their bodies were set aside to be buried decently with the English dead. The others were left to be tipped into vast grave pits dug by the returning peasants.

The French who survived looked about for scapegoats and found them among the foreigners, as they had done after the battle of Sluys six years before. When Philip VI reached Amiens on the morning of 27 August, one of his first acts was to order the massacre of the Genoese 'traitors' wherever they could be found. Many of them were murdered in Amiens and the nearby garrison towns before the King's anger cooled and his orders were countermanded.[69] Longer reflection persuaded most Frenchmen that it was not the crossbowmen but the French heavy cavalry which was at fault for attacking the English lines in impetuous disorder and allowing themselves to be defeated by men fighting on foot and mere archers, 'gens de nulle value' as a monk of Saint-Denis indignantly described them. But his view, although common, was almost as absurd as the one which laid the whole blame for the disaster on the Genoese. The French battle lines had been carefully drawn, and although the Count of Alençon's battalion probably charged too early, there is no reason to suppose that their charge was any more disorderly than a massed cavalry charge necessarily is, or that a charge at any other time would have succeeded better. To rally and reform as often as the French cavalry did at Crécy is no mean feat of horsemanship and discipline. There were two main reasons for their defeat. One was that the English had the incomparable advantage of fighting on the defensive. However powerful the impact of their charge, heavy cavalry in the fourteenth century were generally ineffective against dismounted men fighting in prepared positions. Philip VI was well aware of this. It was the reason why he had refused to attack the English army in 1339 and 1340. He took the risk in 1346 because public opinion demanded it. The second reason for his defeat was the technical superiority of the longbow over the crossbow, which was never more convincingly demonstrated. It may be that in spite of Sluys, Morlaix and Auberoche this came as a surprise to Philip VI, and it was certainly incomprehensible to the rest of his army. The King had invested large sums in hiring contract armies of crossbowmen of unprecedented size drawn from the best source of skilled bowmen in Europe. The crossbow was an ancient and formidable machine, the preferred weapon of bowmen in most European armies since the twelfth century when a Byzantine princess had called it 'diabolical' and the Church had forbidden its use against Christians. The longbow probably never achieved the impact and penetration of the crossbow. But it outranged it by a significant margin and continued to do so until the introduction in the course of the fifteenth century of machines with bows of steel in place of the laminated horn which was usual in the fourteenth. The crossbow never, even in the following centuries, matched its rival's main advantage, which was its speed of fire. Three arrows could be shot from a longbow, according to the Florentine Villani, in the time it took an experienced crossbowman to rearm his weapon once. Modern experiments suggest that the disparity of striking rates was even greater.

Edward III and his army passed the whole of 27 August on the battlefield, the traditional sign of possession and victory. The next two days were spent near Maintenay and at the Cistercian abbey of Valloires. Here Edward buried the French princes, surrounded by all the commanders of his army wearing black, and by walls and altars stripped bare when the monks had fled. On 30 August the English army resumed its march north, advancing across a front stretching from the sea for 20 miles inland. They destroyed everything which would burn. The main walled towns, Hesdin, Montreuil and Boulogne, had been stuffed with garrison troops since Edward's crossing of the Somme. Some of them had been reinforced by men-at-arms escaped from the battlefield. These places lost their crops and suburbs. Étaples was stormed and sacked. The unwalled towns and villages around were reduced to clusters of charred stumps. Wissant, for long the traditional landing place of English travellers to the continent, was obliterated.[70]

On 2 September 1346 Edward III sat down to take stock of his situation with his counsellors and commanders in the village of Wimille, a short distance north of Boulogne. It must have occurred to some of them that they had achieved little of real strategic value in spite of the scale of their victory. 'We have crossed the kingdom of our adversary,' Edward himself wrote to the towns of England; 'we have burned and ruined many castles, manors and towns and killed many of the enemy.'[71] That was all they had done. Crécy was a political catastrophe for the French Crown, but its military consequences were small because Edward III did not have the manpower to set up a permanent occupation in the territory through which he had passed.

There is little doubt that he had originally intended to do so, at least in

Normandy, just as he had done before in Brittany. This was why Godfrey of Harcourt, who had already done homage to Edward in England, did it again on the hill overlooking the bay of La Hougue after the English had landed. It was no doubt also the reason for Edward's orders to his men to abstain from looting and violence. These orders appear to have been issued only while the army was in Normandy. Valognes, the first significant town to be taken after the landings, was 'received within the King's peace' and a small garrison may have been left there. Carentan was certainly occupied after the departure of the army by a garrison of Godfrey's renegade Normans. Edward had sent runners through much of southern Normandy proclaiming that he had come 'not to ravish the land but to take possession of it' and inviting the inhabitants to come over to him. The response was mixed. Some of Edward's runners were lynched as they endeavoured to declare his good intentions to angry villagers. But there were many Normans, particularly at the beginning of the campaign, who took Edward at his word. Great numbers of peasants of the Cotentin arrived in Edward's camp at La Hougue to acknowledge him. The men of Bayeux sent messengers after the invader begging him to accept the surrender of their town and the homage of themselves even though the army had passed them by. Edward's answer was revealing. He refused their offer until he should be in a position to give them his protection, which in the event was not until after he had captured Caen. But the truth was that Edward was never able to protect his newfound subjects in France, as they quickly realized. He could not even protect them against his own troops, and when he had passed through he could not protect them against the reprisals of French soldiers and officials. So, what began as a campaign of conquest became a *chevauchèe*, a great mounted raid passing swiftly through the country before it disappeared. All the places which Edward III and Godfrey of Harcourt occupied were recovered by the French within a short time after the storm had passed overhead. The English garrison of Caen was rounded up and killed by the French troops in the citadel. Godfrey's men in Carentan were surprised and captured by an improvised force of local troops as soon as the English had left. They were sent to Paris to be executed at Les Halles. Edward's march into the north had sealed their fate.[72]

To men like Godfrey of Harcourt the change of strategy was a bitter pill to swallow. Very few of the French malcontents in Edward's allegiance had either the resources or the breadth of local support to maintain themselves without constant assistance from the English. Godfrey's horizons, like those of most of the other dissident noblemen of France, were more narrowly provincial than Edward's own. The decision made at Wimille was to capture the port of Calais and occupy the coast immediately about it.[73] It was a better gateway to France than any Norman port, easier to supply and reinforce from England. It was also closer to the Flemings, who were still Edward's most reliable allies on the continent. Not long afterwards Godfrey himself left the English army and fled to the court of Brabant, where he found friends to work his reconciliation with the French Crown. In December the man who was widely believed to have inspired Edward III's Norman campaign appeared with a halter round his neck and a prayer on his lips to receive his pardon and his Norman lands from Philip VI.[74]

The Siege of Calais
1346–1347

Calais was a minor town of the county of Artois with an awkward, sand-clogged harbour and a population of about 7,000 or 8,000 people living mainly by fishing and piracy. It was not a great commercial port like Dieppe, or an important regional market like Boulogne or Saint-Omer. It was not even a significant staging post for travellers crossing the Channel, who almost invariably embarked and disembarked 10 miles down the coast at Wissant. But because it was only a few miles from the border of Flanders it had become one of the principal fortresses of the north-west. The town was a rectangle with a regular grid of streets and well-designed fortifications dating from the thirteenth century. It was completely surrounded by water. On the north side, towards the sea, lay the harbour, which was separated from the town by a line of walls, a single moat and a long, low, fortified dyke. On the other sides the town was protected by high walls and a broad double moat. In the north-west corner there was a great castle comprising a circular keep and a large square bailey and surrounded by its own independent system of moats and curtain walls. Behind the town, extending for several miles beyond the man-made defences, lay a great expanse of bleak flat marshland crossed by innumerable small rivers and causeways whose course constantly shifted with the accumulation of mud and sand. The ground was so soft that it was impossible to undermine the walls or even to set up siege engines.[1]

Calais had for a long time been viewed as a potential target. It had had a strong garrison since the beginning of the year, and ample stores including stone-throwing and gunpowder artillery. During July and August fears for the security of the town had intensified. Reports from spies in Flanders suggested that the Flemings, who had had designs on the town for many years, were trying to persuade Edward III to attack it and were making their own preparations for a siege. Philip VI did not take these reports seriously. But the local commanders did. In spite of carping from Paris they heavily reinforced and resupplied the garrison in the course of August. The command was given to two men of conspicuous loyalty and

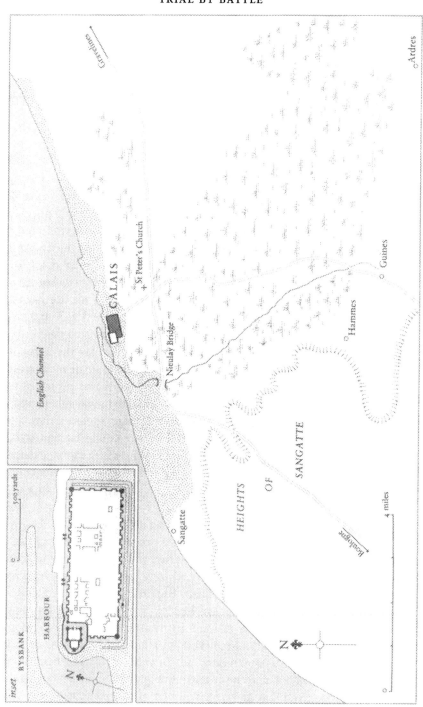

Gravelines

English Channel

CALAIS

+ St Peter's Church

Nieulay Bridge

Sangatte

HEIGHTS

OF

SANGATTE

Boulogne

4 miles

N

Ardres

○ Guines

+ Hammes

INSET

RYSBANK

HARBOUR

500 yards

N

29 Calais

536

ability, both closely associated with the ruler of Artois, Odo, Duke of Burgundy. One of them was the Burgundian knight Jean de Vienne, the other a local knight called Enguerrand de Beaulo. On 14 August 1346 Jean du Fosseux, one of the two lieutenant-governors of Artois, arrived in Calais to take command of the citadel in person. When the first English soldiers appeared across the marsh on 4 September the defenders were well prepared.[2]

Even the most cursory inspection showed that an immediate assault on the town walls was out of the question. The English did not attempt it. Instead, they began to make methodical preparations for what was clearly expected to be a long siege. They set up their main encampment on an island of firm ground around the church of St Peter, which stood by the causeway carrying the road from Boulogne to Gravelines about half a mile south of the town. On the day after their arrival the first English ships appeared off the harbour. These vessels, which had been gathering off Winchelsea and Sandwich while Edward III marched up through Picardy, brought with them most of the reinforcements which the Council had been able to collect in England. Their arrival across the beaches by the town must have brought the strength of the English army to something between 10,000 and 12,000 men. They spread about the three landward sides of the walls and began to dig themselves in, making trenches across the causeways and paths, and constructing improvised fortifications around the bridges to guard themselves against attack from the rear.[3] Within their lines they began, during the following weeks, to build a temporary town along the line of the causeway, which they called Villeneuve-la-Hardie, including mansions of timber for the King and the principal officials and noblemen, market halls, public buildings and stables, and thousands of hovels of brushwood and thatch.

The English troops, who had lived on the uncertain spoils of the French countryside since the end of July, were already hungry and short of clothing and footwear when they arrived. To feed and supply them for a long siege called for a miracle of administrative effort and commercial organization. Villeneuve-la-Hardie served a population larger than any English provincial town and most French ones. Most supplies were brought overland from Flanders via Gravelines, a route which was kept open throughout the siege in spite of the periodic attempts of the French to cut it. But surprisingly large quantities came by sea from England. Proclamations were read in every town of eastern and south-eastern England calling for wholesalers to bring their wares to Calais. All grain exported from the country was reserved for the army on the other side of the

Channel. Immense purchases were made by purveyors and by the Prince of Wales's officers in north Wales and the west country. Orwell, Sandwich and Plymouth became major entrepôts where food was warehoused and shipped on to some hundreds of requisitioned vessels. The operation was a remarkable success. By mid-winter men returning from the siege lines were reporting that the meat and cloth markets of Villeneuve looked just like those of Arras or Amiens.[4]

The siege of Calais, which lasted for eleven months and drew more from the English people than any campaign of the fourteenth century, would not have been possible without the surge of public support in England which followed the victories at Caen and Crécy. Parliament opened at Westminster on 13 September 1346. The commissioners who presided in place of the King gave a highly coloured account of the campaign. 'The whole host of France has been laid low,' they said; 'kings, prelates, dukes, counts, barons, knights and the mighty of their realm have been killed, captured or despoiled.' The document found at Caen, revealing the French King's plans to conquer England, was once again read out. The piratical deeds of the Calais seamen were recounted. There were letters from the leading men of the army calling for special effort and generosity from those at home. The Commons grumbled about past abuses and the strain of continual recruitment, but they voted a subsidy for the coming year and another for the year after that. The Lords agreed to an aid of 40s. per knight's fee to mark the knighting of the Prince of Wales. They did not want Calais to be another Tournai. The less percipient of them hoped that they would have done with the war if they spent enough money on finishing it. Edward's representatives told them that he had committed his honour to the capture of Calais and intended to remain there until it fell. The English King delivered the same message to would-be peacemakers. The two cardinals, who had continued to hover about the armies since July, came into the English camp at Calais soon after Edward had arrived there, but the King refused to receive them. They travelled south to Amiens, where Philip VI had been since the morning after the battle. He would not see them either.[5]

September 1346 was among the most dismal months of Philip VI's reign. It was rainy and unseasonably cold. There was a succession of state funerals as the bodies of the French princes were recovered from the abbey of Valloires and reburied in more fitting surroundings. The King of Bohemia's cortège passed across nothern France to his tomb in Luxembourg, surrounded by the painted arms of fifty knights who had fallen with him. The Count of Alençon's bier was carried through the streets of Paris to be laid to rest in the Dominican church.[6] Philip VI remained for two weeks after the battle of Crécy at Amiens amid the stench of dead horses. Here, inconstant and vacillating as ever, he made a succession of ill-considered decisions. In spite of the firm views of his commanders in Artois and the accurate intelligence which they were receiving, Philip did not at first believe that Edward would embark on a long siege of Calais. He seems to have thought that the English King would bolt into Flanders. On 5 September, the day after the siege began, he dispersed the greater part of the army. Then, on the 7th, he left Amiens for Pont-Sainte-Maxence, his favourite residence by the Oise. On the road he was met by his son, John of Normandy. John had learned of the disaster of Crécy while he was marching across the Limousin. He brought with him the particulars of the complete failure of his own campaign on the Garonne and the disbanding of his army, which had occurred a few days before. From Calais came further news about the elaborate arrangements which the English appeared to be making there. It must have been a gloomy conference. The outcome was a complete change of plan. It was decided to summon a new army to muster at Compiègne, north of Paris, on 1 October. From there it was intended to march to the relief of Calais before the winter. The orders were issued on 9 September 1346, only three weeks before the appointed day. Nothing more clearly illustrated the directionless panic of the French leaders.[7]

The only blow struck for the defenders of Calais in the autumn of 1346 was the work of the despised Genoese. At the beginning of September Philip VI recommissioned the galley fleet, which had been laid up in the Seine since its arrival. On the 17th, the galleys caught the first convoy of victualling ships to cross the Channel since the beginning of the siege and fell upon them just as they were approaching Calais. All twenty-five English vessels were destroyed and their crews killed. This stroke, in addition to damaging the morale of the hungry English, added significantly to the cost of ferrying future cargoes. It became necessary to provide large escorts for convoys and to post strong guards of archers and men-at-arms on every ship.[8]

On land, however, the result of the orders and counter-orders of early September was catastrophic. For the whole of September (and, as it turned out, October) the English had the field to themselves. Against the Earl of Lancaster in the south there was no organized defence at all. The French government distributed every man they had among the garrisons around the marsh of Calais and along the frontier of Flanders, but there were still great gaps in the defences of the north.

The Flemings raised large numbers of men in the three great towns and, joining forces with the rabble which had just returned from Béthune, they poured into the county of Artois, burning their trail towards the great garrison town of Saint-Omer. There they joined forces with the Earl of Warwick, who came up with several hundred English troops from Calais. Leaving enough men behind them to contain the garrison of Saint-Omer, their combined force moved south towards Thérouanne, an ancient ecclesiastical city about 8 miles away which was the site of a famous commercial fair, then in progress. It was virtually defenceless. The Bishop, Raymond Saquet, was in the town with a large military retinue. But Saquet had passed his life in official and diplomatic business about the court and was certainly no soldier. Having no faith in his crumbling Roman walls, he gathered his men and many of the citizens of the town, and marched them out to meet the enemy in open country outside. As a result his scratch army was massacred and he himself was severely wounded. The spoil of the fair filled a large wagon-train and the buildings of the town were so thoroughly sacked that it was several months before the survivors took courage to return and rebuild their homes. The capture of Thérouanne occurred on 19 September 1346. Encouraged by the spoil and the almost complete absence of resistance, the Anglo-Flemish forces spread across north-western Artois from Boulogne to the River Aa. Within a month they had destroyed everything there that would readily burn outside the walled towns and principal castles. At the end of September the Flemings decided that they had had enough. They stopped their raids, abandoned the siege of Saint-Omer and returned home.[9]

Philip VI and his ministers looked on helplessly. Defeat dried up tax revenues and fear made men spend what they had on patching up their walls. The growing desperation of the French government was reflected in the brutal measures which had become necessary to extract even small sums of money. The purveyors of the army, sent about their work without funds, began to take victuals, carts and horses without payment, provoking anger and riots in the northern towns. The richer churches were made to surrender their jewellery and their gold and silver plate. The abbey of Saint-Denis alone gave up 130 pieces worth more than 1,200 *l.p.* The commissioners would have taken the abbey's famous jewelled crucifix presented by Pope Eugenius III 200 years before if there had not been an inscription round the base excommunicating all despoilers. In the provinces some of the *baillis* and seneschals embarked on a heavy-handed campaign of seizures, extracting fines in lieu of military service, and appropriating goods and money for the repair of fortifications and the payment of army wages. The King's need of troops was paramount, said the *bailli* of Chaumont. The public interest would brook no resistance, said the Seneschal of Saintonge; the men would desert if they were not paid.[10]

It is not clear how much Philip VI and his ministers knew about what was happening in the south-west. The immediate result of John of Normandy's withdrawal from Aiguillon had been the collapse of the French position in southern Périgord and most of the Agenais. They held on to their strongholds in the Garonne valley: Port-Sainte-Marie and Agen, where there were strong garrisons; and Marmande, the solitary French garrison downstream of Aiguillon. But the English took firm control of the whole of the Lot valley below Villeneuve in the last few days of August, as well as most of the remaining outposts of French strength between there and the Dordogne. The Earl of Lancaster conducted an effortless military promenade through the region. The towns surrendered without striking a blow.[11]

The task of preserving something of the French Crown's position in the south-west was left to John, Count of Armagnac. He was made royal lieutenant. But he was left with virtually no troops; his treasury was empty; and his attempts to raise money and men were persistently obstructed by orders from the King inconsistent with his own. Within three months of his appointment he was threatening to resign. 'I cannot and will not act as lieutenant and commander,' he wrote, 'for a king who countermands without consulting me the orders that I give for the prosecution of his war.'[12]

On 4 September 1346 the leaders of the Anglo-Gascon army gathered in the castle of La Réole to plan their next move. In view of the absence of organized resistance they decided to divide their forces into three. The 'Archdeacon', Gaillard de Durfort, and the lords of the Agenais were left to hold their own province and conduct raids in the territory east of it. Most of the rest of the Gascon retinues were placed under the command of Bérard and Bernard-Aiz of Albret and sent to complete the reconquest of the Bazadais, south of the Garonne. Lancaster himself, who was more interested in political impact than creeping reconquest, proposed to launch a long-distance raid to the north. On 12 September 1346 he marched out of La Réole with 1,000 men-at-arms and an uncertain number of mounted infantry. About half the men-at-arms and most of the infantry were probably Gascons. Their morale was high. The Gascons had agreed to serve without pay for a month, a sign of the profit they expected to make from ransoms and booty under a much admired commander.

Lancaster's object was to recover the province of Saintonge and the northern approaches to Bordeaux. His method of doing it was characteristically bold. He proposed to strike hard, well north of the disputed region, cutting it off from reinforcement, demoralizing its defenders until they were ready to surrender without serious resistance. Loot may have been the reason why he chose Poitiers, one of the most opulent cities of central France, as his main target.

The Anglo-Gascons marched for eight days without pause from the Garonne to the Charente. On 20 September they arrived at Châteauneuf, within 10 miles of Angoulême. Here the Earl paused to repair the bridge, which the inhabitants had broken on his approach, and was diverted from his purpose by an escapade of Walter Mauny's, not the first nor the last time that this reckless soldier's adventures complicated the course of the war. Mauny had obtained from the Duke of Normandy a safe conduct for himself and twenty companions to cross France and join Edward III's army in the north. He had in effect bought it by remitting the ransom of one of the Duke's friends whom he had captured in a skirmish outside Aiguillon. It was one of those unorthodox transactions at the margin of public and private affairs which were so characteristic of the fourteenth century. Not everyone was willing to take the document at its face value. As Mauny's party travelled up the Bordeaux–Paris road, they were captured by a party of French soldiers and taken into the town of Saint-Jean-d'Angély, where they were thrown into prison. Mauny himself succeeded in escaping with two friends, but the rest of the party were still languishing there when the news of their plight was brought to the Earl of Lancaster. Saint-Jean-d'Angély was about 40 miles north-west of Châteauneuf across the flat plains of Aunis, then one of the richest wine-producing regions of France. It was a small walled town, an important local market and river port lying under the shadow of a Benedictine abbey whose relics, including a head of St John the Baptist, made it one of the great staging posts on the pilgrimage roads to Santiago de Compostela. The walls and barbicans, which were reported a decade later to be broken and crumbling in many places, were probably in even worse condition in 1346. When the English arrived without warning on 22 September 1346 the town fell at the first assault. It was violently sacked. The abbey and most of the warehouses and mansions of the merchants were stripped bare. Those who were spared were subjected to heavy ransoms and indemnities by Lancaster's orders, and made to take oaths of loyalty to their new sovereign. Those who objected were imprisoned and those who fled found their property confiscated after they had gone. But there were not many who fled. The

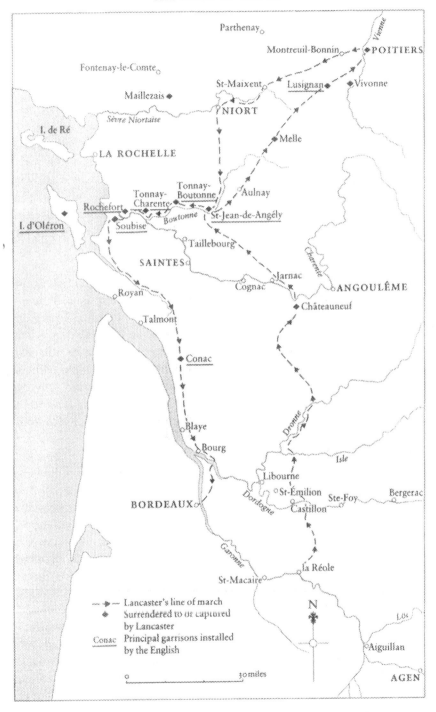

30 The Earl of Lancaster in Poitou and Saintonge, September–October 1346

men of Saint-Jean-d'Angély were stunned by the blow which had fallen on them. Most of them kept their objections to themselves and salved something of their world. In Lancaster's phrase they 'turned English'.[13]

On 30 September Lancaster's army, its strength somewhat reduced by garrison troops needed to hold Saint-Jean-d'Angély, resumed its march at high speed, covering about 20 miles a day. On 2 or 3 October 1346 they stormed the little town of Lusignan a short distance south-west of Poitiers. The resistance of the townsmen was half-hearted. The castle, although it was powerfully constructed and filled with the gentry of the region, who had taken refuge there with their families, offered no resistance at all. The defenders sent out the emissaries to meet the English with the keys. The men of Lusignan, like those of Saint-Jean-d'Angély, reconciled themselves soon enough to the government of King Edward's agents, returning over the following weeks to find the ruins of their homes and buy back their possesions from the soldiers who had pillaged them.[14]

Lusignan fared better than Poitiers. The churches of this great ecclesiastical city were filled with treasures, not only their own but those of many monasteries of the surrounding region whose communities had loaded up their carts and joined the mass of refugees washing into the city as the news of Derby's movements spread. But in spite of its impressive situation at the top of a semicircle of cliffs over the confluence of two rivers, Poitiers was weak. Parts of it were unwalled, the approaches defended only by earthworks and trenches. Where there were walls, they were old and in places ruinous.[15] A garrison had had to be improvised at short notice from the tenants and retainers of some local noblemen.

Lancaster's men arrived outside the city on the evening of 3 October. They launched an immediate assault, which failed. But on the following morning they found a weak point in the defences by the church of St Radegonde in the eastern part of the city, where the rampart had been pierced long ago to allow access to a water mill. The English seized the breach and poured into the town, lighting fires and striking down anyone in their way. There was a terrible massacre. Everyone who could ran to the opposite end of the city with all that they could carry, cramming themselves into the congested streets and fleeing through the gates into the fields outside. Those who fled included the Bishop and four of the five noblemen responsible for the defence of the town. When the initial lust for destruction had died down the English and Gascon soldiers spread through the streets breaking open churches and other buildings and collecting enough booty to fill every cart they could lay hands on: 'sacred vessels, copes, chalices, crucifixes, everything of gold or silver', the cathedral chapter declared when they came to count their losses. The monks of Charroux lost the whole contents of their treasury and much of their muniments, which they had brought into the city for safety. About 600 people died, most of them labourers and petty tradesmen. Men of consequence were spared when they were recognized, but they were ruined by the extortionate ransoms which their captors demanded. And when they returned home, in some cases many months later, it was often to find their houses and furniture burned and their farms occupied by destitute and savage squatters.[16]

It is not difficult to understand why a city like Poitiers should have been so unprepared for this calamity. Although rich and populous it had been a political backwater since the beginning of the thirteenth century. It was more than 100 miles from Bordeaux. The war was now in its tenth year but the lines of battle had ebbed and flowed far away. The municipality was weak and without any real tax-raising powers of its own. Jurisdiction over its defences was uncertainly divided between the city magistrates and three ecclesiastical proprietors. There was nothing unusual about any of this. The breach by which the English entered Saint-Jean-d'Angély was there because of a long-standing quarrel among the citizens about who was to pay to fill it. The same problems were common to most walled towns of France. The surrounding region was as ill prepared as the provincial capital. At the outset of the war, a decade earlier, there had been a survey of royal castles in Poitou, but there is no evidence that it was followed by any significant repairs. During September 1346 Philip VI had sent hurried instructions to the Seneschal of Poitou to repair the walls of three towns of western Poitou, Niort, Saint-Maixent and Fontenay-le-Comte, to serve as refuges for the local population. But it was very late in the day. His letters must have arrived at about the same time as the Earl of Lancaster did.[17]

Some years afterwards the craven terror and helplessness of small provincial towns in the path of the English armies was graphically described in the evidence given for the prosecution at a treason trial in Paris. The accused was the Bishop of Maillezais, which was a minor market town at the edge of the *marais Poitevin* north-east of La Rochelle. Maillezais had no garrison and poor walls, but it was some way from Lancaster's line of march and was reasonably well protected by rivers and marshes. When the first reports of the English campaigns reached the town, the citizens and the monks of the Benedictine abbey began weapon training. They organized themselves in watches, working shifts day and night. But in October the mood changed. The Bishop called the monks before him in the cloister. He described the fate of Saint-Jean-d'Angély and Poitiers. He told them that their town was much weaker than either of those places and that it was folly to defend it against impossible odds. Besides, he said, was not God evidently performing miracles for the English? Was He not showing them plainly that Edward III was their lawful king? Had their own church not been founded by Edward's ancestors? Did they not owe the English King their loyalty? Rather than fight a useless battle at the walls and expose themselves to the revenge of the conquerors, they should meet Lancaster's troops in procession on the road, wearing their finest vestments and carrying the keys of the town. The Bishop then called the citizens before him and made a similar speech to them. He suggested that they should raise funds to buy a suitable gift for the Earl of Lancaster and promised that he would personally make the largest contribution. There were people in Maillezais who had been saying for some time that Edward III would be a better master than Philip VI. Two of these were sent to find the Earl of Lancaster. They presented him with a goshawk and two greyhounds and invited him to come to Maillezais, where he would be received, they said, with honour and joy. Lancaster promised to come and gave them badges bearing his insignia to attach to their clothes. The town began to prepare their welcome. They made banners with the arms of Plantagenet and Lancaster to display at the gates. They laid gold cloth over the tomb of an eleventh-century Duke of Aquitaine in the abbey and surrounded it with lighted candles. In their own evidence the monks and townsmen claimed that they had rejected the Bishop's advice with indignation and had refused to have anything to do with his plan. But there is some doubt about this. The truth seems to be that they supported him, tacitly at least, until the crisis had passed, when they fell to venomous and self-serving recrimination. The Bishop was acquitted. What is interesting is that his defence (which was presumably accepted) stopped a long way short of complete denial. The facts, he said, had been exaggerated by his enemies. But he did not dispute that he had been in favour of treating with the English. His point was that nobody should be blamed for that in the conditions of autumn 1346. He pointed out that there had been virtually no organized bodies of French troops in Poitou when Henry of Lancaster invaded it. There had been no warning of his coming. There were not enough weapons with which to arm the population. The walls of the towns, including Maillezais, were incapable of resisting any determined assault. Other towns and castles of the region had made their peace with the English on whatever terms they could get. What else could they do?[18]

When the English withdrew from Poitiers, on about 12 October 1346, they marched towards Saintonge and Bordeaux, looting, smashing and burning as they went. Resistance was patchy and uncoordinated. Some places, like Maillezais, Melle and Vivonne, officiously thrust their surrenders on the retreating commander. A few resisted ferociously, like the workers of the royal mint at Montreuil-Bonnin just west of Poitiers, many of whom lost their lives on the walls when the place was assaulted. Niort and Saint-Maixent, two of the refuges appointed in September, beat off all the Earl's attacks and survived.[19]

Lancaster made no attempt to occupy Poitou. He left no garrison in the province except at Lusignan, where the castle was well sited and the town small and relatively easy to hold. A hundred men-at-arms and some infantry and archers were left here under the command of the murderous Bertrand de Montferrand and his two brothers. They turned it into a centre of organized banditry from which they terrorized much of western and central Poitou for years. Garrisons like these were not so much intended to control territory as to create chaos and insecurity, tying down many times their own numbers of the enemy. A more serious attempt at permanent occupation was made further south in Saintonge and Aunis. An enormous garrison, 200 men-at-arms and 600 infantry, was installed at Saint-Jean-d'Angély. Regular taxes were imposed on the town, much heavier than those which had previously been paid to the King of France. Gascon officials and judges were brought in to administer the surrounding region.[20] During the second half of October 1346, the English expanded this distant enclave of the duchy by occupying the whole of the valley of the Boutonne from Saint-Jean-d'Angély to the sea, including the great castle and harbour of Rochefort and the island of Oléron. Lancaster himself, however, was in a hurry to return to Bordeaux and he did not have the time or the resources to conquer the whole territory between the Boutonne and the Gironde.[21] Most of the country was brought more or less under the control of the Bordeaux government by seizing the more vulnerable castles and fortifying the larger farms and rural monasteries. These places received small garrisons generally under the command of sympathetic local noblemen. But the French Crown was certainly not driven out of Saintonge. The French hung on to their principal strongholds along the Bordeaux-Paris road, including Saintes, the provincial capital, and Taillebourg, dominating the crossing of the Charente north of it, one of the strongest fortresses of the region. Moreover, they kept most of their garrisons along the north shore of the Gironde, including Blaye, Talmont and Royan.[22] Lancaster's *chevauchée* was therefore only a qualified success.

The result of this stalemate was to condemn the whole province to a permanent and debilitating guerrilla war between neighbouring strongholds of either side, conditions which had already ruined Brittany and much of eastern and southern Gascony. Depopulation, the first symptom, began very soon. On the marches of Poitou and Saintonge towns like La Rochelle and Niort found themselves losing inhabitants at an alarming rate as the burdens of keeping watch twenty-four hours a day and supporting great schemes of fortification made themselves felt, and as fighting on the roads dried up their trade. A constant war of ambushes, murder, arson and vandalism was waged between the English garrison of Saint-Jean-d'Angély and the French garrison of Aulnay across the 10-mile stretch of land which separated them. At Saintes, the citizens declared when they petitioned for money to build a bell tower, that alarms, exercises and calls to arms had now become part of the routine of their daily lives. With the continual danger and insecurity came xenophobia and occasional hysteria, unreasoning suspicion of any stranger who might be spying for the other side, fear of treachery, exaggerated by confessions extracted by torture. Men were hanged as confessed spies or branded on the forehead with the *fleur-de-lys* as suspected ones. The open country beyond the town walls was overrun by the freebooters of both sides, men like the pair of anonymous Gascons described in evocative detail in a contemporary letter of pardon: lightly armed mounted men laden with booty, their satchels stuffed with the recognizances of prisoners of war binding themselves to pay ransom. These two were set upon and one of them killed as they travelled down the road from Saint-Jean-d'Angély to Bordeaux. Such men learned to travel in large bands. Gradually, extensive tracts of this fertile province around the principal towns and roads became uncultivable. Along the coast, land reclaimed from the sea by years of effort was abandoned to the encroaching marsh, a better defence against attack, men said, then firm ground and manned walls.[23]

The French government aggravated the wretched fate of the population by the particular method which they used to recover their lost territory. Having no field army to serve in the south-west and no immediate prospect of raising one, they began to make general grants to freebooters of any English-occupied territory which they could reconquer by their own efforts. These grants were often limited to a specified period, say a year after the recapture, but some of them were indefinite. Important successes were achieved by this method. Oléron, for example, was recaptured by the private enterprise of the lord of Royan within a few months of its fall. But the practice was unfortunate from every other point of view. It set the captors of occupied territory against each other and against the families who had owned them before the occupation, generating vicious local wars between men who might otherwise have been on the same side. It was also one of the seeds of those self-governing private armies owing only tenuous allegiance to either government which were to give the war a momentum of its own in the 1350s and to inflict greater and more continuous misery on the rural population of France than Edward III's periodic expeditions could ever do.[24]

The Earl of Lancaster's troops returned to Bordeaux in early November 1346 and he himself began to prepare for his return to England. But sparks from the fires that he had lit had already started new conflagrations far away. Gaillard de Durfort, whom Lancaster had left in mid-September in command of the lords of the Agenais, embarked soon afterwards on long-distance campaigning of his own. Some of Gaillard's forces occupied themselves in raids into Quercy, penetrating up the valley of the Lot almost as far as Cahors.[25] A force of 400 horsemen under Gaillard's own command turned north. In the last ten days of September they suddenly appeared in the remote and mountainous Corrèze and captured Tulle, the principal market town of the region. This event had an electrifying effect on the neighbouring province of Auvergne, for which tax collectors and recruiting officers had hitherto been distant reflections of a war fought elsewhere. The news reached Montferrand on 30 September 1346, followed within a few days by the first tidings of the sack of Saint-Jean-d'Angély by the Earl of Lancaster. Although Montferrand was 80 miles from Tulle and 180 miles from Saint-Jean-Angély the citizens sent panic-stricken messages in all directions: to Riom to compare reports; to Paris to withdraw an offer of assistance in the relief of Calais; to Poitiers to find out where the Earl of Lancaster had gone after leaving Saint-Jean-Angély; to the neighbouring royal *baillages* to summon help at once. There were anxious inspections of the walls and ditches. The town's ageing stock of crossbows was brought out of store. A barn was taken over to be used for building stone-throwing artillery. The provincial Estates of Auvergne gathered at Riom to raise money and troops for their defence and remained intermittently in session for six weeks. The crisis passed. The Count of Armagnac gathered the troops which he had assembled in Languedoc to reinforce the King's army. He joined forces with the levies of Auvergne and Limousin and laid siege to Tulle in the middle of November. At about Christmas time the intruders surrendered on terms. Their lives were spared. But they were all taken prisoner and ransomed.[26]

It was a Pyrrhic victory. At an absurdly small cost the Gascons had diverted some thousands of French soldiers to the insignificant town of Tulle, depriving Philip VI of part of his army and dislocating the royal administration in central and southern France for three months. While the Count of Armagnac was encumbered with the problems of the Corrèze, the English and their allies tightened their grip on the Agenais and southern Périgord and swept through the Bazadais south-east of Bordeaux, picking up for little or nothing prizes that had eluded them for years. Bazas itself, which had courageously defied Henry of Lancaster after the battle of Auberoche, negotiated attractive commercial terms and opened its gates to the English on 3 January 1347. A wave of treasons, even in regions securely held by the French Cown's officers, signalled the last stages of disillusionment and exasperation with the government's conduct of the southern war: a garrison commander at Aigues-Mortes on the Mediterranean, a bishop of Saint-Papoul in the Toulousain, men with nothing to gain by negotiating with the English unless they really believed that the Valois dynasty was about to be extinguished.[27]

The strongest and best-organized expedition launched from Scotland for many years[28] began on 7 October 1346, three days after the fall of Poitiers. It was a direct response to Edward III's campaign in France: an opportunity for plunder and revenge presented by the King's absence, and the long-delayed answer of the Scottish King to Philip VI's desperate pleas for help. The Scotch army seems to have included a handful of French knights who had arrived in Scotland in the course of the summer.[29] According to reasonably reliable official estimates in England there were about 12,000 men altogether. Some of them had been supplied with modern French weapons and armour, a great improvement on the equipment which Scotch armies usually carried, as English observers noted with dismay.

David II entered England by the western march, north of Carlisle. Although he did not lack courage, David quickly revealed himself to be an inexperienced and mediocre commander with little control over his men. Instead of making progress before the English could organize their defence, the Scots wasted several days in besieging the Peel of Liddell, a powerful natural fortress just over the border on the River Esk. This place was battered down for three days and then taken by assault. The governor, Sir Walter Selby, was butchered unshriven in the presence of the Scotch King. Carlisle, 10 miles south, would probably not even have lasted three days. Its walls and gates were in bad repair and its stores were low.[30] So they paid a heavy indemnity and secured a local truce. Passing the town

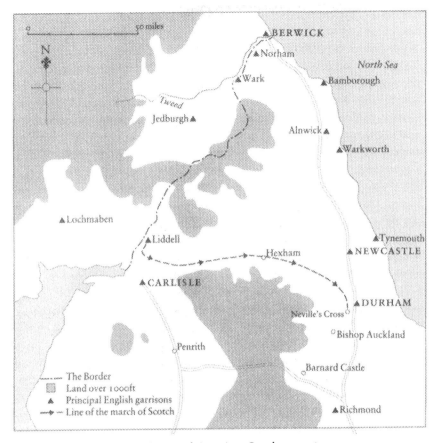

31 The Scotch invasion, October 1346

by, the Scots turned east towards the rich churches and manors of Durham and Yorkshire which had been the magnet of Scotch armies of invasion since the twelfth century. They spread out across a wide front, as Edward had done in northern France, burning whatever lay in front of them. Three days were spent sacking the great priory of Hexham. Then on 16 October, the tenth day of the campaign, they arrived outside Durham and encamped at Beaurepaire, the sumptuous country residence of the priors of the cathedral monastery a short distance west of the city. The monks offered £1,000 protection money, payable on 18 October. The Scots waited.

Philip VI had been wrong to describe the north of England as a 'defenceless void', although it was certainly weak. Persistent Scotch raids over the years had depopulated much of Cumberland, Westmorland and Northumberland, reducing them once more to a patchily cultivated wasteland like the marches of Gascony, Brittany or Flanders. In Cumberland alone (it was probably the worst-affected county) a survey revealed more than a hundred communities reduced to penury during 1345 and 1346. The situation in Northumberland, a larger and better-defended county, may have been marginally more satisfactory. The defence of the border was in the hands of three men: Henry Percy and Ralph Neville, the permanent English commanders of the border; and the warden of the eastern march William de La Zouche, Archbishop of York, a worldly ecclesiastical politician. English spies had been busy in Scotland since August and the general tenor of what the Scots were planning had been known to them for at least six week. Men had already been arrayed and told to wait for their orders. When the Scots crossed the border, therefore, the troops were collected very quickly. The assembly, which was held at Richmond in north Yorkshire, was supervised by the Archbishop of York. But his army, although quickly recruited, was not large. At its greatest strength it probably comprised no more than 3,000 or 4,000 men of Cumberland, Northumberland and Lancashire. Another 3,000 Yorkshiremen had mustered further south and were on their way. No troops were available from south of the Trent, which was still being scoured for fresh reinforcements for the army of Calais.[31]

On 14 October, at about the time that the Scots were passing through Hexham, the Archbishop decided not to wait for the Yorkshiremen and set out with the rest of the northern army across the moorland north of Richmond towards Barnard Castle. Here he drew up his forces in three battalions for the march to Durham. The leaders of the Scots had not anticipated the efficiency of their enemies. They did not learn of the existence of the English army until dawn on 17 October, and then it was by accident. A troop of Scots commanded by William Douglas was engaged in a plundering raid south of Durham when, in the thick morning mist, they suddenly stumbled upon the two rearward divisions of the Archbishop's army. There was a sharp encounter. The Scots were worsted and driven off with heavy losses.

When David II discovered from the survivors how close the English were, he roused his army and led them towards the enemy. He drew them up on high ground at a place called Neville's Cross where there was an old Anglo-Saxon stone cross. He arranged them, like the English, in three battalions, but extremely unskilfully on terrain which was crisscrossed by ditches and walls, where their freedom of movement was very restricted. The Scots remembered Dupplin Moor and Halidon Hill well enough to avoid taking the offensive if they could. So when the English army reached

Neville's Cross, about mid-morning, they remained immobile in their positions. Neither side did anything for several hours. Then, in the middle of the afternoon, the English advanced to within bow range and began to pour arrows into the Scotch line. The Scots, unable to withstand the onslaught, were forced to attack. Their first battalion charged the English lines on foot, keeping their heads down to ward off the arrows with their helmets and shoulder pieces. As they did so, the walls and ditches about the fields broke up their formations. Many of the Scots never reached the English lines. Those who did were forced back by the men-at-arms who had been placed in the front. Seeing this, the second and largest of the Scotch battalions, which was commanded by Robert Stewart and the Earl of March, turned and fled. David II was left with his own battalion to face the whole English army. He and his men fought with ferocious courage. The King himself was badly wounded by an arrow in the face. Towards the end of the afternoon they failed, then turned and fled. David was overtaken and surrounded. He refused to surrender and, in spite of his wounds, knocked out two of his captor's teeth before he was over-powered. The rest of the Scotch army was pursued in the failing light for more than 20 miles across County Durham.

The Sheriff of London did well to hire a barge to carry the first rumours of the battle to Calais. It was an even worse defeat for Scotland than Crécy had been for France. This small country lost in a single day almost all of its leaders and many of its most experienced soldiers. John Randolph, Earl of Moray, who had led the first brave charge into the English lines, had been killed with most of his battalion. The Constable, the Marshal and the Chamberlain of Scotland all perished. Apart from David II, the prisoners included William Douglas, Scotland's most skilful and persistent practi-tioner of guerrilla war, as well as four earls. The English government had learned in France the political value of these great hauls of prisoners. Two of the Scotch earls, Fife and Menteith, who had previously done homage to Edward, were convicted of treason and one of them, Menteith, was drawn, hanged and quartered. As for the other prisoners, Edward III was not prepared to see them released at any price. Orders were given for them to be collected together and placed in the King's custody in the Tower of London. None was to be ransomed without the leave of the Council. These high-handed instructions caused much ill-feeling among the captors, who regarded their prisoners, correctly in point of law, as their property to do with as they pleased. Some captors concealed their prisoners from the King's commissioners. Some made secret bargains with them and then colluded in their 'escape'. Most, however, duly delivered up their captives to the Constable of the Tower in the months which followed the battle, and Edward eventually promised to compensate them for their ransoms. The man who captured David II received a very large annuity, £500 a year, and was promoted to the rank of banneret. David was the most valuable prisoner taken in the war so far. He was kept at Bamburgh Castle for a few weeks while he recovered from his wounds in the care of barber–surgeons brought from York. Then, at the beginning of January 1347, he was brought south under heavy guard to London. They put him on a tall black charger for all to see and paraded him about the streets of the capital. Then they locked him in the Tower. He was to remain in custody for eleven years.[32]

Ten days after the disaster at Neville's Cross, the French government's plans to relieve Calais before the winter collapsed in humiliating confusion. The response of the French military class was late and poor. Hardly any of the troops summoned to Compiègne had arrived by the official muster date, 1 October. Then, as the days passed, news began to arrive of the deeds of the Earl of Lancaster in Saintonge and Poitou and, early in October, of the fall of Poitiers itself. The French ministers probably over-estimated Lancaster's strength, and their first impression was that he was heading for the north. It seemed to them that the English had a grand stretegy for attacking the French army from two directions at once. A succession of panic-stricken decisions was made at Compiègne. On 13 October 1346 the Duke of Normandy announced that he would lead a fresh army against the Earl of Lancaster at the end of the month. Part of this army was to be raised by withdrawing men from the muster of Compiègne; the rest by issuing new military summonses with the utmost urgency. The new summonses called for all available men who were not already on their way to Compiègne to proceed to Orléans, where the Duke would meet them on his march south. The plan was to hold the Anglo-Gascons south of the Loire in Touraine, where the main routes from the south-west converged. These arrangements caused renewed dislocation of the government's recruiting, especially when the Earl of Lancaster turned south again and the Orléans muster was cancelled. In the last ten days of October men were arriving at Orléans only to be redirected to the north.[33]

The Marshals at Compiègne still had only a little over 3,000 men-at-arms by the end of the month of October.[34] To these must be added the troops redirected from Orléans, the forces already deployed in the ring of garrison towns around the marsh of Calais, and an uncertain number of infantry, making perhaps 6,000 to 10,000 men in all. In spite of the desperate expedients to which Philip's officials had resorted, the war treasurers did not even have enough money to pay advances to this modest army. Philip VI, seeing that his campaign was about to fall apart, turned to face-saving diplomacy. He authorized an approach to Edward III through Charles of Bohemia, son of the gallant John. The English King rejected it out of hand. Philip turned to the cardinals. He told them that he was, after all, willing to appoint ambassadors to negotiate with the enemy. It was too late. Edward was persuaded to appoint ambassadors. But his clerks had hardly got beyond the stage of drawing up the formal documents when, on 27 October 1346, Philip suddenly wound up all French naval and military operations in northern France except for the defence of the principal garrison towns. The troops at Compiègne were dispersed without ever leaving the town. New arrivals were turned away. The Genoese galleys were laid up on the banks of the Somme at Abbeville on 31 October and the French ones a week later.[35]

It was the signal for a severe political crisis within the French government, reminiscent in some ways of the English one which had followed the withdrawal of Edward III from Tournai in 1340. Philip, like Edward, blamed his servants. Godemar du Fay was disgraced for failing to stop the English at Blanchetaque; Charles de Montmorency, one of the Marshals present at the battle, was dismissed. Philip dealt harshly with his financial officials, who were blamed for the débâcle of Compiègne. He could not understand, any more than Edward could, that failure to produce money when it was needed could be due to anything other than incompetence or corruption. Pierre des Essarts, one of the principal officials of the Chambre des Comptes, a man who had been at the centre of the French government for more than twenty years, was summarily dismissed and arrested at the end of October 1346. He was charged on the most imprecise counts of embezzling 100,000 *l.t.* On 11 November the entire financial affairs of the Crown were placed in the hands of three commissioners, the abbots of Saint-Denis, Marmoutiers and Corbie. They not only inaugurated a rigid regime for controlling expenditure, but conducted a purge of the financial departments of the administration, dismissing a large number of civil servants great and small and causing some of them to be prosecuted.[36]

Within the King's privy council the same individuals remained in power, but they were divided by rancorous mutual recrimination. There is a good deal of circumstantial evidence that one of the people whom Philip fell out with was his son John of Normandy. Philip had prevented him from taking Aiguillon in August, to no avail for John had failed to arrive in time for the battle of Crécy. But it may well be right, as Jean le Bel suggests, that the occasion for their quarrel was relatively trivial. Walter Mauny, after escaping from prison in Saint-Jean-d'Angély, had been arrested again in early October when passing through Orléans and had been taken to Paris, where he was imprisoned in the Louvre on the instructions of the King. The dishonour of Mauny's safe conduct outraged Edward III and led to retaliatory measures against French prisoners of war in England, some of whom were placed in close confinement unfitting for their rank. John, who had issued the safe conduct in question, was as angry as Edward was and, although he was eventually able to procure Mauny's release, he appears to have withdrawn from court for several months and to have entertained a real (though surely exaggerated) fear that he might be disinherited. Relations between the King and the Duke of Burgundy, John's father-in-law and mentor, were glacial. Artois, the appanage which the Duke governed on behalf of his wife, had now become the principal theatre of the war and and the constitutional niceties which prevented Philip from exercising direct power there were irksome and frustrating. The government tended increasingly to disregard them, appointing its own officials and commanders not only in the march of Calais but in the main towns of the hinterland. In December 1346 Philip suspended the Duke's government in Artois and began to dismiss a large number of his officials.[37]

These were troubling and unaccustomed chinks in the traditional solidarity of the French royal family. Some distanced themselves even more emphatically from the failures of Philip VI as a war leader. Joan of Navarre, Countess of Angoulême and daughter of Louis X, admittedly an embittered and discontented woman, went as far as to conclude a private truce with the Earl of Lancaster. This remarkable document, which was executed in about November 1346, has not survived. But it appears that she obtained protection for her county of Angoulême, granting in return a right of free passage through it for Anglo-Gascon troops, and an undertaking not to build new fortifications in the region or allow old ones to be garrisoned by the French Crown. Philip VI cannot have liked this arrangement, but he was obliged to acquiesce in it. He was in no position to take over Angoulême as he had Artois.[38]

The professional element in the King's Council threw themselves with abrasive vigour into the work of putting his finances on a sound footing for the following year. The winter of 1346–7 was remembered for many years to come for famine, disorder and the heavy exactions of the collectors and farmers of royal taxes. Fresh attempts were made to enforce the *gabelle du sel* and the sales taxes. The government's plan to assess communities for the cost of men-at-arms in proportion to their population, which had been put before the Estates-General as an alternative to these taxes, was now imposed in addition. The French Church was subjected to another tenth, which the Pope authorized, as well as to a variety of more or less illegal impositions which he did not. But these measures were slow in producing money, and as the campaigning season approached the government turned, as it always had done on such occasions, to patchwork expedients. A fresh programme of coinage manipulation began in January 1347, provoking intense discontent. Foreigners and other unpopular minorities were mulcted for all that they were worth. In February, the government confiscated all the asssets of Italian moneylenders in France, including their portfolios of loans, which became repayable (without interest) to the Treasury. Clergymen resident outside France were deprived of their incomes for the profit of the Crown, a measure which might have been decreed in direct imitation of Edward III's proceedings in England a year before. Protests were brushed aside. Every man, Philip told the Pope, had a duty to defend the realm and the place his property and his person at the disposal of the Crown for the common good. If the Queen had had her way, Philip would have gone further and revived the compulsory free military service of the nobility which had not been required in France for many decades. Philip rejected this suggestion. He knew some at least of the limits of his power.[39]

The stagnation of the war around Calais depressed the spirits of both sides during the winter months. The English were unable to blockade the town from the sea, as a result of which supplies and fresh drafts of troops continued to reach it. In the second week of November, just before the foul weather set in, the French got a convoy of requisitioned merchant ships into the harbour with enough food to preserve the garrison until supplies could resume in the spring.[40] For their part, the English received a steady flow of supplies overland from Flanders which the low level of French military strength in the winter months and the poor morale of the Artois garrisons allowed to continue unhindered. The newsletters which the towns of Artois exchanged, sometimes several times a day, reveal their frustration, and shifting moods of fear, anger and despair as they tried to make sense of what was happening only a few miles away. Reports were muffled by ignorance and confusion. It is reported that Edward III has abandoned the siege and withdrawn from Calais. In which direction? Better reports suggest that he is still there. Another assault on the town was attempted this very morning. The earls of Derby and Stafford are on the point of launching a powerful raid into Artois. How many men do they have? Fifty thousand. What route will they take? 'In spite of all the warnings which we and others have given to the King our sovereign,' the councillors of Saint-Omer wrote at the end of February 1347, 'he has done nothing to help us, nothing to bring the battle to the enemy.'[41]

Edward III made a serious attempt to break the deadlock while his enemies' strength was still at its nadir. In the middle of November 1346 an extremely elaborate plan was devised for storming Calais by introducing a fleet of small boats into the moat and scaling the walls from ladders placed on their decks. This enterprise occupied a great deal of energy and ingenuity. Fifty fishing vessels were ordered from England with specially large crews; 25- and 40-foot ladders were obtained. Carpenters were pressed into service in the southern counties. Wooden stone-throwers and at least ten cannon with powder and ammunition were shipped across the Channel. The reinforcements which had been held back in Kent when the French army had dispersed from Compiègne were ordered across the Channel and more were called to arms from their homes. Most of these men reached Calais during the second half of December. But repeated assaults on the walls all failed. The last-known attempt was made on 27 February 1347.[42]

In the intervals between these moments of excitement and the occasional violent foraging raid into the interior, the English army sat about the marsh in the damp and rain, periodically shifting their tents and cabins as neap tides encroached upon their islands of firm ground. Disease diminished their strength and thinned out their numbers. Desertion became a serious problem, particularly among the archers, as men found ways of getting back on victualling ships or through Flanders. Some stole money or plate to get themselves home, or smuggled out valuable prisoners. In England, the sheriffs and councillors were occupied in checking on the homes of long lists of absconders. Some they discovered and punished. Many they found to be wounded or too ill to fight any more.[43]

The French government knew that with the return of fair weather and English ships in the spring Calais would become increasingly difficult to supply. Unfortunately, they no longer had the means of controlling the sea, even locally. The galleys of the Genoese would have been ideal for conducting operations over a limited range around Calais. But either the French did not realize this or else the Genoese, who had only contracted to serve during 1346, declined to stay another year in Philip's service. In view of the treatment which their compatriots had received at the time of the battle of Crécy, neither explanation would be surprising. For whatever reason Grimaldi's shipmasters and crews were paid off in November 1346. The French government bought those of the Genoese galleys which were still seaworthy and laid them up. They then turned from oars to sail, and from Italy to Spain. In the winter of 1346–7 Alfonso XI of Castile and his admiral Giles Boccanegra (he was the brother of the Doge of Genoa) made a business proposal. Castile was becoming an Atlantic power of great importance, with a strong permanent war fleet and a merchant fleet famous for the size and height of its largest vessels. They offered, it seems in their private capacities, to provide the French government with a contract fleet of up to 200 large sailing ships each with a full complement of seamen plus a hundred armed men and twenty-five crossbowmen. Boccanegra visited Vincennes in January 1347 to press this idea on the French King. A contract was signed on the 25th. But the Spanish were no more punctual than the Genoese had been. There may also have been difficulties in paying their mobilization fees and advances, which were high. The result was that the French employed neither the Italians nor the Castilians, and were thrown back on their own maritime resources.[44]

The number of suitable French ships available had been much diminished by the destructions of the English in southern Normandy the year before. But effective use was made of those that there were. The revictualling of Calais was organized by Pierre Flote ('Floton') de Revel, who had been Admiral of France since March 1345. He was no seaman, but he was an intelligent and energetic administrator, scion of one of the great bureaucratic dynasties of the fourteenth century. During February 1347 purveyors scoured north-western France for supplies and dispatched them for carriage downriver to two main collection points on the coast. Supplies found in Normandy and southern Picardy were taken to Dieppe; those from the basin of the Somme and the northern Ile de France were carried by relays of river barges to Abbeville and thence to Saint-Valéry at the mouth of the Somme. At Dieppe and Saint-Valéry they were reloaded on to large ocean-going vessels and sent north. At Boulogne the ships were filled with soldiers, formed into convoys and provided with an escort of galleys and fortified sailing ships. A large number of vessels was engaged in these operations: well over sixty small coasters and river barges, more than two dozen sailing ships, twelve French galleys and oared barges, and a solitary Italian galley from the previous year's campaigns. It represented enormous effort and expenditure by the Crown as well as the maritime towns of Normandy and Picardy. At Dieppe almost all the seafaring community of the town took part including the women, more than 300 of whom volunteered to haul ships with hawsers out of the harbour. The first results were highly satisfactory. Two large convoys successfully got through. The Dieppe convoy of five laden ships and about fifteen escorts reached Calais in the middle of March 1347. The Saint-Valéry convoy, about thirty ships including six laden, entered the harbour at the beginning of April. There was no significant opposition from the English, and no losses except for one ship which foundered in a storm on the way. At least 1,000 tons of stores must have been delivered to the beleaguered town.[45]

Philip VI took the Oriflamme at Saint-Denis on 18 March 1347. he had intended to have his army ready by the end of April and announced his intention of marching against the English early in May. But he was grossly misinformed about the progress of his government's preparations. Recruitment was even slower and patchier than it had been in the previous October. When Philip reached Amiens, there were very few men there. Undaunted, in the second week of May 1347 he left Amiens, marching north 'in short stages to give the troops time to gather'. It was not until he arrived at Arras that his eyes were opened. There were insistent calls for reinforcement, a slow trickle of men in May and a slightly fuller one in June. No serious military operations could be undertaken until July, more than two months late. Even then they had to be conducted on a smaller scale than Philip's first plans had envisaged.[46]

This state of affairs, so entirely uncharacteristic of French military organization before Crécy, was the consequence of the defeat. The battle had been a blow to the authority of the Valois dynasty out of all proportion to its real strategic significance. It was much worse than the aftermath of Courtrai, forty years before. The aggressive efforts of Philip's officials to collect taxes during the winter had largely failed, the result of popular indifference and obstruction. Another more emollient approach was tried in March 1347. A series of assemblies was summoned to agree ways and means with the King's ministers. The towns of Languedoc sent their representatives to Paris in April. There was an ill-attended meeting of the towns of Picardy and the *baillage* of Vermandois, which had to be adjourned when the delegates discovered that they had no authority to agree anything of importance. In provinces across northern and central France local assemblies continued to meet and deliberate during April, May and June. The result was a medley of local taxes, usually involving laborious further negotiations with one community after another. Many districts promised the cost of a specified quota of soldiers. In three districts, Paris, Orléans and Sens, the nobility agreed to fight at their own expense. In the Ile de France there was a property tax. Most of the northern towns were bullied somehow or other into continuing the sales tax. Normandy agreed to a hearth tax. Collection was inordinately slow. Communities far from Calais hardly cared; those closer to the fighting wanted the money spent on their own walls and some of them would raise taxes on no other terms. Reims, for example, that rich city of cloth-makers and ecclesiastical princes, spent some 5,000 *l.t.* on its fortifications between October 1346 and July 1347. In May and June 1347 expenditure was running at more than 1,000 *l.t.* per month and was consuming all the men and stores which the townsmen could lay hands on. They would not pay any taxes to the King's treasury nor send a contingent to his army. Their case was not untypical and their priorities were difficult to fault. An impressive field army had done nothing for Caen or Poissy in 1346.[47]

Graver even than the penury of the Crown was the penury of the nobility on whom it depended for its troops. The French nobility had incurred enormous expenditure over the past decade in equipping themselves for war and had sustained a continuous succession of defeats for two years. Defeat was not only demoralizing. It was costly. Philip's ministers believed that the crushing burden of debt carried by the nobility, and the high rates of interest charged by usurers were prime causes of their difficulty in recruiting troops. They were probably right. The parlous finances of many noble families are revealed in the mass of records generated by the nationalization of the loans of the Italian moneylenders. Jean de Landas and his wife and father had owed between them 5,275 *l.t.* to the Scarampi, bankers of Asti: a sum roughly equal to the entire expenditure of the city of Reims on its fortifications in the year after Crécy. Two-thirds of this was accumulated interest. Jean's brother-in-law, who was the military governor of Artois during the siege of Calais, was so heavily indebted to the Italians that he had had to petition the King for relief in 1346. He was allowed to serve at his own expense with thirty men-at-arms for three months in 1347 just to repay the principal. Jean de Châtillon, lord of Dampierre, who had fought in the battle of Saint-Omer in 1340 and helped to defend Béthune against Hugh Hastings in August 1346, owed 1,400 *l.t.*, most of it interest. This was partly due to the cost of buying horses, a common enough case. Mile de Noyers, the King's minister, whose ostentatious way of life had led him deep into debt even before the war completed his discomfiture, owed 2,000 *l.t.* to the Bardi, representing interest and principal on money borrowed to pay the ransom of his son. The case of Pierre de Messelan is perhaps more striking than any of these, for whereas they were prominent figures with an expensive reputation to maintain, he was a relatively obscure squire from the Gâtinais. This man ruined himself by borrowing from the Italians before he was killed fighting at Crécy. His debts amounted to no less than 14,565 *l.t.* His heirs made the best deal they could with the Treasury before selling up his estates to an acquisitive lawyer and sinking into genteel poverty. Pierre de Messelan bore his burden and died fighting for the King. In the aftermath of defeat men like him became indifferent to the King's military enterprise. Some could no longer afford to fight. Some could not see the point.[48]

Some turned to treason. Edward III had never received as many offers of support from well-placed French noblemen as he did during the eleven months when his army stood immobile outside Calais. Moreover, for the first time their assistance was of real military value. In November 1346 there was a serious rebellion in the county of Burgundy against the authority of the King's brother-in-law, Odo, Duke of Burgundy. The county, legally part of the Empire but belonging to France by language, sentiment and feudal dependence, was a region of fickle political allegiances with an old tradition of aristocratic rebellion. The coalition of Burgundian noblemen who led the rebellion of 1346 had sent their agents into the camp at Calais within two days of the beginning of the siege to concert their plans with Edward III. The subsidy which they received from the English treasury, 45,000 florins (£6,750), was well spent. The rebels devastated much of the county, drained the Duke's funds, and kept the greatest feudatory of the Crown together with most of his retainers and followers in eastern France for virtually all of the year 1347.[49] In March 1347 there was another serious incident when Philip VI's officials uncovered a plot to deliver up the city of Laon on the borders of Champagne and the Ile de France to the English. One of the organizers, an advocate in the Parlement of Paris, was betrayed by an accomplice and arrested before his preparations were complete. The others fled to the castle of Bosmont a few miles outside the city, where they held out under the command of a strange misfit called Jean de Vervins. Like the Burgundians, Jean de Vervins had surreptitiously found his way into the English camp during the winter. Correspondence was intercepted between the ringleaders and Edward's ministers. And when the enterprise misfired, sixty English archers were found among the garrison of Bosmont. This adventure tied up a small army that might otherwise have gone to the aid of Philip VI. It was almost certainly one of the reasons why the towns of Champagne were so reluctant to send their men to Calais. The castle of Bosmont was besieged in May by the *baillis* of Laon and Vermandois and the Count of Roucy. Its garrison eventually surrendered on terms. When they had held out as long as they could, they delivered up Jean de Vervins to the vengeance of the French King, received a safe conduct for themselves and marched away.[50]

These were the most spectacular cases. There were others, too obscure to interest the English or strike a blow for Edward III. The goldsmith of Paris who was quartered and hanged in May for plotting to let in the enemy was probably no more than a discontented loudmouth.[51] Judicial torture could add a great deal of circumstantial detail to what was really only grumbling and careless talk. But incidents like these aggravated the tensions of the crowded populations of the northern towns and the fear of worse ones produced an obsessive preoccupation with the threat of enemies within.

By far the most serious of the many diversions which drew Philip's resources from the main object was the work of the inhabitants of Flanders. The new Count of Flanders had done homage for his territory to the King of France a week after his father's death at Crécy, the lowest point of French fortunes. Louis de Mâle was an intelligent and cunning man with many of the political skills that his father had lacked. He was to become the ablest ruler of Flanders for more than a century. But he was only sixteen years old in the autumn of 1346, entirely without political experience, and destined for the first year of his reign to be manipulated by more powerful politicians: the leaders of the Flemings, for whom he represented the prospect of stability and the legitimacy; the French government, who saw in him the means of reasserting their authority in Flanders; and the English, who perceived very clearly that as long as the Count remained the titular ruler of Flanders and a vassal of Philip VI, Edward's claim to be king there was a mere formula. Soon after Crécy, Philip made lavish offers to the government of the three great towns of Flanders: subsidized supplies of grain, the first call on France's production of raw wool, a protected position in the French cloth market and a variety of fiscal and economic privileges as well as the restoration of the three castleries of Walloon Flanders which had been taken by Philip the Fair. These proposals served mainly to demonstrate Philip's grasp of the factors which bound the Flemings to England. They were firmly rejected. When the English King travelled into Flanders during October 1346 to repair his alliances, the Flemings solemnly renewed them.[52]

But if Philip failed to capture the Flemish oligarchies for his cause, Edward failed just as completely to capture the Count. All three parties for their own purposes urged the new Count to return to Flanders, and when at last he did so at the beginning of October 1346 he was received with much public celebration. But Louis was never allowed to exercise any real power. Within a short time he was as much a prisoner of his subjects as his father had been. He was allowed only two companions of his own choice. Twenty men watched him night and day, 'so closely that he could hardly piss in private' wrote Jean le Bel. His council was packed with nominees of the three great towns, and treaties, letters and public documents were all signed at their dictation. Intolerable pressure was brought to bear on Louis to declare himself publicly for Edward III. They wanted him to seal the alliance permanently by marrying Edward's eldest daughter Isabella.

Louis resisted these demands for as long as he could. He would never, he said, take to his wife the son of the man who had killed his father. But in the middle of March 1347, it seemed that he would be forced to. Edward III returned to Flanders and confronted the young Count at Berghes, a small cloth town in the south-west of the county. There, surrounded by the representatives of Ghent, Bruges and Ypres, Louis solemnly betrothed himself to Isabella. He also undertook to lead an army of Flemings into France in support of the English cause, and accepted a subsidy from the English treasury. About a fortnight after the encounter at Berghes, as the gorgeous preparations for the marriage were nearing completion and the Count was running out of excuses for postponing it, he went out falconing and, slipping his guard to retrieve a bird, bolted southward and escaped into France.[53] His half-brother, a bastard of Louis of Nevers, stayed behind and tried to raise a revolt in Ghent with French money and some Flemish sympathizers. But he was arrested before the arrangements were complete, and beheaded. Fear gave way to hatred as intense in Ghent as it was in Paris. The oligarchy would have had him tortured to death in a public square but for the intervention of the Margrave of Juliers. Some respect, the Margrave said, was surely due to his birth.[54]

The western frontier of Flanders had become vital to both sides. The fall of an important town like Saint-Omer would have been a humiliating blow to Philip VI. Moreover, at a time when he was trying to persuade the northern provinces of his realm to help him with money and men it was unthinkable to allow long-distance raiders to roam freely across the borders. The French King's motives, however, were not entirely defensive. It became clear to him, as it already was to Edward III, that the south-western corner of Flanders was one of the keys to the relief of Calais. The French army would either have to penetrate the marshland fastness of the English around the beleaguered town, a difficult and dangerous undertaking; or starve them out of it, which would involve occupying the roads north of Calais by which the English were receiving most of their supplies.

The dependence of Edward III on these roads was bound to increase as his army was reinforced from England in the course of the summer and the strain of feeding it mounted. Keeping them open was a considerable strategic success, almost entirely due to the Flemings. It was achieved at great cost to themselves, for they were generally outfought by troops who were more experienced, better equipped and better led than they were, and they suffered heavy casualties in consequence. They prevailed by sheer numbers and persistence.

In the absence of Louis de Mâle, the command of the Flemish troops was taken by a disreputable French renegade called Oudart de Renti, the bastard of a distinguished French family from western Artois who had been banished from France for some crime and had temporarily thrown in his lot with the Flemings. Reliable estimates of the strength of his forces are difficult to come by, but it was certainly considerable. By the end of March 1347 there were about 5,000 men from Bruges alone. There must have been at least three times that number from the whole of Flanders, and further contingents continued to arrive during April, May and June.[55]

The French forces in the region consisted of major garrisons at Aire, Saint-Omer, Béthune, Lille and Tournai, and minor ones at less important places. At the beginning of April 1347 they were heavily reinforced, and a mobile border force of several hundred mounted men was created around Aire and Saint-Omer. This was achieved partly by stripping troops from the immense garrison of Boulogne and from other French garrisons further south; and partly by drawing off men from the field army which Philip VI was painfully assembling at Amiens and Arras. Men no sooner arrived there and received their advances than they were sent up to the border. The whole of the western march of Flanders was placed under the control of Charles of Spain, the future Constable of France and one of the ablest of his martial family. At the age of twenty-one, he was exercising his first significant command.[56]

The campaign opened in the middle of April 1347 with a concerted attack on Saint-Omer by detachments from the English and Flemish armies. It was an inauspicious beginning. The two forces mistimed their arrival and were defeated separately. The Flemings came across the Neuve Fosse from the east and were scattered by cavalry outside the town with the loss of several hundred men. The English, who came up from the west about a week later with some 500 mounted men, found themselves heavily outnumbered. They were pursued for several miles back along the Calais road until, caught with their backs to a river near the village of Tournehem, they made a stand and were defeated with some losses.

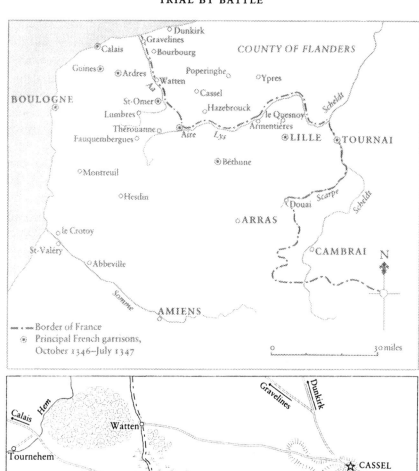

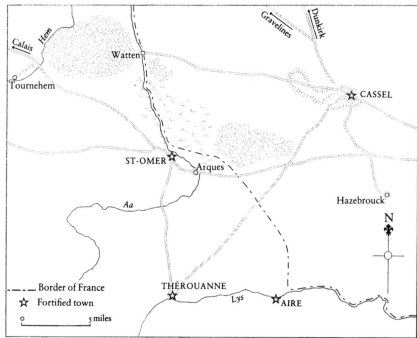

32 The march of Flanders, 1347

A few days after this incident, at the end of April 1347, Charles of Spain took the offensive. His first target was Cassel, an important crossroad town some 15 miles north of the Aa. But his force was not strong enough to take the place. After an unsuccessful attempt to storm it, he withdrew to Saint-Omer. This adventure was followed almost immediately by another, bolder but equally unproductive. The object was to break the dam across the Aa at Watten, north of Saint-Omer, thereby flooding the flats of Bourbourg between Watten and Gravelines and cutting the vital supply road. It almost succeeded. The French approached without warning, the mounted troops coming through the forest of Ham, the infantry arriving in boats from Saint-Omer. The dam was captured and the labourers who had come with them began to cut it. But unfortunately their commander, Moreau de Fiennes, was nervous about a counter-attack and sounded the retreat before the work had been completed. So apart from the loot of the nearby Benedictine abbey, the operation was a waste of effort.

The Flemings regrouped their men in May and shifted their operations further east, attempting a series of hit-and-run raids into eastern Artois and the French provinces of Walloon Flanders. None of them succeeded. Most were sanguinary failures. The first was nipped in the bud when the men who were to take part in it were attacked at their assembly point by the small town of Hazebruck. They formed themselves into battalions when the French arrived and fought it out in front of the town. But although they acquitted themselves better than the French had expected they were routed and most of them were killed. Béthune was probably the destination of this abortive expeditionary force.

Another, a fortnight later, tried to surprise Lille. They did no better. They crossed the River Lys one evening, some 8 miles north of the town. But at dawn on the following morning the Lille garrison attacked them as they passed through the village of Le Quesnoy-sur-Deulle and wiped them out. This was the last service which Oudart de Renti performed for the Flemings. He changed sides a few days afterwards, negotiated his pardon and began a long career as a captain in French service. The French had no particular reason to value his skills. But he could hardly have done more damage to them if he had won victories. His mere presence with a large body of men at unpredictable points on a long border had tied down valuable French troops and forced on them a costly dispersal of effort. The fact that the Lille garrison which finally defeated him was about 800 strong and commanded by Charles de Montmorency, a former Marshal, speaks for itself.[57]

*

Just as defeat had dried up Philip VI's sources of money and men, victory enabled Edward III to mine fresh seams of his subjects' wealth. Edward's representatives called the principal lay and ecclesiastical peers who were still in England to Westminster on 3 March 1347. They told them very plainly that the King needed a great deal of money at once. Unless he received it, they said, everything that had been spent since the beginning of the previous year would be wasted. Faced once more with the spectre of Tournai, the peers agreed to authorize a forced loan of 20,000 sacks of wool to be assessed against every man in the kingdom except the poorest laymen. These were the preliminaries to further monopolistic schemes after the model of 1337. A syndicate of merchants formed by the government's principal bankers undertook the disposal of the wool, paying ready cash and receiving in return a monopoly of the right to export. The Council then sat with the representatives of the seamen to consider the immense resources of shipping which would be required in order to ferry men and horses, equipment and stores across the Channel. In addition to transports, which would be requisitioned in the ordinary way, it was proposed to raise a fighting fleet of 120 ships of 150 tons or more, each carrying sixty seamen and twenty archers. The cost was to be met by a heavy supplementary duty, of doubtful legality, levied on exports. The proceeds of these taxes were anticipated almost at once by a great programme of borrowing. The whole of the wool loan was sold to Walter Chiriton's syndicate for £66,666, which represented a fairly substantial discount on its full value and was payable in instalments over a period of months. A variety of other lenders was found. The Great Crown was mortgaged (again) for £20,000 to a syndicate organized by the London vintner Henry Picard. This great influx of money satisfied the King's needs for a short time.[58]

During the latter half of April 1347 Edward III finally succeeded in surrounding Calais from all sides. The second French victual fleet had entered the harbour at the beginning of the month. Shortly after this event the English seized the Rysbank, which was the narrow tongue of sand extending from the south to enclose the harbour on the seaward side. At the end of it, opposite the town, they built a timber fortification on which they sited cannon and other artillery, and a garrison of 40 men-at-arms and 200 archers. Of the 120 large fighting ships promised by the English seaports, about two-thirds appeared in the second half of April. They were placed under the command of the Earl of Warwick. The English now had more or less complete control of the Channel between Calais and the Kent and Sussex coast.[59]

When it came to reinforcing the army, progress was rather slower. The Council had fixed 2 April 1347 for the assembly of the transport fleets. Embarkation was expected to take place a week later on the 9th at three ports: Sandwich, Dover and Winchelsea. However, none of the men had arrived in France a month later, apart from the personal retinues of a few noblemen. Progress was delayed by a variety of factors, all aggravated by the ambitious scale of the government's plans. The requisitioning of troops did not begin until February and proceeded raggedly throughout the spring months. It was still far from complete at the end of May. The collection of victuals at the ports, which had started at about the same time, was slower still. The King's financial problems, apparently resolved in March, began to reappear towards the end of May, when the shipmasters and the levies of Wales and the English counties demanded their due faster than the King's bankers and collectors could find it.[60]

There were moments of anxiety as news of Philip's progress trickled into the English camp, exaggerated by fear and by respect for the efficiency which had been characteristic of French military organization in the past. A panic at the end of March, when Philip VI took the Oriflamme, subsided when he returned to his mansion on the Oise. Mây was a month of acute alarm on both sides of the Channel. On the 14th, when Philip's departure from Amiens was reported, the French were expected to attack on the 20th. A week later, when he reached Arras, the attack was expected on the 27th.[61] In England, the Council desperately tried to accelerate the receipt of funds. The emergency export duties, which were being paid directly to the paymasters of the army, were now sold to bankers in London and Bruges at a discount in return for ready money. There was another round of forced loans. Well-known merchants from all over England were summoned before the Council to make their proposals for easing the King's difficulties. Commissioners passed from county to county extracting money from monasteries. At Westminster the cash was being laden on to pack animals as soon as it was received and taken down to the ports to pay the men. Henry of Lancaster was abruptly commanded to cross the Channel with every available man, ready or no. He left London and embarked with part of the army of reinforcement, several thousand men, in the last days of May. The others were left behind to follow in relays in the course of June and July. Edward III had no conception of his enemy's difficulties. He only appreciated his own, and those imperfectly.[62]

Philip's major difficulty was that the Flemings had not been humbled by their defeats in April and May nor by the defection of their commander. On the contrary, they had steadfastly reinforced their troops along the Aa and the Lys rivers with levies from the industrial towns. Hardly had one Flemish raiding force been repulsed from Lille by Charles of Montmorency than another larger one appeared in eastern Artois and made for Béthune. They were probably stronger now than they had ever been.

Philip wanted to recall most of his garrison troops to swell his army and then march on Calais. But as matters stood he could do neither. The Flemings would have a free hand to overrun the provinces behind him and then to attack him in the rear as he confronted the English by the coast. The King's dilemma was vigorously debated among his advisers at Arras. The preferred solution, which prevailed until a late stage, was to invade south-western Flanders and come upon the English from the north. This idea had several things to commend it. It would have placed the French army across Edward III's principal lines of supply. It would also, in all probability, have drawn the Flemings away from the French border. The difficulty was that the French army's own line of supply would have had to run through southern Flanders. It would be highly vulnerable there unless the main strongholds along the line of march were captured and securely held. It would also be necessary to clear the main concentrations of Flemish troops in the French rear.

Two large task forces were therefore formed out of the French army at Arras at the beginning of June. The first was placed under the command of Edward de Beaujeu, a rising star in high favour at Philip's court who had distinguished himself at Crécy and was shortly to become a Marshal. Beaujeu joined forces with Charles of Spain at Saint-Omer. His men crossed the Aa into Flanders and made another attempt against Cassel, the second in two months. Cassel was built in a remarkable position, at the summit of a great hill dotted with windmills rising suddenly some 500 feet above the plain of western Flanders. Although its walls had been twice demolished by French armies in the past thirty years and only patchily repaired, it remained a powerful natural fortress. A considerable part of the Flemish border force was concentrated there. They had with them a small troop of English archers. When Charles's army arrived at the base of the hill, early on the morning of 8 June 1347, they found the Flemings waiting for them in prepared positions behind palisades around the summit. The French advanced up the slope. Their crossbowmen went ahead, shooting bolts into the cramped lines of the defenders. Then the French men-at-arms charged the Flemings on foot, trampling down the palisades and pushing them back in hand-to-hand fighting which continued for several hours. At about mid-day, as the Flemings on the hill were beginning to fail, the captain of the town threw in a large body of fresh troops,

Flemish and German mercenaries, which he had kept in reserve. Their arrival was decisive. The French were driven back. They regrouped at the bottom of the hill. Then, finding that their casualties had been heavy and that their crossbowmen had run out of bolts, they retreated and returned to Saint-Omer.

The second French task force fared better, but it did not achieve the shattering victory over the Flemings which Philip needed. The commanders on this occasion were Robert de Waurin, lord of Saint-Venant (one of the Marshals) and the Count of La Marche, Jacques de Bourbon. These two marched to Béthune, the capital of the north-eastern region of Artois. Although Béthune itself was still in French hands the whole of the region around had been overrun by the Flemings. They were still present in force near the town, watching their chances. As soon as they reached Béthune, Bourbon and Saint-Venant collected about them most of the French border forces. There was the garrison of Béthune itself. Charles de Montmorency was recalled from the eastern sector of the border around Lille. Charles of Spain arrived with most of the men from the region of Aire and Saint-Omer. They attacked the Flemings with their combined strength on 13 June 1347. The Flemings' reconnaissance had been careless. They had no advance warning of the attack and, when the French fell on their encampment at night, they were asleep. But most of them escaped in the darkness and confusion into the surrounding fields and, knowing the country better than the French did, were able to regroup their men. They counter-attacked with vigour, causing havoc in the French ranks and killing many of them. Then they melted away, retreating across the Lys and leaving the French to wreak terrible vengeance on their own people, the villagers of north-eastern Artois who had submitted to the invader rather than fight.

In Arras there were still some men about the King who favoured the approach to Calais through Flanders. But the mixed results of Beaujeu's campaign and the fact that the Flemings still held Cassel was enough for most people. The French commanders decided that the English should be attacked from the southern side. The risk of a Flemish invasion behind their backs would have to be accepted. Philip havered for a long time, 'en grant destreche de cuer', before he finally came to agree with them. The border troops and garrisons rejoined the King at Arras. So, on about 20 June 1347, Philip and his army marched towards the coast. On the 23rd, he set up his headquarters at Hesdin, 50 miles south of Calais.[63]

While Philip was on the road to Hesdin, disaster struck his cause in Brittany, a place where few troops were now engaged and which, in the face of greater events elsewhere, had receded from the attention of almost everyone. The French government had no troops of its own in Brittany, although Charles of Blois himself retained several hundred men from other provinces of France as well as some Genoese. Edward III for his part had for some time viewed Brittany as a sideshow whose retention (apart from the important autonomous fortress of Brest) was justified only if it could be achieved without spending money. The system employed was to leave the conduct of operations there to independent captains. These men contracted to carry on the war with their own retainers at their own expense and in their own way. They held their offices at the English King's pleasure but they were only nominally subject to direction from his government. They received almost unlimited civil and military power and all the ordinary revenues of the duchy, which were made over to them together with the profits of war and a lump-sum fee. 'A most convenient and profitable arrangement' Edward III called it, 'considering the great and outrageous sum which the defence of the region has been costing us'.

In Brittany, the first of these military entrepreneurs were Sir Thomas Dagworth and Raoul le Caours, both of whom were appointed in January 1347. Neither was a great nobleman of the kind traditionally appointed to exercise such extensive powers, although Dagworth came nearer to the model than Le Caours did. He was a Suffolk knight who had risen to prominence by marrying a great lady, Eleanor Bohun, sister of the earls of Hereford and Northampton. Northampton had taken Dagworth to Brittany in his retinue in 1345 and left him there as his deputy when he was recalled to England early in the following year. At the time of his appointment, therefore, he had already been in the duchy in one capacity or another for about eighteen months, during which time he had shown himself to be an efficient administrator and a courageous and talented commander who had twice defeated Charles of Blois in the field. Dagworth's army was never very large. He could call on the Breton lords in the occupied parts of the duchy and on their tenants and retainers, sometimes in fair numbers. But the kernel of his strength was a permanent contract army of 300 men-at-arms and 200 archers, a miscellaneous band drawn from his friends, relatives and retainers in England, from pardoned criminals and from soldiers of fortune hired on the continent, mainly in Flanders. In armies like these, few of whose members were gentlemen, the ranks and hierarchies of life at home played a much smaller role than they did in the army of the King. They were professional soldiers, 'making war for their private profit' as one of Dagworth's successors described them, 'neither knights nor squires but men of little worth who will not do a thing without their twelve pence a day and forty marks a year'.[64]

Dagworth's territory covered the whole of Brittany, including Brest and its region but excluding those districts which, although they formed part of the dominions of the dukes, lay south of the Loire estuary and belonged geographically to Poitou. These districts and the territory south of them as far as the Sèvre at Niort were assigned to Raoul le Caours, a shady adventurer of rather similar origin but without the redeeming features of a fine marriage and a chivalrous reputation and without Dagworth's fundamental loyalty to the English Crown. Raoul came from the Guérande peninsula of southern Brittany and owned modest estates in the Vendée. He had already turned his coat at least twice, fighting for John de Montfort in 1342 and 1343, submitting to Charles Blois in 1344, then returning to the Montfortist cause after the English victories of 1345 and 1346. The terms of his appointment were probably similar to Dagworth's. Rather later he was given a fee of £1,000 a year from land to be conquered by him in the territory covered by his captaincy. It was what a man like Raoul really wanted: not to carry home a fortune, like Mauny or Dagworth, but to make a figure in the region where his family had always lived, and to build a great territorial interest transcending any loyalty to this king or that one.[65]

Raoul le Caours was a ruthless but not particularly skilful soldier and his resources were even smaller than Dagworth's. His sole recorded contribution to the English war effort in 1347, apart from the 'excesses, rebellions, murders, rapes and arsons' recorded in the routine formulae of the French Chancery, was to mount a raid on a house where Philip VI's lieutenant in northern Poitou was staying, and to capture him in his bed in the middle of the night. The lieutenant, Louis, Viscount of Thouars, was worth a large ransom but it was otherwise a very minor affair causing more embarrassment than damage to the French.[66]

A few days after this event, towards the end of May 1347, Charles of Blois laid siege to La Roche-Derrien. Richard Totesham, the captain of this long-standing English enclave by the north coast, was an old Brittany hand. He had settled in there with his wife and newborn baby, surrounded by a large permanent garrison. But his hold was precarious. He was a long way from help and, although he seems to have won the support of the townsmen, the English presence was detested by the inhabitants of the surrounding country. For them it meant constant harassment and banditry, and heavy *corvées* by which local men were forced to work on the buildings and fortifications necessary to consolidate the foreigners' position.

Charles of Blois' real purpose was probably to draw Dagworth into battle. The destruction of any significant proportion of Dagworth's small army would have brought the whole of western Brittany (except Brest) into his hands. He had an army which was larger than anything required for the siege of a small town. There were 1,200 men-at-arms, 2,000 crossbowmen and some 600 other infantry in addition to an enormous number of volunteers from the surrounding region armed with sticks and stones who came to join him after his arrival. Trenches and earthworks were constructed around Charles's positions extending more than a mile from the town. Nine siege engines methodically battered at the walls and the buildings. One of them destroyed half of Totesham's house.

Dagworth took almost three weeks to rise to the bait. Most of that time was probably needed for gathering troops from the dispersed garrisons of his command; 700 men were found, 300 cavalry and 400 archers. On 19 June 1347 they arrived within 10 miles of La Roche-Derrien at a deserted Cistercian monastery and made their plans. Careful reconnaissance of the French siege lines had shown that although Charles's army was much larger than their own it had been divided into four separate bodies. They were posted at different sectors of the walls separated from each other by woodland, marsh and waterways. Charles had taken the largest body of troops for himself and encamped with them on the east side of the town. Dagworth decided to send some camp followers with carts and animals round by the west to make a noisy diversion, while he himself and the rest of his men attacked in Charles's sector. To give themselves the advantage of surprise, the English began their march at midnight.

Although they reached La Roche-Derrien well before dawn on the 20th, Dagworth's men found when they got there that their presence had already been detected by Charles's scouts. The French had been drawn up in their battle lines all night, each troop at its own sector of the walls, their armour lit up by torches and candles and the glow of the half-dawn. The camp followers' diversion on the west was a failure. Charles had warned his men about feints and told them to remain in their positions until they were actually attacked. On the east, the English fought their way through the siege works on foot and threw themselves on Charles's men.

There was a confused and bloody battle fought hand to hand in semi-darkness. At first, things went badly for the English. They were pushed back. Several of them were captured, including Dagworth himself. But when the light was strong enough for the two lines to be distinguished, Totesham's garrison rushed out of the gates of the town accompanied by three or four hundred citizens armed with hatchets and home-made weapons. They fell on Charles's men from the rear and overwhelmed them. Dagworth was rescued. Charles of Blois was recognized and cornered near a windmill by a group of Flemish mercenaries. He fought savagely, and was wounded seven times before he finally gave himself up to a Breton knight who made his way through the mêlée to take his surrender. No nobleman of the fourteenth century would willingly surrender to a man too far beneath him. While this was happening, the other three groups of French soldiers remained fixed in their separate positions at the other sectors of the walls as Charles had ordered them to do. None of them was as strong as Charles's group. The English attacked and defeated each of them in turn. It was all over by sunrise.

French casualties in the battle were high. The darkness had made it difficult and dangerous to take prisoners. Large numbers of men had died of hatchet wounds during the indiscriminate slaughter which followed the sortie from the town. The dead included the greatest noblemen of Brittany among Charles's party, the Viscount de Rohan, the lords of Laval, Châteaubriand, Malestroit and Rougé, as well as six or seven hundred knights and squires, more than half the men-at-arms in Charles's army. Of those who survived almost all those of any consequence were taken prisoner. Charles of Blois was a prize of almost incalculable value. The most elaborate precautions were taken to prevent him from being rescued. He was first taken into La Roche-Derrien, then carried secretly from castle to castle before finally ending up in the citadel of Vannes on the south coast.[67] He remained there for several months recovering from his wounds. In the autumn of 1348, when he was well enough to travel, Dagworth shipped him to England and sold him to Edward III for 25,000 écus (£3,500), a very moderate price in the circumstances. In London he joined David II of Scotland and the principal captives of Caen, Crécy and Neville's Cross in the Tower, bargaining counters to be retained against impossible demands for ransom or traded for political concessions in France.[68]

The news of Charles's defeat and capture caused consternation among the French army at Hesdin. At a delicate state of Philip's campaign to relieve Calais the King was forced to devote time, money and scarce troops to shore up his position in Brittany. Philip assumed direct political powers in the duchy. He appointed a royal lieutenant there, Amaury de Craon, a young man of twenty-one years whose family were a great power in Maine on the marches of Brittany and had been closely associated with Charles's cause. Early in July 1347 Amaury was hurriedly dispatched to Brittany with a small army: 600 crossbowmen and less than 100 men-at-arms. Six of the Italian galleys laid up since the winter were recommissioned. They were crewed with more than 1,000 oarsmen forcibly impressed in Normandy and Picardy and then filled up with soldiers and sent at once to Brittany. Ayton Doria, who was still living in France, was persuaded to take command of them.

The battle of La Roche-Derrien did not transform the military balance in Brittany because the English had too few men to contemplate sweeping over northern and eastern Brittany. Indeed La Roche-Derrien itself, which Charles of Blois had failed to capture in three weeks, fell to Amaury de Craon with smaller forces in three days.[69] But there was no longer, now, any prospect of dislodging the English and their allies from the territory which they firmly held in Brittany, without major expenditure by the French Crown. The cause of the house of Blois had lost its leader, on whose powers of inspiration it had always heavily depended. It had lost a generation of its principal supporters, who were dead, imprisoned or financially crippled by the burden of paying their ransoms. With all the principal participants removed from the scene the Breton civil war became more than ever a formless contest of small bands and local enmities and ambitions, of coups and surprises, banditry, intensifying desolation and poverty, and strategic realities essentially unchanged for years.

Inside Calais the defenders were suffering terrible privations. Their stores, which had not been replenished since early April, were approaching exhaustion. There was hardly any grain, wine or meat left. Men were eating cats, dogs and horses. Some of them were reduced to gnawing the leather of their saddles. As the summer lengthened the wells began to dry up; fresh water became scarce and disease took hold among them.[70]

Since the English capture of the Rysbank there had been one attempt, in May, to force the entrance of the harbour with a food convoy. The ships had got as far as Boulogne but when their commander saw the strength of the English fleet lying off the coast, he called off the attempt and sailed south. Towards the end of June, as the royal army was pitching its tents in the forests around Hesdin and the government was grappling with the crisis in Brittany, the seamen made another, more determined attempt which ended in disaster. A large convoy was formed in the mouth of the Seine: ten sailing vessels and a cargo barge all laden with victuals, escorted by ten galleys and twenty-one armed merchantmen, a total of more than fifty ships. On 25 June 1347, as the fleet passed the mouth of the Somme, they were attacked by a much larger fleet of English ships filled with archers and men-at-arms including both English admirals and the earls of

Pembroke and Northampton. The French ships scattered on the enemy's approach. The galleys fled. The crews of the victuallers began to throw their precious cargo overboard to make speed, then leaped into the sea after it, leaving their vessels to drift aimlessly aground.

That evening Jean de Vienne sat down to compose a sombre report to Philip VI. 'We can now find no more food in the town unless we eat men's flesh,' he wrote. None of the officers of the garrison, he said, had forgotten Philip's orders to hold out until they could fight no more. They had agreed that rather than surrender they would burst out of the gates and fight their way through the English siege lines until every one of them was killed. 'Unless some other solution can be found, this is the last letter that you will receive from me, for the town will be lost and all of us that are within it.' This message was entrusted to a Genoese officer. He tried to slip out of the harbour mouth with a few companions in two small boats at first light on the following morning. The English saw them and gave chase. His own boat grounded south of the town, within the siege lines. Before he was captured he attached the letter to an axe and flung it as far as he could into the sea. But the English retrieved it at low tide and took it to Edward III. Edward read it, attached to it his personal seal and forwarded it to Philip VI.

The French King did his best to answer Jean de Vienne's plea. With remarkable courage and persistence the seamen began again. Yet another convoy was formed at Dieppe. Eight barges were loaded up and set out, full of armed men but apparently without escorts, in the middle of July. They hoped to creep into Calais unnoticed. But they were seen, and the whole convoy was captured.[71]

When the commanders in Calais realized that supplies could not be got to them, they rounded up everyone in the town whom they judged to be useless to the defence, women, children, the aged, wounded and infirm, some 500 people in all, and turned them out of the gates. It was the common fate of 'useless mouths' in the last extremity of a long siege. The laws of war imposed no obligation on the besiegers towards these wretches. They had for months defied the King's summons to surrender. Why should the defenders be spared their moral dilemma when they tried to get rid of them to eke out their rations? The English would not let them pass through the lines. They drove them back towards the walls where they remained in the town ditch starving to death within sight of both sides.[72]

Fresh troops from England had now been pouring over the beaches since the end of May, bringing enormous accessions of strength to the English army and making the prospect of relief ever more remote. At its maximum strength, which was probably attained at the end of July, Edward III had more than 5,300 men-at-arms, some 6,600 infantry and 20,000 archers with him, a total of about 32,000 men. It was the largest army that England sent overseas before the end of the sixteenth century. A vast fleet of ships was engaged in ferrying men, horses and stores from the south of England: 699 requisitioned vessels drawn from eighty-three English ports from Bamburgh to Bristol, 37 hired vessels from Bayonne, Castile and the Low Countries. There were more than 15,000 seamen, many of whom could be (and were) deployed on land. In addition to Edward's own men there were the Flemings, who had now placed themselves under the command of William, Margrave or Juliers. An estimated 20,000 of them were gathered by the coast beyond the Aa.[73]

The French army moved north out of Hesdin on 17 July 1347. The English learned about it almost at once from spies sent to hang about the fringes of the enemy's camp. Further information about the enemy's movements came from some English knights, paroled prisoners of war who had been in Hesdin to negotiate about their ransoms. Within the English camp Edward's commanders began to deploy their men. The Earl of Lancaster, who had left with a large body of troops on a foraging raid into Picardy, was recalled. The Margrave of Juliers and his Flemish army crossed the Aa and moved into the English lines. Philip advanced slowly, covering only about 6 to 8 miles a day. In the small town of Lumbres, near Saint-Omer, the army paused while the troops still guarding the Flemish frontier and serving in the garrisons of northern Artois were withdrawn to swell its numbers. At Guines, some 7 miles from Calais, they were joined by the garrison troops who had been stationed for much of the year along the southern flank of the English army, and by infantry levies from the towns of Picardy. There is no reliable evidence of the strength of the French army. The Florentine chronicler Villani, who had good sources and was careful with statistics, reported that there were 11,000 cavalry. He does not offer an estimate of the infantry, but since all of them were concentrated in one of the six battalions into which the French army was divided, they cannot have been very numerous. Philip probably had between 15,000 and 20,000 men under his command. On 27 July 1346 they appeared on the heights of Sangatte, the line of escarpments which abruptly marked the southern edge of the marsh of Calais 6 miles south of the town. Their banners could be clearly seen from the walls by the defenders of the town.[74]

Philip and his entourage were overcome with despondency at what they saw below them. Spread out across the vast extent of the marsh was an army much larger than their own. The only negotiable approaches to the English lines from the south or east were by the beaches and dunes along the shore or by two narrow paths across the marsh. Between the two armies the river Ham meandered towards the sea not far from the escarpment on which the French were standing. There was only one usable bridge, at the hamlet of Nieulay. The English had taken full advantage of these natural obstacles. The beaches were obstructed with palisades and lined from Sangatte to Calais with their ships, filled with archers and artillery. Behind the bridge of Nieulay stood several thousand men in prepared positions under the command of Henry of Lancaster. South of the bridge, by the main approach, there was a tower which the English had surrounded with trenches and filled with soldiers. North of it, behind Lancaster's lines, the English and Flemish encampments could be seen, defended by earth works and trenches across every tongue of passable land.[75]

Skirmishing between the outlying forces of the two armies began as soon as they came within sight of each other. The tower guarding the road to the Nieulay bridge was quickly taken and all the men in it killed. From here, the French sent scouts forward to reconnoitre the English positions. They returned in the early evening of 27 July. Their report was very gloomy. There was not a single approach to the English lines, they said, which could be forced without a massacre worse than Crécy. The terrain was as bad for cavalry as any that could be imagined. Within hours of his arrival Philip had decided that it would not be possible to relieve Calais. He kept his men on the heights of Sangatte for almost a week, time entirely consumed by the search for some diplomatic expedient to mitigate the humiliation. Philip turned, as both he and Edward had done on similar occasions in the past, to the two cardinals, who were never far from the lines of battle. That evening the cardinals passed through the French positions and came to the bridge of Nieulay, where they delivered letters asking for someone of suitable rank to speak to. The earls of Lancaster and Northampton conferred with the King and went out to meet them with a small group of officials. Philip, the cardinals told them, was most anxious to discuss peace. He had some proposals to make which Edward 'ought in all reason to find acceptable'.

The English were very guarded. Opinion in their camp distrusted the cardinals and feared some shabby compromise. But they were willing to agree to a short truce of three days. On the following morning two large pavilions were erected at the edge of the marsh just within the English lines. Lancaster, Northampton, the Margrave of Juliers, Walter Mauny,

Reginald Cobham and Edward's Chamberlain Bartholomew Burghersh represented the English side. The French delegation included the Duke of Bourbon, the Duke of Athens, the Chancellor Guillaume Flote and Geoffrey de Charny, the famous paladin who had once been Northampton's prisoner in England. As soon as the negotiations began, it became clear that the French regarded Calais as lost. Their main concern was to try to get reasonable terms for the garrison and townsmen, guarantees that their lives would be spared and that those who wanted to leave the town could do so with all their goods and chattels. After a great deal of hesitation, they added that they were also authorized to offer a permanent peace. But the terms which they proposed were not attractive. Philip was willing to restore all of Aquitaine but only on the basis on which Edward I had held it, that is as a fief of the French Crown. The French King had already offered these terms three weeks before the battle of Crécy. Edward's representatives would not even discuss them. They said that Calais was as good as theirs in any case. As for the offer of Aquitaine, that seemed 'too small a reward for all their pains'.

On 31 July 1347, after four days of repetitious and unproductive discussion, another delegation arrived with a challenge. They proposed that the English should come out of the march and fight a battle in a 'fitting place' to be chosen by a joint commission of eight knights, four from each side. The proposal was designed to save Philip's face. No sensible person in Edward's strong position could have accepted it, but no one with his reputation could be seen publicly to turn it down. Wealth, brute force and cunning may have decided wars but it was not until the sixteenth century that these were generally recognized as military virtues. Indeed the English King later asserted that he had taken up Philip's challenge 'trusting in God and in our right', and had even issued safe conducts for the four French knights. The French denied it. The truth is obscure and perhaps unimportant, for events passed Philip by. The defenders of the town could not hold out any longer. They had celebrated the arrival of Philip's army with flags, bonfires and trumpets. They could not know what was happening by the bridge of Nieulay, and the delay was more than they could bear. On the evening of 1 August 1347, they took torches to the summit of a tower and signalled to the army on the heights of Sangatte that they intended to surrender. That night the French army burned their tents and equipment and spoiled their stores. Before dawn broke, they marched away.[76]

The commander of the garrison sent a messenger into the besiegers' lines. He asked to speak to Walter Mauny by name, perhaps because he was a Hainaulter with a chivalrous reputation who might be expected to sympathize with their plight. Mauny crossed no-man's land with three other councillors of the King to parley in front of the gates. But his message was bleak. Edward would offer them no terms. He would take everything in the town for his own and ransom or kill whom he pleased. 'You have defied him too long,' the Englishmen said; 'too much money has been spent, too many lives lost.' According to Jean le Bel, Jean de Vienne replied that his men were 'but knights and squires who have served their sovereign as loyally as they could and as you yourself would have done in their place'. Edward's harshness embarrassed his captains. They returned into their lines and remonstrated with him. Their arguments, as Jean le Bel reported them, are interesting. One day, Mauny pointed out, they might be in the same position themselves. 'By Our Lady I say that we shall not go so willingly on your service if you put these men to death, for then they will put us to death though we shall be doing no more than our duty.' Mauny could not have stated more clearly the principle, common to both sides, on which gentlemen were admitted to ransom, not killed. Like many chivalrous conventions it was founded in caste solidarity and mutual self-interest. A very similar argument had persuaded Philip VI to spare the earls of Salisbury and Suffolk when they fell into his hands in April 1340. Edward was habitually more interested in the political than the financial value of prisoners, and chivalrous convention rarely shifted him from his purpose. But he was also sensitive to the political cost of insisting on his own way. 'My friends, I do not want to stand alone against all of you,' he replied. The defenders of Calais were allowed their lives but not their liberty or their possessions. Moreover, there were to be six exceptions, chosen from the most prominent citizens of the town. 'They shall come before me in their shirtsleeves, with nooses round their necks, carrying the keys of the town and they shall be at my mercy to deal with as I please.'

On 3 August, exactly eleven months after Edward III had first laid siege to it, Calais surrendered. It was the occasion of one of the most famous scenes of the middle ages. Jean le Bel's account, written about ten years later, is encrusted with picturesque detail but it is probably substantially accurate. The six 'Burghers of Calais' emerged from one of the gates bearing the keys of the town and dressed exactly as Edward had commanded. The whole of the English army was drawn up in front of the walls, Edward himself seated on a dais in the middle with the Queen, his councillors, allies and commanders. The six threw themselves on the ground before the King, begging for mercy. Edward, however, wanted to teach other towns the consequences of defying him. He called for the executioner and ordered them to be beheaded at once in front of the troops. There was an altercation on the dais. His advisers were shocked. They protested noisily. They pointed out the damage that he would do to his reputation if he killed them in cold blood. But it was only when the Queen began to plead with him that Edward agreed with ill grace to revoke his instructions and allow the six to go free.

When the ceremony was over the marshals of the army entered the town. They raised Edward's standard, the arms of England quartered with those of France, from the battlements and rounded up the citizens, herding them out of the gates. A little later Edward processed through the empty streets towards the citadel with choruses of horns and trumpets. All the movable property in the town was assigned as spoil to the troops as it would have been if the place had been sacked. Every building was meticulously cleared out, money, goods and valuables sorted out from the rest and carried to a central store to be distributed under the supervision of the marshals. Its value exceeded all expectations. Calais, although not a major trading town, was the principal centre of piracy on the Channel coast. Its houses were found to be stuffed with the spoil of years. 'There was not a woman in England of any account who did not enjoy the pickings of Caen, Calais and other places.' Thomas Walsingham wrote; 'coats, furs, quilts and household goods of every kind, table cloths, necklaces, wooden bowls and silver goblets, linen and cloth could be seen in every home.' The knights of the garrison became the King's prisoners. But only a handful of the richest and most prominent, including Jean de Vienne, were held for ransom. They were sent to join the growing crowd of prisoners in the Tower of London and in other castles about England. The rest were allowed to go. The citizens were given doles of bread and wine from the English army's stores. Then, apart from a few favoured exceptions, they were sent away to find whatever home they could.

Philip VI was much shaken by the fate of these refugees, wandering advertisements of his military humiliation. A royal ordinance gave them the rights of residence and citizenship in any town of the kingdom. They were promised cash, grants from the confiscated property of the Italian moneylenders, first call on the proceeds of future forfeitures. Those of them who were qualified were offered appointments to all offices at the disposal of the Crown as they fell vacant. These promises could be honoured only intermittently as circumstances allowed. Nevertheless, for many years after 1347 a committee of ex-citizens kept lists of their fellows in need and distributed the King's largesse as and when it became available. The process was still continuing in the 1360s.[77]

Edward did not propose to rule Calais as King of France but to repopulate it with Englishmen, transforming it into a colony such as Aquitaine had never been. Pulteney, Pole and other well-known English merchants were invited to set up business in the town in the hope that others would follow them. During August and the following months proclamations were published throughout England calling for settlers to cross the Channel and receive free grants of land and houses in Calais. They began to arrive in September. Within ten weeks of the capture of the town nearly 200 people had taken up the offer.[78]

Philip VI assumed that having taken his prize the King of England would now go home with his army, leaving a garrison to hold Calais and allowing the population of north-western France to live in relative peace. He was probably right. A large number of English soldiers was released as soon as Calais had fallen, including some of the King's own household troops and those of the Prince of Wales. The Flemings were paid off. The French government no doubt learned about all this as it was happening. They replaced their garrisons along the Flemish border and in the towns of Artois and northern Picardy. The rest of the army were withdrawn south by the route on which they had come. When they reached Hesdin on 7 August 1347 Philip dispersed them.[79]

It was an act of folly. As soon as Edward III saw his adversary disarmed he seized his opportunity. All further withdrawals from his army were stopped. Messengers were sent after those who had left, recalling them as soon as they could come. Powerful and damaging raids were launched into the French interior. The Prince of Wales took one large mounted raiding party into Artois. Another, led by Henry of Lancaster, captured the town of Fauquembergues, 30 miles south of Calais, five days after the French army had left it. They burned it to the ground. In high alarm the military governor of Artois left Arras for the north on 15 August, taking with him all the troops that he could find.[80]

It was the same mistake as Philip had made a year earlier, after the battle of Crécy, and it had the same results. Some time before the 18th, Philip VI arrived at Pont-Sainte-Maxence. But instead of resting there from his exertions he was obliged to preside over a fresh general summons. The new army was told to be at Amiens on 1 September, less than a fortnight away. Edward, promptly informed as always of the French King's plans, decided to lead a great *chevauchée* into France as soon as he could. He declared that he would leave Calais with his army at the beginning of September.[81] These ambitious schemes proved to be beyond the capabilities of either side.

Philip VI arrived in Amiens from Pont-Sainte-Maxence early in September to find the turnout poor and the war treasury empty. Morale was exceptionally low. Even in provinces close to Calais, which were directly threatened by the invaders, recruitment had to be backed up with threats of imprisonment and forfeiture among noblemen and commoners alike. In Normandy the collection of the hearth tax destined to pay for the new army encountered serious resistance which in some places had to be suppressed by armed force. Philip put off the date of the muster by a month to 1 October 1347.[82]

The morale of the English was higher, but the date which Edward III had set for his *chevauchée* came and went without movement. His own forces and the resources which sustained them were as exhausted as those of the French. His men had been campaigning now for fifteen months. Their difficulties were beginning to accumulate. The weather was very hot and fresh water hard to come by. Food was still plentiful but future supplies uncertain. In England, where the harvest was late, purveyors were having difficulty in buying grain, and the scale of their past purchases was causing severe local shortages. To these troubles and discomforts were added a variety of administrative burdens which Edward had as usual under-estimated when he made his plans. Getting men quickly back to Calais after they had returned home proved to be slow and difficult. Paying them was an even greater problem. The collection of the second year of the Parliamentary subsidy of 1346 was only just beginning. An attempt was made to anticipate it with a fresh round of forced loans, the third in six months. It was extremely badly received.[83]

At the beginning of September 1347 two incidents occurred which dented the self-confidence of Edward's army and reduced their appetite for long-range raiding. The first was a misfortune which overcame the Earl of Warwick. He was conducting a raid around Saint-Omer with a large troop of English and Flemish soldiers when the garrison of the town, reinforced by its citizens, sortied from the gates and fell on them. They were caught off their guard. In the battle which followed Warwick lost 180 men. The rest of his troops were driven in headlong flight back to Calais. At about the same time a fleet of ten ships from England was sailing unescorted towards Calais with victuals, horses and women coming to join their husbands in the encampments. A short distance from the town they were attacked by a French privateer called Marant, a well-known figure, by profession a pirate from Boulogne, in wartime one of Philip VI's more enterprising sea captains. He captured the entire fleet, scuttling half of it and taking the rest as prize into Abbeville. These were unwelcome signs of the continuing capacity of the French to resist. Both of them owed a good deal to private initiative and virtually nothing to their government's direction of affairs.[84]

When, early in September 1347, the cardinals resumed their labours, they found both sides willing to talk in spite of their public professions of bellicosity. A truce was proposed, to last until 7 July 1348. The terms, like those of the truce of Malestroit, were drawn up by the cardinals themselves. Their clerks laboriously journeyed between Calais and Amiens to humour the grievances and reservations of the two kings. The representatives of both sides met on 28 September to convey their formal assent. The terms naturally favoured the victor in possession. Edward III and his allies maintained their present positions everywhere on the march of Calais, in Flanders, Brittany, Aquitaine and Poitou, in Scotland and even in the county of Burgundy, where the coalition of aristocratic malcontents were dignified as allies of England. The Flemings not only preserved their independence but were granted complete liberty to travel and trade in France, while the Flemish royalists in exile in France were prevented from going back to their homes. Both sides swore not to intrigue with the confederates of the other or to tempt or threaten them, a promise profoundly distasteful to the King of France since it prevented him from punishing or even reconciling the traitors of 1346 and 1347. More than any earlier document of its kind the truce of September 1347 recognized Edward III's position as a power in the domestic politics of France.[85]

The news of the truce was received with mixed feelings in the English camp. Some men thought that they had been poised to win the overwhelming victory which would settle the war on whatever terms they should name. Some thought it was a betrayal of Edward's cause which God had favoured with victories. Some regretted the loot which they would have gained on the proposed *chevauchée* into France. But the malcontents saw only a small part of the effort required to maintain an army in the field. Edward and his councillors were more realistic. The truce was short, only nine months. The possession of Calais would make the revival of the war and the choice of moment easier. Public opinion in England was well enough pleased with the victories already won. It was, said the chronicler, 'like the rising of a new sun.'[86]

Few monuments are more evocative of the self-confidence of these victories than the tomb of Sir Hugh Hastings in Elsing Parish Church, Norfolk. The war had raised Hastings from well-born obscurity to great renown, just as it had done for those other East Anglians, Oliver Ingham and Thomas Dagworth. He had fought under Edward III at Sluys and

Tournai and under Henry of Lancaster at Bergerac and Auberoche. He had commanded the Flemish army on the northern border during the Crécy campaign. He had died, probably of disease contracted in the camp at Calais, four days before the town fell.[87] His brass shows him in full plate armour with helmet and visor, the kind of armour which Jean le Bel had been so impressed to see Englishmen wearing in 1337. His soul is borne up by angels to a mounted and armoured figure of St George, patron of soldiers, of chivalry and, shortly, of the Order of the Garter, the saint whose name had become the English King's war-cry. Around the sides of the brass Sir Hugh's companions in arms mourn his passing: Edward III; the Earl of Lancaster; the earls of Warwick and Pembroke; Ralph, Lord Stafford; Amaury, Lord of Saint-Amand. Here was the idealized English soldier of the 1340s and 1350s: the exhibition of wealth, the pride of caste, the relish for war and the utter confidence in the righteousness of those who fought it. Defeat and disappointment were still far away.

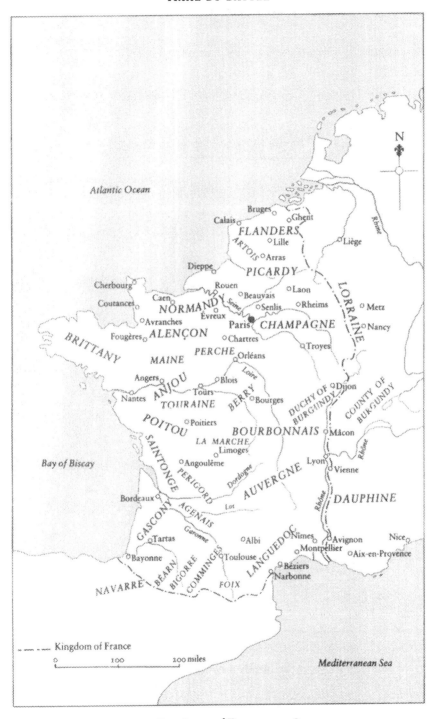

1 Provinces of France, 1328

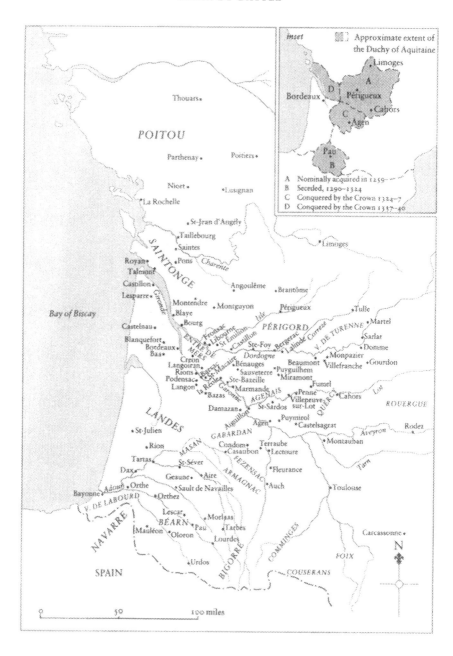

11 South-western France

III England and Wales and the Channel Islands

North Sea

Moray Firth
Forres ○Elgin   Banff
Kinloss
Inverness○   ○Lochindorb
○Lochindorb
○Kildrummy

○Aberdeen
○Dunnotar

Forfar○
Dundee○   ○Arbroath
Perth○   Firth of Tay
Dupplin Moor○ Cupar○ ○St Andrews
FIFE
Stirling○
Dunfermline○   Firth of Forth
Dumbarton○ Linlithgow○   ○Dunbar
Glasgow○ Edinburgh○ Musselburgh
Rothesay○ Bothwell○   Halidon Hill△
Lanark○   ○Peebles   ○Berwick
Islay   ○Selkirk
Arran   Melrose○ ○Roxburgh
ETTRICK   ○Jedburgh

ANNANDALE
○Lochmaben
Dumfries○ ○Annan
GALLOWAY   ○Kirkcudbright

IRELAND   ENGLAND

- - - Boundary of lands ceded by
        Edward Balliol to England
        in 1334
▨ Land over 800 feet
- · - Boundary with England

N

Irish Sea

○————————— 50 miles

IV Scotland

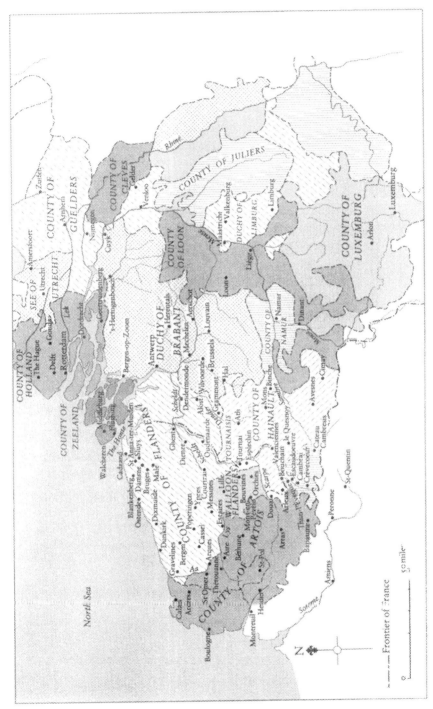

v The Low Countries, 1337–47

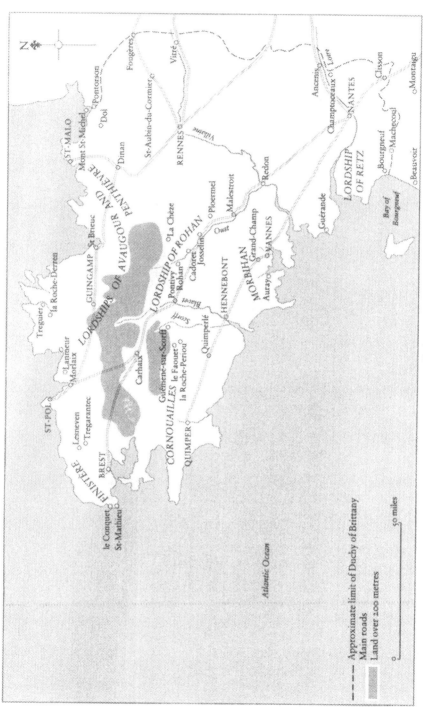

VI Brittany

Atlantic Ocean

- - - Approximate limit of Duchy of Brittany
——— Main roads
▓ Land over 200 metres

0 ————— 50 miles

Abbreviations

Cross-references are to the Bibliography.

ABSHF *Annuaire-Bulletin de la Société de l'Histoire de France*
AD Archives Départmentales
AHG see *Archives historiques . . . de la Gironde*
AHP see *Archives historiques du Poitou*
AHSA see *Archives historiques de la Saintonge . . .*
AHVF see *Atlas historique des villes de France*
AN Archives Nationales (Paris)
AP see *Actes du Parlement de Paris*
BEC *Bibliothèque de l'École des Chartes*
BIHR *Bulletin of the Institute of Historical Research*
BL British Library (London)
BN Bibliothèque Nationale (Paris)
BPH *Bulletin philologique et historique du Comité des Travaux Historiques et Scientifiques*
CCF see *Corpus chronicorum Flandriae*
CCR see *Calendar of close rolls*
CFR see *Calendar of fine rolls*
CIM see *Calendar of inquisitions miscellaneous*
CPR see *Calendar of patent rolls*
DCG see *Documents relatifs au Clos des Galées*
EHR *English Historical Review*
GEC see Cokayne, G. E.
HGL see Vic, C. de and Vaissète, J.
JT see *Journaux du Trésor*
KOF see Froissart, *Œuvres*, ed. Kervyn de Lettenhove [All references are to the documentary appendices]
LC see Philip VI, 'Lettres closes'
LE see *Lettres d'état*
MA *Le moyen age*

PRO	Public Record Office (London)
RBP	see *Register of Edward, the Black Prince*
RDP	see *Reports from the Lords Committees . . .*
RF	see *Foedera . . .*
RH	*Revue historique*
RP	see *Rotuli Parliamentorum*
RS	see *Rotuli Scotiae*
RSG	see *Rekeningen der Stad Gent*
TR	see *Treaty rolls*
TRHS	*Transactions of the Royal Historical Society*
WBN	see *Wardrobe book of William de Norwell*
WSS	see Chaplais, P., *War of Saint-Sardos*

References

Printed sources (Bibliography, Sections B and C) are cited by title or by author/editor and title. Secondary works (Bibliography, Section D) are cited by author alone.

References marked with an asterisk * are to the documentary appendix of the work cited.

CHAPTER I

1 *Louanges de Paris*, 52.
2 *Itinerarium Symonis Semeonis*, ed. M. Esposito (1960), 28–30.
3 *Chron. anon. Par.*, 135–40.
4 Dion, 225.
5 *Layettes du Trésor des Chartes*, iv, ed. E. Berger (1902), no. 5439.
6 Froissart, *Chron.*, i, 117.
7 G. Duby, *L'économie rurale et la vie des campagnes dans l'occident mediévale* (1962), 223–4; Pirenne, i, 263; Fourquin, 106–7.
8 H. van Werveke, 'La famine de l'an 1316 en Flandre', *Revue du Nord*, xli (1959), 5–14; H. S. Lucas, 'The Great European Famine of 1315, 1316, and 1317', *Speculum*, v (1930), 343–77; Desportes, 209–11; Higounet-Nadal, 144–5.
9 H. Laurent, *Un grand commerce d'exportation au moyen age* (1935), 121–2.
10 Laurent, *op.cit.*, 124–6; H. Dubois, *Les foires de Chalon* (1976), 296–309.
11 Joinville, *Hist. de S. Louis*, ed. N. Wailly (1868), 267; *Itinerarium Symonis Symeonis*, ed. M. Esposito (1960), 31; *La Divina Commedia, Inferno*, XXIX:123, ed. N. Sapegno, i (1955), 335n.
12 *Summa curiae regis*, ed. H. Stebbe, *Archiv für kunde osterreichiche Geschichtsquellen*, xiv (1855), 362.
13 Jean de Jandun, *Louanges de Paris*, 60.
14 *Rec. Hist. Fr.*, xxiii, 788–98 (1304); *J. Petit, 395–400 (1323); Contamine (2), 65–74 (1326–40).
15 *Rec. Hist. Fr.*, x, 612.
16 *Coutumes*, ii, 23.
17 E. Martène, *Thesaurus Nov. Anec.*, i (1717), 1331.
18 Digard, *Philippe le Bel et le Saint-Siege*, I (1936), 284.
19 Moranvillé, 'Rapports'; Bautier, 106–7.
20 R. Fédou, *Les hommes de loi Lyonnais* (1964), 34.
21 Lot and Fawtier, ii, 337–8.
22 J. Leclercq, 'Un sermon prononcé pendant la guerre de Flandre', *Revue du moyen age latin*, i (1945), 165–72, esp. 170.
23 Cuttler, 142–6.

24 Henneman, 348; Harriss, 148, 523–5.

25 Henneman, 348.

26 *De regimine judaeorum*, ed. A. P. d'Entrèves, *Selected Political Writings* (1965), 92.

27 Strayer and Taylor, 41.

28 Guilhermoz, 284, 289–99.

29 Strayer and Taylor, 41.

30 E. Petit, *Rec. Anc. Mem.*, 213.

31 *Grandes Chron.*, viii, 299–301.

32 Strayer and Taylor, 58–9.

33 Miskimin, 42–3; Henneman, 331–53.

34 Contamine (1), 137–8, 142–3; Beaumanoir, *Coutumes*, ii, 234; E. Petit, *Rec. Anc. Mem.*, 202; E. Perroy, 'Social Mobility among the French *Noblesse* in the Later Middle Ages', *Études d'histoire mediévale* (1979), 232–5.

35 H. Arbois de Jubainville, *Hist. des ... comtes de Champagne*, iv (1865), 803–11; Guilhermoz, 231–4.

36 *Le mémorial de Robert II duc de Bourgogne*, ed. H. Jassemin (1933), pp. x–xi, xv–xviii; J. Richard, *Les ducs de Bourgogne et la formation du duché* (1954), 317, 364–5, 384–6; J. Petit, 322–5; Cazelles (1), 397.

37 Fourquin, 138–40; *Hist. de la France rurale*, ed. G. Duby and A. Wallon, i (1975), 566–9.

38 A. Brun, *Recherches historiques sur l'introduction du français dans les provinces du Midi* (1923), 29, 31.

39 E. H. Kantorowicz, *The King's Two Bodies* (1957), 250.

40 Jones, 'Documents', 23.

41 P. Jeulin, 'Un grand honneur anglais. Le comte de Richmond', *Annales de Bretagne*, xlii (1935), 265–302; G. A. Knowlson, *Jean V, duc de Bretagne* (1964), 13–15.

42 Lloyd, 6–7, 13, 25–39, 74–5, 99–115.

43 Pirenne, i, 342n.

CHAPTER II

1 *Hist. des ducs de Normandie*, ed. Francisque-Michel (1840), 99–100.

2 Louis: Trokelowe, *Chron.*, ed. H. T. Riley (1866), 79. Glastonbury: R. S. Loomis, 'Edward I, Arthurian Enthusiast', *Speculum*, xxviii (1953), 114–27. Pope: *RF*, i, 932–4. Language: *RF*, i, 827.

3 Froissart, *Chron.*, i, 306.

4 Higden, *Polychron.*, ed. C. Babington, ii (1869), 157–63.

5 Bel, *Chron.*, i, 47.

6 Lloyd, 64–5, 123. *Chron. mon. Melsa*, iii, 48.

7 Froissart, *Chron.*, i, 215.

8 *Red Book of the Exchequer*, ed. H. Hall, iii (1896), 960.

9 Fortescue, *Governance*, 119.

10 Prestwich (1), 206–8.

11 E. B. and N. M. Fryde, 457–8.

12 *Documents Illustrating the Crisis of 1297–98*, ed. M. Prestwich (1980), 159.

13 *Mirror of Justices*, ed. W. J. Whittaker (1895), 155.

14 Froissart, *Chron.*, i, 214; Fortescue, *Governance*, 141.

15 Maddicott (1), 22–3; *Vita Edwardi*, 29.

16 N. Saul, 69, 266; Smyth, i, 304.

17 *Chron.*, i, 257.

18 Philips, 242–5.

19 *Song of Lewes*, l.872, ed. C. L. Kingsford (1890), 28.

20 *Statutes*, i, 15.
21 Maddicott (1), 329–30.
22 Willard and Morris, i, 102–3; N. Saul, 174–5.
23 *Vita Edwardi*, 38.
24 Guisborough, *Chron.*, 289–90.
25 *Statutes*, i, 159.
26 Gilles le Bouvier, *Le Livre de description des pays*, E.-T. Hamy (1908), 119–20.
27 *Ann. Waverley*, ed. H. R. Luard, *Ann. monastici*, ii (1865), 409.
28 Bel, *Chron.*, i, 49.
29 *Vita Edwardi*, 55–6.
30 *Chron. Lanercost*, 242–4; *Brut*, i, 218.
31 *RS*, i, 208.
32 Morris (5), 77–93; Morris (3).
33 Powicke, 189–94.
34 Petrarch, *Le familiari*, XXII:14, ed. V. Rossi, iv (1942), 138; Bel, *Chron.*, i, 155–6; Richard of Bury, *Philobiblon*, ed. M. Maclagan (1960), 106.

CHAPTER III

1 Dion, 365–83; James, 9–10; *RP*, ii, 296.
2 Froissart, *Chron.*, xii, 206; *RF*, i, 554.
3 Renouard (2), 225–8; Boutruche, 81n.
4 Dion, 380–4, 391–2; Renouard (2), 60–3; Champollion-Figeac, *Lettres*, i, 387–8.
5 Guisborough, *Chron.*, 219; *Rôles Gascons 1307–17*, 573; Harriss, 523.
6 TR, i, 37–40; *Registrum epistolarum . . . Johannis Peckham*, ed. C. T. Martin, i (1882), 5; *Purgatorio*, VII:130–2.
7 *RF*, i, 571, 672.
8 *Hist. de St. Louis*, ed. N. de Wailly (1867), 678–9.
9 Trabut-Cussac, 32–4.
10 Gavrilovitch, 69–70, 78–82; Trabut-Cussac, pp. xxi, xxiv.
11 Gardelles, 28–30, 32 and Map II.
12 *Black, 523.
13 Trabut-Cussac, 42–4, 49–52; *RF*, i, 602–3 (notaries); Tucoo-Chala (2), 61–75.
14 *Textes rél. à l'hist. du Parlement*, 121, 145–9; *Rôles Gascons*, iii, pp. xxxii, lv; Renouard (2), 123–4.
15 *Gascon Reg. A*, 206–17.
16 *Olim*, ii, 3–19; *RF*, i, 800; J. Petit, 27–8.
17 *RF*, i. 794–5, 800; Champollion-Figeac, *Lettres*, i. 406–8, 424–9; Chaplais (2), 272; Rishanger, *Chron.*, ed. H. T. Riley (1865), 137–8; Guisborough, *Chron.*, 241–3.
18 Prestwich (1), 171–2.
19 *Rôles Gascons*, iii, pp. cxxxiii–clxvi.
20 Rothwell; *Chaplais (1), 210–1; G. Digard, *Philippe le Bel et le Saint-Siège*, i (1936), 304–7.
21 *Black, 523.
22 Nangis, *Chron.*, i, 324–5; *RF*, i, 952–3; Renouard (2), 206–7.
23 Trabut-Cussac, 111–2, 116–7. Mauléon: *RF*, II, 4. Saintonge, Landes, Bordelais: *Gascon Reg. A*, 38–65, 245–67, 276–311. Defections: *Rôles Gascons*, iii, nos 4059–60. 'No king': PRO, SC1/55/23.
24 Burnell: *RF*, i, 665. Martel: Cuttino, 'Memorandum Book', 96–100.
25 Chaplais (4), 139–40.
26 TR, i, 166–7; *Déprez (1), 20n; Chaplais (4), 144–5, 153–4.
27 Cuttino (2), 87–100; Chaplais (2), 280–4.

28 Chaplais (5), 454, 459–60, 465–6, *469; *Gascon Reg. A*, 679–80; *Doc. rél. à l'Agenais*, ed. E. Langlois (1890), 299–300.

29 *Doc. Pontificaux*, i, 207–11, 213–5; *RF*, ii, 176–7; *AP 1254–1328*, nos 5823–4, 7265; *Textes rél. à l'hist. du Parlement*, 187–98; Champollion-Figeac, *Lettres*, ii, 46–7.

30 Champollion-Figeac, *Lettres*, ii, 40, 54; Gavrilovitch, 102; *RF*, ii, 270.

31 *WSS* 38–9; *RF*, ii, 334.

32 *CCR 1318–23*, 715–6, 721, 722; *AP 1254–1328*, no. 6781.

33 *Rôles Gascons 1307–17*, nos 713–15, 734–5, 797–800, 1081, 1169, 1185; *TR*, i, n. 204–5; PRO SC8/9418, 11657, 11659; Marquette, 420–57.

34 Tucoo-Chala (2), 73–4, 159–60.

35 Gardelles, 217; *WSS*, 91–2, 149–50.

36 *Rôles Gascons 1307–17*, nos 1131–4; *Doc. Pontificaux*, i, 69–71, 119–20; *RF*, ii, 418, 547–8; *Livre des Bouillons*, 169–71. Seneschals: T. F. Tout, *The Place of the Reign of Edward II in English History* (1934), 394–6.

37 *WSS*, pp. x–xi, 253–6; *AP 1254–1328*, ii, nos 5466, 6498, 6980.

38 *WSS*, pp. xi, 1, 8, 36.

39 *WSS*, 3–6, 8, 9, 11–12.

40 *WSS*, 11, 15–17, 22–4, 26–38, 39–41, 186.

41 *RF*, ii, 547; *WSS*, 25, 181–4.

42 *Cal. Pap. R. Letters*, ii, 454; Cheyette, 'Professional Papers', 407–9; *WSS*, 184–7; *RF*, ii, 554–5.

43 *WSS*, 188n.

44 *CPR 1321–4*, 425, 426, 427; *WSS*, 189–92; Cheyette, 'Professional Papers', 410–11; Phillips, 233–4; *RF*, ii, 558–9, 563.

45 *WSS*, 5, 21–2, 49–52, 61–5, 81–2, 101, 153; *RF*, ii, 583–4, 600; Nangis, *Chron.*, ii, 57–9; *Chron. anon. Par.*, 94–6.

46 *WSS*, 131, 151, 154–5, 156–7, 160–2.

47 Coville (2), 266.

48 *WSS*, 195–6; *Cal. Pap. R. Letters*, ii, 463–4. On Isabella and Mortimer: *RF*, ii, 569; Baker, *Chron.*, 15–16, 17; *Fr. Chron. London*, 48; *Chron. Lanercost*, 254; *Vita Edwardi*, 135.

49 *WSS*, 209–10, 222.

50 *WSS*, 202–3; *CPR 1330–4*, 91; *RF*, ii, 601–3.

CHAPTER IV

1 Chaplais (4), 156n; *RF*, ii, 603–4, 605–8; Murimuth, *Chron.*, 44.

2 *WSS*, 243–5, 267–9; Murimuth, *Chron.*, 45–6; Baker, *Chron.*, 20; *Vita Edwardi*, 142; *RF*, ii, 615–6, 623, 630–1.

3 *Vita Edwardi*, 143; *RF*, ii, 615, 622–3, 630, 631; Bel. *Chron.*, i, 12–13.

4 *Chron. anon. Par.*, 104–7; AN JJ 74/577; *RF*, ii, 638.

5 *KOF*, ii, 502–3; *Chronographia*, i, 280.

6 Pipewell chron. quoted in M. V. Clarke, *Medieval Representation and Consent* (1936), 183; Nangis, *Chron.*, ii, 78–9; *Chron. anon. Par.*, 111; Walsingham, *Hist.*, i, 178; *Cal. Pap. R. Letters*, ii, 479; *HGL*, ix, 439–41, 443–4; x, 662–7*; *RF*, ii, 700–1 (treaty).

7 Nangis, *Chron.*, ii, 82–4; *Grandes Chron.*, ix, 72–3, 330–1; Viollet, 125–54; *Confessions*, 46–7, 48 (Flemings).

8 *Chron.*, i, 303.

9 Cazelles (1), 44.

10 Cazelles (1), 71–2.

11 Miret y Sans, 'Negociacions', 327.

12 *KOF*, xviii, 246; Murimuth, *Chron.*, 94; *RF*, ii, 743; *CPR 1327–30*, 338; Nangis, *Chron.*, ii, 105; *Grandes Chron.*, ix, 338.

13 Nangis, *Chron.*, ii, 106; *Grandes Chron.*, ix, 339; Froissart, *Chron.*, i, 90–2; *RF*, ii, 760.

14 *RF*, ii, 761, 765; for the assurances, see the proceedings of April and May 1330, *ibid.*, 791–2. Tournament: *Chronographia*, ii, 12.

15 *RF*, ii, 775, 783, 784, 789; *LE*, no. 25; *Annales Londinienses*, ed. W. Stubbs, *Chronicles of the Reigns of Edward I and Edward II*, i (1882), 247–9.

16 *RF*, ii, 793–4, 797; Mirot and Déprez, *Ambassades*, no. 15.

17 Mirot and Déprez, *Ambassades*, nos 16–17; *CCR 1330–3*, 153; *RF*, ii, 798–9.

18 Nangis, *Chron.*, ii, 122.

19 *Chrons. Abrégées*, in *KOF*, xvii, 2.

20 *RP*, ii, 52–3; Gray, *Scalacronica*, 157.

21 *RF*, ii, 799.

22 Tout (1), v, 247–50.

23 Déprez (1), 71; *RF*, ii, 805–6, 813; Mirot and Déprez, *Ambassades*, no. 21; *CCR 1330–3*, 298; *CPR 1330–4*, 90–5; PRO C47/28/5, 6, C47/30/2(4); Murimuth, *Chron.*, 63.

24 *RF*, ii, 815–8; PRO C47/28/2(10); Murimuth, *Chron.*, 63; *Chron. anon. Par.*, 145; Miret y Sans, 'Negociacions', 69–71; Nangis, *Chron.*, ii, 143.

25 *RP*, ii, 60–1.

26 *WSS*, 130, 176; *RF*, ii, 791, 899; *CPR 1330–4*, 90.

27 BN Ms Lat 3293, fol. 244vo.

28 Cuttino (2), 29–61.

29 Chaplais, *Dipl. Practice*, 306.

30 *RP*, ii, 65; *CPR 1330–4*, 223–4; John XXII, *Lettres*, nos 4109, 5321 (col. 126); PRO C47/28/5 (17, 18, 36, 41, 44, 50), C47/28/9(2), C47/30/7(9) (memoranda).

CHAPTER V

1 *Anglo-Scottish Relations, 1174–1328: Some Selected Documents*, ed. E. L. G. Stones (1965), 161–70; Nicholson (1), 54–6; *Brut*, 251 (tears).

2 Fordun, *Chron.*, i, 354.

3 Nicholson (1), 72–90.

4 *Chron. Lanercost*, 267; *Chron. Melsa*, ii, 362–3; Baker, *Chron.*, 49; *Brut*, 275; Capgrave, *Liber*, 167–8; *RF*, ii, 833, 847–8.

5 *RP*, ii, 66–7; Nicholson (1), 92–4, 96–7.

6 *RF*, ii, 847–8.

7 *Illustrations of Scottish History*, ed. J. Stevenson (1834), 50–4; Gray, *Scalacronica*, 161; *RP*, ii, 67.

8 Nicholson (1), 103–4.

9 *RP*, ii, 69; Gray, *Scalacronica*, 162.

10 *CCR 1333–7*, 109, 113, 129–30, 173–4, 294–5; Tout (1), iii, 56–63.

11 Nicholson (1), 119–38.

12 Murimuth, *Chron.*, 68.

13 Wyntoun, *Cron.*, ii, 404.

14 *RF*, ii, 876–8, 888; Murimuth, *Chron.*, 71; Nicholson (1), 162.

15 Nicholson (1), 139–40.

16 Minot, *Poems*, 1; *Ann. Paulini*, 358–9.

17 Viard (12); Déprez (1), 99; Delaville le Roulx, *La France en Orient*, i (1886), 86–102; Nangis, *Chron.*, ii, 130–1, 134–5, 144, 145.

18 *RF*, ii, 860. The first letter was presumably received at York in January 1333, for a messenger (probably bearing the reply) left for Paris on 7 February 1333: PRO E372/178, m. 42 (Corder).

19 *Déprez (1), 91n; *RF*, ii, 860.

20 Nangis, *Chron.*, ii, 139–40; *DCG*, ii, no. XXIX.
21 PRO SC1/37/134; *Grandes Chron.*, ix, 134.
22 *Ann. Paulini*, 359; *Exch. R. Scot.*, 449, 464; *Grandes Chron.*, ix, 140–1; Nangis, *Chron.*, ii, 141–2.
23 *RF*, ii, 883; PRO E372/179, m. 34 (Stratford); *Grandes Chron.*, ix, 142–3; *Chronographia*, ii, 23; *Cal. Pap. R. Letters*, ii, 584.
24 *Exch. R. Scot.*, i, 449, 450, 456, 464, 465, 466, 479, 506.
25 Baker, *Chron.*, 55–6; *Grandes Chron.*, ix, 143; Benedict XII, *Reg.* (France), no. 90.
26 Cuttino (1); Cuttino (2), 101–10. New commissioners: PRO C47/28/3(11), C47/30/3(15); *RF*, ii, 887.
27 *RF*, ii, 609–10; PRO C61/46, m. 2, C47/30/3(10–12), C47/32/15; cf. PRO C47/27/13(40) (Sept. 1335).
28 *Déprez (1), 407.
29 *CRP 1330–4*, 94. Earlier restraint: PRO C47/30/2(4), C47/28/3(3).
30 Wyntoun, *Cron.*, ii, 414–17; *Chron. Lanercost*, 278; Gray, *Scalacronica*, 164.
31 *RS*, i, 276; *Bridlington Chron.*, 119–20; *Chron. mon. Melsa.*, ii, 372; Gray, *Scalacronica*, 164; Fordun, *Chron.*, i, 357–8.
32 *CFR 1327–37*, 342, 354, 355, 365 (duties); *CCR 1333–7*, 7, 51; Nicholson (1), 115; Harriss, 224.
33 Lay subsidy: *RP*, ii, 447; *Ann. Paulini*, 362; *CPR 1334–8*, 38–40; Willard (2), 345; Willard and Morris, ii, 205–6. Clerical subsidy: *ibid.*, ii, 229–30. Bardi: *CCR 1333–7*, 345, 446, 456–7.
34 *Chron. Lanercost*, 223, 278–9; *Chron. mon. Melsa.*, ii, 373; *Ann. Paulini*, 362–3; *Bridlington Chron.*, 120–1. Reinforcement: *RS*, i, 296, 304–5, 316, 321. Numbers: Nicholson (1), 174–81.
35 *Chron. mon. Melsa.*, ii, 374; *RF*, ii, 899; *Nicholson (1)., 240–1; *Cal. doc. Scot.*, v, no. 734. Bp Avranches: Cazelles (1), 137–8.
36 *Bridlington Chron.*, 121; Fordun, *Chron.*, i, 358; Baker, *Chron.*, 56; *RS*, i, 322–3, 327, 334; *RF*, ii, 904.
37 Fordun, *Chron.*, i, 358; Wyntoun, *Cron.*, ii, 421; *Exch. R. Scot.*, i, 435 *et seq.*
38 *CCR 1333–7*, 468, 469–70; *RS*, i, 352–4.
39 *RS*, i, 350; Fordun, *Chron.*, i, 358.
40 *Bridlington Chron.*, 122; Baker, *Chron.*, 56; *RF*, ii, 908.
41 Nicholson (1), 196–206.
42 Cazelles (1), 93–4, 115–22, 412–3.
43 *Chron. anon. Par.*, 164–5; Nangis, *Chron.*, ii, 145–8; *Grandes Chron.*, ix, 148–50
44 Benedict XII, *Reg.* (France), no. 90 (col. 55); *CPMR*, 92–3; *Chron. anon. Par.*, 164; *Bridlington Chron.*, 124–6.
45 *Exch. R. Scot.*, i, 449, 464. Grants: David II, *Acts*, nos 23–4. Supplies: *RS*, i, 320–1, 322; *CCR 1333–7*, 414, 425.
46 *RF*, ii, 912–3; *CCR 1333–7*, 462, 484–5, 620.
47 *RS*, i, 363–7, 371–4; *RF*, ii, 911–2, 915, 917, 919; *CCR 1333–7*, 411, 426, 434, 435, 521; *CPR 1334–8*, 163, 206, 208.
48 *Chron. Lanercost*, 283.
49 *RF*, ii, 920; *RS*, i, 378; *Chron. Lanercost*, 283.
50 *Bridlington Chron.*, 123–4; Fordun, *Chron.*, i, 359; *Chron. Lanercost*, 282–3; *RF*, ii, 923.
51 Avesbury, *G. Edwardi*, 298–300; *Chron. mon. Melsa.*, ii, 376; Gray, *Scalacronica*, 166; *RS*, i, 381, 388.
52 Nicholson (1), 218–24.
53 Fordun, *Chron.*, i, 357, 359–60; Wyntoun, *Cron.*, ii, 398, 417; *RF*, ii, 856.
54 *RS*, i, 384–7; *RF*, ii, 925, 928, 930, 930–1, 933.

55 Fordun, *Chron.*, i, 359–60; Wyntoun, *Cron.*, 422–7; *Chron. Lanercost*, 284
56 Fordun, *Chron.*, i, 360; Wyntoun, *Chron.*, ii, 428, 436; *RF*, ii, 930–933.
57 *RS*, i, 280–1; *RF*, ii, 924; Nicholson (1), 223, 225–6.
58 *RS*, i, 409; *Chron. Lanercost*, 284.

CHAPTER VI

1 John XXII, *Reg. (France)*, no. 4173.
2 Mollat, 77; Benedict XII, *Reg. (France)*, nos 44, 103.
3 John XXII, *Reg. (France)*, no. 90.
4 Benedict XII, *Reg. (France)*, no. 89, *Reg. (Autres pays)*, nos 467–73. Hugh: John XXII, *Reg. (France)*, nos. 3934, 3939, 3989–90, 4238, 5503, 5519, 5542–3; *RF*, ii, 601; *WSS*, 191–2, 197, 204–7; *Cal. Pap. R. Letters*, ii, 455, 462–7, 469–71, 474–9, 481–2 (he was bishop of Orange until 1328).
5 * Déprez (1), 118n; *RF*, ii, 925–6, 928, 930–1; *RS*, i, 390, 393, 394–5.
6 *Chron. Lanercost*, 284–5; *Bridlington Chron.*, 127; Knighton, *Chron.*, 477; Fordun, *Chron.*, i, 360. Movements of negotiators: *RS*, i, 395–6, 397–8; *RF*, ii, 930.
7 *RF*, ii, 936, 1110; Benedict XII, *Reg. (France)*, no. 167; Knighton, *Chron.*, 477. Subsidy: Murimuth, *Chron.*, 77.
8 *Vitae paparum*, i, 221; Ellis, *Orig. Letters*, i, 30; Benedict XII, *Reg. (Autres pays)*, no. 786, *Reg. (France)*, no. 210; *Vat. Akten, no. 1812*; *Grandes Chron.*, ix, 153.
9 Ellis, *Orig. Letters*, i, 30; AN P2291, p. 219; AN JJ74/74; E. Petit, *Rec. Anc. Mem.*, 204–10.
10 Roncière, i, 189–210, 333–63, 403–9; *DCG*, 27, 31–2 and nos 122, 124, 126.
11 Roncière, i, 390.
12 E. Petit, *Rec. Anc. Mem.*, 204–10.
13 *RF*, ii, 936; BL Cotton Nero C.VIII, fols 240–241, 259–260.
14 *Chron. Lanercost*, 285–6; BL Cotton Nero C.VIII, fol. 276vo.
15 BL Cotton Nero C.VIII, fol. 251; *RS*, i, 411, 414, 416, 417; Ellis, *Orig. Letters*, i, 33; Gray, *Scalacronica*, 166; Wyntoun, Cron., ii, 422–3.
16 BL Cotton Nero C.VIII, fol. 276vo; *RS*, i, 420–5; Ellis, *Orig. Letters*, i, 30–2.
17 *Actes normands*, 142, 144, 146–51; ANJJ74/74; *Chron. anon. Par.*, 165; *RF*, ii, 941; *Exch. R. Scot*, i, 451, 453, 454
18 Coinage: *Ordonnances*, ii, 42, vi, pp.* i–ii; *Rec. doc. monnaies*, i. 49, 219; *Chron. anon. Par.*, 169. Benedict XII, *Reg. (France)*, no. 240; Henneman, 111–2, 350-1
19 *RF*, ii, 940; BL Cotton Nero C.VIII, fols 241–242vo, 243, 243vo–244, 259; Ellis, *Orig. Letters*, i, 34–8; *Cal. doc. Scot.*, v, no. 758; Fordun, *Chron.*, i, 360–1; Baker, *Chron.*, 57; *Chron. Lanercost*, 286–7; Murimuth, *Chron.*, 77; Gray, *Scalacronica*, 166; Wyntoun, *Chron.* ii, 428–31; *Chron. mon. Melsa*, ii, 377; *Anonimalle Chron.*, 7; Knighton, *Chron.*, i, 477.
20 *RF*, ii, 944–5.
21 Scotland: Ellis, *Orig. Letters*, i, 38–9; BL Cotton Nero C.VIII, fol. 240; *Chron. Lanercost*, 287; Fordun, *Chron.*, i, 361. Embassy: *RF*, ii, 941–2; PRO E101/311/120. Galleys: *RS*, i, 438, 440–1, 442.
22 Usomare: *CPR 1307–13*, 378; Lodge, 230–1. Fieschi: *CCR 1313–18*, 589; *CPR 1317–21*, 10. Nicolino: AN J497/11; *RF*, ii, 937, 941, 947; *CPR 1334–8*, 328–9; *CCR 1333–7*, 733.
23 Chaplais, *Dipl. Practice*, 779–80; *RF*, ii, 944–5.
24 *CCR 1337–9*, 43–5; *RS*, i, 450–1, 453.
25 PRO E372/184, m. 39 (Say); PRO E101/19/35; *RS*, i, 419, 427, 438, 440–1, 442, 446, 451.
26 Chaplais, *Dipl. Practice*, 780–1; BL Cotton Nero C.VIII, fols 241–242vo.

27 *RS*, i, 443, 455, 459–60, 463.
28 Taxes: *CCR 1337–9*, 16–17, 118; *Chron. Lanercost*, 287; Knighton, *Chron.*, i, 477. Loans: *CCR 1337–9*, 4, 9–10, 14; *CPR 1334–8*, 322, 332; E. Fryde (9), 48. Crews, levies: *RS*, i, 454–5. Crusade chests: Déprez (1), 131–2; *Bridlington Chron.*, 128; Murimuth, *Chron.*, 78.
29 Bautier, 'Inventaires', no. 202; *RF*, ii, 948.
30 *Chron. Lanercost*, 287–8; Gray, *Scalacronica*, 166–7; BL Cotton Nero C.VIII, fol. 243; Fordun, *Chron.*, i, 361–2, 363; Wyntoun, *Chron.*, ii, 438–9.
31 *RS*, i, 455–6, 457, 466, 467; *RF*, ii, 946, 947; *CCR 1333–7*, 724–5.
32 *RS*, i, 442–3, 452, 457–8, 469–70; E372/184, m. 39 (Say); PRO E101/19/35.
33 *RF*, ii, 953; *CIM*, ii, no. 1588; *RS*, i, 467–8.
34 PRO C47/28/4(4, 6), C47/28/5(46), C47/30/5(14, 17–9), C47/32/14. Blanquefort: *RF*, ii, 936; *AHG*, iv, 91–5. La Sauve: *AP 1328–50*, no. 1246. Saintes: PRO C61/48, m. 5. Blaye: PRO C61/46, m. 8, C61/47, m. 4; BN Coll. Moreau 649, fol. 67. St-Macaire: PRO C61/49, m. 40.
35 *AP 1328–50*, nos 915, 1699, 1709; PRO C47/28/4(8–11), C47/28/5(45–6), C47/30/5(1); *Chron. Norm.*, 37–8; *Chronographia*, ii, 25–6.
36 Foix: AN J332/17; AD Pyr.-Atl. E392. Saintonge: Dupont-Ferrier, v, no. 20061.
37 PRO C61/48, m. 7; Gardelles, 42–3.
38 Benedict XII, *Reg. (France)*, no. 240, 251–2, 260, 264, 280.
39 *Chron.*, i, 100.
40 Nangis, *Chron.*, ii, 111, 124, 126–30, 132–3; *Grandes Chron.*, ix, 126–8, 132; *Chron. anon. Par.*, 156–9; *Chron. Norm.*, 37; *Récits d'un bourgeois*, 156; Cazelles (1), 75–90, 101–2; Lucas, 126–8.
41 Bel, *Chron.*, i, 107–8; *KOF*, ii, 523, xviii, 31; *CPR 1334–8*, 322, 327; *CCR 1337–9*, 24, 36, 42.
42 Benedict XII, *Reg. (France)*, no. 242; *Déprez (1), 414–5.
43 *RF*, ii, 963; *HGL*, x, 795–6; *Chron. Lanercost*, 288; *LC*, no. 69.
44 Jusselin, 'Comment la France se préparait', 234–6.
45 Brooks, 138–9, 148–53.
46 Prestwich (1), 138–9; *RF*, ii, 313.
47 *RS*, i, 115, 116–7; Nicholas, i, 339; *CPR 1330–4*, 258.
48 BL Cotton Nero C.VIII, fols 264–264vo; *RS*, i, 409, 424, 442; *CCR 1333–7*, 692. PRO E403/282, m. 14 (*Cog Edward*).
49 Cinque Ports: Brooks, 79–120; PRO SC1/40/89; *CCR 1341–3*, 263. And Yarmouth: Prestwich (1), 142–8; *WBN*, 366–8, 379–82; *CIM*, iii, no. 14.
50 *CIM*, iii, no. 14.
51 *RS*, i, 474–5, 476–8; *CCR 1333–7*, 737; *RF*, ii, 956.
52 *RF*, ii, 958; *CPR 1334–8*, 341; *CCR 1337–9*, 48; *RS*, i, 482, 483, 484.
53 *RS*, i, 482.
54 *RS*, i, 483, 485; *Bridlington Chron.*, 128; Fordun, *Chron.*, i, 362; *Chron. Lanercost*, 288; *Chron. mon. Melsa*, ii, 378; Wyntoun, *Cron.*, ii, 435.
55 Subsidy: *RDP*, iv, 460–1; *Chron. Lanercost*, 288, 288–9; *RS*, i, 486–7. PRO C61/49, m. 22vo (terms); *CCR 1337–9*, 118.
56 *RF*, ii, 799–800.
57 *Ann. Paulini*, 354–5.
58 Willard and Morris, i, 341; Nicholson (1), 246–54; Morris (5), 93–4.
59 Morgan, 45.
60 Lucas, 182–3.
61 Bel, *Chron.*, i, 155–6; Henry of Grosmont, *Livre*, 72, 77.
62 *Chron. Lanercost*, 288; *Chron. mon. Melsa.*, ii, 379; *Bridlington Chron.*, 128; Murimuth, *Chron.*, 78; *Ann. Paulini*, 366; *CPR 1334–8*, 400, 416–8, 426; Tout (1), iii,

63n; Gray, *Scalacronica*, 167; *RDP*, v, 27–9 (quotation).
63 'Itin. Philippe VI'; *RF*, ii, 966, 995. *Arrière-ban*: *HGL*, x, 764–5; *Arch. admin. Reims*, ii, 782.

CHAPTER VII

1 Pirenne, ii, 65.
2 Froissart, *Chron.*, i, 369; Pirenne, ii, 94 (brutes).
3 Lucas, 113–24, 145–66 (Brabant); Benedict XII, *Reg. (France)*, nos 178, 280.
4 PRO C47/30/4(12, 16–18).
5 *CCR 1337–9*, 44–5; *Chronographia*, ii, 42; *RF*, ii, 948.
6 *RF*, ii, 943, 954–5; *CPR 1334–8*, 315, 333, 337, 340, 351; Lloyd, 144–5; Lucas, 200–2, 219–20.
7 Offler, 615–6; Lucas, 196; Dubrulle, 279–81.
8 Viard (7); Lucas, 196; *KOF*, xviii, 137; *Récits d'un bourgeois*, 74–5; Froissart, *Chron.*, i, 366.
9 John: *CCR 1333–7*, 37–8, 77–8, 200, 265, 345. Juliers: Bock, *Quellen*, nos 36, 44, 100, 106, 128, 153. Woume: *KOF*, xviii, 50–5; *CCR 1333–7*, 110–11, 366, 732; *CPR 1334–8*, 416; PRO E372/182, m. 46 (Woume). Thrandeston: *CPR 1334–8*, 167; *KOF*, xviii, 154–65. Others: e.g. *TR*, ii, 19–20.
10 *KOF*, xviii, 154–8; *RF*, ii, 952, 955; *WBN*, 218–19; *Trautz*, 424–5 (Maldon). Expenditure: *CCR 1333–7*, 640; *CCR 1337–9*, 14–15; Bock, *Quellen*, no. 504.
11 Benedict XII, *Reg. (France)*, no. 341; *Récits d'un bourgeois*, 74–5.
12 *Chronographia*, ii, 32; *Récits d'un bourgeois*, 158; *KOF*, xviii, 158–9.
13 *KOF*, xviii, 158; Bock, *Quellen*, no. 180; *CPR 1334–8*, 416; *RF*, ii, 966–7. Burghersh: Knighton, *Chron.*, ii, 17; Murimuth, *Chron.*, 120.
14 *CIM*, ii, no. 1580; *CCR 1337–9*, 63, 86; *RF*, ii, 968; Bel, *Chron.*, i, 124–5; Klerk, *Van den derden Eduwaert*, 311–12.
15 Bel, *Chron.*, i, 126; *Chronographia*, ii, 32; *Istore de Flandre*, i, 360; *Gedenkwaardigheden Gesch. Gelderland*, i, 368–9; *KOF*, xviii, 30–3. Robert's knight: *CPR 1334–8*, 416.
16 *Chronographia*, ii, 43–4; *Récits d'un bourgeois*, 159. Letter: AN J440/54.
17 *LC*, no. 71; *Arch. admin. Reims*, ii, 781–4; BN Fr. n.a. 7413, fol. 172 (Eu); *KOF*, xviii, 34–7.
18 *Chron. Lanercost*, 291; *Bridlington Chron.*, 124; Walsingham, *Hist.*, i, 198; *CPR 1334–8*, 513, 579; *CCR 1337–9*, 172; PRO E372/182, m. 48 (Ambrose Newburgh); Lennel, i, 79.
19 *TR*, ii, 4–5, 7–8, 8–9, 10, 11–12.
20 Bel. *Chron.*, i, 125; *TR*, ii, 16–18; *KOF*, xviii, 18–19; *RF*, ii, 959, 966, 974–5; PRO E101/20/16. Recruitment: PRO C61/49, mm. 23, 27, 28.
21 *Vat. Akten*, no. 1831; *Trautz*, 425.
22 S. Riezler, 'Urkunden zur bayerischen und deutschen Geschichte, 1256–1343', *Forschungen zur deutschen Geschichte*, xx (1880), 268–71; Schwalm, 'Reiseberichte', 345; *Gedenkwaardigheden Gesch. Gelderland*, i, 361; *TR*, ii, 1–2. These reflect an earlier agreement known in France by 28 June (*Cordey*, 286) and in England by 12 July (*TR*, ii, 2–4).
23 *TR*, ii, 2–4, 5–7, 13–15; BL Cotton Nero C.VIII, fol. 263. Oath: *Chronographia*, ii, 34.
24 *TR*, ii, 1–4, 5–7, 12–5, 18–9, 23–7, 27–9, 30–1.
25 *KOF*, xviii, 38; Bock, *Quellen*, no. 505; *TR*, ii, 2–4, 5–7; Riezler, *op.cit.* (n. 22), 268–71.
26 Roncière, i, 396; *RF*, ii, 977, 981–2, 983; PRO C61/49, mm. 18, 21, 22, 22d, 29d; PRO E372/182, m. 42 (Roos); *KOF*, xviii, 52; *CCR 1337–9*, 159; *Lit. Cant.*, ii, 158–9.

Army: BL Cotton Nero C.VIII, fols 246vo, 263–263vo.

27 GEC, vii, 58–60; Knighton, *Chron.*, ii, 1; PRO SC1/38/176 (jail); *WSS*, 50, 148, 260–6; Walsingham, *Hist.*, i, 178; PRO C61/43, m. 10 (reappointment).

28 *WSS*, 80, 217–8; PRO C61/42, m. 9, C61/46, m. 7; *RF*, ii, 963.

29 PRO E101/166/11, 12, E101/167/3, E404/508.

30 BN Coll. Périgord 10, fols 190–1.

31 PRO C61/52, mm. 7, 2, C61/54, m. 23, C61/55, m. 10, C61/57, m. 6; *RF*, ii, 1236; Guinodie, ii, 482.

32 PRO C61/45, m. 6.

33 Saintes: *RF*, ii, 816–17, 821, 832; PRO C61/46, m. 1; *Grandes Chron.*, ix, 156–7; no garrison pay recorded in PRO E101/166/11. Talmont: PRO C61/50, m. 5; BN Fr. 32510, fol. 140. Montendre: *Confessions*, 165–6, 167. Bourg: PRO C61/50, m. 3. Blaye: *AHG*, iv, 95–7; PRO C61/49, mm. 5, 39, C61/50, m. 12, E101/166/11, mm. 13, 41.

34 *WSS*, 50, 104; PRO C61/49, m. 4. Englishmen: PRO C61/45, m. 6; C61/46, m. 1.

35 PRO C61/49, mm. 38, 38d, 37, 36, 36d; *RF*, ii, 974. Burghersh: *CPR 1334–8*, 403. Opposition: PRO C47/28/5(41).

36 PRO C61/49, mm. 40d, 38d, 34, 34d, 33d, 32d, 31d, 29, 22; *RF*, ii, 974.

37 PRO C61/49, mm. 28, 27, 26d, 23, 23d, 22d. Norwich: GEC, ix, 762–5; McFarlane, 165–6.

38 *Cordey, 286.

39 AN J635/10.

40 BN Fr.n.a. 7413, fols 190–214; BN Fr. 20685, pp. 247–57; BN Coll. Doat 164, fols 154–155. 21,000: Jusselin, 'Comment la France se préparait', 226–8.

41 Villeneuve: AN J880/14; BN Fr. 20685, p. 256 (not previously in English hands: *WSS*, 261, 264, 265). Puymirol: *Chron. Norm.*, 207–9; *AHG*, xxxiii, 91–2; AN JJ73/93.

42 St-Macaire: *Chron. anon. Par.*, 170–1; BN Coll. Doat, 164, fol. 158; *HGL*, x, 827–8; PRO C61/50, m. 1. Tastes, Pommiers: BN Fr. 20685, p. 256; the latter was under siege on 3 and 26 Aug., *Ordonnances*, iv, 39, AN JJ71/32. Civrac: AN JJ82/332.

43 BN Coll. Doat 164, fols 158–9, 164, 165–7; *HGL*, x, 821–2; *KOF*, xviii, 37–8; *LC*, no. 73; *RF*, ii, 1009.

44 PRO C61/49, mm. 21, 20, 18, 17, 16, 15, E101/19/39, m. 1., E101/166/11, m. 1. Assertion of Froissart, *Chron.*, i, 380–8 and *Chron. Norm.*, 38 that Robert of Artois fought in Gascony is probably derived from French royal propaganda and is wrong. He would have outranked J. of Norwich, who was unquestionably in command and second only to Ingham: PRO C61/49, m. 16; *RF*, ii, 1023. No English chronicle and none of the ample English records refer to a campaign of Robert in Gascony and French accounts of his acts conflict with record evidence at every point. Robert's whereabouts are unknown between May 1337 and Nov. 1338 but are thereafter inconsistent with any visit to Gascony: *WBN*, 217, 223, 424.

45 *HGL*, ix, 497n, *x, 827–8; *AHG*, ii, 343.

46 Henneman, 119–20.

47 BN Coll. Doat 186, fols 114–116, 119vo–121; 164, fol. 168; *DCG*, no. 173; Benedict XII, *Reg. (France)*, nos 368–9; *AHG*, ii, 130.

48 *RF*, ii, 990; Gray, *Scalacronica*, 167–8.

49 BL Cotton Nero C.VIII, fols 246vo, 263–263vo; PRO E101/388/5, m. 23. Returns: e.g. PRO C61/49, m. 16.

50 E. Fryde (1), 12–15; *CCR 1337–9*, 148–50; *CPR 1334–8*, 480–2. Pole: E. Fryde (5), 4–7; E. Fryde (9), 44–7.

51 PRO C61/49, mm. 15, 15d, 14, 13, 12; *Ann. Paulini*, 366; Murimuth, *Chron.*, 80; *RF*, ii, 997; *CRP 1334–8*, 530–6; BL Cotton Nero C.VIII, fols 246vo, 263–263vo; PRO E101/388/5, mm. 19–23.

52 PRO E101/388/5, mm. 20, 23; Knighton, *Chron.*, ii, 2.

53 *RF*, ii, 997; PRO E101/388/5, m. 22. Border: *Chron. Lanercost*, 305–6, 307–8; Gray, *Scalacronica*, 168; *RS*, i, 499, 501–13; PRO E101/388/5, mm. 19–23.

54 *Cordey, 287–9; LC, no. 78. Spies: BN PO 998 (Deuilly, 2); Froissart, *Chron.*, i, 404.

55 Benedict XII, *Reg.* (*France*), no. 370. Thames: *CCR 1337–9*, 197.

56 Nangis, *Chron.*, ii, 159; *Grandes Chron.*, ix, 161; *Chronographia*, ii, 56; BN Fr. n.a. 7413, fol. 214vo.

57 *Chron. anon. Par.*, 171; Nangis, *Chron.*, ii, 157; AN JJ74/195.

58 PRO E101/388/5, mm. 20, 23; Muisit, *Chron.*, 112; *Grandes Chron.*, ix, 163; *Chron. anon. Par.*, 172; *Chronographia*, ii, 44–5; *RF*, ii, 1123; *KOF, xviii, 297–9.

59 *Gedenkwaardigheden Gesch. Gelderland*, i, 371–4; Cuttler, 145–6; *Chron. anon. Par.*, 171–2.

60 *Vitae Paparum*, i, 200; *RF*, ii, 1002–3, 1006; *CPR 1334–8*, 546; *Chronographia*, ii, 55–6; Murimuth, *Chron.*, 81.

61 Chaplais, *Dipl. Practice*, 287–8; Walsingham, *Hist.*, i, 222; Benedict XII, *Reg.* (*France*), nos 305–35 (powers); *RDP*, iv, 488–91; *RF*, ii, 1007, 1009.

62 PRO E101/388/31, m. 3; Lloyd, 149–50; Lucas, 246; E. Fryde (2), 17–23; Chaplais, *Dipl. Practice*, 293–4.

63 Chaplais, *Dipl. Practice*, 288–91.

64 Sturler, 353–4; Bel, *Chron.*, i, 135–6.

65 *RF*, ii, 989–90, 994–5; Grandisson, *Reg.*, i, 300–2.

66 Benedict XII, *Reg.* (*France*), no. 389; *Lit. Cant.*, ii, 158–9; Gray, *Scalacronica*, 168; E. Fryde (7), 257.

67 Murimuth, *Chron.* 82; Knighton, *Chron.*, ii, 3; *TR*, ii, 44–5, 46–9, 50–62, 62–3, 72–3, 73–4; E. Fryde (7), 260–1; *Déprez, 418.

68 *Ménard, ii (*Preuves*), 103; *CCR 1337–9*, 391.

69 *Ménard, ii (*Preuves*), 103–4.

70 AN JJ73/194–5, 197, 200; *Ordonnances*, xii, 61.

71 E.g. PRO C61/47, m. 6, C61/48, m. 2, C61/49, m. 12; *Doc. Durfort*, nos 631–2, 637.

72 BN PO 226 (de la Baume-Montrevel, 2); AN JJ71/170, 230, 382, JJ72/456, 497, 517.

73 *AHG*, iv, 98; *HGL*, ix, 497–501.

74 *Doc. Durfort*, nos 617, 721, 749–51, 759, 789, 792, 817–18, 1021–2; *CPR 1338–40*, 25.

75 Tholin, 19–30; M. J. de Bourrousse de Lafforre, *Nobiliaire de Guienne*, iv (1883), 289–90; *HGL*, ix, 497–50; AN JJ71/77, 229, 230, 317. For his changes of allegiance in 1340s: AN JJ74/754; BN Clairambault 7/385; PRO C61/67, m. 15.

76 Geaune, Aire: BN Coll. Doat 186, fols 160–161vo, 162–162vo; *HGL*, ix, 500–1, 506n, 512; AN JJ73/38; *AHG*, iv, 101. Cazaubon: PRO E101/166/12, m. 11vo; AN JJ71/60.

77 AN JJ71/45, 246; AD Pyr.-Atl. E511.

78 AN JJ71/47, 49, 79, 92, 182, JJ72/4, JJ73/333.

79 Knighton, *Chron.*, ii, 3; Hemingburgh, *Chron.*, ii, 315; Nangis, *Chron.*, ii, 158; *Bridlington Chron.*, 135; *DCG*, no. 185; *CCR 1339–41*, 479; *RF*, ii, 1027–8, 1042, 1067; *TR*, ii, 171–2; Godfray, 'Documents', 31.

80 PRO C61/50, m. 7; *RF*, ii, 1055; *TR*, ii, 101, 102–103, 162–4; *CPR 1338–40*, 180–1; *CCR 1339–41*, 226; Hewitt, 6–11.

81 Grandisson, *Reg.*, i, 301; PRO C61/50, m. 8d; *TR*, ii, 172; compare *TR*, ii, 172–4 and *WBN*, 358–62.

82 Jusselin, 'Comment la France se préparait', 233–4.

83 *Chron. Norm*, 210–3; *Doc. Monaco*, 219–30, 286; *Cron. D. Alfonso XI*, 285. Philip had 22 French galleys in 1340: *DCG*, no. XXVIII(331–3, 468, 503). Pay stop: *JT*, no. 5661.

84 PRO E356/8 (enrolled customs accts). *CPR 1334–8*, 578–9; *CCR 1333–7*, 643–4;

CCR 1337–9, 90, 229–30, 557; PRO E372/182, m. 48 (Reppes).

85 Chronographia, ii, 42–3; Bel, Chron., i, 132–3. Pensions: RF, ii, 1034; JT, nos 5337, 5602.

86 Kervyn, iii, 172–5; Lucas, 224–7, 260; Chronographia, ii, 46.

87 *KOF, xviii, 53.

88 Lucas, 263–8.

89 Grandes Chron., ix, 164.

90 Brussel, 824n (summons). Kervyn, iii,. 188–9; Lucas, 269–72; *KOF, xviii, 54; Bel, Chron., i, 131–2; Grandes Chron., ix, 164–5. Terms formally executed on 10 June 1338: TR, ii, 117–20.

91 Lucas, 273–9; Muisit, Chron., 113–4; Nangis, Chron., ii, 159; Grandes Chron., ix, 162–3, 165–6; Chronographia, ii, 43–4, 52–4; *KOF, xviii, 62–3, xxi, 208–11. Impressment: Inventaire AD P.-de-Calais, ii, 23.

92 Froissart, Chron., i, 403–5; Chronographia, ii, 38–40. Date of letter (19 Oct 1337) corresponds with Edward's itinerary and sittings of Parliament but chronicler's date for presentation (1 Nov. 1337) is wrong. Philip not in Paris between 10 Oct. and 19 Nov. 1337 ('Itin. Philippe VI'). K. of Navarre, said to have been present, was at Boulogne (BN Fr. n.a. 7413, fol. 214vo). Burghersh's known movements rule out visit to France before March 1338 (PRO E101/311/31; *KOF, xviii, 53–4). Letter probably overtaken by cancellation of invasion in Nov. 1337. Most likely date of delivery between c.6 May 1338, when Edward repudiated informal truce (TR, ii, 91–2), and c.21 May 1338, when Philip VI referred to it in summons of his army (Chron. anon. Par., 174).

93 WSS, 92; Benedict XII, Reg. (France), no. 432; PRO C61/50, mm. 1, 2, 4d, 13, 14, 16; AHG, lv, 22–4, 25; PRO E101/21/3, E101/166/10.

94 DCG, no. 173, 180, 186; PRO E101/166/11, mm. 32, 33; Cron. D. Alfonso XI, 285. Bayonne fight: PRO C81/240/10405; PRO C61/50, m. 5; RF, ii, 1005. Talmont fight: PRO C61/50, m. 16, C61/51, m. 3.

95 James, 15, 32; PRO E101/166/11 (Exchequer subsidy: m. 7). J. of Norwich: CCR 1337–9, 318, 323; PRO E101/166/11, m. 19. Riots, desertion: PRO C61/50, mm. 1, 3d.

96 Scotland: Prince (1), 358–60; RS, i, 501–12, 521–2. Low Countries: TR, ii, 61–4, 66–72. Gascony: RF, ii, 1018, 1020; PRO C61/50, mm. 3, 4, 6.

97 PRO C61/50, m. 4; RF, ii, 1012, 1022, 1033, 1038; AHG, ii, 126–7; Marquette, 478–81.

98 HGL, ix, 502.

99 Plans: DCG, no. 180, 186. Savary: Anselme, viii, 763; Rec. doc. Poitou, ii, 159n. Blainville: Anselme, vi, 758. Blaye, Montlaur: PRO E101/166/11, mm. 11, 22; Trés. Chartes Albret, i, 530. Montendre: ibid., 530–1; BN Fr. 2598, fol. 50; BN Clairam-bault, 31, p. 2305, 54, p. 4123, 87, p. 6887; Confessions, 165–6.

100 PRO C61/50, mm. 4, 8, 10, 12d, C47/2/30; CCR 1337–9, 355; TR, ii, 93, 82–3.

101 Chron. Lanercost, 297–8; Fordun, Chron., i, 362–3; Gray, Scalacronica, 168.

102 Walsingham, Hist., i, 222–3; CCR 1337–9, 499; PRO E101/166/10 (for 'July' read 'June').

103 AHG, iv, 98–101, 102; BN Coll. Doat 186, fols 123–125vo; LC, nos. 92, 94, 97–100.

104 RF, ii, 1047; AHG, ii, 127–30; AN JJ71/46; BN PO 24 (Albret 2, 3).

CHAPTER VIII

1 RF, ii, 1050; TR, ii, 73–4, 82–3; Bel, Chron., i, 137. Numbers: WBN, 325–86. Pay: Powicke, 210–12.

2 TR, ii, 145–8; RF, ii, 1045; Murimuth, Chron., 83; PRO E101/311/36; Benedict XII, Reg. (France), nos 472, 481, 495, 538.

3 LC, nos 91–100; *AHG*, ii, 127–30, 131–2; *Cordey, 292; *Lescot, *Chron.*, 215–16; *Chron. anon. Par.*, 176; Muisit, *Chron.*, 115, 116, 117; Benedict XII, *Reg.* (*France*), nos 464–7; 'Itin. Philippe VI', 527–8; Contamine (3), 34.

4 PRO E101/311/35, 36.

5 PRO C81/250/11439; *WBN*, 240.

6 *TR*, ii, 80, 104–9, 113, 116, 117, 156–62; *RF*, ii, 1031–2; *Déprez(1), 418–19; *WBN*, 363; *KOF*, xviii, 64–5; E. Fryde (6), 1149–50, 1160–1; E. Fryde (9), 86.

7 Bel. *Chron.*, i, 137–8; Baker, *Chron.*, 61–2; Murimuth, *Chron.*, 83–4.

8 E. Fryde (6), 1154–7; *TR*, ii, 156–62; *KOF*, xviii, 64–5.

9 *CCR 1337–9*, 511–2, 526; *RF*, ii, 1051; *TR*, ii, 193–202, 203–15, 220–25.

10 Bel. *Chron.*, i, 139–42.

11 Schwalm, 'Reiseberichte', 350–2; *WBN*, 417. Negotiations with France: AN J918/25, J919/13; LC, no. 99; Benedict XII, *Reg.* (*France*), 496.

12 *WBN*, 69, 85–91, 212, 219, 221–3, 242–4, 417, 446; Murimuth, *Chron.*, 84–5; *Récits d'un bourgeois*, 165–6; Knighton, *Chron.*, ii, 5–6. Vicariate: Bock, *Quellen*, nos 530–2; *KOF*, ii, 548–9.

13 Bock, *Quellen*, nos 533–4; Hocsem, *Chron.*, 282; Bel, *Chron.*, i, 148–9; *WBN*, 246; Knighton, *Chron.*, ii, 6–7; Benedict XII, *Reg.* (*France*), no. 518, *Reg.* (*Autres pays*), 2082–93.

14 Bel. *Chron.*, i, 138–9; *CPR 1338–40*, 187; *WBN*, 241–2, 247, 248–9, 251, 252.

15 PRO E101/311/35, 36; *WBN*, 278, 282, 460; *RF*, ii, 1065; *Chronographia*, ii, 1064–5; *Chron. anon. Par.*, 177; Benedict XII, *Reg.* (*France*), no. 588.

16 Dispersal: *Chron. anon. Par.*, 177; BN Coll. Doat 186, fols 161vo–162. Winter dispositions: *Chronographia*, ii, 60–4; *Chron. Norm.*, 214–16; Jusselin, 'Comment la France se préparait', 228–9.

17 BN Fr. 2598, fol. 50. Spies: PRO E101/166/11, m. 36; *WBN*, 60; PRO E101/311/35. Edward's supplies: e.g. *TR*, ii, 204–5, 218–19; *WBN*, 218.

18 *RF*, ii, 969; *TR*, ii, 171–2; *Chron. anon. Par.*, 173–4; PRO E372/191, m. 52 (Ferrers); *Chronographia*, ii, 28; French *Chron. London*, 74; *Actes Normands*, 217, 219.

19 PRO E372/191, m. 55(Weston), C62/115, m. 5.

20 *WBN*, 213, 363; PRO C81/249/11331; Nangis, *Chron.*, ii, 161; *Chron. anon. Par.*, 178; Murimuth, *Chron.*, 87; Baker, *Chron.*, 62, 69; Minot, *Poems*, 8–9.

21 *RF*, ii, 1060; *TR*, ii, 252, 297.

22 *TR*, ii, 226, 252, 297–300, 313–4; *DCG*, nos. 221, 223; *RF*, ii, 1070; *CPR 1338–40*, 149–50, 180–1; *CPR 1340–3*, 4, 572, 579; *CPR 1345–8*, 298–9; *CCR 1337–9*, 183, 184, 286; *CCR 1339–41*, 104, 143, 477–8; *CFR 1337–47*, 97; Murimuth, *Chron.*, 87; Baker, *Chron.*, 62–3; *Chronographia*, ii, 93–4; Platt, 108, 111–12.

23 *DCG*, nos 218–23; *TR*, ii, 228, 231–5, 305, 307–8; *RF*, ii, 1061, 1062; *RS*, i, 552; French *Chron. London*, 74; *CCR 1337–9*, 537; *Cal. Letter Books*, F, 1, 16, 28; *Cal. Plea Mem.* R, 176–7.

24 *RP*, ii, 104; *Nicholas, ii, 469–73; *CCR 1337–9*, 199, 339; *TR*, ii, 181, 228, 310; PRO E372/184, m. 50 (Stephen de Padyham); *RF*, ii, 958; *WBN*, 385; *RS*, i, 515; Tinniswood.

25 *RF*, ii, 947, 1008, 1058, 1066, 1104; *WBN*, 3, 428.

26 *CPR 1338–40*, 190, 195; *RF*, ii, 1066–7; *Doc. Monaco*, i, 270–1.

27 Brown *et al.*, 589, 592–3, 638–9, 724–5, 779, 788–9. Pevensey: *CPR 1338–40*, 208, 236–7. Winchester: *TR*, ii, 311; *RF*, ii, 1077; *CCR 1337–9*, 579. Dover: PRO C76/14, m. 10. Chichester: PRO C76/14, mm 10, 11. Southampton: PRO E101/22/7, 11, 12, 34, 77; *CPR 1338–40*, 237; *CFR 1337–47*, 129–30; *RF*, ii, 1077; PRO C76/15, m. 31, SC1/41/177 (E. of Warwick).

28 Murimuth, *Chron.*, 88–9; Maddicott (2), 50–2.

29 Maddicott (2), 31, 53–9, 66.

30 E. Fryde (7), 258–64; E. Ames, 'The Sterling Crisis of 1337–9', *J. Econ.H.*, xxv (1965),

496–522; Maddicott, 48–50, 62–4, 69. Disorder: *Bridlington Chron.*, 138; *Chron. mon. Melsa*, ii, 387; *Rot. Parl. ined.*, 268–9.

31 Tout (1), iii, 90–8; *E. Fryde (1), 77.

32 E. Fryde (7), 262–3; *Year Books 14–15 Edward III*, ed. L. O. Pike (1889), 258–62; *French Chron. London*, 87; Aspin, *Political Songs*, 112.

33 *Rot. Parl. ined.*, 269; Knighton, *Chron.*, ii, 3; E. Fryde (7), 262–3; Aspin, *Political Songs*, 105–15; *RF*, ii, 1070; Gray, *Scalacronica*, 168.

34 *Doc. Durfort*, no. 811; AN JJ68/35; *HGL*, ix, 508; *AHG*, xxxiii, 93–4.

35 Bock, *Quellen*, nos 538, 541; Benedict XII, *Reg. (France)*, nos 553, 555; *Chron. anon. Par.*, 179; Muisit, *Chron.*, 117–18; Muevin, *Chron.*, 470; *Chronographia*, ii, 62; *E. Petit (2), 259; BN Fr.n.a. 9236, p. 26. Spies: PRO E101/311/35; *WBN*, 228.

36 *Doc. Durfort*, no. 762; *AHG*, xxxiii, 93–4; BN Fr.n.a. 9236–7, pp. 28, 88, 350, 755; PRO E101/166/11, mm. 14, 23, 29–30; AN JJ71/169, 174, 220, JJ72/52.

37 Contamine (2), 68; BN Fr.n.a. 9237, pp. 705–7, 750, 751, 769–74.

38 Penne: BN Fr.n.a. 9236, pp. 74–88 (arrivals at Penne). Caumont: BN Fr.n.a. 9237, pp. 574–5, 584, 708, 750; PRO E101/166/11, m. 35. Puyguilhem: BN PO 1120 (de Fays, 2), PO 1172 (Foix, 9), PO 2188 (la Palu, 2, 3, 5), PO 2739 (Sussa, 2); BN Fr.n.a. 9237, p. 781.

39 Penne: BN Fr.n.a. 9237, pp. 549–51, 755, 756; PRO E101/166/11, m. 23. Bourg, Blaye: PRO E101/166/11, mm. 21, 22, 32, C61/52, m. 3; *Chron. anon. Par.*, 180; BN Fr. 2598, fol. 50vo; *Chron. Norm.*, 220; AN JJ72/63 (epilogue); BN Fr.n.a. 9237, pp. 678–97 (garrison).

40 Devaluation: Boutruche, 265–7. Gordon: PRO C61/52, m. 20. Quotation: SC1/38/174.

41 *Actes Normands*, 196–9, 212–13, 218–21; DCG, nos 229–45; *RF*, ii, 1072.

42 'Ancient Petitions' ayant trait aux îles de la Manche, 67–9; PRO E372/191, m. 52 (Ferrers); BN Fr. 2598. fol. 50.

43 *RF*, ii, 1078; Murimuth, *Chron.*, 88; Baker, *Chron.*, 63; PRO C81/254/11807.

44 *RF*, iii, 76; AN J210/4, 5, 7; *Ordonnances*, vi, 549–50; Nangis, *Chron.*, ii, 162.

45 *RF*, ii, 1078; DCG, no. 248. Articles: Murimuth, *Chron.*, 257–61.

46 *CPR 1338–40*, 206, 212, 279; *CCR 1339–41*, 19, 40, 55, 71, 79, 87, 106, 121, 190, 233, 236; *RF*, ii, 1076, PRO C76/14, mm. 18d, 11, 10d, 8, 8d; PRO E101/21/32, mm. 3–7.

47 May raids: Murimuth, *Chron.*, 89–90; Baker, *Chron.*, 63–4; Knighton, *Chron.*, ii, 8–9. I. of Wight: PRO E101/21/32, m. 7. Hastings: *CPR 1338–40*, 258, 287; *CCR 1339–41*, 215, 293–4, 298, 333.

48 PRO C76/14, mm. 12d, 13d. Cinque Ports: PRO E372/184, m. 42 (E. of Huntingdon).

49 *Chron. anon. Par.*, 180; *CPR 1338–40*, 372–3, 491–2; *CPR 1340–3*, 319; *WBN*, 216, 258; PRO C76/14, mm. 8, 7, 7d, 6; PRO E101/22/8. Crabbe: *Cal. doc. Scot.*, iii, nos 417, 673, 1086, 1090; *Exch. R. Scot.*, i, 64, 311; *CCR 1337–9*, 223–4; *CCR 1339–41*, 11, 139; *Bridlington Chron.*, 109.

50 DCG, nos 254, 257; *Actes Normands*, 205–8; Knighton, *Chron.*, ii, 9; *CCR 1339–41*, 452, 650; Roncière, i, 432; Guesnon, 'Documents', 226.

51 Giorgio Stella, *Annales Genuenses*, ed. G. P. Balbi (1975), 128–9; DCG, nos 249–50, 265, 275; *Actes Normands*, 221–8. Grimaldi paid off: AN JJ72/72. Doria's treason: *CPR 1340–3*, 330; PRO C49/7/15.

52 *Chronographia*, ii, 67; Nangis, *Chron.*, ii, 163; *Cart. S. Michel du Tréport*, pp. xlix–l; AN JJ73/72; CIM, iii, no. 14 (p. 6) (Poitou); C. Guibert, *Méms. p. servir à l'hist. de Dieppe*, ed. M. Hardy, i (1878), 24.

53 PRO C76/14, mm. 11d, 10d, 5, 5d, 4. Convoys: *ibid.*, mm. 5d, 4d; PRO E372/184, m. 42 (Swanlond); *Hughes, 242.

54 *RF*, ii, 1080; Harriss, 244n.

55 Captaincies: E. Petit, *Rec. Anc. Mem.*, 63, 174–6, 177–8; *Inventaire AD P.-de-Calais*, ii,

28 (Boulonnais); *DCG*, no. XXVII(140); BN Fr. 9501, fols 153–153vo (S. of Seine); *Rec. doc. Poitiers*, 343, 345 (Poitou). Reinforcements inland: Guesnon, 'Documents', 224; *Inventaire AD P.-de-Calais*, ii, 28.

56 This section: E. Fryde (6), 1157–75, 1194–1216; E. Fryde (4), 17; E. Fryde (9), 121–9; and other references below.

57 *RF*, ii, 1080.

58 *Hughes, 243.

59 Benedict XII, *Reg. (France)*, no. 531; AN JJ71/352–3.

60 *RF*, ii, 1080.

61 Jusselin, 'Comment la France se préparait', 228–32; Henneman, 153, 350, 355. Normandy: *RF*, iii, 76. Paris, *arrière-ban*: Timbal, *Registres*, 54–7.

62 Ménard, ii (*Preuves*), 110; *LE*, no. 117; *Chronographia*, ii, 66–7.

63 BN Fr.n.a. 9236, pp. 71, 140; cf. pp. 37, 38, 43, 46, 86. Bordeaux: *ibid.*, 197, 263–4, 266.

64 *Cal. doc. Scot.*, iii, no. 1307; *RS*, i, 557–70; Fordun, *Chron.*, i, 364; Bower, *Supp.*, ii, 330; Wyntoun, *Cron.*, ii, 451–2; *Chron. Lanercost*, 317–18.

65 *KOF, xx, 414–18; E. Fryde (6), 1173–4; BN Fr. 2598, fol. 50.

66 Benedict XII, *Reg. (France)*, nos 560, 588, *Reg. (Autres pays)*, nos 2184, 3401; Stengel, *N. Alemanniae*, i, 388–90; Schwalm, 'Reiseberichte', 352–4, 359; *RF*, ii, 1088; *WBN*, 417.

67 Robert: *RF*, ii, 1066; *WBN*, 216–7, 223, 268, 424; PRO E101/311/36 (conspirators); Benedict XII, *Reg. (France)*, no. 603; *Trautz, 285, 340; Bock, *Quellen*, no. 551; *CCR 1339–41*, 288, 291. Philip: *Lescot, *Chron.*, 220.

68 *Chron. anon. Par.*, 181; Walsingham, *Hist.*, i, 225–6; *AHG*, iv. 102–3; BN Fr.n.a. 9236–7, pp. 37–286, 343–502, esp. 87–8, 189, 263–4, 343, 533, 678–97, 779, 781; PRO E101/166/12, mm. 7, 7d.

69 Fordun, *Chron.*, i, 364; *RS*, i, 571; Bower, *Supp.*, ii, 330–1; Wyntoun, *Cron.*, ii, 452–6; *RF*, ii, 1094. Relief force: *RF*, ii, 1093; PRO SC1/42/94A, E372/184, m. 45 (Bp of Carlisle); *CCR 1339–41*, 289.

70 *WBN*, 282, 284, 285, 460; PRO E101/311/35, 36; *RF*, ii, 1084; Benedict XII, *Reg. (France)*, 620, 644.

71 E. Fryde (6), 1168–9, 1173; *RF*, ii, 1085, 1088; *WBN*, 232; Bock, *Quellen*, nos 549–51; *Gedenkwaardigheden Gesch. Gelderland*, i, 399–402; *Actes . . . intérressant la Belgique*, 130–8; Murimuth, *Chron.*, 91; Avesbury, *G. Edwardi*, 307.

72 Bel. *Chron.*, i, 151–3 (place and dates wrong); *Lescot, *Chron.*, 206; Bock, *Quellen*, no. 551.

73 *Lescot, *Chron.*, 223–4.

74 Campaign of Sept.–Oct. 1339: (a) English official record, *KOF, xviii, 84–93; (b) Edward III's letter to his son (1 Nov. 1339) in Avesbury, *G. Edwardi*, 304–6; (c) itineraries of Edward III (*Lescot, *Chron.*, 206) and Philip VI ('Itin. Philippe VI'); (d) principal chroniclers, Bel, *Chron.*, i, 153–65, *Chronographia*, ii, 62, 68–85; (e) minor chroniclers, Hocsem, *Chron.*, 288–90, *Récits d'un bourgeois*, 167–70, Muisit, *Chron.*, 118–19, Baker, *Chron.*, 64–6, BN Fr. 2598, fols 50vo–51; (f) other chroniclers are substantially based on (a), (b) and (d) and unreliable so far as they add to them, but some material is supplied by Murimuth, *Chron.*, 101–3, Gray, *Scalacronica*, 169, Lescot, *Chron.*, 49, Nangis, *Chron.*, ii, 163–5; (g) accts of papal almoners in Carolus-Barré, 'Mission charitable'; (h) other references below.

75 Finance: *KOF, xx, 54–6, 413–31; E. Fryde (6), 1171, 1174; *RF*, ii, 1091.

76 Benedict XII, *Reg. (France)*, no. 648.

77 Denifle, 10.

78 Froissart, *Chron.*, i, 162.

79 Numbers: *RP*, ii, 103 (Edward's estimate); Prince (1), 360–1, whose figures do not include allied contract armies.

80 *RF*, ii, 1092.

81 BN PO 226 (Baume, 5, 6).
82 AN J624/31; *KOF, xviii, 38.
83 Ordonnances, iv, 239.
84 WBN, 216.
85 AN JJ72/318.
86 Froissart, Chron., i, 179.
87 PRO E101/166/12, m. 10; Knighton, Chron., ii, 14; RF, ii, 1101; Johnson, 'An Act'. French numbers: Contamine (2), 68; BN Fr.n.a. 9236-7, pp. 429, 432, 441-7, 659, 660, 762, 807-8.
88 RP, ii, 103-6; RF, ii, 1091, 1098; E. Fryde (7), 266-7.
89 Jousts: Chronographia, ii, 85. Pope: RF, ii, 1103.

CHAPTER IX

1 RF, ii, 1117; Bock, Quellen, no. 596.
2 Wright, Political Poems, i, 1-25; Chronographia, ii, 35-8; Bel, Chron, i, 119-20, 124; Froissart, Chron., i, 359-60.
3 F. H. Russell, The Just War in the Middle Ages (1975), 131-47; Honoret Bonet, The Tree of Battles, tr. G. W. Coopland (1949), 128-9, 139, 171; E. Chaplais, 'Some Documents Regarding . . . the Treaty of Brétigny', Camden Miscellany, xix (1952), 51-78, esp. 70-8.
4 BN Fr. 2598, fol. 49vo (France); Oxford, MS Bodley 462 (England).
5 Faucogney: WBN, 282; U. Plancher, Hist. de Bourgogne, ii (1741), 192-3; E. Petit (1), vii, 225-6, 228-9. Henry: CPR 1338-40, 454. Guy: RF, ii, 1123. 'Various': WBN, 298.
6 Gray, Scalacronica, 167.
7 RF, ii, 966, 994; Urkudenbuch für die Geschicte des Niederrheins, ed. T. Lacomblet, iii (1855), 247.
8 TR, ii, 1-2, 33, 40-3, 118; CPR 1334-8, 551, 557, 561; CPR 1338-40, 5, 7, 13, 29, 30; CCR 1337-9, 327, 360, Defiance: Froissart, Chron., i, 404.
9 TR, ii, 145-8; RF, ii, 1051, 1065-6; Benedict XII, Reg. (France), no. 560. Arras debate: ibid., no. 644; RF, ii, 1107; Murimuth, Chron.,91-100.
10 E.g. WBN, 214, 247, 261, 272-3, 274, 416, 444, 446; CPR 1338-40, 280, 372-3, 387; CCR 1339-41, 105.
11 WBN, 268, 275, 278, 279, 280; CPR 1338-40, 189, 196; CCR 1339-41, 105; PRO E101/311/35 (chaplain).
12 Chronographia, ii, 85-6.
13 Lucas, 309-14, 316, 319-22, 325-6, 339-45.
14 *KOF, 11, 549-51.
15 Hocsem, Chron., 290-2; Arch. S. Quentin, ii, 122; RSG, i, 306, 403, 471-5; WBN, 260, 286; Chron. Norm., 42. Louis: Chronographia, ii, 85-6; RSG, i, 402, cf. 383, 396, 402, 428.
16 WBN, 288; Avesbury, G. Edwardi, 306; RSG, i, 403-4; RF, ii, 1097. Louis: Lucas, 346.
17 *KOF, iii, 492-4.
18 Bel, Chron., i, 166-8; WBN, 268; RF, ii, 1106; Benedict XII, Reg. (France), nos 677-82. Cf. Bock, Quellen, no. 597; RF, ii, 1117; Murimuth, Chron., 103.
19 Chronographia, ii, 88-9; RSG, i, 431; Guesnon, 'Documents', 218-20.
20 *KOF, xviii, 110-29, ratifying earlier agreement, see RF, ii, 1107. Land operations: Bock, Quellen, nos 596-7; Récits d'un bourgeois, 170.
21 WBN, 455; Bock, Quellen, no. 596.
22 RF, ii, 1108-9, 1111; Chronographia, ii, 91-3.
23 Benedict XII, Reg. (France), nos 677-82; Budt, Chron., 326.
24 Guesnon, 'Documents', 218-20, 221-2, 225-6; Inventaire AD P.-de-Calais,ii, 28, 29, 30, 31, 32.
25 Economic sanctions: Bock, Quellen, no. 596; *E. Petit (1), 282; AN JJ73/110; Guesnon.

'Documents', 220–1. Interdict: Lucas, 367–70, 372–3. Appeal: AN JJ72/285; Muisit, *Chron.*, 122; *KOF*, xxi, 211–47.

26 *RF*, ii, 1115.
27 *RP*, ii, 107–8; *Harriss, 518–20.
28 *CPR 1338–40*, 398, 408–9; PRO C76/14, mm. 3, 2; *Déprez (1), 419–20; *RF*, ii, 1109; *Gedenkwaardigheden Gesch. Gelderland*, i, 413–16.
29 *RF*, ii, 1100, 1115; *French Chron. London*, 73; *Chron. mon. Melsa*, iii, 43.
30 Loans: *RF*, ii, 1116; *Cal. Letter Books F*, 43–50; *Cal. Plea Mem. R*, 120. Parlt.: *RP*, ii, 112–16; *CCR 1339–41*, 468.
31 *Chron. Lanercost*, 333.
32 Grants: AN P2291, pp. 549–52, 809–12; *Doc. Parisiens*, ii, 81–3; Henneman, 141–53. Crusade: Benedict XII, *Reg. (France)*, 708, 713. Devaluation: *Ordonnances*, vi, p.* vii; *Rec. doc. monnaies*, i, 15, 37, 236.
33 Henneman, 153. War wages: Contamine (2), 95–6. Non-payment: BN Fr.n.a. 9239, fols 271vo–272, 273.
34 *Ordonnances*, vi, 356–7; BN Fr.n.a. 9238, fols 89vo–117vo (garrison); *Chron.Norm.*, 214–6; *Chronographia*, ii, 95.
35 *Récits d'un bourgeois*, 168, 171–2, 173; *Chronographia*, ii, 86–7, 95; Bel, *Chron.*, i, 170–1; *KOF*, xviii, 138–9; *Chron. Norm*, 216.
36 Benedict XII, *Reg. (France)*, nos 708, 713 (cols 434, 439); LC, nos 122–3; *Actes Normands*, 265.
37 *WBN*, 266, 326–7, 328, 362, 440; PRO C76/15, m. 32, E101/22/39.
38 *Chronographia*, ii, 96–7.
39 *KOF*, xviii, 136–40; *Chronographia*, ii, 104–6; *Récits d'un bourgeois*, 173–5; Bel, *Chron.*, i, 171–2; *Grandes Chron.*, ix, 174; BN Fr. n.a. 9239, fol. 210; Carolus-Barré, 'Mission charitable', 185–6.
40 *WBN*, 328; *Chronographia*, ii, 98–104; BN Fr. 2598, fol. 51; Bel, *Chron.*, i, 168–9; Baker, *Chron.*, 67–8; Murimuth, *Chron.*, 104–5; *French Chron. London*, 73–4; Knighton, *Chron.*, ii, 17. Armentières: *E. Petit (1), vii, 244. Godemar: Dupont-Ferrier, ii, no. 6821. Fate of prisoners: BN Fr.n.a. 9239, fol. 269; *KOF*, iii, 485.
41 Muisit, *Chron.*, 121–2; *Chronographia*, ii, 97–8, 102–3; *RSG*, i, 482–9.
42 *Chronographia*, ii, 107–8; BN Fr. 2598, fol. 51; BN Fr.n.a. 9239, fol. 273.
43 *Chronographia*, ii, 108–20; *Récits d'un bourgeois*, 175–80; Muisit, *Chron.*, 123–5; Bel, *Chron.*, i, 172–7; *Grandes Chron.*, ix, 178–80; Hocsem, *Chron.*, 294–5; BN Fr. 2598, fol. 51; BN Fr. 9239, fols 272vo–274 (abstract of correspondence of Ch. des Comptes); *ibid.*, fols 127–129vo, 172, 210vo–235 (numbers and chronology of advance); and other references below.
44 *RSG*, i, 419.
45 Froissart, *Chron*, ii, 197.
46 BN Fr.n.a. 9239, fol. 211.
47 E. Petit (1), vii, 277.
48 Count: *RSG*, i, 419–20; *Récits d'un bourgeois*, 175; PRO E372/194, m. 45 (Stury). Louis: Bock, *Quellen*, no. 601.
49 *RSG*, i, 495–501.

CHAPTER X

1 *Cal. Letter Books*, F, 41; *RP*, ii, 107(5), 108(11–13); PRO C76/15, mm. 32, 31, 29, 28, 27; *WBN*, 297–8.
2 Venice: *Cal. State Papers Venice, 1202–1509*, ed. R. Brown (1864), 8–9. Fieschi: *RF*, ii, 1111, 1126; Benedict XII, *Reg. (France)*, nos 715, 720–2, 727–8, 730, 734; *Vitae Paparum*, i, 205–6, 213–14.

3 *Doc. Monaco*, i, 270–1; AN P2291, pp. 549–52; Bock, *Quellen*, no. 282; *CCR 1339–41*, 410, 431.

4 *DCG*, nos 278, XXVII (331–3, 468, 503).

5 *Chron. mon. Melsa*, iii, 43; Murimuth, *Chron.*, 103–4; Baker, *Chron.*, 67; Nangis, *Chron.*, ii, 165; *Grandes Chron.*, ix, 174; BN Fr. 2598, fol. 51; *DCG*, no. XXVII (502–3).

6 *DCG*, no. XXVII (329, 331–3, 394–401, 423, 432–3, 441–2, 468, 473, 475, 477).

7 BN Fr. 2598, fol. 51; *Cart. S.-Michel du Tréport*, pp. l–li.

8 *DCG*, no. XXVII (12, 647); *Actes Normands*, 264–8; *Ordonnances*, vi, 549.

9 PRO C76/15, mm. 29, 29d, 28d, 26, 25d, 23, C62/117, m. 6, E101/22/25. Hainault knight: *WBN* 266.

10 *DCG*, no. XXVII (12–20, 166–505, 617–41); BN Fr. 2598, fol. 51vo.

11 Murimuth, *Chron.*, 105; Avesbury, *G. Edwardi*, 310.

12 Avesbury, *G. Edwardi*, 310–2; Walsingham, *Hist. Angl.*, i, 226–7; Gray, *Scalacronica*, 170; *RF*, ii, 1130; PRO C76/15, mm. 22, 19.

13 Avesbury, *G. Edwardi*, 311; *RF*, ii, 1129.

14 Sluys: (a) Edward III's letters, *RF*, ii, 1129, 1130, *KOF*, xviii, 166–7; (b) English chronicles, Murimuth, *Chron.*, 105–7, 109, Baker, *Chron.*, 68–9, Avesbury, *G. Edwardi*, 312, Knighton, *Chron.*, ii, 17–8, *French Chron. London*, 76–7, *Chron. mon. Melsa*, iii, 45, *Chron. Lanercost*, 333–4; (c) continental chronicles, *Chronographia*, ii, 121–4, Nangis, *Chron.*, ii, 168–70, *Grandes Chron.*, ix, 180–4, *Chron. Quatre Valois*, 10–11, BN Fr. 2598, fol. 51vo, *Chron. Norm.*, 44–5, Villani, *Hist.*, XI. 109, cols 836–7. French fleet: Edward III's figures after the battle were 190 captured and 23 escaped, *KOF*, xviii, 167; compare 202 in pay of French war treasurers, *DCG*, no XXVII (166–449); the difference probably represents French allies rather than miscounting; for these, see Murimuth, *Chron.*, 106 (Spanish), and PRO C76/15, m. 10d (Flemish).

15 French survivors: *DCG*, no. XXVII (331–5, 394, 397–8, 401, 468, 525–9, 531, 534, 536–8).

16 Froissart, *Chron.*, ii, 37.

17 BN Fr. 9501, fols 153–154vo, Fr.n.a. 7413, fols 296–302, Fr. 32510, fols 178–178vo; AN K43/14bis.

18 *Actes Normands*, 268; AN JJ74/694, JJ81/202; Froissart, *Chron.*, ii, 226.

19 Minot, *Poems*, 17; Avesbury, *G. Edwardi*, 312; Raine, *N. Reg.*, 379–80. Coin: *Chron. mon. Melsa*, iii, 45; C. Oman, *The Coinage of England* (1931), 170–2.

20 BN Coll. Doat 186, fols 248–50 (alliances); BN PO 1839 (Marchi, 2); *HGL*, x, 896–7; AP 1328–50, no. 2330.

21 *AHG*, ii, 126–7 (misdated); BN Coll. Doat 186, fols 251–4; Marquette, 479.

22 BN Coll. Doat, 186, fols 248–250, 187, fols 114–115. Tartas: Marquette, 487–8.

23 Marquette, 281–327, 485–6; AD Pyr.-Atl. E799 ('capital enemies'); BN Coll. Doat 243, fols 75–76vo (*lèse-majesté* pardoned).

24 BN Fr.n.a. 9239, fols 228, 231. Overtures: Armagnac: BN Coll. Doat 187, fols 194–195vo (1340), 114 (1341); Foix: PRO E101/167/3, m.6 (1342).

25 Knighton, *Chron.*, ii, 13–4.

26 Knighton, *Chron.*, ii, 13; *WBN*, 265; *RF*, ii, 1105. Hugh: *RF*, ii, 975; *WBN*, 315, 328–9; P. Duparc, *Le comté de Genève* (1955), 279–81.

27 Money: PRO SC1/38/73, E101/166/12, mm. 2d, 3, 6. Allies: Marquette, 490–1. Armagnac: BN Coll. Doat 187, fols 194–195vo.

28 PRO E101/166/12, mm. 9d, 12. Caumont: BN Fr.n.a. 9237, p. 792, Ste-Bazeille: AN JJ73/51; BN Fr.n.a. 9237, pp. 587, 763–4. Gontaut: AN JJ74/683; BN Fr.n.a. 9237, pp. 576–7. Monségur: AN JJ71/374, JJ73/203.

29 Communications: BN Fr.n.a. 9237, pp. 772–3, 782–3. Agen: *ibid.*, pp. 765, 766, 778, 779.

30 BN Coll. Doat 187, fols 194–195vo. Montréal: AN JJ73/171, 294, JJ74/183.
31 BN Fr.n.a. 9237, p. 468; HGL, ix, 523.
32 AN JJ73/234–5; BN Fr.n.a. 9237, p. 701. Raymond: WSS, 220; BN Fr.n.a. 9237, p. 451; AD Pyr.-Atl. E626; BN Coll. Périgord 10, fol. 39vo; PRO C61/55, m. 5, SC1/38/73.
33 Mézin: *Lacabane (2), 120–2, 124. Condom: AD Herault A4/110–1; BN Fr.n.a. 9237, pp. 772, 818–21; AN JJ73/190, 212.
34 Armagnac: Auvillar, Lectoure and Lomagne promised by Edward III (BN Coll. Doat, fols 194–195vo) and granted by Philip VI (AN J293/12). Garrisons, troops: BN Fr.n.a. 9237, pp. 528–705; Contamine (2), 68–9. Languedoc diversions: *HGL, x, 864–6. Eu: BN Fr.n.a. 9237, p. 796, Fr.n.a. 7413, fols 248–249vo. Louis: BN Clairambault 43/3235, 97/7549. Correspondence: BN Fr.n.a. 9237, pp. 772–3, 812, 815.
35 *Lescot, Chron., 207; RSG, i, 422. RF, ii, 1130; PRO C76/15, m. 17; Grandes Chron., ix, 185–6; Chronographia, ii, 124–5.
36 Chron. Norm., 45–6; 'Itin. Philippe VI'; Arch. S.-Quentin, ii, 141. Numbers: Contamine (2), 69.
37 A. Giry, 'Registre', 250–1. Campaign of S.-Omer; Grandes Chron., ix, 187–97; Chronographia, ii, 127–35; Gray, Scalacronica, 171; Murimuth, Chron., 108; Bel, Chron., i, 188–90; BN Fr.n.a. 9239, fol. 274 (Ch. des Comptes, abstract of correspondence).
38 BN Fr.n.a. 9239, fol. 274; G. Canestrini, 'Alcuni documenti', Archivio Storico Italiano, series I, vii, 358.
39 Grandes Chron., ix, 185; Récits d'un bourgeois, 183.
40 RP, ii, 103–4(4); E. Fryde (9), 146–7; Harriss, 276–8. Penniless: *KOF, xxv, 343–4.
41 RP, ii, 117–22.
42 N. Sea: CR 1339–41, 560, 629. Houdetot; DCG, nos XIX, XXVII (133, 138, 140–65, 525–47, 604, 609, 635, 650); CPR 1340–3, 476; PRO C76/15, mm. 17, 10d.
43 N. Seas: CCR 1339–41, 503–4. Ch. Islands: PRO E372/191, m. 52 (Ferrers); CCR 1339–41, 499; CPR 1340–3, 20.
44 BN Fr.n.a. 9239, fol. 274; PRO C76/15, mm 10d, 9, 8, 7d; Baker, Chron., 70; Murimuth, Chron., 109n; CCR 1339–41, 637, 641.
45 PRO C76/15, mm. 17, 10d, 9, 8, 7, 7d, 6, 6d; RF, ii, 1133, 1156, 1185, iii, 1; DCG, no. XXVII (140).
46 Cal. doc. Scot., iii, no. 1338, v, no. 809; RS, i, 600–2.
47 PRO C76/15, mm. 16, 15, 14, 14d, 13; RP, ii, 120(18); Lloyd, 157–8. Enforcement: Harriss, 279–81; CRP 1340–3, 96; CCR 1339–41, 532, 536; French Chron. London, 83 (quotation).
48 Récits d'un bourgeois, 183; *Lescot, Chron., 207; *KOF, xxv, 344; RSG, i, 502–5, ii, 87–8. Challenge: RF, ii, 1131.
49 Siege of Tournai: (a) two chronicles of Tournai in *KOF, xxv, 344–65; (b) other continental chronicles, Muisit, Chron., 127–36, Bel, Chron., i, 191–212, Chronographia, ii, 135–62, Grandes Chron., ix, 200–11, Récits d'un bourgeois, 181–5, Hocsem, Chron., 295–6; (c) English chronicles (less well informed), French Chron. London, 77–82, Baker, Chron., 70–1, Murimuth, Chron., 109–16, Avesbury, G. Edwardi, 314–7; (d) Ch. des Comptes, abstract of correspondence at BN Fr.n.a. 9239, fol. 274–274vo. Philip's movements: 'Itin. Philippe VI'. Numbers: Contamine (2) 69 (French Army); BN Fr.n.a. 9238–9, fols 44–77vo, 127vo–177vo, 211–4, 231vo, 232vo (Tournai garrison).
50 *KOF, xxv, 365.
51 Suppliques Clément VI, no. 1016; AN JJ72/178, JJ73/189, 327.
52 BN Fr.n.a. 9238, fol. 140.
53 Cart. des Artevelde, 235–8.
54 PRO C81/269/13359; Fowler, 35.
55 BN Fr.n.a. 9239, fol. 274vo; Benedict XII, Reg. (Autres pays), no. 2926.
56 Bock, Quellen, no. 603.

57 *RF*, ii, 1135–7, **KOF*, xviii, 176–7.

58 Déprez (1), 356.

59 Jousts: *Grandes Chron.*, ix, 209. Council: *CCR 1339–41*, 625–7; PRO C76/15, m. 6. Distress: Déprez (1), 355n, 357. Borrowing: Fowler, 35–7; *CCR 1339–41*, 639–40; E. Fryde (6), 1165–6. Falkenburg: Déprez (1), 357n. Ghent conference: *ibid.*, 356.

60 **Varenbergh, 346–7; *French Chron. London*, 83–6. Stratford: Benedict XII, *Reg. (Autres pays)*, no. 2981; *Vitae Arch. Cantaur.*, 20. Borrowing: *CCR 1339–41*, 649; *CCR 1341–3*, 225, 231, 286–7. D. of Brabant: **KOF*, xx, 56–7.

61 *RF*, ii, 1141; *French Chron. London*, 83–6; Murimuth, *Chron.*, 116; Avesbury, *G. Edwardi*, 323–4; *CPR 1340–3*, 110–1; BN Fr.n.a. 9239, fol. 274vo (French report).

62 *Vitae Arch, Cantaur.*, 21.

63 *Chronographia*, ii, 155–6; **KOF*, xviii, 186–8; *Actes intérressant la Belgique*, 146–8; *RF*, ii, 1166, 1167; Trautz, 313.

64 Ch. Islands: PRO E372/191, m. 52 (Ferrers). Scots: Fordun, *Chron.*, i, 365; BL Add. Chart. 4147.

65 Tout (1), iv, 104–9; the charges of the allies must be added to Cusance's account of 1340–1.

66 E. Fryde (6), 1142, 1165–6 and Table B; E. Fryde (4), 23; Villani, *Hist.*, XI: 88.

67 *French Chron. London*, 84–90; Murimuth, *Chron.*, 118–9; *Vitae Arch. Cantaur.*, 20–38.

68 Benedict XII, *Reg. (France)*, nos 830, 843–4, 852.

69 Henneman, 339–40.

70 Timbal, *Registres*, pp. 73–4, 81–6, 89–103.

71 Surveys: AN P2291, p. 767; BN PO 2525 (de Rogne, 2); *Arch. admin. Reims*, iii, 246. Noyon: Timbal, *Registres*, 175–9. Reims: Desportes, 528–9, 540–1. St-Quentin: *Arch. S.-Quentin*, ii, 99–104, 117, 122–4, 138–40, 142–3, 192. Artois: *Inventaire AD Pas-de-Calais*, i, 111, 111–12, ii, 22, 24, 27, 28, 29, 30, 31.

72 Desportes, 539–40 (Aubenton); BN Fr.n.a. 2598, fol. 50vo (La Capelle); Giry, 'Registre', 250–1 (S.-Omer); Timbal, *Régistres*, 185–8 (Lille); *Inventaire AD P.-de-Calais*, ii, 29 (Aire); *ibid.*, ii, 24 (bridges).

73 AN JJ73/145 (squire); **KOF*, xxv, 346 (castellan); *Chronographia*, ii, 158 (temper); Coville (2), 265 (verse).

CHAPTER XI

1 *Chron.*, ii, 86.

2 Jones, 'Documents', 15–70.

3 Nangis, *Chron.*, ii, 144; *Chron. anon. Par.*, 161. Marriage: **Duchesne, 118–20; Jones, 'Documents', 49–50.

4 Jones, 'Documents', 18, 52–3; Morice, *Preuves*, i, 1398.

5 B. d'Argentre, *Hist. de Bretagne*, 3rd edn (1618), 355; Jones, 'Documents', 27, 50.

6 Morice, *Preuves*, i, 1457.

7 Froissart, *Chron.*, ii, 318; *Chronographia*, ii, 167.

8 John's conquest of Brittany, May-Aug. 1341: Bel, *Chron.*, i, 248–59 (much exaggerated); *Chronographia*, ii, 166–75, 193; *Chron. Norm.*, 48–9. Nantes treasury: *RF*, ii, 1164. Champtoceaux: *Istore de Flandre*, ii, 2. St-Aubin: *Chron. Norm.*, 50. PRO E372/187, m. 48 (Swaffham) reveals John's presence in Nantes on 10 July.

9 **Duchesne, 120; *Chronographia*, ii, 176–80.

10 HGL, ix, 528–30, 536–7; Bock, *Quellen*, nos 561, 563; **Lecoy, ii, 296, 306–8. Occupation: BN Fr.n.a. 9236, pp. 193–6, 211–17.

11 *Confessions*, 167–9; *CPR 1345–8*, 546; PRO E101/166/12, m. 16, C61/54, mm. 18, 7, C61/59, m. 10; *RF*, ii, 1167. Date: BN Fr. 9237, pp. 628–97 (French garrison pay

records). Treason: AN X2a/4, fols 82, 82vo. La Motte family: PRO C61/52, mm. 20, 17; AN JJ72/457, JJ76/395.

12 BN Coll. Doat, 187, fols 202–204vo; BN Fr.n.a. 9237, p. 766; Trés. Chartes Albret, i, 529.

13 REP, ii, 126–34; Bridlington Chron., 38–41; French Chron. London, 89–90; RF, ii, 1177.

14 CFR 1337–47, 258; RP, ii, 126–7. Expedition: RF, ii, 1150, 1151; PRO C76/16, mm. 28, 28d, 27, 26d, 19, 16; PRO C47/2/33; Prestwich (2); CCR 1341–3, 302 (Antwerp destination).

15 RF, ii, 1160, 1165; Déprez (1), 378n; Cart. Hainault, i, 139–41. Ships, troops: PRO C76/14, mm. 19, 18, 17, 16.

16 H. Lot, 'L'avocat du Breuil', RH, 5th series, iv (1863), 137. Garrisons: Jassemin, 'Papiers', 193–7. Ships: DCG, no. XXVII (59–109, 571, 594–5, 652–3). Summons: Rec. doc. Poitiers, 351., South: Contamine (2), 68.

17 Petit Chron. Guyenne, 398–9; Gray, Scalacronica, 181–2; BN Fr.n.a. 9237, 696, 697, 752, 759; Très Chartes Albret, i, 529. French garrisons expelled; Bazas: RF, ii, 1188; PRO C61/54, m. 32; Ste-Bazeille: PRO C61/54, m. 22d; Damazan, Vianne, Durance: *HGL, x, 904–6; AN JJ68/234.

18 Henneman, 155–62, 340, 350; AN P2291, pp. 565–7.

19 Chronographia, ii, 180; *Anselme, vii, 912–3 (misdated 1342); DCG, no. XXVII (573–4, 652–3). Muster fixed for 26 Sept. (BN Fr.n.a. 7413, fol, 452); six weeks' notice normally required.

20 Conference: PRO E101/311/40; Muisit, Chron., 136–7; Cart. Hainault, i, 147–51; RF, ii, 1175. English preparations: PRO C76/16, m. 14d; *Déprez (1), 382n. Ship numbers: 213 requisitioned between London and Bristol, 3 April–26 May (PRO E101/22/39), adjusted down for desertions and up for contribution of Cinque Ports. Bayonne: RF, ii, 1173. Proceedings: Chron. Norm., 49; Chronographia, ii, 180; Bel, Chron., i, 260–1; Jones, 'Documents', 15–16, 70–1; PRO E372/187, m. 48 (Swaffham).

21 Jones, 'Documents', 15–70, 75–8; BN Fr. 22338, fols 117–55; Morice, Preuves, i, 1421–4; Grandes Chron., ix, 219–20; Chronographia, ii, 181–2; Bel, Chron., i, 261–4; RF, ii, 1176. Army: BN Fr.n.a. 7413, fol. 452.

22 RF, ii, 929, 1159; CFR 1337–47, 37–8; CCR 1337–9, 89–90, 94, 169, 171, 185; CCR 1339–41, 429; CCR 1341–3, 356; CPR 1334–8, 479; CPR 1338–40, 93; Borderie, iii, 404–7.

23 PRO E372/187, m. 48 (Swaffham), E101/23/5; RF, ii, 1176.

24 Murimuth, Chron., 121; PRO C76/16, m. 7d.

25 PRO C76/16, m. 10d; RF, ii, 1175, 1177; Cart. Hainault, i, 152–3.

26 Jones, 'Documents', 72 (recital); PRO C76/16, mm. 8d, 7, 7d, 4, 3, E403/323, m. 17; RF, ii, 1177, 1181.

27 PRO E101/22/39, C76/16, mm. 5d, 4, 3.

28 Brittany campaign, Sept.–Nov. 1341: Chronographia, ii, 183–95; Chron. Norm., 51–3; Bel, Chron., i, 264–71; Grandes Chron., ix, 220–1. Army: DCG, nos 396, XXI, XXII. Instructions: LC, no. 143. Other references below.

29 Dates: BN Fr.n.a. 7413, fols 417, 419; JT, no. 4723.

30 Date: cf. DCG, no. XXII.

31 Morice, Preuves, i, 1426–8; AN J241/43bis.; Murimuth, Chron., 131 (recital in truce of Malestroit). Imprisonment: Grandes Chron., ix, 220–1; Chron. Norm., 53.

32 Grandes Chron., ix, 21; Bel Chron., i, 270; Chron. Norm., 53; Morice, Preuves, i, 1429–30; AN J241/42 (pardons).

33 Morice, Preuves, i, 1428, 1429–30, 1431; AN J241/42.

34 Bel, Chron., i, 271–2; Chronographia, ii, 195.

35 Jones, 'Documents', 72–4; PRO C76/17, mm. 47, 47d, 44, E101/22/39, C62/119, m. 10;

RF, ii, 1187, 1189; *CFR 1337–47*, 270. Tournament, council: Murimuth, *Chron.*, 123–4.

36 AN J241/41, 43, 43bis.; Morice, *Preuves*, i, 1430, 1431.

37 *CCR 1341–3*, 536, 545–6; *CPR 1340–3*, 451, 454.

38 PRO E101/22/39, C76/17, mm. 43, 44; *CCR 1341–3*, 504, 505.

39 PRO C76/17, m. 43, E101/22/39.

40 *RF*, ii, 1190, 1191; PRO E36/204, p. 161. French summons: *Cordey, 298.

41 PRO C76/17, m. 44d.

42 Genoese: AN JJ74/685; *Chronographia*, ii, 196–7; Bel, *Chron.*, i, 307, 311, 323.
    Spaniards: *Cart. Rays*, i, pp. xxv–xxvi; *Chronographia*, ii 196–7; Bel, *Chron.*, i, 307, 311,
    321, 323, 327.

43 Bel, *Chron.*, i, 306–7; *Chron. Norm.*, 50–1.

44 Murimuth, *Chron.*, 125; Knighton, *Chron.*, ii, 23–4; Morice, *Preuves*, i, 7; *Grandes
    Chron.*, ix, 221–2. Dates, numbers: PRO E36/204, p. 210; Hervé's capture known in Paris
    by 2 June: *KOF, iii, 524–6. Vannes: *Denifle, 21n.

45 Tournament: Murimuth, *Chron.*, 124. Conference: PRO E36/204, p. 161; *RF*, ii, 1196;
    Muisit, *Chron.*, 137. Orders: *RF*, ii, 1195; PRO C76/17, m. 40.

46 *Grandes Chron.*, ix, 222–3; Bel, *Chron.*, i, 307–15, 319–20 (partly fictional); Charles was
    still at Hennebont on 13 June, Maitre, 'Repertoire', 247.

47 Murimuth, *Chron.*, 125; Knighton, *Chron.*, ii, 24; PRO E36/204, p. 210.

48 *Vitae Paparum*, i, 263; Lescot, *Chron.*, 57.

49 Clément VI, *L. Cl. (France)*, nos 94–6; PRO E403/326, m. 15; Murimuth, *Chron.*, 125–6;
    Lescot, *Chron.*, 58; *Grandes Chron.*, ix, 226–7.

50 Clément VI, *L. Cl. (France)*, no. 157, *Lettres*, no. 567; *Cart. Hainault*, i, 180–2; Muisit,
    Chron., 138; Lescot, *Chron.*, 58; *Grandes Chron.*, ix, 226–7.

51 BN Fr. 25996, no. 189.

52 Agenais: AN JJ68/234, JJ77/5; BN Fr. 7877, fols 219–219vo, 232; BN Clairambault
    70/5479, 5744; *HGL, x, 916–7. Ste-Bazeille: PRO C61/54, m. 22d; BN PO 2215 (Paule,
    3); BN Clairambault: 26/1877, 35/2615, 54/4085, 56/4251, 69/5401, 70/5479, 103/177,
    113/25, 114/119. Numbers: Contamine (2), 69.

53 Army: BN Fr.n.a. 7413, fols 453vo–456vo; BN PO 750 (du Chillot, 2). Covering force: BN
    Fr.n.a. 20025, fols 140–3; *Chronographia*, ii, 200. Ships: DCG, no. XXVII (571, 599,
    653). Blockade: *RF*, ii, 1210; *CPR 1340–3*, 562, 575, 579.

54 Bel, *Chron.*, i, 322–5; Murimuth, *Chron.*, 126; DCG, no. XXVII (653).

55 Numbers: E36/204, pp. 211–40, where the figures for troops exclude R. of Artois'
    contingent and those for ships exclude some which sailed in August and deserted before
    next passage. Reinforcements: PRO E372/190, m. 41 (Watenhull). Bohun: *RF*, ii, 1206.

56 PRO E403/326, mm. 15, 16, 17, 29, C61/54, m. 5, E36/204, p. 211; *CCR 1341–3*, 562–3,
    571, 653; *CCR 1343–6*, 209–10; *CPR 1340–3*, 567–8, 591.

57 PRO E372/187, m. 48 (Baddeby), C76/17, mm. 35d, 32, 31, E204/36, p. 211; Murimuth,
    Chron., 125.

58 Portsmouth: *RF*, ii, 1210; *CPR 1340–3*, 562, 575, 579. Brest: Murimuth, *Chron.*, 126–7.
    Charles went to Guingamp: DCG, no. XXVI. Louis' retreat: see below.

59 PRO C76/17, m. 33; Déprez (2), 63–4. Numbers: *CCR 1341–3*, 564; PRO E36/204,
    pp. 211–20.

60 Murimuth, *Chron.*, 127; *CPR 1343–5*, 33 (wrong date, see PRO C81/287/15131).
    Morlaix topography: *AHVF Morlaix*; Leguay, 174–5, 252.

61 PRO C76/17, mm. 30, 28, 22, 19, 17, 16, 16d, 15, 14, E36/204, pp. 211–20, E403/327, m.
    17; *CCR 1341–3*, 597–8, 621–5, 628–31, 651–2, 646, 686–90; *CCR 1343–6*, 70;
    Murimuth, *Chron.*, 227.

62 *Chronographia*, ii, 199–200; Murimuth, *Chron.*, 127–8; *RSG*, ii, 152–3, 204, 207, 254;
    Kervyn, iii, 275. Troop movements: BN Fr.n.a. 7413, fols 456vo–458vo; BN Clairambault
    7/369, 10/617, 41/3109, 44/3249, 76/5937.

63 Knighton, *Chron.*, ii, 25–6; Murimith, *Chron.*, 127, 128–9; Baker, *Chron.*, 76; *Doc. Monaco*, 315–6; *CPR 1343–5*, 130.

64 AN JJ74/53, 118; *Confessions*, 169; *Bertrandy, 280n; *AHP*, iv, 424.

65 PRO E101/167/3, mm. 8, 9, 15, 16, 18; BN Clairambault 6/275, 326, 7/323, 27/2017. French numbers: Contamine (2), 69.

66 Brittany campaign, Oct. 1342–Jan. 1343: (a) itineraries, Edward's reconstructed from PRO E36/204, pp. 65–84 and *Lescot, *Chron.*, 207–8, and 'Itin Philippe VI'; (b) Edward's letter to his son in Avesbury, *G. Edwardi*, 340–4; (c) English chroniclers, Murimuth, *Chron.*, 127–35, Knighton, *Chron.*, 26–7, *French Chron. London*, 91–2; (d) accounts of French spy Jobelin in *Lescot, *Chron.*, 228–30; (e) French chroniclers (unreliable in detail), *Chronographia*, ii, 196–204, *Chron. Norm.*, 54–9, Venette, *Chron.*, ii, 192, Lescot, *Chron.*, 58–9, *Grandes Chron.*, ix, 227–30, Bel, *Chron.*, ii, 10–21; (f) other references below. Mutinies of English fleet: *CCR 1343–6*, 128–33; PRO E372/192, m. 29 (Montgomery).

67 Death of R. of Artois: cf. *RF*, ii, 1215; Déprez (2), 65–6.

68 Artillery: cf. PRO E36/204, pp. 164, 220; *RF*, ii, 1213, 1215.

69 Protection money: PRO E36/204, p. 34.

70 PRO E36/204, p. 211, C76/17, mm. 20, 19, 18d, 17, 16, 15, 14d; *RF*, ii, 1213. Gloucester, Pembroke: E101/23/22, E372/190, m. 41 (Watenhull); *CPR 1343–5*, 494; *CIM*, ii, 489. Dec. plans: *RF*, ii, 1216, 1218; PRO C76/17, mm. 15d, 13, 13d, 12, 11, 11d.

71 AN K43/23; BN PO 1757 (Toubert, 8); BN Fr.n.a. 7413, fol. 466.

72 Murimuth, *Chron.*, 129–35; Avesbury, *G. Edwardi*, 343; Lescot, *Chron.*, 59, *230; *Grandes Chron.*, ix, 230; AN J636/18, 18bis (custody of Vannes).

73 Miret y Sans, 'Lettres closes', no. 11; *RP*, ii, 136(8).

74 Gray, *Scalacronica*, 299; Fordun, *Chron.*, i, 365; *Cal. doc. Scot.*, iii, no. 1383.

75 PRO E36/204, pp. 82–4; *RF*, ii, 1220.

76 Murimuth, *Chron.*, 135; PRO E372/203, m. 41 (Fraunkes, Haukesden); Borderie, iii, 488–91.

77 Hardeshull: *Bel, *Chron.*, ii, 334; *CCR 1343–5*, 131. Victuals: *RF*, iii, 3. Drafts: PRO C76/18, m. 4, C76/19, m. 23, E101/24/10. Galleys: PRO C76/19, m. 20. Brest: *RF*, ii, 1240; PRO C76/27, m. 13; Jones (1), 144–5.

78 Coupegorge: *CCR 1337–9*, 393; *CCR 1339–41*, 334; *CPR 1338–40*, 30; *CPR 1340–3*, 147, 162; *CPR 1343–5*, 351; PRO C76/19, m. 23. Brefs: *RF*, ii, 1241; PRO C61/56, mm. 7, 5d. Impositions: *RF*, ii, 1242; *KOF*, xviii, 342. Coinage: Planiol, iii, 388–9.

79 *KOF*, xviii, 339.

CHAPTER XII

1 Moranvillé, 'Rapports', 388; AN JJ75/135, 141, JJ76/338; *AP 1328–50*, no. 4176.

2 Avesbury, *G. Edwardi*, 140; *Confessions*, 151–2, 153–4; *Chronographia*, ii, 205–6. On Retz and Machecoul: A. Guillotin de Corson, 'Les grandes seigneuries de Haute Bretagne', *Bull. Soc. Arch. Nantes*, xxxvii, 201, 208–9; Touchard, 10–13. La Rochelle: AN X2a/5, fols 4vo, 7. Wife: *Chron. Norm.*, 61; AN X2a/4, fols 107vo, 113vo.

3 *Grandes Chron.*, ix, 236–7; Lescot, *Chron.*, 60, *230; *Delisle, 87–8, 95–106, 109–12; *AP 1328–50*, nos 4871–?; *Actes Normands*, 288; BN Fr.n.a. 7413, fol. 468; other references below.

4 *Confessions*, 151–2, 153–4; *Grandes Chron.*, ix, 242.

5 *Chronographia*, ii, 202–3, 208; *Grandes Chron.*, ix, 247–8; *Confessions*, 154–5.

6 *Grandes Chron.*, ix, 248. Seal: Bautier, 328. Council: Cazelles (1), 120–4. Queen: Froissart, *Chron.*, iii, 249.

7 Henneman, 152, 223; *Doc. Par.*, ii, 27; Cazelles (1), 394–8.

8 Daumet (2), 41 (Louis); *Chron. Norm.*, 220 (Eu).

9 Geoffroy de Paris, *Chron. Métrique*, ed. A. Diverres (1956), 208.

10 *JT*, nos 5399, 5650, 5942; *Cart. de . . . Bricquebec*, ed C. Breard (1908), 289–95; AN JJ66/837, J211/24. Taissons: Moranvillé, 'Rapports', 388.

11 Coville (1), 43–54, 58; Bois, 198–9, 218–20; *Chron. Quatre Valois*, 8–9.

12 AN P2291, pp. 599, 791, 793; Henneman, 167–9; Cazelles (1), 163.

13 *HGL*, x, 933; Coville (1), 58; Cazelles (1), 165–6; Henneman, 171–6.

14 *Ordonnances*, ii, 191; *Grandes Chron.*, ix, 245; BN Fr. 2598, fol. 53. Sales taxes: Henneman, 177–9.

15 AN P2291, pp. 585–8.

16 Hansa: E. Fryde (3), 2–3. Crown: CCR 1343–6, 292, 373–4; *Ancient Calendars and Inventories of the Exchequer*, ed. F. Palgrave, i (1836), 156. Breton campaign: Tout (1), iv, 111; PRO E403/327, 328, 331, 332, *passim*.

17 BN PO 1675 (de Laye, 4); *LC*, no. 165.

18 Baker, *Chron.*, 73; *RF*, ii, 1222.

19 *RF*, ii, 1145, 1183; PRO C49/7/15; Murimuth, *Chron.*, 121–2.

20 1342: PRO E403/326, mm. 15, 16, 17, 29, C61/54, m. 5; *RF*, ii 1204. 1343: *RF*, ii, 1222, 1229; PRO E101/167/3, mm. 8, 10; CCR 1343–6, 128; GEC, vii, 60.

21 Albret: CPR 1340–3, 255, 263; PRO E101/507/22. June 1344; CCR 1343–6, 389. Special grants: CCR 1341–3, 455, 562–3; CCR 1343–6, 128; PRO C61/54, m. 23.

22 *RF*, ii, 1229, 1236; PRO E403/331, m. 6 (Hugh).

23 PRO SC8/293/14603, 14613, C61/55, mm. 8, 7; *RF*, ii, 1235.

24 Caumont: AN JJ74/750; *AHG*, iv, 108–9. Bayonnais: *RF*, ii, 1149, 1180, iii, 23; CCR 1341–3, 548–9; PRO C61/53, m. 12, C61/56, m. 7d, E101/167/3, m. 1. Escort: *RF*, iii, 8.

25 Henneman, 167–77; *HGL*, ix, 546n.

26 Private war: AN JJ78/45 (Albigeois); *Ordonnances*, ii, 61–3. Routiers: *Ménard, ii, 126–8; *HGL*, ix, 546n. Agen, Condom: 'Chartes d'Agen', 113; *Ordonnances*, iii, 234–6.

27 St-Astier: BN Fr.n.a. 9237, pp. 752, 759. Montencès: *Inventaire AC Périgueux*, 78–9; *Maj. Chron. Lemovicensis, Rec. Hist. Fr.*, xxi, 788; AN JJ75/346. Mussidan: PRO C61/54, m. 29. Périgueux: AN JJ74/257.

28 *Confessions*, 164–72.

29 *AHP*, iv, 413–24, esp. 422, 424.

30 'Guyenne!': AN X2a/5, fols 204vo–205. Toulousain: *RF*, ii, 1101; Johnson, 'An Act'. Belcayre: *Inventaire AD Aveyron (Ser. G)*, 189. Mende: BN Fr.n.a. 9237, p. 759.

31 *HGL*, x, 988–97. Bourg: BN Fr.n.a. 9237, pp. 678–97; PRO C61/54, mm. 23, 21, 16. Ste-Bazeille: PRO C61/54, m. 22d.

32 *Confessions*, 170.

33 'Chartes d'Agen', 139–45; Viard (3), 362n; Cazelles (1), 195–6; *HGL*, ix, 563–4, 566–7, 571–3.

34 *RF*, ii, 1224; Murimuth, *Chron.*, 148; Jean du Tillet, *Recueil des guerres et des traitez* (1618), 235; *Grandes Chron.*, ix, 243; AN JJ76/248 (sureties).

35 Vannes: *RF*, ii, 1242, iii, 54; Clément VI, *L. Cl. (France)*, no. 2726 (col. 219). Redon: *RF*, ii, 1242 (it had been in French hands in Jan. 1343: 'Itin. Phillipe VI', 551). Ambush: *Chronographia*, ii, 206–7; *Istore de Flandre*, ii, 10; *Chron. Norm.*, 61; *Grandes Chron.*, ix, 245–7; BN Clairambault 68/41 (place).

36 *RF*, ii, 1242, iii, 1; PRO C76/19, mm. 23, 22, E403/331, mm. 29, 30, 36, E101/24/10.

37 *KOF*, xviii, 204–5.

38 *RF*, iii, 54; Knighton, *Chron.*, ii, 29; *Chronographia*, ii, 208–9; *Mon. procès de canonisation*; Morice, *Preuves*, i, 7–8; *Chron. Norm.*, 62; BN Fr. 2598, fols 53, 53vo; *Confessions*, 154–5, 156.

39 *RF*, iii, 11, 15, 16, 17; PRO C76/19, mm. 16, 5, SC1/56/8; Murimuth, *Chron.*, 158, 159–60.

40 PRO C76/19, mm. 15, 2d, E403/332, mm. 24, 25. Vannes: PRO E403/332, mm. 25, 27;

*KOF, xviii, 238. Submissions. AN JJ75/148–61, 235–6.

41 Morice, *Preuves*, i, 1442–7, 1452, 1457; BN Fr. 2598, fol. 53vo; Murimuth, *Chron.*, 164, 243; AN JJ68/219, JJ75/421, 471, JJ76/248, 260, JJ77/4.

42 Murimuth, *Chron.*, 136–8, 143, 148–9; *RF*, iii, 54; PRO E101/312/3,7.

43 Clément VI, *L. Cl. (France)*, nos 593–4, 743.

44 Derby embassy: PRO C70/20, m. 2; Clément VI, *L. Cl. (France)*, nos 864, 899, 1155–8; *RF*, iii, 54; *Grandes Chron.*, ix, 248–9; JT, no. 165; Murimuth, *Chron.*, 158–9. Bateman embassy: *RF*, iii, 18–19; Clément VI, *L. Cl. (France)*, no. 1039. French: *KOF, xviii, 226.

45 Miret y Sans, 'Lettres closes', 68. Bias: Clément VI, *L. Cl. (France)*, no. 743; *KOF, xviii, 203; *RF*, iii, 54. Marriage: *RF*, ii, 1140, iii, 32, 35; Clément VI, *L. Cl. (France)*, nos 1308, 1327, 1701; cf. similar assurances by Benedict XII in 1339, Benedict XII, *Reg. (France)*, no. 624.

46 Murimuth, *Chron.*, 138–40, 142–3, 149, 175, 229–30; *RP*, ii, 141, 143–5, 162; *RF*, ii, 1232, 1233–4; *KOF, xviii, 204, 206–7, 229–33.

47 Conference, diary of proceedings: *KOF, xviii, 202–72.

48 J. Stevenson, *Letters and Papers Illustrative of the Wars of the English in France during the Reign of Henry VI*, ii (1864), 577.

49 Murimuth, *Chron.*, 159–60; *KOF, xviii, 229, 230; PRO C70/20, m. 2; *RF*, iii, 25.

50 *RF*, iii, 32; Clément VI, *L. Cl. (France)*, nos 1574, 1590, 1591; Murimuth, *Chron.*, 163.

51 Knighton, *Chron.*, ii, 2–3; *RF*, ii, 982; CFR 1337–47, 26, 27, 28–36, 37–8, 144, 175–7, 191, 206, 207, 222, 235; on the change of policy, *ibid.*, 254, 258, 259, 261, 267, 268, 269, 271–5; CCR 1343–6, 48–9. Cf. *Actes Normands*, 344–5 (Dives); AN JJ74/74 (Eu).

52 Confiscations: *Lit. Cant.*, ii, 271; CIM,, ii, no. 1763; AN JJ68/46, JJ72/7, 296; *AP* 1328–50, no. 5504. Expatriates: *Chron. anon. Par.*, 175; *Arch. St.-Quentin*, ii, 122; *Doc. Par.*, ii, 107.

53 *AP* 1328–50, nos 2653, 4192, 4671; AN X2a/4, fols 119vo, 121; AN JJ72/285, JJ74/122, 454, JJ78/252; A. Thierry, *Recueil des monuments inédits du l'histoire de tiers état*, i (1850), 475.

54 CCR 1343–6, 82, 207, 267–8, 410–1, 428–9; CPR 1345–8, 30, 97. Calais: *Inventaire AD P.-de-Calais*, ii, 26, 29. Ships: *RF*, ii, 1138; PRO C76/18, m. 13; CPR 1343–5, 92. Timber: *RF*, ii, 1223. Horses: *RF*, iii, 30.

55 Bautier, 'Inventaires', no. 202; *Chron. anon. Par.*, 176; *Arch. St.-Quentin*, ii, 122. Somme: *Chron. mon. Melsa*, iii, 57.

56 *RF*, ii, 1061, 1190, 1213; CCR 1339–41, 458; CCR 1343–6, 158; *RP*, ii, 161(27).

57 *Doc. Amiens*, i, 441–3; CIM, ii, no. 1990.

58 AN X1a 31, fols 155–6; AN JJ78/60, 67.

59 France: *Doc. Par.*, ii, 106–7; AN JJ68/353, JJ74/577, JJ78/85, 149. England: CCR 1337–9, 94, 167, 169; CCR 1343–6, 511; CPR 1334–8, 488; *RF*, ii, 989; CPR 1340–3, 312; CIM, ii, no. 1763; 'Ancient Petitions' . . . ayant trait aux Iles de la Manche, 66. Cusance: CCR 1337–9, 165; CPR 1345–8, 89; *Doc. Par.*, ii, 34–5.

60 Salisbury: Gransden. Language: *RP*, ii, 147; *RF*, iii, 67, 72. Turks: RBP, i, 5. Invasion plans: Murimuth, *Chron.*, 211–12; *RP*, ii, 158. Preaching: *RF*, iii, 72, 81.

61 CPR 1343–5, 293–4, 513; CPR 1345–8, 112–13.

62 Eling: *Nonarum inquisitiones in curia scaccarii* (1807), 126. Yarmouth: CPR 1345–8, 213, 397; CIM, iii, no. 14. Chichester: CPR 1340–3, 587.

63 RDP, v, 43–4.

64 Davies, 80–4; Evans, 46–70, 75–7, *102–5; Willard and Morris, i, 342–3; RBP, i, 13, 14–15, 49–50, 55–6, 68, 80; *RF*, ii, 1216–17; *Cal. A. C. Wales*, no. XLII: 118.

65 *Cal. A. C. Wales*, nos LIV: 53, 102.

66 Lancaster: *RF*, iii, 5. Tournaments: *ibid.*; Murimuth, *Chron.*, 123, 146, 155–6, 231–2; J. Vale, 172–4.

67 CCR 1343–6, 190, 217; *RP*, ii, 136–8, 140, 147–8; Murimuth, *Chron.*, 156.

68 PRO C76/20, mm. 35, 32, 31, 30, 29, 27, 23, 22, 21, 13.
69 Montfort: Murimuth, *Chron.*, 243. Harcourt: PRO C76/20, m. 16; *RF*, iii, 44. Others: *RF*, iii, 35, 44. Third army: *RF*, iii, 36, 37, 38–9, 42; PRO E101/25/6, m. 1 (Harcourt).
70 *RF*, iii, 44, 45, 53–5; Murimuth, *Chron.*, 165–8. Armies: *RF*, iii, 44, 50; PRO E101/25/6, m. 1, E101/25/7, E101/25/9, mm. 4, 5; Murimuth, *Chron.*, 164, 168, 169–70.

CHAPTER XIII

1 *Chron.*, iii, 44.
2 Fowler, 222–4, *230–2; *RF*, iii, 32, 34–5, 37–8.
3 *HGL*, ix, 572.
4 Henneman, 181–4, 187–8.
5 Arras army: AN P2291, pp. 833, 841–3 (postponed in June to 8 Aug., *Grandes Chron.*, ix, 254); BN Fr. 25998/437. Spain, Portugal: *HGL*, x, 971; *Arch. admin. Reims*, ii, 949–51; Daumet (1), 10–17, *132–47. La Rochelle: *LE*, no. 240. Ships: *DCG*, nos 421, XXXII (21, 22); Roncière, i, 472, 474. Saintonge: BN Clairambault 5/229, 21/1501, 1675, 46/3419, 65/5023, 76/5937, 5981, 87/6889, 6895. Agenais, Languedoc: *HGL*, ix, 572, 580; Dupont-Ferrier, iii, no. 13671. Funds: *Bertrandy, 23n; *HGL*, ix, 572–3, 573n, *x, 969–72.
6 PRO E372/191, m. 54 (Lancaster); *RF*, iii, 58.
7 *Bertrandy, 24n; *Jurades d'Agen*, 21; AN JJ78/60 (Monbreton); *HGL*, ix, 580; BN Clairambault 212/9435.
8 Blaye: *Chronographia*, ii, 214. Langon: *Chron. Bazas*, 43. Périgord: AN JJ68/187, 199, 428, JJ78/148; AD Pyr.-Atl. E608; *Bertrandy, 50n.
9 *Chron. Norm.*, 66; *HGL*, x, 973; *Bertrandy, 32n; *Chron. Bazas*, 43. Bishop: BN Clairambault 5/229; *JT*, nos 910, 2751.
10 *RF*, iii, 44; Morice, *Preuves*, i, 8; PRO E101/25/6 (Ferrers).
11 PRO E372/191, m. 54 (Lancaster). Defence: *JT*, no. 185; *LE*, nos 244, 247; BN Clairambault 29/2121, 41/3099, 71/5507. 'Itin. Philippe VI'.
12 Lucas, 493–505, 509–11.
13 Lucas, 481–93; Werveke, 87–95.
14 Lucas, 511–7. Edward's visit to Sluys, death of van Artevelde: *RF*, iii, 50, 53, 55–6; Murimuth, *Chron.*, 169–70; *Récits d'un bourgeois*, 198–201; *Chron. Com. Flandrensium*, 216–17; *RSG*, ii, 391–3, *CPR 1374–7*, 508 (Appendix); *Chronographia*, ii, 211–12; *Chron. Norm.*, 63–5; *Istore de Flandre*, ii, 32–3; Villani, *Hist.* XII: 46, col. 926; Lucas, 519–27. Artevelde's family: PRO E403/336, mm. 10, 12, 15, 16, 20–1, 27, 33.
15 *RF*, iii, 55–6; Murimuth, *Chron.*, 170. Bourbon: *Ordonnances*, iii, 160.
16 Bergerac campaign: *Chron. Bazas*, 43–4: *Petit Chron. Guyenne*, 400; *Chronographia*, ii, 214–5; *Chron. Norm.*, 66–7; Murimuth, *Chron.*, 189; Knighton *Chron.*, ii, 118. Topography: *AHVF Bergerac*.
17 *Chron. Bazas*, 43; Knighton, *Chron.*, ii, 32.
18 *HGL*, ix, 579–81; E. Petit (1), viii, 4–5; *Titres Bourbon*, no. 2418; *LE*, nos 248–50, 258–60, 262, 264, and lists of French combatants at Auberoche in *Petit Chron. Guyenne*, 401, and Murimuth, *Chron.*, 190, 249–50.
19 S. Périgord: *Bertrandy, 33n, 36n , 44n; *HGL*, x, 973. March to Périgueux: Villani, *Hist.* XII: 46, col. 927; Knighton, *Chron.*, ii, 32; *Bertrandy, 97n (Maurens), 72n, 75 (St.-Astier); Murimuth, *Chron.*, 251 (St-Front de Pradoux, Sourzac); Avesbury, *G. Edwardi*, 356 (St-Louis, Lisle, Montagrier).
20 Avesbury, *G. Edwardi*, 356; *Rec. titres Périgueux*, 251, 253. Murimuth, *Chron.*, 251 (Biras, Bonneval); AN JJ68/428 (Ans); *Bertrandy, 77n, 105n (St-Privat, St-Raphaël). Topography: Higounet-Nadal, 25–7, 31–9; *AHVF Périgueux*.
21 *HGL*, ix, 581. Auberoche campaign: Bertrandy, 16; Villani, *Hist*, XII: 46, col. 927;

Chron. Bazas, 44; *Petit Chron. Guyenne*, 401; Murimuth, *Chron.*, 190, 249-50; Avesbury, *G. Edwardi*, 356-7; Clément VI, *L. Cl. (France)*, nos 2608-10. On occupation of Auberoche by English: *Bertrandy, 105n; AN JJ68/157, JJ80/699.

22 Keen (1), 156-74; Timbal, *Registres*, 305-74; *CPR 1345-8*, 468 (courts). Mauny: PRO E403/270 (Crabbe); *RF*, ii, 1123 (Guy, etc.); Knighton, *Chron.*, ii, 24, and *KOF*, iii, 525 (Bretons).

23 Montricoux: *Bertrandy, 51n, 117n; *HGL*, ix, 575-6; Anselme, ii, 195. Nephew: Clément VI, *L. Cl. (France)*, no. 2608. Galard: AN JJ68/79. Derby: Knighton, *Chron.*, ii, 118; Villani, *Hist.* XII:46, col. 927.

24 Villani, *Hist.* XII:46, col. 927; Bertrandy, 265-71; *JT*, nos 2265, 2270, 3187, 3368, 3649, 4311, 4535; E. Petit (1), viii, 5n. Seneschal: *HGL*, x, 973.

25 PRO E101/25/6.

26 BN Fr. 25998/437; *JT*, no. 278.

27 BL Add. Chart, 3323-4; Morice, *Preuves*, i, 8, 113; *Grandes Chron.*, ix, 255-6; Murimuth, *Chron.*, 189.

28 *RDP*, iv, 556-7; Murimuth, *Chron.*, 176-7; PRO C76/21, m.4.

29 *Grandes Chron.*, ix, 260-4. Guningamp: Leguay, 43. Roche-Derrien: Touchard, 324.

30 Murimuth, *Chron.*, 190-2; *Bertrandy, 64n; *Chron. Bazas*, 45.

31 *Avesbury, G. Edwardi*, 356: *Bertrandy, 64n; *Chron. Bazas*, 45.

32 Chron. Bazas, 44; *Chron. Norm.*, 69-70; *Grandes Chron.*, ix, 259; *AHG*, i, 302-3. Bourbon: *Doc. Millau*, 82; BN Col. Doat 189, fol. 183. Topography; *AHV La Réole*. Rewards: *Bertrandy, 168n; *RF*, iii, 125; PRO C61/57, m. 2, C61/59, mm. 12, 10, 9, 8, 7, 6, SC8/243/12141, 12154-55.

33 PRO E372/191, m. 54 (Pembroke), E372/202, m. 37 (Audley), E101/24/20.

34 Angoulême (not an error for Agen or Aiguillon): *Chron. Norm.*, 70-1; Bel, *Chron.*, ii, 43-4, 50-4. Toulouse: AD Hérault A1/12, 16, 17, 19, 20; Bertrandy, 298-9. Limoges: *Bertrandy, 223n; *LE*, no. 296. Rouergue: Débat, 'Trois lettres', 73-6.

35 Froissart, *Chron.*, iii, 77, 303. Ste-Foy; *Chron. Norm.*, 67. Bazas: *JT*, no. 1366; *Chron. Bazas*, 43. Langon: Knighton, *Chron.*, ii, 32. Ste-Bazeille: Bel, *Chron.*, ii, 40. Other conquests: Murimuth, *Chron.*, 251.

36 *Doc. Durfort*, pp. xxvii-xxx, nos 918-19, 931, 947, 949-54.

37 Anarchy: *Jurades d'Agen*, 31. Tonneins, Damazan, Villefranche de Queyran: *Chron. Norm.*, 69; Bel, *Chron.*, ii, 43. Castelsagrat, Beauville, Balamont, Montclar, Montagnac: *Jurades d'Agen*, 60. Miramont, St-Sardos, Pressas: Murimuth, *Chron.*, 251. Villeneuve: Muisit, Chron., 151. Montpezat: *Bertrandy, 227n; *Chronographia*, ii, 217; *Chron. Norm.*, 68; Bel. *chron., ii, 42. Castelmoron: *Jurades d'Agen*, 98. Moissac: *Doc. Durfort*, no. 929. Port Ste-Marie: *Bertrandy, 317n.

38 *Jurades d'Agen*, 32-8, 40-7, 53-4, 60, 68-9, 72, 79-80; 'Chartes d'Agen', 150-1, 153-5; Tholin, 25-8; *AHVF Agen*.

39 *Bertrandy, 295n.

40 Guesnon, 'Documents', 233-6; *Arch. admin. Reims*, ii, 977, 1019; *Grandes Chron.*, ix, 265; *Ordonnances*, ii, 238-41; *H. Hervieu, *Recherches sut les premiers États-Généreaux* (1879), 244-5; AN P2291, pp. 55-8; Henneman, 191-202.

41 *HGL*, x, 976-80, 984-7.

42 Aragon: *LC*, no. 175. Ships, bowmen: *DCG*, XXII (34, 81, 84-791, 1016-17, 1022, 1041-2); *Doc. Monaco*, i, 330-1; AN P2291, pp 553-7; Roncière, i, 4/4-6, *JT*, nos 2198, 4874.

43 Compositions, forced loans: Henneman, 189, 206-7. Queen: AN J357/14bis; *JT*, no. 268. John: BN Chairambault 67/5245. Pope: Clément VL, *L. Cl. (France)*, nos 1852, 2180; *Bertrandy, 292n, 293n, 294n; *HGL*, x, 1019-20; 'Inventarium instrumentorum', 71-2, 76; *Faucon, 572-4.

44 *HGL*, x, 980-2.

45 BN Fr. 32510, fol. 185–7; *LE*, nos 272–428; E. Petit (1), viii, 6–7; *Jurades d'Agen*, 60; *HGL*, ix, 583, 585n, 586–8; Anselme, vi, 701–2; *JT*, no. 380; Bertrandy, 309–10; *DCG*, no. XXXII (1016). Siege train: *HGL*, ix, 583; Lacabane, 43. *Arrière-ban*: AD Hérault A4/178.

46 Siege of Aiguillon, to June: *Chron. Norm.*, 71–3; *Chronographia*, ii, 220–1; *Istore de Flandre*, ii, 35–7; Villani, *Hist.*, XII: 46, col. 928; Bel, *Chron.*, ii, 49–50, 56–64; Knighton, *Chron.*, ii, 40; Murimuth, *Chron.*, 249; Baker, *Chron.*, 78. Other references below.

47 AD Hérault A4/178.

48 Keen (1), 131–3.

49 Lancaster: Fowler, 264. Reinforcements: PRO E101/25/9; *RF*, iii, 77.

50 Topography: Gardelles, 83–4; *Rôles Gascons 1307–17*, no. 1709; *Bertrandy, 365n; Knighton, *Chron.*, ii, 41; Bel, *Chron.*, ii, 62.

51 Chain: *Jurades d'Agen*, 70.

52 Ransom: Bertrandy, 326–7.

CHAPTER XIV

1 *RDP*, iv, 556–7; 'Compte de P. de Ham', 244–5 (Flemings); PRO E403/336, m. 40 (Bretons).

2 *CCR 1346–9*, 46–7, 72–4, 186–7; *CFR 1337–47*, 463–5; E. Fryde (3), 3–8, 11–16.

3 *CPR 1343–5*, 414–16, 427–8; PRO C76/22, mm. 2, 13, 16, 34d; *RF*, iii, 77–8; *RP*, ii, 160; *CPR 1345–8*, 112–13; Murimuth, *Chron.*, 192–3, 198.

4 Hewitt, 54–8, 64–6, 68–9; *CCR 1346–9*, 44; *CPR 1345–8*, 113; *CFR 1337–47*, 486; Murimuth, *Chron.*, 245; Knighton, *Chron.*, ii, 32.

5 *RF*, iii, 67, 72.

6 *RF*, iii, 71, 78; PRO C76/22, m. 6.

7 *RF*, iii, 67–8; PRO C76/22, mm. 3, 3d, 16; *Cal. A. C. Wales*, nos LIV:53, 93.

8 Border: *RS*, i, 680–1; *Baldwin, 483–4. Coast: *RF*, iii, 72, 77, 81; PRO C76/22, mm. 10, 12.

9 Aliens: *CIM*, ii, nos 1946, 1990; *RP*, ii, 161(27). Spies: 'Compte de P. de Ham', 244–5, 246–7; *Bel, *Chron.*, ii, 338.

10 Northampton: Prince (1), 370–1. Gascony: *Fowler, 232; Murimuth, *Chron.*, 200.

11 *Jones (2), 637.

12 Crossbowmen: *Acta bellicosa*, 159. Piles: *Chron. anon. Cant.*, 187. Merchant ships: *DCG*, no. XXXII(76); *JT*, no. 1959; Avesbury, *G. Edwardi*, 358, 359–60; Roncière, i, 475–6. Galleys: AN P2291, pp. 553–6; *DCG*, nos 427, XXXII (84–758); *Lecoy, ii, 354.

13 *Grandes Chron.*, ix, 265–9; Lescot, *Chron.*, 69–70.

14 Galbraith, 'Hist. aurea', 213–14; *Jones (2), 637–9.

15 Bertrandy, 329–30, 332–3, *334n, *341n; Knighton, *Chron.*, ii, 40–1; *HGL*, x, 1002; Bel, *Chron.*, ii, 62–4.

16 Murimuth, *Chron.*, 198; PRO C76/22, mm. 10d, 17, 18; *RF*, iii, 78.

17 Baker, *Chron.*, 79; Froissart, *Chron.*, iii, 131 (tr. based on Berners, i, 277); the decision was probably made at the same time as the decision to send Hastings to Flanders, see below. Earlier interest in Normandy: *KOF, xviii, 38; *CPR 1338–40*, 454.

18 *RF*, iii, 83, 86; PRO C76/22, m. 25, C76/23, m. 23, E372/191, m. 49 (Wendyngburgh); 'Compte de P. de Ham', 247; Knighton, *Chron.*, ii, 34–5. Mautravers: *RF*, iii, 56; *KOF, xxii, 189. Flemish deliberations: *RSG*, ii, 492; Muisit, *Chron.*, 151; Lucas, 547–8.

19 *Bel, *Chron.*, ii, 337–8; *RF*, iii, 85; Murimuth, *Chron.*, 201; Baker, *Chron.*, 79; Villani, *Hist.* XII:62, col. 944.

20 BN Fr.n.a. 7413, fols 472–5; *DCG*, nos 431–2, XXXII(1016); *Acta bellicosa*, 159.

21 *RP*, ii, 147; *RS*, i, 664–7; *CIM*, ii, no. 2051; *Chron. Lanercost*, 341; Walsingham, *Ypod. Neustr.*, 285; Murimuth, *Chron.*, 189; *Anonimalle Chron.*, 19.

22 Text in Hemingburgh, *Chron.*, ii, 420–2.

23 Noyal, 'Fragments', 253; AN JJ75/425; Muisit, *Chron.*, 171; *Grandes Chron.*, ix, 269–70.

24 *Bel, *Chron.*, ii, 337–8; *RF*, iii, 85; *Acta bellicosa*, 157–8; Murimuth, *Chron.*, 198–9, 200; Avesbury, *G. Edwardi*, 360. Genoese: *DCG*, no. XXXII(105).

Crécy campaign, July–Sept. 1346: (a) *Acta bellicosa*, a detailed eyewitness account to 20 Aug.; (b) two letters from Edward III (1. PRO C81/314/17803, of which extracts, edited by the Council, at *Chron. Lanercost*, 342–3, *KOF*, xviii, 285–7, *RF*, iii, 89–90; 2. *Chandos Herald, *The Black Prince*, ed. H. A. Coxe, 1842, 351–5), and letters from members of the army and household, Thomas Bradwardine, Michael Northburgh and Richard Wynkeley (Murimuth, *Chron.*, 200–4, 212–17, Avesbury, *G. Edwardi*, 358–63, 367–72); (c) Edward's itinerary in *Baker, *Chron.*, 252–7; (d) English chronicles, Baker, *Chron.*, 79–86, *Chron. anon. Cant.*, 187–92, Knighton, *Chron.*, ii, 32–9, *Eulogium hist.*, iii, 206–11, *Chron. Lanercost*, 341–4, *Anonimalle Chron.*, 20–3, Chandos Herald, *Vie*, 51–9, *Chron. mon. Melsa*, iii, 55–60; (e) French chroniclers, *Chron. Norm.*, 75–83, *Chronographia*, ii, 223–35, *Istore de Flandre*, i, 23–6, 39–46 (valuable for the preliminaries of the battle), Lescot, *Chron.*, 71–5, Venette, *Chron.*, 196–203, *Grandes Chron.*, ix, 270–85 (important); (f) 'neutral' chroniclers, Bel, *Chron.*, ii, 70–110 (the principal continental account based, for the battle, on John of Hainault), Muisit, *Chron.*, 151–66 (laconic, very accurate), *Récits d'un bourgeois*, 214–36, Villani, *Hist.* XII:62–7, cols 944–52 (probably based not on Genoese accounts but on Florentine newsletters from London and Bruges, in turn based on newsletters from the English army); (g) 'Itin. Philippe VI'. Other references below.

25 *JT*, nos 1959, 2583.

26 *RF*, iii, 89; *Acta bellicosa*, 160. Courts: cf. in an earlier period, *Cal. doc. Scot.*, ii, no. 822; Guisborough, *Chron.*, 246.

27 Denifle, 36; *JT*, nos 1963, 3736.

28 BN Fr.n.a. 7413, fol. 472, Fr. 20363, fol. 175; *JT*, no. 1539.

29 Hastings: PRO E372/191, m. 49 (Wendyngburgh); 'Compte de P. de Ham', 247.

30 Text in Hemingburgh, *Chron.*, ii, 422–3.

31 *RS*, i, 672–3; *Baldwin, 483–4; *Chron. Lanercost*, 341; *Anonimalle Chron.*, 19; Knighton, *Chron.*, ii, 32–3; Raine, *N. Reg.*, 387–9.

32 Norman knights (Roland de Verdon, Nicholas de Grouchy): PRO E403/336, mm. 21, 26, 30, E403/339, m. 46, E403/340, m. 7; Cazelles (1), 152.

33 Desertions: PRO C76/23, m. 21.

34 Topography of Caen: Prentout, 20–5; AN JJ68/220; Denifle, 37n.

35 *Chron.*, iii, 147.

36 Holland's Baltic crusade (Bel, *Chron.*, ii, 82) is confirmed by *Cal. Pap. R. Letters*, iii, 252.

37 AN JJ68, fol. 439 (struck out).

38 Reinforcements, supplies: PRO C76/23, mm. 22, 22d, 21, 20, 19; *RF*, iii, 87. Le Crotoy: PRO C81/314/17803.

39 Eu: *RF*, iii, 126; Avesbury, *G. Edwardi*, 414. Tancarville: *Accounts Chamberlains of Chester*, 126; *RBP*, i, 28, 33, 45, 48, 60, 62, iv, 14; AN JJ77/216, JJ79A/32; *JT*, nos 1018, 1245, 2640, 2651, 2935.

40 *RP*, ii, 158–9; Murimuth, *Chron.*, 211–12.

41 Cardinals: Clément VI, *L.Cl. (France)*, nos 2726, 2760; *RF*, iii, 88.

42 'Compte de P. de Ham', 248; *Inventaire AD P.-de-Calais*, i, 115; PRO E372/191, m. 49 (Wendyngburgh); Muisit, *Chron.*, 151–2; Knighton, *Chron.*, ii, 34–5; *Chron. Com. Flandrensium*, 219.

43 Bel, *Chron.*, ii, 63–4.

44 'Chartes d'Agen', 152; *Jurades d'Agen*, 71, 73, 75–6, 88–9, 90–3; *JT*, no. 4358.
45 *Arrière-ban*: *Arch. admin. Reims*, ii, 1124. Genoese: cf. *DCG*, XXXII(106).
46 Pont-l'Évêque: AN JJ79A/14.
47 Call for authority: Oxford, MS Bodley 462, fol. 28vo.
48 Cf. *Actes Normands*, 347.
49 Genoese: *DCG*, no. XXXII(611, 768). Pay records show only about 5 per cent casualties among galley crew; they cannot therefore have fought at Crécy: *DCG*, no. XXXII(84–768).
50 *KOF*, iv, 496–7.
51 Genoese: *Inventaire AD P.-de-Calais*, i, 115.
52 Avesbury, *G. Edwardi*, 372–3; Knighton, *Chron.*, ii, 40–1; Bel, *Chron.*, ii, 117; Baker, *Chron.*, 78; Murimuth, *Chron.*, 249. John's itinerary after Aiguillon: AN JJ77/313; BN Coll. Doat 189, fol. 263.
53 *CPR 1345–8*, 516–17.
54 Somme army: *JT*, nos 806, 936, 2276, 3206, 3340, 3370, 4433, 4527, 4540.
55 Hangings: Froissart, *Chron.*, iii, 151–2.
56 Gates: cf. AN JJ77/384.
57 *Inventaire AD P.-de-Calais*, i, 115.
58 Townsmen: *Inventaire AD P.-de-Calais*, i, 115; *Ordonnances*, iv, 143–5; Loisne, 'Ordonnances', 708–10.
59 Runners: PRO E372/191, m. 49 (Wendyngburgh).
60 Noyelles: *LE*, no. 467. Crotoy: cf. AN JJ100/151. Reinforcements, supplies: PRO C76/23, mm. 19, 19d, 18, 18d, 14d.
61 Hence Baker's nine 'turmae', *Chron.*, 82.
62 Tout (2), 237–9, 254, 258–62. Berwick: Nicholson (1), 121–2.
63 Froissart, *Chron.*, iii, 177.
64 War-cries: Contamine (2), 666 (French); *Récits d'un bourgeois*, 220 (English).
65 Holland: *RBP*, i, 45.
66 *Chron.*, iii, 183 (tr. Berners, i, 300).
67 Cf. Léger, 'Poème tchèque', 326–7.
68 Cf. Moranvillé (1); Clément VI, *L.Cl. (France)*, no. 2790.
69 Cf. JJ107/310.
70 Wissant: *Suppliques de Clément VI*, no. 1470.
71 *RF*, iii, 89.
72 Valognes: *Acta bellicosa*, 161. Carentan: *Grandes Chron.*, ix, 271, 290; *Lescot, Chron.*, 71n. Runners: AN JJ76/393. Peasants: Murimuth, *Chron.*, 200. Bayeux: Avesbury, *G. Edwardi*, 360. Caen: *Chronographia*, ii, 225–6.
73 Muisit, *Chron.*, 166.
74 *Grandes Chron.*, ix, 290; *Delisle, 109–11; *CFR 1337–47*, 490, 495.

CHAPTER XV

1 P. Bougard and C. Wyffels, *Les finances de Calais* (1966), 11, 198–221; Brown *et al.*, 423–50; Patourel (2); Baker, *Chron.*, 89.
2 *JT*, nos 661–3, 854, 893, 1922, 1935, 2239–42, 4614, 5025; 'Compte de P. de Ham', 246–8; *Inventaire AD P.-de-Calais*, i, 115. J. de Vienne: Anselme, vii, 806.
3 Venette, *Chron.*, ii, 203; Muisit, *Chron.*, 166.
4 *RF*, iii, 89–90; *RBP*, i, 57–8, 85; PRO C76/23, mm. 17d, 15d, 12d, 8, 7, 5, 4, 3, E403/339, mm. 24, 27, 33; Avesbury, *G. Edwardi*, 369; Bel, *Chron.*, ii, 112; *Grandes Chron.*, ix, 285–6; Lescot, *Chron.*, 75; *Istore de Flandre*, ii, 61; Baker, *Chron.*, 89.
5 Parlt.: *RP*, ii, 157–63(5–14, 18–19, 45). Cardinals: Muisit, *Chron.*, 166.
6 *Grandes Chron.*, ix, 286–7.

7 *DCG*, no. XXXII (792–921); *JT*, nos 420, 750, 796, 806, 936, 1771, 2269, 2276, 3206, 3340, 3370, 4433, 4527, 4540, 4635, 5030; 'Itin. Philippe VI'; *Recits d'un bourgeois*, 237; *Arch. St.-Quentin*, ii, 198; AN P2291, p. 779; *Arch. admin. Reims*, ii, 1124.

8 Muisit, *Chron.*, 167; Murimuth, *Chron.*, 217; *RF*, iii, 91; PRO C76/23, mm. 18, 17, 14d; *DCG*, no. XXXII(37).

9 *Chron. Norm.*, 83–4; *RSG*, iii, 121–30; Muisit, *Chron.*, 164–7; *Chron. Com. Flandriae*, 219–20; *Istore de Flandre*, ii, 58–9; Knighton, *Chron.*, ii, 39; *Récits d'un bourgeois*, 240; *JT*, no. 672; AN JJ68/329.

10 *Arch. St.-Quentin*, ii, 199; *JT*, no. 290; *Grandes Chron.*, ix, 288; Viard (2); Timbal, *Registres*, 63–4, 67, 97–8.

11 Avesbury, *G. Edwardi*, 373; Murimuth, *Chron.*, 217.

12 *HGL*, ix, 595–8.

13 Avesbury, *G. Edwardi*, 373–4; Bel, *Chron.*, ii, 118–19; Muisit, *Chron.*, 167–8; *Grandes Chron.*, ix, 287; Bertrandy, 377; *CPR 1345–8*, 562; *Reg. St.-Jean d'A*, i, 134–6, 138; *Ordonnances*, xviii, 690–1; Clément VI, *L. Cl. (France)*, no. 2901.

14 Avesbury, *G. Edwardi*, 374; *Chron. Norm.*, 69; *Istore de Flandre*, ii, 60–1; *Rec. doc. Poitou*, iii, 1–3.

15 *Rec. doc. Poitiers*, ii, 90–1, 94–5, 97–8; Favreau, 150–1.

16 Avesbury, *G. Edwardi*, 374; Bel, *Chron.*, ii, 123–4; *Rec. doc. Poitou*, ii, 332–5, 356–8, 370–5, 429–34, iii, 58–60; *Chartes . . . de l'abbaye de Charroux*, ed. D.P. de Montsabert, *AHP*, xxxix, 308–9; Favreau, 153.

17 S.-Jean d'A.: *Chron. Quatre Valois*, 12–13. Survey: BN Clairambault 163/4765. Refuges: *Cartulaire de N.D. des Chatelliers*, ed. L. Duval, *Mems. Soc. Stat. Sci. et Arts Deux-Sèvres*, 2e serie, vii (1867), 134–5, 137.

18 *Rec. doc. Poitou*, ii, pp. xxx–xxxvi.

19 Avesbury, *G. Edwardi*, 374; *Chron. Maillezais*, 166–7; Bel, *Chron.*, ii, 122–3; *Rec. doc. Poitou*, ii, p. xxxv.

20 Avesbury, *G. Edwardi*, 373–4; *Chron. Maillezais*, 167; PRO C61/60, mm. 36, 39 (S.-Jean d'A.); AN X2a/5, fols 180, 189 (Lusignan).

21 Tonnay-Charente: AN JJ76/321, JJ86/37; PRO C61/60, mm. 1, 3, 19, 20, 41. Soubise: PRO C61/60, mm. 12, 16, 41; *Rec. doc. Poitou*, ii, 331. Tonnay-Boutonne: PRO C61/60, m. 17. Rochefort: *CPR 1345–8*, 560. Oléron: *AHSA*, vi, 229–30; AN JJ77/192.

22 Coiron: *AHSA*, xli, 244–6. Conac: PRO C61/60, m. 7; *CPR 1345–8*, 546. Cheray: Denifle, 33. Saintes, Talmont: Bertrandy, 380. Taillebourg: *Rec. doc. Poitou*, ii, 331.

23 La Rochelle: AN JJ77/80, 194. Niort: *Rec. doc. Poitou*, ii, 343. Aulnay: *LE*, nos 527, 629. Saintes: AN JJ77/233. Spies: AN JJ76/321; *Inventaire AC Périgueux*, 80. Freebooters: AN JJ76/380. Marsh: *Reg. S.-Jean d'A.*, i, 116–30; *JT*, no. 241.

24 *Rec. doc. Poitou*, ii, 329–30; *AHSA*, vi, 230.

25 AN JJ76/303; *Doc. Durfort*, nos 943–6.

26 *Inventaire AC Clermont-F.*, i, 368–9; *Doc. Durfort*, no. 946; *HGL*, ix, 598; *JT*, no. 3649; Baluze, 199, *717–18; *Jurades d'Agen*, 94.

27 Bazadais: *Jurades d'Agen*, 98; Bertrandy, 181–3, 185. Treasons: *HGL*, ix, 598–601.

28 Neville's Cross campaign: *CIM*, ii, no. 2051; *CCR 1346–9*, 448–9; *Chron. Lanercost*, 344–51; Baker, *Chron.*, 86–9; *Anonimalle Chron.*, 23–8; Murimuth, *Chron.*, 218–19, 252–3; Knighton, *Chron.*, ii, 41–4; Letters of Thomas Samson (*KOF*, v, 489–92) and Prior of Durham (Raine, *N. Reg.*, 387–9, 392–5); Fordun, *Chron.*, i, 367; Bower, *Chron.*, ii, 339–40, 341–3; Wyntoun, *Oryg. Chron.*, ii, 470–7. Other references below.

29 Cf. *RS*, i, 685.

30 *Cal. doc. Scot*, v, nos 802–3.

31 Spies: *RS*, i, 673–4. Numbers: Morris (5), 98–9.

32 Barge: PRO E403/339, mm. 17–18. Prisoners: *RS* i, 675–6, 677–9, 680, 684, 685, 688; *RF*, iii, 99, 102–3 ; *CCR 1346–9*, 332–3; *CPR 1345–8*, 225; Morris (5), 102.

33 AD Hérault A1/15; *Baluze, 717–18; BN Fr.n.a. 9421, fols 95, 102–54; JT, no. 373.
34 BN Fr.n.a. 9241, fols 102–54; Arch. admin. Reims, ii, 1124n.
35 Ludewig, Reliquiae, v, 465–7; RF, iii, 92; DCG, no. XXXII (34, 84, 947).
36 Godemar: Froissart, Chron., iii, 437 (derived from J. of Hainault). Montmorency: Cazelles (1), 178. Financial officials: Grandes Chron., ix, 288–9; Cazelles (1), 181–9, *460–3.
37 John, Mauny: Bel, Chron., ii, 128–9; Muisit, Chron., 168; Récits d'un bourgeois, 243–4; RBP, i, 33; Ludewig, Reliquiae, v, 450–1; Cazelles (1), 201–5. D. of Burgundy: Cazelles (1), 196–201; LE, no. 502.
38 BN Coll. Périgord 13, fol. 298; AN JJ76/380; RF, iii, 157. Cf. LC, no. 203.
39 Venette, Chron., ii, 204–5; Lescot, Chron., 75; Grandes Chron., ix, 291; Ordonnances, ii, 252–7, 262–3; HGL, ix, 602; Rec. doc. Poitou, ii, 361–3; Viard (9), 169n; LC, no. 185.
40 DCG, nos 441, XXXII(1032, 1156, 1199, 1239, 1243–4); JT, nos 2302, 2913, 3134.
41 Guesnon, 'Documents', 237–40.
42 *Bel, Chron., ii, 338–40; RF, iii, 93–5, 98; Knighton, Chron., ii, 39; Tout (2), 241–2, 259–60, 261; PRO E372/191, mm. 11, 7 (Surrey, Sussex, Essex) (ladders), E403/339, m. 33 (troops), C76/23, m. 8 (carpenters); Guesnon, 'Documents', 239–40.
43 RF, iii, 94, 96; CPR 1345–8, 308–9; PRO C76/23, mm. 4d, 3d, 3.
44 DCG, nos XXXII (1126bis–1152); AN J602/46–7; JT, nos 1981–3.
45 JT, nos 1157, 1163, 1207, 1752, 1898; DCG, no. XXXII (922–46, 950–9, 1008–9, 1020–1, 1025–9, 1034, 1038–9, 1048, 1153–1301); Récits d'un bourgeois, 245; Knighton, Chron., ii, 46–7.
46 Grandes Chron., ix, 291; Arch. admin. Reims, ii, 1124n, 1152–4; LC, nos 182, 185; Viard (9), 168n, 169n; 'Itin. Philippe VI'; JT, nos 1035, 1097, 1372, 1749, 1799, 2236, 2250, 3098, 4526, 4529, 4534, 4541, 4681, 4728, 4753.
47 Taxes: Henneman, 216–27; Ordonnances, ii, 262; Arch. admin. Reims, ii, 1145, 1151; LC, nos 181–2; Actes Normands, 322–5, Reims: Arch. admin. Reims, ii, 1153; Desportes, 541–4.
48 AN X2a/5, fol. 97. Landas: AN JJ68/262; Anselme, vi, 166. Châtillon: AN JJ68/324; Duchesne, 380. Noyers: E. Petit (2), 279. Messelan: AP 1328–50, no. 8479; AN JJ76/225.
49 Burgundy: CPR 1345–8, 517; Bock, 'English Register', 366; E. Petit (1), viii, 17–24.
50 Muisit, Chron., 172–3, 174–5; Grandes Chron., ix, 293–6; Chronographia, ii, 241; Noyal, 'Fragments', 253–4; Moranvillé (2); AN JJ77/183, JJ80/396; Arch. admin. Reims, ii, 1153–4.
51 Grandes Chron., ix, 296.
52 Avesbury, G. Edwardi, 383; Muisit, Chron., 168.
53 AN JJ77/42; Bel, Chron., ii, 136–9; Muisit, Chron., 169–70; Venette, Chron., ii, 208–9; Chronographia, ii, 237–9; Chron. Com. Flandriae, 222; Chaplais, Dipl. Practice, 503–7.
54 Récits d'un bourgeois, 247–8; Muisit, Chron., 176.
55 Muisit, Chron., 171; Chron. Norm., 86.
56 LE, nos 456–7, 462–3, 472–3, 475; JT, nos 332, 761, 2093, 2219, 2725, 3291; Philip VI, 'Nouvelles LC', 177–8; Récits d'un bourgeois, 249; Chron. Norm., 86.
57 Istore de Flandre, ii, 51–2, 53–4, 61, 63–5; Muisit, Chron., 173–4, 176; Chron Norm., 86, 87–8; Chronographia, ii, 240–1, 242–3; RSC, iii, 133–6; JT, no 562 (Renti).
58 Councils: RDP, iv, 562–3; CFR 1347–56, 1–10; RF, iii, 112–13, 115; RP, ii, 166(11); CPR 1345–8, 264. Loans: CCR 1346–9, 290–1; E. Fryde (3), 11–12; RF, iii, 102; Harriss, 450–1.
59 Bel, Chron., ii, 152, *344–5; Knighton, Chron., ii, 47.
60 PRO C76/24, mm. 23, 18, 16, 15, 14, 11, 8d; RF, iii, 114, 121; *Bel, Chron., ii, 344–8.
61 RF, iii, 114, 120; RBP, i, 81; *KOF, xviii, 301–2.

62 RDP, iv, 563–5; RF, iii, 122, 124 –5; *Bel, Chron., ii, 346–7; Knighton, Chron., ii, 47. Lancaster: RBP, i, 81; PRO C81/319/18383B.

63 RSG, iii, 136–41, 244–9; Kervyn, iii, 325; Muisit, Chron., 178–9; Istore de Flandre, 66–8; Recits d'un bourgeois, 251–2; Avesbury, G. Edwardi, 384; 'Itin. Philippe VI'.

64 GEC, iv, 27–8; *Prince (1), 370–1; RF, iii, 100, 169; *Bel, Chron., ii, 340–1; PRO E101/25/19; *KOF, xviii, 340–1; Avesbury, G. Edwardi, 389, and Lescot, Chron., 8on (Flemings); Jones (1), 144–5.

65 RF, iii, 100–1, 168; AN JJ75/154; Rec. doc. Poitou, iii, 26–30.

66 AN JJ80/8; Grandes Chron., ix, 296; LE, nos 479, 529; JT, no. 381.

67 Avesbury, G. Edwardi, 388–9 (Dagworth's report); Grandes Chron., ix, 298–306; Lescot, Chron., 77–81.

68 *Bel, Chron., ii, 353–4; CCR 1346–9, 570.

69 JT, no. 2226, 2228; DCG, no. XXXII(1011); Grandes Chron., ix, 306–9.

70 Avesbury, G. Edwardi, 386; Chronographia, ii, 244–5, 245n.

71 Istore de Flandre, ii, 65; Avesbury, G. Edwardi, 384–6; Knighton, Chron., ii, 47–8; DCG, nos. 453–5, 457; Muisit, Chron., 180.

72 Knighton, Chron., ii, 48; cf. Bel, Chron., ii, 113.

73 Champollion-Figeac, Lettres, ii, 82–92; Morris (5), 97–8; RSG, iii, 72; Muisit, Chron., 179–80; Istore de Flandre, ii, 69; Villani, Hist. XII: 95, col. 973.

74 Istore de Flandre, ii, 68–9; Knighton, Chron., ii, 49–50; Coll. gén. doc. français, 73–4; Doc. historiques inédits, ed. L.-A. Champollion-Figeac, ii (1843), 181–3; JT, nos 371, 419. Numbers: Villani, Hist. XII:95, cols 973–4.

75 Bel, Chron., ii, 156; Villani, Hist. XII:95, cols 973–4.

76 Bel, Chron., ii, 157–9; Chron. Norm., 89–90; Avesbury, G. Edwardi, 392–3; Knighton, Chron., ii, 50–1; Baker, Chron., 90–1; Récits d'un bourgeois, 257; Muisit, Chron., 182; Anonimalle Chron., 29.

77 Bel, Chron., ii, 161–9; Récits d'un bourgeois, 258–60; Chron. Norm., 90; John of Reading, Chron., 105. Spoil, prisoners: Bel. Chron., ii, 168; Avesbury, G. Edwardi, 396; Muisit, Chron., 274; Knighton, Chron., ii, 53; Istore de Flandre, ii, 70; Villani, Hist. XII:95, col. 974; Walsingham, Hist., i, 272. Citizens: Ordonnances, iv, 606–9; AP 1328–50, nos 8921, 9028; Molinier, 'Documents'.

78 RF, iii, 130; *Bel, Chron., ii, 349; CPR 1345–8, 549, 563–8; Venette, Chron., ii, 207.

79 RF, iii, 130; Knighton, Chron., ii, 52; Villani, Hist. XII:95, Cols 974–5; Bel, Chron., ii, 169–70; JT, no. 375, cf. nos 1009, 1021, 1282, 1372, 1389, 1446, 2896, 3174, 4176, 4507, 4529–30, 4534; DCG, no. XXXII(40); 'Itin. Philippe VI'.

80 RF, ii, 130; Knighton, Chron., ii, 52; Muisit, Chron., 186; Guesnon, 'Documents', 241.

81 'Itin. Philippe VI'; Récits d'un bourgeois, 261–2; Guesnon, 'Documents', 242; Arch. admin. Reims, ii, 1159–61; RF, iii, 130.

82 Arch. admin. Reims, ii, 1159–61; *Delisle, 114–15; Actes Normands, 351–2; JT, no. 375.

83 RF, iii, 130–5; CFR 1347–56, 44–5; Knighton, Chron., ii, 53. Shortages: PRO C76/25, mm. 26d, 24, 23.

84 Knighton, Chron., ii, 53; Muisit, Chron., 187–8.

85 Clément VI, L.Cl. (France), no. 3486; RF, iii, 136–8.

86 Wright, Political Songs, i, 53–8; Walsingham, Hist., i, 272.

87 GEC, vi, 352–4.

Bibliography

A MANUSCRIPTS

London: Public Record Office

Chancery
C.47/27–32 Chancery Miscellanea (Diplomatic documents)
C.49/6–7, 45–6, 66–7 Council and Parliamentary Proceedings
C.61/32–3, 35–60 Gascon Rolls [1317–49]
C.62/114–24 Liberate Rolls [1337–49]
C.70/15–23 Roman Rolls [1337–48]
C.76/14–25 Treaty Rolls [1339–48]
C.81/179–236 Chancery Warrants [1337–48]

Exchequer
E.30 Treasury of Receipt (Diplomatic documents)
E.36/204 Wardrobe account (Richard Eccleshale), 12.7.1342–1.4.1344
E.101 Accounts Various
    E.101/18/28–25/34, 531/23: Army, navy and ordnance [1327–48]
    E.101/89/17–8: Channel Islands, Keepers' and lieutenants' accounts [1338–40, 1345]
    E.101/166/10: Gascony, account of John Ellerker, receiver of victuals [1338]
    E.101/166/11–167/3: Gascony, Constables' and Controllers' accounts [1338–43]
    E.101/309/36–312/29: *Nuncii* [messengers and diplomatic agents] [1327–47]
    E.101/388/1–391/20: Wardrobe and household [1337–47]
E.372 Pipe Rolls (enrolled accounts)
E.403/282–339 Issue Rolls [1335–48]
E.404/508 Debentures and vouchers, Constable of Bordeaux

Special Collections
SC.1/37–42, 51–6 Ancient Correspondence
SC8 Ancient Petitions

London: British Library

Cotton Nero C.viii, fols 179–325:
    Wardrobe Book (Richard Ferriby), July 1334–August 1337
Additional Charters
    1–208 (Collection Courcelles)
    232–505, 1397–1516, 2028–4578 (Collection Joursanvault)
    11318–12468

Oxford: Bodleian Library

Ms. Bodley 462, fols 21–34
    Fragments of Latin chronicle of England, 1339–47

Paris: Archives Nationales

Série J   Trésor des Chartes, Layettes
  240–6: Bretagne
  292–4: Guyenne
  497: Genoa
  519–20: Hainault
  521: Camrai
  Guelders and Juliers
  601–2: Castile
  6●●: Fiefs and homages
  635: Angleterre
Série JJ   Trésor des Chartes, Registres
  65A–79B Principal series [1328–50]
  259 Supplementary registers, Dettes et créances de Raoul, comte d'Eu
Série K   Cartons des Rois
  42–5: Philippe VI
Série P   Chambre des Comptes
  2291–2: Mémoriaux B, C [1330–58]
Série X   Parlement de Paris
  X1a/31, fols 155–156: Parlement civil, Jugés et arrêts [1383]
  X2a/2–5: Parlement criminel, Régistres [1319–50]

Paris: Bibliothèque Nationale

Collection Clairambault (Titres scellés)
Collection Doat (Languedoc):
  164: Counts of Foix
  186–9: Houses of Foix, Armagnac and Albret [1336–46]
  243: Counts of Périgord
Collection du Périgord:
  9–10: Counts of Périgord
  13: Périgueux
  15: Various seigneurial archives
  47: Mussidan
  87: Miscellaneous acts
Manuscrits français:
  2598: Continuation of Chronicle of Guillaume de Nangis
  7877, fols 217–66: War Treasurers' accounts, Gascony, 1341–3
  9501, fols 153–154 vo: War accounts (Robert Bertrand, 1340)
  20685, pp. 247–74: War accounts (Count of Eu)
  22338, fols 117–55: Proceedings against John de Montfort (1341)
  25996–8: Quittances et pièces diverses
  32510: War accounts (various)
  n.a. 7413: War accounts (various)
  n.a. 9236–7: War Treasurers' accounts (Barthélémy du Drach and François de l'Hôpital),
    Guyenne, 1338–41
  n.a. 9238–9: War Treasurers' accounts (Barthélémy du Drach), northern France, November
    1339–October 1341
  n.a. 9240: War Treasurers' accounts (Jean du Cange), northern France, 1340
  n.a. 9241, fols 95–161: War Treasurers' accounts (Barthélémy du Drach), armies of
    Compiègne and Orléans, October 1346

n.a. 20025, fols 140–3: War accounts (Count of Eu)
Pièces Originales [PO]

Montpellier: Archives Départmentales de l'Hérault

Série A 1–16, 231–43:
Administrative orders (seneschalsies of Beaucaire and Toulouse)

Pau: Archives Départmentales des Pyrénées-Atlantiques

Série E:
13–236: Albret
237–87: Armagnac
288–367: Béarn
391–484: Foix
600–881: Périgord, Limousin

B PRINTED RECORD SOUCES

Accounts of the Chamberlains and Other Officers of the County of Chester, 1301–1360, ed. R. Stewart-Brown (1910)

Actes du Parlement de Paris, 1e série, de l'an 1254 à l'an 1328, ed. E. Boutaric, 2 vols (1863–7); *2e série, de l'an 1328 à l'an 1350*, ed. H. Furgeot, 3 vols (1920–75)

Actes du Parlement de Paris. Parlement criminel, règne de Philippe VI de Valois, ed. B. Labat-Poussin, M. Langlois and Y. Lanhers (1987)

Actes et documents anciens intérressant la Belgique conservés aux Archives de l'État à Vienne, ed. H. Laurent (1933)

Actes Normands de la Chambre des Comptes sous Philippe de Valois, ed. L. Delisle (1871)

Actes royaux des Archives de l'Hérault, i, 1151–1422, ed. A. Caramel (1980)

'Ancient petitions of the Chancery and the Exchequer' *ayant trait aux îles de la Manche*, Société Jersiaise (1902)

Archives administratives de la ville de Reims, ed. P. Varin, 5 vols (1839–48)

Archives anciennes de la ville de Saint-Quentin, ed. E. Lemaire, 2 vols (1888–1910)

Archives historiques de la Saintonge et de l'Aunis, 50 vols (1874–1967)

Archives historiques du Département de la Gironde, 58 vols (1859–1932)

Archives historiques du Poitou, 61 vols (1872–1982)

Bautier, R.-H., 'Inventaires de comptes royaux particuliers de 1328 à 1351', *BPH* (1960), 773–837

Benedict XII, *Lettres closes et patentes interressant les pays autres que la France*, ed. J.-M. Vidal and G. Mollat, 2 vols (1913–35)

Benedict XII, *Lettres closes, patentes et curiales se rapportant à la France*, ed. G. Daumet (1920)

Bock, F., 'An Unknown English Register of the Reign of Edward III', *EHR*, xlv (1930), 353–72

Bock, F., *Das deutsch–englische Bundniss von 1335–1342, i (Quellen)* (1956)

Calendar of Ancient Correspondence Concerning Wales, ed. J. G. Edwards (1935)

Calendar of Close Rolls, 45 vols (1892–1954)

Calendar of Documents Relating to Scotland, ed. J. Bain, 5 vols (1881–1988)

Calendar of Entries in the Papal Registers Relating to Great Britain and Ireland. Papal Letters, ed. W. H. Bliss and C. Johnson, 14 vols (1894–1961)

Calendar of Fine Rolls, 22 vols (1911–63)

Calendar of Inquisitions Miscellaneous, 7 vols (1916–69)

Calendar of Letter Books of the City of London, ed. R. R. Sharpe, 11 vols (1899–1912)

Calendar of Patent Rolls, 70 vols (1891–1982)

Calendar of Plea and Memoranda Rolls of the City of London, 1323–1364, ed. A. H. Thomas (1926)

Carolus-Barré, L., 'Benoit XII et la mission charitable de Bertrand Carit dans les pays devastés du nord de la France . . . 1340', *Mélanges d'archéologie et d'histoire*, lxii (1950), 165–232

Cartulaire de l'abbaye de Saint-Michel du Tréport, ed. P. Laffleur de Kermaingent (1880)

Cartulaire des comtes de Hainault, ed. L. Devillers, 6 vols (1881–96)

Cartulaire des sires de Rays (1160–1449), ed. R. Blanchard, AHP, xxviii, xxx (1898–9)

Cartulaire historique et généalogique des Artevelde, ed. N. de Pauw (1920)

Catalogue de comptes royaux des règnes de Philippe VI et de Jean II, 1328–1364, ed. R. Cazelles, 1ère partie (1984)

Champollion-Figeac, L.-A., *Lettres de rois, reines et autres personnages des cours de France et d'Angleterre*, 2 vols (1839–43)

Chaplais, P., *English Medieval Diplomatic Practice*, i, *Documents and Interpretation* (1982)

Chaplais, P., *The War of Saint-Sardos (1323–1325). Gascon Correspondence and Diplomatic Documents* (1954)

'Chartes d'Agen se rapportant au règne de Philippe VI de Valois (1328–1350)', ed. G. Tholin, *AHG*, xxxiii (1985), 75–177

Cheyette, F. L., 'Paris B. N. Ms. latin 5954. The Professional Papers of an English Ambassador on the Eve of the Hundred Years War', *Économies et sociétés au moyen age. Mélanges offerts à Edouard Perroy* (1973), 400–13

Clément VI, *Lettres closes, patentes et curiales se rapportant à la France*, ed. E. Deprez, J. Glenisson and G. Mollat (1901–61)

Clément VI, *Lettres closes, patentes et curiales interressant les pays autres que la France*, ed. E. Déprez and G. Mollat (1960–1)

Clément VI, *Lettres de Clément VI (1342–1352)*, ed. P. van Isacker and U. Berlière (1924)

'Compte de Pierre de Ham, dernier bailli de Calais (1346–1347)', ed. J.-M. Richard, *Mems. Comm. Dep. des Mons. Hist. du Pas-de-Calais*, i(3) (1893), 241–58

Confessions et jugements de criminels au Parlement de Paris (1319–1350), ed. M. Langlois and Y. Lanhers (1971)

Cuttino, G. P., 'Another Memorandum Book of Elias Joneston', *EHR*, lxiii (1948), 90–103

David II, *The Acts of David II, King of Scots*, ed. B. Webster (1982)

Débat, A., 'Trois lettres de Gilbert de Cantobre pour la défense du Rouergue, 18 et 20 avril 1347', *Procès-verbaux Soc. Lettres, sciences et arts de l'Aveyron*, xliv (1983), 66–77

Documents historiques . . . rélatifs à la seigneurie de Monaco, ed. G. Saige, i (1905)

Documents inédits concernant la ville et le siège du baillage d'Amiens extraits des registres du Parlement de Paris et du Trésor des Chartes, ed. E. Maugis, i, XIVe siècle (1296–1412) (1908)

Documents Parisiens du règne de Philippe VI de Valois (1328–1350), ed. J. Viard (1899–1900)

Documents pontificaux sur la Gascogne. Pontificat de Jean XXII, ed. L. Guérard, 2 vols (1896–1903)

Documents rélatifs au clos des galées de Rouen et aux armées de la mer des rois de France de 1293 à 1418, ed. A. Chazelas, 2 vols (1977–8)

Documents sur la maison de Durfort, ed. N. de la Pena (1977)

Documents sur la ville de Millau, ed. J. Artières, *Arch. Hist. Rouergue*, vii (1930)

Ellis, H., *Original Letters Illustrative of English History*, 3rd series, 4 vols (1846)

Exchequer Rolls of Scotland, ed. J. Stuart *et al.*, 23 vols (1878–1908)

Foedera, conventiones, literae et acta publica, ed. T. Rymer, n.e. A. Clarke *et al.*, 7 vols (1826–69)

Gascogne (La) dans les registres du Trésor des Chartes, ed. C. Samaran (1966)

Gascon Calendar of 1322, ed. G. P. Cuttino (1949)

Gascon Register A (Series of 1318–1319), ed. G. P. Cuttino, 3 vols (1975–6)
Gedenkwaardigheden uit de Geschiedenis van Gelderland, ed. A. Nijhoff, 7 vols (1830–75)
Géraud, H., *Paris sous Philippe le Bel* (1837)
Giry, A., 'Analyse et extraits d'un registre des archives de Saint-Omer', *Mems. Soc. Antiquaires de Morinie*, xv (1876), 65–316
Godfray, H. M., 'Documents rélatifs aux attaques sur les îles de la Manche, 1338–1345', *Bull. de la Soc. Jersiaise*, iii (1897), 11–53
Grandisson, John de, *The Register of John de Grandisson, Bishop of Exter (A.D. 1327–1369)*, ed. F. C. Hingeston-Randolph, 3 vols (1894–9)
Guesnon, A., 'Documents inédits sur l'invasion anglaise et les états au temps de Philippe VI et Jean le Bon', *BPH* (1897), 208–59
Inventaire des Archives Communales de la ville d'Aurillac antérieures à 1790, ed. G. Esquier, 2 vols (1906–11)
Inventaire des sceaux de la Collection Clairambault à la Bibliothèque Nationale, ed. G. Demay, 2 vols (1885–6)
Inventaire-sommaire des Archives Communales antérieures à 1790. Ville de Clermont-Ferrand. Fonds de Montferrand, ed. E. Teilhard de Chardin, 2 vols (1922)
Inventaire-sommaire des Archives Communales antérieures à 1790. Ville de Périgueux, ed. M. Hardy (1897)
Inventaire-sommaire des Archives Départmentales antérieures à 1790. Aveyron. Archives ecclesiastiques. Série G (Evêché de Rodez), ed. C. Estienne and L. Lempereur (1934–58)
Inventaire-sommaire des Archives Départmentales antérieures à 1790. Basses-Pyrénées, ed. P. Raymond, 6 vols (1863–76)
Inventaire-sommaire des Archives Départmentales antérieures à 1790. Pas-de-Calais. Archives Civiles, Série A, ed. J.-M. Richard, 2 vols (1878-87)
'Inventarium instrumentorum camerae apostolicae', ed. E. Göller, *Romische Quartalschrift, Geschichte*, 65–109
'Itinéraire de Philippe VI de Valois', ed. J. Viard, *BEC*, lxxiv (1913), 74–128, 524–94, lxxxiv (1923), 166–70
Jassemin, H., 'Les papiers de Mile de Noyers', *BPH*, Année 1918 (1920), 174–226
John XXII, *Lettres secrètes et curiales . . . rélatifs à la France*, ed. A. Coulon and S. Clémencet (1900–in progress)
Johnson, C., 'An Act of Edward III as Count of Toulouse', *Essays in History Presented to Reginald Lane Poole*, ed. H. W. C. Davis (1927), 399–404
Jones, M., 'Some Documents Relating to the Disputed Succession to the Duchy of Brittany, 1341', *Camden Miscellany*, xxiv (1972), 1–78
Journaux du Trésor de Philippe VI de Valois, ed. J. Viard (1899)
Jurades de la ville d'Agen (1345–1355), ed. A. Magen (1894)
Jusselin, M., 'Comment la France se préparait à la guerre de cent ans', *BEC*, lxxiii (1912), 209–36
Languedoc (Le) et le Rouergue dans le Trésor des Chartes, ed. Y. Dossat, A.-M. Lemasson and P. Wolff (1983)
'Lettres d'état enregistrées au Parlement de Paris sous le règne de Philippe de Valois', *ABSHF*, xxxiv (1897), 193–267, xxxv (1898), 177–249
Literae Cantuarienses, ed. J. B. Sheppard, 3 vols (1887–9)
Livre des bouillons (Archives municipales de Bordeau, i) (1867)
Livre des coutumes, ed. C. Barckhausen (*Archives municipales de Bordeau, v*) (1890)
Loisne, Cte de, 'Ordonnances inédites du roi de France Philippe VI rélatives au siège de Béthune de 1346', *Bull. Hist. de la Soc. des Antiquaires de la Morinie*, x (1902), 703–10, 742–50
Ludewig, P. de, *Reliquiae manuscriptorum*, v (1723)
Maître, L., 'Répertoire analytique des actes de Charles de Blois', *Bull. Soc. Arch. Nantes*, xlv (1904), 247–73

Miret y Sans, J., 'Lettres closes des premiers Valois', *MA*, xx (1917–18), 53–88

Miret y Sans, J., 'Negociacions diplomatiques d'Alfons III de Catalunya-Arago als el rey de Franca per la croada contra Grenada (1328–1332)', *Institut d'Estudis Catalans*, Anuari 1908

Mirot, L. and Déprez, E., *Les ambassades anglaises pendant la guerre de cent ans. Catalogue chronologique (1327–1450)* (1900)

Molinier, E., 'Documents rélatifs aux Calésiens expulsés par Edouard III', *Le cabinet historique*, xxiv (1878), 254–80

Monuments du procès de canonisation du bienheureux Charles de Blois duc de Bretagne, 1320–64, ed. F. Plaine (1921)

Moranvillé, H., 'Rapports à Philippe VI sur l'état de ses finances', *BEC*, xlviii (1887), 380–95, liii (1892), 111–14

Morice, P. H., *Mémoires pour servir de preuves à l'histoire ecclesiastique et civile de Bretagne*, 3 vols (1742–6)

Olim, ou registres des arrêts rendus par la cour du roi, ed. Beugnot, 3 vols (1839–48)

Ordonnances des rois de France de la troisième race, ed. D. Secousse *et al.*, 22 vols (1729–1849)

Petit, E., Gavrilovitch, M., Maury, P., and Teodoru, C. *Essai de restitution des plus anciens mémoriaux de la Chambre des Comptes* (1889)

Philip VI, 'Lettres closes, lettres "de par le roi" de Philippe de Valois', ed. R. Cazelles, *ABSHF*, Années 1956–7 (1958), 61–225

Philip VI, 'Nouvelles lettres closes et "de par le roi" de Philippe VI de Valois', ed. P. Gasnault, *BEC*, cxx (1962), 172–8

Raine, J., *Historical Papers and Letters from the Northern Registers* (1873)

Recueil de documents concernant la commune et la ville de Poitiers, ed. E. Audouin, ii, 1328–1380, *AHP*, xlvi (1928)

Recueil de documents rélatifs à l'histoire des monnaies frappées par les rois de France, ed. L. F. J. C. de Saulcy, 4 vols (1879–92)

Recueil des documents concernant le Poitou contenus dans les registres de la Chancellerie de France, ii, 1334–8, iii, 1348–69, ed. P. Guérin, *AHP*, xiii, xvii (1883–6)

Recueil de titres et autres pieces justificatives employées dans le Mémoire sur la constitution politique de la ville de Périgueux (1775)

Register of Edward the Black Prince, 4 vols (1930–3)

Registres de l'échevinage de Saint-Jean d'Angély, ed. D. d'Aussy, 3 vols, *AHSA*, xxiv, xxvi, xxxii (1895–1902)

Registres du Trésor des Chartes. Inventaire analytique, iii, *Règne de Philippe de Valois*, ed. J. Viard and A. Vallée, 3 vols (1978–84)

Rekeningen der Stad Gent. Tijdvak van Jacob van Artevelde, 1336–1349, ed. N. de Pauw and J. Vuylsteke, 3 vols (1874–80)

Reports from the Lords Committees . . . Touching the Dignity of a Peer, 5 vols (1820–9)

Rôles Gascons, ed. F. Michel, C. Bémont and Y. Renouard, 4 vols (1885–1962)

Rotuli Parliamentorum, 7 vols (1767–1832)

Rotuli Parliamentorum Angliae hactenus inediti, ed. H. G. Richardson and G. O. Sayles (1935)

Rotuli Scotiae, ed. D. Macpherson *et al.*, 2 vols (1814)

Schwalm, J., 'Reiseberichte, 1894–1896 (ii)', *Neues Archiv des Gesellschaft für altere deutsche Geschichtskunde*, xxiii (1898), 291–374

Statutes of the Realm, ed. A. Luders *et al.*, 11 vols (1810–28)

Stechele, W., 'England und der Niederrhein bei Beginn der Regierung Konig Edwards III', *Westdeutsche Zeitschrift für Geschichte und Kunst*, xxvii (1908), 98–151, 441–73

Stengel, E. E., *Nova Alemanniae*, i (1921)

Suppliques de Clément VI (1342–1352). Textes et analyses, ed. U. Berlière (1906)

Textes rélatifs à l'histoire du Parlement depuis les origines jusqu'en 1314, ed. C.-V. Langlois (1888)

Timbal, P.-C., *La guerre de cent ans vue à travers les registres du Parlement (1337–1369)* (1961)

Titres de la maison ducale de Bourbon, ed. A. Huillard-Bréhollés, 2 vols (1867–74)

Treaty Rolls, 2 vols (1955–in progress)

Trésor des Chartes d'Albret, ed. J. Marquette, i, *Les archives de Vayres* (1973)

Vatikanische Akten zur deutschen Geschichte in der Zeit Kaisers Ludwigs des Baiers, ed. S. Riezler (1881)

Wardrobe Books of William de Norwell, 12 July 1338 to 27 May 1340, ed. M. Lyon, B. Lyon and H. S. Lucas (1983)

Wrottesley, G., *Crécy and Calais from the Public Records* (1897)

C PRINTED NARRATIVE AND LITERARY SOURCES

Asterisks * mark editions having important documentary appendices

Acta bellicosa ... Edwardi regis Angliae, ed. J. Moisant, *Le Prince Noir en Aquitaine* (1894), 157–74, corrected by Barber, R., *Edward, Prince of Wales and Aquitaine* (1978), 253–4, from Cambridge Corpus Christi College Ms. 370

Annales Paulini, ed. W. Stubbs, *Chronicles of the Reign of Edward I and Edward II*, i (1882), 255–370

Anonimalle chronicle, 1333–1381, ed. V. H. Galbraith (1927)

Anonymous of Canterbury: *see* Reading, John of

Aspin, I. S. T., *Anglo-Norman Political Songs* (1953)

Avesbury, Robert of, *De gestis mirabilibus regis Edwardi tertii*, ed. E. M. Thompson (1889)

Baker, Geoffrey le, *Chronicon*, ed. E. M. Thompson (1889)

Beaumanoir, Philipppe de, *Coutumes de Beauvaisis*, ed. A. Salmon, 2 vols (1900)

*Bel, Jean le, *Chronique*, ed. J. Viard and E. Déprez, 2 vols (1904–5)

Bower, Walter, *Joannis de Fordun Scottichronicon cum supplementis et continuatione Walter Boweri*, 2 vols (1759)

Bridlington Chronicle, ed. W. Stubbs, *Chronicles of the Reign of Edward I and Edward II*, ii (1883), 23–151

Brut (The), ed. F. W. D. Brie 2 vols (1906–8)

Budt, Adrian de, *Chronicon Flandriae*, CCF, i, 261–367

Chandos Herald, *La vie du Prince Noir*, ed. D. B. Tyson (1975)

Chronicon anonymi Cantuariensis: *see* Reading, John of

Chronicon Comitum Flandrensium, CCF, i, 34–257

Chronicon de Lanercost, ed. J. Stevenson (1839)

Chronicon monasterii de Melsa, ed. E. A. Bond, 2 vols (1866–8)

Chronique anonyme Parisienne de 1316 à 1339, ed. A. Héllot, Mems. Soc. Hist. Paris, xi (1885), 1–207

Chronique de Bazas, AHG, xv (1874), 1–67

Chronique de Maillezais, ed. P. Marchegay, BEC, ii (1840–1), 148–68

Chronique des quatre premiers Valois (1327–1393), ed. S. Luce (1862)

Chronique Normande du XIVe siècle, ed. A. and E. Molinier (1882)

Chronographia regum Francorum, ed. H. Moranville, 3 vols (1891–7)

Corpus chronicorum Flandriae, ed. J. J. de Smet, 4 vols (1837–65)

Cronicas del rey don Alfonso XI, ed. F. Cerda y Rico, *Biblioteca de autores espanoles*, lxvi (1875)

Eulogium historiarum, ed. F. S. Haydon, 3 vols (1858–63)

Fordun, John, *Chronica gentis Scotorum*, ed. W. F. Skene, 2 vols (1871)

Fortescue, Sir John, *The Governance of England*, ed. C. Plummer (1885)

French Chronicle of London, ed. G. J. Aungier (1844)

Froissart, Jean, *Chroniques de J. Froissart*, ed. S. Luce, 15 vols (1869–1975) [all citations of the text are to this edition]

*Froissart, Jean, *Œuvres de Froissart. Chroniques*, ed. Kervyn de Lettenhove, 25 vols (1867–77)

Froissart, Jean, *The Chronicle of Froissart Translated out of French by Sir John Bourchier, Lord Berners, annis 1523–25*, 6 vols (1901–3)

Galbraith, V. H., 'Extracts from the Historia Aurea and a French Brut (1317–47)', *EHR*, xliii (1948), 203–17

Grandes chroniques de France, ed. J. Viard, 10 vols (1920–53)

Gray, Sir Thomas, of Heton, *Scalacronica*, ed. J. Stevenson (1836)

Guisborough, Walter of, *Chronicle*, ed. H. Rothwell (1957)

Hemingburgh, Walter of, *Chronicon*, ed. H. C. Hamilton, 2 vols (1948–9)

Henry of Grosmont, Earl of Lancaster, *Le livre de seyntz medecines*, ed. E.-J. Arnould (1940)

Higden, Ranulph, *Polychronicon*, ed. J. R. Lumby and C. Babington, 9 vols (1865–86)

Hocsem, Jean de, *La chronique de Jean de Hocsem*, ed. G. Kurth (n.d.)

Istore et croniques de Flandres, ed. Kervyn de Lettenhove, 2 vols (1879–80)

Jandun, Jean de, *Traité des louanges de Paris*, ed. Le Roulx de Lincy, *Paris et ses historiens* (1867), 33–79

Klerk, Jean de, *Les gestes des ducs de Brabant*, ed. J.-F. Willems and J.-H. Bormans, 3 vols (1839–69)

Klerk, Jean de, *Van den derden Eduwaert, coninc van Engelant*, ed. J.-F. Willems, *Belgisch Museum*, iv (1840)

Knighton, Henry, *Chronicon*, ed. J. R. Lumby, 2 vols (1889–95)

Léger, L., 'Un poème tchèque sur la bataille de Crécy', *Journal des Savants* (1902), 323–31

*Lescot, R., *Chronique*, ed. J. Lemoine (1896)

Minot, Laurence, *The Poems of Laurence Minot*, ed. J. Hall (1887)

Muevin, Jacob, *Chronicon*, CCF, ii, 455–71

Muisit, Gilles li, *Chronique et annales*, ed. H. Lemaître (1906)

Murimuth, Adam, *Continuatio chronicorum*, ed. E. M. Thompson (1889)

Nangis, Guillaume de, *Chronique latine de Guillame de Nangis de 1113 à 1300 avec les continuations de 1300 à 1368*, ed. H. Géraud (1843)

Noyal, Jean de, 'Fragments inédits de la chronique de Jean de Noyal', *ABSHF*, Année 1883, 246–75

Petit chronique de Guyenne, ed. V. Barckhausen, *Archives municipales de Bordeux*, v (1890), 395–402

Reading, John of, *Chronica Johannis de Reading et Anonymi Cantuariensis, 1346–1367*, ed. J. Tait (1914)

Recits d'un bourgeois de Valenciennes (XIVe siècle), ed. Kervyn de Lettenhove (1877)

Recueil des Historiens des Gaules et de la France, ed. M. Bouquet et al., 24 vols (1734–1904)

Venette, Jean de, *Continuatio Chronici Guillelmi de Nangiaco*, in Nangis, G. de, *Chronique*, ii, 178–378

Villani, Giovanni, *Historia universalis*, ed. L. A. Muratori, *Rerum Italicarum scriptores*, xiii (1728)

Vitae archiepiscoporum Cantuariensium, ed. H. Wharton, *Anglia sacra*, i (1691), 1–48

Vita Edwardi secundi, ed. N. Denholm-Young (1957)

Vitae paparum Avenionensium, ed. S. Baluze, n.e. G. Mollat, 4 vols (1916–22)

Walsingham, Thomas, *Historia Anglicana*, ed. H. T. Riley, 2 vols (1863–4)

Walsingham, Thomas, *Ypodigma Neustriae*, ed. H. T. Riley (1876)

Wright, T., *Political Poems and Songs*, 2 vols (1859–61)

Wyntoun, Andrew of, *Orygynale cronykil of Scotland*, ed. D. Laing, 3 vols (1872–9)

D SELECTED SECONDARY WORKS

Asterisks * mark works having important documentary appendices

Alban, J. R., 'English Coastal Defence: Some Fourteenth-Century Modifications Within the System', *Patronage, the Crown and the Provinces in Late Medieval England*, ed. R. A. Griffiths (1981), 57–78

Anselme, Le P., *Histoire généalogique et chronologique de la maison royale de France*, 3rd edn, 9 vols (1726–33)

Artonne, A., *Le mouvement de 1314 et les chartres provinciales de 1315* (1912)

Atlas historique des villes de France (1982–in progress)

*Baldwin, J. F., *The King's Council in England During the Middle Ages* (1913)

*Baluze, S., *Historiae Tutelensis libri tres* (1717)

Barber, R., *Edward Prince of Wales and Aquitaine* (1978)

Barnie, J., *War in Medieval English Society. Social Values in the Hundred Years War, 1377–99* (1974)

Bautier, R. H., 'Recherches sur la Chancellerie royale au temps de Philippe VI', *BEC*, cxxii (1964), 89–176; cxxiii (1965), 313–459

*Bertrandy, M., *Étude sur les chroniques de Froissart. Guerre de Guienne, 1345–1346* (1870)

*Black, J. G., 'Edward I and Gascony in 1300', *EHR*, xvii (1902), 518–25

Bois, G., *Crise du féodalisme* (1976)

Borderie, A. le Moyne de la, *Histoire de Bretagne*, 6 vols (1905–14)

Boutruche, R., *La crise d'une société. Seigneurs et paysans du Bordelais pendant la querre de cent ans* (1963)

Brooks, F. W., *The English Naval Forces, 1199–1272* (n.d.)

Brown, R. A., Colvin, H. M. and Taylor, A. J., *The History of the King's Works*, i, *The Middle Ages* (1963)

*Brussel, N., *Nouvel examen de l'usage générale des fiefs en France* (1750)

Burley, S. J., 'The Victualling of Calais, 1347–65', *BIHR*, xxxi (1958), 49–57

Burne, A. H., *The Crécy War* (1955)

Campbell, J., 'Scotland and the Hundred Years War in the 14th Century', *Europe in the Late Middle Ages*, ed. J. Hale, R. Highfield and B. Smalley (1965), 184–216

Cazelles, R. (1), *La société politique et la crise de la royauté sous Philippe de Valois* (1958)

Cazelles, R. (2), 'Quelques reflexions à propos des mutations de la monnaie royale française (1295–1360)', *MA*, lxxii (1966), 83–105, 251–78

Cazelles, R. (3), *Nouvelle histoire de Paris de la fin du règne de Philippe Auguste à la mort de Charles V, 1223–1380* (1972)

*Chaplais, P. (1), 'English Arguments Concerning the Feudal Status of Aquitaine in the Fourteenth Century', *BIHR*, xxi (1948), 203–13

*Chaplais, P. (2), 'Règlements des conflits internationaux franco-anglais au XIVe siècle (1293–1377)', *MA*, lvii (1951), 269–302

Chaplais, P. (3), 'Le traité de Paris de 1259 et l'inféodation de la Gascogne allodiale' *MA*, lxi (1955), 121–37

Chaplais, P. (4), 'Le duché-pairie de Guyenne. L'homage et les services féodaux', *Annales du Midi*, lxix (1957), 5–38, 135–60

*Chaplais, P. (5), 'La souveraineté du roi de France et le pouvoir legislatif en Guyenne au début du XIVe siècle', *MA*, lxix (1963), 449–69

Cokayne, G. E., *The Complete Peerage*, ed. V. Gibbs *et al.*, 12 vols (1910–59)

Contamine, P. (1), 'The French Nobility and the War', *The Hundred Years War*, ed. K. Fowler (1971), 135–62

Contamine, P. (2), *Guerre, état et société à la fin du moyen age. Étude sur les armées des rois de France, 1337–1494* (1972)

Contamine, P. (3), *L'Oriflamme de St.-Denis aux XIVe et XVe siècles* (1975)

Contamine, P. (4), *La vie quotidienne pendant la guerre de cent ans* (1976)

Contamine, P. (5), 'Les fortifications urbaines en France à la fin du moyen age: aspects financiers et économiques', *RH*, cclx (1978), 23–47

Contamine, P. (6), *La guerre au moyen age* (1980)

*Cordey, J., *Les comtes de Savoie et les rois de France pendant la guerre de cent ans* (1911)

*Coville, A. (1), *Les états de Normandie. Leurs origines et leur développement au XIVe siècle* (1894)

Coville, A. (2), 'Poèmes historiques de l'avènement de Philippe de Valois au Traité de Calais (1328–1361)', *Histoire Littéraire de la France*, xxxviii (1949), 259–333

*Cuttino, G. P. (1), 'The Process of Agen', *Speculum*, xix (1944), 161–78

Cuttino, G. P. (2), *English Diplomatic Administration*, 2nd edn (1971)

Cuttler, S. H., *The Law of Treason and Treason Trials in Later Medieval France* (1981)

*Daumet, G. (1), *Étude sur l'alliance de la France et la Castille au XIVe et au XVe siècles* (1898)

Daumet, G. (2), 'Louis de la Cerda ou d'Espagne', *Bull. Hispanique* (1913), 38–67

Davies, R. R., *Lordship and Society in the March of Wales, 1282–1400* (1978)

*Delisle, L., *Histoire du château et des sires de Saint-Sauveur-le-Vicomte* (1867)

Denholm-Young, N. (1), *The Country Gentry in the Fourteenth Century* (1969)

Denholm-Young, N. (2), 'Feudal Society in the Thirteenth Century. The Knights', *Collected Papers* (1969), 83–94

Denifle, H., *La guerre de cent ans et les désolations des églises, monastères et hôpitaux en France, i, Jusqu'à la mort de Charles V (1380)* (1899)

*Déprez, E., (1), *Les préliminaires de la guerre de cent ans. La papauté, la France et l'Angleterre (1328–1342)* (1902)

*Déprez, E. (2), 'La mort de Robert d'Artois', *RH*, xciv (1907), 63–6

*Déprez, E. (3), 'La double trahison de Godefroi de Harcourt (1346–1347)', *RH*, xcix (1908), 32–4

Déprez, E. (4), 'La conférence d'Avignon (1344)', *Essays in Medieval History Presented to Thomas Frederick Tout* (1925), 301–20

Desportes, P., *Reims et les Remois aux XIIIe et XIVe siècles* (1979)

Dessalles, L., *Histoire du Périgord*, 3 vols (1883–5)

Diller, G. T., *Attitudes chevaleresques et réalités politiques chez Froissart* (1984)

Dion, R., *Histoire de la vigne et du vin en France des origines au XIXe siècle* (1959)

Drouyn, L., *La Guyenne militaire*, 3 vols (1865)

Dubrulle, H., *Cambrai à la fin du moyen age (XIIIe–XVe siècle)* (1903)

*Duchesne, A., *Histoire de la maison de Châtillon-sur-Marne* (1621)

Dupont-Ferrier, G., *Gallia Regia ou état des officiers royaux des baillages et des sénéchaussés de 1328 à 1515*, 7 vols (1942–65)

Evans, D. L., 'Some Notes on the Principality of Wales in the Time of the Black Prince', *Trans. Hon. Soc. Cymmrodorion* (1925–6), 25–110

*Faucon, M., 'Prêts faits aux rois de France par Clément VI, Innocent VI et le comte de Beaufort (1345–1360)' *BEC*, xl (1879), 570–8

Favreau, R., *La ville de Poitiers à la fin du moyen age* (1978)

Fourquin, G., *Les campagnes de la région Parisienne à la fin du moyen age* (1964)

*Fowler, K., *The King's Lieutenant. Henry of Grosmont Duke of Lancaster, 1310–1361* (1969)

*Fryde, E. B., (1), 'Dismissal of Robert de Woodhouse from the Office of Treasurer, December 1338', *EHR*, lxvii (1962), 74–8

Fryde, E. B. (2), 'Edward III's Wool Monopoly: A Fourteenth-Century Royal Trading

Venture', *History*, n.s., xxxvii (1952), 8–24

Fryde, E. B. (3), 'The English Farmers of the Customs', *TRHS*, 5th series, ix, (1959), 1–17

Fryde, E. B. (4), 'The Last Trials of Sir William de la Pole', *Econ. Hist. Rev.*, xv (1962), 17–30

*Fryde, E. B. (5), 'The Wool Accounts of William de la Pole', *St. Anthony's Hall Publications*, no. 25 (1964)

Fryde, E. B. (6), 'Financial Resources of Edward III in the Netherlands, 1337–40', *Revue Belge de philologie et d'histoire*, xlv (1967), 1142–1216

Fryde, E. B. (7), 'Parliament and the French War, 1336–40', *Essays in Medieval History Presented to Bertie Wilkinson* (1969), 250–69

Fryde E. B. (8), 'The Financial Policies of the Royal Government and Popular Resistance to them in France and England, c.1270–c.1420', *Revue Belge de philologie et d'histoire*, lvii (1979), 824–60

Fryde, E. B. (9), *William de la Pole, Merchant and King's Banker (d.1366)* (1988)

Fryde, E. B. and N.M., 'Public Credit With Special Reference to North-Western Europe', *Cambridge Economic History of Europe*, iii, ed. M. M. Postan, 430–553

Fryde, N., *The Tyranny and Fall of Edward II* (1978)

Funck-Brentano, F., *Les origines de la guerre de cent ans. Philippe le Bel en Flandre* (1896)

Gardelles, J., *Les châteaux du moyen age dans la France du sud-ouest* (1972)

*Gavrilovitch, M., *Étude sur le traité de Paris de 1259* (1899)

Gransden, A., 'The Alleged rape by Edward III of the Countess of Salisbury', *EHR*, lxxxvii (1972), 333–44

Guilhermoz, P., *Essai sur les origines de la noblesse en France au moyen age* (1902)

Guinodie, R., *Histoire de Libourne*, 3 vols (1845)

*Harriss, G. L., *King, Parliament and Public Finance in Medieval England, to 1369* (1975)

Henneman, J. B., *Royal Taxation in Fourteenth-Century France. The Development of War Financing, 1322–1356* (1971)

Hewitt, H. J., *The Organisation of War Under Edward III, 1338–62* (1966)

Higounet, C., 'Bastides et frontières', *MA* (1948), 113–30

Higounet-Nadal, A., *Périgueux aux XIVe et XVe siècles. Étude de démographie historique* (1978)

Holmes, G. A., *The Estates of the Higher Nobility in Fourteenth-Century England* (1957)

*Hughes, D., *A Study of the Social and Constitutional Tendencies in the Early Years of Edward III* (1915)

James, M. J., *Studies in the Medieval Wine Trade* (1971)

Jones, M. (1), *Ducal Brittany, 1364–1399* (1970)

*Jones, M. (2), 'Sir Thomas Dagworth et la guerre civile en Bretagne au XIVe siècle: quelques documents inédits', *Annales de Bretagne*, lxxxvii (1980), 621–39

Jones, M. (3), 'Bons bretons et bons francoys. The Language and Meaning of Treason in Late-Medieval France', *TRHS*, 5th series, xxxii (1982), 92–112

Jones, M. (4), 'Edward III's Captains in Brittany', *England in the Fourteenth Century. Proceedings of the Harlaxton Symposium*, ed. W. M. Ormrod (1986), 99–118

Jones, M. (5), 'Sir John Hardreshull, King's Lieutenant in Brittany, 1343–5', *Nottingham Medieval Studies*, xxxi (1987), 76–97

Keen, M. (1), *The Laws of War in the Late Middle Ages* (1965)

Keen, M. (2), *Chivalry* (1984)

Keeney, B. C., 'Military Service and the Development of Nationalism in England, 1272–1327', *Speculum*, xxii (1947), 534–49

*Kervyn de Lettenhove, *Histoire de Flandre*, 6 vols (1847–50)

Kicklinger, J. A. (1), 'French Jurisdictional Supremacy in Gascony: An Aspect of the Ducal Government's Response', *J. Med. Hist.*, iii (1979), 127–34

Kicklinger, J. A. (2), 'English Bordeaux in Conflict: The Execution of Pierre Vigier de la

Rousselle and Its Aftermath, 1312–14', *J. Med. Hist.*, ix (1983), 1–14

King, D. J. C., *Castellarium Anglicanum*, 2 vols (1983)

Lacabane, L. (1), 'De la poudre à canon et de son introduction en France', *BEC*, 2e série, i (1844), 28–57

*Lacabane, L. (2), 'Mémoire sur les deux prétendues delivrances de Condom en 1369 et 1374', *BEC*, 3e série, ii (1851), 97–130

*Lecoy de la Marche, A., *Les rélations politique de la France avec le royaume de Majorque*, 2 vols (1892)

Leguay, J.-P., *Un réseau urbain au moyen age: les villes du duché de Bretagne aux XIVe et XVe siècles* (1981)

Lehugeur, P., *Histoire de Philippe le Long, roi de France (1316–1322)*, 2 vols (1897–1931)

Lennel, F., *Histoire de Calais*, 3 vols (1908–13)

Lewis, N. B. (1), 'The Organisation of Indentured Retinues in Fourteenth-Century England', *TRHS*, 4th series, xxvii (1945), 29–39

Lewis, N. B. (2), 'Recruitment and Organisation of a Contract Army. May to November 1337', *BIHR*, xxxvii (1964), 1–19

Lloyd, T. H., *The English Wool Trade in the Middle Ages* (1977)

Lodge, E. C., 'The Constables of Bordeaux in the Reign of Edward III', *EHR*, l (1935), 225–41

Lot, F. and Fawtier, R. (ed.), *Histoire des institutions françaises au moyen age*, 3 vols (1957–62)

Lucas, H. S., *The Low Countries in the Hundred Years War, 1326–1347* (1929)

Luce, S., 'Les préliminaires de la bataille de l'Écluse', *Bull. Soc. Antiq. Normandie*, xiii (1885), 3–41

Maddicott, J. R. (1), *Thomas of Lancaster, 1307–1322* (1970)

Maddicott, J. R. (2), *The English Peasantry and the Demands of the Crown, 1294–1341, Past and Present*, Supplement no. 1 (1975)

Marquette, J.-B., *Les Albrets* (1975–9)

McFarlane, K. B., *The Nobility of Later Medieval England* (1973)

McNeill, P. and Nicholson, R., *An Historical Atlas of Scotland* (1975)

*Ménard, L., *Histoire civile, ecclésiastique et littéraire de la ville de Nîmes*, 7 vols (1744–58)

Miller, E. (1), *War in the North. The Anglo-Scottish Wars of the Middle Ages* (1960)

Miller, E. (2), 'War, Taxation and the English Economy in the Late 13th and Early 14th Centuries', *War and Economic Development. Essays in Memory of David Joslin*, ed. J. M. Winter (1975), 11–31

Miskimin, H., *Money, Prices and Foreign Exchange in Fourteenth-Century France* (1963)

Mollat, G., *Les papes d'Avignon*, 10th edn (1964)

Moranvillé, H. (1), 'Philippe VI à la bataille de Crécy', *BEC*, l (1889), 295–7

Moranvillé, H. (2), 'La trahison de Jean de Vervins', *BEC*, liii (1892), 605–11

*Morel, O., *La grande Chancellerie royale* (1900)

Morgan, P., *War and Society in Medieval Cheshire, 1277–1403* (1987)

Morris, J. E. (1), 'The Archers at Crécy', *EHR*, xii (1897), 427–36

Morris, J. E. (2), *The Welsh Wars of Edward I* (1901)

Morris, J. E. (3), 'Cumberland and Westmorland Military Levies in the Time of Edward I and Edward II', *Trans. Cumberland and Westmorland Archit. and Archaeol. Soc.*, n.s., ii (1903), 307–27

Morris, J. E. (4), *Bannockburn* (1913)

Morris, J. E. (5), 'Mounted Infantry in Medieval Warfare', *TRHS*, 3rd series, viii (1914), 77–102

*Nicholas, N. H., *A History of the Royal Navy*, 2 vols (1847)

*Nicholson, R. (1), *Edward III and the Scots* (1965)

Nicholson, R. (2), *Scotland. The Later Middle Ages* (1974)

639

Offler, H. S., 'England and Germany at the Beginning of the Hundred Years War', *EHR*, liv (1939), 608–31

Palmer, J. J. N. (ed.)., *Froissart: Historian* (1981)

Patourel, J. Le (1), *The Medieval Administration of the Channel Islands, 1199–1399* (1937)

Patourel, J. Le (2), 'L'occupation anglaise de Calais', *Revue du Nord* xxxiii (1951), 228–41

Patourel, J. Le (3), 'Edward III and the Kingdom of France', *History*, xliii (1958), 173–89

Patourel, J. Le (4), 'The King and the Princes in Fourteenth-Century France', *Europe in the Late Middle Ages*, ed. J. Hale, R. Highfield and B. Smalley (1965), 155–83

Patourel, J. Le (5), 'The Origins of the War', *The Hundred Years War*, ed. K. Fowler (1971), 28–50

Pena, N. de la, 'Vassaux Gascons au service du roi d'Angleterre dans la première moitié du XIV siècle', *Annales du Midi*, xxxviii (1976), 5–21

Perroy, E., *The Hundred Years War* (1945)

*Petit, E. (1), *Histoire des ducs de Bourgogne de la race Capétienne*, 9 vols (1885–1905)

*Petit, E. (2), *Les sires de Noyers* (1874)

*Petit, J., *Charles de Valois (1270–1325)* (1900)

Phillips, J. R. S., *Aymer de Valence, Earl of Pembroke, 1307–1324* (1972)

Pirenne, H., *Histoire de Belgique*, 4th edn, 6 vols (1947)

Planiol, M., *Histoire des institutions de la Bretagne*, 5 vols (1921–4)

Platt, C., *Medieval Southampton* (1973)

Power, E., *The Wool Trade in English Medieval History* (1941)

Powicke, M., *Military Obligation in Medieval England* (1962)

Prentout, H., 'La prise de Caen par Edouard III, *Mems. Acad. Nat. Caen* (1904)

Prestwich, M. (1), *War, Politics and Finance Under Edward I* (1972)

Prestwich, M. (2), 'English Armies in the Early Stages of the Hundred Years War: A Scheme in 1341', *BIHR*, lvi (1983), 102–13

Prestwich, M. (3), 'Cavalry Service in Fourteenth-Century England', *War and Government in the Middle Ages. Essays in Honour of J. O. Prestwich*, ed. J. Gillingham and J. C. Holt (1984), 147–58

Prince, A. E. (1), 'The Strength of English Armies in the Reign of Edward III', *EHR*, xlvi (1931), 353–71

Prince, A. E. (2), 'The Importance of the Campaign of 1327', *EHR*, l (1935), 299–302

Prince, A. E. (3), 'The Payment of Army Wages in Edward III's Reign', *Speculum*, xix (1944), 137–60

Renouard, Y. (1), 'Conjectures sur la population du duché d'Aquitaine en 1316', *MA* (1963), 471–8

Renouard, Y. (2), *Bordeaux sous les rois d'Angleterre* (1965)

Richardson, H. G., 'Illustrations of English History in the Medieval Registers of the Parlement of Paris', *TRHS*, 4th series, x (1927), 55–85

Rigaudière, A., 'Le financement des fortifications urbaines en France du milieu du XIVe siècle à la fin du XVe siècle', *RH*, cclxxiii (1985), 19–95

Roncière, C. de la, *Histoire de la marine française*, 6 vols (1899–1932)

Rothwell, H., 'Edward I's Case Against Philip the Fair over Gascony in 1298', *EHR*, xlii (1927), 572–82

Saul, A., 'Great Yarmouth and the Hundred Years War in the Fourteenth Century', *BIHR*, lii (1979), 105–15

Saul, N., *Knights and Esquires. The Gloucester Gentry in the Fourteenth Century* (1981)

Scammell, 'Robert I and the North of England', *EHR*, lxxiii (1958), 385–403

*Sibertin-Blanc, C., 'La levée du subside de 1337 en Rouergue et l'hôpital d'Aubrac au début de la guerre de cent ans', *BPH* (1963–4), 301–38

Smyth, J., *The Lives of the Berkeleys*, ed. J. Maclean, 2 vols (1883–5)

Strayer, J. R. and Taylor, C. H., *Studies in Early French Taxation* (1931)

Studd, R., 'The *Privilegiati* and the Treaty of Paris, 1259', *La 'France Anglaise' au moyen age. Actes du IIIe congrès nationale des sociétés savantes* (Poitiers, 1986), *Section d'histoire médiévale et de philologie*, i (1988), 175–89

Sturler, J. de, *Les rélations politiques et les échanges commerciaux entre le duché de Brabant et l'Angleterre au moyen age* (1936)

Templeman, G., 'Edward III and the Beginnings of the Hundred Years War', *TRHS*, 5th series, ii (1952), 69–88

*Tholin, G., *Ville libre et barons. Essai sur les limites de la juridiction d'Agen* (1886)

Thrupp, S. L., *The Merchant Class of Medieval London* (1948)

Tinniswood, J. T., 'English Galleys, 1272–1377', *Mariners' Mirror*, xxxv (1949), 276–315

Touchard, H., *Le commerce maritime breton à la fin du moyen age* (1967)

Tout, T. F. (1), *Chapters in the Administrative history of Medieval England*, 6 vols (1920–37)

Tout, T. F. (2) 'Firearms in England in the Fourteenth Century', *Collected Papers*, ii (1934), 233–75

Tout, T. F. (3), 'The Tactics of the Battles of Boroughbridge and Morlaix', *Collected Papers*, ii (1934), 221–5

Trabut-Cussac, J. P., *L'administration anglaise en Gascogne sous Henri III et Edourd I de 1254 à 1307* (1972)

*Trautz, F., *Die Konige von England und das Reich, 1272–1377* (1961)

Tucoo-Chala, P. (1), *Gaston Fébus et la vicomté de Béarn* (1959)

Tucoo-Chala, P. (2), *La vicomté de Béarn et le problème de la souveraineté* (1961)

Vale, M. G. A., 'The Gascon Nobility and the Anglo-French War, 1294–98', *War and Government in the Middle Ages. Essays in Honour of J. O. Prestwich*, ed. J. Gillingham and J. C. Holt (1984), 134–46

Vale, J., *Edward III and Chivalry* (1982)

*Varenbergh, E., *Histoire des rélations diplomatiques entre le comte de Flandre et l'Angleterre au moyen age* (1874)

Viard, J. (1), 'Les ressources extraordinaires de la royauté sous Phillippe VI de Valois', *Rev. quest. hist.*, xciv (1888), 167–218

*Viard, J. (2), 'Geoffroy de Nancy', *Bull. Soc. Hist. et Arch. de Langres*, iii (1887–92), 430–76

Viard, J. (3) 'La France sous Philippe VI de Valois, État géographique et militaire', *Rev. quest. hist.*, lix (1896), 337–402

Viard, J. (4), 'Henri le Moine de Bâle à la bataille de Crécy', *BEC*, lxvii (1906), 89–96

Viard, J. (5), 'La Cour (Curia) au commencement du XIVe siècle', *BEC*, lxxiv (1916), 74–87

Viard, J. (6), 'Philippe de Valois. La succession à la couronne de France', *MA*, xxiii (1921), 219–22

Viard, J. (7), 'L'Ostrevant. Enquêtes au sujet de la frontière française sous Philippe VI de Valois', *BEC*, lxxxii (1921), 316–29

Viard, J. (8), 'La campagne de juillet-août 1346 et la bataille de Crécy', *MA*, 2e serie, xxvii (1926), 1–84

Viard, J. (9), 'Le siège de Calais: 4 septembre 1346–4 août 1347', *MA*, 2e série, xxx (1929), 9–189

Viard, J. (10), 'La Chambre des Comptes sous le règne de Philippe VI de Valois', *BEC*, xciii (1932), 331–59

Viard, J. (11), 'Philippe de Valois. Le début du règne', *BEC*, xcv (1934), 259–83

Viard, J. (12), 'Les projets de croisade de Philippe VI de Valois', *BEC*, xcvii (1936), 305–16

*Vic, C. de and Vaissète, J., *Histoire générale de Languedoc*, 16 vols (1874–1905)

Viollet, P., 'Comment les femmes ont été exclués en France de la succession à la couronne', *Mems. Acad. Incr. et Belles Lettres*, xxxiv(2) (1895), 125–78

Werveke, H. van, *Jacques van Artevelde* (1942)

Willard, J. F. (1), 'The Scotch Raids and the Fourteenth-Century Taxation of Northern England', *University of Colorado Studies*, v. (1907–8), 237–42

Willard, J. F. (2), *Parliamentary Taxes on Personal Property, 1290 to 1334* (1934)

Willard, J. F. and Morris, W. A. (ed), *The English Government at Work*, 3 vols (1940–50)

Wood, C. T., *The French Apanages and the Capetian Monarchy* (1966)

Index

CPSIA information can be obtained
at www.ICGtesting.com
Printed in the USA
BVHW04s1224100718
521275BV00006B/167/P